PQ

French, Italian, Spanish, and Portuguese Literatures

Library of Congress Classification 2008

Prepared by the Cataloging Policy and Support Office
Library Services

LIBRARY OF CONGRESS
Cataloging Distribution Service
Washington, D.C.

This edition cumulates all additions and changes to Subclass PQ through Weekly List 2008/24, dated June 11, 2008. Additions and changes made subsequent to that date are published in weekly lists posted on the World Wide Web at

<http://www.loc.gov/aba/cataloging/classification/weeklylists/>

and are also available in *Classification Web*, the online Web-based edition of the Library of Congress Classification.

Library of Congress Cataloging-in-Publication Data

Library of Congress.
Library of Congress classification. PQ. French, Italian, Spanish, and Portuguese literatures / prepared by the Cataloging Policy and Support Office Library Services. — 2008 ed.
p. cm.
"This edition cumulates all additions and changes to Subclass PQ through Weekly list 2008/24, dated June 11, 2008. Additions and changes made subsequent to that date are published in weekly lists posted on the World Wide Web ... and are also available in *Classification Web*, the online Web-based edition of the Library of Congress classification"—T.p. verso.
Includes index.
ISBN 978-0-8444-1221-4
1. Classification, Library of Congress. 2. Classification—Books—French literature. 3. Classification—Books—Italian literature. 4. Classification—Books—Spanish literature. 5. Classification—Books—Portuguese literature. I. Library of Congress. Cataloging Policy and Support Office. II. Title. III. Title: French, Italian, Spanish, and Portuguese literatures.
Z696.U5P77 2008 025.4'684—dc22 2008030561

For sale by the Library of Congress Cataloging Distribution Service,
101 Independence Avenue, S.E., Washington, DC 20541-4912.
Product catalog available on the Web at **www.loc.gov/cds**.

PREFACE

Class P: Subclass PQ, Part 1, *French Literature*, was originally published in 1936 and was reprinted in 1966 with supplementary pages of additions and changes. A second edition was published in 1992. Subclass PQ, Part 2, *Italian, Spanish, and Portuguese Literatures*, was published in 1937 and reprinted in 1965 with supplementary pages. A 1998 edition combined the two parts into a single volume. A 2004 edition cumulated changes that were made between 1998 and 2004. This 2008 edition cumulates changes made since the 2004 edition was published.

Classification numbers or spans of numbers that appear in parentheses are formerly valid numbers that are now obsolete. Numbers or spans that appear in angle brackets are optional numbers that have never been used at the Library of Congress but are provided for other libraries that wish to use them. In most cases, a parenthesized or angle-bracketed number is accompanied by a "see" reference directing the user to the actual number that the Library of Congress currently uses, or a note explaining Library of Congress practice.

Access to the online version of the full Library of Congress Classification is available on the World Wide Web by subscription to *Classification Web*. Details about ordering and pricing may be obtained from the Cataloging Distribution Service at

<http://www.loc.gov/cds/>

New or revised numbers and captions are added to the L.C. Classification schedules as a result of development proposals made by the cataloging staff of the Library of Congress and cooperating institutions. Upon approval of these proposals by the weekly editorial meeting of the Cataloging Policy and Support Office, new classification records are created or existing records are revised in the master classification database. Weekly lists of newly approved or revised classification numbers and captions are posted on the World Wide Web at

<http://www.loc.gov/aba/cataloging/classification/weeklylists>

Milicent Wewerka, senior cataloging policy specialist in the Cataloging Policy and Support Office, is responsible for coordinating the overall intellectual and editorial content of class P and its various subclasses. Kent Griffiths, assistant editor, creates new classification records and their associated index terms, and maintains the master database.

Barbara B. Tillett, Chief
Cataloging Policy and Support Office

July 2008

OUTLINE

PQ1-3999	French literature
PQ1-771	History and criticism
PQ1-150	General
PQ151-221	Medieval. Old French
PQ226-317	Modern
PQ400-491	Poetry
PQ500-591	Drama
PQ601-771	Prose and prose fiction
PQ(781)-(841)	Folk literature
PQ845	Juvenile literature
PQ1100-1297	Collections
PQ1100-1145	General
PQ1160-1193	Poetry
PQ1211-1241	Drama
PQ1243-1297	Prose
PQ1300-1595	Old French literature
	To ca. 1500/1550
PQ1300-1391	Collections
	Individual authors and works
PQ1411-1545	To 1350/1400
PQ1551-1595	(14th-) 15th century (to ca. 1525)
PQ1600-2726	Modern literature
	Individual authors
PQ1600-1709	16th century
PQ1710-1935	17th century
PQ1947-2147	18th century
PQ2149-2551	19th century
PQ2600-2651	1900-1960
PQ2660-2686	1961-2000
PQ2700-2726	2001-
PQ3800-3999	Provincial, local, colonial, etc.
PQ4001-5999	Italian literature
PQ4001-4199.5	History and criticism
PQ4001-4063	General
PQ4064-4075	Early to 1500
PQ4077-4088	Modern
PQ4091-(4131)	Poetry
PQ4133-4160	Drama
PQ4161-4185	Prose
PQ(4186)-(4199)	Folk literature
PQ4199.5	Juvenile literature (General)
PQ4201-4263	Collections
PQ4201-4204	General

OUTLINE

- Italian literature
  - Collections - Continued
    - PQ4205-4206 Translations
    - PQ4207-4225 Poetry
    - PQ4227-4245 Drama
    - PQ4247-4263 Prose
  - PQ4265-4556 Individual authors and works to 1400
  - PQ4561-4664 Individual authors, 1400-1700
  - PQ4675-4734 Individual authors, 1701-1900
  - PQ4800-4851 Individual authors, 1900-1960
  - PQ4860-4886 Individual authors, 1961-2000
  - PQ4900-4926 Individual authors, 2001-
  - PQ5901-5999 Regional, provincial, local, etc.
- PQ6001-8929 Spanish literature
  - PQ6001-6168 History and criticism
    - PQ6001-6056 General
      - PQ6056 Moorish-Spanish literature
    - PQ6058-6060 Early to 1500
    - PQ(6061)-6073 Modern
    - PQ6075-6098 Poetry
    - PQ6098.7-6129 Drama
    - PQ6131-6153 Prose
    - PQ(6155)-(6167) Folk literature
    - PQ6168 Juvenile literature (General)
  - PQ6170-6269 Collections
    - PQ6170-6174.9 General
    - PQ6174.95-6215 Poetry
    - PQ6217-(6241) Drama
    - PQ6247-6264 Prose
    - PQ(6265)-6269 Translations
  - PQ6271-6498 Individual authors and works to 1700
  - PQ6500-6576 Individual authors, 1700-ca. 1868
  - PQ6600-6647 Individual authors, 1868-1960
  - PQ6650-6676 Individual authors, 1961-2000
  - PQ6700-6726 Individual authors, 2001-
  - PQ7000-8929 Provincial, local, colonial, etc.
    - PQ7081-8560 Spanish America
- PQ9000-9999 Portuguese literature
  - PQ9000-9129 History and criticism
    - PQ9000-9034 General
    - PQ9035-9055 Special periods
    - PQ9061-9081 Poetry
    - PQ9083-9095 Drama

	Portuguese literature
	History and criticism - Continued
PQ9097-9119	Prose
PQ(9121)-(9128)	Folk literature
PQ9129	Juvenile literature (General)
PQ9131-9188	Collections
PQ9131-9144	General
PQ9137	Translations
PQ9149-9163	Poetry
PQ9164-9170	Drama
PQ9172-9188	Prose
PQ9189	Individual authors and works to 1500
PQ9191-9255	Individual authors and works, 1500-1700
PQ9261	Individual authors, 1701-1960
PQ9262-9288	Individual authors, 1961-2000
PQ9300-9326	Individual authors, 2001-
PQ9400-9999	Provincial, local, colonial, etc.
PQ9500-9698.36	Brazil

	French literature
	Literary history and criticism
	Periodicals
1	American and English
2	French
3	German
5	Italian
7	Scandinavian
8	Spanish and Portuguese
9	Other
	Yearbooks see PQ1+
	Societies
21	American and English
22	French
23	German
25	Italian
27	Scandinavian
28	Spanish and Portuguese
29	Other
31	Congresses
33	Museums. Exhibitions
	Collections
35	Monographs, studies, etc., by various authors
36.A-Z	Festschriften. By honoree, A-Z
41	Encyclopedias. Dictionaries
45	Theory of the study of French literature Including philosophy, psychology, esthetics
47	History of literary history
	Study and teaching
51	General
53	General special
	By period
55	Middle Ages to 1600
57	17th-18th centuries
59	19th century
61	20th century
63.A-Z	By region or country, A-Z
65.A-Z	By school, A-Z
	Biography of teachers, critics, and historians
67.A2	Collective
67.A3-Z	Individual, A-Z Subarrange each by Table P-PZ50
	Criticism
(69)	Periodicals see PN80
71	Treatises. Theory. Canons
75	History

Literary history and criticism
Criticism -- Continued
79 Special topics (not A-Z)
e.g. Textual criticism
81 Collections of essays in criticism
By period
Middle ages to 1600
82 Treatises. Theory. History
83 Special topics
84 Specimens. Selections
17th century
85 Treatises. Theory. History
86 Special topics
87 Specimens. Selections
18th century
88 Treatises. Theory. History
89 Special topics
90 Specimens. Selections
19th century
91 Treatises. Theory. History
92 Special topics
93 Specimens. Selections
20th century
94 Treatises. Theory. History
95 Special topics
96 Specimens. Selections
History of French literature
General works
100 Early works to 1800
1801-
101 French
103 English
105 German
107 Italian
109 Other
Compends
French
115 Through 1900
116 1901-
English
118 Through 1900
119 1901-
German
121 Through 1900
122 1901-
Italian
124 Through 1900

Literary history and criticism
History of French literature
Compends
Italian -- Continued
125 1901-
Other
127 Through 1900
128 1901-

135 Outlines. Syllabi. Tables. Charts
141 Single addresses, essays, lectures, etc.
141.5.A-Z Awards, prizes, A-Z
141.5.G6 Prix Goncourt
142 Relations to history, civilization, culture, etc.
Relations to foreign literatures and countries
143.A2 General
Special
143.A3 Ancient
143.A4-Z Modern
Subdivide by language or country
e. g.
143.D8 Dutch
143.E5 English
143.G3 German
143.I5 Italian
143.S2 Scandinavian
143.S5 Spanish
143.U6 United States
144 Translations (General)
144.5 French literature by foreign authors (General)
For individual authors see PQ1410.2+
145 Miscellaneous aspects, forms, etc.
Including evolution of the different forms, poetry, drama, etc.; psychology; moral aspects
Special subjects, classes, etc., not limited to one period or form
145.1 A - N
145.1.A25 Accidents
145.1.A3 Adolescence
145.1.A54 Animals
145.1.A77 Art
145.1.A87 Atreus, House of (Greek mythology)
Autobiography see PQ145.6.S32
145.1.B53 Bible
145.1.B57 Birds
Body, Human see PQ145.1.H8
145.1.B64 Books and reading
145.1.B67 Boredom

Literary history and criticism
History of French literature
Special subjects, classes, etc., not limited to one period or form
A - N -- Continued

145.1.C35 Cannibalism
145.1.C38 Castles
145.1.C4 Characters and characteristics
145.1.C44 Children
145.1.C46 Cities and towns
145.1.C48 Civilization
145.1.C5 Classicism
145.1.C6 Collectors and collecting
145.1.C68 Courtship
145.1.C75 Crime
145.1.C78 Cruelty
145.1.D33 Death
145.1.D37 Description
145.1.D4 Devil
145.1.D52 Dialect literature
145.1.D73 Dreams
145.1.E56 Emotions
145.1.E6 Epicureanism
145.1.E63 Equality
145.1.E65 Erotica
145.1.E7 Errors and blunders
145.1.E83 Ethics
145.1.E94 Existentialism
Exoticism see PQ145.7.A2
145.1.F32 Fantasy
145.1.F4 Fear
145.1.F56 Flowers
145.1.G34 Games
145.1.G35 Gastronomy
145.1.G6 God
145.1.H35 Happiness
145.1.H4 Heroes
145.1.H57 History
145.1.H66 Homosexuality
145.1.H8 Human body
145.1.I43 Illusion
145.1.I45 Imagination
145.1.I47 Imitation
145.1.I48 Impotence
145.1.I5 Incest
145.1.I55 Incongruity
145.1.J68 Journalism

Literary history and criticism
History of French literature
Special subjects, classes, etc., not limited to one period or form
A - N -- Continued

145.1.L26	Landscape
145.1.L3	Laughter
145.1.L46	Light and darkness
145.1.L55	Loneliness
145.1.L6	Love
145.1.M26	Male friendship
145.1.M28	Masculinity
145.1.M35	Melancholy
145.1.M37	Mental illness
145.1.M4	Meteorology
145.1.M5	Mirrors
145.1.M57	Money
145.1.M6	Monsters
145.1.M65	Morality
145.1.M84	Music
145.1.M89	Myth
145.1.M9	Mythology
145.1.N35	Names
145.3	Nature
145.4	Nat - Rel
145.4.O65	Orientalism
145.4.O75	Other (Philosophy)
145.4.P35	Pastoral literature
145.4.P48	Philosophy
145.4.P64	Polemics
145.4.P65	Politics
145.4.P66	Popular literature
145.4.P7	Prisons
145.4.P73	Protest
145.4.R33	Race relations
145.4.R4	Realism
145.5	Religion
145.6	Rel - Z
145.6.R57	Rites and ceremonies
145.6.R8	Ruins
145.6.S25	Salt
145.6.S315	Sea
145.6.S32	Self. Autobiography
145.6.S34	Setting
145.6.S36	Sick
145.6.S38	Slavery
145.6.S43	Society

Literary history and criticism
History of French literature
Special subjects, classes, etc., not limited to one period or form
Rel - Z -- Continued

145.6.S5 Staircases
145.6.S57 Sugar
145.6.S58 Suicide
145.6.S6 Supernatural
145.6.S63 Survival after airplane accidents, shipwrecks, etc.
145.6.T34 Tales
145.6.T38 Taxation
145.6.T44 Telephone
145.6.T46 Theater
145.6.T5 Time
145.6.T7 Travel
145.6.U5 Unicorns
145.6.U6 Utopias
145.6.V44 Veils
145.6.V5 Violence
145.6.V54 Visions
145.6.V64 Volcanoes
Wit and humor see PQ751
145.6.W54 Wine

Regions, countries and races
145.7.A2 General (Exoticism)
145.7.A3-Z Special, A-Z
145.7.A35 Africa
Algeria
145.7.A4 General works
145.7.A42A-.A42Z Local, A-Z
145.7.A5 America
145.7.B3 Barbaresques
Belgium
145.7.B4 General works
145.7.B42A-.B42Z Local, A-Z
145.7.B99 Byzantine Empire
145.7.E2 The East
Egypt
145.7.E3 General works
145.7.E32A-.E32Z Local, A-Z
France
145.7.F7 General
145.7.F8A-.F8Z Local, A-Z
145.7.F8P3 Paris
Germany
145.7.G4 General works

Literary history and criticism
History of French literature
Special subjects, classes, etc., not limited to one period or form
Regions, countries and races
Special, A-Z
Germany -- Continued

145.7.G42A-.G42Z	Local, A-Z
	Great Britain
145.7.G74	General works
145.7.G742A-.G742Z	Local, A-Z
	India
145.7.I47	General works
145.7.I472A-.I472Z	Local, A-Z
145.7.I6	Indochina
	Italy
145.7.I7	General
145.7.I72A-.I72Z	Local, A-Z
145.7.I72S37	Sardinia
	Japan
145.7.J3	General works
145.7.J32A-.J32Z	Local, A-Z
145.7.J4	Jews
	Morocco
145.7.M6	General works
145.7.M62A-.M62Z	Local, A-Z
	Persia
145.7.P4	General works
145.7.P42A-.P42Z	Local, A-Z
	Poland
145.7.P6	General works
145.7.P62A-.P62Z	Local, A-Z
145.7.R5	Riviera
	Russia
145.7.R87	General works
145.7.R872A-.R872Z	Local, A-Z
145.7.S6	Slavs
	Spain
145.7.S7	General works
145.7.S8A-.S8Z	Local, A-Z
	Turkey
145.7.T9	General works
145.7.T92A-.T92Z	Local, A-Z
	United States
145.7.U5	General works
145.7.U52A-.U52Z	Local, A-Z
145.7.V55	Vikings

Literary history and criticism
History of French literature
Special subjects, classes, etc., not limited to one period or form
Regions, countries and races
Special, A-Z -- Continued
145.7.W47 West Indies, French
145.8.A-Z Special classes, A-Z
145.8.A25 Actresses
(145.8.J48) Jews
see PQ145.7.J4
145.8.M68 Mothers
145.8.N8 Nuns
145.8.P7 Priests
145.8.S35 Saints
145.8.S47 Servants
145.8.W6 Women
145.9.A-Z Special persons or characters, A-Z
145.9.A76 Artemis
145.9.D65 Don Juan
145.9.M43 Medea (Greek mythology)
145.9.O64 Ophelia
145.9.P53 Phaedra
Biography of French authors (Collected)
146 General
Individual
see PQ1411+
147 Memoirs. Letters
147.5 Relations to women. Love, marriage, etc.
147.9 Iconography: Portraits, monuments, etc.
148 Literary landmarks. Homes and haunts of authors
149 Women authors. Literary relations of women
Cf. PQ147.5 Love, marriage, etc.
150.A-Z Special classes of authors, A-Z
150.C3 Catholic authors
150.C53 Children
150.J4 Jewish authors
150.L3 Laboring class authors
150.L5 Literary prize winners
150.M46 Mentally ill
150.N67 North African authors
Class here works about French literature written in France by authors of North African origin or ancestry
150.P4 Physicians
150.P7 Protestant authors
150.S65 Soldiers
By period

Literary history and criticism
History of French literature
By period -- Continued
Medieval. Old French

151 General works
155.A-Z Special subjects, A-Z
155.A44 Allegory
Arms see PQ155.M6
155.C53 Children
155.C55 Chivalry
155.C65 Closure (Rhetoric)
155.C7 Costume
155.C73 Courtesy
155.C74 Courtly love
155.C76 Courts and courtiers
155.C86 Crusades
155.D47 Desire
155.D7 Dreams
155.E2 The East
155.E25 Economics
155.E6 Ermanaric
155.E7 Estates (Social orders)
155.F29 Fairies
155.F3 Faith
155.F33 Falconry
155.F47 Festivals
155.F66 Food
155.F67 Forests and forestry
155.F84 Funeral rites and ceremonies
155.G4 Ganelon
155.G44 Gawain
Gender identity see PQ155.S48
155.G5 Germany
155.G64 Gold
155.H32 Heart
155.H35 Hell
155.H38 Heresy
155.H8 Hunting
155.I35 Identity (Psychology)
155.I74 Irony
155.J4 Jesus Christ
155.L47 Lesbians
155.L57 Lists
155.L7 Love
155.M2 Magic
155.M27 The marvelous
155.M3 Mary, Blessed Virgin, Saint

Literary history and criticism
History of French literature
By period
Medieval. Old French
Special subjects, A-Z -- Continued

155.M4 Matriarchy
155.M5 Medicine
155.M52 Melancholy
155.M53 Mental illness
155.M54 Merchants
155.M55 Messengers
155.M6 Military science, arms, and armor
155.M88 Music
155.M94 Mythology
155.N2 Names
155.N24 Narration
155.N28 Nature
155.N65 Nonsense
155.P65 Political poetry
155.P7 Polyphemus
155.P72 Poverty
155.P8 Proverbs
155.R4 Religion
155.R45 Repentance
155.R48 Rewards
155.S46 Senses and sensation
155.S48 Sex. Sex role. Gender identity
155.S53 Sick
155.S56 Silence
155.S7 Social conditions
155.S76 Sound
155.S94 Symbolism
155.T38 Taverns (Inns)
155.T48 Textual criticism
155.T56 Time
155.V5 Villain, villeinage (Fuedalism)
155.W34 War
155.W36 Water
155.W5 Wit and humor
155.W6 Women

Special periods
To 1328/50
156 Treatises
158 Special subjects, poetry, etc. (not A-Z)
To 1000/50. Origins. Sources
166 Treatises
168 Special subjects, poetry, etc. (not A-Z)

Literary history and criticism
History of French literature
By period
Medieval. Old French
Special periods
To 1328/50 -- Continued
11th century
171 Treatises
173 Special subjects, poetry, etc. (not A-Z)
12th century
176 Treatises
178 Special subjects, poetry, etc. (not A-Z)
13th century to 1328/50
181 Treatises
183 Special subjects, poetry, etc. (not A-Z)
1328/50-1483. 14th-15th centuries
186 Treatises
188 Special subjects, poetry, etc. (not A-Z)
14th century
191 Treatises
193 Special subjects, poetry, etc. (not A-Z)
15th century
196 Treatises
198 Special subjects, poetry, etc. (not A-Z)
199 Trouvères and jongleurs
Cf. PC3304+ Provençal
Special forms
Epics
201 General. National epics. Chansons de geste
203 Special groups, cycles, etc.
e.g. Celtic, Arthurian, Greco-Roman
203.5 Hero legends, A-Z
203.5.A77 Arthur
203.5.C45 Charlemagne
204 Beast epics
205 Special subjects (not A-Z)
207 Narrative poetry. Lais. Fabliaux
211 Lyric poetry
216 Didactic and other
Drama, see PQ511+
221 Prose romances
Modern
226 General works
Renaissance. 16th century
230 Periodicals. Societies
231 General works
Special periods

Literary history and criticism
History of French literature
By period
Modern
Renaissance. 16th century
Special periods -- Continued
235 To 1550
237 1550-1600
Special topics
La Pléiade see PQ1661+
239 Other special (not A-Z)
17th century
241 General works
245 Topics not limited to the special periods
Including Précieux
247 1600-1650
249 1650-1715
Querelle des anciens et modernes
251.A2 Contemporary authors
251.A3-Z Modern authors
18th century
261 General works
265 Special topics (not A-Z)
273 Memoirs. Correspondence. Sources
276 Revolution, Empire, Restoration, 1789-1815/30
19th century, ca. 1789-1900
281 General works
283 Special topics not limited to shorter periods
1789-1850/70
285 General works
Special topics
287 Romanticism
288 Other special (not A-Z)
1789-1830, see PQ276
289 Memoirs, letters, journals of contemporaries illustrating the history of the period
1830/50-1860/70
290 General works
292 Special topics (not A-Z)
1850/70-1900
293 General works
295.A-Z Special topics, A-Z
295.A53 Androgyny (Psychology)
295.B6 Boredom
295.C6 Classicism
295.C7 Cruelty
295.D37 Dandies

Literary history and criticism
History of French literature
By period
Modern
19th century, ca. 1789-1900
1850/70-1900
Special topics, A-Z -- Continued

295.D4 Decadents
295.D47 Despair
295.D73 Dreams
295.H47 Heredity
295.H65 Homosexuals
295.I44 Illusion
295.J36 Japan
295.M37 Marginality, Social
295.M5 Middle Ages
295.M63 Modernism
295.M64 Money
295.M66 Mothers
295.M9 Mysticism
295.M92 Myth
295.N17 Narcotics
295.N18 Narrations (Rhetoric)
295.N2 Naturalism, Realism
295.P35 Paris
Parnassiens, see PQ437+
295.P65 Populism
295.P7 Psychology, ethics, etc. of literature
295.R4 Religious thought
295.S3 Salome
295.S9 Symbolism
295.W33 Wagner, Richard, 1813-1883
295.W6 Women

1870/80-1900

296 General works
298 Special topics (not A-Z)
299 Memoirs, letters, sources

20th century

305 General works
307.A-Z Special topics, A-Z
307.A45 Africa
307.A47 Aging
307.A52 AIDS
307.A56 Anti-clericalism
307.A57 Antisemitism
307.A575 Apathy
307.A58 Aphorisms. Apothegms

Literary history and criticism
History of French literature
By period
Modern
20th century
Special topics, A-Z -- Continued
Authors and readers see PQ307.R37

307.A63 Authorship
307.A65 Autobiography
307.B35 Banality (Philosophy)
307.B63 Body, Human
(307.C3) Catholic authors
see PQ307.R37
307.C47 Censorship
307.C54 Colonies
307.C56 Commitment (Psychology)
307.C57 Communities
307.C58 Concentration camps
307.C59 Confession
307.C6 Conservatism
307.C74 Cries
307.D3 Dadaism
307.D54 Diseases
307.D73 Dreams
307.E36 Ego (Psychology)
307.E77 Erotic literature
307.E87 Evil
307.E9 Existentialism
307.E94 Exoticism
307.E95 Experimental literature
307.F23 Fables
307.F3 Fascism
307.F43 Feminism
307.F87 Futurism
307.G35 Gender identity
307.G4 Germany
307.G59 Gnosticism
307.G6 God
307.G75 Grief
307.H4 Heroes
307.H6 Homosexuals
307.H65 Hospitality
307.H8 Humanism
307.H84 Hussards
307.I54 Identity (Psychology)
307.I56 Indochina
307.I58 Invention (Rhetoric)

Literary history and criticism
History of French literature
By period
Modern
20th century
Special topics, A-Z -- Continued

307.L53 Libertarian literature
Lockouts see PQ307.S75
307.M3 Macedonia
307.M37 Masculinity
307.M45 Melancholy
307.M55 Minimalism (Literature)
307.M63 Modernism
307.M67 Mothers
307.M68 Motion pictures
307.M87 Murder
307.N44 Negation (Logic)
307.N54 Nihilism
307.N67 North Africans
307.O43 Old age
307.P26 Pacifism
307.P3 Paris
307.P47 Philosophy
307.P52 Place (Philosophy)
307.P64 Politics
307.P65 Popular literature
307.P66 Postmodernism
307.P68 Prisons
307.P7 Proletarian literature
307.P77 Psychoanalysis
307.R37 Readers and authors. Reader-response criticism
307.R39 Regionalism
307.R4 Religion
307.R45 Restaurants, etc.
307.R47 Revolution
307.R6 Romanticism
307.S35 Sanatoriums
307.S42 Sea
307.S49 Sex
307.S54 Silence
307.S6 Social problems
307.S63 Socialist realism
307.S66 Spanish Civil War
307.S69 Sports
307.S73 Stereotype (Psychology)
307.S75 Strikes and lockouts
307.S9 Suffering

Literary history and criticism
History of French literature
By period
Modern
20th century
Special topics, A-Z -- Continued
307.S95 Surrealism
307.T73 Travel
307.T85 Tunisia
307.U5 Unanimism
307.U6 United States
307.V55 Violence
307.V57 Vision
307.W28 War (General)
307.W3 War literature (World War I)
307.W4 War literature (World War II)
(307.W6) Women authors
see PQ149
310 Memoirs, letters, sources
21st century
315 General works
317.A-Z Special topics, A-Z
Poetry
For philosophy, esthetics see PN1031+
400 Periodicals. Societies
401 General works
By period
Medieval see PQ151+
Modern
General
411 Treatises
413 Special topics (not A-Z)
Renaissance. 16th century
416 Treatises
418 Special topics (not A-Z)
17th-18th centuries
421 Treatises
423 Special topics (not A-Z)
18th century
426 Treatises
428 Special topics (not A-Z)
19th century
431 Treatises
433 Special topics (not A-Z)
To 1850. Romanticism
434 Treatises
436 Special topics (not A-Z)

Literary history and criticism
History of French literature
Poetry
By period
Modern
19th century -- Continued
1850-1900. Realism, etc.

437 Treatises
439 Special topics (not A-Z)
20th century
441 Treatises
443 Special topics (not A-Z)
21st century
444 Treatises
444.5 Special topics (not A-Z)
Special forms
445 Chanson. Chanson populaire
447 Epic
Lyric poetry
451 General works
Special by form
456 Pastoral. Idylls
459 Elegiac
Chanson see PQ445
466 Sonnet
469 Ode (Palinode)
471.A-Z Other, A-Z
471.B3 Ballade
471.E64 Epistolary poetry
471.F74 Free verse
471.H35 Haiku
471.P3 Pastourelles
471.R7 Rondeau
473.A-Z Special. By subject, A-Z
473.E57 Erotic poetry
481 Didactic
491 Other
e.g. Society verse
498 Dialogue
Drama
For technique see PN1660+
For history of the French theater see PN2620+
General works
500 Early through 1800
501 1801-
509 Special topics (not A-Z)
By period

Literary history and criticism
History of French literature
Drama
By period -- Continued
Medieval. Origins to 1500
511 General
512 General special
513 Mysteries, Moralities, Passion plays, etc.
514 Théâtre comique
515 Other
Modern
General works
516 Treatises
518 Special topics (not A-Z)
Special periods
Renaissance. 16th century
521 Treatises
523 Special topics (not A-Z)
17th-18th centuries
526 Treatises
528 Special topics (not A-Z)
18th century
536 Treatises
538 Special topics (not A-Z)
19th century
541 Treatises
543 Special topics (not A-Z)
To 1850. Romanticism
546 Treatises
548 Special topics (not A-Z)
1850-1900. Realism, etc.
551 Treatises
553 Special topics (not A-Z)
20th century
556 Treatises
558 Special topics (not A-Z)
Special forms
Tragedy
561 General works
563 Special topics (not A-Z)
Comedy
566 General works
568 Special topics (not A-Z)
571 Historical drama
573 Religious drama
576 Tragicomedy
578 Pastoral drama

Literary history and criticism
History of French literature
Drama
Special forms -- Continued
580 Romantic drama
582 Melodrama
584 Farce
586 Other
591 Special subjects, A-Z
591.D6 Don Juan
591.J4 Jeanne d'Arc
591.O7 Orestes
591.S54 Silence
Prose and prose fiction
601 General works
By period
607 Medieval
For prose romances, see PQ221
Modern
611 General works
613 Renaissance. 16th century
17th-18th centuries
615 General works
618 18th century
19th century
621 General works
624 To 1850
627 1850-1900
629 20th century
Special
Prose fiction
For technique see PN3355+
631 General works
636 Short stories
637.A-Z Special topics, A-Z
637.A28 Adaptations
637.A36 Adultery
637.A37 Adventure stories
637.A39 Africa
637.A77 Art
637.A96 Autobiographic fiction
637.C37 Causation
637.C48 Christian fiction
637.C58 Classicism
637.C62 Closure (Rhetoric)
637.C64 Colonies
637.D37 Description

Literary history and criticism
History of French literature
Prose and prose fiction
Special
Prose fiction
Special topics, A-Z -- Continued

637.D38	Desire
637.D4	Detective and mystery stories
637.D53	Didactic fiction
637.E6	Epistolary fiction
637.E76	Erotic stories
637.E86	Ethics
637.F27	Fairy tales
637.F29	Family
637.F3	Fantastic fiction
637.F57	First person narrative
637.G35	Gender identity
637.G37	Genres
637.G4	Germany
637.H56	Historical fiction
637.H65	Homosexuality
637.I48	India
637.J4	Jews
637.L32	Labor. Working class
637.L34	Landscape
637.L53	Libertinism
637.L68	Love
637.M53	Middle East
637.M55	Minimalism (Literature)
637.M6	Mountains
	Mystery stories see PQ637.D4
637.M98	Myth
637.N37	Narration
637.P35	Peasants
637.P4	Philosophy
637.P68	Popular fiction
637.R4	Realism
637.R43	Regionalism
637.S34	Science fiction
637.S4	Sea stories
637.S42	Secrecy
637.S43	Seduction
637.S64	Social classes
637.S65	Space and time
637.S96	Sympathy
637.T44	Technology
637.T73	The tragic

Literary history and criticism
History of French literature
Prose and prose fiction
Special
Prose fiction
Special topics, A-Z -- Continued
637.U76 Utopias
637.V56 Violence
637.V7 Voyages, Imaginary
637.V73 Voyeurism
637.W35 War stories
637.W64 Women
637.Y6 Youth
(641) Medieval
see PQ221
643 Renaissance. 16th century
645 17th century
648 18th century
19th century
651 General works
653 Special topics (not A-Z)
Special periods
1789-1850/70. Romanticism
655 General works
657 Special topics (not A-Z)
1850/70-1900. Realism, etc.
661 General works
663 Special topics (not A-Z)
20th century
671 General works
673 Special topics (not A-Z)
21st century
681 General works
683 Special topics (not A-Z)
Other prose forms
701 Oratory
711 Letters
731 Essays
Fables see PN984.A2+
751 Wit and humor
Cf. PQ155.W5 Medieval
771 Miscellaneous
Folk literature
For general works on folk literature, see subclass GR
(781) Periodicals. Societies. Collections
(783) Treatises
By period

Folk literature
By period -- Continued
(787) Origins
(788) Middle Ages
(789) Modern
By form
Poetry
791 General works
793 Special topics (not A-Z)
Prose
see subclass GR
(795) General works
(797) Special topics (not A-Z)
Collections of texts
(801) General collections
see subclass GR
Chapbooks
Collections
803 Reprints
804 Originals (Collections of separates bound together)
Separate chapbooks
Including originals and reprints
805 Prose tales
806 Poetry. Ballads
(811-813) Legends
see subclass GR
(821) Fairly tales
see subclass GR
(831) Special characters, heroes, fairies, etc.
see subclass GR
(841) Individual tales
see subclass GR
845 Juvenile literature
For special genres, see the genre
Collections of French literature
1100 Periodicals
General (not limited to special periods)
1101 Before 1800
1103 19th century
1104 20th century
1107 Selections from women authors
1109 Selections. Anthologies
Cf. PC2112.9+ Readers
1109.5.A-Z Special classes of authors, A-Z
1109.5.C3 Catholics
1109.5.C5 Children
1109.5.C64 College students

Collections of French literature
General (not limited to special periods)
Special classes of authors, A-Z -- Continued

1109.5.J48	Jews
1109.5.M46	Mentally ill
1109.5.P4	Physicians
1109.5.P7	Prisoners
1109.5.Y6	Youth
1110	Special topics, A-Z
1110.A47	Aeronautics
1110.A9	Aunis
1110.B48	Beverages
1110.B53	Blacks
1110.B7	Brittany
1110.C48	Christmas
1110.C55	Cities and towns
1110.C65	Columbus, Christopher
1110.C67	Conversation
1110.D4	Death
1110.D54	Didactic literature
1110.D63	Dogs
1110.D7	Dreams
1110.E7	Erotic literature
1110.E8	Evil
1110.F3	Fantastic literature
1110.F7	France
1110.G47	Germany
1110.H4	Heroes
1110.H8	Hunting
1110.I8	Islam
1110.J48	Jesus Christ
1110.L3	Labor. Working class
1110.L55	Loire River
1110.L6	Love
1110.M35	Marginality, Social
1110.M45	Melancholy
1110.M57	Moon
1110.N36	Nature
	Negroes see PQ1110.B53
1110.P35	Paris
1110.P37	Pastoral literature
1110.P4	Peasants
1110.P58	Politics
1110.P62	Popular literature
1110.P64	Portraits
1110.P7	Primitivism
1110.R35	Railroads

Collections of French literature
General (not limited to special periods)
Special topics, A-Z -- Continued
1110.R37 Rats
1110.R53 Richard I, Duke of Normandy, 932-996
1110.S4 Sea
1110.S6 Sports
1110.V6 Vosges Mountains
1110.W37 War
Working class see PQ1110.L3
1110.Y84 Yugoslavia
Quotations see PN6086+
Translations from foreign literatures
(1111.A2) From several languages
see PN6021+
(1111.A5-Z) From special languages, A-Z
see PA-PT
Translations of French literature into foreign languages
1112 Polyglot
1113 English
1114 German
1115 Italian
1116 Other languages, A-Z
By period
Old French to ca. 1500, see PQ1300+
(15th to) 16th century
1121 General
Special
La Pléiade see PQ1661+
1125 Other (not A-Z)
17th century
1126 General
1130.A-Z By subject, A-Z
1130.E8 Ethics
1130.L5 Libertinage
Cf. B1818.L5 Libertines
1130.P7 Précieuses
18th century
1131 General
1135.A-Z By subject, A-Z
1135.E7 Erotic literature
1135.F2 Facetiae
1135.S4 Sentimentalism
19th century
1136 General
Special
1137 1789-1850/70. Romanticism

Collections of French literature
By period
19th century
Special -- Continued
1138 1850/70-1900. Naturalism. Realism. Symbolism
1139.A-Z By subject, A-Z
1139.B34 Balloons
1139.C45 Characters and characteristics
1139.D43 Death
1139.E74 Erotic literature
1139.P3 Paris
20th century
1141 General
1145.A-Z By subject, A-Z
1145.C56 Christmas
1145.D34 Dancing
1145.D43 Death
1145.E94 Experimental literature
1145.G45 Geography
1145.H38 Hate
1145.L6 Love
1145.L96 Lyon (France)
1145.M32 Machinery
1145.M6 Mothers
1145.M64 Motion pictures
1145.N37 Nature
1145.P37 Paris
1145.P46 Petra (Ancient city)
1145.R4 Religion
1145.R47 Réunion
1145.R65 Roses
1145.S25 Savoy
1145.S8 Surrealism
1145.T7 Travel
1145.W3 World War II
21st century
1147 General
1148.A-Z By subject, A-Z
1148.E94 Experimental literature
1148.N54 Nihilism
Local collections see PQ3800
Poetry
1160 Periodicals
General
1161 Through 1800
1163 1801-
1165 Selections, anthologies, etc.

Collections of French literature
Poetry -- Continued
1165.3 Anthologies of poetry for children
1166 Concordances, indexes, etc.
1167 Selections from women poets
1168 Other special collections
Including poets laureate
(1169) Translations from foreign literature
see PN6103
Translations of French poetry into foreign languages
1170.A2 Polyglot
1170.A5-Z By language, A-Z
By period
(1171) Old French,
see PQ1300+
Modern
(1172) General
see PQ1161+
1173 15th-16th centuries
1175 17th century
1177 18th century
19th century
1181 General
Special
1182 To 1850/60
1183 1850/60-
1184 20th century
1185 21st century
Special. By form
1187 Epic
Cf. PQ1309+ Old French
1189 Chansons. Chansons populaires
1191 Other forms, A-Z
1191.A3 Acrostiche
1191.A6 Air
1191.B3 Ballade
1191.B4 Bergrette
Cf. PQ1191.R6 Rondel or Rondeau
Bouts rimés see PQ1191.S7
1191.C4 Chant-royale. Serventois
1191.E6 Epigram
1191.G6 Glose
1191.I2 Iambe
1191.L3 Lai
1191.N7 Noel
1191.P3 Pantoum
1191.P4 Pastourelles

Collections of French literature
Poetry
Special. By form
Other forms, A-Z -- Continued

1191.R6 Rondel or Rondeau
1191.S4 Sestine
1191.S7 Sonnet
1191.T7 Triolet
1191.V3 Vaudeville
1191.V5 Virelai
1193.A-Z Special. By subject, A-Z
1193.A35 Aging
1193.A43 Alchemy
1193.A6 Anacreontic
1193.B74 Bread
1193.C63 City and town life
1193.C66 Cosmology
1193.C68 Colors
1193.D4 Death
1193.D5 Didactic
1193.D7 Drinking songs
1193.E7 Erotic
1193.F35 Family
1193.F56 Flowers
1193.F74 Freemasonry
1193.F8 Fugitive
1193.G3 Gastronomy
1193.H3 Happiness
1193.H6 Historical. Patriotic. Political
1193.H63 Holidays
1193.H64 Homeland
1193.I74 Islands
1193.L52 Liberty
1193.L7 Love
1193.M6 Military
1193.M65 Mills and millwork
1193.M66 Monuments
1193.M67 Motion pictures
1193.M68 Mountains
1193.M87 Music
1193.N3 Narrative
1193.N4 Nature
1193.P3 Paris
Patriotic see PQ1193.H6
1193.P45 Perfumes
Political see PQ1193.H6
1193.R4 Religious

Collections of French literature
Poetry
Special. By subject, A-Z -- Continued
Revolutionary see PQ1193.H6
1193.S3 Satirical
1193.S4 Sea
1193.S43 Seasons
1193.S7 Spring
1193.T54 Time
1193.T72 Transportation
1193.T74 Trees
1193.W37 War
1193.W5 Wine
Drama
Comprehensive collections
1211 Early through 1800
1213 1801-
1215 Selected plays. Anthologies
By period
(1217) Medieval
see PQ1341+
1219 Renaissance. 16th century
1220 17th century
1221 18th century
1222 19th century
1223 20th century
(1223.Z9) Copyright deposit, uncataloged
(1223.Z99) Plays in typewritten form
1224 21st century
Special forms
1227 Tragedies
1229 Comedies
1231 Special types, A-Z
1231.I5 Comédie italienne
1231.L3 Comédie larmoyante
1231.T7 Tragicomedy
Historical and romantic dramas
1233 General works
1235.A-Z Special types, A-Z
1235.E7 Erotic
1235.H5 Historical
1235.P2 Pastoral
1235.R4 Religious
1235.R7 Romantic
1237.A-Z Minor forms, A-Z
1237.F2 Farces
1237.F6 Théâtre de la Foire

Collections of French literature
Drama
Minor forms, A-Z -- Continued
1237.H67 Horror plays
1237.I5 Interludes. One-act plays
1237.M4 Melodramas
1237.P7 Proverbs dramatiques. Charades
1238 Amateur drama. Juvenile drama
(1239) Translations from foreign literature
(1239.A2) From several languages
see PN6113
(1239.A5-Z) From special languages, A-Z,
see classes PA - PT
Translations into foreign languages
1240.A2 Polyglot
Special languages
English
1240.E5 General
1240.E6 Tragedies
1240.E7 Comedies
1240.E8 Other
German
1240.G5 General
1240.G6 Tragedies
1240.G7 Comedies
1240.G8 Other
Italian
1240.I5 General
1240.I6 Tragedies
1240.I7 Comedies
1240.I8 Other
Portuguese
1240.P5 General
1240.P6 Tragedies
1240.P7 Comedies
1240.P8 Other
Spanish
1240.S5 General
1240.S6 Tragedies
1240.S7 Comedies
1240.S8 Other
1241.A-Z Other languages, A-Z
Prose
General works
1243 Early through 1800
1245 1800-
1247 Selections, anthologies, etc.

Collections of French literature
Prose -- Continued
By period
(1249) Old French
see PQ1391
1251 (15th-) 16th century
1252 17th century
1253 18th century
1254 19th century
1255 20th century
Prose fiction
General works
1261 Early through 1800
1262 1801-
1264 Selections. Anthologies, etc.
By period
(1265) Old French
see PQ1391
1266 (15th-) 16th century
1267 17th century
1268 18th century
1269 19th century
1271 20th century
Short stories
1274 Serials. Collections
1275 Minor collections (including school texts)
1276.A-Z Special forms, subjects, etc., A-Z
1276.B74 Brittany
1276.C34 Canada
1276.C5 Christmas
1276.D34 Decadence (Literary movement)
1276.D4 Detective and mystery stories
1276.E75 Erotic literature
1276.F3 Fantastic fiction
1276.F73 France
1276.H65 Horses
1276.M68 Mountaineering
1276.M88 Music
1276.P62 Popular literature
1276.P7 Provence
1276.R4 Religious
1276.R7 Romantic
1276.S35 Science fiction
1276.S4 Sea stories
1276.V3 Vacations
1276.V45 Vendée (France)
(1277) Translations from foreign literatures

Collections of French literature
Prose
Translations from foreign literatures -- Continued
(1277.A2) From several languages
see PN6021+
(1277.A5-Z) From special languages, A-Z,
see PA-PT
Translations into foreign languages
1278 English
1279.A-Z Other languages, A-Z
Oratory
1281 Through 1800
1283 1801-
1284 Diaries
Letters
1285 Through 1800
1286 1801-
1288 Special, A-Z
1288.L8 Love letters
For guides to writing of love letters see HQ801.5
Essays
1290 Through 1800
1291 1801-
(1293) Fables (in prose)
see PN984
1295 Wit and humor
For minor works see PN6183+
1297 Miscellaneous collections
Old French literature
Class here Old French literature to ca. 1500/1550
Collections
1300 Société des anciens texts
(1300.A5) Texts
Classify by subject
1300.B7 Bulletins
1300.B8 Compte rendu
1300.Z3 Miscellaneous publications
1300.Z5 Works about the society
1301 Comprehensive collections
Translations
1302.A2 Modern French
1302.A5-Z Other languages, A-Z
1303 General special
Including collections of wit and humor, satire, etc., in prose and verse
Special periods
1304 To 1300/50

Old French literature
Collections
Special periods -- Continued
14th-15th centuries
1305 General works
1306 15th century
Poetry
1307 General collections
Translations
1308.A2 Modern French
1308.A5-Z Other. By language
Epic and narrative
1309 General
Special
1310 National. Chansons de geste
1310.5 Franco-Italian chansons de geste
Collections of French poems, popularized in a hybrid idiom by Italian authors
For separate editions of any of these poems, see French poems
For collections of French poems, by Italian authors of this period see PQ1320
For collections of Franco-Italian poetry see PQ4213.A3Z5
1311 Épopées of the crusades
1312 Rimed chronicles
1313 Romances of antiquity
1314 Arthurian and other romances of the Épopée courtoise
1315 Romances of adventure
1316 Allegoric-didactic romances
Tales in verse
1317 Lays (Lais)
1318 Animal epics
1319 Fabliaux, contes, etc.
1320 Collections of French poems composed by Italian authors
Cf. PQ1310.5 Franco-Italian chansons de geste
Cf. PQ4213.A3Z5 Franco-Italian poetry
Lyric
1321 "Chansonniers"
Medieval collections to be arranged alphabetically by place and library
1322 Modern collections or selections
1323.A-Z Special forms of lyric verse
1323.B3 Ballades
1323.C7 Contrafacta
1323.D4 Descorts

Old French literature
Collections
Poetry
Lyric
Special forms of lyric verse -- Continued
1323.E7 Estampies
1323.J4 Jeux-partis
1323.L3 Lais (Lyric)
Cf. PQ1317 Epic poetry
1323.M7 Motets
1323.P3 Parodies
1323.P33 Pastourelles
1323.R7 Rondeaux
1323.S4 Serventois
1323.T4 Tensons
1324 Didactic (Religious, moral, allegoric-satirical, etc.)
Religious
1325.A1 General collections
1325.B5 Bible story in verse
1325.E6 Épitres farcies
Legends of saints and miracles
1325.L4 General
Special see PQ1410.2+
Legends of the Virgin see PQ1492.A1+
1325.R5 Rimed sermons
Moral
1327.A1 General collections
1327.B4 Bestiaires
1327.D5 Dits
1327.L3 Lapidaires
1328 Proverbs
Cf. PN6450+ Modern literature
1329 Fables
For special authors and works, see PQ1410.2+
Cf. PN984.A2+ Fables in the French language
1333 Allegoric-satirical
1339 Concordances, dictionaries, indexes, etc.
Drama
1341 General collections
Translations
1342.A2 Modern French
1342.A5-Z Other. By language, A-Z
Special
Mysteries and miracle plays
1343 General
Separate plays and groups of plays
12th century

Old French literature
Collections
Drama
Special
Mysteries and miracle plays
Separate plays and groups of plays
12th century -- Continued

1345.A2-.A3	Adam (Mystery)
	13th century
1346.N5	Saint Nicolas (by Jean Bodel)
1346.R4	Résurrection du Sauveur (Fragment)
1346.T5	Théophile (by Rutebeuf)
	14th century
	Miracles de Notre Dame
1347.A1	Collections
1347.A3-Z	Criticism
1348.A-Z	Separate plays, A-Z
1349.A-Z	Other special, A-Z
1349.C48	Saint Christopher
1349.G7	Griselda (Griseldis) (Mystery)
1349.J68	Jour du jugement
	15th century
	Mystère du Vieux Testament
1351	General collections
1353.A-Z	Separate mysteries, A-Z
1353.E7	Esther
1353.J6	Job (De la pacience de Job)
1353.J8	Judith
1353.O3	Octavien
1353.S5	Sibylles
1353.S8	Suzanne et Daniel
1353.T5	Tobie
1354	Job (not a part of the cycle)
	Mystère du Nouveau Testament
	Seven mysteries that contain in more or less different versions the story of Christ and that are known as "Passions"
1356	General
1357	Special parts
1357.N2	Nativité
1357.P2	Passion
	e. g.
1357.P2G8	Le mystère de la passion, by Arnoul Greban
1357.R4	Résurrection
1359	Actes des Apôtres, by Arnoul and Simon Greban
	Mysteries relating to the saints

Old French literature
Collections
Drama
Special
Mysteries and miracle plays
Separate plays and groups of plays
15th century
Mysteries relating to the saints -- Continued
Collections see PQ1343

1361.A-Z Special saints, A-Z
1361.B5 Bernard de Menthon
1361.C6 Clement
1361.D4 Denis
1361.F5 Fiacre
1361.G5 Genesius (Genis)
1361.M3 Martin
1361.N3 Nicolas
1361.Q8 Quentin
1361.R45 Remigius of Rheims
1362.A-Z Other mysteries. By author or title, A-Z
1362.M5 Milet, Jacques. Destruction of Troye
1362.M6 Criticism
1362.P74 Prophètes du Christ
1362.S2 La sainte hostie
1362.S6 Siège d'Orléans
16th century
About 20 mysteries including the Mystère de Saint Louis, by Gringore
Collections see PQ1343
1365.A-Z Special, A-Z
e. g.
1365.M6 Mystère de la passion joué à Mons, 1501
Moralities. Farces. Sotties. Monologues. Sermons joyeux, etc.
General collections
1371 To 1800
1372 1801-
Special
Moralities
For work of Adam de la Halle see PQ1411.A1+
For Le jeu du pelerin see PQ1411.A37
For Eustache Dechamps see PQ1455
1375 Collections
1377.A-Z Separate plays, A-Z
Farces and sotties
1381 Collections
1383.A-Z Separate plays, A-Z

Old French literature
Collections
Drama
Special
Moralities. Farces. Sotties. Monologues. Sermons joyeux, etc.
Special
Farces and sotties
Separate plays, A-Z -- Continued

1383.G2 Le Garçon et l'aveugle
1385 Monologues and sermons joyeux
1391 Prose

Individual authors and works
To 1350/1400
Subarrange individual works by Table P-PZ43 unless otherwise specified
Subarrange each author by Table P-PZ40 unless otherwise specified
Adam (Mystery) see PQ1345.A2+
Adam de la Halle, ca. 1235-ca. 1288 (Adam le Bossu)

1411.A1 Collected works. By date
1411.A2 Poems (Canchons, partures, etc.). By date
Single poems
1411.A23 Le congé
1411.A25 Le dit d'amour
1411.A27 Le vers de la mort
1411.A3 Plays (Collected)
1411.A33 Le jeu de la feuillée (Li jus Adan)
1411.A35 Le jeu de Robin et Marion
Spurious works
1411.A37 Le jeu du pélerin
1411.A4-.A7 Translations (Collected)
1411.A8-Z Biography and criticism
1412.A2 Adam de Saint-Victor, d. 1192 (Table P-PZ38)
1413 Adenet le Roi
1413.A1 Collected works
Separate works
(1413.A2) Berte aus grans pies
see PQ1431.B2
Bueves de Commarchis (Chanson de geste)
Title varies: Bovon de Commarcis, etc.
Cf. PQ1533.S4+ Siège de Barbastre
1413.A3 Editions of the text. By date
1413.A3A2 Modern French version
1413.A3A5-.A3Z3 Other translations. By language and translator
1413.A3Z5-.A3Z9 Criticism
Clèomadès

Old French literature
Individual authors and works
To 1350/1400
Adenet le Roi
Separate works
Clèomadès -- Continued

1413.A4 Editions of the text. By date
1413.A4A2 Modern French version
1413.A4A5-.A4Z3 Other translations. By language and translator
1413.A4Z5-.A4Z9 Criticism
(1413.A45) Enfances Ogier
see PQ1459.E6
1413.A5-.Z3 Biography and criticism
1413.Z5 Language. Style
Adgar. Legends of the Virgin see PQ1492.A1+
Aesopus see PQ1459.E82+
1417 Aimeri de Narbonne (Chanson de geste) (Table P-PZ41)
Attributed to Bertrand de Bar-sur-Aube
Aimon, Les quatre fils see PQ1503.Q2+
1419.A4-.A43 Aiol (Chanson de geste) (Table P-PZ43)
1419.A5 Alard de Cambrai, 13th cent. (Table P-PZ40)
Alberic de Besançon see PQ1421.A8
1419.A7 Alberic de Trois-Fontaines (Table P-PZ40)
Alexandre, author of Athis et Prophilias see PQ1425.A59+
Alexandre de Bernay see PQ1421.A5
1419.A8 Alexandre du Pont, 13th cent. (Table P-PZ40)
Roman de Mahomet see PQ1491.M3+
Alexandre le Grand (Poems and romances)
1421.A1 Collections. By date
1421.A11-.A19 Collections. By editor
1421.A3-.A39 Selections. By editor
1421.A4-.A49 Translations (Collections). By language
1421.A5 Roman d'Alexandre, by Lambert le Tort and Alexandre de Bernay
1421.A6 Translations. By language, A-Z
1421.A7-Z Other poems
1421.A7 Fragments in decasyllables
1421.A8 Alberic de Besançon
1421.P7 Prise de Defur
1421.V4 Vengement Alixandre, by Gui de Cambrai
1421.V6 Venjance Alixandre, by Jean le Névelon (Jean de Venelais)
Other continuations
see under their special titles

Old French literature
Individual authors and works
To 1350/1400
Alexandre le Grand (Poems and romances) -- Continued

1422 Prose romances
Translations of the Epitome of Julius Valerius and of the letter of Alexander to Aristoteles
Translations of the Historia de preliis (Published under title: L'histoire du noble et tres vaillant Alexandre le Grand)
L'histoire de Jean Wauquelin (Livre des conquestes et faits d'Alexandre le Grand)

1423 History and criticism

1424.A4-.A8 Alexius, Saint. Legend

1424.A4 Editions of the Chanson, ascribed to Tetbald, Thibaud, or Tibaud de Vernon, chanoine de Rouen, ca. 1050, and later revisions. By editor, A-Z

1424.A5 Later poems, based upon the Latin vita

Dramatizations, Medieval see PQ1361.A+

Dramatizations, Modern
see the authors, e.g. PQ1794.D39, Desfontaines

1424.A6 Prose versions (Medieval)

Criticism (of poems listed under .A4 only)

1424.A7 General

1424.A71 Language, metrics, etc.

1424.A72 Glossaries, lexicographic studies

1424.A8 Criticism of later poems and prose versions (the texts of which are in .A5 and .A6)

1425.A22-.A24 Aliscans (Chanson de geste) (Table P-PZ43a)

1425.A3-.A33 Amadas et Idoine (Table P-PZ43)

Amadís de Gaula see PQ6275.F1+

1425.A34 Ambroise, fl. ca. 1196 (Table P-PZ40)
L'estoire de la guerre sainte, histoire en vers

1425.A35-.A37 Amis et Amiles (Table P-PZ43a)

1425.A4 André de Coutances (Table P-PZ38 modified)

1425.A4A61-.A4A78 Separate works. By title
e.g. Roman des François
Roman de la résurrection (Évangile de Nicodème) see PQ1459.E92+

Anglure, Ogier, seigneur d', d. 1412? see PQ1533.S13+

1425.A44-.A442 Anseïs de Carthage (Chanson de geste) (Table P-PZ43a)

1425.A46-.A463 Anseïs de Metz (Table P-PZ43)

1425.A48-.A483 Antioche (Chanson de geste) (Table P-PZ43)

Apollonius of Tyre see PQ1485.H44+

Aquin, Roman d' see PQ1453.C57+

1425.A5-.A53 Ars d'Amour (Table P-PZ43)

Old French literature
Individual authors and works
To 1350/1400 -- Continued

	Artus, Mort d' see PQ1496.M75+
1425.A55-.A553	Artus de Bretagne (Table P-PZ43)
1425.A57-.A573	Aspremont (Chanson de geste) (Table P-PZ43)
1425.A59-.A6	Athis et Prophilias (Table P-PZ43a)
1425.A605-.A6053	Atre périlleux (Table P-PZ43)
1425.A61-.A613	L'Auberée (Fabliau) (Table P-PZ43)
1425.A62-.A623	Auberi (Chanson de geste) (Table P-PZ43)
1425.A625-.A6253	Auberi le Bourgoing (Chanson de geste) (Table P-PZ43)
1425.A63-.A633	Auberon (Chanson de geste) (Table P-PZ43)
1426	Aucassin et Nicolette
	Texts
1426.A2	By date
1426.A3A-.A3Z	By editor
	Translations
1426.A5A-.A5Z	Modern French
1426.E5A-.E5Z	English
1426.G5A-.G5Z	German
1426.I5A-.I5Z	Italian
1426.S5A-.S5Z	Spanish
1426.Z5A-.Z5Z	Criticism
1427.A74-.A743	Audigier (Poem) (Table P-PZ43)
1427.A8-.A83	Aye d'Avignon (Chanson de geste) (Table P-PZ43)
1427.B4-.B43	Barlaam and Joasaph (Table P-PZ43)
1427.B45	Barthélemy, réclus de Molliens (Table P-PZ40)
1427.B5-.B512	Bastart de Bouillon (Chanson de geste) (Table P-PZ43a)
(1427.B52)	La bataille de trente see PQ1453.C45
1427.B53-.B533	Bataille Loquifer (Chanson de geste) (Table P-PZ43)
1427.B54	Baude de la Quarière, fl. 1250 (Table P-PZ40)
1427.B55	Baudouin d'Avesnes, d. 1289 (Table P-PZ40) For chronicles attributed to him, see subclass DH
1427.B56	Baudoin de Condé (Table P-PZ40)
1427.B57	Baudoin de Flandres (Table P-PZ40)
1427.B6-.B63	Baudoin de Sebourg (Chanson de geste) (Table P-PZ43)
(1427.B7)	Beaudous see PQ1513.R7+
	Beaumanoir, Philippe de Remi, sire de, ca. 1250-1296 see PQ1501.P42
1427.B718-.B72	Belle Hélène (Romance) (Table P-PZ43a)
1429	Benoît de Sainte-More, 12th. cent.
	Roman de Troie
1429.A1	Editions. By date
1429.A15	Selections. By date

Old French literature
Individual authors and works
To 1350/1400
Benoît de Sainte-More, 12th. cent.
Roman de Troie -- Continued
1429.A18 Episodes
e.g. Troilus et Briseïda
Prose versions. Translations. Adaptations, etc.
1429.A2 French, Old. By date
1429.A25 French, Modern. By author
(1429.A26) Latin
see PA8310.C6, Colonne, Guido delle; PA8360.J7, Joseph of Exeter
1429.A27 Italian
For Medieval versions, see subclass PQ, Italian literature
1429.A3 English
For Medieval versions, see subclass PR, English literature
1429.A33 German
For Medieval versions, see subclass PT, German literature
1429.A34-.A39 Other. By language (Alphabetically)
Doubtful works
1429.A4 Histoire des ducs de Normandie, by "Maistre Beneeit"
Roman de Thèbes, see PQ1533.T5+
Énéas, Roman d' see PQ1459.E35+
1429.A7-Z Criticism
(1430.B5) Béroul (Bérol)
see PQ1537
Berte aus grans pies
1431.B2 Early texts. By date
1431.B2A3 Modern French texts. By date
1431.B2A5-.B2Z3 Other languages, A-Z
1431.B2Z5-.B2Z9 Criticism
1431.B22 Berzé, Hugues de, 1170?-1216 (Table P-PZ40)
Bertrande de Bar-sur-Aube see PQ1417
1431.B23 Béthune, Conon de, fl. 1180-1220 (Table P-PZ40)
1431.B25-.B26 Beuve de Hanstone (Chanson de geste) (Table P-PZ43a)
Beuves de Commarchis see PQ1413.A3
(1433) Bible (Translations in Old French)
see BS228
Blancandin (Romance)
1435.B2 Editions. By date
1435.B23 Prose versions. By editor, A-Z, or date
1435.B25 Criticism

Old French literature
Individual authors and works
To 1350/1400 -- Continued

1435.B3 Blondel de Nesle, 12th cent. (Table P-PZ40)
1437 Bodel, Jean, 12th cent. (Table P-PZ39 modified)
1437.A61-.Z48 Separate works. By title
Subarrange each by Table P-PZ43
Jeu Saint Nicolas see PQ1346.N5
Les Saisnes (Chansons des Saxons) see PQ1533.S2+
1439.B25 Bozon, Nicole, fl. 1300-1320 (Table P-PZ38)
1439.B27-.B273 Braies au cordelier (Table P-PZ43)
1439.B28-.B283 Branche d'armes (Table P-PZ43)
1439.B3-.B33 Brendan, Saint. Legend (Table P-PZ43)
1439.B44 Brisebarre Le Court, Jean, d. ca. 1340 (Table P-PZ40)
1439.B5-.B53 Brun de la Montaigne (Romance) (Table P-PZ43)
Bueve de Commarchis see PQ1413.A3
Bueve de Hanstone see PQ1431.B25+
Bueves de Commarchis see PQ1413.A3
1440.C26-.C263 Cantilène de sainte Eulalie (Table P-PZ43)
1440.C27-.C273 Cantique des cantiques (12th cent. poem) (Table P-PZ43)
Carité (Roman) see PQ1427.B45
Castellan de Coucy see PQ1453.C59
1440.C3-.C33 Catharina, Saint, of Alexandria. Legend (Table P-PZ43)
Les cent ballades see PQ1489.L53+
Chançun de Guillelme see PQ1477.G8+
Chanson d'Antioche see PQ1425.A48+
Chanson de Roland, see PQ1517+
1441.C3 Chardri (Anglo-Norman poet), 13th cent. (Table P-PZ38)
Charité (Roman) see PQ1427.B45
(1441.C4) Charlemagne (Chanson de geste)
see PQ1463.G7
1441.C43-.C433 Charlemagne. Voyage à Jérusalem et à Constantinople (Table P-PZ43)
1441.C44-.C45 Charles le Chauve (Chanson de geste) (Table P-PZ43a)
Charrette, Conte de la see PQ1445.L3+
1441.C5-.C513 Charroi de Nîmes (Chanson de geste) (Table P-PZ43a)
1441.C52-.C523 La chasse du cerf (Table P-PZ43)
1441.C526-.C5263 Chastie-musart (Table P-PZ43)
1441.C53-.C533 Chastoiement d'un père à son fils (Table P-PZ43)
Châtelain de Coucy (Lyric poet) see PQ1453.C59
1441.C54-.C543 Le châtelain de Coucy (Romance) (by Jakemon Sakesep) (Table P-PZ43)
1441.C55-.C553 La châtelaine de Saint Gille (Table P-PZ43)
1441.C56-.C563 La châtelaine de Vergi (Table P-PZ43)
1441.C57-.C573 Chétifs (Table P-PZ43)

Old French literature
Individual authors and works
To 1350/1400 -- Continued

1441.C58-.C583	Chevalerie Vivien (Chanson de geste) (Table P-PZ43)
1441.C6-.C612	Chevalier à l'épées (Poem) (Table P-PZ43a)
1441.C618-.C6183	Chevalier as deux épées (Romance) (Table P-PZ43)
1441.C62-.C623	Chevalier au barisel (Table P-PZ43)
1441.C63-.C6312	Chevalier au cygne (Chanson de geste) (Table P-PZ43a)
1441.C632-.C6323	Chevalier au cygne et Godefroid de Boullion (Table P-PZ43)
	Chevalier au lyon see PQ1445.Y8+
1441.C64-.C643	Chevalier de la Charrette (Prose Romance) (Table P-PZ43)
1441.C65-.C653	Chevalier du papegau (Romance) (Table P-PZ43)
	Chrestien de Troyes, 12th cent.
	Collected works
1443.A1	By date
1443.A3-Z	By editor
1444	Selections
	Translations see PQ1446+
1445.A-Z	Separate works, A-Z
	Chevalier au lyon see PQ1445.Y8+
	Chevalier de la Charratte see PQ1445.L3+
1445.C5-.C6	Cligés (Table P-PZ43a)
1445.E6-.E7	Érec et Énide (Table P-PZ43a)
1445.G2-.G3	Guillaume d'Angleterre (Table P-PZ43a)
	Ivain see PQ1445.Y8+
1445.L3-.L5	Lancelot; ou, Le chevalier de la Charrette (Table P-PZ43a)
1445.P2	Perceval le Gallois; ou, Le conte du Graal, and continuations
1445.P23	Élucidation (Prologue to the conte du Graal)
1445.P25	v. 10601-ca 21916 (Gauvain's adventure, by an unknown author)
1445.P28	v. 21916-34934 (Perceval's adventures and arrival at the castle of the Grail, by Gauchier de Dourdan or Wauchier de Denain)
1445.P3	v. 34935-45378 (Perceval's further adventures and death, by Manessier)
1445.P35	Interpolation between Gauchier's and Manessier's continuation (ca. 15,000 verses by Gerbert de Montreuil. Perceval's adventures)
1445.P4	Old and early French prose versions
1445.P7	Criticism
1445.P8-.P83	Philomena (Table P-PZ43)
1445.Y8-.Y83	Yvain; ou, Le chevalier au Lyon (Table P-PZ43)

Old French literature
Individual authors and works
To 1350/1400
Chrestien de Troyes, 12th cent. -- Continued
Translations
For translations of separate works, see the work

1446 Modern French. By translator
1447.A-Z Other languages, A-Z
Subarrange by translator, if given, or date
1447.E5 English
1447.G5 German
Criticism
1448 General (including authorship)
1449 Textual
1450.A-Z Special. By subject, A-Z
1450.C5 Civilization
1450.L6 Love
1450.M35 The marvelous
1450.R44 Religious and ethics
1450.S94 Symbolism
1450.W6 Women
1451 Language, style, etc.
1451.Z5 Glossaries, vocabulary, etc. By date
Chrestien Legouais de Sainte-Maure see PQ1445.P8+
1452.C57-.C573 Chrétienté Corbaran (Table P-PZ43)
1453.C15-.C153 Chronique saintongeaise (Table P-PZ43)
1453.C16-.C163 Ci commence doctrinal de latin en roumanz ... (Table P-PZ43)
1453.C2-.C23 Claris et Laris (Table P-PZ43)
1453.C3-.C33 Clarisse et Florent (Chanson de geste) (Table P-PZ43)
1453.C35-.C353 Clef d'amors (Anglo-Norman) (Table P-PZ43)
1453.C37 Clemence, de Barking, 12th cent. (Table P-PZ40)
Cléomadès see PQ1413.A4+
1453.C38 Clerc de Vaudoy (Table P-PZ40)
Cligès see PQ1445.C5+
1453.C45-.C453 Combat des trente (Table P-PZ43)
1453.C5-.C53 Comte de Poitiers (Romance) (Table P-PZ43)
Comtesse de Ponthieu (Romance) see PQ1485.H4+
Conon de Béthune see PQ1431.B23
1453.C56-.C563 Conquête d'Irlande (Table P-PZ43)
1453.C57-.C573 Conquête de la Bretagne (Roman d'Aquin) (Table P-PZ43)
1453.C575-.C5753 Constant Du Hamel (Fabliau) (Table P-PZ43)
Conte del Graal see PQ1465+
1453.C585-.C5853 Cort d'Amor (Table P-PZ43)
1453.C59 Coucy, Gui, châtelainde, fl. 1186-1203 (Table P-PZ40)
1453.C595 Couldrette, 14th cent. (Table P-PZ40)

Old French literature
Individual authors and works
To 1350/1400 -- Continued

1453.C6-.C613 Couronnement de Louis (Chanson de geste) (Table P-PZ43a)
Couronnement Renart see PQ1506.R2+
1453.C63-.C633 Coutois d'Arras (a play) (Table P-PZ43)
Covenant Vivien see PQ1441.C58+
1453.C7-.C73 Cristal et Clarie (Romance) (Table P-PZ43)
1453.C75-.C753 Croissant (Middle French prose version) (Table P-PZ43)
1453.C76-.C763 Croissant (Romance) (Table P-PZ43)
1453.C87 Cuvelier, trouvère, 14th cent. (Table P-PZ40)
De Thaon, Philippe see PQ1501.P44
1453.D3-.D33 Débat des hérauts d'armes de France et d'Angleterre (Table P-PZ43)
1453.D35-.D353 Débat du corps et de l'âme (Table P-PZ43)
Cf. PR1968.D6+ Middle English poem
1453.D5-.D53 Délivrance du peuple d'Israël (Table P-PZ43)
1453.D6-.D63 Denis Piramus, 12th cent. La vie seint Edmund (Table P-PZ43)
1453.D7-.D73 Départment des fils d'Aimeri (Département des enfans Aimeri) (Table P-PZ43)
Cf. PQ1496.N3+ Les Narbonnais
1455 Deschamps, Eustache, d. 1406? (Table P-PZ37)
1457.D22-.D223 Destructioun de Rome (Table P-PZ43)
1457.D25-.D252 Deu le omnipotent (Table P-PZ43a)
Dime de pénitence see PQ1486.J4
1457.D27-.D273 Dit de Guillaume d'Engleterre (Table P-PZ43)
1457.D3-.D33 Doctrinal Sauvage (Table P-PZ43)
1457.D5-.D53 Doon de la Roche (Chanson de geste) (Table P-PZ43)
Doon de Mayence (Chanson de geste)
1457.D6 Early texts. By date
1457.D6A3 Modern French texts. By date
1457.D6A5-.D6Z3 Other languages, A-Z
1457.D6Z5-.D6Z9 Criticism
1457.D7-.D73 Doon de Nanteuil (Chanson de geste) (Table P-PZ43)
1457.D74 Douin de Lavesne, 13th cent. (Table P-PZ40)
1457.D77 Dupin, Jean, 1302-1374 (Table P-PZ40)
1457.D78-.D8 Durmart le Gallois (Table P-PZ43a)
1457.D93-.D933 Dyalogue Saint Gregore (Table P-PZ43)
1459.E15-.E153 Échecs amoureux (Table P-PZ43)
Edmund, Vie de Seint see PQ1453.D6+
1459.E2 Edmund Rich, Saint, Abp. of Canterbury, d. 1240 (Table P-PZ40)
1459.E3-.D313 Élie de Saint-Gille (Chanson de geste) (Table P-PZ43a)
1459.E35-.E353 Énéas (Romance) (Table P-PZ43)

Old French literature
Individual authors and works
To 1350/1400 -- Continued

1459.E4-.E413 Enfances Garin de Montglane (Chanson de geste) (Table P-PZ43a)
1459.E43-.E433 Enfances Godefroi (Chanson de geste) (Table P-PZ43)
1459.E45-.E453 Enfances Guillaume (Chanson de geste) (Table P-PZ43)
1459.E6-.E63 Enfances Ogier (Chanson de geste) (Table P-PZ43)
1459.E7-.E73 Enfances Vivien (Chanson de geste) (Table P-PZ43)
1459.E74-.E75 Entrée d'Espagne (Chanson de geste) (Table P-PZ43a)
Éracle see PQ1463.G4
1459.E76 Erart, Jean (Table P-PZ40)
Erec (by Chrestien de Troyes) see PQ1445.E6+
1459.E77-.E773 Érec (Anonymous medieval work) (Table P-PZ43)
1459.E79-.E793 Esclarmonde (Table P-PZ43)
1459.E797-.E7973 Escommeniement au lecheor (Table P-PZ43)
1459.E8-.E813 Escoufle (Table P-PZ43a)
Esope, Ysopets
Old French translations of Aesop
Cf. PN984.A2+ Collections of fables in French
Cf. PQ1494.F2 Ysopets of Marie de France
1459.E82 Collected and selected works
1459.E83-.E834 Special works
1459.E83 Ysopet of Lyons
Paraphrase of Anonymous Neveleti
1459.E831 Ysopet I (Ysopet-Avionnet)
Paraphrases of Anonymous Neveleti and Avianus
1459.E832 Ysopet II
Paraphrase of the Novus Aesopus, by Alexander Neckham
1459.E833 Ysopet of Chartres
Another version of Ysopet II
1459.E835 Criticism. By date
Estoire dou Graal see PQ1515.A3
1459.E85 Étienne de Fougéres, Bp. of Rennes, d. 1178 (Table P-PZ40)
1459.E857 Eustache d'Amiens, 13th cent. (Table P-PZ40)
Eustache Deschamps see PQ1455
1459.E86-.E863 Eustache le Moine (Romance) (Table P-PZ43)
1459.E87-.E873 Eustachius, Saint. Legend (Table P-PZ43)
1459.E9-.E912 Évangile aux femmes (Table P-PZ43a)
Évangilede l'enfance see PQ1463.G95+
1459.E92-.E923 Évangile de Nicodème (versions rimées) (Table P-PZ43)
1459.E95 Évrat, 12th cent. (Table P-PZ40)
1461.F19-.F192 Faits des Romains (Table P-PZ43a)
1461.F196 Fantosme, Jordan, fl. 1158-1174 (Table P-PZ40)
1461.F2-.F23 Fauvel (Table P-PZ43)

Old French literature
Individual authors and works
To 1350/1400 -- Continued

1461.F25 Ferrières, Henri de, fl 1377 (Table P-PZ40)
1461.F3-.F33 Fierabras (Chanson de geste) (Table P-PZ43)
Floire et Blancheflor
1461.F4 Early texts. By date
1461.F4A3 Modern French texts. By date
1461.F4A5-.F4Z3 Other languages, A-Z
1461.F4Z5-.F4Z9 Criticism
1461.F47-.F473 Floire et Jeanne (Table P-PZ43)
1461.F5-.F513 Floovent (Chanson de geste) (Table P-PZ43a)
1461.F53-.F533 Florence de Rome (Chanson de geste) (Table P-PZ43)
1461.F55-.F553 Florent et Octavien (Chanson de geste) (Table P-PZ43)
1461.F56-.F563 Floriant et Florete (Roman) (Table P-PZ43)
1461.F59-.F593 Fou (Table P-PZ43)
1461.F6-.F63 Foulque de Candie (Romance) (Table P-PZ43)
1461.F64 Fournival, Richard de, fl. 1246-1260 (Table P-PZ40)
Freine, Simon de see PQ1533.S5
1461.F8 Froissart, Jean, 1338?-1410 (Table P-PZ40)
Cf. D, History
1461.F9-.F93 Fulk Fitz-Warine (Romance) (Table P-PZ43)
1463.G18 Gace Brulé, fl. 1200 (Table P-PZ40)
1463.G19 Gaimar, Geoffroy, 12th cent. (Table P-PZ40)
1463.G2-.G22 Galien (Romance) (Table P-PZ43a)
1463.G23-.G233 Garin de Montglane ("Guérin de Montglave") (Chanson de geste) (Table P-PZ43)
1463.G25-.G253 Garin le Loherain (Chanson de geste) (Table P-PZ43)
Cf. PQ1496.M8+ Mort Garin le Loherain
(1463.G26) Gauchier de Dourdan (Wauchier de Denain?), 13th cent. see PQ1545.W4
1463.G27-.G273 Gaufrey (Chanson de geste) (Table P-PZ43)
1463.G4 Gautier d'Arras, 12th cent. (Table P-PZ38)
1463.G42 Gautier de Belleperche, 13th cent. (Table P-PZ38)
1463.G43 Gautier de Châtillon, fl. 1170-1180 (Table P-PZ40)
1463.G44 Gautier de Coincy, 1177?-1236 (Table P-PZ40)
1463.G45 Gautier de Dargies, 13th cent. (Table P-PZ40)
1463.G48-.G483 Gaydon (Chanson de geste) (Table P-PZ43)
Gérard de Nevers see PQ1463.G5A5+
Gerbert de Montreuil, 13th cent.
Interpolation in Perceval see PQ1445.P35
Le roman de la violette
1463.G5 Editions. By date
Translations
1463.G5A2 Modern French. By date
1463.G5A21 English. By date
1463.G5A22 German. By date

Old French literature
Individual authors and works
To 1350/1400
Gerbert de Montreuil, 13th cent.
Le roman de la violette
Translations -- Continued
1463.G5A23-.G5A29 Other. By language (Alphabetically)
1463.G5A3 Criticism. By date
Prose versions (Medieval). By date
1463.G5A5-.G5Z5 French
Histoire de Gérard de Nevers et de Euryant sa mie
1463.G5A5 Editions of 1520 and reprints
1463.G5A7 Later, 1600-
1463.G5A8-.G5Z3 Translations of French prose versions. By language, A-Z
1463.G5Z5 Criticism. By date
1463.G53-.G533 Geste francor di Venezia (Table P-PZ43)
1463.G54 Gielée, Jacquemars, fl. 1280 (Table P-PZ40)
Renart le Nouvel see PQ1512.R6+
1463.G55-.G553 Gilion de Trasignyes (Romance) (Table P-PZ43)
1463.G57 Gillebert de Berneville, 13th cent. (Table P-PZ40)
1463.G6-.G63 Gilles de Chin (Romance) (Table P-PZ43)
Gilles de Trasignyes see PQ1463.G55+
1463.G7 Girard d'Amiens, 13th cent. (Table P-PZ40)
1463.G75-.G753 Girard de Roussillon (Table P-PZ43)
Cf. PC3328.G6+ Provençal literature
Cf. PC3328.G6+ Provençal literature
1463.G78-.G783 Girard de Viane (Chanson de geste) (Table P-PZ43)
1463.G8-.G83 Girnert de Metz (Chanson de geste) (Table P-PZ43)
1463.G85-.G853 Gliglois (Table P-PZ43)
1463.G86-.G863 Godefroi de Bouillon (Table P-PZ43)
1463.G87-.G873 Godin (Chanson de geste) (Table P-PZ43)
1463.G9-.G93 Gormont et Isembart (Table P-PZ43)
1463.G95-.G953 Gospels of infancy (Table P-PZ43)
1463.G98 Gower, John, 1325?-1408 (Table P-PZ40)
Grail. Legend
See also special parts of the cycle; e.g. PQ1487.J5, Joseph d'Arimathie; PQ1489.L2, Lancelot; PQ1496.M4, Merlin; PQ1496.M42, Suite de Merlin; PQ1475, La queste del saint graal; PQ1496.M75, Mort Artu
Cf. PN686.G7 Medieval literature (General)
Cf. PQ1445.P2 Chrestien de Troyes
Cf. PQ1515.A3+ Robert de Boron
1465 General collections
Prose versions
1466 Collections. By editor

Old French literature
Individual authors and works
To 1350/1400
Grail. Legend
Prose versions -- Continued

1467 Le grand Saint-Graal
1468 Le petit Saint-Graal
1472 Criticism
1475 Grail. La queste de Saint Graal (Table P-PZ41)
1476.G4 Granson, Oton de, d. 1397 (Table P-PZ40)
1476.G7-.G73 Grégoire, Vie de Saint (Table P-PZ43)
1476.G8 Grosseteste, Robert, d. 1253 (Table P-PZ38)
Guérin de Montglave see PQ1463.G23+
1477.G45 Guernes de Pont-Sainte-Maxence, 12th cent. (Table P-PZ38)
1477.G455-.G4553 Guerre de Metz en 1324 (Table P-PZ43)
1477.G5-.G53 Gui de Bourgogne (Chanson de geste) (Table P-PZ43)
1477.G55 Gui de Cambrai, 13th cent. (Table P-PZ40)
Vengement Alixandre see PQ1421.V4
1477.G6-.G63 Gui de Nanteuil (Chanson de geste) (Table P-PZ43)
1477.G65-.G653 Gui de Warwick (Romance) (Table P-PZ43)
1477.G7-.G73 Guibert d'Andreas (Chanson de geste) (Table P-PZ43)
1477.G8-.G83 Guillaume (Chanson de geste) (Table P-PZ43)
Poem of the 11th century in Norman French; also known as "Chancun de Willame"
Guillaume d' Angleterre (Metrical romance) see PQ1445.G2+
Guillaume d'Orange (Cycle of Chansons de geste)
see also special chansons of the cycle: e. g. PQ1453.C6 Couronnement de Louis; PQ1459.E45 Enfances Guillaume; PQ1477.G8 Guillaume (Chanson de geste)
1481.A2 Collections. By date
1481.A3 Collections. By editor
1481.A5-.Z4 Translations. By language, A-Z
1481.Z5 Criticism
1483.G2 Guillaume de Berneville, 12th cent. (Table P-PZ40)
Guillaume de Deguilleville, 14th cent.
Separate works
Le pélerinage de vie humaine
1483.G3A2 1st ed. (13540 verses)
1483.G3A3 2nd ed. (18126 verses)
1483.G3A4 Le pélerinage de l'âme
1483.G3A5 Le pélerinage de Jhésu Crist
1483.G3A55 Le roman des trois pèlerinages (Le pelèrinage de l'homme)
Version by Pierre Virgin
Translations

Old French literature
Individual authors and works
To 1350/1400
Guillaume de Deguilleville, 14th cent.
Translations -- Continued

1483.G3A6-.G3A9 French (Early and modern later)
1483.G3A6 Le pèlerinage de vie humaine
1483.G3A7 Le pèlerinage de l'âme
1483.G3A8 Le pèlerinage de Jhèsu Crist
1483.G3A9 Le roman des trois pèlerinages
1483.G3D6-.G3D9 Dutch
1483.G3E4-.G3E7 English
1483.G3G4-.G3G7 German
1483.G4A-.G4Z Criticism
1483.G45-.G453 Guillaume de Dole (Romance) (Table P-PZ43)
1483.G5-.G5Z Guillaume de Machaut, d. 1377 (Table P-PZ38 modified)
Collected works
Including editions of "Poésies"
1483.G5 By date
1483.G5A11-.G5A19 By editor, if given
Separate works. By title
1483.G5A67 Fonteinne amoureuse
1483.G5A68 Jugement dou roy de Behaingne
1483.G5A7 Le livre du Voir-dit
1483.G5A71 Selections
1483.G5A73 La prise d'Alexandrie
1483.G6-.G613 Guillaume de Palerne (Romance) (Table P-PZ43a)
1483.G68 Guillaume, le clerc, 13th cent. (Table P-PZ40)
1483.G7 Guillaume le Clerc, de Normandie, 13th cent. (Table P-PZ40)
1483.G75-.G753 Guillaume le Maréchal, L'histoire de (Table P-PZ43)
1483.G76 Guillaume Le Vinier, d. 1245 (Table P-PZ40)
1483.G78 Guiot de Dijon, 13th cent. (Table P-PZ40)
1483.G8 Guiot de Provins, fl. 1200 (Table P-PZ38)
1483.G83-.G833 Guiron le courtois (Table P-PZ43)
Guy of Warwick see PQ1477.G65+
1483.H3-.H33 Havelok le Danois (Romance) (Table P-PZ43)
1483.H37-.H373 Hector et Hercule (Table P-PZ43)
1483.H42-.H423 Heldris de Cornuaille (Table P-PZ43)
Hélias see PQ1441.C63+
1485.H25-.H253 Hélinandus, Cistercian monk of Froidmont, d. ca. 1229. Vers de la mort (Table P-PZ43)
1485.H28 Henri d'Andeli, 13th cent. (Table P-PZ38)
1485.H284 Henri d'Arci, 13th cent. (Table P-PZ38)
Heraclius see PQ1463.G4
1485.H286 Herbert, 13th cent. (Table P-PZ40)
1485.H288 Herman de Valenciennes, 12th cent. (Table P-PZ40)

Old French literature
Individual authors and works
To 1350/1400 -- Continued

1485.H29-.H293 Hernaut de Beaulande (Chanson de geste) (Table P-PZ43)
1485.H3-.H33 Hervis de Metz (Chanson de geste) (Table P-PZ43)
Histoire d'outre mer (La fille du comte de Pontieu)
1485.H4 Editions. By date
1485.H4A-.H4Z3 Translations. By language
1485.H4Z5 Criticism. By date
1485.H44-.H443 Histoire du noble roy Apolonie (Table P-PZ43)
1485.H53 Hue de Rotelande, fl. 1170-1190 (Table P-PZ40)
1485.H55-.H553 Hugues de Lincoln (Anglo-Norman ballad) (Table P-PZ43)
1485.H57-.H573 Hunbaut (Table P-PZ43)
1485.H58 Huon, de Saint-Quentin, 13th cent. (Table P-PZ40)
1485.H6-.H63 Huon Capet (Chanson de geste) (Table P-PZ43)
1485.H7-.H73 Huon d'Auvergne (Chanson de geste) (Table P-PZ43)
Huon de Bordeaux (Chanson de geste)
1485.H8 Editions. By date
Prose versions
French
1485.H8A2 Early to 1600. By date
1485.H8A3 Later, 1600- . By date
1485.H8A5-.Z3 Other. By language, A-Z
Subarrange by translator
1485.H8Z5-.Z99 Criticism
1485.H82 Huon de Méri, fl. 1234 (Table P-PZ40)
1485.H83 Huon le Roi, de Cambrai, 13th cent. (Table P-PZ40)
1485.H9-.H93 L'Hystore Job (Table P-PZ43)
1486.I18-.I183 Ider (Romance) (Table P-PZ43)
1486.I5-.I53 Image du monde (Table P-PZ43)
Isopets see PQ1459.E82+
Istoire d'outre mer see PQ1485.H4
Ivain see PQ1445.Y8+
1486.J16 Jacques d'Amiens, 13th cent. (Table P-PZ38)
1486.J18 Jacques de Baisieux (Table P-PZ40)
1486.J19 Jacques de Cambrai, 13th cent. (Table P-PZ40)
Jakemon Sakesep see PQ1441.C54+
Jean Bodel see PQ1437
Jean Clopinel de Meun see PQ1486.J5
1486.J25 Jean d'Arras (Table P-PZ40)
1486.J26 Jean de Conde, d. ca. 1345 (Table P-PZ40)
1486.J4 Jean de Journi, fl. 1288 (Table P-PZ40)
1486.J45 Jean de la Mote (Belgian), 14th cent. (Table P-PZ40)

Old French literature
Individual authors and works
To 1350/1400 -- Continued

1486.J5 Jean de Meun (Jean Clopinel de Meun), d. 1305? (Table P-PZ38)
Cf. PQ1527+ Roman de la Rose
Cf. PQ1545.V25+ L'art de chevallerie

1486.J55 Jean le Marchant, fl. 1262 (Table P-PZ38)

Jean le Névelon, 13th cent. Le venjance Alixandre see PQ1421.V6

Jean le Seneschal see PQ1489.L53+

Jean Priorat de Besançon see PQ1501.P7

1486.J7 Jean Renart, fl. ca. 1190-1210 (Table P-PZ40)
Cf. PQ1459.E8+ Escoufle
Cf. PQ1483.G45+ Guillaume de Dole (Romance)

1486.J8-.J83 Jehan de Lanson (Chanson de geste) (Table P-PZ43)

1486.J84 Jehan de Saint-Quentin (Table P-PZ40)

1487.J4-.J413 Jérusalem (Chanson de geste) (Table P-PZ43a)

1487.J43-.J433 Jeu d'amour (Table P-PZ43)

1487.J44-.J443 Jeu des Trois Rois (Table P-PZ43)

1487.J46-.J463 John the Evangelist (Interlude) (Table P-PZ43)

Jongleur de Notre Dame see PQ1534.T4+

1487.J47-.J473 Joseph, Histoire de (Table P-PZ43)

1487.J5-.J52 Joseph d'Arimathie (Table P-PZ43a)
Cf. PQ1515.A3 Robert de Boron

1487.J53-.J533 Joufroi de Poitiers (Table P-PZ43)

1487.J55-.J553 Jourdains de Blaivies (Chanson de geste) (Table P-PZ43)

1487.K2-.K23 Karleto (Chanson de geste) (Table P-PZ43)

Kyot see PQ1483.G8

Lai d'Havelok see PQ1483.H3+

1487.L3-.L33 Lai de l'oiselet (Table P-PZ43)

Lai de l'ombre see PQ1486.J7

1487.L35-.L353 Lai di Eliduc (Table P-PZ43)

1487.L4-.L43 Lai du cor (Table P-PZ43)

1487.L5-.L52 Le laie Bible (Table P-PZ43a)

Lambert le Tort see PQ1421.A5

1487.L53-.L533 Lassez jouer jeunes gens (Table P-PZ43)

1489.L2-.L213 Lancelot (Table P-PZ43a)
Including the Lancelot prose romance and the Lancelot-Grail prose cycle
Cf. PQ1445.L3+ Chrestien de Troyes

1489.L23-.L233 Lapidaire chrétien (Medieval French poem) (Table P-PZ43)

Lapidaires see PQ1327.L3

1489.L24 Latini, Brunetto, 1220-1295 (Table P-PZ40)

1489.L38 Leduc, Herbert de Dammartin, 13th cent. (Table P-PZ40)

Old French literature
Individual authors and works
To 1350/1400 -- Continued

1489.L4 LeFèvre, Jehan, de Ressons, 14th cent. (Table P-PZ40)
1489.L47-.L473 Lion de Bourges (Table P-PZ43)
Livre d'Artus see PQ1496.M4
Livre de chasse du roi Modus see PQ1459.E35+
Livre de la loi au Sarrazin see PQ1489.L55+
1489.L49-.L493 Livre de Sibile (Table P-PZ43)
1489.L5-.L513 Livre del juise (Table P-PZ43a)
1489.L53-.L533 Livre des cent ballades (Table P-PZ43)
Livre des manieres see PQ1459.E85
1489.L55-.L553 Livre du gentil et des trois sages (Table P-PZ43)
(1489.L6) Livre du roy Modus
see PQ1461.F25
1489.L65-.L653 Lohier et Mallart (Chanson de geste) (Table P-PZ43)
1489.L7-.L8 Les Lorrains (Geste des Lorrains) (Cycle of Chansons de geste) (Table P-PZ43a)
See also special chansons of the cycle, e.g., Garin de Loherain PQ1463.G25
1491.M18-.M183 Mabrien (Table P-PZ43)
1491.M2-.M213 Macaire (Chanson de geste) (Table P-PZ43a)
1491.M23 Macé de la Charité, curé, 13th cent. (Table P-PZ40)
1491.M28 Mahieu le Poirier (Table P-PZ40)
1491.M3-.M33 Mahomet, Roman de (Table P-PZ43)
1491.M4-.M413 Mainet (Chanson de geste) (Table P-PZ43a)
Maisières, Païens de see PQ1501.P13
1491.M42 Malkaraume, Jehan (Table P-PZ40)
(1491.M7) Manessier (Manecier, Mannecier, Mennessier), 13th cent.
Continuation of Perceval see PQ1445.P3
1491.M85 Marie, Anglo-Norman nun, 13th cent. (Table P-PZ40)
Marie la Vierge (Legends)
1492.A1 Collections and selections of various legends
(1492.A3-Z) Particular legends
See individual titles; e.g. PQ1501.P55, Plaintes de la Vierge
Marie de France, 12th cent.
Collected editions
1494.A1 By date
1494.A11-.A19 By editor
Translations
1494.A2A-.A2Z Modern French. By translator
1494.A3A-.A3Z English. By translator
1494.A4A-.A4Z German. By translator
1494.A5A-.A5Z Other. By language
Separate works

Old French literature
Individual authors and works
To 1350/1400
Marie de France, 12th cent.
Separate works -- Continued

1494.F2 Fables (Ésope, Ysopet)
1494.F3A-Z Translations
1494.F5A-Z Special fables, A-Z
1494.F7A-Z Criticism
1494.L2 Lais
1494.L3A-Z Translations
1494.L5A-Z Separate lais, A-Z
Évangile aux femmes see PQ1459.E9+
1494.L7A-Z Criticism
1494.P3 Purgatoire de Saint Patrice
1495 Biography and criticism
1496.M2-.M23 Marie l'Égyptienne, Vie de Sainte (Table P-PZ43)
1496.M25-.M253 Marie-Madeleine, Vie de Sainte (Table P-PZ43)
1496.M3-.M33 Marques de Rome (Romance) (Table P-PZ43)
1496.M35-.M353 Maugis d'Aigremont (Chanson de geste) (Table P-PZ43)
1496.M39-.M393 Méliadus de Leonnoys (Table P-PZ43)
Méraugis de Portlesguez see PQ1505.R22A2
1496.M4 Merlin (Prose romance)
Cf. PQ1515.A4 Robert de Boron
1496.M42 Suite de Merlin
1496.M44 Prophecies de Merlin
1496.M47 Milet, Jacques, d. 1466 (Table P-PZ40)
Destruction de Troye see PQ1362.M5
Miserere de réclus de Molliens see PQ1427.B45
1496.M6-.M63 Moniage Guillaume (Chanson de geste) (Table P-PZ43)
1496.M65-.M653 Moniage Rainouart (Chanson de geste) (Table P-PZ43)
1496.M7-.M73 Mort Aimeri de Narbonne (Chanson de geste) (Table P-PZ43)
1496.M75-.M753 Mort Artu (Table P-PZ43)
1496.M8-.M83 Mort Garin le Loherain (Chanson de geste) (Table P-PZ43)
Cf. PQ1463.G25+ Garin le Loherain
1496.M85 Mousket, Philippe, 13th cent. (Table P-PZ40)
Mule sans frain see PQ1501.P13
1496.M95 Muset, Colin, 13th cent. (Table P-PZ40)
1496.N27-.N273 La Naissance du Chevalier au cygne (Table P-PZ43)
1496.N3-.N313 Les Narbonnais (Chanson de geste) (Table P-PZ43a)
Cf. PQ1453.D7+ Département des fils d'Aimeri
1496.N33-.N333 Narcissus (Table P-PZ43)
1496.N37 Niccoló, da Verona, fl. 1343 (Table P-PZ40)
Nicodème, Évangile de see PQ1459.E92+
Nicole Bozon see PQ1439.B25

Old French literature
Individual authors and works
To 1350/1400 -- Continued

1497.N4	Nicole de Margival (Table P-PZ40)
1499.O2-.O23	Octavian, empereur de Rome (Romance) (Table P-PZ43)
1499.O3-.O33	Ogier le Danois (Chanson de geste) (Table P-PZ43)
	Cf. PQ1459.E6+ Enfances Ogier
1499.O4-.O43	Orson de Beauvais (Chanson de geste) (Table P-PZ43)
1499.O5-.O53	Otinel (Chanson de geste) (Table P-PZ43)
1499.O9-.O93	Ovide moralisé (Table P-PZ43)
1501.P13	Païens de Maisières, 13th cent. (Table P-PZ40)
1501.P15-.P153	Palamède (Romance) (Table P-PZ43)
1501.P18	Paris, Matthew, 1200-1259 (Table P-PZ40)
1501.P2-.P23	Parise la duchesse (Chanson de geste) (Table P-PZ43)
1501.P25-.P253	Partonopeus de Blois (Table P-PZ43)
1501.P27-.P273	Passion de Jesu Christ (Old French poems) (Table P-PZ43)
1501.P2745-.P27453	Passion des jongleurs (Table P-PZ43)
1501.P275-.P2753	La Passiun de Seint Edmund (Table P-PZ43)
1501.P28-.P283	Pénitence d'Adam (Table P-PZ43)
1501.P3-.P32	Perceforest (Table P-PZ43a)
1501.P33-.P333	Perceval ("Didot-Perceval") (Table P-PZ43)
	Perceval le Gallois see PQ1445.P2
1501.P35-.P353	Perlesvaus (Romance) (Table P-PZ43)
1501.P38	Perrin d'Angicourt, 13th cent. (Table P-PZ40)
1501.P42	Philippe de Remi, sire de Beaumanoir, d. 1296 (Table P-PZ38)
1501.P44	Philippe de Thaon, fl. 1120 (Table P-PZ40)
1501.P46	Philippe de Vitry, 1291-1361 (Table P-PZ40)
	Cf. PQ1499.O9+ Ovide moralisé
	Philippe Mousket see PQ1496.M85
1501.P5	Philippe, of Novara, 13th cent. (Table P-PZ40)
	For memoirs see D181.P5
1501.P52	Pierre de Beauvais, 13th cent. (Table P-PZ40)
1501.P53-.P533	Pierre de Provence et Maguelonne (Table P-PZ43)
1501.P55-.P553	Plaintes de la Vierge (Table P-PZ43)
1501.P59-.P593	La Poissance d'amours (Table P-PZ43)
1501.P6-.P63	Ponthus et Sidoine (Table P-PZ43)
1501.P7	Priorat, Jean, d. 1290? (Table P-PZ40)
1501.P75-.P753	Prise d'Orange (Chanson de geste) (Table P-PZ43)
1501.P8-.P83	Prise de Cordres et de Sebille (Chanson de geste) (Table P-PZ43)
1501.P85-.P853	Prise de Pampalune (Chanson de geste) (Table P-PZ43)
1501.P87-.P873	Pseudo-Turpin. Anglo-Norman and early French translations (Table P-PZ43)
1501.P9-.P93	Pyrame et Thisbé (Piramus et Tisbé) (Table P-PZ43)
1503.Q2-.Q23	Quatre fils Aimon (Chanson de geste) (Table P-PZ43)

Old French literature
Individual authors and works
To 1350/1400 -- Continued

1503.Q3-.Q4 Quatre livres des Rois (Table P-PZ43a)
Quête saint graal, see PQ1475
Rainouart (Chanson de geste) see PQ1481.A2+
1505.R18 Raoul, trouvère, 13th cent. (Table P-PZ40)
1505.R2-.R213 Raoul de Cambrai (Chanson de geste) (Table P-PZ43a)
1505.R22 Raoul de Houdenc, 13th cent.
1505.R22A2 Meraugis de Portlesguez
1505.R22A3 La vengeance de Raguidel
1505.R22A4-.R22A7 Translations. By language, A-Z
1505.R22A8-.R22Z Criticism (regardless of individual works)
1505.R42-.R423 Récits d'un ménestrel de Reims (Table P-PZ43)
1506.R2-.R23 Renart, Couronnement de (Table P-PZ43)
Renart, Roman de
1507.A1 Editions. By date
1507.A3 Selections. By editor, A-Z
1508.A1-.A26 Special branches. By date
Translations
1508.A3 Modern French. By translator, A-Z
1508.A5-Z Other languages, A-Z
1509 Criticism
1510 Language. Versification
1511 Glossaries
Renart bestourné see PQ1532.R7
1512.R4-.R43 Renart le contrefait (Table P-PZ43)
1512.R6-.R63 Renart le Nouvel (by Jacquemars Gielée) (Table P-PZ43)
1512.R8 Renaud de Beaujeu (Table P-PZ40)
Renaut de Montauban see PQ1503.Q2+
1513.R2-.R23 Renier (Chanson de geste) (Table P-PZ43)
1513.R3-.R313 Renier de Genève (Gennes) (Chanson de geste) (Table P-PZ43a)
(1513.R32) Résurrection
see PQ1346.R4; PQ1357.R4
1513.R33 Richard, le Pèlerin, 12th cent. (Table P-PZ40)
Richard de Fournival see PQ1461.F64
1513.R34-.R343 Richard sans peur (Romance) (Table P-PZ43)
1513.R345-.R3453 Richars li Biaus (Table P-PZ43)
1513.R348-.R3483 Richeut (Table P-PZ43)
1513.R5-.R53 Rigomer (Romance) (Table P-PZ43)
Robert Biguet (Biket), 13th cent. see PQ1487.L4+
Robert de Blois, 13th cent.
1513.R7 Collected works. By date
Separate works
1513.R7A2 Beaudous
1513.R7A3 Chastiement des dames

Old French literature
Individual authors and works
To 1350/1400
Robert de Blois, 13th cent.
Separate works -- Continued
1513.R7A4 Enseignement des princes
1513.R7A5 Floris et Liriope
Translations
1513.R7A7 Modern French. By date
1513.R7A8-.R7Z Other. By language and date
1513.R8 Biography and criticism
Robert de Boron, 13th cent.
1515.A3 Roman de l'Estoire dou Graal. Joseph d'Arimathie (Romance in verse)
1515.A4 Merlin (Romance in verse)
1515.A5 Prose romances (Spurious)
Joseph d'Arimathie, Merlin, etc., see PQ1487.J5, PQ1496.M42, etc.
1515.A6 Translations. Adaptations, etc. By language and date
1515.A7-Z Biography and date
1516.R3 Robert de Ho, 13th cent. (Table P-PZ40)
1516.R6 Robert de Rains, called La Chievre (Li Kievre), 13th cent. (Table P-PZ40)
1516.R7-.R73 Robert le Diable (Romance) (Table P-PZ43)
1516.R8 Roger d'Andeli, fl. 1200 (Table P-PZ40)
Roland (Chanson de Roland)
1517 Editions
1517.A2 By date
1517.A5-Z By editor, A-Z
1518 Selections, extracts, etc.
Translations
1520.A-Z Modern French. By author, A-Z
1521.A-Z Other. By language and translator, A-Z
1521.E5 English
1521.G3 German
Criticism
1522 General
1523 Special. Textual, etc.
1524.A-Z Special topics, A-Z
1524.C4 Characters
1524.C65 Combat
1524.D7 Dreams
1524.E8 Ethos
1524.G35 Ganelon (Legendary character)
1524.G46 Geography
1524.L3 Law
1524.N8 Numbers

Old French literature
Individual authors and works
To 1350/1400
Roland (Chanson de Roland)
Criticism
Special topics, A-Z -- Continued

1524.S67 Spain
1525 Language, grammar, versification
1525.A-.Z3 Treatises
1525.Z7A-Z Versifications
1525.Z9 Glossaries. By date

Roman d' Auberon see PQ1425.A63+

1526.R6-.R63 Roman de Cardenois (Table P-PZ43)
1526.3 Roman de Jules César (Table P-PZ41)

Roman de Floriant et Florete see PQ1461.F56+

Roman de la Rose
Editions

1527.A1 By date
1527.A2-.A49 By editor
1527.A5 Parts, selections, etc.

Translations

1528.A2-.A29 Modern French
1528.A4-.A49 English
1528.A5-.A59 German
1528.A6-.A69 Other. By language

Criticism

1528.A8-Z General
1529 Special
e.g. Social life and customs
1530.A3A-.A3Z Textual. Manuscripts, etc.
1530.A6-Z Grammar. Metrics. Style
1531 Dictionaries. Glossaries

Roman de la Rose, ou Guillaume de Dole see PQ1483.G45+
Roman de la violette see PQ1463.G492+

1532.R3-.R33 Roman de Laurin (Table P-PZ43)
1532.R34-.R343 Roman de messire Charles de Hongrie (Table P-PZ43)

Roman de Mahomet see PQ1491.M3+
Roman de Renart see PQ1507+
Roman de sept sages de Rome see PQ1533.S3+

1532.R6-.R613 Roman du lis (Table P-PZ43a)
1532.R62-.R623 Romance du Sire de Créqui (Table P-PZ43)
1532.R625-.R6253 Rosarius (Table P-PZ43)

Rose, Roman de la see PQ1527+

1532.R64-.R643 Rossignol (Table P-PZ43)
1532.R65 Rusticiano da Pisa, 13th cent. (Table P-PZ40)
1532.R7 Rutebeuf, 13th cent. (Table P-PZ38)

	Old French literature
	Individual authors and works
	To 1350/1400
	Rutebeuf -- Continued
	Théophile see PQ1346.T5
1533.S126-.S1263	St. Patrick's Purgatory (Legend) (Table P-PZ43)
	Cf. PQ1494.P3 Marie de France
1533.S13-.S133	Saint voyage de Jherusalem du Seigneur d'Anglure (Table P-PZ43)
	La sainte hostie (Mystère) see PQ1362.S2
1533.S2-.S213	Les Saisnes (Chanson des Saxons) (Table P-PZ43a)
1533.S3-.S33	Sept sages de Rome (Table P-PZ43)
	Cf. PA8430.A1 Latin versions
1533.S34-.S343	Sermone di Valenciennes (Table P-PZ43)
	Seven sages of Rome see PQ536+
	Siège d'Orléans (Mystère) see PQ1362.S6
1533.S4-.S43	Siège de Barbastre (Chanson de geste) (Table P-PZ43)
	Cf. PQ1413.A3+ Adenet le Roi's Bueves de Commarchis
	Siège de Narbonne (Chanson de geste) see PQ1496.N3+
1533.S45-.S453	Simon de Pouille (Table P-PZ43)
1533.S5	Simund de Freine, fl. 1200 (Table P-PZ40)
1533.S55-.S553	Sires de Gavre (Table P-PZ43)
1533.S64-.S643	Sone de Nansay (Roman d'aventures) (Table P-PZ43)
1533.T4-.T43	Terrier l'Evêque (Table P-PZ43)
1533.T5-.T52	Thèbes (Romance) (Table P-PZ43a)
1533.T53-.T533	Theobaldus of Provins, Saint, d. 1066. Legend (Table P-PZ43)
1533.T6	Thibaud I, king of Navarre, 1201-1253 (Table P-PZ40)
	Thibaud IV, conte de Champagne see PQ1533.T6
1533.T62	Thibaut, Messire, 13th cent. (Table P-PZ40)
1533.T63	Thibaut de Blaison, d. 1229 (Table P-PZ40)
1533.T65	Thierry de Vaucoulerus, 13th cent. (Table P-PZ40)
	Thomas, Anglo-Norman poet see PQ1544.T3+
1533.T735	Thomas, Mestre (Table P-PZ40)
1533.T74	Thomas of Kent, fl. 13th cent. (Table P-PZ40)
1533.T75-.T753	Tombel de Chartrose (Table P-PZ43)
	Tombeor Nostre Dame
1534.T4	Editions. By date
1534.T4A2	Modern French
1534.T4E5	English translations
1534.T5	Criticism
	Tristan
1535	Collections and selections
1537	Poem by Béroul (Bérol) (Table P-PZ41)
1538	Poem by Thomas (Table P-PZ41)

Old French literature
Individual authors and works
To 1350/1400
Tristan -- Continued

1539 La folie Tristan (Table P-PZ41)
1540.A-Z Other poems, A-Z
1541 Prose romances. By editor or date
1542 Translations. Paraphrases, etc.
1542.A2A-Z Modern French
1542.E5A-Z English
1542.G3A-Z German
1543 History and criticism
1544.T3-.T33 Tristan de Nanteuil (Chanson de geste) (Table P-PZ43)
1544.T83-.T833 Trois morts et trois vifs (Table P-PZ43)
1545.V25-.V253 Vegetius Renatus, L'art de chevalerie (Translation by Jean de Meun) (Table P-PZ43)
1545.V3-.V33 Vengeance de la mort de Nostre Seigneur (Table P-PZ43)
1545.V4-.V413 Vengence de Raguidel (Table P-PZ43a)
Vengement Alixandre see PQ1421.V4
1545.V42-.V423 Ver de Couloigne (Table P-PZ43)
1545.V424-.V4243 Ver del juïse (Table P-PZ43)
1545.V426-.V4263 Vie de Marine d'Egipte viergene (Table P-PZ43)
1545.V427-.V4273 Vie de saint Evroul (Table P-PZ43)
1545.V428-.V4283 Vie de saint Georges (Table P-PZ43)
1545.V43-.V433 Vie de saint Laurent (Table P-PZ43)
1545.V434-.V4343 Vie de Sainte Marguerite (Table P-PZ43)
1545.V44-.V443 Vie des anciens pères (Table P-PZ43)
1545.V445-.V4453 La Vie Saint Jehan-Baptiste (Table P-PZ43)
1545.V45-.V453 La vie Saint Julien martir (Table P-PZ43)
1545.V47-.V473 Vilain mire (Fabliau) (Table P-PZ43)
1545.V475 Villehardouin, Geoffroi de, d. ca 1212 (Table P-PZ40)
Conquête de Constantinople. Biography and criticism only. Texts to be classed in D164.A3V
Violette, Roman de la see PQ1463.G492+
1545.V5-.V53 Vita Pylati (Table P-PZ43)
1545.V54-.V543 Vivien de Monbranc (Table P-PZ43)
1545.V63-.V633 Voeux du héron (Table P-PZ43)
Voyage de Charlemagne à Jérusalem et à Constantinople see PQ1441.C43+
1545.V68-.V683 Voyage du puys Sainct Patrix (Table P-PZ43)
1545.W2 Wace, fl. 1170
1545.W2A6 Roman de Brut
1545.W2A7 Roman de Rou
1545.W2A77 Vie de St. Nicolas
1545.W2A8-Z Biography and criticism

Old French literature
Individual authors and works
To 1350/1400 -- Continued

1545.W4 Wauchier de Denain (= Gauchier de Dourdan?) 13th cent. (Table P-PZ40)
Gauchier de Dourdan's continuation of Perceval see PQ1445.P3
Willame (Chanson de geste) see PQ1477.G8+
1545.Y4-.Y43 Yde et Olive (Table P-PZ43)
Yder (Romance) see PQ1486.I18+
1545.Y5-.Y53 Yon (Chanson de geste) (Table P-PZ43)
Yonet, Yonnet de Metz, etc.
1545.Y8-.Y83 Ystoire de la passion (Old French poem) (Table P-PZ43)
Yzopet see PQ1459.E82+

(14th-) 15th century (to ca. 1525)
Subarrange individual works by Table P-PZ43 unless otherwise specified
Subarrange each one-number author by Table P-PZ37 unless otherwise specified
Subarrange each Cutter-number author by Table P-PZ38 unless otherwise specifiec

1551.A2-.A23 L'abusé en court (Table P-PZ43)
1551.A4 Antitus, d. ca. 1501 (Table P-PZ40)
1551.A4 Alexis, Guillaume, prieur de Bucy, d. 1486 (Table P-PZ40)
L'amant rendu cordelier see PQ1571.M3A3
Antoine de la Sale see PQ1567+
1551.A9 Aubert, David, fl. 1458-1479 (Table P-PZ40)
Auvergne, Martial see PQ1571.M3
1551.B28-.B283 The Baptism and temptation of Christ (Table P-PZ43)
1551.B3 Basselin, Olivier, 15th cent. (Table P-PZ38)
1551.B4 Baude, Henri, 15th cent. (Table P-PZ40)
1551.B7 Bonet, Honoré, fl. 1378-1398 (Table P-PZ40)
1551.B9 Bueil, Jean de comte de Sancerre, 1406-1477 (Table P-PZ40)
1553.C3-.C33 Cent nouvelles nouvelles (Table P-PZ43)
1553.C45 Champier, Symphorien, 1472?-ca. 1535 (Table P-PZ40)
1553.C5 Charles d'Orléans, 1394-1465 (Table P-PZ38)
Chartier, Alain, 15th cent.
Collected works
1557.A1 By date
1557.A11-.A19 By editor
1557.A2A-Z Modern French. By translator
Translations
1557.A3A-.A3Z English. By translator
1557.A4A-.A4Z German. By translator
1557.A5A-.A5Z Other. By translator

Old French literature
Individual authors and works
(14th-) 15th century (to ca. 1525)
Chartier, Alain, 15th cent. -- Continued

1557.A6-Z Separate works
1557.B3-.B4 Belle dame sans merci (Table P-PZ43a)
1557.B5-.B7 Breviaire des nobles (Table P-PZ43a)
1557.C5-.C53 Complainte contre la mort (Table P-PZ43)
Consolation des trois vertus see PQ1557.E5+
1557.C8-.C83 Le curial (Table P-PZ43)
1557.D3-.D33 De plaisance (Table P-PZ43)
1557.D4-.D43 Debat des deux fortunés d'amours (Table P-PZ43)
1557.D5-.D53 Debat du reveille-matin (Table P-PZ43)
1557.E5-.E6 L'esperance; ou, Consolation des trois vertus (Table P-PZ43a)
1557.E9-.E93 Excusation (Table P-PZ43)
1557.L2-.L23 Lai de la paix (Table P-PZ43)
1557.L5-.L6 Livre des quatre dames (Table P-PZ43a)
1557.Q2-.Q23 Quadrilogue invectif (Table P-PZ43)
1558 Biography and criticism
1559.C5 Chastellain, Georges, 1405?-1475 (Table P-PZ38)
Collected works and Chroniques see DC611.B78
1559.C52 Chastellain, Pierre, b. ca. 1408 (Table P-PZ38)
1559.C525 Chevalet, maistre (Claude), 15th-16th cent. (Table P-PZ38)
1559.C53-.C533 Chevalier aux dames
Christine de Pisan see PQ1575
1559.C55-.C553 Cleriadus et Meliadice
1559.C56 Col, Gontier, 1354?-1418 (Table P-PZ38)
1559.C59-.C593 Concil de Basle (Table P-PZ43)
1559.C6 Coquillart, Guillaume, ca. 1450-1510 (Table P-PZ38)
Crétin Guillaume Dubois, called see PQ1607.C7
1561.D36-.D363 Dance of death (Table P-PZ43)
1561.D58-.D583 Dit du prunier (Table P-PZ43)
1561.E93-.E94 Evangiles de Quenouilles (Table P-PZ43a)
1561.F4 Fillastre, Guillaume, d. 1473 (Table P-PZ38)
1561.G37 Garin, François, ca. 1413-ca. 1460 (Table P-PZ40)
1561.H33 Hauteville, Pierre de, 1376-1448 (Table P-PZ40)
1561.H45-.H453 Heures de la Passion
Histoire de Gérard de Nevers see PQ1463.G5A5+
1561.H57-.H58 Histoire de la première destruction de Troie (Table P-PZ43a)
1563.J3-.J33 Jean de Paris (Romance) (Table P-PZ43)
1563.J34-.J343 Jehan d'Avennes (Romance) (Table P-PZ43)
1565.L2 La Marche, Olivier de, d. 1502
1565.L2A6-.L2A79 Separate works
1565.L2A65 Le chevalier deliberé

Old French literature
Individual authors and works
(14th-) 15th century (to ca. 1525)
La Marche, Olivier de, d. 1502
Separate works
Le chevalier deliberé -- Continued
1565.L2A68 Spanish translation
Le parement des dames see PQ1565.L2A75
1565.L2A75 Le triumphe des dames
Mémoires see DC611.B781
Vie de Philippe le Hardi see DC611.B78
1565.L2A8-Z Biography and criticism
La Sale, Antoine de, b. 1388
Collected editions
1567.A1 By date
1567.A11-.A19 By editor
Translations
1567.A2A-.A2Z Modern French. By translator
1567.A3A-.A3Z English. By translator
1567.A4A-.A4Z German. By translator
1567.A5A-.A5Z Other. By translator
Separate works
Cent nouvelles nouvelles see PQ1553.C3+
1567.H2-.H9 L'histoire et plaisante chronique du petit Jehan de Saintré
1567.H2 Editions. By date
Translations
1567.H2A-.H2Z Modern French. By translator
1567.H3A-.H3Z English. By translator
1567.H4A-.H4Z German. By translator
1567.H7A-.H7Z Other. By translator
1567.H9 Criticism
1567.J2-.J23 La journée d'onneur et de prouesse (Table P-PZ43)
La Salade see D17
Les quinze joyes de mariage
1567.Q2 Editions. By date
Translations
1567.Q2A-.Q2Z Modern French. By translator
1567.Q3A-.Q3Z English. By translator
1567.Q4A-.Q4Z German. By translator
1567.Q7A-.Q7Z Other. By translator
1567.Q9 Criticism
1568 Biography and criticism
1569.L2 La Vigne, André de, ca. 1457-ca. 1527 (Table P-PZ40)
1570 Lefèvre, Raoul, fl. 1460 (Table P-PZ37 modified)
1570.A7 Recueil des hystoires de Troyes
1570.A75 Roamn de Jason et Médée

Old French literature
Individual authors and works
(14th-) 15th century (to ca. 1525) -- Continued

1571.L3 Le Franc, Martin, d. 1461 (Table P-PZ40)
1571.L417-.L4173 Livre de Alixandre, empereur de Constentinoble et de Cligés son filz (Table P-PZ43)
1571.L42-.L423 Le Livre de l'amoureuse alliance (Table P-PZ43)
1571.L5-.L53 Le livre du faulcon (Table P-PZ43)
Lemaire de Belges, Jean see PQ1628.L5
1571.L55-.L553 Livre des fais du bon messire Jehan Le Maigre, dit Bouciquaut (Table P-PZ43)
1571.M3 Martial d'Auvergne, d. 1508
1571.M3A3 L'amant rendu cordelier
1571.M3A33 English translations
1571.M3A34 German translations
1571.M3A35 Other translations
1571.M3A4 Arrests d'amour
1571.M3A5 Grant danse macabre des femmes
1571.M3A7 Louanges à la Vierge Marie
1571.M3A76 Vigilles de la mort du roy Charles VII
Martial de Paris see PQ1571.M3
Martin le Franc see PQ1571.L3
1571.M4 Meschinot, Jean, sieur des Mortières, ca. 1420-1491 (Table P-PZ38)
1571.M45 Michault, Pierre, 15th cent. (Table P-PZ40)
1571.M47 Michault, Taillevent, d. ca. 1450 (Table P-PZ40)
1571.M5 Michel, Jean, fl. 1486 (Table P-PZ38)
1571.M52 Miélot, Jean, 15th cent. (Table P-PZ40)
1571.M6-.M63 Le miroir aux dames (Table P-PZ43)
1571.M7 Molinet, Jean, d. 1507 (Table P-PZ38)
1571.M8 Montgesoie, Amé de, 15th cent. (Table P-PZ38)
1571.M83-.M833 Moralité des blasphémateurs de Dieu (Table P-PZ43)
1571.M85-.M853 Le mors de la põme (Table P-PZ43)
1571.M95-.M953 Mystère de Judith et Holofernés (Table P-PZ43)
1571.M97-.M973 Mystère de sainte Venice (Table P-PZ43)
1572.N4 Nesson, Pierre de, 1383-1439? (Table P-PZ40)
1572.O6-.O63 Olivier de Castille (Table P-PZ43)
1572.P355-.P3553 Pas de Saumur (Table P-PZ43)
1572.P36-.P363 Passion de Semur (Table P-PZ43)
1572.P37-.P373 Pastoralet (Table P-PZ43)
1572.P4-.P43 Le pâté et la tarte (Farce) (Table P-PZ43)
1573 Pathelin (Maistre Pierre Pathelin, farce, ca. 1469)

Old French literature
Individual authors and works
(14th-) 15th century (to ca. 1525)
Pathelin (Maistre Pierre Pathelin, farce, ca. 1469) -- Continued

1573.A1 Editions. By date
Including editions containing also Nouveau Pathelin and Testament de Pathelin
Facsimile reproductions by date of original with addition of letters a, b, c, etc., for century of reproduction, d for 19th e for 20th etc.

1573.A2-.A29 Editions without date
Arrange by place of publication

1573.A3 Le nouveau Pathelin (ca 1474)

1573.A35 Le testament de Pathelin (end of 15th century)

Imitations. Adaptations. Librettos, etc.
see the author

1573.A5-.A69 Translations. By language and date

1573.A55 English

1573.A7-Z Criticism

1574.P53 Pierre, de la Cépède, 15th cent. (Table P-PZ38)

1575 Pisan, Christine de, ca. 1363-ca. 1431 (Table P-PZ39)

1577.P8-.P83 Le prisonnier desconforté du château de Loches (Table P-PZ43)

1577.P87-.P873 Purgatoire d'amours (Table P-PZ43)

1577.R34 Raffaele, da Verona, fl. 1379-1407 (Table P-PZ40)

1579 René I, d'Anjou, king of Naples and Jerusalem, 1409-1480

1579.A1 Collected works. By date

1579.A6-.A79 Separate works

1579.A8-Z Criticism

1580.R6 Robertet, Jean, d. 1503 (Table P-PZ38)

1580.S4 Saint-Gelais, Octovien de, 1468-1502 (Table P-PZ38)

1581.S25 Sala, Pierre, ca. 1457-1529 (Table P-PZ38)

(1581.S8) Surville, Clotilde de, 1405-1492
Original poems lost
For the poems purporting to have been written by her see PQ2066.S9

1581.T45 Thomas III, marquis de Saluces, ca. 1356-1416 (Table P-PZ38)

1581.T76-.T763 Trois fils de rois (Table P-PZ43)

1581.V35-.V353 Valentin et Orson (French romance) (Table P-PZ43)

1581.V4-.V5 Vie de Sainte Valérie (Table P-PZ43a)

1581.V54 Villebresmes, Berthault de, 15th cent. (Table P-PZ38)

Villon, François, b. 1431

1590.A15 Facsimiles of manuscripts. By date of facsimile

Works (Collections and selections)

Old French literature
Individual authors and works
(14th-) 15th century (to ca. 1525)
Villon, François, b. 1431
Works (Collections and selections) -- Continued

1590.A2 By date
1590.A21 By editor
Separate works
1590.A3 Jargon (Jobelin). By date
1590.A4 Le grant testament. By date
1590.A5 Le petit testament (Les lais). By date
1590.A6A-.A6Z Other works, A-Z
Translations
1590.A7 Modern French. By translator, A-Z
1590.A8-Z Other languages. By language and translator (regardless of individual works)
1590.E5P3 English by John Payne
1593 Biography and criticism
1595.V55-.V553 Visio Tnugdali (Table P-PZ43)

Modern French literature
Collections see PQ1121
Individual authors
16th century

1600 Anonymous works (Table P-PZ28 modified)
1600.A6A-.A6Z Works by authors indicated by a descriptive phrase. By first word of phrase, A-Z
Satyre Menippée see PQ1704
1601.A2 Abundance, Jehan d', 16th cent. (Table P-PZ40)
Alcripe, Philippe d' 16th cent. see PQ1628.L57
1601.A4 Alione, Giovanni Giorgio, ca. 1460-ca. 1521 (Table P-PZ38)
1601.A46 Amboise, François d', 1550-1620 (Table P-PZ38)
Amyot, Jacques, Bp. of Auxerre, 1513-1593
Including translations of Greek works
1601.A5 Editions (Comprehensive, or selected works). By date
Separate works
1601.A5A3 Translation of Diodorus. Sept livres des histoires
1601.A5A4 Translation of Heliodorus. L'histoire éthiopique ... amours de Thëagenes et Chariclée
1601.A5A5 Translation of Longus. Les amours pastorales de Daphnis et de Chloé
Translations of Plutarch
1601.A5A6 Comprehensive or selected works
1601.A5A7 Oeuvres morales
1601.A5A73 Selected treatises
1601.A5A75 Selections. Passages. Thoughts

Modern French literature
Individual authors
16th century
Amyot, Jacques, Bp. of Auxerre, 1513-1593
Editions (Comprehensive, or selected works). By date
Separate works
Translations of Plutarch
Oeuvres morales -- Continued
1601.A5A8-.A5Z Separate treatises (by French title)
e. g.
1601.A5D4 Sur les délais de la justice divine
Les vies des hommes illustres grecs et romains
1601.A6 Editions. By date
1601.A6A3 Selections
1601.A6A5-.A6Z Separate parts (by first named subject)
1601.A7 Biography and criticism
1601.A74 Aneau, Barthélemy, d. 1561 (Table P-PZ38)
1602.A37 Arena, Antoine d', d. 1544 (Table P-PZ38)
1602.A4 Artus, Thomas, sieur d' Embry, 16th cent. (Table P-PZ38)
1603 Aubigné, Théodore Agrippa d', 1552-1630 (Table P-PZ37)
Baïf, Jean Antoine de, 1532-1589, see PQ1665+
Bartas, Guillaume de Salluste, seigneur du see PQ1613+
1605.B25 Bassecourt, Claude de, 1570?-ca. 1608 (Table P-PZ38)
1605.B3 Beaulieu, Eustorg de, d. 1552 (Table P-PZ38)
Bellay, Joachim du, see PQ1668+
Belleau, Remy see PQ1666
1605.B34 Belleforest, Françoise de, 1530-1583 (Table P-PZ38)
1605.B37 Béreau, Jacques (Table P-PZ38)
1605.B4 Béroalde de Verville, François, 1556-ca. 1612 (Table P-PZ38)
1605.B5 Bèze, Théodore de, 1519-1605 (Table P-PZ38)
1605.B6 Billon, François de, 16th cent. (Table P-PZ38)
1605.B62 Birague, Flaminio de, 16th cent. (Table P-PZ38)
Bonaventure Despériers, see PQ1609.D3
1605.B7 Bosquier, Philippe, 1562-1636 (Table P-PZ38)
1605.B74 Bouchet, Guillaume, sieur de Brocourt, 1513-1593 (Table P-PZ38)
1605.B75 Bouchet, Jean, 1476-ca. 1550 (Table P-PZ38)
1605.B76 Bounin, Gabriel, fl. 1554-1586 (Table P-PZ38)
1605.B768 Bouquet, Simon, 16th cent. (Table P-PZ38)
1605.B77 Bourdigne, Charles de, 16th cent. (Table P-PZ38)
1605.B8 Brantôme, Pierre de Bourdeille, seigneur de, d. 1614 (Table P-PZ38)
1605.B82 Bretog, Jean (Table P-PZ38)

Modern French literature
Individual authors
16th century -- Continued

1605.B85 Brisset, Roland, sieur du Sauvage, 1560-1643? (Table P-PZ38)
1605.B86 Brodeau, Victor, ca. 1500-1540 (Table P-PZ38)
1605.B88 Bugnyon, Philibert, ca. 1530-1590 (Table P-PZ38)
1605.B89 Busche, Alexandre van den, 1535?-1585? (Table P-PZ38)
1607.C3 Cartigny, Jean de, 1520?-1578 (Table P-PZ38)
1607.C48 Chassignet, Jean-Baptiste, 1570?-1635? (Table P-PZ38)
1607.C56 Coignard, Gabrielle de, d. 1586 (Table P-PZ38)
1607.C57 Collerye, Roger de, 1468-ca. 1540 (Table P-PZ38)
1607.C6 Corrozet, Gilles, 1510-1568 (Table P-PZ38)
1607.C65 Crenne, Hélisenne de (Table P-PZ38)
1607.C7 Crétin, Guillaume Dubois, called, d. ca. 1525 (Table P-PZ38)
1607.C74 Crignon, Pierre, ca. 1464-1540 (Table P-PZ38)
1607.D25 Denisot, Nicolas, 1515-1559 (Table P-PZ38)
1607.D3 Deslauriers (Table P-PZ38)
1607.D4 Des Masures, Louis, 1523?-1574 (Table P-PZ38)
1609.D3 Despériers, Bonaventure, 1500?-1544 (Table P-PZ40)
1609.D4 Desportes, Philippe, d. 1606 (Table P-PZ38)
1609.D49 Des Roches, Catherine and Madeleine (Table P-PZ38)
1609.D5 Des Roches, Catherine (Table P-PZ38)
1609.D51 Des Roches, Madeleine (Table P-PZ38)
1611 Dolet, Étienne, 15508-1546 (Table P-PZ39)
Dorat, Jean, 1508?-1588, see PQ1667
1612.D4 Dorléans, Louis, 1542-1629 (Table P-PZ38)
Du Bartas, Guillaume de Salluste, seigneur, 1544-1590
Collected works
1613.A1 To 1800. By date
1613.A11-.A19 1801-. By editor
Selections. Anthologies
1613.A2 To 1800. By date
1613.A21-.A29 1801-. By editor
Separate works
1614 La semaine, ou Creation du monde
Complete editions
1614.A1 To 1800. By date
1614.A11-.A19 1801- . By editor
1614.P2 Première semaine
1614.P31-.P37 Special days, 1-7
1614.S2 Seconde semaine
1614.S31-.S34 Special days, 1-4
1614.S4A-.S4Z Special parts. By name, A-Z
e. g.

	Modern French literature
	Individual authors
	16th century
	Du Bartas, Guillaume de Salluste, seigneur, 1544-1590
	Separate works
	La semaine, ou Creation du monde
	Seconde semaine
	Special parts. By name, A-Z -- Continued
1614.S4E4	Eden
1615.A-Z	Minor works, A-Z
1615.C2	Cantique sur la victoire d'Ivry
1615.J8	Judith
1615.T7	Triomphe de la foi
1615.U6	L'Uranie
1616.A-Z	Translations. By language, A-Z
	English
1616.E2	Collected works. By translator, A-Z
	e. g.
1616.E2S8	Sylvester
1616.E3	Première semaine
1616.E31-.E37	Special days, 1-7
1616.E5	Seconde semaine
1616.E51-.E54	Special days, 1-4
1616.E6A-.E6Z	Special parts, A-Z. By English name
	e. g.
1616.E6B3	Babilon
1616.E6S3	Sacrifice of Isaac
1616.E7A-.E7Z	Other works, A-Z
1617	Biography and criticism
	Du Bellay, Joachim, ca. 1525-1560, see PQ1668+
1619.D2	Du Doc, Fronton, 1558-1624 (Table P-PZ38)
1619.D3	Du Fail, Noël, 1520?-1591 (Table P-PZ38)
1619.D35	Du Guillet, Pernette, 1520?-1545 (Table P-PZ38)
1619.D39	Du Saix, Antoine, 1505-1579 (Table P-PZ38)
1619.D4	Du Tour, Henri, d. 1580 (Table P-PZ38)
1619.D6	Du Tronchet, Étienne, ca. 1510-ca. 1585 (Table P-PZ38)
1620.D6	DuVair, Guillaume, 1556-1621 (Table P-PZ38)
1620.E8	Espinay, Charles d', bp., 1531?-1591 (Table P-PZ38)
	Essars, Nicolas de Herberay des see PQ1627.H45
1621	Estienne, Henir (Table P-PZ39)
1622	Est - Ez
1623.F2	Fabri, Pierre, fl. 1483-1515 (Table P-PZ38)
1623.F33	Favre, Antoine, 1557-1624 (Table P-PZ38)
1623.F5	Filleul, Nicolas, 1530-1575 (Table P-PZ38)
1623.F6	Flore, Jeanne (Table P-PZ38)
1623.F73	Forcadel, Étienne, 1534-1579 (Table P-PZ38)
	Fronton du Duc see PQ1619.D2

Modern French literature
Individual authors
16th century -- Continued

1625.G17 Gamon, Christofle de, 1574-1621 (Table P-PZ38)
1625.G2 Garnier, Robert, 1544?-1590 (Table P-PZ38)
1625.G6 Grévin, Jacques, 1538?-1570 (Table P-PZ38)
1625.G7 Gringore, Pierre, ca. 1475-1538? (Table P-PZ38)
1625.G84 Gueroult, Guillaume (Table P-PZ38)
1627.H4 Henri IV, King of France, 1553-1610 (Table P-PZ38)
1627.H45 Herberay, Nicolas de, sieur des Essars, 16th cent. (Table P-PZ40 modified)
1627.H45A61-.H45Z458 Separate works. By title
His translation of Amadis de Gaula see PQ6275.F1+
1627.H5 Héroët, Antoine, d. 1568 (Table P-PZ38)
1627.H55 Heyns, Peeter, 1537-1598 (Table P-PZ38)
1627.J3 Jamyn, Amadis, d. 1592 or 3 (Table P-PZ38)
Jodelle, Étienne, 1532-1573 see PQ1672
1628.L2 Labé, Louise Charly, called, 1526?-1566 (Table P-PZ38)
1628.L23 La Boétie, Estienne de, 1530-1563 (Table P-PZ38)
1628.L234 La Ceppède, Jean de, 1548 (ca)-1623 (Table P-PZ38)
1628.L236 Ladam, Nicaise, 1465-1547 (Table P-PZ38)
1628.L237 La Gessée, Jean de, ca. 1551-cd. 1596 (Table P-PZ38)
1628.L238 La Noue, François de, 1531-1591 (Table P-PZ38)
1628.L24 La Perrière, Guillaume de, 1499-1565 (Table P-PZ38)
1628.L25 La Péruse, Jean de, 1529-1554 (Table P-PZ38)
1628.L27 Larcher, Jean de, fl. 1600 (Table P-PZ38)
1628.L3 Larivey, Pierre de, ca. 1550-1612 (Table P-PZ38)
1628.L33 La Roque, Siméon-Guillaume de, ca. 1550-ca. 1615 (Table P-PZ38)
1628.L34 La Taille, Jacques de, 1542-1562 (Table P-PZ38)
1628.L35 La Taille, Jean de, 1533?-1611 or 12 (Table P-PZ38)
1628.L355 La Tayssonière, Guillaume de (Table P-PZ38)
1628.L358 L'Aubespine, Madeleine de, 1546-1596 (Table P-PZ38)
1628.L367 Laval, Pierre de, 16th cent. (Table P-PZ38)
1628.L38 Le Fèvre de la Boderie, Guy, 1541-1598 (Table P-PZ38)
1628.L395 Le Jars, Louis (Table P-PZ38)
1628.L4 Le Loyer, Pierre, sieur de la Brosse, 1550-1634 (Table P-PZ38)
1628.L5 Lemaire de Belges, Jean, 1473-1515 or 16 (Table P-PZ38)
1628.L57 Le Picard, Philippe, 16th cent. (Table P-PZ38)
1628.L6 Le Vasseur, Jacques, 1571-1638 (Table P-PZ38)
1628.L65 Lingendes, Jean de, 1580?-1616 (Table P-PZ38)
1629.M3 Magny, Olivier de, d. ca. 1560 (Table P-PZ38)
1629.M5 Margaretha, of Austria, 1480-1530 (Table P-PZ38)
Cf. DH183 Biography

Modern French literature
Individual authors
16th century -- Continued
1631-1632 Marguérite d'Angoulême, queen of Navarre, 1492-1549
Works
1631.A1 By date
1631.A11-.A19 By editor
Translations
1631.A2-.A29 English
1631.A3-.A39 German
1631.A4-.A49 Other. By language
Selected works
1631.A5 Marguerites de la Marguerite des princess. By date
1631.A6 Other selected works. By date
1631.A7-Z Separate works
1631.C2 Chansons spirituelles
1631.C66 La comédie de Mont-de-Marsan
1631.D5 Dialogue en forme de vision nocturne
1631.H3-.H4 L'Heptaméron
1631.H3 Texts. By date
1631.H3A-Z Translations. By language
1631.H3E5 English
1631.H4 Criticism
1631.M5 Le miroir de l'âme pécherresse
1631.T7 Le triomphe de l'Agneau
Biography and letters, see DC112.M2
1632 Criticism
Marguerite d'Autriche, 1480-1530 see PQ1629.M5
1635 Marot, Clément, 1495?-1544 (Table P-PZ37 modified)
1635.A61-.A78 Separate works. By title
Les Pseavmes mis en rime françoise see BS1443.A+
1637.M3 Marot, Jean, 1467?-1527? (Table P-PZ38)
1637.M36 Mary, Queen of Scots, 1542-1587 (Table P-PZ38)
1637.M38 Matthieu, Pierre, 1563-1621 (Table P-PZ38)
1637.M53 Maugin, Jean, 16th cent. (Table P-PZ38)
Montaigne, Michel Eyquem de, 1533-1592
Cf. JC139 Political science
Cf. LB475.M6+ Education
1641.A1 Collected works, essays. By date
1641.A2 Selected essays. By editor, A-Z
1641.A3 Particular essays. By name
1641.A5 Selections. By editor, A-Z
1641.A7-Z Other works
1641.J68 Journal de voyage en Italie
1641.L2 Lettres
1642.A-Z Translations. By language, A-Z
1642.A5 Modern French

Modern French literature
Individual authors
16th century
Montaigne, Michel Eyquem de, 1533-1592
Translations. By language, A-Z -- Continued
English

1642.E5 Collections. By translator
1642.E6 Selected essays. By editor
1642.E7 Other works, A-Z
Biography and criticism
1643.A2 Societies. Periodicals. Collections
1643.A3 Dictionaries, indexes, etc.
1643.A5-Z General works
1644 Minor works
1645 Miscellaneous. Special
1647.M4 Montchrétien, Antoine de, ca. 1575-1621 (Table P-PZ38)
1647.M5 Montreux, Nicolas de, b. 1561? (Table P-PZ38)
1649.N5 Nicolas de Troyes, fl. 1535 (Table P-PZ38)
1649.N67 Nostredame, César de, 1553-1629 (Table P-PZ38)
1651 O - Oz
Ollenix du Mont Sacré, pseud. see PQ1647.M5
1653.P25 Palissy, Bernard, 1510?-1590
Biography see NK4210.P3
1653.P252 Palma-Cayet, Pierre-Victor (Table P-PZ38)
1653.P253 Papillon, Marc de, seigneur de Lasphrise, b. 1555 (Table P-PZ38)
1653.P27 Papon, Loys, ca. 1535-1599 (Table P-PZ38)
1653.P3 Pasquier, Étienne, 1529-1615 (Table P-PZ38)
1653.P35 Passerat, Jean, 1534-1602 (Table P-PZ38)
1653.P4 Peletier, Jacques, 1517-1582 (Table P-PZ38)
1653.P455 Philippe de Vigneulles, 1471-1527 or 8 (Table P-PZ38)
1653.P46 Pibrac, Guy du Faur, seigneur de, 1529-1584 (Table P-PZ38)
1653.P7 Plantin, Christophe, 1514-1589
Biography see Z232.P71
The Pléiade
1661.A1-.A3 Collections
1661.A1 Marty-Laveaux, La Pléiade françoise
1662.A-Z Translations. By language, A-Z
1663.A-Z Selections. By language, A-Z
1664 Criticism
Separate authors
1665 Baïf, Jean Antoine de, 1532-1589 (Table P-PZ37)
1666 Belleau, Remy, 1527?-1577 (Table P-PZ39 modified)
1666.A61-.Z48 Separate works. By title
1666.A75-.A753 Les amours et nouveaux changes des pierres précieuses (Table P-PZ43)

Modern French literature
Individual authors
16th century
The Pléiade
Separate authors
Belleau, Remy, 1527?-1577
Separate works. By title -- Continued

1666.A8-.A83	Anacreon (Table P-PZ43)
1666.B4-.B43	La bergerie (Table P-PZ43)
1666.E3-.E33	Ecclesiates (Table P-PZ43)
1666.E4-.E43	Eclogues sacrées prises du Cantique des Cantiques (Table P-PZ43)
1667	Dorat, Jean, 1508?-1588 (Table P-PZ39)
	Du Bellay, Joachim, ca. 1525-1560
1668.A1	Collected works. By date
1668.A5	Selections
	Separate works
	Antiquez de Rome, see PQ1668.P7
(1668.D3)	La deffence et illustration de la langue françoyse see PC2079
1668.D5	Discours au roi sur la posie
1668.D7	Divers jeux rustiques et autres oeuvres poétiques
1668.E3	Eneïde
	Huit sonnets, see PQ1668.S5
1668.L3	Lettres
	Nouvelle manière de faire son profit des lettres, see PA8585.T8
1668.O3	L'olive et quelques autres oeuvres poétiques
1668.P7	Premier livre des antiquitez de Rome
1668.P8	Translations
1668.R3	Recueil de poésie
1668.R4	Les regrets
1668.S5	Sonnets
1668.S6	Translations
1668.S9	Criticism
1669	Biography and criticism
1672	Jodelle, Étienne, 1532-1573 (Table P-PZ39)
	Pontus de Tyard see PQ1679
	Ronsard, Pierre de, 1524-1585
	Collected works
1674.A1	Reproductions of manuscript editions in facsimile
1674.A2	Printed editions. By date
1674.A3	Editions. By editor, A-Z
1674.A5	Selected works. By editor, A-Z
(1674.A8-Z)	Posthumous works see PQ1674.A5

Modern French literature
Individual authors
16th century
The Pléiade
Separate authors
Ronsard, Pierre de, 1524-1584 -- Continued

1675.A-Z Translations. By language, A-Z
e. g.
1675.E5 English
1676 Separate works
Abregé de l'art poétique see PN1043
1676.A6 Les amours
1676.A65 Les amours de Marie
1676.B6 Le bocage
1676.D5 Discours des misres de ce temps
1676.E6 Élégies, mascarades et bergerie
1676.E7 Épitaphes
Folastries see PQ1676.L6
1676.F7 La Franciade
1676.G3 Les gayetez
1676.H7-.H9 Hymnes
1676.H8 L'hymne des Daimons
1676.L6 Livret des folastries
1676.M5 Les meslanges
1676.O2-.O3 Odes
1676.P3 La paix
1676.S7 Sonnets
1676.S8 Sonnets pour Hélène
1677 Biography and criticism
1678 Criticism
1678.Z8 Versification
1678.Z9 Glossaries, indexes
1679 Tyard, Pontus de, 1521-1605 (Table P-PZ39)
1680.P6 Poupo, Pierre, ca. 1552-ca. 1591
Rabelais, François, 1490 (ca.)-1533?
Collected works
Complete works (including editions of Gargantua and Pantagruel)
1681 Early, 1553-1691. By date
1682 Later, 1711- . By editor
1682.A1 Anonymous. By date
1682.Z5 Selections. By editor
1683 Separate works
1683.C5 Les chroniques de Gargantua. By date
Epîtres see PQ1693.A2+
1683.G5 Gargantua. La vie du grand Gargantua, père de Pantagruel

Modern French literature
Individual authors
16th century
Rabelais, François, ca. 1490-1533?
Separate works -- Continued

1683.G6 Selections from Gargantua. By editor
1683.P2 Pantagruel. Les horribles et espouëtables faictz & prouesses du tresrenome Pantagruel roy des Dipsodes
1683.P3 Le tiers livre. (Tiers livre des faictz et dictz heroïques du noble Pantagruel)
1683.P4 Le quart livre. (Le quart livre des faictz & dictz heroques du noble Pantagruel)
1683.P5 Le cinquième livre. (Cinquiesme & dernier livre des faicts & dicts heroïques du bon Pantagruel)
First published with title: L'isle sonante
1683.P6 Selections from Pantagruel
1683.P7 Le disciple de Pantagruel
1683.P8 Prognostication (Pantagrueline prognostication)
1683.S4 La sciomachie & festins fait à Rome au palais de mon seigneur reverendissme cardinal du Bellay
1683.Z9 Spurious works, A-Z

Translations
Including translations of Gargantua and Pantagruel or any of the parts
1684 Modern French
1685 Other languages. By language and translator
e. g.
1685.E5 English
1685.G5 German
1685.S7 Spanish
1687 Illustrations

Biography and criticism
1692.A1-.A6 Periodicals. Societies. Collections
1692.A8-Z Dictionaries, indexes, etc.
For linguistic glossaries, etc. see PQ1699.Z8

Biographical sources
1693.A2 Letters. By date of publication
1693.A3 Letters addressed to Rabelais. By date of publication
1693.A5-.Z6 General works. Literary biography. Life and works
1693.Z7 Manuscripts. Autographs
1693.Z8 Iconography. Monuments

Criticism
1693.6.A-Z Biography of Rabelais scholars, A-Z

Modern French literature
Individual authors
16th century
Rabelais, François, ca. 1490-1533?
Biography and criticism
Criticism -- Continued

1694 General (including treatises on Gargantua and Pantagruel, or any of the parts)
Criticism of the minor works classed with the works

1695 Textual criticism
Special topics
1696 Sources of Rabelais' works
1697.A-Z Other topics, A-Z
1697.A8 Architecture
1697.C34 Canada
1697.C5 Characters
1697.E4 Education
1697.F38 Fathers. Father figures
1697.G4 Geography
1697.G53 Giants
1697.L3 Laughter
1697.L52 Liberty
1697.M4 Medicine
1697.N3 Natural history
1697.P47 Performing arts
1697.P6 Political and social views
1697.P63 Popular culture
1697.R4 Religion and ethics
1697.V85 Vulgarity
Language, style, etc.
1698 General
1699.A-Z Special, A-Z
1699.F5 Figures of speech
1699.N35 Names
1699.N37 Narration
1699.P37 Paradox
1699.Z8 Glossaries, indexes, etc. By date
1700.R36 Rapin, Nicolas, ca. 1540-1608 (Table P-PZ38)
1701 Régnier, Mathurin, 1573-1613 (Table P-PZ37)
1702.R6 Romieu, Marie de (Table P-PZ38)
Ronsard see PQ1674+
1702.R68 Rougeart, Jucquel, 1558-1588 (Table P-PZ38)
1703.S2 Saint-Gelais, Mellin de, d. 1558 (Table P-PZ38)
1703.S4 Sainte-Marthe, Charles de, 1512-1555 (Table P-PZ38)
1703.S43 Salel, Hugues, 1504 (ca.)-1553 (Table P-PZ38)
1704 Satyre Ménippée (Table P-PZ38)
1705.S5 Scève, Maurice, 16th cent. (Table P-PZ38)

Modern French literature
Individual authors
16th century -- Continued

1705.S6	Sillac, Jacques de, d. ca. 1569 (Table P-PZ38)
1705.S7	Sponde, Jean de, 1557-1595 (Table P-PZ38)
1705.T15	Tabourot, Estienne, 1549-1590 (Table P-PZ38)
1705.T2	Tahureau, Jacques, 1527-1555 (Table P-PZ38)
1705.T23	Taillemont, Claude de, b. 1526 or 7 (Table P-PZ38)
1705.T68	Tournebu, Odet de, d. 1581 (Table P-PZ38)
1705.T69	Toutain, Charles, 16th cent. (Table P-PZ38)
	Troyes, Nicolas de see PQ1649.N5
	Tyard, Pontus de see PQ1679
1707.U68	Urfé, Anne d', 1555-1621 (Table P-PZ38)
1707.U7	Urfé, Honor d', 1567-1625 (Table P-PZ38 modified)
1707.U7A61-.U7A78	Separate works
1707.U7A62	L'Astrée
1707.U7A65	Les epistres morales
1707.U7A7	La Savoysiade
1707.U7A73	Le sireine
1707.U7A75	La Sylvanire
1707.V3	Vatel, Jean, 16th cent. (Table P-PZ38)
1707.V35	Vauquelin de la Fresnaye, Jean, 1536-1606 or 8 (Table P-PZ38)
1707.V46	Vermeil, Abraham de (Table P-PZ38)
	Verville, François Béroalde de see PQ1605.B4
1707.V6	Viret, Pierre, 1511-1571 (Table P-PZ38)
1707.V64	Virey, Claude-Enoch, 1566-1636 (Table P-PZ38)
1709.Y6	Yver, Jacques, 1520-1572 (Table P-PZ38)
	17th century
	Subarrange each author by Table P-PZ40 unless otherwise indicated
1710	Anonymous works (Table P-PZ28)
1711.A25	Abeille, Gaspard, 1648-1718 (Table P-PZ40)
1711.A47	Ancelin, Hubert (Table P-PZ40)
1711.A5	Angot, Robert, sieur de l'Eperonnière, b. 1581 (Table P-PZ40)
1711.A63	Argonne, Bonaventure d', 1634-1704 (Table P-PZ40)
1711.A65	Arnauld d'Andilly, Robert, 1588-1674 (Table P-PZ40)
1711.A7	Assoucy, Charles Coypeau d', 1605-1675 (Table P-PZ40)
1711.A73	Astros, J.-G. d' (Jean-Géraud), 1594-1648 (Table P-PZ40)
1711.A8	Aubignac, Franois Hedelin, abbé, d', 1604-1676 (Table P-PZ38)
1711.A82	Audiffret, Hercule, 1603-1659 (Table P-PZ40)
1711.A84	Audin, prieur de Thermes, 17th century (Table P-PZ40)

Modern French literature
Individual authors
17th century -- Continued

1711.A85 Aulnoy, Marie Catherine Jumelle de Berneville, comtesse d', d. 1705 (Table P-PZ40)
1711.A87 Auvray, fl. 1628-1633 (Table P-PZ40)
1711.A88 Auvray, Jean, d. 1622 (Table P-PZ40)
1711.B3 Bachaumont, François Le Coigneux de, 1624-1702 (Table P-PZ40)
1713 Balzac, Jean Louis Guez, sieur de, d. 1654
1713.A6-.Z3 Separate works
1713.A8 Aristippe; ou, De la cour
1713.B2 Le Barbon
1713.E3 Entretiens de feu M. de Balzac
1713.E4 Les derniers entretiens de M. du Mas avec M. Balzac
1713.H2 Harangues panégyriques
1713.L2 Lettres (1624)
1713.L25 Lettres, 2me partie
1713.L3 Lettres. Suite de la 2me partie
1713.L4 Recueil des nouvelles lettres
1713.L5 Lettres choisies
1713.L6 Lettres familières à M. Chapelain
1713.L7 Lettres à M. Conrart
1713.L8 Lettres inédites
1713.L9 Translations of letters. By language
1713.L9E5 English
1713.S7 Socrate chrestien
1713.Z5 Biography. Criticism
1714.B2 Bardou, Pierre, 1662?-1724 (Table P-PZ40)
1714.B23 Baron, Michel Boyron, called, 1653-1729 (Table P-PZ40)
1714.B25 Barrin, Jean, ca. 1640-1718 (Table P-PZ40)
1714.B3 Bayle, Pierre, 1647-1706 (Table P-PZ40)
1715 Benserade, Isaac de, 1613-1691 (Table P-PZ37)
1716.B14 Bernard, Catherine, 1662-1712 (Table P-PZ40)
1716.B22 Berthod, sieur, fl. 1650 (Table P-PZ40)
1716.B3 Beys, Charles de, 1610 (ca)-1659 (Table P-PZ40)
1716.B56 Billard, Claude, seigneur de Courgenay, 1550 (ca.)-1618 (Table P-PZ40)
1716.B6 Billaut, Adam, 1602-1662 (Table P-PZ40)
1716.B68 Blessebois, Pierre Corneille, 1646?-1700? (Table P-PZ40)
1716.B9 Boileau, Gilles, 1631-1669 (Table P-PZ40)
Boileau-Despréaux, Nicolas, 1636-1711
1719 Collected works
1719.A1 To 1800. By date
1719.A2 After 1800. By date
1720 Selections

Modern French literature
Individual authors
17th century
Boileau-Despréaux, Nicolas, 1636-1711
Selections -- Continued

1720.A1 Anonymous editors. By date
1721.A-Z Separate works, A-Z
1721.A7 L'Art poétique (in verse)
1721.B6 Boileau aux prises avec les jésuites
1721.E7 Épitres
1721.H5 Les héros de roman
1721.L7 Lutrin
1721.L8 Translations. By language
1721.L9 Criticism
1721.S3 Satires
1722 Biography
1723 Criticism
1724.B3 Bois-Robert, François le Métel de, 1592-1662 (Table P-PZ40)
1724.B6 Bonnecorse, Balthasar de, d. 1706 (Table P-PZ40)
Bossuet, Jacques Bénigne, bp. of Meaux, 1627-1704
Collected works
1725.A1 To 1800
1725.A2 1800-
1725.A5 By editor
Cf. BX890 Religious works
Cf. BX1756.A1+ Sermons
1725.A6-Z Translations, by language, subarranged by translator
1726 Selections, anthologies, etc.
1727.A-Z Separate works. By title, A-Z
1728 Letters
1728.A4 Collections
1728.A5-Z Letters to special persons, A-Z
Biography see BX4705.B7
1729 Criticism
1731.B47 Bouchard, Jean Jacques, 1606-1641? (Table P-PZ40)
1731.B65 Bouhours, Dominique, 1628-1702 (Table P-PZ40 modified)
1731.B65A61-.B65Z458 Separate works. By title
1731.B65E6 Les entretiens d'Ariste et d'Eugene
1731.B65M3 La maniére de bien penser
1731.B7 Boursault, Edme, 1638-1701 (Table P-PZ40 modified)
1731.B7A61-.B7Z458 Separate works. By title
1731.B7A67 Artemise et Poliante
1731.B7C6 La comédie sans titre, ou Le Mercure galant
1731.B7E8 Ésope à la cour, comédie héroique

Modern French literature
Individual authors
17th century
Boursault, Edme, 1638-1701
Separate works. By title -- Continued

1731.B7F3 Les fables d'Ésope, ou Ésope à la ville
1731.B7L5 Lettres nouvelles, accompagnées de fables, de contes [etc.]
1731.B7M3 Le marquis de Chavigny
1731.B7M4 Le médicin volante
Le Mercure galant see PQ1731.B7C6
1731.B7M8 Les mots à la mode
1731.B7N4 Ne pas croire oe qu'on void
1731.B7P4 Phaéton
1731.B7P7 Le portrait du peintre
1731.B7P8 Le prince de Condé
1731.B74 Boyer, Claude, 1618-1698 (Table P-PZ40)
1731.B8 Brébeuf, Georges de, 1617?-1661 (Table P-PZ40)
1731.B82 Brécourt, Guillaume Marcoureau de, d. 1685 (Table P-PZ40)
1731.B835 Brémond, Gabriel de (Table P-PZ40)
1731.B87 Brillon, Pierre Jacques, 1671-1736 (Table P-PZ40)
1731.B89 Brosse, 17th cent. (Table P-PZ40)
1731.B9 Brueys, David Augustin de, 1640-1723 (Table P-PZ40)
1731.B95 Bussières, Jean de, 1607-1678 (Table P-PZ40)
Bussy, Roger de Rabutin, comte de, 1618-1693
1733.A6 Selected works. Selections. By date
1733.A61-.Z48 Separate works. By title
1733.C2-.C23 Carte géographique de la cour et autres galantries (Table P-PZ43)
1733.D5-.D53 Discours sur le bon usage des adversitez (Table P-PZ43)
1733.L2-.L23 Lettres (Table P-PZ43)
Amours des dames illustres de France see DC128
Histoire amoureuse des Gaules see DC128
Biography and memoirs see DC130.B9
1735.C2 Campistron, Jean Galbert de, 1656-1723 (Table P-PZ38)
1735.C3 Camus, Jean Pierre, bp., 1584-1652 (Table P-PZ40)
1735.C33 Cantenac, fl. 1662-1665 (Table P-PZ40)
1735.C35 Carel, Jacques, sieur de Sainte-Garde, ca. 1620-1684 (Table P-PZ40)
1735.C4 Cassagnes, Jacques, 1635-1679 (Table P-PZ40)
1735.C5 Caumont de La Force, Charlotte Rose de, d. 1724 (Table P-PZ38)
1735.C53 Caylus, Marie Marguerite Le Valois de Vilette de Muray, comtesse de, 1673-1729 (Table P-PZ40)
Cf. DC130.C2 French history

Modern French literature
Individual authors
17th century -- Continued

1735.C7 Chapelain, Jean, 1595-1674 (Table P-PZ40)
1735.C8 Chapelle, Claude Emmanuel Lhuillier, 1626-1686 (Table P-PZ40)
Chapelle, Jean de la see PQ1805.L35
1735.C83 Chapelon, Jean, 1647-1694 (Table P-PZ40)
1735.C9 Chappuzeau, Samuel, 1625-1701 (Table P-PZ40)
Charron, Pierre, 1541-1603
see B, BJ, etc.
1737.C4 Chaulieu, Guillaume Amfrye de, 1636?-1720 (Table P-PZ40)
Chesnay, Claude-Ferdinand Guillemay Du, fl. 1686-1718 see PQ1914.R597
1737.C58 Coeffeteau, Nicolas, 1574-1623 (Table P-PZ40)
1737.C65 Colletet, Guillaume, 1598-1659 (Table P-PZ40)
Corneille, Pierre, 1606-1684
1741 Collected works. By date
1742 Selected works
1742.A1 Dramatic works. By date
1742.A2 Comedies. By date
1743 Miscellaneous works
1744 Anthologies. Selections
1744.A3 School editions. By editor
1745.A-Z Translations (Collected). By language, A-Z
e. g.
1745.E5 English
Subarrange by tranlator, A-Z, if known, or by date
1745.G5 German
Subarrange by tranlator, A-Z, if known, or by date
1745.I5 Italian
Subarrange by tranlator, A-Z, if known, or by date
1745.S5 Spanish
Subarrange by tranlator, A-Z, if known, or by date
Separate works
1746.A4 Agésilas
1746.A6 L'ami du Cid à Claveret
1747 Andromède (Table P-PZ41)
1748.A7 Atilla
1748.A8 L'aveugle de Smyrna
Le Cid
1749.A1 Texts. By date
1749.A2 School texts. By editor, A-Z
1749.A5-Z Translations. By language, A-Z
Criticism
1750 Contemporary ("Querelle du Cid")

Modern French literature
Individual authors
17th century
Corneille, Pierre, 1606-1684
Separate works
Le Cid
Criticism -- Continued

1751 Other
1752 Cinna (Table P-PZ41)
1753.C6 Clitandre
1753.C7 Comédie des Tuileries
1753.D6 Don Sanche d'Aragon
Excuse d'Ariste see PQ1750
1753.G3 La galerie du Palais
1753.H4 Héraclius
1754 Horace (Table P-PZ41)
1755.I5 L'illusion comique
L'imitation de Jésus-Christ see BV4823.C7
Louanges de la Sainte Vièrge see PA8290
1755.M5 Médée
1755.M7 Mélite
1756 Le menteur (Table P-PZ41)
1757.M2 La suite du Menteur
1757.M6 La mort de Pompée
1757.N5 Nicomède
Occasion perdue recouverte see PQ1764.O4
1757.O4 Oedipe
1757.O8 Othon
1758.P4 Pertharite
1758.P5 La place royale
Plainte de la France à Rome see PQ1764.A+
1759 Polyeucte (Table P-PZ41)
Pompée see PQ1757.M6
1760.P8 Psyché
1760.P9 Pulchérie
1760.R6 Rodogune
1761.S4 Sertorius
1761.S6 Sophonisbe
La suite du Menteur see PQ1757.M2
1761.S8 La suivant
1761.S9 Suréna
1761.T4 Théodore
1761.T5 Tite et Bérénice
1761.T7 La toison d'or
1761.V4 La veuve
1764.A-Z Doubtful or spurious works, A-Z
1764.A45 Alidor, ou, L'indifférent

Modern French literature
Individual authors
17th century
Corneille, Pierre, 1606-1684
Doubtful or spurious works, A-Z -- Continued

1764.O4 L'occasion perdue recouverte
1764.P6 Plainte de la France à Rome
1765 Imitations, paraphrases, adaptations
1766 Parodies on Corneille's works
1767 Translations of Corneille (as subject)
1768 Illustrations to the works
Biography and criticism
1770 Periodicals. Societies. Collections
1771 Dictionaries. Indexes, etc.
Class here general encyclopedic dictionaries only
For special dictionaries, see the subject
For concordances, language dictionaries see PQ1789.Z9
1772.A2-.A4 Autobiography. Journals, letters, memoirs
1772.A5-Z General works (Literary biography, life and works)
1774 Relations to contemporaries
1775 Homes and haunts. Local associations. Landmarks
1776 Anniversaries. Celebrations, etc. Iconography
1777 Authorship
Including manuscripts, forgeries, sources, etc.
1778 Chronology of works
Criticism and interpretation
1779 General works. Genius, etc.
Dramatic art and theories. Technique. Representation on the stage
1780 General. Structure. Plots. Unity of action, time and place
1781 Characters
1782 Groups. Classes
e.g. Women. Heroines of Corneille
Individual
see the special play
1783 Corneille as a librettist
1784 Representation on the stage
Cf. PQ1778 Chronology
1785.A-Z Treatment and knowledge of special subjects, A-Z
1785.H57 History
1785.L6 Love
1785.P6 Politics
1785.P65 Power
1785.P78 Prudence
History of study and appreciation

Modern French literature
Individual authors
17th century
Corneille, Pierre, 1606-1684
Criticism and interpretation
History of study and appreciation -- Continued
1786 General
1787.A-Z By country, A-Z
Cf. PQ1767 Translations as subject
1788 By individual persons
Language, style, etc.
1789 General, including grammar and syntax
1789.Z5 Versification
1789.Z9 Glossaries. Indexes. Concordances. By date
1791 Corneille, Thomas, 1625-1709
1791.A1 Collected works. By date
1791.A14 Selected works. By date
1791.A7-.Z4 Separate works, A-Z
1791.Z5 Biography and criticism
1792.C35 Costar, Pierre, 1603-1660
1792.C4 Cotin, Charles, 1604-1681
1792.C5 Cotolendi, Charles, d. ca. 1710 (Table P-PZ40)
1792.C7 Coulanges, Philippe Emmanuel, marquis de, 1633-1716
Biography see DC130.C77
1792.C85 Courtilz de Sandras, Gatien, 1644-1712 (Table P-PZ40)
1792.C87 Courtin, Nicolas, fl. 1666-1687 (Table P-PZ40)
1792.C89 Cramail, Adrien de Montluc, comte de, 1646 (Table P-PZ40)
1793 Cyrano de Bergerac, Savinien, 1619-1655
1793.A1 Editions. By date
Including the older editions up to 1741 (whether complete or not)
1793.A14 Selected works. By date
1793.A15 Selections. Thoughts
1793.A19 Minor works (Collected)
Single works
L'Autre monde see PQ1793.A2
1793.A2 Histoire comique des tats et empires de la lune
(Editions of the first part or first and second parts together)
1793.A27 Histoire comique. 2d part
1793.A3 Letters. By date
(Including Lettres satyriques, Lettres diverses, Lettres d'amour)
1793.A4-.A49 Mazarinades
1793.A4 Collections
1793.A41 Le conseiller fidèle

Modern French literature
Individual authors
17th century
Cyrano de Bergerac, Savinien, 1619-1655
Single works
Mazarinades -- Continued

1793.A42 Le gazettier des-intéressé
1793.A43 Le gazettier des-intéressé et le testament de Jules Mazarin
1793.A44 Lettre de consolation envoyée à madame de Chastillon
1793.A45 Lettre de consolation envoyée à madame la duchesse de Rohan
1793.A46 Le ministre d'Estat, flambé
1793.A47 Le ministre d'Estat flambé. Jouxte la coppie imprimée à Paris
1793.A48 Remonstrances des trois estats
1793.A49 La sibylle moderne, ou, L'oracle du temps
1793.A5 La mort d'Agrippine
1793.A7 Le pédant joué
Voyage dans la lune, see PQ1793.A2
Voyages fantastiques, see PQ1793.A2
1793.A8-Z Biography and criticism
1794.D3 Dancourt, Florent Carton, sieur d'Ancourt, called, 1661-1725 (Table P-PZ40)
Dassoucy, M. (Charles, 1605-1677 see PQ1711.A7
1794.D35 Dehénault, Jean, 1611 (ca).-1682 (Table P-PZ40)
1794.D37 Des Barreaux, Jacques Vallée, sieur, 1599-1673 (Table P-PZ40)
1794.D39 Desfontaines, fl. 1637-1649 (Table P-PZ40)
1794.D4 Deshoulières, Mme. Antoinette (Du Ligier de la Garde) 1638?-1694 (Table P-PZ40)
1794.D5 Desjardins, Marie Catherine Hortense, known as Mme. de Villedieu, d. 1683 (Table P-PZ38)
1794.D6 Desmarets de Saint Sorlin, Jean, 1595-1676 (Table P-PZ38)
1794.D65 Donneau de Visé, Jean, 1638-1710 (Table P-PZ40)
1794.D657 Dorimon, b. 1628 (Table P-PZ40)
Du Chesnay, Claude-Ferdinand Guillemay, fl. 1686-1718 see PQ1914.R597
1794.D69 Du Four de La Crespelière, Jacques (Table P-PZ40)
1794.D7 Dufresny, Charles, sieur de la Rivière, ca. 1654-1724 (Table P-PZ40)
1794.D78 Du Lorens, Jacques, 1580?-1655 (Table P-PZ40)
1794.D788 Du Plaisir, fl. 1682-1684 (Table P-PZ40)
1794.D795 Durand, Etienne, 1586-1618 (Table P-PZ40)
1794.D8 Du Ryer, Pierre, d. 1658 (Table P-PZ38)

Modern French literature
Individual authors
17th century -- Continued

1794.F7 Favier, Claude, fl. 1624 (Table P-PZ40)

Fénelon, François de Salignac de la Mothe-, 1651-1715

1795.A1-.A4 Collected works

Cf. BX890 Religions works

Cf. BX2183 Meditations, etc.

1795.A1 By date

1795.A11-.A19 By editor

Including selections, anthologies, thoughts

Translations

1795.A2A-.A2Z English

1795.A3A-.A3Z German

1795.A4A-.A4Z Other. By language

Separate works

1795.A5 Abrégé des vies des anciens philosophes

1795.A7 Aventures d'Aristonoüs

1795.A8 Aventures de Mélésichthon

Aventures de Télémaque see PQ1795.T5+

Demonstration de l'existence de Dieu see BT100

1795.D4 Dialogues des morts

Dialogues sur l'éloquence see PN4105

Éducation des filles see LC1422

Explication des maximes des saints see BX2183

1795.F3 Fables

Letters

1795.L5 General collections

Lettres spirituelles see BX2183

1795.L7 Lettres inédites

1795.L9 Individual letters, alphabetically by person addressed

Télémaque

1795.T5 Texts. By date

1795.T5A1-.T5A29 Paraphrases, adaptations, etc.

1795.T5A3 Translations, Polyglot

1795.T5A4-Z Translations. By language

1795.T6 Criticism

1796 Biography and criticism

Cf. PQ1795.L5+ Letters

1797.F27 Ferrand, Anne Bellinzani, ca. 1657-1740 (Table P-PZ40)

1797.F3 Ferrier de La Martinière, Louis, 1652-1721 (Table P-PZ40)

1797.F7 Fontenelle, Bernard Le Bovier de, 1657-1757

Separate works

Amusements sérieux et comiques see PQ1794.D7

1797.F7B4 Bellérophon

Modern French literature
Individual authors
17th century
Fontenelle, Bernard le Vovier de, 1657-1757
Separate works -- Continued

1797.F7C6 La comète
1797.F7D4-.F7D6 Dialogues des morts
1797.F7D7-.F7D9 Nouveaux dialogues des morts
1797.F7D92 Jugement de Pluton, sur les deux parties des Nouveaux dialogues des morts
Éloges des academiciens de l'Académie royale des sciences see Q141
1797.F7E6 Endymion, pastorale héroique
1797.F7E7 Énée et Lavinie
Entretiens sur la pluralité des mondes see QB54
Histoire des oracles see BF1761
1797.F7L4 Lettres galantes
Nouveaux dialogues des morts see PQ1797.F7D7+
1797.F7P6 Poésies pastorales
1797.F7P8 Psyché
1797.F7R4 La republique des philosophes
1797.F7T4 Thétis et Pelée
Vie de Corneille see PQ1772.A2+
1797.F7Z5-.F7Z99 Biography. Criticism
1797.F74 Forest, Geneviève, fl 1676-1683 (Table P-PZ40)
1797.F8 Frénicle, Nicolas, 1600-1661 (Table P-PZ40)
1797.F9 Furetière, Antoine, 1619-1688
1797.F9A6 Furetiriana
Separate works
L'Apothéose du Dictionnaire de l'Académie see PC2617
Les couches de l'Académie, see PC2617
L'enterrement du Dictionnaire de l'Académie see PC2617
1797.F9A63 Fables morales et nouvelles
1797.F9A65 Nouvelle allégorique, ou Histoire des derniers troubles arrivez au royaume d'éloquence
Les paraboles de l'Évangile, traduites en vers see BT374
Plan et dessein du poëme ... intitulé: Le couches de l'Académie, poème allegorique et burlesque see PC2617
Les preuves par écrit see PC2617
1797.F9A67 Poésies diverses
Recueil des factums contre quelques-uns de cette Académie see PC2617
1797.F9A7 Le roman bourgeois

Modern French literature
Individual authors
17th century
Furetière, Antoine, 1619-1688
Separate works -- Continued

1797.F9A8 Le voyage de Mercure
1799.G17 Galaut, Jean, d. 1605 (Table P-PZ40)
1799.G2 Garasse, François, 1584-1631 (Table P-PZ40)
1799.G3 Gaultier-Garguille, Hugues Guéru, known as, d. 1633 (Table P-PZ40)
1799.G315 Gay, Geoffroy (Table P-PZ40)
1799.G32 Genest, Charles Claude, 1639-1719 (Table P-PZ40)
1799.G36 Gilbert, Gabriel, 1620(ca.)-1680? (Table P-PZ40)
1799.G37 Gillet de La Tessonerie, b. ca. 1620 (Table P-PZ40)
1799.G374 Gillot de Beaucour, Louise-Geneviève de Gomès de Vasconcellos, 17th cent. (Table P-PZ40)
1799.G4 Godeau, Antoine, bp., 1605-1672 (Table P-PZ40)
1799.G6 Gombauld, Jean Ogier de, 1570(ca.)-1666 (Table P-PZ40)
1799.G62 Gomberville, Marin Le Roy, sieur du Parc et de, 1600-1674 (Table P-PZ40)
1799.G64 Gougenot, 17th cent. (Table P-PZ40)
1799.G65 Gournay, Marie Le Jars de, 1565-1645 (Table P-PZ40)
1799.G77 Grignan, Françoise Marguerite de Sévigné, comtesse de, 1646-1705 (Table P-PZ38)
1799.G79 Guerin de Bouscal, Daniel, 1613?-1675 (Table P-PZ40)
Guerin de Bouscal, Guyon see PQ1799.G79
1799.G793 Guérin de la Pinerlière, Pierre (Table P-PZ40)
1799.G795 Guilleragues, Gabriel Joseph de Lavergne, vicomte de, 1628-1685 (Table P-PZ40)
1799.G8 Guyon, Jeanne Marie (Bouvier de La Motte) 1648-1717
Biography see BX4705.G8
1801.H2 Hardy, Alexandre, fl. 1595-1631 (Table P-PZ40)
1801.H25 Hauteroche, Noël Le Breton, sieur de, 1617-1707 (Table P-PZ40)
1801.H67 Horry, Nicolas (Table P-PZ40)
1801.H83 Huet, Pierre-Daniel, 1630-1721 (Table P-PZ40)
1801.J2 Jacques, Jacques, fl. 1657-1673 (Table P-PZ40)
1801.J73 John of Saint Samson, 1571-1636 (Table P-PZ40)
1803 La Bruyère, Jean de, 1645-1696 (Table P-PZ37 modified)
1803.A6 Caractères
Including editions with his translation of Theophrastus prefixed
1805.L3 La Calprenède, Gaultier de Coste, siegneur de, d. 1663 (Table P-PZ40)
1805.L32 La Calprenède, Madeleine de, 1668 (Table P-PZ40)

Modern French literature
Individual authors
17th century -- Continued

1805.L35 La Chapelle, Jean De, 1651-1723 (Table P-PZ40)
1805.L4 La Fare, Charles Auguste, marquis de, 1644-1712 (Table P-PZ40)
1805.L5 La Fayette, Marie Madeleine (Pioche de La Vergne) comtesse de, 1634-1693
Separate works
1805.L5A62 La comtesse de Tende
Histoire de Madame Henriette d'Angleterre see DC130.L2
Mémoires de la cour de France see DC126
1805.L5A68 La princesse de Montpensier
1805.L5A7-.L5A779 La princesse de Clèves
1805.L5A78 Zayde
1805.L5A8 Letters
1805.L5A81-.L5Z Biography and criticism
La Fontaine, Jean de, 1621-1695
1806 Collected works. By date
Selected works. Posthumous works
1807.A1 By date
1807.A3-Z By editor
1808 Fables
1808.A1 By date
(1808.A11) By editor
Selected, School editions, etc.
1808.A2 By date
1808.A3 By editor
1808.A5 Editions without date or editor. By place, A-Z
(1808.A6) Adaptations. Imitations
1808.A7-.Z3 Criticism
(1808.Z9) Illustrations. By illustrator, A-Z
1809 Contes et nouvelles
1810.A-Z Other works, A-Z
1810.A3 Adonis
1810.A5 Amours de Psyché et de Cupidon
1810.A8 Astrée
1810.C6 La coupe enchantée
1810.D5 Discours à Madame de la Sablière
1810.F6 Le Florentin
1810.J4 Je vous prens sans verd
1810.P6 Poëme du quinquina
1810.S6 Le songe de Vaux
1810.V6 Voyage de Paris en Limousin
1811.A-Z Translations. By language, A-Z
e. g.

Modern French literature
Individual authors
17th century
La Fontaine, Jean de, 1621-1695
Translations. By language, A-Z -- Continued
English

1811.E1 Collected works
1811.E2 Selected works
1811.E3 Fables. By translator, A-Z
1811.E4 Contes et nouvelles
1811.E5-.E9 Other works
e. g.
1811.E6 Loves of Cupid and Psyche
1812 Biography and criticism
1814.L3 La Fosse, Antoine de, sieur d'Aubigny, 1653-1708 (Table P-PZ40)
1814.L36 La Garenne, Sieur de (Humbert de Guillot de Goulet), 1590-1660? (Table P-PZ40)
Lagrange-Chancel, Franois Joseph Chancel, known as, 1677-1758
1814.L4 Collected works. By date
1814.L4A2 English translations
1814.L4A3 German translations
1814.L4A4-.L4A49 Other translations. By language (Alphabetically)
1814.L4A5-.L4Z4 Separate works, A-Z
1814.L4Z5-.L4Z99 Biography and criticism
1814.L47 La Mesnardière, Hippolyte Jules Pilet de, 1610-1663 (Table P-PZ40)
1814.L5 La Monnoye, Bernard de, 1641-1728 (Table P-PZ40)
1814.L57 La Mothe de Vayer, Franois de, 1583-1672 (Table P-PZ40)
Cf. AC21 Collected works
(1814.L6) La Motte, Antoine Houdar de, 1672-1731
see PQ1993.L46
1814.L7 La Roche-Guilhem, Mlle. de, d. ca. 1710 (Table P-PZ40)
1815 La Rochefoucauld, François, duc de, 1613-1680
1815.A1 Works. By date
1815.A15 Selections. By date
1815.A7 Refléxions et maximes
1815.A72 English translations
1815.A73 Other languages, A-Z
1815.A8-Z Biography and criticism
1817.L2 La Sablière, Antoine de Rambouillet, sieur de, 1624-1679 (Table P-PZ40)
1817.L25 La Serre, Jean Puget de, 1593?-1665 (Table P-PZ40)

Modern French literature
Individual authors
17th century -- Continued

1817.L3 La Suze, Henriette (de Coligny) comtesse de, 1618-1673 (Table P-PZ40)
Cf. PQ1126 Pièces galantes (by comtesse de la Suze and others)
1817.L36 Le Boulanger de Chalussay, fl. 1669-1672 (Table P-PZ40)
1817.L45 Le Laboureur, Louis, 1615 (ca.)-1679 (Table P-PZ40)
1817.L47 Le Moyne, Pierre, 1602-1671 (Table P-PZ40)
1817.L5 Lenoble, Eustache, baron de Saint Georges et de Tenneliére, 1643-1711 (Table P-PZ40)
1817.L54 Le Noir, Philippe, sieur du Crevain, fl. 1650-1680 (Table P-PZ40)
1817.L6 Le Pays, René, sieur du Plessis-Villeneuve, 1636-1690 (Table P-PZ40)
1817.L65 Le Petit, Claude, 1638 (ca.)-1662 (Table P-PZ40)
1817.L654 Lesconvel, Pierre de, 1650?-1722 (Table P-PZ40)
1817.L66 L'Estoile, Claude de 1597-1652 (Table P-PZ40)
1817.L7 Longepierre, Hilaire Bernard de Requeleyne, baron de, 1659-1721 (Table P-PZ40)
1818.M3 Magnon, Jean, d. 1662 (Table P-PZ40)
1818.M4 Mailly, chevalier de, d. ca. 1724 (Table P-PZ40)
1818.M6 Mairet, Jean de, 1604-1686 (Table P-PZ40)
1819 Malherbe, François de, 1555-1628
1819.A1 Works. By date
1819.A6 Poetical works
1819.A7 Letters
1819.A8-Z Biography and criticism
1820.M15 Malleville, Claude de, 1597-1647 (Table P-PZ40)
1820.M23 Marbeuf, Pierre de, 1596-1645 (Table P-PZ40)
1820.M24 Mareschal, André, fl. 1631-1646 (Table P-PZ40)
1820.M3 Maynard, François de, 1582?-1646
1820.M3A6-.M3A79 Separate works
1820.M3A8-.M3Z Biography and criticism
1820.M5 Ménage, Gilles, 1613-1692 (Table P-PZ40)
Cf. PN6252 Menagiana
1820.M77 Millot, Michel, fl. 1655 (Table P-PZ40)
Molière, Jean Baptiste Poquelin, 1622-1673
1821 Collected works. By date
1821.A3-Z Collected works. By editor
1823 Minor collections
1825 Translations. By language, A-Z
e. g.
1825.E5 English
1825.H8 Hungarian

Modern French literature
Individual authors
17th century
Molière, Jean Baptiste Poquelin, 1622-1673
Translations. By language, A-Z -- Continued

1825.P5 Portuguese

Separate works

1826.A2-.A3 Les amans magnifiques
1826.A5-.A6 L'amour médecin
1826.A7-.A8 Amphitryon
1827 L'avare (Table PQ11)
1828.B3-.B4 Le ballet des ballets
1828.B5-.B6 Le ballet des muses
1829 Le bourgeois gentilhomme (Table PQ11)
1830.C4-.C5 La comtesse d'Escarbagnas
1830.C6-.C7 La critique de l'école des femmes
1830.D4-.D5 Le dépit amoureux
1830.D6-.D7 Le divertissement du roy
Le docteur amoureux see PQ1844.D6+
1830.D8-.D9 Dom Garcie de Navarre
1831 Dom Juan, ou Le festin de pierre (Table PQ11)
1832.E3-.E4 L'école des femmes
1832.E5-.E6 L'école des maris
1832.E7-.E8 L'étourdi
1832.F3-.F4 Les fâcheux
1833 Les femmes savantes (Table PQ11)
Les festin de pierre, see PQ1831
1834.F5-.F6 Les fêtes de l'amour et de Bacchus
1834.F7-.F8 Les fourberies de Scapin
1834.G4-.G5 George Dandin, ou Le mari confondu
1834.G6-.G7 La gloire du Val-de-Grâce
Le grande divertissement royal, see PQ1834.G4+
L'imposteur, ou le Tartuffe, see PQ1842
1834.I4-.I5 L'impromptu de Versailles
1834.I6-.I7 Les incompatibles (Ballet)
1834.J2-.J3 La jalousie de Barbouillé
Joguenet see PQ1834.F7+
1835 La malade imaginaire (Table PQ11)
1836.M2-.M3 Le mariage forcé
1836.M4-.M5 Le médicin malgré lui
1836.M6-.M7 Le médicin volant
1836.M8-.M9 Mélicerte
1837 Le misanthrope (Table PQ11)
1837.M7-.M8 Monsieur de Pourceaugnac
Le plaisirs de l'île enchantée, see PQ1840.P2+
1839 Les précieuses ridicules (Table PQ11)
1840.P2-.P3 La princesse d'Élide

Modern French literature
Individual authors
17th century
Molière, Jean Baptiste Poquelin, 1622-1673
Separate works -- Continued

1840.P6-.P7 Psyché
1840.S3-.S4 Sganarelle, ou Le cocu imaginaire
1840.S7-.S8 Le Sicilien, ou L'amour peintre
1842 Le Tartuffe, ou L'imposteur (Table PQ11)
1843 Paraphrases. Adaptations. Tales from Molière
1844 Doubtful or spurious works
1844.D6-.D7 Le docteur amoureux
1844.L6-.L7 Le le livre abominable de 1665
1845 Imitations and parodies of the work of Molière
1846 Molière in poetry, drama, burlesque, etc.
1847 Translations of Molière (as subject)
1848 Illustrations to the works of Molière

Biography and criticism
1850 Periodicals. Societies. Collections
1851 Dictionaries, indexes, etc.
see also the special subject
For concordances and language dictionaries see PQ1867
1852.A1-.A3 Autobiography. Journals, letters, memoirs
1852.A4-Z General works (Literary biography. Life and works)
1853 Special periods and phases
Early life. Education
Love and marriage. Relations to women
Later life. Death
1854 Molière and his troupe
1855 Relations to contemporaries. Milieu. Age of Molière
Cf. PQ1860.A2 Criticism
1856 Homes and haunts. Local associations. Landmarks
1857 Anniversaries. Celebrations
1857.5 Iconography. Relics
1857.5.A5 Portraits
1857.5.Z7 Monuments
1857.5.Z9 Relics
(1857.9) Fiction, drama, etc. based on life of Molière
Class with author
1858 Authorship
Including manuscripts, forgeries, sources, etc.
1859 Chronology of works
Criticism and interpretation
1860.A2 Criticism by his contemporaries
1860.A3-Z General works. Genius. Philosophy
1861 Characters

Modern French literature
Individual authors
17th century
Molière, Jean Baptiste Poquelin, 1622-1673
Biography and criticism
Criticism and interpretation
Characters -- Continued

1862.A-Z Individual, A-Z
1863 Plots. Scenes. Time, etc.
1864.A-Z Treatment and knowledge of special subjects, A-Z
1864.C37 Carnival
1864.F4 Fear
1864.G36 Gastronomy
1864.L4 Law
1864.M35 Marriage
1864.P53 Play
1864.P6 Political and social views
Social views see PQ1864.P6
1864.W7 Women
1865 Textual criticism, commentaries, etc.
1866 Language, style, etc.
1867 Dictionaries. Concordances
1868 Grammar
1869 Versification
1871 Stage history
1875.M4 Monléon, Monsieur de, 17th cent. (Table P-PZ40)
1875.M6 Montausier, Charles de Saint-Maure, duc de, 1610-1690 (Table P-PZ40)
1875.M64 Montfleury, Antoine Jacob, called, 1640-1685 (Table P-PZ40)
1875.M74 Montreuil, Mathieu de, 1620-1691 (Table P-PZ40)
1875.M75 More, Alexandre, 1616-1670 (Table P-PZ40)
1875.M76 Motin, Pierre, ca. 1566-ca.1614 (Table P-PZ40)
1875.M8 Murat, Henriette Julie (de Castelnau) comtesse de, 1670-1716 (Table P-PZ40)
1875.N46 Nerveze, Antoine de, ca. 1570-ca. 1622 (Table P-PZ40)
1875.N5 Nicole, Pierre, 1625-1695 (Table P-PZ40)
1875.N7 Nouvelon, Nicolas L'Héritier, sieur de, 1613 (ca.)-1680 (Table P-PZ40)
1875.O3 Octavie, fl. 1658 (Table P-PZ40)
1875.O9 Oudin, César François, sieur de Préfontaine, fl. 1660-1671 (Table P-PZ40)
1876.P25 Palaprat, Jean, sieur de Bigot, 1650-1721 (Table P-PZ40)
1876.P3 Pascal, Blaise, 1623-1662 (Table P-PZ40)
1876.P66 Péchantrè, 1638-1708 (Table P-PZ40)
Péchantrès, Nicolas de, 1638-1708 see PQ1876.P66

Modern French literature
Individual authors
17th century

1876.P75 Pellisson-Fontanier, Paul, 1624-1693 (Table P-PZ40)
1877 Perrault, Charles, 1628-1703 (Table P-PZ37)
1879.P3 Perrin, Pierre, d. 1675 (Table P-PZ40)
1879.P34 Petit, Louis, 1614 (ca.)-1693 (Table P-PZ40)
1879.P35 Pichou, 1597-1631? (Table P-PZ40)
1879.P36 Picot, Antoine, baron de Puiset (Table P-PZ40)
1879.P45 Pinchesne, Étienne Martin, sieur de 1616-1680 (Table P-PZ40)
1879.P49 Prade, Jean le Royer, sieur de, fl. 1648-1677 (Table P-PZ40)
1879.P5 Pradon, Jacques, 1644-1698 (Table P-PZ40)
1879.P6 Préchac, Jean de, 1647?-1720 (Table P-PZ40)
1879.P65 Prévost, Jean, ca. 1580-1622 (Table P-PZ40)
1879.P87 Pure, Michel de, 1620-1680 (Table P-PZ40)
1880.Q6 Quennes, sieur de, fl. 1651 (Table P-PZ40)
1881 Quinault, Philippe, 1635-1688 (Table P-PZ39)
Rabutin, Roger de see PQ1733+
1883 Racan, Honorat de Bueil, marquis de, 1589-1670 (Table P-PZ37)
Racine, Jean Baptiste, 1639-1699
1885 Collected works. By date
1887.A-Z Selections. By editor, A-Z
1888.A-Z Translations. By language, A-Z
e. g.
1888.E5 English
Separate works
1889 Alexandre le Grand (Table P-PZ41)
1890 Andromaque (Table P-PZ41)
1891 Athalie (Table P-PZ41)
1892 Bajazet (Table P-PZ41)
1893 Bérénice (Table P-PZ41)
1894 Britannicus (Table P-PZ41)
1895 Esther (Table P-PZ41)
1896 Iphigénie (Table P-PZ41)
1897 Mithridate (Table P-PZ41)
1898 Phèdre (Table P-PZ41)
1899 Les plaideurs (Table P-PZ41)
1900 La Thébaïde (Table P-PZ41)
1901 Other works
1901.C23 Cantique spirituel
1901.L4 Lettres
1901.P6 Poésies
1902 Apocryphal, spurious works
1903 Dictionaries, indexes, etc.

Modern French literature
Individual authors
17th century
Racine, Jean Baptiste, 1639-1699 -- Continued
Biography and criticism

1904 General works
1904.5 Anniversaries. Celebrations
Criticism
1905 General
1906 Textual
Special
1907 Sources
1908.A-Z Other, A-Z
1908.A7 Appreciation in other countries
1908.B5 Bible
1908.C45 Characters
1908.G84 Guilt
1908.J35 Jansenists
1908.M43 Mediation
1908.N37 Narration (Rhetoric)
1908.S7 Stage history
1908.T7 Translations (as subject)
1908.W37 War
1909 Language. Grammar. Style
1912.R5 Ramberviller (Table P-PZ40)
1912.R75 Ravaud, Abraham, 1600-1646 (Table P-PZ40)
1913 Regnard, Jean François, 1655-1709 (Table P-PZ39)
1914.R4 Regnier-Desmarais, François Sraphin, abbé, 1632-1713 (Table P-PZ40)
1914.R57 Richelieu, cardinal (as author) (Table P-PZ40)
1914.R597 Rosidor, fl. 1686-1718 (Table P-PZ40)
1914.R6 Rosset, François de, b. ca. 1570 (Table P-PZ40)
1915 Rotrou, Jean, 1609-1650 (Table P-PZ39 modified)
1915.A61-.Z48 Separate works. By title
1915.A64-.A643 Agésilan de Colchos (Table P-PZ43)
1915.A7-.A73 Amélie (Table P-PZ43)
1915.A8-.A83 Antigone (Table P-PZ43)
1915.B3-.B33 La bague de l'oubli (Table P-PZ43)
1915.B4-.B43 Bélisaire (Table P-PZ43)
1915.B5-.B53 La belle Alphrède (Table P-PZ43)
1915.C2-.C23 Les captifs, ou Les esclaves (Table P-PZ43)
1915.C3-.C33 La Céliane (Table P-PZ43)
1915.C4-.C43 Célie, ou Le vice-roi de Naples (Table P-PZ43)
1915.C5-.C53 La Célimène (Table P-PZ43)
1915.C6-.C63 Clarice, ou L'amour constant (Table P-PZ43)
1915.C7-.C73 Cléagénor et Doristée (Table P-PZ43)
1915.C8-.C83 Clorinde (Table P-PZ43)

Modern French literature
Individual authors
17th century
Rotrou, Jean, 1609-1650
Separate works. By title -- Continued

1915.C9-.C93 Cosroès (Table P-PZ43)
1915.C95-.C953 Crisante (Table P-PZ43)
1915.D3-.D33 Les deux pucelles (Table P-PZ43)
Les deux Sosies see PQ1915.S7+
1915.D5-.D53 La Diane (Table P-PZ43)
1915.D7-.D73 Dom Bernard de Cabèrre (Table P-PZ43)
1915.D8-.D83 Dom Lope de Cardone (Table P-PZ43)
Doristée see PQ1915.C7+
1915.F5-.F53 Le filandre (Table P-PZ43)
1915.F6-.F63 Florimonde (Table P-PZ43)
1915.H4-.H43 Hercule mourant (Table P-PZ43)
1915.H5-.H53 L'heureuse Constance (Table P-PZ43)
1915.H6-.H63 L'heureux naufrage (Table P-PZ43)
1915.H8-.H83 L'hypochondriaque, ou Le mort amoureux (Table P-PZ43)
1915.I5-.I53 L'illustre amazone (Table P-PZ43)
1915.I6-.I63 L'innocente infidélité (Table P-PZ43)
1915.I7-.I73 Iphigénie en Aulide (Table P-PZ43)
1915.L3-.L33 Laure persécutée (Table P-PZ43)
1915.M4-.M43 Les Ménechmes (Table P-PZ43)
1915.O3-.O33 Les occasions perdues (Table P-PZ43)
1915.P4-.P43 La pèlerine amoureuse (Table P-PZ43)
1915.S3-.S33 Saint-Genest (Table P-PZ43)
1915.S6-.S63 La soeur (Table P-PZ43)
1915.S7-.S73 Les Sosies (Table P-PZ43)
1915.V4-.V43 Venceslas (Table P-PZ43)
Le véritable Saint-Genest see PQ1915.S3+
1917.S2 Sabatier, de, fl. 1687 (Table P-PZ40)
1917.S25 Sablé, Madeleine (de Souvré) marquise de, 1599-1678 (Table P-PZ40)
1917.S3 Saint-Amant, Marc Antoine Gérard, sieur de, 1594-1661? (Table P-PZ40)
1917.S5 Saint-Évremond, Charles de Marguetel de Saint Denis, seigneur de, 1613-1703 (Table P-PZ40 modified)
1917.S52 Spurious and doubtful works
1917.S53 Saint-Gilles, Charles de L'Enfant, chevalier de, fl. 1690-1706 (Table P-PZ40)
1917.S533 Saint-Glas, Pierre de, d. 1699 (Table P-PZ40)
1917.S542 Saint-Réal, Csar Vichard de, 1639-1692 (Table P-PZ40)
1917.S55 Santeul, Jean de, 1630-1697 (Table P-PZ40)
1917.S6 Sarasin, Jean François, 1614-1654 (Table P-PZ40)
1919 Scarron, Paul, 1610-1660 (Table P-PZ39 modified)

Modern French literature
Individual authors
17th century
Scarron, Paul, 1610-1660 -- Continued
1919.A61-.Z48 Separate works. By title
1919.A7-.A73 L'adultère innocente (Table P-PZ43)
1919.D6-.D63 Dom Japhet d'Arménie (Table P-PZ43)
1919.E6-.E63 Epistre chagrine à Mgr. de Mareschal d'Albret (Table P-PZ43)

1919.E8-.E83 L'escolier de Salamanque, ou Les généreux ennemis (Table P-PZ43)
1919.F3-.F33 La fausse apparence (Table P-PZ43)
1919.F6-.F63 La foire Sainct-Germain en vers burlesque (Table P-PZ43)
1919.G3-.G33 Le gardien de soy-mesme (Table P-PZ43)
Les généreux ennemis see PQ1919.E8+
1919.H4-.H43 L'héritier ridicule, ou La dame interessée (Table P-PZ43)
1919.J6-.J63 Jodelet, ou Le maître valet (Table P-PZ43)
1919.J7-.J73 Jodelet duelliste (Table P-PZ43)
1919.L4-.L43 Lettre en vers sur le mariage de Mlle. de Rohan (Table P-PZ43)
1919.M3-.M33 Le marquis ridicule, ou La comtesse faite à la haste (Table P-PZ43)
1919.M5-.M53 Les médecins au 17e siècle (Table P-PZ43)
1919.P5-.P53 Plus d'effets que de paroles (Table P-PZ43)
1919.P7-.P73 Le prince corsaire (Table P-PZ43)
1919.R4-.R43 La rélation véritable de tout ce qui s'est passé en l'autre monde, ou Combat des parques et des poëtes (Table P-PZ43)
Le romant comique
1919.R5 Texts. By date
1919.R5A-.R5Z Translations. By language, A-Z
1919.R6 Paraphrases. Adaptations, etc.
1919.R7 Criticism
Les trois Dorotées, ou Jodelet souffleté see PQ1919.J7+
1919.T8-.T83 Typhon, ou La gigantomachie (Table P-PZ43)
1920.S3 Schelandre, Jean de, 1585?-1635 (Table P-PZ40)
Scudéry, Georges de, 1601-1667
1921.A1 Collected works. By date
1921.A6-.Z4 Separate works
1921.A7 Alaric, ou Rome vaincue
1921.A75 L'amant libéral
1921.A8 L'amour tyrannique
1921.A85 Andromire
1921.A9 Arminius, ou Les frères ennemis

Modern French literature
Individual authors
17th century
Scudéry, Georges de, 1601-1667
Separate works -- Continued

1921.C6 La comédie des comédiens
Curia politiae see JC155
1921.D5 Didon
Discours politiques des rois see JC155
1921.E8 Eudoxe
1921.F5 Le fils supposé
1921.I3 Ibrahim, ou L'illustre Bassa (Play)
Cf. PQ1922.I3
1921.L5 Ligdamon et Lidias, ou La resemblance
1921.M6 La mort de César
Observations sur el Cid see PQ1750
1921.O4 Ode sur le retour de Mgr. le prince
1921.O6 L'ombre du grand Armand
1921.O7 Orante
1921.P6 Poésies diverses
1921.P7 Le prince déguisé
1921.S3 Salomon instruisant le roy
1921.T7 Le trompeur puny
1921.V3 Le vassal généreux
1921.Z5 Biography and criticism

Scudéry, Madeleine de, 1607-1701
Including her works published under name of Georges de Scudry

1922.A1 Collected works. By date
Separate works
1922.A6 Almahide
1922.A7 Amaryllis to Tityrus
1922.A8 Artamène, ou Le grand Cyrus
1922.C5 Clélie, histoire romaine
1922.C7 Les conversations sur divers sujets
1922.F4 Les femmes illustres, ou Les harangues heroïques
Le grand Cyrus see PQ1922.A8
1922.I3 Ibrahim, ou L'illustre Bassa (Novel)
1922.L4 Lettres
1922.M3 Mathilde
1922.Z4 Zelinda
1922.Z5 Biography and criticism
1924.S3 Segrais, Jean Regnauld de, 1624-1701 (Table P-PZ40)
1924.S4 Selve, Lazare de, ca. 1550-1622 (Table P-PZ40)
1924.S6 Sénecé, Antoine Bauderon de, 1643-1737 (Table P-PZ40)

Modern French literature
Individual authors
17th century -- Continued
Sévigné, Marie (de Rabutin Chantal) marquise de, 1626-1698
Lettres
1925.A1 Comprehensive collections
Translations (including selections). By translator
1925.A2-.A29 English
1925.A3-.A39 German
1925.A4-.A49 Other languages, alphabetically
(1925.A5) Posthumously published letters
see PQ1925.A6
1925.A6 Selections. By editor
1925.A7-.A89 Letters to special persons, alphabetically
1925.A9-Z Biography and criticism
1926.S6 Somaize, Antoine Bandeau de, b. ca. 1630 (Table P-PZ40)
1926.S7 Sonnet, Thomas, sieur de Courval, 1577-1627? (Table P-PZ40)
Sorel, Charles, 1602?-1674
1927.A1 Collected works
1927.A6-.A79 Separate works
1927.A64 Le berger extravagant
1927.A65 Cleagenor et Doristée
1927.A67 Histoire comique de Francion
1927.A68 La jeunesse de Francion
1927.A7 Les nouvelles françoises
1927.A73 Polyandre
1927.A75 Relation véritable de ce qui s'est passé au royaume de Sophie
1927.A8-Z Biography and criticism
1928.S7 Subligny, Adrien Thomas Perdou de, b. ca. 1640 (Table P-PZ40)
1928.T3 Tabarin, Jean Salomon, known as, d. 1633 (Table P-PZ40)
1928.T5 Testu, Jacques, 1626 (ca.)-1706 (Table P-PZ40)
Théophile see PQ1933
1928.T7 Torche, Antoine de, 1631-1675 (Table P-PZ40)
1929 Tristan l'Hermite, François, 1601-1655
1929.A1 Collected works. By date
Separate works
1929.A7 Les amours
1929.L8 La lyre
1929.M3 La Mariane
1929.M7 La mort de Sénèque
1929.P8 Les plaintes d'Acante

Modern French literature
Individual authors
16th century
Tristan l'Hermite, Francois
Separate works
Vers heroïque see PQ1929.A1

1929.Z8 Biography and criticism
1930.T5 Troterel, Pierre, sieur d'Aves (Table P-PZ40)
1930.T9 Tyssot de Patot, Simon, b. 1655 (Table P-PZ40)
1930.V28 Valincour, Jean Baptiste Henri du Trousset de, 1653-1730 (Table P-PZ40)
1930.V3 Vallée, fl. 1656-1662 (Table P-PZ40)
Vallée, Jacques, sieur des Barreaux see PQ1794.D37
1930.V5 Vauquelin, Nicolas, sieur des Yveteaux, 1567-1649 (Table P-PZ40)
Vauquelin de la Fresnaye, Jean, 1536-1606 or 8 see PQ1707.V35
1931 Vergier, Jacques, 1655-1720 (Table P-PZ39)
1932 Ver - Via
1933 Viau, Théophile de, known as Théophile, 1590-1626
1933.A1 Collected works
1933.A6-.A79 Separate works
1933.A63 Apologie de Théophile
1933.A67 La maison de Silvie
1933.A7 Pasiphaé
1933.A73 La pénitence de Théophile
1933.A75 Pyrame et Thisbé
1933.A8-Z Biography and criticism
Villedieu, Mme. de see PQ1794.D5
1935.V3 Villiers, Claude Deschamps, sier de, 1600?-1681 (Table P-PZ40 modified)
1935.V3A61-.V3Z458 Separate works. By title
1935.V3A67 Le festin de pierre, ou Le fils criminel
1935.V5 Villiers, Pierre de, 1648-1728 (Table P-PZ40)
1935.V6 Voiture, Vincent, 1597-1648 (Table P-PZ38)
Yveteaux see PQ1930.V5
18th century
Subarrange by Table P-PZ40 or Table P-PZ43 unless otherwise specified
1947 Anonymous works (Table P-PZ28)
Affichard, Thomas l' see PQ1993.L25
1951.A5 Aignan, Étienne, 1773-1824 (Table P-PZ40)
1951.A7 Aïssé, Charlotte Élisabeth, 1695?-1733 (Table P-PZ40)
1951.A76 Alègre, d'. (Table P-PZ40)
1951.A8 Allainval, Léonor Jean Christine Soulas d', abbé, d. 1753 (Table P-PZ40)

Modern French literature
Individual authors
18th century -- Continued

1953	Allarde, Marie Franois Denis Thérésa Leroi, baron d', 1778-1840 (Table P-PZ39)
1954.A5	Andrieux, François Guillaume Jean Stanislas, 1759-1833 (Table P-PZ40)
1954.A52	Aquin de Chateau-Lyon, Pierre Louis d', 1720-1796 (Table P-PZ40)
1954.A54	Argens, Jean Baptiste de Boyer, marquis d', 1704-1771 (Table P-PZ40)
1954.A57	Argenson, Marc Antoine René de Voyer, marquis de Paulmy d', 1722-1787 (Table P-PZ40)
1954.A6	Argenson, René Louis de Voyer de Paulmy, marquis d', 1694-1757 (Table P-PZ40)
1954.A7	Arnaud, Franois Thomas Marie de Baculard d', 1718-1803 (Table P-PZ38)
1954.A8	Auvigny, Jean du Castre d', 1712-1743
	Baculard d' Arnaud see PQ1954.A7
1955.B39	Barbé-Marbois, Franois, Marquis de, 1745-1837 (Table P-PZ40)
1955.B4	Barbier, Marie Anne, d. 1742 (Table P-PZ40)
	Barré, M., 1749-1832 see PQ1955.B58
1955.B58	Barré, Pierre Yves, 1749-1832 (Table P-PZ40)
1955.B6	Barrett, Paul, 1728-ca. 1795 (Table P-PZ40)
1955.B65	Barthe, Nicolas, Thomas, 1736-1785 (Table P-PZ40)
1955.B68	Barthélemy, Jean Jacques, 1716-1795 (Table P-PZ40)
1955.B7	Barthélemy, Louis, 1759-1815 (Table P-PZ40)
1955.B715	Bastide, Jean-François de, 1724-1798 (Table P-PZ40)
1955.B718	Baudouin, 18th cent. (Table P-PZ40)
1955.B75	Beauchamps, Pierre-François Godart de, 1689-1761 (Table P-PZ40)
1955.B8	Beauharnais, Fanny (Mouchard de Chaban) comtesse de, 1737-1813 (Table P-PZ40)
1956	Beaumarchais, Pierre Augustin Caron de, 1732-1799 (Table P-PZ37, modified)
1956.A61-.A78	Separate works. By title
1956.A63	Le barbier de Séville
1956.A66	Eugénie
1956.A7	Le mariage de Figaro
1956.A76	Le tartare á la légion
1957.B25	Beaunoir, Alexandre Louis Bertrand, 1746-1823 (Table P-PZ40)
1957.B27	Beaurieu, Gaspard Guillard de, 1728-1795 (Table P-PZ38)
1957.B29	Beckford, William, 1760-1844 (Table P-PZ40)

Modern French literature
Individual authors
18th century -- Continued

1957.B3 Beffroy de Reigny, Louis Abel, 1757-1811 (Table P-PZ40)
1957.B326 Belin de Ballu, Jacques Nicolas, 1753-1815 (Table P-PZ40)
1957.B33 Belloy, Pierre Laurent Buyrette de, 1727-1775 (Table P-PZ40)
1957.B4 Bernard, Pierre Joseph, known as Gentil-Bernard, 1710-1775 (Table P-PZ40)
Bernardin de Saint Pierre see PQ2065
1957.B45 Bernis, François Joachim de Pierre de, comte de Lyon, cardinal, 1715-1794 (Table P-PZ40)
1957.B455 Berquin, M. (Arnaud), 1747-1791 (Table P-PZ40)
1957.B46 Bertin, Antoine, chevalier de, 1752-1790 (Table P-PZ40)
1957.B4613 Bertin d'Antilly, A.-L. (Auguste-Louis), 1763-1804 (Table P-PZ40)
1957.B462 Besenval, Pierre Victor, baron de, 1721-1791 (Table P-PZ40)
1957.B47 Bilderbeck, Ludwig Benedict Franz, freiherr von, b. 1766 (Table P-PZ40)
1957.B5 Billardon de Sauvigny, Edme Louis, 1736-1812 (Table P-PZ40)
1957.B52 Bitaubé, Paul Jérémie, 1732-1808 (Table P-PZ40)
1957.B535 Blin de Sainmore, Adrien Michel Hyacinthe, 1733-1807 (Table P-PZ40)
1957.B539 Boindin, Nicolas 1676-1751 (Table P-PZ40)
1957.B55 Boissy, Louis de, 1694-1758 (Table P-PZ40)
1957.B59 Bonardy, Jean Baptiste (Table P-PZ40)
1957.B6 Bonnard, Bernard, chevalier de, 1744-1784 (Table P-PZ40)
1957.B65 Borde, Charles, 1711-1781 (Table P-PZ40)
1957.B67 Bordelon, Laurent, 1653-1730 (Table P-PZ40)
1957.B7 Boufflers, Stanislas Jean de, marquis, 1738-1815 (Table P-PZ40)
1957.B72 Bougeant, Guillaume Hyacinthe, 1690-1743 (Table P-PZ40)
1957.B75 Bourdon, Louis Gabriel, 1741-1795 (Table P-PZ40)
Bourlin, Jean André see PQ1981.D8
1957.B78 Boutet de Monvel, Jacques Marie, 1745-1812 (Table P-PZ40)
1957.B8 Bret, Antoine, 1717-1792 (Table P-PZ40)
1957.B83 Bricaire de La Dixmerie, Nicolas, d. 1791 (Table P-PZ40)
1959.C23 Cailhava d'Estendoux, Jean François, 1730-1813 (Table P-PZ40)
1959.C237 Cailleau, André-Charles, 1731-1798 (Table P-PZ40)

Modern French literature
Individual authors
18th century -- Continued

1959.C3 Caracciolì, Louis Antoine de, 1721-1803 (Table P-PZ40)
1959.C33 Carbon de Flins des Oliviers, Claude Marie Emmanuel, 1757-1806 (Table P-PZ40)
1959.C4 Carmontelle, Louis Carrogis, known as, 1717-1806 (Table P-PZ40)
1959.C45 Carolet, d. 1739 (Table P-PZ40)
1959.C5 Cartier de Saint-Philip (Table P-PZ40)
1959.C6 Casanova, Giacomo, 1725-1798
For biography see D285.8.C4
For literary works in Italian see PQ4687.C274
1959.C7 Castéra, Jean Henri, b. ca. 1755 (Table P-PZ40)
1959.C8 Castillon, Jean Louis, 1720-ca. 1793 (Table P-PZ40)
1960 Catharine II, empress of Russia (and others) (Table P-PZ39)
1961.C27 Caux, Monsieur de (Gilles), 1682-1733 (Table P-PZ40)
1961.C4 Caylus, Anne Claude Philippe, comte de, 1692-1765 (Table P-PZ40)
1961.C5 Cazotte, Jacques, 1719-1792 (Table P-PZ38)
1961.C6 Cérou, Pierre (Table P-PZ40)
Chabannes, Marc Antoine Jacques Rochon de see PQ2027.R5
1963.C3 Chabanon, Michel Paul Gui de, 1730-1792 (Table P-PZ40)
1963.C35 Challes, Robert, 1659-ca. 1720 (Table P-PZ40)
1963.C4 Chamfort, Sébastien Roch Nicolas, called, 1740?-1794 (Table P-PZ40)
1963.C45 Chansierges (Table P-PZ40)
1963.C5 Charlemagne, Armand, 1753-1838 (Table P-PZ40)
1963.C55 Charriére, Isabella Agneta (Van Tuyll) de, d. 1805 (Table P-PZ40)
1963.C7 Chaussard, Pierre Jean Baptiste, 1766-1823 (Table P-PZ40)
1963.C8 Chavannes de La Giraudière, H. de (Table P-PZ40)
1965 Chénier, André Marie, 1762-1794 (Table P-PZ37)
1966 Chénier, Marie Joseph Blaise, 1764-1811 (Table P-PZ39)
1968.C4 Chevrier, François Antoine, 1721-1762 (Table P-PZ40)
Choderlos de Laclos see PQ1993.L22
1968.C54 Clément, Pierre, 1707-1767 (Table P-PZ40)
1968.C8 Colardeau, Charles Pierre, 1732-1776 (Table P-PZ40)
1969 Collé, Charles, 1709-1783 (Table P-PZ39)
1971.C3 Collin d' Harleville, Jean François, 1755-1806
1971.C355 Constant, Samuel de (Table P-PZ40)

Modern French literature
Individual authors
18th century -- Continued

1971.C357 Constant de Rebecque, David-Louis-Constant de, 1722-1785 (Table P-PZ40)

Cottin, Marie (Risteau), called Sophie see PQ2211.C412

1971.C6 Crébillon, Claude Prosper Jolyot de, 1707-1777 (Crébillon fils) (Table P-PZ40)

1971.C7 Crébillon, Prosper Jolyot de, 1674-1762 (Table P-PZ40)

1971.C76 Crouzet, Pierre, 1753-1811 (Table P-PZ40)

1971.C8 Cubières, Michel de, known as Cubières-Palmezeaux, 1752-1820 (Table P-PZ40)

Damaniant, Antoine Jean Bourlin see PQ1981.D8

1972.D2 Danchet, Antoine, 1671-1748 (Table P-PZ40)

1972.D35 Daubenton, Mme. (Maguerite), 1720-1788 (Table P-PZ40)

1973.D4 Decremps, Henri, 1746-1826? (Table P-PZ40)

1973.D6 Delacroix, Jacques Vincent, 1743-1832 (Table P-PZ40)

1975 Delille, Jacques Montanier, called, 1738-1813 (Table P-PZ39 modified)

1975.A61-.Z48 Separate works. By title

1975.B4-.B5 Bagatelles (Table P-PZ43a)

1975.C2-.C3 Catacombes de Rome (Table P-PZ43a)

1975.C6-.C7 La conversation (Table P-PZ43a)

1975.D4-.D5 Le départ d' Eden (Table P-PZ43a)

1975.D6-.D7 Discours de réception (Table P-PZ43a)

1975.D8-.D9 Dithyrambe sur l'immortalité de l'âme (Table P-PZ43a)

L'Énéide see PA6809

1975.E6-.E7 Epître sur la ressource qu' offre la culture des arts et des lettres (Table P-PZ43a)

Les Géorgiques françaises see PA6809

1975.H5-.H6 L'homme des champs, ou les Géorgiques françaises (Table P-PZ43a)

1975.I4-.I5 L'imagination (Table P-PZ43a)

1975.J3-.J4 Les jardins; ou, l'art d'embellir les paysages (Table P-PZ43a)

Le malheur et la pitié see PQ1975.P5+

1975.P5-.P6 La pitié (Table P-PZ43a)

1975.T6-.T7 Les trois règnes de la nature (Table P-PZ43a)

Delisle de la Drévetière see PQ1993.L24

1977.D32 Demoustier, Charles Albert, 1760-1801 (Table P-PZ40)

1977.D33 Denon, Dominique Vivant, baron, 1747-1825 (Table P-PZ38)

1977.D4 Desboulmiers, Jean Auguste Julien, known as, 1731-1771 (Table P-PZ40)

1977.D46 Desfontaines, M. l'abbé, 1685-1745 (Table P-PZ40)

Modern French literature
Individual authors
18th century -- Continued

	Desfontaines, Pierre François Guyot, 1685-1745 see PQ1977.D46
1977.D48	Desfontaines de La Vallée, Guillaume François Fouques Deshayes, 1733-1825 (Table P-PZ40)
1977.D5	Desforges, Pierre Jean Baptiste Choudard-, 1746-1806 (Table P-PZ40)
1977.D52	Desforges-Maillard, Paul, 1699-1772 (Table P-PZ40)
1977.D63	Deslandes, André François Boureau, 1690-1757 (Table P-PZ40)
1977.D65	Desmahis, Joseph François Édouard de Corsembleu, 1722-1761 (Table P-PZ40)
1977.D66	Desorgues, Théodore, 1763-1808 (Table P-PZ40)
1977.D67	Despréaux, Jean Étienne, 1748-1820 (Table P-PZ40)
1977.D683	Destival de Braban (Table P-PZ40)
1977.D7	Destouches, Philippe Néricault, 1680-1754 (Table P-PZ38) Cf. B2010+ Philosophy
	Diderot, Denis, 1713-1784
1979.A1-.A19	Collected works
1979.A6-.A79	Separate works e. g.
1979.A64	Le fils naturel
1979.A66	Le neveu de Rameau
1979.A73	Le paradox sur le comédien
1979.A74	Le père de famille
1979.A75	La pièce et la prologue
1979.A76	La religieuse
1979.A8	Memoirs, letters, etc.
1979.A85-Z	Biography and criticism
1981.D12	Didot, Pierre, 1761-1853 (Table P-PZ40)
1981.D2	Dionis, Mlle. (Table P-PZ40)
1981.D3	Dominique, i.e. Pierre Franois Biancolelli, called, 1680-1734 (Table P-PZ40)
1981.D35	Dorat, Claude Joseph, 1734-1780 (Table P-PZ40)
1981.D4	Dorvigny, Louis Archambault, called, 1742?-1812 (Table P-PZ40)
1981.D45	Dreux, Pierre Lucien Joseph, 1756-1827 (Table P-PZ40)
1981.D48	Du Boccage, Mme Marie Anne (Le Page) Fiquet, 1710-1802 (Table P-PZ40)
1981.D5	Dubois-Fontanelle, Jean Gaspard, 1737-1812 (Table P-PZ40)
1981.D53	Dubuissen, Pierre Ulric, 1746-1794 (Table P-PZ40)
1981.D55	Du Châtelet-Lomont, Gabrielle Émilie (Le Tonnelier de Breteuil) marquise, 1706-1749 (Table P-PZ40)

Modern French literature
Individual authors
18th century -- Continued

1981.D6 Ducis, Jean François, 1733-1816 (Table P-PZ40)
1981.D63 Duclos, Charles Pinot, 1704-1772 (Table P-PZ38)
1981.D65 Du Deffand de La Lande, Marie Anne (De Vichy Chamrond) marquise, 1697-1780 (Table P-PZ38)
1981.D75 Dulaurens, Henry Joseph, 1719-1797 (Table P-PZ40)
1981.D8 Dumaniant, Antoine Jean Bourlin, called, 1752-1828 (Table P-PZ40)
1981.D895 Du Terrail, Joseph Durey de Sauroy, marquis, 1712-1770 (Table P-PZ40)
1981.D9 Duveyrier, Honoré Marie Nicolas, baron, 1753-1839 (Table P-PZ40)
1981.E44 Elie de Beaumont, Mme. (Anmne-Louise Morin-Dumesnil), 1729-1783 (Table P-PZ40)
1982.E8 Esménard, Joseph Étienne, 1767-1811 (Table P-PZ40)
1982.E87 Evra (Table P-PZ40)
1982.F3 Fagan, Christophe Barthélemy, 1702-1755 (Table P-PZ40)
1982.F4 Falbaire de Quinqey, Charles Georges Fenouillot de, 1727-1800? (Table P-PZ40)
1982.F8 Fauques. Marianne-Agnès Pillement, dame de, ca. 1720-ca. 1777 (Table P-PZ40)
1983.F3 Favart, Charles Simon, 1710-1792 (Table P-PZ40)
1983.F34 Favre, de, abbé, of the Société littéraire of Metz (Table P-PZ40)
Favre, Jean Baptiste Castor, 1727-1783 see PC3401.F3
Fenouillot de Falbaire de Quingey see PQ1982.F4
Flahaut, Adélaïde, Marie Émile, comtesse de see PQ2429.S6
1983.F6 Florian, Jean Pierre Claris de, 1755-1794 (Table P-PZ40)
1983.F7 Fontaines, Marie Louis Charlotte de Pelard (de Givry) comtesse de, d. 1730 (Table P-PZ40)
1983.F75 Fougeret de Monbron, Louis Charles, ca. 1720-1761 (Table P-PZ40)
1983.F825 Fréron, Elie-Catherine, 1718-1776 (Table P-PZ40)
1983.F83 Friedrich II, der Grosse, king of Prussia, 1712-1786
Collected works see DD405
1983.F85 Fromaget, Nicolas, d. 1759 (Table P-PZ40)
1983.F9 Fuzelier, Louis, 1672-1752 (Table P-PZ40)
1985.G2 Gacon, François, 1667-1725 (Table P-PZ40)
1985.G3 Gaillard de La Bataille, Pierre Alexandre, 1708-1779 (Table P-PZ40)
1985.G33 Galiani, Ferdinando, 1728-1787 (Table P-PZ40)
1985.G346 Gallet, chansonnier et auteur dramatique, 1698?-1757 (Table P-PZ40)

Modern French literature
Individual authors
18th century -- Continued

1985.G4 Gayot de Pitaval, Franois, 1673-1743 (Table P-PZ40)
Genest, Charles Claude, 1639-1719 see PQ1799.G32
1985.G5 Genlis, Stéphanie Félicité, comtesse de, 1746-1830 (Table P-PZ38)
1985.G56 Gérard, Philippe Louis, 1737-1813 (Table P-PZ40)
1985.G564 Gervaise de Latouche, Jean-Charles, 1715-1782 (Table P-PZ40)
1985.G57 Gilbert, Nicolas Joseph Laurent, 1751-1780 (Table P-PZ40)
1985.G58 Giraud, Claude Marie, 1711-1780 (Table P-PZ40)
1985.G62 Giuseppina, di Lorena, principessa di Carignano, 1735-1797 (Table P-PZ40)
1985.G65 Godard d'Aucour, Claude, 1716-1795 (Table P-PZ40)
1985.G68 Goldoni, Carlo, 1707-1793 (Table P-PZ40)
Cf. PQ4693+ Italian literature
1985.G7 Gomez, Madeleine Angélique (Poisson) de, 1684-1770 (Table P-PZ40)
1985.G8 Gorjy, Jean Claude, 1753-1795 (Table P-PZ40)
1985.G83 Gorsas, Antoine Joseph, 1752-1793 (Table P-PZ40)
1985.G86 Gouges, Olympe de, 1748-1793 (Table P-PZ40)
1986 Graffigny, Françoise d'Issembourg d'Happoncourt de, 1695-1758
1986.A1 Collected works. By date
1986.A6-.Z4 Separate works
1986.Z5 Biography. Criticism
1987.G13 Grainville, Jean Baptiste François Xavier Cousin de, 1746-1805 (Table P-PZ40)
1987.G15 Grandval, Charles François Racot de, 1710-1784 (Table P-PZ40)
1987.G2 Grécourt, Jean Baptiste Joseph Willart de, 1683-1743 (Table P-PZ40)
1987.G3 Gresset, Jean Baptiste Louis, 1709-1777 (Table P-PZ40)
1987.G4 Grivel, Guillaume, 1735-1810 (Table P-PZ40)
1987.G43 Grosley, Pierre Jean, 1718-1785 (Table P-PZ40)
1987.G45 Guénard, Élisabeth, baronne de Méré, 1751-1829 (Table P-PZ40)
1987.G49 Gueudeville, Nicolas, ca. 1654-ca. 1721 (Table P-PZ40)
1987.G5 Gueulette, Thomas Simon, 1683-1766 (Table P-PZ40)
1987.G6 Guyot de Merville, Michel, 1696-1755 (Table P-PZ40)
1987.G7 Guyton de Morveau, Louis Bernard, baron, 1737-1816 (Table P-PZ40)
1988.H3 Hamilton, Anthony, count, 1645?-1719 (Table P-PZ38)
For his Mémoires de la vie du comte de Gramont see DA447.G7

Modern French literature
Individual authors
18th century -- Continued

1988.H4 Henrion, M. (Charles), d. 1808 (Table P-PZ40)
1988.H42 Henzi, Samuel, ca. 1700-1749 (Table P-PZ40)
1988.H45 Hérault de Séchelles, Marie Jean, 1759-1794 (Table P-PZ40)
1988.H5 Hilliard d'Auberteuil, Michel René, 1751-1789 (Table P-PZ40)
Houdart, de Lamotte, Antoine see PQ1993.L46
1989.I6 Imbert, Barthélemi, 1747-1790 (Table P-PZ40)
1989.J8 Julien Scopon, de, fl. 1728 (Table P-PZ40)
1989.L3 La Beaumelle, Laurent Angliviel de, 1726-1773 (Table P-PZ40)
1993.L2 La Chaussée, Pierre Claude Nivelle de, 1692-1754 (Table P-PZ40)
1993.L22 Laclos, Pierre Ambroise François Choderlos de, 1741-1803 (Table P-PZ40)
1993.L24 La Drévetière, Louis François, sieur de l'Isle, 1682-1756 (Table P-PZ40)
1993.L25 Laffichard, Thomas, 1698-1753 (Table P-PZ40)
1993.L3 Lafont, Joseph de, 1686-1725 (Table P-PZ40)
Lagrange-Chancel, François Joseph Chancel, known as, 1677-1758 see PQ1814.L4
1993.L35 Laguérie, Jean Tesson de, 1744-1776 (Table P-PZ40)
1993.L4 La Harpe, Jean François de, 1739-1803 (Table P-PZ40)
1993.L426 Lamarteliere, M. (Jean Henri Ferdinand), 1761-1830 (Table P-PZ40)
1993.L428 Lambert, Anne Thérèse de Marguenat de Courcelles, marquise de, 1647-1733 (Table P-PZ40)
1993.L43 Lambert, Claude François, 1705-1765 (Table P-PZ40)
1993.L433 Lambert, L.-T. (Table P-PZ40)
1993.L45 Lamorlière, Jacques Rochette de, 1719-1785 (Table P-PZ40)
1993.L46 La Motte, Antoine Houdar de, 1672-1731 (Table P-PZ40)
1993.L5 Lancelin, 18th cent. (Table P-PZ40)
1993.L55 La Noue, Jean Sauvé de, 1701-1761 (Table P-PZ40)
1993.L6 Lantier, Étienne François de, 1734-1826 (Table P-PZ40)
1993.L63 Lattaignant, Gabriel Charles de, 1697-1779 (Table P-PZ40)
1993.L65 Lavallée, Joseph, marquis de Bois-Robert, 1747-1816 (Table P-PZ40)
1993.L667 Laya, J.L. (Jean Louis) 1761-1833 (Table P-PZ40)
1993.L67 Leblanc de Guillet, Antoine Blanc, called, 1730-1799 (Table P-PZ40)
1993.L7 Le Brun, Antoine Louis, 1680-1743 (Table P-PZ40)

Modern French literature
Individual authors
18th century -- Continued

1993.L75 Le Brun, Ponce Denis Écouchard, 1729-1807 (Table P-PZ40)
1993.L8 Le Clerc, Laurent-Josse, 1677-1736 (Table P-PZ40)
Lefranc, Jean Jacques, marquis de Pompignan see PQ2019.P8
1995.L4 Legay, Louis Pierre Prudent, 144-1826 (Table P-PZ40)
1995.L45 Léger, François Pierre Auguste, 1766-1823 (Table P-PZ40)
1995.L5 Legouvé, Gabriel Marie Jean Baptiste, 1764-1812 (Table P-PZ40)
1995.L6 Legrand, Marc Antoine, 1673-1728 (Table P-PZ40)
1995.L62 Lejeune, Augustin, fl. 1800 (Table P-PZ40)
1995.L65 Le Mierre, Antoine Marin, 1723-1793 (Table P-PZ40)
1995.L7 Léonard, Nicolas Germain, 1744-1793 (Table P-PZ40)
1995.L75 Le Prince de Beaumont, Marie, 1711-1780 (Table P-PZ40)
1995.L8 Le Roy de Lozembrune, François Candide, 1751-1801 (Table P-PZ40)
1997 Le Sage, Alain René, 1688-1747
1997.A1 Collected works. By date
1997.A11-.A14 Collected works. By editor
1997.A5-.Z3 Separate works
Cf. ML, Music
1997.A5-.A6 Les amants jaloux
1997.A7-.A8 Aventures de M. Robert Chevalier, dit de Beauchêne
1997.B3-.B4 Le bachelier de Salamanque
1997.B7-.B8 La boite de Pandore
1997.C7-.C8 Crispin, rival de son maître
1997.D5-.D6 Le diable boiteux
Gil Blas
1997.G5 Texts. By date
1997.G6 Translations. By language
1997.G7 Criticism
1997.J6-.J7 Une journée des Parques
1997.P4-.P5 Les pèlerins de la Mecque
1997.T6-.T7 Turcaret
1997.V34-.V343 Valise trouvée (Table P-PZ43)
1997.Z4A-.Z4Z Spurious works, by title, A-Z
1997.Z5A-.Z5Z Biography. Criticism
1999.L3 Le Tourneur, Pierre Prime Félicien, 1737-1788 (Table P-PZ40)
1999.L35 Lezay-Marnézia, Claude-François-Adrien, marquis de, 1735-1800 (Table P-PZ40)

Modern French literature
Individual authors
18th century -- Continued

1999.L4 L'Héritier de Villandon, Marie Jeanne, 1664-1734 (Table P-PZ40)
1999.L47 Ligne, Charles Joseph, prince de, 1735-1814 (Table P-PZ40)
1999.L48 Loaisel de Tréogate, Joseph Marie, 1752-1812 (Table P-PZ40)
1999.L49 Longchamps, Ch. de (Charles), 1768-1832 (Table P-PZ40)
1999.L5 Longchamps, Pierre de, d. 1812 (Table P-PZ40)
Lore see PQ1982.E87
1999.L6 Louvet de Couvrai, Jean Baptiste, 1760-1797 (Table P-PZ40)
1999.L7 Luchet, Jean Pierre Louis de La Roche du Maine, marquis de, 1740-1792 (Table P-PZ40)
1999.L8 Lussan, Marguerite de, 1682-1758 (Table P-PZ40)
1999.L87 Luynes, Louis-Joseph d'Albert de, prince de Grimbergen, 1672-1758 (Table P-PZ40)
2001.M2 Maimieux, Joseph de, 1753-1820 (Table P-PZ40)
2001.M3 Mainvilliers, Genu Soalhat de, d. 1776 (Table P-PZ40)
2001.M4 Malfilâtre, Jacques Charles Louis, 1733-1767 (Table P-PZ40)
2001.M434 Mannequins
2001.M48 Marchant, François, 1761-1793 (Table P-PZ40)
2001.M5 Maréchal, Pierre Sylvain, 1750-1803 (Table P-PZ40)
2003 Marivaux, Pierre Carlet de Chamblain de, 1688-1763
2003.A1 Collected works. By date
2003.A11-.A14 Collected works. By editor
2003.A6-.Z3 Separate works
2003.A6-.A63 Annibal (Table P-PZ43)
2003.A7-.A73 Arlequin poli par l'amour (Table P-PZ43)
2003.A8-.A83 Les aventures de ... ou, Les effets surprenants de la sympathie (Table P-PZ43)
2003.C3-.C33 Le cabinet du philosophe (Table P-PZ43)
2003.C6-.C63 La commére (Table P-PZ43)
2003.D55-.D553 La dispute (Table P-PZ43)
2003.D6-.D63 La double inconstance (Table P-PZ43)
2003.E7-.E73 L'épreuve (Table P-PZ43)
2003.F3-.F33 Les fausses confidences (Table P-PZ43)
2003.H7-.H73 L'Homère travesti (Table P-PZ43)
2003.I4-.I43 L'île des esclaves (Table P-PZ43)
2003.I44-.I443 L'indigent philosophe (Table P-PZ43)
2003.J4-.J43 Le jeu de l'amour et du hasard (Table P-PZ43)
2003.L4-.L43 Le legs (Table P-PZ43)
2003.L47-.L473 Lettres sur les habitants de Paris (Table P-PZ43)

Modern French literature
Individual authors
18th century
Marivaux, Pierre Carlet de Chamblain de, 1688-1763
Separate works -- Continued

2003.P3-.P33 Le paysan parvenu (Table P-PZ43)
2003.P4-.P43 Pharsamon (Table P-PZ43)
2003.S4-.S43 La seconde surprise de l'amour (Table P-PZ43)
2003.S5-.S53 Les sincères (Table P-PZ43)
2003.S6-.S63 Le spectateur français (Table P-PZ43)
2003.S8-.S83 La surprise de l'amour (Table P-PZ43)
2003.T4-.T43 Le Télémaque travesti (Table P-PZ43)
2003.T75-.T753 Le triomphe de l'amour (Table P-PZ43)
2003.V5-.V53 La vie de Marianne (Table P-PZ43)
2003.V7-.V73 Le voiture embourbée (Table P-PZ43)
2003.Z5 Biography and criticism
2004 Mari - Marm
2004.M37 Marmion, Nicolas, 1751-1837 (Table P-PZ40)
2005 Marmontel, Jean François, 1723-1799 (Table P-PZ39 modified)
Cf. ML50.2 Literature on music
2005.A7-.Z48 Separate works. By title
e. g.
2005.B4-.B5 Bélisaire (Table P-PZ43a)
2005.B6-.B63 La bergère des Alpes (Table P-PZ43)
2005.C5-.C6 Contes moraux (Table P-PZ43a)
2005.I5-.I6 Les Incas (Table P-PZ43a)
2005.M4-.M5 Mémoires (Table P-PZ43a)
2007.M15 Marsollier des Vivetières, Benoît Joseph, 1750-1817 (Table P-PZ40)
2007.M2 Marteau, François Joseph, b. 1732 (Table P-PZ40)
2007.M25 Masson, Alexandre Frédéric Jacques de, marquis de Pezay, 1741-1777 (Table P-PZ40)
2007.M3 Maucomble, Jean François Dieudonné, 1735-1768 (Table P-PZ40)
2007.M4 Mayer, Charles Joseph, 1751-1825? (Table P-PZ40)
2007.M5 Melon, Jean François, 1675-1738 (Table P-PZ40)
2007.M54 Mérard de Saint-Just, Anne Jeanne Félicité (d'Ormoy) b. 1765 (Table P-PZ40)
2007.M55 Mérard de Saint-Just, Simon Pierre, 1749-1812 (Table P-PZ40)
2007.M58 Mercier, Claude François Xavier, 1763-1800 (Table P-PZ40)
2007.M6 Mercier, Louis Sébastien, 1740-1814 (Table P-PZ38)
2007.M7 Michel (de Saint-Sauveur-le-Vicomte) (Table P-PZ40)
2007.M75 Mirabeau Honoré Gabriel Riquetti, comte de, 1749-1791 (Table P-PZ40)

Modern French literature
Individual authors
18th century -- Continued

2007.M8 Moissy, Alexandre Guillaume Mouslier de, 1712-1777 (Table P-PZ40)

2007.M85 Moncrif, François Augustin Paradis de, 1687-1770 (Table P-PZ40)

Montesquieu, Charles Louis de Secondat, baron de la Brède et de, 1689-1755

2011.A1 Collected works. By date

2011.A11-.A19 Collected works and selections. By editor

Translations

2011.A2 English

2011.A3 German

2011.A4 Other. By language, A-Z

2011.A6-Z Separate works

2011.A7-.A8 Arsace et Ismnie

Défense de l'Esprit des lois see JC179

Esprit des lois see JC179

2011.H5-.H6 Histoire véritable

2011.L5-.L6 Lettres persanes

2011.T4-.T5 Le temple de Gnide

2012 Biography. Criticism

2012.A4 Correspondence

2013.M2 Montesson, Charlotte Jeanne Béraud de la Hale de Riou, marquise de, 1737-1806 (Table P-PZ40)

2013.M3 Montjoie, Christophe Félix Louis Ventre de La Touloubre, called Galart de, 1746-1814 (Table P-PZ40)

Monvel, Jacques Marie Boutet de see PQ1957.B78

2013.M45 Morel de Chefdeville, Étienne, 1747-1814 (Table P-PZ40)

2013.M5 Morel de Vindé, Charles Gilbert Terray, vicomte, 1759-1842 (Table P-PZ40)

2013.M6 Morelly (Table P-PZ40)

2013.M65 Mouhey, Charles de Fieux, chevalier de, 1701-1784 (Table P-PZ40)

2013.M8 Murville, Pierre Nicolas André, called, 1754-1815 (Table P-PZ40)

2015.N3 Nadal, Augustin, 1664-1740 (Table P-PZ40)

2015.N312 Napoleon I, Emperor of the French, 1769-1821 (Table P-PZ40)

For biography of Napoleon I see DC203+

2015.N35 Nerciat, André Robert, known as Andréa de, 1739-1800 (Table P-PZ40)

2015.N4 Nivernais, Louis Jules Barbon Mancini Mazarini, duc de, 1716-1798 (Table P-PZ40)

2015.N5 Nogaret, Franois Félix, 1740-1831 (Table P-PZ40)

Modern French literature
Individual authors
18th century -- Continued

2015.N6	Nougaret, Pierre Jean Baptiste, 1742-1823
2015.N6A6-.N6Z3	Separate works
	e. g.
	Anecdotes des beaux-arts see ND1155
	Anecdotes secrètes du dix-huitième siècle see PQ273
2015.N6A8	Les astuces de Paris, anecdotes parisiennes
2015.N6H7	Honorine Clarins
2015.N6M6	Les mille et une folies; contes français
2015.N6P3	Paris, ou le rideau levé; anecdotes
2015.N6P8	Le plaiser et l'illusion
2015.N6S7	Spectacle et tableau mouvant de Paris, ou varietés amusantes
2015.O6	Olivier, abbé, 18th cent. (Table P-PZ40)
2019.P2	Pagés, François Xavier, 1745-1802 (Table P-PZ40)
2019.P22	Pajon, Henri, d. 1776 (Table P-PZ40)
2019.P25	Palissot de Montenoy, Charles, 1730-1814 (Table P-PZ40)
2019.P3	Pannard, François Charles, 1689-1765 (Table P-PZ40)
2019.P33	Parny, Évariste Désiré de Forges, vicomte de, 1753-1814 (Table P-PZ40)
2019.P35	Patrat, Joseph, 1732-1801 (Table P-PZ40)
2019.P4	Perreau, Jean André, 1749-1813 (Table P-PZ40)
2019.P418	Pesselier, Charles Étienne, 1712-1763 (Table P-PZ40)
	Pezay, Alexandre Frédéric Jacques de Masson, marquis de see PQ2007.M25
2019.P5	Picard, B. A. (Table P-PZ40)
2019.P56	Piis, Pierre-Antoine-Augustin de, 1755-1832 (Table P-PZ40)
2019.P6	Piron, Alexis, 1689-1773 (Table P-PZ38)
2019.P65	Plancher-Valcour, Philippe Alexandre Louis Pierre, called Aristide, ca. 1751-1815 (Table P-PZ40)
2019.P7	Poinsinet, Antoine Alexandre Henri, 1735-1769 (Table P-PZ40)
2019.P72	Poinsinet de Sivry, Louis, 1733-1804 (Table P-PZ40)
2019.P75	Poisson, Philippe, 1682-1743 (Table P-PZ40)
2019.P78	Pommereul, François René Jean, baron de, 1745-1823 (Table P-PZ40)
2019.P8	Pompignan, Jean Jacques Lefranc, marquis de, 1709-1784 (Table P-PZ40)
2019.P85	Pont de Veyle, Antoine de Ferriol, comte de, 1697-1774 (Table P-PZ40)
2019.P87	Potocki, Jan, hrabia, 1761-1815 (Table P-PZ40)

Modern French literature
Individual authors
18th century -- Continued
2021 Prévost, Antoine François, called Prévost d'Exiles, 1697-1763
Separate works
2021.C3 Campagnes philosophiques, ou Mémoires de M. de Montcal
2021.C7 Contes, avantures et faits singuliers
2021.D6 Le doyen de Killerine
2021.H4 Histoire d'une grecque moderne
Histoire de Marguerite d'Anjou, reine d'Angleterre see DA247.M3
Histoire de M. Cleveland see PQ2021.P5
Histoire du chevalier des Grieux et de Manon Lescaut see PQ2021.M3
2021.L4 Lettres de à Mentor un jeune, tr. de l'anglois
2021.M3 Manon Lescaut
2021.M5 Mémoires et avantures d'un homme de qualité
2021.M6 Mémoires pour servir à l'histoire de Malte
2021.M7 Le monde moral, ou Mémoires pour servir à l'histoire du coeur humain
Le pour et contre see AP20
2021.P5 Le philosophe anglois, ou Histoire de Monsieur Cleveland, fils naturel de Cromwell
Voyages de capitaine Robert Lade en différentes parties de l'Afrique, de l'Asis et de l'Amérique see G560
2022.P7 Puisieux, Madeleine (d'Arsant) de, 1720-1798 (Table P-PZ40)
2023.R2 Racine, Louis, 1692-1763 (Table P-PZ40)
2023.R4 Ramsay, Andrew Michael, 1686-1743 (Table P-PZ40)
2023.R45 Rémond de Saint-Mard, Toussaint, 1682-1757 (Table P-PZ40)
2023.R5 Renout, Jean Julien Constantin, 1725-1785 (Table P-PZ40)
Restif de la Bretonne, Nicolas Edme, 1734-1806
2025.A1-.A19 Collections
2025.A19 Collected plays
2025.A6-.Z3 Separate works
2025.A7 L'an deux-mille
L'andrographe see HN101+
2025.A75 L'année des dames nationales
2025.C6 Les contemporaines
2025.C7 Contr'avis aux gens de lettres
Les dangers de la ville see PQ2025.P45
2025.D4 La découverte australe

Modern French literature
Individual authors
18th century
Restif de la Bretonne, Nicolas Edme, 1734-1806
Separate works -- Continued

2025.D5 La dernière aventure d'un homme de quarante-cinq ans
2025.D7 Le drame de la vie
2025.E4 L'école de la jeunesse
2025.E5 L'école des pres
2025.F2 La famille vertueuse
2025.F3 La femme dans les trois états
2025.F4 La femme infidèle
2025.F5 La fille entretenue et vertueuse
2025.F6 La fille naturelle
Les filles du Palais-Royal see PQ2025.P2
2025.F8 Les Françaises
Les gynographes see HQ1201
2025.H5 Histoire des campagnes de Maria
Idées singulières
see the individual works: L'andrographe, HN428; Les gynographes, HQ1201; La mimographe, PN2633; Le pornographe, HQ121
2025.I6 Ingenue Saxancourt
2025.L4 Lettres d'une fille à son père
2025.L8 Lucile, ou Les progrès de la vertu
2025.M3 La malédiction paternelle
2025.M4 Le marquis de T ...
2025.M5 Le ménage parisien
Mes inscripcions, journal intime see PQ2025.Z45
La mimographe see PN2633
2025.M7 Monsieur Nicolas
2025.N5 Nouveaux mémoires d'un homme de qualité
2025.N6 Le nouvel Abeilard
2025.N7 Les nouvelles contemporaines; ou, Histoires de quelques femmes du jour
2025.N8 Les nuits de Paris, ou La spectateur nocturnale
2025.P2 Le palais royal
2025.P3 Les Parisiennes
2025.P4 Le paysan perverti
2025.P45 La paysane pervertie
2025.P47 Philosophie de M. Nicolas
2025.P5 Le pied de Fanchette, ou Le soulier couleur de rose
Le pornographe, ou Idées d'un honnête homme sur un project de réglement pour les prostituées see HQ121
2025.P7 Les posthumes

PQ1-3999

Modern French literature
Individual authors
18th century
Restif de la Bretonne, Nicolas Edme, 1734-1806
Separate works -- Continued

2025.P8 La prévention nationale
Les provinciales see PQ2025.A75
2025.Q3 Le quadragénaire
2025.R48 Les Revies
Le ruses, supercheries, artifices et machinations des filles publiques see HQ115
2025.T2 Tableau des moeurs
2025.T3 Tableaux de la bonne campagnie
2025.T5 Tableaux de la vie
Théâtre, collected plays see PQ2025.A19
Le thesmographe
see class K
2025.V6 La vie de mon père
2025.V7 Les viellées du marais
2025.V78 Voyages de Multipliandre
Biography. Criticism
2025.Z4-.Z49 Autobiography. Letters. Journals
2025.Z45 Mes inscripcions, journal intime
Cf. PQ2025.M7 Monsieur Nicolas
Cf. PQ2025.N7 Nuits de Paris
Cf. PQ2025.V6 Vie de mon père
2025.Z5 Biography and criticism
2027.R2 Reyrac, François Philippe de Laurens de, 1734-1781 (Table P-PZ40)
2027.R28 Riccoboni, Francesco, 1707-1772 (Table P-PZ40)
2027.R3 Riccoboni, Marie Jeanne (de Heurles Laboras de Mézières) 1713-1792 (Table P-PZ40 modified)
2027.R3A61-.R3Z458 Separate works. By title
Les caquets see PQ2027.R28
2027.R3H2 Histoire d'Adélaïde de Dammartin, comtesse de Sancerre
2027.R3H3 Histoire d'Aloïse de Livarot
2027.R3H4 Histoire d'Ernestine
2027.R3H5 Histoire de Christine de Suabe
2027.R3H6 Histoire de Miss Jenny
2027.R3H7 Histoire de M. le marquis de Cressy
2027.R3L4 Lettres d'Élisabeth-Sophie de Vallière
Letters de la comtesse de Sancerre see PQ2027.R3H2
2027.R3L5 Lettres de mistriss Fanni Butlerd
2027.R3L6 Lettres de mylady Juliette Catesby
2027.R3L7 Lettres de mylord Rivers

Modern French literature
Individual authors
18th century -- Continued

2027.R32 Riflé de Garouville, Savinien, 17th cent. (Table P-PZ40)
2027.R35 Rivarol, Antoine, 1753-1801 (Table P-PZ40)
2027.R4 Robert, Marie Anne de Roumier, dame, 1705-1771 (Table P-PZ40)
2027.R44 Robespierre, Maximilien, 1758-1794 (Table P-PZ40)
2027.R5 Rochon de Chabannes, Marc Antoine Jacques, 1730-1800 (Table P-PZ40)
2027.R55 Romagnesi, Jean Antoine, 1690-1742 (Table P-PZ40)
2027.R7 Roucher, Jean Antoine, 1745-1794 (Table P-PZ40)
Rouget de Lisle see PQ2389.R25+
2029 Rousseau, Jean Baptiste, 1670-1741
2029.A1 Complete works, by date, including collections of poems
2029.A2-.A29 Collections of his dramatic works. By editor
Translations
2029.A3-.A39 English. By translator
2029.A4-.A49 German. By translator
2029.A5-.A59 Other. By language
2029.A6-.Z3 Separate works
2029.C3 Le caffé
2029.C4 Le capricieux
2029.E6 Épîtres
2029.F6 Le flatteur
2029.H9 L'hypocondre
2029.J3 Jason
2029.L5 Lettres
2029.M3 Marianne
2029.V4 Vénus et Adonis
2029.Z5 Biography. Criticism
Rousseau, Jean Jacques, 1712-1778
2030 Collected works. By date
Selected works
Including posthumous works
2032.A1 By date
2032.A5-Z By editor
Letters see PQ2037
2033 Selections. Extracts. Quotations
Translations
English
2034.A3 Anonymous. By date
2034.A5-Z By translator
2035.A-Z Other languages, A-Z
Subarrange by translator
2036-2041 Separate works

Modern French literature
Individual authors
18th century
Rousseau, Jean Jacques, 1712-1778
Separate works -- Continued

2036 Confessions
2036.A1 Texts. By date
2036.A2 Texts. By editor
2036.A3 School texts
2036.A4 Selections, extracts, etc.
Translations
English
2036.A5 Anonymous. By date
2036.A51-.A59 By translator
2036.A6-.A69 German
2036.A7-.A79 Other languages (Alphabetically)
2036.A8-Z Criticism
Du contrat social see JC179
Émile; ou, De l'éducation, see LB511+
Émile et Sophie, see LB511+
Julie; ou, La nouvelle Héloïse see PQ2039
2037 Letters
For treatises in form of letters, see the treatise
2037.A1 Collections. By date
(2037.A3) Posthumously published letters, collected
see PQ2037.A1
To special persons see PQ2037.A5+
2037.A5-.Z3 Letters to special persons, A-Z
2038 Lettres écrites de la montagne (Table P-PZ41)
2039 La nouvelle Héloïse
2039.A1 Texts. By date
2039.A2 Selections. By date
Translations
2039.A4-.A49 English. By translator
2039.A5-.A59 German. By translator
2039.A7-.A79 Other, by language (Alphabetically)
2039.A8-Z Criticism
2040.A-Z Minor works, A-Z
2040.D4 La découverte du nouveau monde
2040.D5 Le devin du village
2040.D55 Discours...la vertu la plus nécessaire aux héros
Discours sur l'origine ... de l'inégalité see JC179
2040.D6-.D7 Discours sur les sciences et les arts
2040.I6 Iphis
Lettre à Christophe de Beaumont, archevêque de Paris (On the condemnation of Émile), see LB511+

Modern French literature
Individual authors
18th century
Rousseau, Jean Jacques, 1712-1778
Separate works
Minor works, A-Z -- Continued
Lettre à d'Alembert sur les spectacles see PN2051
2040.L4 Lettres sur la vertu et la bonheur

2040.L5 Le Lévite d'Éphraim
2040.L8 Lucrèce
2040.M8 Muses galantes
2040.N3 Narcisse
Le nouveau Dédale see TL516
2040.P4 Pensées d'un esprit droit
2040.P6 Profession de foi du vicaire savoyard
2040.P9 Pygmalion, scène lyrique
2040.R4 La reine fantasque
2040.R5 Les reveries du promeneur solitaire
2040.R8 Rousseau juge de Jean Jacques
2041 Doubtful, spurious works
Letters of an Italian nun and an English gentlemen see PR3291
Lettre à J.F. de Montillet (By P.F. Lacroix) see BX3701+
2041.T4 Le testament de Jean Jacques Rousseau
2042.A2 Societies. Periodicals. Collections
2042.A3-Z Dictionaries. Indexes, etc.
2042.5 History of the study and appreciation of Rousseau
Biography and criticism
2043 General works
2044 Sources
Autobiography see PQ2036
2045 Early life. Education
2046 Love. Relations to women
2047 Later life and death, including works on his mental and physical conditions
2048 Relations to his contemporaries. Milieu. Age of Voltaire and Rousseau
Cf. PQ2105.A2+ Voltaire
2049 Homes and haunts. Local associations. Landmarks
2049.A2 General
2049.A3-Z Special, A-Z
2049.B47 Besançon
2049.C48 Chambéry
2049.C5 Les Charmettes
2049.E6 England
2049.E8 Ermenonville

Modern French literature
Individual authors
18th century
Rousseau, Jean Jacques, 1712-1778
Biography and criticism
Homes and haunts. Local associations. Landmarks
Special, A-Z -- Continued

2049.G4 Geneva
2049.M37 Maubec (Isère)
2049.M6 Montmorency
2049.N48 Neuchâtel (Principality)
2049.T7 Val de Travers
2050 Anniversaries. Celebrations
2051 Memorial addresses. Poetry
2052 Iconography. Portraits. Monuments
Criticism
General
2053.A2-Z Contemporary works
2053.A2 Compilations
2053.A3A-.A3Z Special authors, A-Z
2053.A5-Z Later criticism
2054 Textual criticism
Special
2055 Sources
2056.A-Z Special topics, A-Z
2056.A38 Aesthetics
2056.D7 Drama
2056.E6 English influence
2056.E85 Ethics
2056.G5 German influence
2056.G7 Greco-Roman world
2056.M66 Montaigne's influence
2056.M8 Music
2056.M94 Myth
2056.N3 Nature
2056.P6 Political science
2056.P7 Psychology
2056.R4 Religion
2056.S92 Subjectivity
2057.A2 Influence in general
2057.A3-Z Influence in special countries, A-Z
2057.E5 England
2057.P7 Poland
2057.R8 Russia
2057.S9 Switzerland
2058 Language. Grammar
2061.R4 Roy, Pierre Charles, 1683-1764 (Table P-PZ40)

Modern French literature
Individual authors
18th century -- Continued

2061.R8 Rustaing de Saint-Jory, Louis, de. 1752 (Table P-PZ40)
2063.S12 Sabatier de Castres, abbé (Antoine), 1742-1817 (Table P-PZ40)
2063.S2 Sacy, Claude Louis Michel de, 1746-1790 (Table P-PZ40)
2063.S3 Sade, Donatien Alphonse Franois, comte, called marquis de, 1740-1814 (Table P-PZ38 modified)
2063.S3A61-.S3A78 Separate works. By title
2063.S3A62 Aline et Valcour
2063.S3A65 Les crimes de l'amour
2063.S3A655 Dialogue entre un prêtre et un moribond
2063.S3A657 English translations
2063.S3A66 Dorci
2063.S3A67 Historiettes, contes et fabliaux
2063.S3A68 Juliette
2063.S3A69 Justine
2063.S3A71 Le marquise du Gange
2063.S3A73 Oxtiern
2063.S3A75 Pauline et Belval
2063.S3A76 Le philosophie dans le boudoir
Saint-Aubin, M.C. Cammaille see PQ2203.C38
2063.S4 Saint-Foix, Germain François Poullain de, 1698-1776 (Table P-PZ40)
2063.S45 Saint-Hyacinthe, Hyacinthe Cordonnier, known as chevalier de Thmiseul de, 1684-1746 (Table P-PZ40)
Saint-Jory, Louis Rustaing de see PQ2061.R8
2063.S7 Saint-Lambert, Jean François, marquis de, 1716-1803 (Table P-PZ40)
2063.S8 Saint-Marc, Jean Paul André de Razins, marquis de, 1728-1818 (Table P-PZ40)
2063.S84 Saint-Martin, Louis Claude de, 1743-1803 (Table P-PZ40)
2065 Saint-Pierre, Jacques Henry Bernardin de, 1737-1814 (Table P-PZ40)
Complete works
2065.A1 By date
2065.A11-.A19 By editor
Selected works. Selections. Posthumous works
2065.A2 Anonymous. By date
2065.A21-.A29 Others. By editor
Translations
2065.A3-.A39 English
2065.A4-.A49 German
2065.A5-.A59 Other. By language

Modern French literature
Individual authors
18th century
Saint-Pierre, Jacques Henri Bernardin de, 1737-1814 -- Continued
Separate works
2065.A7 L'Arcadie
2065.C4 La chaumière indienne
2065.E6-.E7 Études de la nature
2065.H3-.H4 Harmonies de la nature
2065.M6 Le mort de Socrate
2065.P3-.P4 Paul et Virginie
2065.Z5 Biography and criticism
2066.S38 Salverte, Aglaé Baconnière de, d. 1828 (Table P-PZ40)
2066.S4 Saumery, Pierre Lambert de, ca. 1690-ca. 1767 (Table P-PZ40)
2066.S5 Saurin, Bernard Joseph, 1706-1781 (Table P-PZ40)
2066.S6 Sedaine, Michel Jean, 1719-1797 (Table P-PZ40)
2066.S75 Ségur, Alexandre Joseph Pierre, vicomte de, 1756-1805 (Table P-PZ40)
2066.S8 Sénac de Meilhan, Gabriel, 1736-1803 (Table P-PZ38)
2066.S82 Sérieys, A. (Antoine), 1755-1829 (Table P-PZ40)
2066.S86 Staal, Marguerite-Jeanne, baronne de, 1684-1750 (Table P-PZ40)
2066.S87 Suard, Jean Baptiste Antoine, 1734-1817 (Table P-PZ40)
2066.S9 Surville, Joseph Étienne, marquis de, 1755-1798 (Table P-PZ40)
Here are classed the editions of poems purporting to have been written in the 15th century by Clotilde de Surville. The authorship of these poems has been ascribed to the marquis de Surville
2067.T2 Tencin, Claudine Alexandrine Guérin de, 1682-1749 (Table P-PZ38)
2067.T25 Terrasson, Jean, 1670-1750 (Table P-PZ40)
2067.T277 Thibouville, Henry Lambert d'Erbigny, marquis de, 1710-1784 (Table P-PZ40)
2067.T28 Thiroux d'Arconville, Marie Geneviève Charlotte (Darlus) dame, 1720-1805 (Table P-PZ40)
2067.T3 Thomas, Antoine Léonard, 1732-1785 (Table P-PZ40)
2067.T4 Tiphaigne de la Roche, Charles François, 1729-1774
Separate works
2067.T4A62 Amilec
2067.T4A63 L'amour devoilé
Les bigarrures philosophique see B2147.T5+
L'empire des Zaziris see BF1552
2067.T4A66 Giphantie
2067.T4A68 Histoire des Galligènes

Modern French literature
Individual authors
18th century
Tiphaigne de la Roche, Charles Francois, 1729-1774
Separate works
2067.T4A7 Sanfrein
2067.T4A8-Z Biography and criticism
2067.T45 Toussaint, François Vincent, d. 1772 (Table P-PZ40)
2067.T48 Tressan, abbé de, 1747-1809 (Table P-PZ40)
2067.T5 Tressan, Louis Élisabeth de la Vergne de Broussin, comte de, 1705-1783 (Table P-PZ38)
Separate editions of his prose versions of medieval epic poems are classed with the originals
2067.T6 Tschudi, Jean Baptiste Louis Théodore, baron de, 1734-1784 (Table P-PZ40)
Tyssot de Patot, Simon see PQ1930.T9
2067.U7 Ussieux, Louis d', 1744-1805 (Table P-PZ40)
2068.V2 Vadé, Jean Joseph, 1719-1757 (Table P-PZ40)
2068.V25 Varennes de Mondasse, de (Table P-PZ40)
2068.V27 Vasselier, Joseph, 1735-1790 (Table P-PZ40)
Vergier, Jacques, 1655-1720 see PQ1931
2068.V33 Viel, Etienne-Bernard-Alexandre, 1736-1821 (Table P-PZ40)
2068.V34 Vigée, M. (Louis-Jean-Baptiste-Etienne), 1758-1820 (Table P-PZ40)
2068.V4 Villeneuve, Gabrielle Suzanne Barbot, dame de, 1695?-1755
Separate works
2068.V4A62 Le beau-frère supposé
2068.V4A627 La belle et la bête
2068.V4A63 Les belles solitaires
2068.V4A64 Les contes de cette année
Les contes marins see PQ2068.V4A68
2068.V4A66 La jardinière de Vincennes
2068.V4A68 La jeune Ameriquaine et Les contes marins
2068.V4A7 Le juge prévenu
2068.V4A72 Mesdemoiselles de Marsange
2068.V4A74 Le phénix conjugal
2068.V48 Vixouze, François-Xavier Pagès de, 1745-1802 (Table P-PZ40)
2068.V5 Voisenon, Claude Henry de Fusée, abbé de, 1708-1775 (Table P-PZ40)
Voltaire, François Marie Arouet de, 1694-1778
Complete works
2070 By date
2071 By editor

Modern French literature
Individual authors
18th century
Voltaire, François Marie Arouet de, 1694-1778 -- Continued

2072 Selected works. By editor
Including posthumous works

2073 Collections of minor works, including works in part written and in part edited by Voltaire
e. g.

2073.E8 L'Évangile du jour

2074 Selections. Extracts. Quotations

Translations
General collections and selections from various groups

2075 English translations. By date

2075.A-Z Other translations. By language and translator
Anonymous translations. By language and date

Dramatic works

2076.A1 Collections. By date

(2076.A11-.A19) Collections. By editor

Selected plays

2076.A2 By date

2076.A21-.A29 By editor

2076.A3-Z Translations. By language, A-Z
e. g.

2076.E5 English

2076.G5 German

2076.I5 Italian

2076.S5 Spanish

2077.A-Z Separate plays, A-Z

2077.A3 Adélaïde du Guesclin

2077.A4 Agathocle

2077.A5-.A6 Alzire, ou Les Américains (Table P-PZ43a)

2077.A7 Amulius et Numitor

2077.A8 Artémire

2077.B2 Le Baron d'Otrante

2077.B7 Brutus

2077.C2-.C3 Le caffé, ou L'Écossaise (Table P-PZ43a)

Catalina, ou Rome sauvée, see PQ2077.R6+

2077.C4 Charlot, ou La comtesse de Givri

2077.C5 Le comte de Boursoufle, ou Les agréments du droit d' anesse
"Le petit Boursoufle"

2077.C6 Le comte de Boursoufle, ou Mademoiselle de la Cochonnière
(Another version of the preceding)

2077.C7 Criticism of the preceding (both versions)

Modern French literature
Individual authors
18th century
Voltaire, François Marie Arouet de, 1694-1778
Dramatic works
Separate plays, A-Z -- Continued

2077.D2 Le dépositaire
2077.D3 Les deux tonneaux
2077.D4 Divertissement pour le mariage du roi Louis XV
2077.D5 Don Pèdre, roi de Castille
2077.D6 Le droit du seigneur
2077.D8 Le duc d'Alençon, ou Les frères ennemis
2077.D9 Le duc de Foix
L'échange, ou Quand est-ce qu'on me marie, see PQ2077.C5
L'Écossaise see PQ2077.C2+
2077.E3 L'écueil du sage
2077.E4 L'enfant prodigue
2077.E6 L'envieux
2077.E7 Eriphile
Le fanatisme, ou Mahomet, le prophète, see PQ2077.M2+
2077.F4 La femme qui a raison
2077.G8 Les Guèbres, ou La tolérance
2077.H4 L'Héraclius espagnol, ou La comédie fameuse
2077.H5 Hérode et Mariamne
2077.H7 L'hôte et l'hôtesse
2077.I5 L'indiscret
2077.I7 Irène
Jules César see PR2779.A+
2077.L6 Les loix de Minos, ou Astérie
2077.M2-.M3 Mahomet, ou Le fanatisme (Table P-PZ43a)
Mariamne, see PQ2077.H5
2077.M5-.M53 Le Mérope française (Table P-PZ43)
2077.M7 Le mort de César
2077.N3 Nanine, ou Le préjugé vaincu
2077.O2 Octave et le jeune Pompée, ou Le triumvirat
2077.O3-.O4 Oedipe (Table P-PZ43a)
2077.O5 Olimpie
2077.O6 Oreste
2077.O7 Les originaux, ou Monsieur du Cap-Vert
(Also entitled Le comte de Boursoufle or Boursoufle. Called "Le grand Boursoufle" to distinguish from the play with title: Le comte du Boursoufle, ou Les agréments du droit d' aînesse)
2077.O8-.O9 L'orphelin de la Chine (Table P-PZ43a)
2077.P4 Pandore

Modern French literature
Individual authors
18th century
Voltaire, François Marie Arouet de, 1694-1778
Dramatic works
Separate plays, A-Z -- Continued

2077.P5 Les Pélopides, ou Atrée et Thieste
2077.P7 La princesse de Navarre
2077.P8 La prude, ou La gardeuse de cassette
2077.R6-.R7 Rome sauvée (Table P-PZ43a)
2077.S2 Samson
2077.S3-.S4 Saül (Table P-PZ43a)
2077.S5 Les Scythes
2077.S6 Sémiramis
2077.S7 Socrate
2077.S8 Sophonisbe
2077.T2-.T3 Tancrède (Table P-PZ43a)
2077.T4 Tanis et Zélide, ou Les rois pasteurs
2077.T5 Le temple de la gloire
2077.T6 Thérèse
2077.Z3-.Z4 Zaïre (Table P-PZ43a)
2077.Z8 Zulime

Poetical works
Collections and selections
2079.A1 Collections. By date
Selected poems
2079.A2 By date
2079.A21-.A29 By editor
2079.A3-Z Translations. By language, A-Z
e. g.
2079.E5 English
2079.G5 German
2079.I5 Italian
2079.S5 Spanish

Separate works
2080.C7 Contes de Guillaume Vadé
2080.H4-.H5 La Henriade (Table P-PZ43a)
2080.P54-.P55 Poème sur le désastre de Lisbonne (Table P-PZ43a)
2080.P7-.P8 La pucelle d'Orléans (Table P-PZ43a)
2080.T3-.T4 Le temple du goût (Table P-PZ43a)

Prose fiction
Collections and selections
2081.A1 Collections. By date
Selected prose fiction
2081.A2 By date
2081.A21-.A29 By editor

Modern French literature
Individual authors
18th century
Voltaire, François Marie Arouet de, 1694-1778
Prose fiction
Collections and selections -- Continued

2081.A3-Z Translations. By language, A-Z
e. g.
2081.E5 English
2081.G5 German
2081.I5 Italian
2081.S5 Spanish

Separate works, A-Z
2082.A7 Avanture de la mémoire
2082.A8 Avanture indienne
2082.A9 Les aveugles juges des couleurs
2082.B3 Bababec et les fakirs
2082.B6 Le blanc et le noir
2082.C3-.C4 Candide (Table P-PZ43a)
2082.C5 Cosi-Sancta
2082.C7 Le crocheteur borgne
2082.D4 Les deux consolés
2082.E6 Éloge historique de la raison
2082.H3 Histoire d'un bon Bramin
2082.H4 Histoire de Jenni
2082.H5 Histoire des voyages de Scarmentado
2082.H6 L'homme aux quarante écus
Le Huron, ou L'ingenu see PQ2082.I5+
2082.I5-.I7 L'ingénu (Table P-PZ43a)
2082.J4 Jeannot et Colin
2082.L4 Les lettres d'Amabed
2082.M4 Memnon
Not to be confused with Zadig, originally called Memnon
2082.M5 Micromégas
2082.M7 Le monde comme il va
2082.O5-.O6 Les oreilles du comte de Chesterfield et le chapelain Goudman (Table P-PZ43a)
2082.P7 La princesse de Babylone
2082.S6 Songe de Platon
2082.T3 Le taureau blanc

Zadig, ou La destinée
2082.Z3 Editions. By date
2082.Z4 School editions. By editor
2082.Z5 Translations. By language, A-Z
2082.Z6 Criticism

Letters

Modern French literature
Individual authors
18th century
Voltaire, François Marie Arouet de, 1694-1778
Letters -- Continued

2084.A1 Collections. By date
2084.A2 Selections
Including collections of posthumously published letters
2084.A3 School editions. By editor, A-Z
2084.A6-.Z3 Letters to special persons, A-Z
2084.B5 Biord, J.P., prince-bishop of Geneva (including editions containing the "Confession de foi")
2084.C3 Catharine II, Empress of Russia
2084.F7 Frederick the Great
2084.R6 Rousseau
2084.Z4 English translations. By translator, A-Z
2084.Z5 Other translations. By language, A-Z
2084.Z9 Letters addressed to Voltaire
2084.Z9A2 Collections. By date
2084.Z9A5-Z By special persons, A-Z
If the letters deal with a special subject, see the subject
(2085) Historical works
For historical works, see subclasses D, DC, DD, etc.
2086 Other prose works
Confession de foi, see PQ2084.B5
2086.D4 La défense de mon oncle
Dictionnaire philosophique see B42
2086.D5-.D52 Discours prononcez dans l'Académie françoise, le lundi 9 mai 1746, à la réception de M. de Voltaire (Table P-PZ43a)
2086.L2-.L3 Lettres chinoises, indiennes et tartares (Table P-PZ43a)
2086.L4-.L5 Lettres philosophiques (Table P-PZ43a)
Le philosophe ignorant see B2170+
Le sermon des cinquante see BL2773
2086.S7 Le sottisier
Traité sur la tolérance see BR1610+
(2089.A-.Z3) Books edited by Voltaire (By author, A-Z)
(2089.Z5) Books annotated by Voltaire (By author, A-Z)
Spurious or doubtful works
2090.A2 Collections and selections
2090.A5-Z Separate works
2091 Imitations of Voltaire
2092 Parodies of Voltaire's works
History of the study and appreciation of Voltaire
2093 General

Modern French literature
Individual authors
18th century
Voltaire, François Marie Arouet de, 1694-1778
History of the study and appreciation of Voltaire -- Continued

2094 Translations (as subject; comparative studies)
2095 Dramatization of Voltaire's novel, etc.
For studies of Voltaire's relation to the stage and performances of his plays on the stage in France or in other countries see PQ2123
2095.9 Illustrations to the works
Biography and criticism
2097 Periodicals. Societies. Collections
2098 Dictionaries, indexes, etc.
General dictionaries only. Special dictionaries with subject, e.g. PQ2126, Characters; PQ2139-2140, Concordances and language dictionaries
2099 General works
Autobiography. Journals. Memoirs. Letters see PQ2084.A1+
Sources of biography
2100.Z5 Collections. By date
2100.Z5A-.Z5Z Separate documents
Letters see PQ2084.A1+
Confession de foi see PQ2084.B5
2101 Family. Ancestry. Name
2102 Early life. Education
Relation to women
2103.A2 General
2103.A3-Z Individual
2104 Later life
Relations to his contemporaries. Milieu. Age of Voltaire
Cf. PQ2119.A2+
2105.A2 General
2105.A3-Z Individual
2105.F8 Frederick the Great
2105.R6 Rousseau
2105.5 Anecdotes. By editor
Homes and haunts. Local associations. Landmarks
2106.A2 General
2106.A3-Z Special
2106.B4 Berlin
2106.E5 England
2106.F47 Ferney
2106.G4 Geneva

Modern French literature
Individual authors
18th century
Voltaire, François Marie Arouet de, 1694-1778
Biography and criticism -- Continued

2107 Anniversaries. Celebrations
2108 Memorial addresses
Iconography
2111 Portraits
2112 Monuments
2113 Relics
2114 Authorship
2115 Manuscripts
2116 Forgeries, etc.
Cf. PQ2091 Imitations of Voltaire
Sources
2117.A2 General
2117.A3-Z Special
e. g.
2117.P7 Pope
Followers. Circle. School
Cf. PQ2105.A2+
2119.A2 General
2119.A3-Z Individual
2120 Allusions
2121 Chronology of works
Criticism and interpretation
2122 General works. Genius, etc.
2122.A2 Contemporary works to 1800. By date
Special classes of works
2123 Drama
2124 Poetry
2125 Other
Philosophy see PQ2130
Characters
2126 General
2126.5.A-Z Special classes, A-Z
2126.5.W6 Women
2127 Individual, A-Z
2129 Plots. Scenes. Time, etc.
Treatment and knowledge of special subjects
2130 Philosophy and Religion
2131 Law. Politics, etc.
2132 History
2133 Art
2134 Nature
2135 Science

Modern French literature
Individual authors
18th century
Voltaire, François Marie Arouet de, 1694-1778
Criticism and interpretation
Treatment and knowledge of special subjects -- Continued

2136 Other
2137 Textual criticism
2138 Language, style, etc.
2139 Dictionaries
2140 Concordances
2141 Grammar
Special
2142 Use of words
2143 Syntax
2144 Versification
2147.W3 Walef, Blaise Henri de Corte, baron de, 1661-1734 (Table P-PZ40)

19th century
Subarrange by Table P-PZ39 or Table P-PZ40 unless otherwise specified

2149 Anonymous works (Table P-PZ28)
2150.A25 Abany, Marie-Thérèse Péroux d' (Table P-PZ40)
2151 About, Edmond François Valentin, 1828-1885 (Table P-PZ39)
2152.A2 Achard, Louis Amédée Eugène, 1814-1875 (Table P-PZ40)
2152.A24 Ackermann, Louise, 1813-1890 (Table P-PZ40)
2152.A3 Adam, Mme. Juliette, 1836- (Table P-PZ40)
2152.A32 Adam, Paul Auguste Marie, 1862-1920 (Table P-PZ40)
2152.A35 Aderer, Adolphe, 1855-1923 (Table P-PZ40)
2152.A38 Agoult, Marie Catherine Sophie (de Flavigny), comtesse d', 1805-1876 ("Daniel Stern") (Table P-PZ40)
2152.A4 Aicard, Jean François Victor, 1848-1921 (Table P-PZ40)
2152.A45 Aigueperse, Mathilde, 1854- (Table P-PZ40)
2152.A5 Aimard, Gustave, 1818-1883 (Table P-PZ40)
2152.A53 Aimery de Pierrebourg, Marguerite, (Thomas-Galline), baronne, 1858- (Table P-PZ40)
2152.A7 Allart de Méritens, Hortense, 1801-1879 (Table P-PZ40)
2152.A77 Amiel, Henri Frédéric, 1821-1881 (Table P-PZ40)
2152.A8 Ampère, Jean Jacques Antoine, 1806-1864 (Table P-PZ40)
2153.A2 Ancelot, Jacques Arsène Polycarpe François, 1794-1854 (Table P-PZ40)
2153.A3 Ancelot, Marguerite Louise Virgine (Chardon), dame, 1792-1875 (Table P-PZ40)

Modern French literature
Individual authors
19th century -- Continued

2153.A33	Ancey, Georges (Table P-PZ40)
	Andrieux, François Guillaume Jean Stanislas see PQ1954.A5
2153.A357	Anglemont, Édouard d, 1798-1876 (Table P-PZ40)
2153.A36	Anicet-Bourgeois, Auguste, 1806-1871 (Table P-PZ40)
2153.A422	Arago, Jacques, 1790-1855 (Table P-PZ40)
2153.A43	Arbouville, Sophie de Bazancourt Loyré d', 1810-1850 (Table P-PZ40)
2153.A44	Arcelin, Adrien, 1838-1904 (Table P-PZ40)
2153.A5	Arène, Paul Auguste, 1843-1896 (Table P-PZ40)
2153.A6	Arlincourt, Charles Victor Prévôt, vicomte d, 1789-1856 (Table P-PZ40)
2153.A65	Arnault, Antoine Vincent, 1766-1834 (Table P-PZ40)
2153.A7	Arnould, Arthur, 1833-1895 (Table P-PZ40)
2153.A8	Arvers, Félix, 1806-1850 (Table P-PZ40)
2153.A9	Assollant, Alfred, 1827-1886 (Table P-PZ40)
	Aubanel, Théodore, 1829-1886 see PC3402.A8
2154.A3	Aubryet, Xavier, 1827-1880 (Table P-PZ40)
2154.A4	Audebrand, Philibert, 1816-1906 (Table P-PZ40)
2154.A5	Auger, Édouard (Table P-PZ40)
2154.A53	Auger, Hippolyte Nicolas Just, 1797-1881 (Table P-PZ40)
2154.A56	Augeron, Monsieur, 19th cent. (Table P-PZ40)
2154.A6	Augier, Émile, 1820-1889 (Table P-PZ40)
2154.A63	Augustin, Marie (Table P-PZ40)
2154.A67	Aulnay, Louise d', b. ca. 1830 (Table P-PZ40)
2154.A7	Auriac, Jules Berlioz d', 1820- (Table P-PZ40)
2154.A75	Auriol, George, 1863- (Table P-PZ40)
2154.A8	Autran, Joseph Antoine, 1813-1877 (Table P-PZ40)
2154.A86	Aymard, J. (Table P-PZ40)
2156.B27	Badin, Adolphe, 1839- (Table P-PZ40)
2156.B4	Ballanche, Pierre Simon, 1776-1847 (Table P-PZ40)
	Balzac, Honoré de, 1799-1850
2157	Collected works. By date letter e. g.
2157.E75	1875
2157.F12	1912
2158	Collected drama
2158.A4-.A49	English translations
2159	Selected works
2159.A2	Miscellaneous collections. By editor
2159.A3	School editions. By editor
2159.C7	Comédie humaine see note above PQ2163.A5

Modern French literature
Individual authors
19th century
Balzac, Honoré de, 1799-1850
Selected works -- Continued
Correspondence see PQ2179
Théâtre see PQ2158

2160 Selections. Extracts. Quotations

Translations

2161 English. By translator (or publisher)

2162 Other. By language, subarranged by translator (or publisher)

Separate works

The several subseries of the Comédie humaine, e.g. Scènes de la vie privée, are classified under the title of the subseries provided that these collections have the series title for the main title-page and the volumes are numbered under it consecutively. Individual works or volumes with the series title (Scènes, etc.) as a mere caption are to be classified as separate works

2163.A5-.A52 Albert Savarus (Table P-PZ43a)

2163.A7-.A72 L'amour masqué (Table P-PZ43a)

2163.A85-.A86 L'auberge rouge (Table P-PZ43a)

Autre étude de femme see PQ2165.E57+

2163.B3-.B32 Le bal de sceaux (Table P-PZ43a)

Balthazar Claës see PQ2169.R3+

2163.C2-.C22 Le cabinet des antiques (Table P-PZ43a)

2163.C25-.C26 Les célibataires (Table P-PZ43a)

2163.C3-.C32 César Birotteau (Table P-PZ43a)

2163.C4-.C42 Le chef-d'oeuvre inconnu (Table P-PZ43a)

2163.C5-.C6 Les Chouans (Table P-PZ43a)

2163.C7-.C72 Le colonel Chabert (Table P-PZ43a)

Comédie humaine see PQ2159.C7

2163.C8-.C82 La confidence des Ruggieri (Table P-PZ43a)

2164 Contes drôlatiques (Table P-PZ41 modified)

Translations

(2164.A31-.A39) These numbers not used

2164.A4-.A49 English

2165.C2-.C22 Contes philosophiques (Table P-PZ43a)

Contains the twelve stories following La peau de chagrin in the series "Romans et contes philosophiques"

2165.C3-.C32 Le contrat de mariage (Table P-PZ43a)

2165.C4-.C42 Le cousin Pons (Table P-PZ43a)

2165.C5-.C52 Le cousine Bette (Table P-PZ43a)

2165.C7-.C72 Le curé de Tours (Table P-PZ43a)

Modern French literature
Individual authors
19th century
Balzac, Honoré de, 1799-1850
Separate works -- Continued

2165.C8-.C82 Le curé de village (Table P-PZ43a)
Les dangers de l'inconduite see PQ2167.G6+
2165.D2-.D22 Un début dans la vie (Table P-PZ43a)
Le dernier Chouan see PQ2163.C5+
2165.D4-.D42 Les deux jeunes mariées (Table P-PZ43a)
Dinah Piédefer see PQ2167.M9+
2165.D5-.D52 Le doigt de Dieu (Table P-PZ43a)
2165.D6-.D62 Une double famille (Table P-PZ43a)
2165.D8-.D82 La Duchesse Langeais (Table P-PZ43a)
2165.E4-.E42 L'école des menages (Table P-PZ43a)
2165.E43-.E44 L'élixir de longue via (Table P-PZ43a)
2165.E46-.E47 Les employés (Table P-PZ43a)
2165.E48-.E49 L'enfant maudit (Table P-PZ43a)
2165.E494-.E4942 L'envers de l'histoire contemporaine (Table P-PZ43a)
2165.E5-.E52 Esther heureuse (Table P-PZ43a)
2165.E55-.E56 Étude de femme (Table P-PZ43a)
2165.E57-.E58 Autre étude de femme (Table P-PZ43a)
2165.E6-.E62 Études analytiques (Table P-PZ43a)
see note above PQ2163.A5
2165.E7-.E72 Études de moeurs au 19e siècle (Table P-PZ43a)
see note above PQ2163.A5
2165.E8-.E82 Études philosophiques (Table P-PZ43a)
see note above PQ2163.A5
2165.E9-.E92 Études sociales (Table P-PZ43a)
see note above PQ2163.A5
2166 Eugénie Grandet (Table P-PZ41 modified)
2166.A3 School texts
2167.F2-.F22 Facino Cane (Table P-PZ43a)
Faiseur see PQ2167.M5+
2167.F27-.F28 Falthurne (Table P-PZ43a)
Les fantaisies de Claudine see PQ2169.P65+
2167.F3-.F32 Les fantaisies de la Gina (Table P-PZ43a)
2167.F37-.F38 La femme abandonneé (Table P-PZ43a)
2167.F4-.F42 La femme de trente ans (Table P-PZ43a)
La femme supériere see PQ2165.E46+
La femme vertueuse see PQ2165.D6+
2167.F45-.F46 Ferragus (Table P-PZ43a)
2167.F5-.F52 La fille aux yeux d'or (Table P-PZ43a)
2167.F6-.F62 Une fille d'Eve (Table P-PZ43a)
La fleur des pois see PQ2165.C3+
Gloire et malheur see PQ2167.M25+
2167.G6-.G62 Gobseck (Table P-PZ43a)

Modern French literature
Individual authors
19th century
Balzac, Honoré de, 1799-1850
Separate works -- Continued

2167.G68-.G682 Grand homme de province à Paris (Table P-PZ43a)
2167.G69-.G692 Grande Bretèche (Table P-PZ43a)
2167.G7-.G72 Le grenadière (Table P-PZ43a)
2167.H3-.H32 Histoire de l'empereur (Table P-PZ43a)
Extract from Le médicin de la campagne
Histoire de la grandeur et de la décadence de César Birotteau see PQ2163.C3+
2167.H5-.H52 Histoire des treize (Table P-PZ43a)
Histoire intellectuelle de Louis Lambert see PQ2167.L7+
2167.I6-.I62 Illusions perdues (Table P-PZ43a)
2167.L5-.L52 Le livre des douleurs (Table P-PZ43a)
Comprises: I, Gambara; II, Les proscrits. Massimilla Doni I
2167.L6-.L62 Le livre mystique (Table P-PZ43a)
2167.L7-.L72 Louis Lambert (Table P-PZ43a)
2167.L8-.L82 Le lys dans la vallée (Table P-PZ43a)
2167.M2-.M22 Madame Firmiani (Table P-PZ43a)
2167.M25-.M26 La maison de chat qui pelote (Table P-PZ43a)
2167.M3-.M32 La maison Nucingen (Table P-PZ43a)
2167.M35-.M36 Maître Cornélius (Table P-PZ43a)
2167.M377-.M3772 Maranas (Table P-PZ43a)
2167.M4-.M42 Massimilla Doni (Table P-PZ43a)
2167.M45-.M46 Le médicin de campagne (Table P-PZ43a)
Cf. PQ2167.H3+ Histoire de l'empereur
Même histoire see PQ2165.E46+
2167.M5-.M52 Mercadet (Comédie) (Table P-PZ43a)
2167.M55-.M56 Le message (Table P-PZ43a)
2167.M6-.M62 La messe de l'athée (Table P-PZ43a)
2167.M7-.M72 Modeste Mignon (Table P-PZ43a)
2167.M8-.M82 Montriveau (Table P-PZ43a)
2167.M9-.M92 La muse du départment (Table P-PZ43a)
2167.N6-.N62 Nouveaux contes philosophiques (Table P-PZ43a)
2167.N7-.N72 Nouvelles scènes de la vie de province (Table P-PZ43a)
2167.O7-.O72 Où mènent les mauvais chemins (Table P-PZ43a)
2167.P17-.P172 Paris marié (Table P-PZ43a)
2167.P2-.P3 Les paysans (Table P-PZ43a)
2167.P5-.P6 La peau de chagrin (Table P-PZ43a)
2168 Le père Goriot (Table P-PZ41)
2169.P2-.P3 Petites misères de la vie conjugale (Table P-PZ43a)
2169.P4-.P5 Physiologie du mariage (Table P-PZ43a)

Modern French literature
Individual authors
19th century
Balzac, Honoré de, 1799-1850
Separate works -- Continued

2169.P6-.P62 Pierrette (Table P-PZ43a)
2169.P65-.P66 Une prince de la Bohême (Table P-PZ43a)
Profil de marquise see PQ2165.E55+
2169.P7-.P8 Les proscrits (Table P-PZ43a)
2169.R3-.R4 La recherche de l'absolu (Table P-PZ43a)
Le rendez-vous see PQ2165.E46+
2169.R5-.R6 Le réquisitionnaire (Table P-PZ43a)
2169.R7-.R8 Romans et contes philosophiques (Table P-PZ43a)
see note above PQ2163.A5
Cf. PQ2165.C2+ Contes philosophiques
Rosalie see PQ2163.A5+
2169.S3-.S4 Sarrasine (Table P-PZ43a)
2170.S3-.S32 Scènes de la vie de campagne (Table P-PZ43a)
see note above PQ2163.A5
2170.S5-.S52 Scènes de la vie de province (Table P-PZ43a)
see note above PQ2163.A5
2170.S6-.S62 Scènes de la vie de militaire (Table P-PZ43a)
see note above PQ2163.A5
2170.S7-.S72 Scènes de la vie de parisienne (Table P-PZ43a)
see note above PQ2163.A5
2170.S8-.S82 Scènes de la vie de vie politique (Table P-PZ43a)
see note above PQ2163.A5
2170.S9-.S92 Scènes de la vie de vie privée (Table P-PZ43a)
see note above PQ2163.A5
2171 Sc - Ser
Le secret de Ruggieri see PQ2163.C8+
2172 Séraphita (Table P-PZ41)
2173 S - Th
2173.S5-.S52 Les souffrances inconnues (Table P-PZ43a)
2173.S6-.S7 Splendeurs et misères des courtisanes (Table P-PZ43a)
see note above PQ2163.A5
2173.S9-.S93 Sur Catherine de Medicis (Table P-PZ43a)
Théâtre see PQ2158
2175 Th - Z
La torpille see PQ2165.E5+
2175.T6-.T62 Traité de la prière (unfinished work) (Table P-PZ43a)
2175.T7-.T8 Traité de la vie élégante (Table P-PZ43a)
2175.U8-.U82 Ursule Mirouët (Table P-PZ43a)
2175.V38-.V382 Vautrin (Table P-PZ43a)
2175.V4-.V5 El verdugo (Table P-PZ43a)

Modern French literature
Individual authors
19th century
Balzac, Honoré de, 1799-1850
Separate works
Th - Z -- Continued

2175.V68-.V682 Voyage de Paris à Java (Table P-PZ43a)
2176 Doubtful, spurious works
(2176.5) Imitations. Adaptations. Dramatizations
see special author in subclasses PA - PZ
Biography and criticism
2177.A2 Societies. Periodicals. Collections
2177.A3-Z Dictionaries, indexes, etc.
2178 General works
Love. Marriage. Relation to women
2178.3 General
2178.32 Hanska, Eveline, ca. 1800-1881 or 2
Madame Honoré de Balzac
2179 Autobiography. Journals. Letters. Memoirs
2179.A2 Collected letters
2179.A4 English translations
2179.A6-Z Special correspondents, A-Z
2179.5 Homes and haunts. Literary landmarks and journeys
(2180) Balzac in fiction, poetry, drama
Criticism
2180.3 History of criticism
2180.6.A-Z Biography of Balzac scholars, A-Z
2181 General
2182 Textual
2183 Sources
2184.A-Z Special topics, A-Z
2184.A36 Adolescence
2184.A47 Altruism
2184.A7 Art
2184.A9 Authorship
2184.C5 Characters
2184.D54 Digression
2184.E27 Economics
2184.E37 Education
2184.E76 Eroticism. Sex
2184.F32 Fairy tales
2184.F34 Family
2184.F54 Film and video adaptations
2184.F7 France
2184.G46 Geography
2184.H55 History
2184.I8 Italy

Modern French literature
Individual authors
19th century
Balzac, Honoré de, 1799-1850
Biography and criticism
Criticism
Special topics, A-Z -- Continued

2184.L3 Law
2184.M3 Marriage
2184.M4 Medicine
2184.M8 Music
2184.M95 Mysticism
2184.N3 Nature
2184.P3 Paris
2184.P34 Peasants
2184.P4 Philosophy
2184.S32 Self
Sex see PQ2184.E76
2184.S58 Social views
2184.S6 Spain
2184.T55 Time
2184.W57 Wit and humor
2185 Language, grammar, style
Cf. PQ2177.A3+ Dictionaries, indexes
2186 Bal - Ban
2187-2188 Banville, Théodore Faullain de, 1823-1891 (Table P-PZ36)
2189.B25 Baour-Lormian, Pierre Marie François Louis, 1770-1850 (Table P-PZ40)
2189.B319 Barante, Amable Guillaume Prosper Brugière, baron de, 1782-1866 (Table P-PZ40)
2189.B3196 Barbara, Charles, 1817-1866 (Table P-PZ40)
2189.B32 Barbey d'Aurevilly, Jules Amédée, 1808-1889 (Table P-PZ40)
2189.B325 Barbiano di Belgiojoso, Cristina Trivulzio, principessa, 1808-1871 (Table P-PZ40)
2189.B33 Barbier, Auguste, 1805-1882 (Table P-PZ40)
2189.B5 Barrière, Théodore, 1823-1877 (Table P-PZ40)
2189.B6 Barthélemy, Auguste Marseille, 1796-1867 (Table P-PZ40)
2189.B63 Barthélemy-Hadot, Marie Adèle, 1763-1821 (Table P-PZ40)
2189.B64 Barthet, Armand, 1820-1874 (Table P-PZ40)
2191 Baudelaire, Charles Pierre, 1821-1867 (Table P-PZ39)
2193.B163 Bauer, Henry, b. 1852 (Table P-PZ40)
2193.B17 Baumaine, Felix (Table P-PZ40)

Modern French literature
Individual authors
19th century -- Continued

2193.B18 Bawr, Alexandrine Sophie (Goury de Champgrand), baronne de, 1773-1860 (Table P-PZ40)
2193.B2 Bayard, Jean François Alfred, 1796-1853 (Table P-PZ40)
2193.B3 Bazin, René, 1853-1932 (Table P-PZ40)
2193.B324 Beaucourt, Raymond, 1867-1925 (Table P-PZ40)
2193.B332 Beaujoint, Jules, 1830-1893 (Table P-PZ40)
2193.B4 Becque, Henri, 1837-1899 (Table P-PZ40)
2193.B5 Bégon, Fanny, comtesse de ("Mme. de Stolz") (Table P-PZ40)
Belgioioso, Cristina, 1808-1871 see PQ2189.B325
2193.B58 Bellemare, Gabriel de, 1846- ("Gabriel Ferry") (Table P-PZ40)
2193.B6 Bellemare, Louis de, 1809-1852 ("Gabriel Ferry") (Table P-PZ40)
2193.B65 Bellin de La Liborlière, Louis-François-Marie, 1774-1847 (Table P-PZ40)
2193.B7 Belot, Adolphe, 1829-1890 (Table P-PZ40)
2193.B72 Bemmel, Eugène van, 1824-1880 (Table P-PZ40)
2193.B74 Bénédit, G. (Gustave), 1802-1870 (Table P-PZ40)
2193.B84 Benoît, Eulalie (Table P-PZ40)
Bentzon, Théodore see PQ2197.B6
2195 Béranger, Pierre Jean de, 1780-1857 (Table P-PZ39)
2196.B2 Berchoux, Joseph de, 1762-1838 (Table P-PZ40)
2196.B3 Bergerat, Émile, 1845-1923 (Table P-PZ40)
2196.B34 Berjot, Eugène (Table P-PZ40)
2196.B4 Bernard, Charles de, 1804-1850 (Table P-PZ40)
Bernadin de St. Pierre see PQ2065
2196.B73 Berthet, Élie Bertrand, 1818-1891 (Table P-PZ40)
2196.B8 Bertrand, Louis Jacques Napolon, called Alosius, 1807-1841 (Table P-PZ40)
2196.B86 Betances, Ramón Emeterio, 1827-1898 (Table P-PZ40)
Beyle, Marie Henri see PQ2435+
2197.B26 Bignan, A (Table P-PZ40)
2197.B4 Bilhaud, Paul, 1854- (Table P-PZ40)
2197.B5 Bisson, Alexandre Charles Auguste, 1848-1912 (Table P-PZ40)
2197.B6 Blanc, Mme. Marie Thérèse (de Solms), 1840-1907 (Table P-PZ40)
2197.B64 Blanchemain, Prosper, 1816-1879 (Table P-PZ40)
2197.B7 Blaze de Bury, Ange Henri, 1813-1888 (Table P-PZ40)
2197.B75 Blémont, Émile, 1839- (Table P-PZ40)
2197.B9 Blouët, Paul, 1848-1903 ("Max O'Rell") (Table P-PZ40)
2198.B18 Bloy, Léon, 1846-1917 (Table P-PZ40)
2198.B19 Blum, Ernest, 1836-1905 (Table P-PZ40)

Modern French literature
Individual authors
19th century -- Continued

2198.B325 Boissonneau, F. (Francois), b. 1831 (Table P-PZ40)
2198.B375 Bonjean, Albert, 1858-1939 (Table P-PZ40)
2198.B379 Bonnejoy-Pérignon, Mme. (Eugénie) (Table P-PZ40)
2198.B38 Bonnetain, Paul, 1858-1899 (Table P-PZ40)
2198.B4 Borel, Petrus, i.e. Pierre Joseph Borel d'Hauterive, 1809-1859 (Table P-PZ40)
2198.B5 Bornier, Henri, vicomte de, 1825-1901 (Table P-PZ40)
2198.B55 Bory d'Arnex, Mme. Angèle (Dussaud), 1850- ("Jacques Vincent") (Table P-PZ40)
2198.B57 Boucher de Crèvecoeur de Perthes, Jacques, 1788-1868 (Table P-PZ40)
2198.B6 Bouchor, Maurice, 1855-1929 (Table P-PZ40)
2198.B63 Bouilhet, Louis, 1822-1869 (Table P-PZ40)
2198.B65 Bouilly, Jean Nicolas, 1763-1842 (Table P-PZ40)
Bourgeois, Auguste Anicet see PQ2153.A36
2198.B72 Bourgeois, Emmanuel, 1826-1877 (Table P-PZ40)
2198.B73 Bourges, Elemir, 1852-1925 (Table P-PZ40)
2199 Bourget, Paul Charles Joseph, 1852-1935 (Table P-PZ39)
2201.B35 Bovet, Marie Anne de, 1860- (Table P-PZ40)
2201.B363 Boyer, Philoxène, 1829-1867 (Table P-PZ40)
2201.B365 Brazier, Nicolas, 1783-1838 (Table P-PZ40)
2201.B47 Brèthel, Alexandre, 1834-1901 (Table P-PZ40)
2201.B5 Brieux, Eugène, 1858- (Table P-PZ40)
2201.B52 Brifaut, Charles, 1781-1857 (Table P-PZ40)
2201.B54 Brillaud-Laujardidre, Charles (Table P-PZ40)
2201.B556 Brizeux, Julien Auguste Pglage, 1806-1858 (Table P-PZ40)
2201.B56 Brontë, Emily Jane, 1818-1848 (Table P-PZ40)
2201.B57 Brot, Alphonse, i.e. Charles Alphonse, b.1809 (Table P-PZ40)
Bruant, Aristide see PQ2603.R9
2201.B7 Brun, Adrien, b. 1800 (Table P-PZ40)
2201.B78 Buffenoir, Hippolyte, 1847-1928 (Table P-PZ40)
2201.B8 Bungener, Felix, 1804-1874 (Table P-PZ40)
2201.B85 Busnach, W. (William) (Table P-PZ40)
2203.C2 Cadol, Édouard, 1831-1898 (Table P-PZ40)
2203.C3 Cahun, David-Léon, 1841-1900 (Table P-PZ40)
2203.C33 Caigniez, Louis Charles, 1762-1842 (Table P-PZ40)
2203.C35 Cairon, Claude Antoine Jules, called Jules Noriac, 1827-1882 (Table P-PZ40)
2203.C37 Calmettes, Fernand, 1846- (Table P-PZ40)
2203.C38 Cammaille-Saint-Aubin, M.C., ca. 1750-1830 (Table P-PZ40)

Modern French literature
Individual authors
19th century -- Continued

2203.C456 Cannizzaro, Tommaso, 1838-1916 (Table P-PZ40)
2203.C6 Capendu, Ernest, 1826-1868 (Table P-PZ40)
2203.C65 Cappeau, Placide (Table P-PZ40)
2203.C7 Capus, Alfred, 1858-1922 (Table P-PZ40)
2203.C73 Carlier, Thodore, 1802-1839 (Table P-PZ40)
2204.C22 Caro, Pauline (Cassin), 1835-1901 (Mme. Elme Marie Caro) (Table P-PZ40)
2204.C35 Carré, Michel, 1819-1872 (Table P-PZ40)
2204.C4 Case, Jules, 1856 (Table P-PZ40)
2204.C7619 Cazalis, Henry, 1840-1909 (Table P-PZ40)
2204.C7673 Chabrillat, Henri, 1842-1893 (Table P-PZ40)
2204.C7678 Chambrier, Alice de, 1861-1882 (Table P-PZ40)
Champfleury see PQ2252.A61+
Champsaur, Félicien see PQ2605.H325
2204.C775 Chancel, Ausone de, 1808-1878 (Table P-PZ40)
2204.C8 Chandeneux, Emma Branger, 1836-1881 ("Claire de Chandeneux") (Table P-PZ40)
2204.C93 Chastenet de Puysgur, A.-M.-J. (Armand-MarieJacques), 1751-1825 (Table P-PZ40)
2205 Chateaubriand, Frangois Auguste Ren, vicomte de, 1768-1848 (Table P-PZ39)
For editions of his Mémoires d'outre-tombe see DC255.C4
2207.C16 Châtelain, Auguste, 1838-1923 (Table P-PZ40)
2207.C18 Chatelain, Jean Baptiste François Ernest de, chevalier, 1801-1881 (Table P-PZ40)
Chatrian, Alexandre see PQ2238
2207.C3 Chênedollé, Charles Julien Lioult de, 1769-1833 (Table P-PZ40)
Chénier, Marie Joseph Blaise see PQ1966
2207.C4 Cherbuliez, Victor, 1829-1899 (Table P-PZ40)
2207.C45 Chevalier, H.-Émile (Henri-Émile), 1828-1879 (Table P-PZ40)
2207.C454 Chevigné, Louis Marie Joseph Le Riche, comte de, 1793-1876 (Table P-PZ40)
2207.C54 Cladel, Lon Alpinien, 1834?-1892 (Table P-PZ40)
2207.C56 Clairville, Louis Frangois Nicolaie, called, 1811-1879 (Table P-PZ40)
2207.C58 Clarens, Jean Paul (Table P-PZ40)
2207.C6 Claretie, Jules, 1840-1913 (Table P-PZ40)
2207.C63 Claretie, Léo, 1862-1924 (Table P-PZ40)
2207.C85 Cluzeaux, P.-C. (Pierre C.), b. 1808 (Table P-PZ40)
2209.C4 Cogniard, Hippolyte and Théodore (1831-1876) (Table P-PZ40)

Modern French literature
Individual authors
19th century -- Continued

2209.C45 Coiffier de Moret, Simon, 1764-1826 (Table P-PZ40)
2209.C6 Colet, Mme. Louise (Revoil), 1810-1876 (Table P-PZ40)
2210.C65 Combettes-Labourelié, Louis de, 1817-1881 (Table P-PZ40)
2211.C24 Constant de Rebecque, Henri Benjamin, 1767-1830 (Benjamin Constant) (Table P-PZ38)
2211.C3 Coppée, François, 1842-1908 (Table P-PZ40)
2211.C318 Corbiére, Édouard, 1793-1875 (Table P-PZ40)
2211.C32 Corbire, Tristan, 1845-1875 (Table P-PZ40)
2211.C4 Coster, Charles Théodore Henri de, 1827-1879 (Table P-PZ40)
2211.C412 Cottin, Marie (Risteau), called Sophie, 1770-1807 (Table P-PZ40)
2211.C4146 Courchamps, comte de, 1783-1849 (Table P-PZ40)
2211.C42 Courier de Méré, Paul Louis, 1772-1825 (Table P-PZ40)
2211.C43 Courmont, Louis de, 1828-1900 (Table P-PZ40)
2211.C5 Craven, Pauline Marie Armande Agla (Ferron de La Ferronays), 1808-1891 (Table P-PZ40)
Mrs. Augustus Craven
2211.C57 Crémieux, Hector Jonathan, 1828-1892 (Table P-PZ40)
2211.C6 Creuz de Lesser, Augustin Frangois, baron, 1771-1839 (Table P-PZ40)
2211.C612 Crevel de Charlemagne, Louis, b. 1806 (Table P-PZ40)
2211.C63 Croiset, Paul, 1860- (Table P-PZ40)
2211.C65 Cros, Charles, 1842-1888 (Table P-PZ40)
2211.C8 Curel, François, vicomte de, 1854-1930 (Table P-PZ40)
2211.C85 Custine, Astolphe Louis Léonard, marquis de, 1790-1857 (Table P-PZ40)
2211.C87 Cuvelier, J.-G.-A. (Jean-Guillaume-Antoine), 1766-1824 (Table P-PZ40)
2215.D3 Darzens, Rodolphe, 1865- (Table P-PZ40)
2215.D33 Daniel, abbe (J.) (Table P-PZ40)
2215.D34 Dasconaguerre, J.B. (Table P-PZ40)
Dash, La comtesse see PQ2390.S5
2216 Daudet, Alphonse, 1840-1897
2216.A1-.A59 Collected works
2216.A1 Collected works. By date
2216.A14A-.A14Z Selected works. By editor, A-Z
2216.A19 Collected plays
2216.A2-.A29 English translations
Alphabetically by translator or publisher
2216.A3-.A39 German translations
Alphabetically by translator or publisher

Modern French literature
Individual authors
19th century
Daudet, Alphonse, 1840-1897
Collected works -- Continued

2216.A5-.A59 Other translations, alphabetically by language e. g.
2216.A56 Polish
2216.A6-.Z3 Separate works
2216.A63 Les absents (Opéra-comique)
2216.A7 Les amoureuses, poèmes et fantasies
2216.A8 L'Arlésienne (Drame)
2216.A86 Audiberte
Aventures prodigieuses de Tartarin de Tarascon see PQ2216.T4
2216.B4 La Belle-Nivernaise
2216.C3 Le char (Opéra-comique)
2216.C4 Les cicognes, legendes rhénane
2216.C5 La comtesse Irma
2216.C6 Contes choisis
2216.C65 Contes d'hiver
2216.C7 Contes de lundi
2216.D4 La défense de Tarascon
2216.D5 La dernière idole
2216.E5 L'enterrement d'une étoile
2216.E6 Entre les frises et la rampe
2216.E8 L'évangéliste
2216.F4 La Fédor
2216.F5 Les femmes d'artistes
2216.F6 Le frère aîne (Drame)
2216.F8 Fromont jeune et Risler aîné
Histoire d'un enfant see PQ2216.P4
2216.I4 L'immortel
2216.J3 Jack
Lettres à un absent see PQ2216.Z5A6
2216.L5 Lettres de mon moulin
2216.L6 Lise Tavernier
2216.L8 La lutte pour la vie (Drame)
2216.M4 La meneuse (Drame)
2216.N2 Le nabab, moeurs parisiennes
2216.N3 Le nabab (Drame)
2216.N6 Notes sur la vie
2216.N8 Numa Roumestan; moeurs parisiennes
2216.N9 Numa Roumestan (Drame)
2216.O3 L'obstacle (Drame)
2216.O4 L'oeillet blanc (Comédie)

Modern French literature
Individual authors
19th century
Daudet, Alphonse, 1840-1897
Separate works -- Continued

2216.P4 Le petit chose, histoire d'un enfant
Also published with title: Histoire d'un enfant, Le petit chose
2216.P5 Le petite paroisse: moeurs conjugales
2216.P7 Port-Tarascon
2216.P8 Premier voyage, premier mensonge, souvenirs de mon enfance
2216.P9 Les prunes; poèsie
2216.R6 Robert Helmont
2216.R7 Les rois en exil
2216.R75 Le roman du Chaperon Rouge
2216.R8 Rose et Ninette
2216.S2 Le sacrifice (Comédie)
2216.S3 Sapho; moeurs parisiennes
2216.S4 Sapho (Play)
Le secret de maître Cornille see PQ2216.L5
2216.S5 Le siège de Berlin
2216.S8 Soutien de famille
Souvenirs d'un homme de lettres see PQ2216.Z5A2
2216.T4 Tartarin de Tarascon
2216.T5 Tartarin sur les Alpes
Théâtre see PQ2216.A19
Trente ans de Paris; à travers ma vie et mes livres see PQ2216.Z5
2216.T7 Le tresor d'Arlatan
2216.T8 Trois souvenirs: Au Fort-Montrouge; à la Salpêtrière; Une leçon
2216.Z5 Biography. Criticism
e. g.
2216.Z5A2 Souvenirs d'un homme de lettres
2216.Z5A6 Lettres à un absent
2217.D2 Daudet, Ernest, 1837-1921 (Table P-PZ40)
2217.D25 Daudet, Julia Rosalie Cleste (Allard), 1847- (Table P-PZ40)
2217.D27 Dautrevaux, Clophas Reimbold (Table P-PZ40)
2217.D3 David, Jules Antoine (Table P-PZ40)
2217.D4 David, Marie (de Saffron), 1831-1885 (Table P-PZ40)
2217.D58 Decourcelle, Adrien, 1824-1892 (Table P-PZ40)
2217.D6 Decourcelle, Pierre, 1856-1926 (Table P-PZ40)
2217.D617 Defontenay, Charlemagne Ischir, 1814-1856 (Table P-PZ40)
Delarue, Gabriel Jules see PQ2445.S7

Modern French literature
Individual authors
19th century -- Continued

2217.D8 Delavigne, Jean Franois Casimir, 1794-1843 (Table P-PZ40)
2217.D9 Deleutre, Paul Charles Philippe Eric, 1856- (Table P-PZ40)
2218.D2 Delpit, Albert, 1849-1893 (Table P-PZ40)
2218.D3 Delpit, douard, 1844-1900 (Table P-PZ40)
2218.D34 Deltuf, Paul, 1825-1871 (Table P-PZ40)
2218.D4 Denis, Ferdinand, 1798-1890 (Table P-PZ40)
2218.D54 Dennery, Adolphe Philippe, 1811-1899 (Table P-PZ40)
2218.D6 Depré, Ernest, 1854- (Table P-PZ40)
2218.D63 Dépret, Louis, 1837- (Table P-PZ40)
2218.D7 Déroulède, Paul, 1846-1914 (Table P-PZ40)
2218.D73 Désaugiers, Marc Antoine Madeleine, 1772-1827 (Table P-PZ40)
2218.D75 Desbordes-Valmore, Marceline Félicité Josèphe, 1786-1859 (Table P-PZ40)
2218.D8 Descaves, Lucien, 1861- (Table P-PZ40)
2218.D87 Deschamps, Émile, 1791-1871 (Table P-PZ40)
2219.D2 Deschanel, Émile Auguste tienne Martin, 1819-1904 (Table P-PZ40)
2219.D3 Des Essarts, Alfred Stanislas Langlois, 1811-1893 (Table P-PZ40)
2219.D35 Des Essarts, Emmanuel, 1839- (Table P-PZ40)
2219.D4 Deslys, Charles Collinet, 1821-1885 (Table P-PZ40)
2219.D526 Desprez, Louis, 1861-1885 (Table P-PZ40)
2219.D528 Destrée, Jules, 1863-1936 (Table P-PZ40)
2219.D56 Deulin, Charles, 1827-1877 (Table P-PZ40)
2219.D7 Dierx, Léon, 1838-1912 (Table P-PZ40)
2219.D73 Dieulafoy, Jane, 1851-1916 (Table P-PZ40)
2219.D75 Dieulafoy, Joseph Marie Armand Michel, 1762-1823 (Table P-PZ40)
2219.D8 Dinaux (Table P-PZ40)
Joint pseudonym of J.F. Beudin and P.P. Goubaux
2220.D2 Dodillon, Émile, 1848- (Table P-PZ40)
2220.D3 Dorchain, Auguste, 1857-1930 (Table P-PZ40)
2220.D315 Dossion, Étienne-Auguste, 1770-1832 (Table P-PZ40)
2220.D32 Double, Henriette Marie Adelaide Biard d'Aunet, baronne, 1848-1897 (Table P-PZ40)
2220.D33 Doucet, Camille, 1812-1895 (Table P-PZ40)
2220.D345 Dovalle, Charles, 1807-1830 (Table P-PZ40)
2220.D36 Driant, Émile Augustin Cyprien, 1855-1916 (Table P-PZ40)
2220.D4 Droz, Gustave, 1832-1895 (Table P-PZ40)

Modern French literature
Individual authors
19th century -- Continued

2220.D6 Du Boisgobey, Fortuné Hippolyte Auguste, 1821-1891 (Table P-PZ40)
2220.D67 Dubut de Laforest, Jean Louis, 1853-1902 (Table P-PZ40)
2220.D7 Du Camp, Maxime, 1822-1894 (Table P-PZ40)
2220.D716 Ducancel, C.-P. (Charles Pierre), 1766-1835 (Table P-PZ40)
2220.D72 Du Cange, Victor Henri Joseph Brahain, 1783-1833 (Table P-PZ40)
2220.D723 Ducasse, Isadore Lucien, 1846-1870 (Table P-PZ40)
2220.D74 Ducos, Florentin, 1789-1873 (Table P-PZ40)
2220.D75 Ducray-Duminil, M. (François Guillaume), 1761-1819 (Table P-PZ40)
2220.D8 Dujardin, Edouard, 1861- (Table P-PZ40)
2220.D9 Dumanoir, Philippe Fraois Pinel, called, 1806-1865 (Table P-PZ40)

Dumas, Alexandre, père, 1802-1870

2221 Collected works. By date (date letter)
2222 Selected works. By editor

Translations

2223 English. By translator or publisher
2224 Other. By language, A-Z, subarranged by translator

Separate works

2225.A2 L'abbaye de Peyssac
2225.A3 Acté
2225.A4 L'alchimiste

Andrée de Taverney see PQ2227.M5

2225.A5 Ange Pitou
2225.A7 Antony
2225.A75 Aventures de John Davys
2225.C15 Caligula
2225.C18 Le capitaine Pamphile
2225.C2 Le capitaine Paul (Novel)

Cf. PQ2227.P2 Paul Jones (Play)

2225.C25 Cathèrine Howard
2225.C3 Charles VII
2225.C4 La chasse et l'amour
2225.C5 Le chevalier d' Harmental
2225.C6 Le chevalier de Maison-Rouge (Play)
2225.C7 Le chevalier de Maison-Rouge (Novel)
2225.C734 Le chevalier de Sainte-Hermine
2225.C75 Chroniques de France
2225.C8 Le collier de la reine
2225.C9 Les compagnons de Jéhu

Modern French literature
Individual authors
19th century
Dumas, Alexandre, pere, 1802-1870
Separate works -- Continued

2226 Le comte de Monte-Cristo (Novel) (Table P-PZ41)
Monte-Cristo (Play) see PQ2227.M8
2227.C2 La comtesse de Charny
2227.C3 La comtesse de Salisbury
2227.C4 La conscience (Novel)
2227.C5 La conscience (Play)
Crimes célèbres see HV6211
2227.D2 La dame de Monsoreau
2227.D4 Les demoiselles de Saint-Cyr
2227.D5 Les deux Diane
2227.D53 Les deux reines
2227.D6 Dieu dispose
2227.D7 Don Juan de Marana, ou La chute d'un ange
2227.D8 Les drames de la mer
2227.E3 Emma Lyonna
2227.E4 L'envers d'une conspiration
2227.F3 Une fille du régent (Novel)
2227.F35 Une fille du régent (Play)
2227.F44 Les fils de l'emigré
2227.F5 Les fréres corses
Le garde-forestier see PQ2338.L43
2227.G8 La guerre des femmes (Series of novels)
see also the individual titles
Hamlet, prince de Danemarck see PR2779.A+
2227.H4 Henri III et sa cour
2227.H5 Histoire d'un cabanon et d'un chalet
2227.H68 Homme au masque de fer (Novel)
2227.H69 Homme au masque de fer (Play)
(2227.I4) Impressions de voyage
see classes G and D
Impressions de voyage en Russia see DK26
2227.I6 L'invitation à la valse
2227.I7 Isable de Bavière
Jehanne la Pucelle see DC103.A3+
Joseph Balsamo see PQ2227.M5
2227.K3 Kean
2227.L7 Louise Bernard
2227.M2 Mademoiselle de Belle-Isle
2227.M3 Massacres de midi. Urbain Grandier
2227.M4 Les Médicis
2227.M5 Mémoires d'un médecin
2227.M51 1. partie: Joseph Balsamo

Modern French literature
Individual authors
19th century
Dumas, Alexandre, pere, 1802-1870
Separate works
Mémoires d'un médecin -- Continued

2227.M52	2. partie: Andrée de Tavernay
	Mes mémoires see PQ2230.A2
2227.M6	Les mille et un fantômes
2227.M7	Les Mohicans de Paris (Novel)
2227.M75	Les Mohicans de Paris (Play)
	Monsieur Coumbes see PQ2227.H5
2227.M77	Monseigneur Gaston Phoebus
	Monte-Cristo, Le comte de, (Novel) see PQ2226
2227.M8	Monte-Cristo (Play)
2227.M81	1: partie: 1. soirée
2227.M82	2: partie: 2. soirée
2227.M83	3: partie: Le conte de Morcerf
2227.M84	4: partie: Villefort, 4e soirée de Monte-Cristo
	Monte-Cristo, journal hebdomadaire de romans, d'histoire, de voyages et de poésie see PQ1
2227.M9	Les mousquetaires (Play)
	Cf. PQ2228 Les trois mousquetaires (Novel)
2227.N15	Nanon de Lartigues
2227.N2	Napoléon Bonaparte, ou Trente ans de l'histoire de France
2227.N6	La noce et l'enterrement
2227.N7	Nouvelles contemporaines
(2227.N8)	Nouvelles impressions de voyage
	see class D
2227.O6	Olympe de Clèves
2227.O8	Othon l'archer
2227.P15	Le page du duc de Savoie
2227.P2	Paul Jones (Play)
	Cf. PQ2225.C2 Le capitaine Paul (Novel)
2227.P4	Pélérinage de Hadji-Abd-el-Hamid Bey
2227.P7	Praxede
2227.P8	Le pribonnier de la Bastille, fin des mousquetaires
2227.Q2	Les quarante-cinq
2227.R3	La reine Margot (Novel)
2227.R35	La reine Margot (Play)
2227.R76	La royale Maison de Savoie
2227.S2	La salle d'armes
2227.S3	La San-Felice
	Cf. PQ2227.E3 Emma Lyonna
2227.S4	Le séducteur et la mari
2227.S6	Souvenirs d'Antony

Modern French literature
Individual authors
19th century
Dumas, Alexandre, pere, 1802-1870
Separate works -- Continued

2227.S7 Souvenirs d'une favorite
Souvenirs de 1830 à 1842 see PQ2230.A2
Souvenirs dramatiques see PQ501
2227.S78 Stockholm, Fontainebleau, et Rome, trilogie dramatique
2227.S8 Les Stuarts
2227.S9 Sylvandire
Le tasse see PQ2235.D8
2227.T3 Térésa
2227.T6 Le tour de Nesle
2228 Les trois mousquetaires (Novel) (Table P-PZ41)
Cf. PQ2227.M9 Les mousquetaires
2229.T7 Le trou de l'enfer
2229.T8 La tulipe noire
2229.V4 Le vicomte de Bragelonne
2229.V46 La vicomtesse de Cambes
2229.V5 Une vie artiste
2229.V55 La Villa Palmire
Villefort see PQ2227.M84
2229.V6 Vingt ans apres
2230 Biography and criticism
2230.A2 Autobiography, journals, letters, memoirs
2231 Dumas, Alexandre, fils, 1824-1895
2231.A19 Collected plays
2231.A6-.Z3 Separate works
2231.A63 Affaire Clémenceau
2231.A65 L'ami des femmes
2231.A68 Antonine
2231.A7 Atala
2231.A8 Aventures de quatre femmes et d'un perroquet
2231.B7 La boîte d'argent
2231.C2 Un cas de rupture
2231.C3 Ce que llon voit tous les jours
2231.C4 Césarine
2231.C6 La comtesse Romani
2231.C7 Contes et nouvelleb
2231.D2 La dame aux camélias (Novel)
La dame aux camélias (Play)
2231.D3 Texts. By date
2231.D32 English translations. By date
2231.D33 Polyglot translations. By date
2231.D34 Criticism

Modern French literature
Individual authors
19th century
Dumas Alexandre, fils, 1824-1895
Separate works -- Continued

2231.D37 La dame aux perles
Les Danicheff see PQ2320.K7
2231.D4 Le demimonde
2231.D5 Denise
2231.D6 Les deux reines
2231.D7 Diane de Lys et Grangette (Novel)
2231.D75 Diane de Lys (Play)
2231.D8 Discours de réception a l'Académie
2231.D9 Le docteur Servans
2231.E4 Entr'actes
2231.E42 Nouveau entr'actes
2231.E7 L'étrangère
2231.F3 La femme de Claude
2231.F4 Les femmes qui tuent et les femmes qui votent
Le filleul de Pompignac see PQ2311.J17
2231.F5 Le fils naturel
2231.F7 Francillon
2231.H4 Héloïse Paranquet
2231.H5 Histoire du supplice d'une femme
L'homme-femme see HQ31
2231.I3 Les ides de Mme. Aubray
2231.I6 Ilka
2231.L4 Une lettre sur les choses du jour
2231.M3 Les madeleines repenties
2231.M7 Monsieur Alphonse
Nouveau entr'actes see PQ2231.E42
2231.N6 Nouvelle lettre sur les choses du jour
2231.P4 Péchés de jeunesse
2231.P5 Un père prodigue
2231.P7 La princesse de Bagdad
2231.P8 La princesse Georges
2231.Q4 La question d'argent
2231.R4 Le régent Mustel
Revenants see PQ2231.R4
2231.R6 Le roman d'une femme
2231.R65 La Route de Thèbes
2231.S7 Sophie Printems
Le supplice d'une femme (Play) see PQ2260.G68
Théâtre see PQ2231.A19
2231.T4 Thérèse
2231.T7 Tristan le Roux
2231.T8 Trois hommes forts

Modern French literature
Individual authors
19th century
Dumas Alexandre, fils, 1824-1895
Separate works -- Continued

2231.V4 La vie à vingt ans
2231.V7 Une visite de noces
2231.Z5 Biography. Criticism
2235 Dumas - Dz
2235.D3 Dumersan, Théophile Marion, 1780-1849 (Table P-PZ40)
2235.D38 Dumot d'Urville, Jules-Sébastien-César, 1790-1842 (Table P-PZ40)
Dumur, Louis see PQ2607.U76
2235.D42 Dupaty, Louis Emmanuel Félicité Charles Mercier, 1775-1851 (Table P-PZ40)
2235.D46 Duplessis, Paul, 1815-1865 (Table P-PZ40)
2235.D492 Dupond, Jean Louis Nicolas, 1831-1902 (Table P-PZ40)
2235.D5 Dupont, Pierre, 1821-1870 (Table P-PZ40)
2235.D54 Dupouy, Georges (Table P-PZ40)
Duquesnel Félix see PQ2607.U813
2235.D6 Durand, Alice Marie Céleste (Fleury), 1842-1902 (Table P-PZ40)
2235.D65 Duras, Claire de Durfort, duchesse de, 1777-1828 (Table P-PZ40)
2235.D665 Duruy, George, 1853-1918 (Table P-PZ40)
2235.D8 Duval, Alexandre, 1767-1842 (Table P-PZ40)
2235.D9 Duval, Georges, 1847- (Table P-PZ40)
2235.D93 Duval, Paul Alexandre Martin, 1856-1906 (Table P-PZ40)
2235.D96 Duveyrier, Anne Honoré Joseph, 1787-1865 (Table P-PZ40)
2237.E13 Eberhardt, Isabelle, 1877-1904 (Table P-PZ40)
2237.E2 Eekhoud, Georges, 1854-1927 (Table P-PZ40)
2237.E22 Eggis, Étienne, 1830-1867 (Table P-PZ40)
2237.E25 Elisabeth, Queen of Romania, 1843-1916 (Table P-PZ40)
2237.E5 Énault, Louis, 1824-1900 (Table P-PZ40)
Ennery, A.P. d' see PQ2218.D54
2238 Erckmann, Émile, 1822-1899, and Chatrian, Alexandre, 1826-1890 (Table P-PZ39)
2240.E7 Esquuios, Alphonse, 1812-1876 (Table P-PZ40)
2240.E8 Étienne, Charles Guillaume, 1777-1845 (Table P-PZ40)
Etincelle, ca. 1840-1897 see PQ2220.D32
2241.F2 Fabié, François Joseph, 1846-1928 (Table P-PZ40)
2241.F3 Fabre, Ferdinand, 1830-1898 (Table P-PZ40)

	Modern French literature
	Individual authors
	19th century -- Continued
2241.F36	Fabre d'Olivet, Antoine, 1767-1825 (Table P-PZ40)
2241.F44	Fargèze, Félicien, 1836-1920 (Table P-PZ40)
2241.F514	Favre, Louis, 1822-1904 (Table P-PZ40)
2241.F597	Féré, Charles Octave Moget, called, 1815-1875 (Table P-PZ40)
	Ferry Gabriel see PQ2193.B6
2241.F68	Fertiault, Frangois, 1814-1915 (Table P-PZ40)
2242	Feuillet, Octave, 1821-1890 (Table P-PZ39)
2243	Feuillet, Valérie Marie Elvire (Dubois) (Table P-PZ39)
2244.F2	Féval, Paul Henri Corentin, 1817-1887 (Table P-PZ40)
2244.F27	Feydeau, Ernest Aimé, 1821-1873 (Table P-PZ40)
	Feydeau, Georges, 1862-1921 see PQ2611.E86
2244.F68	Figuier, Juliette (Bouscaret), 1829-1879 (Table P-PZ40)
2244.F7	Figuier, Louis, 1819-1894 (Table P-PZ40)
2244.F9	Flammarion, Camille, 1842-1925 (Table P-PZ40)
	Flaubert, Gustave, 1821-1880
2246.A1	Works. By date
	Translations
2246.A2-.A29	English
2246.A3-.A39	German
2246.A5-.A59	Other. By language (Alphabetically)
2246.A6-Z	Separate works
	e. g.
2246.M2-.M3	Madame Bovary (Table P-PZ43a)
2246.S3-.S4	Salammbô (Table P-PZ43a)
2246.T4-.T5	La tentation de Saint Antoine (Table P-PZ43a)
	Biography and criticism
2247.A2	Journals, letters, memoirs
2247.A3-Z	General works
2248	Authorship. Sources
	Criticism
2249	General. Genius, philosophy, characters, plots, etc.
2250	Other special: Language, etc.
2251.F58	Fleurigny, Henry de, 1846-1916 (Table P-PZ40)
2251.F6	Fleury, Hippolyte de Saint-Anthoine, comte de (Table P-PZ40)
	Fleury, Jules, 1821-1889
2252.A61-.Z48	Separate works, A-Z
2252.Z5A-.Z5Z	Biography. Criticism
2253.F18	Floupette, Ador (Table P-PZ40)
	Joint pseudonym of Henri Beauclair and Gabriel Vicaire
2253.F415	Fontanes, Louis, marquis de, 1757-1821 (Table P-PZ40)
2253.F614	Forneret, Xavier, 1809-1884 (Table P-PZ40)

Modern French literature
Individual authors
19th century -- Continued

2253.F63 Fortia de Piles, A. (Alphonse), comte de, 1758-1826 (Table P-PZ40)
2253.F64 Fos, Léonde, 1798-1869 (Table P-PZ40)
2253.F8 Foudras, Theodore Louis Auguste, marquis de, 1800-1872 (Table P-PZ40)
2253.F83 Fouinet, Ernest, 1799-1845 (Table P-PZ40)
France, Anatole, 1884-1924
2254.A1 Collected works. By date
2254.A14 Miscellaneous collections, ouevres inédites, etc.
2254.A17 Collected poems
Translations
2254.A2-.A29 English
2254.A3-.A39 German
2254.A4-.A49 Spanish
2254.A5-.A59 Other. By language (Alphabetically)
2254.A6-.A64 Selections
2254.A62 English
2254.A625 German
2254.A63 Spanish
2254.A65-.Z2 Separate works
2254.Z3 Conversations, table-talk, etc. By editor, A-Z
2254.Z4 Letters
2254.Z5 Biography. Criticism
2256.F36 Frémine, Aristide, 1837-1897 (Table P-PZ40)
2256.F37 Frémine, Charles (Table P-PZ40)
2256.F5 Fromentin, Eugène, 1820-1876 (Table P-PZ40)
2256.F8 Fuster, Charles, 1866-1929 (Table P-PZ40)
2257.G2 Gaboriau, Émile, 1835-1873 (Table P-PZ40)
2257.G26 Gagnebin, Suzanne (Table P-PZ40)
2257.G3 Gaillardet, Frédéric, 1808-1882 (Table P-PZ40)
2257.G363 Galoppe d'Onquaire, Jean Hyacinthe Adonis, 1810-1867 (Table P-PZ40)
2257.G47 Garreau, Louis-Armand, 1817-1864 (Table P-PZ40)
2257.G5 Gasparin, Catherine valrie (BoisBier), comtesse de, 1813-1894 (Table P-PZ40)
2257.G6 Gastine, Louis Jules, 1858- (Table P-PZ40)
2257.G7 Gaugiran-Nanteuil, P. Charles, 1778-1830 (Table P-PZ40)
2257.G8 Gauthier-Villars, Henry, 1859-1931 (Table P-PZ40)
2257.G9 Gautier, Judith, 1846-1917 (Table P-PZ40)
2258 Gautier, Théophile, 1811-1872 (Table P-PZ39)
2260.G25 Gay, Sophie (Nichault de Lavalette), 1776-1852 (Table P-PZ40)
2260.G3 Gebhart, Émile, 1839-1908 (Table P-PZ40)

Modern French literature
Individual authors
19th century -- Continued

	Genlis, Stéphanie Félicité Ducrest de Saint Aubin, comtesse de, 1746-1830 see PQ1985.G5
2260.G35	Geoffroy, Louis, 1803-1858 (Table P-PZ40)
2260.G36	Gérard de Nerval, Gérard Labrunie, known as, 1808-1855 (Table P-PZ40)
2260.G362	Géraud, Edmond, 1775-1831 (Table P-PZ40)
2260.G4	Germain, Auguste, 1862-1915 (Table P-PZ40)
2260.G44	Gilkin, Iwan, 1858-1924 (Table P-PZ40)
	Gille, Valère see PQ2613.I5
2260.G5	Ginisty, Paul, 1855- (Table P-PZ40)
2260.G62	Girard, Charles François, 1811-1876 (Table P-PZ40)
2260.G67	Girardin, Delphine (Gay) de, 1804-1855 (Table P-PZ40)
2260.G68	Girardin, Émile de, 1806-1881 (Table P-PZ40)
2260.G7	Girardin, Jules, 1832-1888 (Table P-PZ40)
2260.G75	Glatigny, Albert Alexander, 1839-1873 (Table P-PZ40)
	Glouvet, Jules de see PQ2384.Q6
2260.G89	Gobineau, Joseph Arthur, comte de, 1816-1882
2260.G9	Biography. Criticism
2261	Goncourt, Edmond and Jules de (Table P-PZ39)
2263	Goncourt, Edmond Louis Antoine Huot de, 1822-1896 (Table P-PZ39)
2265.G2	Gondinet, Pierre Edmond Julien, 1828-1888 (Table P-PZ40)
2265.G5	Gonzalès, Emmanuel, 1815-1887 (Table P-PZ40)
2265.G57	Gosse, Étienne, 1773-1834 (Table P-PZ40)
2265.G6	Gosselin, Louis Léon Théodore, 1857-1935 (Table P-PZ40)
2265.G66	Gouët, Siméon, 1835-1880 (Table P-PZ40)
2265.G68	Gouraud, Julie (Table P-PZ40)
2265.G69	Gourdon, Georges, 1852- (Table P-PZ40)
2266	Gourmont, Rémy de, 1858-1915 (Table P-PZ39)
2268	Gozlan, Léon, d. 1866 (Table P-PZ39)
2269.G25	Gramont, Ferdinand de, comte, 1815-1897 (Table P-PZ40)
2269.G31	Grandmougin, Charles Jean, 1850-1930 (Table P-PZ40)
2269.G39	Gras, Louis Pierre, 1833-1873 (Table P-PZ40)
2269.G5	Grenet-Dancourt, Ernest, 1858-1913 (Table P-PZ40)
2269.G53	Grenier, Édouard, 1819-1901 (Table P-PZ40)
	Gréville, Henry see PQ2235.D6
2269.G7	Grousset, Paschal, 1844-1909 (Table P-PZ40)
2270.G25	Guébhard, Caroline (Rémy), 1855- (Table P-PZ40)
2270.G29	Guérin, Eugéne Louis, 1807-1848 (Table P-PZ40)
2270.G3	Guérin, Eugénie de, 1805-1848 (Table P-PZ40)
2270.G32	Guérin, Maurice de, 1810-1839 (Table P-PZ40)

Modern French literature
Individual authors
19th century -- Continued

2270.G34	Guéroult, Constant, 1816-1882 (Table P-PZ40)
	Guiches, Gustave see PQ2613.U4
2270.G5	Guiraud, Pierre Marie Thérèse Alexandre, baron, 1788-1847 (Table P-PZ40)
2271.G2	Guizot, Élisabeth Charlotte Pauline de Meulan, 1773-1827 (Table P-PZ40)
2271.G7	Guttinguer, Ulric, 1785-1866 (Table P-PZ40)
	Gyp see PQ2347.M6
2272.H3	Halévy, Léon, 1802-1883 (Table P-PZ40)
2273	Halévy, Ludovic, 1834-1908 (Table P-PZ39)
	For works written with Henri Meilhac see PQ2359.M3
	Haraucourt, Edmond see PQ2615.A7
2274.H6	Hasdeu, Iulia, 1869-1888 (Table P-PZ40)
2274.H7	Hasselt, André Henri Constant van, 1806-1874 (Table P-PZ40)
2275.H24	Hennique, Léon, 1851- (Table P-PZ40)
2275.H3	Heredia, José María de, 1842-1905 (Table P-PZ40)
2275.H47	Héricault, Charles d', 1823-1899 (Table P-PZ40)
	Hermant, Abel see PQ2615.E7
2275.H7	Hervieu, Paul Ernest, 1857-1915 (Table P-PZ40)
2275.H74	Hervilly, Ernest d', 1839-1911 (Table P-PZ40)
2275.H8	Hetzel, Pierre Jules, 1814-1886 (Table P-PZ40)
	Hinzelin, Émile see PQ2615.I4
2276.H6	Hoffmann, François Benoît, 1760-1828 (Table P-PZ40)
2276.H7	Houssaye, Arsène, 1815-1896 (Table P-PZ40)
2276.H74	Huart, Louis, 1813-1865 (Table P-PZ40)
2276.H8	Hugo, Charles Victor, 1826-1871 (Table P-PZ40)
	Hugo, Victor Marie, comte, 1802-1885
	Collected works
2279	By date (date letters)
	e. g.
2279.E85	1885
2279.F04	1904
(2280)	By editor
	see PQ2279
	Selected works. By editor
2281.A1-.A9	General
	Including posthumous works
2281.D1-.D9	Drama
2281.P1-.P9	Poetry
2281.Z1-.Z9	Miscellaneous special
2282	Selections. Extracts. Quotations
	Translations
	English. By translator

Modern French literature
Individual authors
19th century
Hugo, Victor Marie, comte, 1802-1885
Translations
English. By translator -- Continued

2283.A1-.A9 General
Including posthumous works
2283.D1-.D9 Drama
2283.P1-.P9 Poetry
2283.Z1-.Z9 Miscellaneous special
2284.A-Z Other. By language, A-Z
Subarrange by translator

Separate works
2285.A3 Amy Robsart
2285.A4 L'âne
2285.A5 Angelo
2285.A6 L'année terrible
2285.A8 L'art d'être grand-père
2285.A9 L'aumône
2285.B8 Bug-Jargal
2285.B9 Les burgraves
2285.C2 Les chansons des rues et des bois
2285.C3 Les chants du crépuscle
2285.C4 Les châtiments
Choses vues see PQ2294
2285.C7 Claude Gueux
2285.C8 Les contemplations
2285.C89 Cromwell
2285.D4 Le dernier jour d'un condamné
2285.D5 Dernière gerbe
2285.D6 Dieu
Discours pour Voltaire see PQ2108
2285.E5 Les enfants (le livre des mères)
2285.E7 La Esmeralda
Étude sur Mirabeau see DC146.M7
2285.F4 Les feuilles dlautomne
2285.F5 La fin de Satan
2285.H2 Han d'Islande
2285.H3 Hernani
2285.H8 L'homme qui rit
2285.J8 Les jumeaux
2285.L15 La légende des siècles
2285.L2 1. Série
2285.L3 2. Série
2285.L4 3. Série
2285.L5 Criticism

Modern French literature
Individual authors
19th century
Hugo, Victor Marie, comte, 1802-1885
Separate works -- Continued
Lettres see PQ2294
Lettres à la fiancée see PQ2294

2285.L6	Littérature et philosophic mêlées
2285.L8	Lucrèce Borgia
2285.M4	Marie Tudor
2285.M5	Marion Delorme
2285.M64-.M643	Mille francs de recompense (Table P-PZ43)
2286	Les Misérables (Novel) (Table P-PZ41)
2287.M5	Les Misérables (Play)
2288	Notre-Dame de Paris (Table P-PZ41)
2289.O4	Odes et ballades
2289.O7	Les orientales
2289.P2	Le pape
2289.P5	La pitié suprême
2289.P7	Post-scriptum de ma vie
2289.P8	Pour un soldat
2289.Q2	Quatre vents de l'esprit
2289.Q3	Quatrevingt-treize
2289.R3	Les rayons et les ombres
2289.R4	Religions et religion
2289.R7	Le roi s'amuse
2289.R8	Ruy Blas
2289.T4	Le théâtre en liberté
2289.T5	Torquemada
2289.T6	Toute la lyre
2289.T7	Travailleurs de la mer
2289.V6	Les voix intérieures
2289.Z4	Periodicals, serials, etc., edited by Victor Hugo
2290	Doubtful, spurious works
2291	Imitations. Parodies
2291.5	Translations (as subject)
2291.9	Illustrations
2292.A2	Societies. Periodicals. Collections
2292.A3-Z	Dictionaries, indexes, etc.
2293	Biography and criticism
2294	Autobiography. Journal. Letters. Memoirs
2295	Details of his life e.g. Love and marriage; Relations to women; Later life and death
2295.7	Family. Ancestry, etc.
2296	Relations to contemporaries. Milieu
2297	Homes and haunts. Local associations. Landmarks

Modern French literature
Individual authors
19th century
Hugo, Victor Marie, comte, 1802-1885
Biography and criticism -- Continued
2298 Anniversaries. Celebrations. Memorial addresses
2299 Iconography. Portraits. Monuments
2300 Authorship. Manuscripts. Sources. Associations. Followers. Circle. School
Criticism and interpretation
2301 General works. Genius, etc.
Philosophy see PQ2301
2302 Characters. Plots. Scenes. Time, etc.
2304.A-Z Treatment and knowledge of special subjects, A-Z
2304.A69 Art
2304.C55 China
2304.E38 Education
2304.G4 Germany
2304.G73 Great Britain
2304.H5 History
2304.L28 Laughter
2304.L5 Literature
2304.M83 Music
2304.M88 Myth
2304.O25 Occultism
2304.O74 Orient
2304.P45 Philosophy
2304.P65 Poland
2304.P67 Portugal
2304.R4 Religion
2304.S3 The Sea
2304.T43 Technology
2304.T47 Theater
2304.W37 War
2305 Language. Grammar
2306 Versification
2307 Dictionaries. Concordances
2309.H244 Huguenin, Oscar, 1842-1903 (Table P-PZ40)
2309.H245 Hugues, Clovis, 1851-1907 (Table P-PZ40)
Humilis, 1851-1920 see PQ2376.N88
2309.H4 Huysmans, Joris Karl, 1848-1907 (Table P-PZ40)
2310.I44 Imbert de Bourdillon, M. le marquise d' (Raymond Maurice), 1789-1865 (Table P-PZ40)
Ivoi, Paul d', 1856-1915 see PQ2217.D9
Jacob, P.L. see PQ2323.L32
2311.J17 Jalin, Alphonse de (Table P-PZ40)
Joint pseudonym of Alphonse François and A. Dumas, fils

Modern French literature
Individual authors
19th century -- Continued

2311.J2 Janin, Jules Gabriel, 1804-1874 (Table P-PZ40)
2311.J3 Janvier, Ambroise, or Janvier de la Motte, called Beauvallon, 1852-1905 (Table P-PZ40)
Jasmin, Jacques Boé, 1798-1864 see PC3402.J27
2311.J42 Jaugey, Louis (Table P-PZ40)
2311.J62 Jenna, Marie, 1834-1887 (Table P-PZ40)
2311.J7 Joliet, Charles, 1832-1910 (Table P-PZ40)
2311.J73 Joubert, Joseph, 1754-1824 (Table P-PZ40)
2311.J75 Jouy, Étienne de, 1764-1846 (Table P-PZ40)
2311.J76 Jouy, Jules Théodore Louis, 1855-1897 (Table P-PZ40)
2311.J78 Jullien, Jean, 1854-1919 (Table P-PZ40)
2311.J8 Julliot, François de (Table P-PZ40)
2311.J94 Jurion, Séraphin, 1837-1929 (Table P-PZ40)
2313 Jussieu, Laurent Pierre de, 1792-1866 (Table P-PZ39)
Kahn, Gustave see PQ2621.A3
2315 Karr, Alphonse, 1808-1890 (Table P-PZ39)
2316 Karr - Ko
Kéroul, Henri, 1857-1921 see PQ2621.E7
2318 Kock, Charles Paul de, 1794-1871 (Table P-PZ39)
2320.K2 Kock, Henry de, 1819-1892 (Table P-PZ40)
2320.K7 Korvin-Krukovskii, Petr, 1844-1899 (Table P-PZ40)
2320.K8 Krüdener, Barbara Juliane von vietinghoff, Freifrau von, 1764-1824 (Table P-PZ40)
2320.L45 Labenskil, Ksaverii Ksaverievich, 1800-1855 (Table P-PZ40)
2321 Labiche, Eugène Marin, 1815-1888 (Table P-PZ39)
2323.L2 Laboulaye, Édouard René Lefebvre de, 1811-1883 (Table P-PZ40)
2323.L26 Lacaussade, Auguste, 1817-1897 (Table P-PZ40)
2323.L265 Lachambeaudie, Pierre, 1806-1872 (Table P-PZ40)
2323.L27 Lacretelle, Pierre Henri de, b. 1815 (Table P-PZ40)
2323.L3 Lacroix, Jules, 1809-1887 (Table P-PZ40)
2323.L32 Lacroix, Paul, 1806-1884 (Table P-PZ40)
2323.L5 Lafarge, Marie Fortunée (Cappelle) Pouch-, 1816-1852 (Table P-PZ40)
2323.L6 Lafenestre, Georges Édouard, 1837-1919 (Table P-PZ40)
2323.L8 Laforgue, Jules, 1860-1887 (Table P-PZ40)
Lamartine, Alphonse Marie Louis de, 1790-1869
Cf. DC255.A3+
Collections
2325.A1 Collected works
2325.A16 Collected essays, miscellaneous, etc.
Translations

Modern French literature
Individual authors
19th century
Lamartine, Alphonse Marie Louis de, 1790-1869
Translations -- Continued
2325.A2-.A29 English
2325.A4-.A49 German
2325.A5-.A59 Other languages (Alphabetically)
2325.A6 Selections
2325.A7-Z Separate works
Biography
2326.A1-.A29 Journals. Letters. Memoirs
2326.A3-Z Literary biography. "Life and works"
2327 Authorship. Sources, etc.
Criticism
2328 General. Genius. Philosophy. Characters. Plots, etc.
2329 Other special. Language, etc.
2330.L2 Lambert, Albert, 1847- (Table P-PZ40)
2330.L3 Lamothe-Langon, Étienne Léon, baron de, 1786-1864 (Table P-PZ40)
2330.L319 Lance, Paul (Table P-PZ40)
2330.L4 Lapauze, Jeanne (Loiseau), 1860-1921 (Table P-PZ40)
2330.L44 Laprade, Victor de, 1812-1883 (Table P-PZ40)
2330.L465 Larocque, Jean, 1836-1891 (Table P-PZ40)
2330.L48 Lassailly, Charles (Table P-PZ40)
2330.L5 Latouche, Henri de, 1785-1851 (Table P-PZ40)
Lautréamont, comte de see PQ2220.D723
2330.L7 Lavedan, Henri Léon Émile, 1859- (Table P-PZ40)
2330.L75 Le Braz, Anatole, 1859-1926 (Table P-PZ40)
2330.L77 Lebreton, Théodore-Eloi, 1805-1883 (Table P-PZ40)
2330.L8 Lebrun, Pierre Antoine, 1785-1873 (Table P-PZ40)
Lebrun, Pigault see PQ2382.P2
2330.L89 Le Comte, F.H., b. 1859 (Table P-PZ40)
2330.L9 Lecomte, Jules François, 1814-1864 (Table P-PZ40)
Leconte de Lisle, Charles Marie René, 1818-1894
2332.A1-.A19 Collected works
2332.A6 Selected works. Selections. By date
2332.A7-Z Separate works
2333.A2 Journals. Letters. Memoirs
2333.A3-Z Literary biography. "Life and works"
2334 Authorship. Sources, etc.
Criticism
2335 General. Genius. Philosophy. Characters. Plots, etc.
2336 Other special. Language, etc.
2337.L17 Le Fèvre-Deumier, Jules, 1797-1857 (Table P-PZ40)
2337.L23 Legouvé, Ernest, 1807-1903 (Table P-PZ40)
2337.L24 Legrand, Henry, 1814-1876 (Table P-PZ40)

Modern French literature
Individual authors
19th century -- Continued

2337.L3 Lemaître, Jules, 1853-1914 (Table P-PZ40)
2337.L34 Lemercier, Louis Jean Népomucène, 1771-1840 (Table P-PZ40)
2337.L4 Lemonnier, Camille, 1844-1913 (Table P-PZ40)
2337.L43 Lemoyne, André, 1822-1907 (Table P-PZ40)
2337.L5 Lepelletier, Edmond Adolphe de Bouhelier, 1846-1913 (Table P-PZ40)
2337.L52 L'Epine, Ernest-Louis-victor-jules, 1826-1893 (Table P-PZ40)
2337.L6 Lermina, Jules Hippolyte, 1839-1915 (Table P-PZ40)
Le Roux Hugues, 1860-1925 see PQ2623.E63
2337.L62 Leroux, Pierre, 1797-1871 (Table P-PZ40)
2338.L24 Le Roy, Eugène, 1836-1907 (Table P-PZ40)
2338.L273 Lescot, Madame (Marie Meusy), 1837-1902 (Table P-PZ40)
Lesueur, Daniel see PQ2330.L4
2338.L4 Létang, Louis, 1855- (Table P-PZ40)
2338.L43 Leuven, Adolphe de, 1800-1884 (Table P-PZ40)
2338.L45 Levavasseur, Gustave, 1819-1896 (Table P-PZ40)
2338.L8 Lonlay, Eugène, marquis de, 1815-1866 (Table P-PZ40)
Lorrain, Jean see PQ2235.D93
(2339) Loti, Pierre
see PQ2472
Louÿs, Pierre, 1870-1925 see PQ2623.O8
2340.L6 Luce de Lancival, Jean Charles Julien, 1764-1810 (Table P-PZ40)
Maeterlink, Maurice see PQ2625.A3+
2342.M17 Mahalin, Paul, 1838-1899 (Table P-PZ40)
2342.M25 Maindron, Maurice Georges René, 1857-1911 (Table P-PZ40)
2342.M28 Maistre, Joseph Marie, comte de, 1753-1821 (Table P-PZ40)
2342.M3 Maistre, Xavier, comte de, 1763-1852 (Table P-PZ40)
Maizeroy, René see PQ2452.T6
2342.M56 Malato, Charles, 1857-1938 (Table P-PZ40)
2344 Mallarmé, Stéphane, 1842-1898 (Table P-PZ39)
2345.M3 Mallefille, Jean Pierre Félicien, 1813-1868 (Table P-PZ40)
Malot, Hector Henri, 1830-1907
2346.A1 Collected works
2346.A6-.Z3 Separate works
2346.Z5 Biography. Criticism
2347.M12 Malot, Mme. Hector Henri (Table P-PZ40)
2347.M2 Manual, Eugène, 1823-1901 (Table P-PZ40)

Modern French literature
Individual authors
19th century -- Continued
2347.M25 Maquet, Auguste, 1813-1888 (Table P-PZ40)
2347.M283 Marcel, B. (Table P-PZ40)
2347.M285 Marchangy, Louis Antoine François de, 1782-1826 (Table P-PZ40)
2347.M3 Margueritte, Paul and Victor (Table P-PZ40)
2347.M32 Margueritte, Paul, 1860-1918 (Table P-PZ40)
2347.M33 Margueritte, Victor, 1866- (Table P-PZ40)
2347.M34 Mariaker, Élie (Table P-PZ40)
2347.M35 Mariéton, Paul, 1862-1911 (Table P-PZ40)
2347.M4 Marmier, Xavier, 1809-1892 (Table P-PZ40)
2347.M6 Martel de Janville, Sybille Gabrielle Marie Antoinette de Riquetti de Mirabeau, comtesse de, 1849-1932 (Table P-PZ40)
2347.M655 Martin, Louis Aimé, 1786-1847 (Table P-PZ40)
2347.M68 Mary, Jules, 1851-1922 (Table P-PZ40)
2347.M7 Mary-Lafon, Jean Bernard Lafon, called, 1812-1884 (Table P-PZ40)
2347.M757 Massard, Émile Nicolas, 1857-1932 (Table P-PZ40)
2347.M77 Massiac, Théodore (Table P-PZ40)
Matthey, A. see PQ2153.A7
Maupassant, Guy de, 1850-1893
Works
2349.A1 Collected. By date
2349.A2 Selected. By date
2349.A4 Translations. By language, A-Z
2349.A5-.Z3 Novels and short stories, A-Z
2349.Z5A-Z Selections for colleges, etc. By editor, A-Z
Chroniques
2349.5 Collected
2349.6.A-Z Individual, A-Z
2350.A-Z Voyages. Miscellaneous, A-Z
2351.A-Z Poésies, A-Z
2351.A2 Collected
2352 Théâtre, A-Z
2352.A2 Collected
Biography
2353 General works
2354 Special. Details
2355 Authorship. Sources
Criticism
2356 General
2357 Special
2358 Language
2359.M228 Mayeux, M. (Table P-PZ40)

Modern French literature
Individual authors
19th century -- Continued

2359.M29 Meilhac, Henri, 1831-1897 (Table P-PZ40)
2359.M3 Meilhac, Henri, and Halévy, Ludovic
Collected plays. By date
2359.M31 Meilhac, Henri, with other collaborators (Table P-PZ40)
2359.M35 Melegari, Dora, 1849-1924 (Table P-PZ40)
Mélesville, Anne Honoré Joseph, called see PQ2235.D96
2359.M5 Mendès, Catulle, 1841-1909 (Table P-PZ40)
2359.M53 Mengin, Urbain, 1864-1955 (Table P-PZ40)
2359.M6 Mérat, Albert, 1840 (Table P-PZ40)
Mercier, Louis Sébastien, 1740-1814 see PQ2007.M6
2359.M62 Mercoeur, Eliza, 1809-1835 (Table P-PZ40)
2362 Merimée, Prosper, 1803-1870 (Table P-PZ39)
2364.M12 Merle, Jean Toussaint, 1785-1852 (Table P-PZ40)
2364.M15 Merrill, Stuart, 1863-1915 (Table P-PZ40)
2364.M2 Méry, Joseph, 1797-1865 (Table P-PZ40)
2364.M27 Méténier, Oscar, 1859-1913 (Table P-PZ40)
2364.M29 Métivier, Adolphe, ca. 1850-1931 (Table P-PZ40)
2364.M35 Meurice, Paul, 1820-1905 (Table P-PZ40 modified)
2364.M35A61-.M35Z458 Separate works. By title
Les deux Diane see PQ2227.D5
2364.M366 Michel, Louise, 1830-1905 (Table P-PZ40)
2364.M37 Michelet, Jules, 1798-1874 (Table P-PZ40)
Cf. DC36.98.M5
2364.M4 Michon, Jean Hippolyte, 1806-1881 (Table P-PZ40)
2364.M6 Millevoye, Charles Hubert, 1782-1816 (Table P-PZ40)
2364.M65 Millien, Achille, 1838-1917 (Table P-PZ40)
2364.M68 Minier, Hippolyte, b. 1813 (Table P-PZ40)
2364.M7 Mirbeau, Octave, 1850-1917 (Table P-PZ40)
2364.M9 Mirecourt, Eugène de, 1812-1880 (Table P-PZ40)
Mistral, Frédéric, 1830-1914 see PC3402.M5
2366.M25 Mockel, Albert, 1866- (Table P-PZ40)
Moinaux, Georges, 1860-1929 see PQ2605.O7677
2366.M32 Molènes, Louis Marie Antoinette Alix (de Bray) Gaschon de, 1838-1892 (Table P-PZ40)
2366.M39 Monnier, Antoine, 1846- (Table P-PZ40)
2366.M42 Monnier, Henri Bonaventure, 1799-1877 (Table P-PZ40)
2366.M425 Monnier, Marc, 1827-1885 (Table P-PZ40)
2366.M5 Monselet, Charles, 1825-1888 (Table P-PZ40)
2366.M74 Montégut, Émile, 1826-1895 (Table P-PZ40)
2366.M75 Montégut, Maurice, 1855-1911 (Table P-PZ40)
2366.M77 Montépin, Xavier Aymon, comte de, 1826?-1902 (Table P-PZ40)

Modern French literature
Individual authors
19th century -- Continued
Montesquiou-Fezensac, Robert, comte de, 1855-1921 see PQ2625.O39

2366.M82 Montifaud, Marc de, b. 1850 (Table P-PZ40)
2366.M85 Montolieu, Isabelle, i.e. Elisabeth Jeanne Pauline (Polier) de, 1751-1832 (Table P-PZ40)
2367.M3 Moréas, Jean, 1856-1910 (Table P-PZ40)
2367.M4 Moreau, Charles François Jean Baptiste, 1783-1832 (Table P-PZ40)
2367.M47 Moreau, Elise, b. 1813 (Table P-PZ40)
2367.M5 Moreau, Émile, 1852-1922 (Table P-PZ40)
2367.M54 Moreau, Eugène, 1806-1876 (Table P-PZ40)
2367.M6 Moreau, Hégésippe, 1810-1838 (Table P-PZ40)
2367.M62 Morency, Suzanne G. de, b. 1770 (Table P-PZ40)
Morice, Charles, 1861-1919 see PQ2625.O76
2367.M68 Mortier, Arnold, 1843-1885 (Table P-PZ40)
2367.M8 Mounet-Sully, Jean, 1841-1916 (Table P-PZ40)
2367.M84 Mouton, Eugéne, 1823-1902 (Table P-PZ40)
2367.M85 Muller, Eugéne, 1826-1913 (Table P-PZ40)
2367.M9 Muret, Théodore César, 1808-1866 (Table P-PZ40)
2367.M94 Murger, Henri, 1822-1861 (Table P-PZ40)
Musset, Alfred de, 1810-1857
Collected works
2369.A1 General collections. By date
2369.A14 Selected works. Selections. Posthumous works, etc. By date
2369.A15 Collected novels and tales. By date
2369.A17 Collected poems. By date
2369.A19 Collected plays. By date
Translations
Separate works see PQ2369.A6+
2369.A2-.A29 English. By translator
2369.A3-.A39 German. By translator
2369.A4-.A49 Italian. By translator
2369.A5-.A59 Other languages (Alphabetically)
2369.A6-Z Separate works, A-Z
e. g.
2369.C6 La confession d'un enfant du siècle
Biography
2370.A17 Ancestry
2370.A2 Journals. Letters. Memoirs
2370.A3-Z Literary biography. "Life and works"
2371 Authorship. Sources, etc.
2372 Criticism (General). Genius. Philosophy, etc.
2373 Other special. Language, etc.

Modern French literature
Individual authors
19th century -- Continued

2374.M2 Musset, Paul Edme de, 1804-1880 (Table P-PZ40)
2376.N2 Nadaud, Gustave, 1820-1893 (Table P-PZ40)
2376.N23 Nadejda, 19th cent. (Table P-PZ40)
Nerval, Gérard de see PQ2260.G36
Newsky, Pierre see PQ2320.K7
2376.N35 Nibor, Yann (Table P-PZ40)
Nicolaie, Louis François see PQ2207.C56
2376.N6 Nodier, Charles, 1780-1844 (Table P-PZ40)
Noriac, Jules see PQ2203.C35
2376.N7 Normand, Jacques Clary Jean, 1848-1931 (Table P-PZ40)
2376.N87 Noussanne, Henri de, 1865- (Table P-PZ40)
2376.N88 Nouveau, Germain, 1851-1920 (Table P-PZ40)
2378.O3 Ohnet, Georges, 1848-1918 (Table P-PZ40)
2378.O42 Olivier, Juste, 1807-1876 (Swiss) (Table P-PZ40)
2378.O43 Olivier, Urbain, 1810-1888 (Table P-PZ40)
O'Monroy, Richard, 1850-1916 see PQ2390.S35
Onquaire, Jean Hyacinthe Adonis CLéon Galoppe d' see PQ2257.G363
O'Rell, Max see PQ2197.B75
2380.P2 Pailleron, Édouard Jules Henri, 1834-1899 (Table P-PZ40)
2380.P36 Parfait, Paul, 1841-1881 (Table P-PZ40)
2380.P37 Parodi, Dominique Alexandre, 1842 (Table P-PZ40)
2380.P38 Parseval-Grandmaison, François Auguste, 1759-1834 (Table P-PZ40)
2380.P44 Pavie, Théodore, 1811-1896 (Table P-PZ40)
2380.P5 Péladan, Joséphin, 1859-1918 (Table P-PZ40)
2380.P6 Pelletan, Eugène, 1813-1884 (Table P-PZ40)
2380.P8 Perret, Paul, 1838-1904 (Table P-PZ40)
2380.P87 Petrucelli della Gattina, Ferdinando, 1816-1890 (Table P-PZ40)
Cf. PQ4730.P25 (Italian)
2380.P89 Peyrat, Napoléon (Table P-PZ40)
Peyrebrune, Georges de see PQ2380.P9
2380.P9 Peyrebrune, Mathilde Georginia Élisabeth de, 1848-1917 (Table P-PZ40)
Picard, Louis Benoit, 1769-1828
Cf. PT2468.N3+ Der neffe als onkel
Cf. PT2468.P2+ Der parasit
2381.A6-.Z3 Separate works
2381.Z5 Biography. Criticism
2382.P15 Picquenard, Jean-Baptiste, d. 1826 (Table P-PZ40)
2382.P18 Pifteau, Benjamin, 1836-1890 (Table P-PZ40)

Modern French literature
Individual authors
19th century -- Continued

2382.P2 Pigault-Lebrun, Charles Antoine Guillaume Pigault de Épinoy, called, 1753-1835 (Table P-PZ40)
2382.P25 Pigeon, Amédée, b. 1851 (Table P-PZ40)
2382.P32 Pimpurniaux, Jérôme, 1741-1838 (Table P-PZ40)
2382.P4 Pixérécourt, René Charles Guilbert de, 1773-1844 (Table P-PZ40)
2382.P65 Poictevin, Francis, 1854- (Table P-PZ40)
2382.P72 Poitevin, Prosper, 1805-1884 (Table P-PZ40)
2382.P8 Pomairols, Charles de, 1843- (Table P-PZ40)
2382.P87 Ponchon, Raoul, 1848-1937 (Table P-PZ40)
2382.P9 Ponsard, François, 1814-1867 (Table P-PZ40)
2383.P2 Ponson du Terrail, Pierre Alexis, vicomte de, 1829-1871 (Table P-PZ40)
2383.P25 Pontmartin, Armand, comte de, 1811-1890 (Table P-PZ40)
2383.P4 Porto-Riche, Georges de, 1849-1930 (Table P-PZ40)
2383.P415 Potocki, Arthur, comte, 1787 or 8-1832 (Table P-PZ40)
2383.P42 Pottier, Eugene, 1816-1887 (Table P-PZ40)
2383.P434 Poullet, Ch. (Table P-PZ40)
2383.P44 Pouvillon, Émile, 1840-1906 (Table P-PZ40)
2383.P5 Pressensé, Élise Françoise Louise de Plessis-Gouret de, 1826-1901 (Table P-PZ40)
2383.P6 Prévost, Marcel, 1862- (Table P-PZ40)
Prudhomme, Sully see PQ2448.A1+
2383.P63 Psicharis, Ioannis, 1854-1929 (Table P-PZ40)
2383.P9 Puliga, Henriette Consuelo (Sansom), contessa di (Table P-PZ40)
2383.P95 Pyat, Aimé Felix, 1810-1889 (Table P-PZ40)
Quatrelles, 1826-1893 see PQ2337.L52
2384.Q4 Quellien, Narcisse, 1848-1902 (Table P-PZ40)
2384.Q5 Quesnay de Beaurepaire, Jules, 1838-1923 (Table P-PZ40)
2384.Q6 Quinet, Edgar, 1803-1875 (Table P-PZ40)
2384.Q7 Quioc, Mme. Louis, 1861- (Table P-PZ40)
2385.R15 Raban, Louis François, 1795-1870 (Table P-PZ40)
2385.R17 Rabbe, Alphonse, 1786-1830 (Table P-PZ40)
2385.R19 Rabou, Charles, 1803-1870 (Table P-PZ40)
2385.R2 Rabusson, Henry, 1850- (Table P-PZ40)
Rachilde see PQ2643.A323
2385.R27 Raimes, Gaston de, b. 1859 (Table P-PZ40)
2385.R29 Rameau, Jean, 1852-1931 (Table P-PZ40)
2385.R3 Rameau, Jean, 1859- (Table P-PZ40)
2385.R5 Rattazzi, Marie Lestizia (Bonaparte-Wyse), b. 1830 (Table P-PZ40)

Modern French literature
Individual authors
19th century -- Continued

2385.R55 Ravrio, Antoine André, 1759-1814 (Table P-PZ40)
2385.R6 Raynouard, François Juste Marie, 1761-1836 (Table P-PZ40)
2386.R15 Rebell, Hugues, 1867-1905 (Table P-PZ40)
2386.R2 Reboul, Jean, 1796-1864 (Table P-PZ40)
2386.R24 Reepmaker, M., 1858- (Table P-PZ40)
2386.R3512 Régnier-Destourbet, Hippolyte François, 1804-1832 (Table P-PZ40)
2386.R36 Rémusat, Charles François Marie, comte de, 1797-1875 (Table P-PZ40)

Renan, Ernest, 1823-1892

Here are classed those works of Renan that belong to French literature proper, and such selections from his other works as are published for literary purposes. Classification with the subject is preferred wherever selected or particular works or letters are restricted to a definite subject

Editions. By date

(2386.R37) Collected and selected works,
see subclass AC

2386.R37A1 Collected works (Literature proper). By date
(2386.R37A14) Posthumous works (Collected)
see PQ2386.R37A1 for literary collections
see subclass AC for nonliterary collections without a subject focus
see the subject in classes B-Z for collections on a subject

Collected plays see PQ2386.R37D7

2386.R37A19 Collected discourses, essays, necrologues
2386.R37A2-.R37A59 Translations (Collected). By language (Alphabetically)

Particular works

2386.R37A6 L'abbesse de Jouarre
2386.R37C2 Cahiers de jeunesse
2386.R37C3 Nouveaux cahiers de jeunesse
2386.R37C4 Caliban
2386.R37D4 Dialogues et fragments philosophiques
2386.R37D7 Drames philosophiques
2386.R37E2 L'eau de jouvence
2386.R37F4 Feuilles détachées
2386.R37F8 Fragments intimes et romanesques

Lettres see PQ2386.R38

Lettres philosophiques
see class B

Nouveaux cahiers de jeunesse see PQ2386.R37C3

Modern French literature
Individual authors
19th century
Renan, Ernest, 1823-1892
Editions. By date
Particular works -- Continued

2386.R37P7 Prière de Némi
2386.R37P8 Prière sur l'Acropole
2386.R37S6 Souvenirs d'enfance et de jeunesse
2386.R37V5 Vingt jours en Sicile
Correspondence
Miscellaneous
2386.R38 Collections and selections. By date
(2386.R38A14) Posthumously published letters (Collected)
see PQ2386.R38
By period
2386.R38A15 Lettres du séminaire
2386.R38A16 Lettres de 1848
2386.R38A17 Lettres d'Italie, 1849-50
By subject
see the subject
Translations
2386.R38A2 English. By date
2386.R38A21-.R38A29 Other. By language (Alphabetically)
2386.R38A4-.R38Z Special correspondents
2386.R38A4-.R38A69 Henriette Renan (sister of R., d. 1861)
2386.R38A4 Correspondence intime (reprinted with title "Lettres intimes")
2386.R38A41 Nouvelles lettres intimes
Translations
2386.R38A5 English. By date
2386.R38A51-.R38A69 Other. By language (Alphabetically)
2386.R38A8-.R38Z Other, A-Z
2386.R39 Biography. Criticism
2386.R39A1-.R39A5 Societies. Collections, etc.
2386.R39A6-.R39Z Individual authors
2386.R4 Renard, Georges François, 1847- (Table P-PZ40)
2386.R414 Renard, Michel, 1829-1904 (Table P-PZ40)
2386.R5 Retté, Aldolphe, 1863- (Table P-PZ40)
2386.R62 Réveroni Saint Cyr, Jacques Antoine, baron de, 1767-1829 (Table P-PZ40)
2386.R74 Rey, Roize H. (Henry), baron (Table P-PZ40)
2386.R8 Reybaud, Henriette Étienette Fanny (Arnaud), 1802-1871 (Table P-PZ40)
2386.R9 Reybaud, Louis, 1799-1879 (Table P-PZ40)

Modern French literature
Individual authors
19th century -- Continued

2386.R93	Reymond, Lucien (Table P-PZ40)
2386.R95	Rhéal, Sébastien, 1815-1863 (Table P-PZ40)
	Ribaux, Adolphe see PQ2635.I17
2387.R3	Ricard, Jules, 1848-1903 (Table P-PZ40)
2387.R32	Ricard, Louis Xavier de, 1843-1911 (Table P-PZ40)
2387.R37	Richebourg, Émile, i.e. Jules Émile, 1833-1898 (Table P-PZ40)
2387.R4	Richepin, Jean, 1849-1926 (Table P-PZ40)
2387.R48	Ricquebourg, Jean (Table P-PZ40)
2387.R5	Rimbaud, Jean Nicolas Arthur, 1854-1891 (Table P-PZ40)
2387.R53	Rimbaud, Vitalie, 1858-1875 (Table P-PZ40)
	Robert, Louis de see PQ2635.O17
2388.R27	Robida, Albert, 1848-1926 (Table P-PZ40)
	Robin, Albert Auguste see PQ2376.N35
2388.R3	Rochefort-Luçay, Victor Henri, marquis de, 1831-1913 (Table P-PZ40)
2388.R4	Rod, Édouard, 1857-1910 (Table P-PZ40)
2388.R413	Rodenbach, Georges, 1855-1898 (Table P-PZ40)
2388.R416	Roederer, Antoine-Marie, baron, 1782-1865 (Table P-PZ40)
2388.R425	Roger, Jean François, 1776-1842 (Table P-PZ40)
	Rolland, Romain see PQ2635.O5
2388.R428	Rollinat, Maurice, 1846-1903 (Table P-PZ40)
2388.R47	Rosny, Léon de, 1837-1914 (Table P-PZ40)
	Rosny see PQ2635.O559
2388.R5	Rossel, Virgile, 1858- (Table P-PZ40)
	Rostand, Edmond see PQ2635.O58+
	Rouget de Lisle, Claude Joseph, 1760-1836
2389.R25 date	Collected works
2389.R25A61-.R25Z458	Separate works, A-Z
	Biography see ML410.R85
	History of the Marseillaise see ML3621.M37
	Roumanille, Joseph, 1818-1891 see PC3402.R6
2389.R595	Rousseau, Henri Julien Félix, 1844-1910 (Table P-PZ40)
2389.R69	Roux, Marius (Table P-PZ40)
2389.R8	Roy, J.-J.-E. (Just-Jean-Etienne), 1794-1871 (Table P-PZ40)
2389.R85	Rulins, C. Malraison de (Table P-PZ40)
2390.S33	Saint-Aulaire, A. de (Anatole), comte, b. 1842 (Table P-PZ40)
2390.S35	Saint-Geniès, Richard, vicomte de, 1850-1916 (Table P-PZ40)

Modern French literature
Individual authors
19th century -- Continued

2390.S36 Saint-Génois, Jules Ludger Dominique Ghislain, baron de, 1813-1867 (Table P-PZ40)
Saint-Georges de Bouhélier see PQ2637.A28
2390.S5 Saint-Mars, Gabrielle Anne Cisterne de Courtiras, vicomtesse de, 1804-1872 (Table P-PZ40)
2390.S68 Saint-Saëns, Camille, 1835-1921 (Table P-PZ40)
Biography see ML410.S15
Sainte-Beuve, Charles Augustin, 1804-1869
2391.A1 Collected works. By date
2391.A15 Selected works. Selections
2391.A2 Poetical works (Collected and separate). By date
Romans
2391.A3 Collected
2391.A4 Arthur
2391.A5 Clou d'or
2391.A6 Mme. de Pontivy
2391.A7 Pendule
2391.A8 Volupté
2391.C2 Causeries du lundi
2391.C3 Nouveaux lundis
2391.C4 Premiers lundis
2391.C5 Chroniques parisiennes
2391.C7 Critiques et portraits littéraires
2391.G3 Galerie des femmes
2391.G4 Nouvelle galerie des femmes
2391.G5 Galerie des grand écrivains français
2391.G6 Nouvelle galerie des grands écrivains français
2391.G7 Galeri des portraits historiques
2391.G8 Galerie des portraits littéraires
2391.L3 La Bruyère et La Rochefoucauld ...
2391.O7 Originaux et beaux esprits
2391.P3 Portraits contemporains
2391.P5 Portraits de femmes
2391.P7 Portraits littéraires
2391.P8 Derniers portraits littéraires
Translations (Collected)
2391.Z2 English. By translator
2391.Z3 German. By translator
2391.Z35 Japanese. By translator
2391.Z4 Slavic. By translator
2391.Z5 Biography and criticism
2391.Z5A3 Correspondence
2391.Z7 Indexes
2392.S2 Sainte-Croix, Camille de, 1859- (Table P-PZ40)

Modern French literature
Individual authors
19th century -- Continued

2392.S5 Saintine, Joseph Xavier Boniface, known as, 1798-1865 (Table P-PZ40)
2392.S6 Sales, Pierre, 1856-1914 (Table P-PZ40)
2392.S64 Salle, Eusèbe de (Table P-PZ40)
2392.S65 Salm-Reifferscheid-Dyck, Constance Marie (de Théis), princesse de, 1767-1845 (Table P-PZ40)
2392.S7 Salvandy, Narcisse Achille, comte de, 1795-1856 (Table P-PZ40)
2392.S9 Samain, Albert Victor, 1858-1900 (Table P-PZ40)
Sand, George, 1804-1876
2393 Collected works. By date
2394 Selected works. By editor
Including posthumous works
2395 Selections. Extracts. Quotations
Dramatic works
2396.A3 Collected
2396.A5-Z Separate plays, A-Z
Translations
2397 English. By translator (or publisher)
2398 Other. By language
Subarrange by translator
Separate works
2399.A3 Adriani
2399.A38 Albine Fiori
Les amours de l'âge d'or see PQ2401.E8
2399.A5 André
2399.A6 Antonia
2399.A8 Autour de la table
L'autre see PQ2396.A3+
2399.B3 Le beau Laurence
2399.B4 Les beaux messieurs de Bois-Doré (Novel)
Les beaux messieurs de Bois-Doré see PQ2396.A3+
2399.C2 Cadio
2399.C3 Césarine Dietrich
2399.C4 Le château des désertes
Claudie see PQ2396.A3+
Comme il vous plaira see PR2779.A+
2399.C5 Le compagnon du Tour de France
2399.C6 La comtesse de Rudolstadt
2399.C7 La confession d'une jeune fille
2399.C8 Constance Verrier
2400 Consuelo (Table P-PZ41)
2401.C3 Contes d'une grandlmère
2401.C4 Contes vénitiens

Modern French literature
Individual authors
19th century
Sand, George, 1804-1876
Separate works -- Continued

	Correspondance see PQ2412.A3
	Cosima see PQ2396.A3+
2401.C7	La coupe
2401.D2	Les dames vertes
2401.D3	Daniella
	Le démon du foyer see PQ2396.A3+
2401.D4	Le dernier amour
2401.D45	La dernière Aldini
2401.D5	Dernières pages
2401.D55	Les deux frères
2401.D6	Le diable aux champs
	Le drac see PQ2396.A3+
2401.E3	Elle et lui
2401.E8	Evenor et Leucippe
2401.F2	La famille de Germandre
2401.F3	La filleule
2401.F4	Flamarande
	Flaminio see PQ2396.A3+
2401.F5	Flavie
2401.F7	Francia
2402	François le Champi (Nouvelle) (Table P-PZ41)
	François le Champi (Play) see PQ2396.A3+
	Françoise see PQ2396.A3+
	Gabriel see PQ2396.A3+
	Histoire de ma vie see PQ2412.A2
2403.H5	Histoire du véritable Gribouille
	Un hiver à Majorque see DP302.B27
2403.H7	L'homme de neige
2403.H8	Horace
	Impressions et souvenirs see PQ2412.A2
2404	Indiana (Table P-PZ41)
2405.I3	Isidora
2405.J2	Jacques
2405.J3	Jean de la Roche
2405.J5	Jeanne
2405.L3	Laura
2405.L5	Légendes rustiques
2406	Lélia (Table P-PZ41)
2407.L2	Leone Leoni
	Lettres à A. de Musset à Sainte-Beuve see PQ2412.A4A+
2407.L4	Lettres au peuple

Modern French literature
Individual authors
19th century
Sand, George, 1804-1876
Separate works -- Continued

	Le lis du Japon see PQ2396.A3+
	Lucie see PQ2396.A3+
2407.M2	Ma soeur Jeanne
2407.M3	Mademoiselle La Quintinie
2407.M4	Mademoiselle Merquem
	Maître Favilla, see PQ2396.A3+
2407.M5	Maîtres mosaïstes
2407.M6	Maîtres sonneurs
2407.M7	Malgrétout
2408	La mare au diable (Table P-PZ41)
	Marguérite de Sainte-Gemme see PQ2396.A3+
	Le mariage de Victorine see PQ2396.A3+
2409.M4	Marianne
2409.M5	Le marquis de Villemer (Novel)
	Le marquis de Villemer (Play) see PQ2396.A3+
2409.M6	Marquise
2410	Mauprat (Novel) (Table P-PZ41)
	Mauprat (Play) see PQ2396.A3+
2411.M3	Melchior
2411.M35	Métella
2411.M4	Le meunier d'Angibault
2411.M6	Les Mississipiens
	Molière see PQ2396.A3+
2411.M8	Monsieur Sylvestre
2411.M9	Mont-Revêche
2411.N2	Nanon
2411.N4	Narcisse
2411.N6	Le noce de campagne
	Nouvelles lettres d'un voyageur see PQ2412.A33+
2411.P17	Pages choisies
2411.P2	Pauline
2411.P3	Pèché de M. Antoine
2411.P4-.P5	La petite Fadette
2411.P6-.P7	Le Piccinino
2411.P75	Pierre qui roule
	Le pressoir see PQ2396.A3+
2411.P87	Procope le grand
2411.P9	Promenades autour d'un village
2411.Q4	Questions d'art et de littérature
2411.Q5	Questions politiques et sociales
2411.R6	Romans champêtres
2411.R8	Rose et Blanche

Modern French literature
Individual authors
19th century
Sand, George, 1804-1876
Separate works -- Continued

2411.S2 Le secrétaire intime
2411.S3 Les sept cordes de la lyre
2411.S4 Simon
2411.S7 Souvenirs de 1848
Souvenirs et idées see PQ2412.A2
2411.S8-.S9 Spiridion
2411.T2 Tamaris
2411.T4 Teverino
Théâtre see PQ2396.A3+
Le théâtre de Nohant see PQ2396.A3+
2411.T8 La tour de Percemont
2411.U7 L'uscoque
2411.V2 Valentine
2411.V4 Valvèdre
2411.V6 La ville noire
Biography and criticism
Biography
2412.A2 Autobiography. Journals. Memoirs
Letters
2412.A3 Collections and selections. By date
2412.A3A-.A3Z Translations. By language and date
Lettres d'un voyageur
2412.A32 Editions. By date
2412.A32A-.A32Z Translations. By language, A-Z
Nouvelles lettres d'un voyageur
2412.A33 Editions. By date
2412.A33A-.A33Z Translations. By language, A-Z
2412.A4A-.A4Z Letters to particular persons. By addressee and date
2412.A5-Z Literary biography. "Life and works"
2413 Details of life. Early life. Education
2414 Relation to contemporaries
2415 Homes and haunts
2416 Authorship. Sources, etc.
Criticism
2417 General. Genius. Philosophy, etc.
2418 Characters, plots, etc.
2419 Other special
2420 Language
2421.S15 Sand, Maurice, 1823-1889 (Table P-PZ40)
2421.S2 Sandeau, Jules, 1811-1883 (Table P-PZ40)
2421.S4 Sarcey, Francisque, 1827-1899 (Table P-PZ40)

Modern French literature
Individual authors
19th century -- Continued

2422 Sardou, Victorien, 1831-1908
2422.A8-.Z3 Separate works
2422.Z5 Biography. Criticism
2423.S32 Saunière, Paul, 1829-1894 (Table P-PZ40)
2423.S348 Scherder, Sophie de, 18th/19th cent. (Table P-PZ40)
2423.S38 Scholl, Aurélien, 1833-1902 (Table P-PZ40)
2423.S4 Schultz, Jeanne (Table P-PZ40)
2423.S6 Schuré, Édouard, 1841-1929 (Table P-PZ40)
2423.S8 Schwob, Marcel, 1867-1905 (Table P-PZ40)
2425 Scribe, Augustin Eugène, 1791-1861
2425.A1 Collected works. By date (date letters)
2425.A15 Novels, stories, etc.
2425.A6-Z Separate works, A-Z
e. g.
2425.A7 Adrienne Lecouvreur
2425.B3 Bataille de dames
2425.B5 Bertrand et Raton, ou L'art de conspirer
2425.B7 La Bohémienne, ou L'Amérique en 1775
2425.C2 La camaraderie, ou La courte échelle
2425.C4 Une chaîne
2425.C6 Les contes de la reine de Navarre
2425.D7 Les doigts de feé
2425.F5 Le filleul d'Amadis
2425.F6 Fleurette
2425.L8 La lune de miel
2425.M3 Le mariagé d'argent
2425.P5 Piquillo Alliaga
2425.S6 Le solliciteur
2425.V3 Valérie
2425.V5 Le verre d'eau
2427.S2 Séché, Léon, 1848-1914 (Table P-PZ40)
2427.S3 Ségalas, Anaïs Ménard, dame, 1814-1895 (Table P-PZ40)
2427.S4 Ségur, Anatole Henri Philippe, marquis de, 1823-1902 (Table P-PZ40)
2427.S45 Ségur, Louis Philippe, comte de, 1753-1830 (Table P-PZ40)
2427.S5 Ségur, Sophie (Rostopchine), comtesse de,1799-1874 (Table P-PZ38)
2427.S7 Sénancour, Étienne Pivert, de, 1770-1846 (Table P-PZ40)
Séverin, Fernand see PQ2637.E9
2427.S8 Sewrin, Charles Augustin, 1771-1853 (Table P-PZ40)
2428.S35 Signoret, Emmanuel, 1872-1900 (Table P-PZ40)

Modern French literature
Individual authors
19th century -- Continued

2428.S6 Silvestre, Paul Armand, 1837-1901 (Table P-PZ40)
2428.S7 Simon, Jules, 1814-1896 (Table P-PZ40)
2428.S75 Siraudin, Paul, 1813-1883 (Table P-PZ40)
2428.S8 Sirven, Alfred, 1838-1900 (Table P-PZ40)
2429.S4 Sorel, Albert, 1842-1906 (Table P-PZ40)
2429.S47 Soulary, Josephine Marie, called Joséphin. 1815-1891 (Table P-PZ40)
2429.S5 Soulié, Frédéric, 1800-1847 (Table P-PZ40)
2429.S53 Soumet, Alexandre, 1788-1845 (Table P-PZ40)
2429.S6 Sousa Botelho Mourão e Vasconcellos, Adélaïde Marie Émilie (Filleul), comtesse Flahaut, marqueza do, 1761?-1836 (Table P-PZ40)
2429.S7 Souvestre, Émile, 1806-1854 (Table P-PZ40)
2429.S88 Stackelberg, Ernest, comte, 1813?-1870 (Table P-PZ40)
2431 Staël Holstein, Anne Louise Germaine (Necker), baronne de, 1766-1817 (Table P-PZ39)
Commonly called Madame de Stael
Stahl, P.J. see PQ2275.H8
2433.S4 Stapleaux, Léopold Louis Lambert, 1831-1891 (Table P-PZ40)
Stendhal, 1783-1842
Works
2435.A1 Collected works. By date
2435.A11-.A14 Collected works. By editor
2435.A2 Selections. By editor, A-Z
Translations
2435.A3 English. By translator, A-Z
2435.A4 Other. By language, A-Z
2435.A6-Z Separate works
Biography and criticism
2436.A15 Dictionaries, indexes, etc.
2436.A2 Journals. Letters. Memoirs
2436.A3-Z Literary biography. "Life and works"
2437 Details of life
2438 Relations to contemporaries
2439 Homes and haunts
2439.5 Museums, relics, etc.
2440 Authorship. Sources, etc.
Criticism
2441 General. Genius. Philosophy, etc.
2442 Characters, plots, etc.
2443 Other special
2444 Language
Stern, Daniel see PQ2152.A38

Modern French literature
Individual authors
19th century -- Continued

2445.S54 Stevens, Mathilde (Table P-PZ40)
Stolz, Mme. de see PQ2193.B5
2445.S7 Strada, J., 1821-1902 (Table P-PZ40)
2445.S8 Suberwick, Mme. de (Table P-PZ40)
Sue, Eugène, 1804-1857
2446.A1 Collected works. By date
2446.A2-.A29 English translations
2446.A3-.A39 German translations
2446.A6-.Z3 Separate works
2446.Z5 Biography. Criticism
2447.S3 Suès-Ducommun, Mme. (Table P-PZ40)
Sully-Prudhomme, René François Armand, 1839-1907
2448.A1 Collected works. By date
2448.A2-.A29 English translations
2448.A3-.A39 German translations
2448.A6-.Z3 Separate works
2448.Z5 Biography. Criticism
Tailhade, Laurent, 1854-1919 see PQ2639.A5
2449.T3 Taine, Hippolyte Adolphe, 1828-1893 (Table P-PZ40)
2449.T4 Talmeyr, Maurice, 1850- (Table P-PZ40)
2449.T6 Tardieu, Jules Romain, 1805-1868 (Table P-PZ40)
2449.T7 Tastu, Mme. Amable (Voïart), 1798?-1885 (Table P-PZ40)
2449.T92 Thackeray, William Makepeace, 1811-1863 (Table P-PZ40)
2450.T14 Théaulon de Lambert, Marie Emmanuel Guillaume Marguerite, 1787-1841 (Table P-PZ40)
2450.T16 Thérèse, Saint, 1873-1897 (Table P-PZ40)
2450.T2 Theuriet, André, 1833-1907 (Table P-PZ40)
Thibault, Jacques Anatole see PQ2254.A1+
2450.T4 Thiboust, Lambert, 1826-1867 (Table P-PZ40)
2450.T57 Thuez, Caroline (Table P-PZ40)
2450.T584 Thyes, Félix, 1830-1855 (Table P-PZ40)
2450.T59 Tiercelin, Louis, 1849-1915 (Table P-PZ40)
2450.T6 Tillier, Claude, 1801-1844 (Table P-PZ40)
2450.T67 Tinan, Jean de, 1874-1898 (Table P-PZ40)
2450.T7 Tinseau, Léon de, comte, 1844-1921 (Table P-PZ40)
Tiutchev, Fedor Ivanovich, 1803-1873 see PG3361.T5Z4+
2452.T2 Toepffer, Rodolphe, 1799-1846 (Table P-PZ40)
2452.T5 Toudouze, Gustave, 1847-1904 (Table P-PZ40)
2452.T6 Toussaint, René Jules Jean, baron, 1856-1918 (Table P-PZ40)
2452.T7 Travers, Julien Gilles, 1802-1888 (Table P-PZ40)

Modern French literature
Individual authors
19th century -- Continued

2452.T9 Truinet, Charles Louis Étienne, 1828-1899 (Table P-PZ40)
2454.U3 Uchard, Mario, 1824-1893 (Table P-PZ40)
2454.U5 Ulbach, Louis, 1822-1889 (Table P-PZ40)
2454.U8 Uzanne, Louis Octave, 1852- (Table P-PZ40)
2458.V28 Vachette, Eugène, 1827-1902 (Table P-PZ40)
2458.V3 Vacquerie, Auguste, 1819-1895 (Table P-PZ40)
2458.V4 Valabrègue, Albin, 1853- (Table P-PZ40)
2458.V7 Vallès, Jules Louis Joseph, 1832-1885 (Table P-PZ40)
Valvor, Guy see PQ2459.V75
Vandérem, Fernand see PQ2643.A35
Van Hasselt, André see PQ2274.H7
2459.V5 Vast-Ricouard (Table P-PZ40)
Collective name of Vast, Raoul, 1850-1889 and Ricouard, Gustave, 1853-1887
2459.V7 Vaucaire, Maurice, 1863?-1918 (Table P-PZ40)
2459.V75 Vayssière, Georges André, 1853-1904 (Table P-PZ40)
Verhaeren, Émile, 1855-1916
2459.V8A1-.V8A19 Collected works
Translations
2459.V8A2-.V8A29 English
2459.V8A3-.V8A39 German
2459.V8A5-.V8A59 Other. By language (Alphabetically)
e. g.
2459.V8A57 Spanish
2459.V8A6-.V8Z Separate works
2459.V9 Biography and criticism
2461 Verh - Verl
Verlaine, Paul Marie, 1844-1896
2463.A1-.A19 Collected works. By editor
Translations
2463.A2-.A29 English. By translator
2463.A3-.A39 German. By translator
2463.A5-.A59 Other. By language and date
2463.A6 Selected works. By date
2463.A61-Z Separate works. By title
Biography
2464.A2 Journals, letters, memoirs
2464.A3-Z Literary biography. "Life and works"
2465 Authorship. Sources
Criticism
2466 General. Genius. Philosophy
2467 Special
2468 Verl - Vern

Modern French literature
Individual authors
19th century -- Continued

2469 Verne, Jules, 1828-1905 (Table P-PZ39)
2471.V4 Véron, Pierre, 1833-1900 (Table P-PZ40)
2471.V6 Vervins, Nicolas Alfred de (Table P-PZ40)
2471.V7 Veuillot, Louis François, 1813-1883 (Table P-PZ40)
2471.V9 Vial, Jean Baptiste Charles, 1771-1834 (Table P-PZ40)

Viaud, Julien, 1850-1923
2472.A1 Collected works
Translations
2472.A2-.A29 English
2472.A3-.A39 German
2472.A6-.Z3 Separate works
Biography. Criticism
Autobiography. Journals, etc.
2472.Z5 Collections. By date
Roman d'un enfant
2472.Z5A1 Editions. By date
2472.Z5A11-.Z5A29 Translations. By language, A-Z and date
Prime jeunesse
2472.Z5A3 Editions. By date
2472.Z5A31-.Z5A49 Translations. By language, A-Z and date
Un jeune officier pauvre
2472.Z5A5 Editions. By date
2472.Z5A51-.Z5A69 Translations. By language, A-Z and date
Journal intime, 1878-1881
2472.Z5A7 Editions. By date
2472.Z5A71-.Z5A89 Translations. By language, A-Z and date
Journal, 1885-1901
2472.Z5A9 Editions. By date
2472.Z5A91-.Z5A95 Translations. By language, A-Z and date
Correspondence
2472.Z6 General. By date
2472.Z6A-.Z6Z Special correspondents, A-Z
2472.Z8 General works
2473.V3 Vicaire, Gabriel, 1849-1900 (Table P-PZ40)
Cf. PQ2253.F18 Adoré Floupette
Vielé-Griffin, Francis see PQ2643.I3
2473.V5 Viennet, Jean Pons Guillaume, 1777-1868 (Table P-PZ40)
Vigny, Alfred Victor, comte de, 1797-1863
2474.A1-.A19 Collected works
Translations
2474.A2-.A29 English
2474.A3-.A39 German
2474.A5-.A59 Other. By language (Alphabetically)

Modern French literature
Individual authors
19th century
Vigny, Alfred Victor, comte de, 1797-1863
Translations
Other. By language (Alphabetically) -- Continued
2474.A57 Spanish
2474.A6 Selections
2474.A7-.Z4 Separate works
2474.Z5 Biography. Criticism
2476.V3 Villers, Charles François Dominique de, 1765-1815 (Table P-PZ40)
2476.V4 Villiers de l'Isle-Adam, Jean Marie Mathias Philippe Auguste, comte de, 1838-1889 (Table P-PZ40)
2476.V42 Vinçard, Pierre (Table P-PZ40)
Vincent, Jacques see PQ2198.B55
2479.W2 Wafflard, Alexis Jacques Marie, 1787-1824 (Table P-PZ40)
2479.W4 Weill, Alexandre, originally Abraham, 1811-1899 (Table P-PZ40)
Cf. PT2553.W7 German literature
2479.W8 Wey, Francis Alphonse, 1812-1882 (Table P-PZ40)
Wilde, Oscar, 1854-1900. Salomé see PR5820.S2+
2480.W6 Wolff, Albert, 1835-1891 (Table P-PZ40)
Wolff, Pierre see PQ2645.O6
Xanrof, Léon see PQ2611.O8
2484.Y6 Yriarte, Charles Émile, 1832-1898 (Table P-PZ40)
2484.Z2 Zaccone, Pierre, 1817-1895 (Table P-PZ40)
2484.Z4 Zévaco, Michel, 1860-1918 (Table P-PZ40)
Zola, Émile, 1840-1902
Collected works
2489 By date
By editor see PQ2489
2491 Selected works. By editor
Including posthumous works
2492 Selections. Extracts. Quotations
Translations
2493 English. By translator or publisher. Anonymous. By date
2494.A-Z Other. By language, A-Z
Subarrange by translator
Separate works
L'affaire Dreyfus see DC354+
2495.A5 L'argent
2496 L'assommoir (Novel) (Table P-PZ41)
2497.A2 L'assommoir (Play)
2497.A5 L'attaque du moulin (Nouvelle)

Modern French literature
Individual authors
19th century
Zola, Émile, 1840-1902
Separate works -- Continued

2497.A6 L'attaque du moulin (Play)
2497.A8 Au bonheur des dames
2498 La bête humaine (Table P-PZ41)
2499.B6 Le bouton de rose
2499.C2 Une campagne
2499.C3 Le capitaine Burle
2499.C5 La confession de Claude
2499.C6 La conquête de Plassans
2499.C7 Contes à Ninon
2499.C75 Nouveaux contes a Ninon
2499.C8 Les coquillages de M. Chabre
Correspondence, Lettres de jeunesse see PQ2529.A2
2499.C9 La curée
2500 La débâcle (Table P-PZ41)
2501.D3 Le docteur Pascal
2501.E6 L'enfant roi
2501.F3 La faute de l'abbé Mouret
2502 Fécondité (Table P-PZ41)
2503.F4 La fête à Coqueville
2503.F7 La fortune des Rougon
2504 Germinal (Novel) (Table P-PZ41)
2505.G2 Germinal (Play)
2505.H4 Les héritiers Rabourdin
2505.J3 Jacques Damour
2505.J4 Jean Gourdan
2505.J7 La joie de vivre
2506 Lourdes (Table P-PZ41)
2507.M2 Madame Neigeon
2507.M3 Madeleine Férat
2507.M4 Mes haines
2508 Messidor (Table P-PZ41)
2509.M6 La mort d'Olivier Bécaille
2509.M8 Les mystères de Marseille
2509.N3 Naïs Miscoulin
2510 Nana (Novel) (Table P-PZ41)
2511.N2 Nana (Play)
2511.N3 Nantes
La naturalisme au théâtre see PQ295.N2
Nos auteurs dramatiques see PQ541
Nouveaux contes à Ninon see PQ2499.C75
2511.N6 Nouvelle campagne

Modern French literature
Individual authors
19th century
Zola, Émile, 1840-1902
Separate works -- Continued

2511.O4 L'oeuvre
2511.O8 L'ouragan
2511.P2 Une page d'amour
2512 Paris (Table P-PZ41)
2513 Paris-Pot-bouille
2514.P6 Pot-bouille (Novel)
2515.P2 Pot-bouille (Play)
2515.P5 Pour une nuit d'amour
2515.Q3 Les quatre Évangiles (Series of novels)
2515.R2 Renée
La République française et la littérature see PQ293
2515.R3 Retour de voyage
2515.R4 Le rêve
Le roman expérimental see PQ661
Les romanciers naturalistes see PQ295.N2
2516 Rome (Table P-PZ41)
2518 Les Rougon-Macquart, histoire naturelle et sociale d'une famille sous le second empire (Series of novels) (Table P-PZ41)
see also the individual titles
2519.S3 Sidoine et Médéric
2519.S5 Les soirées de Médan
2519.S7 Son excellence Eugène Rougon
2520 La terre (Table P-PZ41)
2521.T3 Thérèse Raquin (Novel)
2521.T4 Thérèse Raquin (Play)
2521.T5 Travail
2521.T7 Les trois villes
2521.V3 Le ventre de Paris
2521.V4 Vérité
2521.V6 Le voeu d'une morte
2522 Doubtful, spurious works
2523 Imitations. Parodies
2524 Translations
2525 Illustrations to the works
Biography and criticism
2526 Periodicals. Societies. Collections
2527 Dictionaries, indexes, etc.
General encyclopedic dictionaries only. Special dictionaries with subject, e.g. PQ2539, Characters, PQ2544, Concordance and language dictionaries
2528 General biography. "Life and works"

Modern French literature
Individual authors
19th century
Zola, Émile, 1840-1902
Biography and criticism
General biography. "Life and works" -- Continued

2529.A2 Journals. Memoirs
Letters
2529.A3 Collections and selections. By date
2529.A3A-Z Translations. By language and date
2529.A4A-Z Letters to particular persons. By addressee and date
2532 Relations to contemporaries
2533 Homes and haunts. Local associations. Landmarks
2535 Iconography. Portraits. Monuments
2536 Authorship
Including manuscripts, forgeries, sources, etc.
2537 Chronology of works
Criticism and interpretation
2538 General works. Genius, philosophy, etc.
Characters
2539.A2 General
2539.A3-Z Special
2539.C59 Clergy
2539.W7 Women
2540 Criticism of dramatic works
2541.A-Z Treatment and knowledge of special subject, A-Z
2541.A78 Art
2541.C56 Clothing and dress
2541.C6 Coal mines and mining
2541.H47 Heredity
2541.M53 Middle classes
2541.N3 Naturalism
2541.N33 Nature
2541.P3 Paris
2541.P66 Politics
2541.R4 Religion
2541.S28 Scapegoat
2541.W6 Woman
2542 Textual criticism, commentaries, etc.
2543 Language, style, etc.
2544 Dictionaries. Concordances
2545 Grammar
2547 Versification
2548 Dialect, etc.
2551.Z5 Zorelli, Sylvia (Table P-PZ40)

Modern French literature
Individual authors -- Continued
1900-1960
The author number is determined by the second letter of the name
Subarrange each author by Table P-PZ40 unless otherwise indicated
Including usually authors beginning to publish about 1890, flourishing after 1900

2600 Anonymous works (Table P-PZ28)
2601 A
2601.C4 Acker, Paul, 1874-1915 (Table P-PZ40)
2601.G7 Agraives, Jean d' (Table P-PZ40)
2601.J3 Ajalbert, Jean, 1863 (Table P-PZ40)
Ajar, Émile see PQ2613.A58
Alain-Fournier see PQ2611.O85
2601.L3 Alanic, Mathilde, 1864- (Table P-PZ40)
2601.L53 Alibert, François Paul, 1873- (Table P-PZ40)
2601.L6 Allais, Alphonse, 1855-1905 (Table P-PZ40)
2601.M55 Amiel, Denys (Table P-PZ40)
2601.R27 Ardel, Henri, 1863-1938 (Table P-PZ40)
2601.R55 Arland, Marcel, 1899- (Table P-PZ40)
2601.R565 Arman de Caillavet, Gaston, 1869-1915 (Table P-PZ40)
2601.R566 Armand, Émile, 1872-1962 (Table P-PZ40)
2601.R57 Armandy, André, 1882- (Table P-PZ40)
2601.R615 Arnaud, Robert, 1873- (Table P-PZ40)
2601.R62 Arnoux, Alexandre, 1884- (Table P-PZ40)
2601.R7 Artus, Louis Charles, 1870- (Table P-PZ40)
2601.U334 Aubry, Octave, 1881- (Table P-PZ40)
2601.U4 Audoux, Marguerite (Table P-PZ40)
Aurel see PQ2625.O77
2603 B
2603.A2 Bachelin, Henri, 1879- (Table P-PZ40)
2603.A24 Baillon, André, 1875-1932 (Table P-PZ40)
2603.A25 Bailly, Auguste, 1878- (Table P-PZ40)
2603.A32 Barbusse, Henri, 1874-1935 (Table P-PZ40)
Barde, André see PQ2603.O78
Bargone, Charles, 1876-1957 see PQ2611.A78
Bargy, Gilles, 1919- see PQ2623.A834
2603.A52 Barrès, Maurice, 1862-1923 (Table P-PZ40)
2603.A6 Basset, Serge, 1865-1917 (Table P-PZ40)
2603.A7 Bataille, Henry, 1872-1922 (Table P-PZ40)
2603.A82 Baudouin, Charles, 1893- (Table P-PZ40)
Bazin, Hervé, 1911- see PQ2615.E772
2603.E26 Beaume, Georges, 1861- (Table P-PZ40)
2603.E3 Beaunier, André, 1869-1925 (Table P-PZ40)

Modern French literature
Individual authors
1900-1960
B -- Continued

2603.E56 Benjamin, René, 1885- (Table P-PZ40)
2603.E583 Benoît, Pierre, 1886- (Table P-PZ40)
2603.E585 Béraud, Henri, 1885- (Table P-PZ40)
2603.E586 Berger, Marcel, 1885- (Table P-PZ40)
2603.E59 Bernard, Jean Jacques, 1888- (Table P-PZ40)
2603.E6 Bernard, Tristan, 1866- (Table P-PZ40)
2603.E62 Bernède, Arthur, 1871- (Table P-PZ40)
2603.E65 Bernstein, Henry, 1876- (Table P-PZ40)
2603.E7 Berr, Georges, 1867- (Table P-PZ40)
2603.E72 Berr de Turique, Julien, 1863-1923 (Table P-PZ40)
Bertheroy, Jean, see PQ2623.E17
2603.E73 Berton, René (Table P-PZ40)
2603.E74 Bertrand, Louis, 1866- (Table P-PZ40)
2603.E897 Beuve, Louis, 1869-1949 (Table P-PZ40)
2603.I24 Bibescu, Marthe, ca. 1887-1973 (Table P-PZ40)
2603.I45 Billotey, Pierre (Table P-PZ40)
2603.I5 Binet-Valmer, Gustave, 1875- (Table P-PZ40)
2603.I65 Birabeau, André (Table P-PZ40)
2603.L32 Blanche, Jacques-Émile, 1861-1942 (Table P-PZ40)
2603.L35 Bloch, Jean Richard, 1884- (Table P-PZ40)
Boëx brothers see PQ2635.O559
2603.O6 Bordeaux, Henry, 1870- (Table P-PZ40)
2603.O625 Borel, Marguerite (Appell) (Table P-PZ40)
2603.O75 Boulenger, Marcel, 1873- (Table P-PZ40)
2603.O78 Bourdonneau, André, 1874- (Table P-PZ40)
2603.O8 Boutet, Frédéric, 1874- (Table P-PZ40)
Boutin, Joseph, 1903- see PQ2623.E4634
2603.O86 Bouzinac-Cambon, Joseph, 1881- (Table P-PZ40)
2603.O9 Boylesve, René, 1867-1926 (Table P-PZ40)
2603.R28 Bramson, Karen (Adler), 1875- (Table P-PZ40)
2603.R3 Brandenburg, Albert Jacques, 1878- (Table P-PZ40)
Bréte, Jean de la see PQ2605.H6
2603.R43 Bringer, Rodolphe, 1871- (Table P-PZ40)
2603.R45 Brisson, Adolphe, 1860-1925 (Table P-PZ40)
2603.R9 Bruant, Aristide, 1857-1925 (Table P-PZ40)
2603.R924 Bruller, Jean, 1902- (Table P-PZ40)
2603.R95 Bruyère, André (Table P-PZ40)
2603.U6 Burnat-Provins, Marguerite, 1872- (Table P-PZ40)
2605 C
2605.A325 Calvet, Jean, 1874-1965 (Table P-PZ40)
2605.A35 Cami, Henri, 1884- (Table P-PZ40)
2605.A36 Cammaerts, Émile (Table P-PZ40)
2605.A4 Canudo, Ricciotto, 1879-1923 (Table P-PZ40)

Modern French literature
Individual authors
1900-1960
C -- Continued

2605.A55 Carco, Francis, 1886-1958 (Table P-PZ40)
2605.A82 Cauvain, Henry, 1847-1899 (Table P-PZ40)
2605.E5 Celarié, Henriette (Table P-PZ40)
Céline, Louis-Ferdinand, 1894-1961 see PQ2607.E834
2605.H167 Chabrier, Agnès, 1914- (Table P-PZ40)
2605.H325 Champsaur, Félicien, 1859- (Table P-PZ40)
Chantepleure, Guy see PQ2607.U845
Charles, Geo see PQ2613.E638
2605.H4218 Chavannes, Fernand, 1868-1936 (Table P-PZ40)
2605.H47 Chepfer, George, 1870-1945 (Table P-PZ40)
2605.H5 Chérau, Gaston, 1872- (Table P-PZ40)
2605.H6 Cherbonnel, Alice, 1854- (Table P-PZ40)
Christophe, 1856-1945 see PQ2605.O35
2605.L2 Claudel, Paul, 1868-1955 (Table P-PZ40)
2605.L4 Clemenceau, Georges Eugène Benjamin, 1841-1929 (Table P-PZ40)
2605.L42 Clement, Colette Grunbaum (Table P-PZ40)
2605.O15 Cocteau, Jean, 1889-1963 (Table P-PZ40)
2605.O28 Colette, Sidonie Gabrielle, 1873- (Table P-PZ40)
Coline, Constance, 1898- see PQ2605.L42
2605.O35 Colomb, Georges, 1856-1945 (Table P-PZ40)
2605.O475 Constantin-Weyer, Maurice, 1881- (Table P-PZ40)
2605.O5 Coolus, Romain, 1868- (Table P-PZ40)
2605.O55 Coquiot, Gustave, 1865-1926 (Table P-PZ40)
2605.O6 Corday, Michel, 1870- (Table P-PZ40)
Corthis, André see PQ2623.E364
Coulevain, Pierre de see PQ2611.A9
2605.O76 Coulomb, Jeanne de, 1864- (Table P-PZ40)
2605.O7677 Courteline, Georges (Table P-PZ40)
2605.R38 Crémieux, Albert (Table P-PZ40)
2605.R75 Croisset, Francis de, 1877- (Table P-PZ40)
2607 D
2607.A3 Daireaux, Max, 1883- (Table P-PZ40)
2607.A594 Darien, Georges, 1862-1921 (Table P-PZ40)
2607.A8 Daudet, Léon, 1867-152 (Table P-PZ40)
2607.A83 Daudet, Lucien Alphonse, 1883- (Table P-PZ40)
2607.A927 David-Néel, Alexandra, 1868-1969 (Table P-PZ40)
2607.A93 Davignon, Henri, 1879- (Table P-PZ40)
Deauwille, Max, 1881-1966 see PQ2607.U96
2607.E13 Deberly, Henri, 1882- (Table P-PZ40)
2607.E2 Degée, Olivier, 1890-1944 (Table P-PZ40)
2607.E22 Dekobra, Maurice, 1885- (Table P-PZ40)
2607.E24 Delarue-Mardrus, Lucie, 1875-1945 (Table P-PZ40)

Modern French literature
Individual authors
1900-1960
D -- Continued

2607.E2478 Delbousquet, Emmanuel, 1874-1909 (Table P-PZ40)
2607.E28 Delhaye de Marnyhac, Thérèse, 1875- (Table P-PZ40)
2607.E32 Delly (Table P-PZ40)
Pseudonym of Frédéric Henri Joseph Petitjean de la Rosière and Jeanne Marie Henriette Petitjean de la Rosière
2607.E37 Delteil, Joseph, 1894- (Table P-PZ40)
2607.E4 Demolder, Eugène, 1862-1919 (Table P-PZ40)
2607.E54 Deprat, Jacques, 1880-1935 (Table P-PZ40)
2607.E57 Derennes, Charles, 1882-1930 (Table P-PZ40)
2607.E6717 Descamps, Édouard Éugène François, baron, 1847-1933 (Table P-PZ40)
Descaves, Lucien see PQ2218.D8
2607.E68 Deschard, Marie (Table P-PZ40)
2607.E7 Des Gachons, Jacques, 1868- (Table P-PZ40)
2607.E834 Destouches, Louis Ferdinand, 1894-1961 (Table P-PZ40)
2607.E875 Deval, Jacques, 1894- (Table P-PZ40)
Deville, René see PQ2613.A58
2607.E98 Dezeuze, François (Table P-PZ40)
2607.I3 Dieudonné, Robert Félix Edmond, 1879- (Table P-PZ40)
2607.O43 Doff, Neel, 1858-1941 (Table P-PZ40)
Dominique, Pierre see PQ2623.U37
2607.O5 Donnay, Maurice Charles, 1859- (Table P-PZ40)
2607.O64 Dorgelès, Roland, 1886- (Table P-PZ40)
2607.O7 Doucet, Jérôme, 1865- (Table P-PZ40)
2607.O75 Doumic, René, 1860- (Table P-PZ40)
2607.R5 Drieu La Rochelle, Pierre, 1893- (Table P-PZ40)
2607.R57 Drouilly, José Germain, 1884- (Table P-PZ40)
Dubrau, Louis, 1904- see PQ2619.A56
2607.U3 Duchêne, Ferdinand (Table P-PZ40)
2607.U53 Duhamel, Georges, 1884- (Table P-PZ40)
2607.U76 Dumur, Louis, 1860- (Table P-PZ40)
2607.U764 Dunan, Renée (Table P-PZ40)
2607.U766 Dungis, Dominique (Table P-PZ40)
Duplaix, Georges, b. 1895 see PQ2627.I378
Dupont de Menet, 1919- see PQ2623.A834
2607.U813 Duquesnel, Félix, 1839-1915 (Table P-PZ40)
2607.U83 Durtain, Luc, 1881- (Table P-PZ40)
2607.U845 Dussap, Jeanne (Violet), 1875- (Table P-PZ40)
2607.U9 Duvernois, Henri, 1875-1937 (Table P-PZ40)
2607.U96 Duwez, Maurice, 1881-1966 (Table P-PZ40)

Modern French literature
Individual authors
1900-1960
D -- Continued
2607.Y97 Dyvonne (Table P-PZ40)
2609 E
Ebreuil, Luc d', 1919- see PQ2623.A834
2609.D5 Edinger, Gaston (Table P-PZ40)
Elder, Marc see PQ2639.E5
2609.L7 Elskamp, Max, 1862-1931 (Table P-PZ40)
2609.N45 Enne, Francis, b. 1844 (Table P-PZ40)
2609.Q55 Equilbecq, Victor François,1872-1917 (Table P-PZ40)
Erlande, Albert see PQ2603.R3
2609.R45 Ermengem, Frédéric van, 1881-1972 (Table P-PZ40)
2609.S55 Esménard, Jean d', vicomte, 1893- (Table P-PZ40)
2609.S8 Estaunié, Édouard, 1862- (Table P-PZ40)
2611 F
2611.A2 Fabre, Émile, 1870- (Table P-PZ40)
Farigoule, Louis, 1885-1972 see PQ2635.O52
2611.A78 Farrère, Claude, 1876-1957 (Table P-PZ40)
2611.A8 Fauchois, René, 1882- (Table P-PZ40)
2611.A86 Faure, Élie, 1873- (Table P-PZ40)
2611.A9 Favre de Coulevain, Hélène, d. 1913 (Table P-PZ40)
2611.E8 Féval, Paul, 1860- (Table P-PZ40)
2611.E83 Fèvre, Henry, 1864-1937 (Table P-PZ40)
2611.E86 Feydeau, Georges Léon Jules Marie, 1862-1921 (Table P-PZ40)
2611.I7 Fischer, Max, 1880- (Table P-PZ40)
2611.L32 Fleg, Edmond, 1874- (Table P-PZ40)
2611.L4 Flers, Robert de, 1872-1927 (Table P-PZ40)
2611.O6 Foleÿ, Charles, 1861- (Table P-PZ40)
2611.O65 Fonson, Jean François, 1871-1924 (Table P-PZ40)
2611.O745 Forbin, Victor, 1864- (Table P-PZ40)
2611.O78 Fort, Paul, 1872- (Table P-PZ40)
2611.O8 Fourneau, Léon, 1867- (Table P-PZ40)
2611.O85 Fournier, Alain, 1886-1914 (Table P-PZ40)
Franc-Nohain, 1873-1934 see PQ2623.E415
2611.R3225 Frans, Charles (Table P-PZ40)
2611.R33 Frapié, Léon, 1863- (Table P-PZ40)
2611.R35 Frappa, Jean José, 1882- (Table P-PZ40)
Fraudet, René see PQ2611.R6
2611.R6 Frondaie, Pierre, 1884-2613 (Table P-PZ40)
2613 G
2613.A58 Gary, Romain (Table P-PZ40)
Gauthier-Villars, Henry see PQ2257.G8
2613.A8 Gavault, Paul, 1867- (Table P-PZ40)
2613.A93 Gayet-Tancrède, Paul, 1907- (Table P-PZ40)

Modern French literature
Individual authors
1900-1960
G -- Continued

2613.E55 Genevoix, Maurice, 1890- (Table P-PZ40)
2613.E6 Géniaux, Charles, 1873-1931 (Table P-PZ40)
2613.E62 Géniaux, Claire (Table P-PZ40)
2613.E63 Génin, Auguste, 1863- (Table P-PZ40)
2613.E638 Géo-Charles, 1892-1963 (Table P-PZ40)
2613.E72 Géraldy, Paul, 1885- (Table P-PZ40)
2613.E736 Gérbidon, Marcel, 1868- (Table P-PZ40)
Germain, José see PQ2607.R57
2613.H2 Ghéon, Henri, 1875- (Table P-PZ40)
2613.H47 Ghika, Marie Chassaigne, princesse, 1869-1950 (Table P-PZ40)
2613.H495 Ghil, René, 1862-1925 (Table P-PZ40)
2613.I2 Gide, André Paul Guillaume, 1869-1951 (Table P-PZ40)
2613.I3 Gilbert de Voisins, Auguste, comte, 1877- (Table P-PZ40)
Gilkin, Iwan, 1858-1924 see PQ2260.G44
2613.I5 Gille, Valère, 1867- (Table P-PZ40)
2613.I66 Girard, Maxime (Table P-PZ40)
2613.I74 Giraudoux, Jean, 1882- (Table P-PZ40)
2613.O28 Godoy, Armand, 1880- (Table P-PZ40)
Gonzaque de Pont-Royal, 1919- see PQ2623.A834
2613.O7 Gorsse, Henry Joseph Auguste de, 1868- (Table P-PZ40)
2613.O77 Gourdon, Pierre, 1869- (Table P-PZ40)
Gray, Daniel, 1914- see PQ2605.H167
2613.R3 Green, Julien, 1900- (Table P-PZ40)
2613.U2 Guérin, Charles, 1873-1907 (Table P-PZ40)
2613.U4 Guiches, Gustave, 1860- (Table P-PZ40)
2613.U43 Guillaumin, Émile, 1873-1951 (Table P-PZ40)
2613.U485 Guillot de Saix, Léon, 1885- (Table P-PZ40)
2613.U56 Guitry, Sacha, 1885- (Table P-PZ40)
Guyot, Charles, 1892-1963 see PQ2613.E638
2615 H
2615.A25 Hamp, Pierre, 1876- (Table P-PZ40)
2615.A7 Haraucourt, Edmond (Table P-PZ40)
2615.A8 Harry, Myriam (Table P-PZ40)
Hellens, Franz see PQ2609.R45
2615.E35 Hémon, Louis, 1880-1913 (Table P-PZ40)
2615.E4 Hennequin, Maurice, 1863-1926 (Table P-PZ40)
2615.E47 Henriot, Émile, 1889- (Table P-PZ40)
2615.E7 Hermant, Abel, 1862- (Table P-PZ40)
2615.E75 Herold, A. Ferdinand, 1865- (Table P-PZ40)

Modern French literature
Individual authors
1900-1960
H -- Continued

2615.E772 Hervé-Bazin, Jean Pierre Marie, 1911- (Table P-PZ40)
2615.I4 Hinzelin, Émile, 1858- (Table P-PZ40)
2615.I6 Hirsch, Charles Henry, 1870- (Table P-PZ40)
Houville, Gérard d', 1875-1963 see PQ2635.E35
2615.U8 Huzard, Antoinette (de Bergevin), 1874- (Table P-PZ40)
2617 I
2617.M3 Imann, Georges, 1889- (Table P-PZ40)
2617.S85 Istrati, Panait, 1884- (Table P-PZ40)
2619 J
2619.A2 Jacques, Henry, 1886- (Table P-PZ40)
2619.A4 Jaloux, Edmond, 1878- (Table P-PZ40)
2619.A5 Jammes, Francis, 1868- (Table P-PZ40)
2619.A56 Janson, Louise (Scheidt), 1904- (Table P-PZ40)
Jarneze, Roland, 1919- see PQ2623.A834
2619.A65 Jarry, Alfred, 1873-1907 (Table P-PZ40)
2619.O53 Jolinon, Joseph, 1887- (Table P-PZ40)
Joris, Françoise Mallet-, 1930- see PQ2625.A7124
2619.O754 Jouglet, René, 1884- (Table P-PZ40)
2619.O76 Jouhandeau, Marcel, 1888- (Table P-PZ40)
2619.O77 Jourda, Daniel (Table P-PZ40)
2619.O78 Jouve, Pierre Jean, 1887- (Table P-PZ40)
Jullien, Jean see PQ2311.J78
2621 K
Kacew see PQ2613.A58
2621.A3 Kahn, Gustave, 1859- (Table P-PZ40)
Kassef, Romain see PQ2613.A58
2621.E5 Keim, Albert, 1876- (Table P-PZ40)
2621.E66 Kérouan, Jean (Table P-PZ40)
2621.E7 Kéroul, Henri, 1857-1921 (Table P-PZ40)
2621.E77 Kessel, Joseph, 1898- (Table P-PZ40)
2621.E9 Keyser, Édouard de, 1883- (Table P-PZ40)
2621.I7 Kistemaeckers, Henry Hubert Alexandre, 1872- (Table P-PZ40)
2621.R35 Kremer, Raymond Jean Marie de, 1887-1964 (Table P-PZ40)
2623 L
2623.A27 La Fouchardière, Georges de, 1874- (Table P-PZ40)
2623.A44 Lamandé, André, 1886-1933 (Table P-PZ40)
2623.A5 Landay, Maurice, 1873- (Table P-PZ40)
2623.A53 Landre, Jeanne, 1874- (Table P-PZ40)
2623.A63 Laparcerie, Marie (Table P-PZ40)
2623.A67 Larrouy, Maurice, 1882- (Table P-PZ40)

Modern French literature
Individual authors
1900-1960
L -- Continued

2623.A834 Laurent, Jacques, 1919- (Table P-PZ40)
Laurent-Cély, 1919- see PQ2623.A834
2623.A936 Lavergne, Antonin, 1863-1941 (Table P-PZ40)
2623.A94 La Ville de Mirmont, Jean de, 1886-1914 (Table P-PZ40)
2623.E113 Le Febvre, Yves (Table P-PZ40)
2623.E14 Léautaud, Paul, 1872-1956 (Table P-PZ40)
2623.E17 Le Barillier, Berthe, 1868-1927 (Table P-PZ40)
2623.E22 Lebey, André, 1877- (Table P-PZ40)
2623.E23 Leblanc, Georgette (Table P-PZ40)
2623.E24 Leblanc, Maurice, 1864- (Table P-PZ40)
2623.E26 Leblond, Marius, 1877- (Table P-PZ40)
2623.E29 Lebreton, B. (Table P-PZ40)
2623.E34 Leclercq, Marie (Table P-PZ40)
2623.E342 Leclère, Léon, 1874- (Table P-PZ40)
2623.E364 Lécuyer, Andrée (Husson), 1885- (Table P-PZ40)
2623.E386 Léger, Alexis Saint-Léger, 1889-1975 (Table P-PZ40)
2623.E39 Le Goffic, Charles, 1863- (Table P-PZ40)
2623.E4147 Legrand, Marc, b. 1865 (Table P-PZ40)
2623.E415 Le Grand, Maurice, 1873-1934 (Table P-PZ40)
2623.E44 Le Maire, Éveline (Table P-PZ40)
2623.E4625 Le Marguet, Claude, d. 1933 (Table P-PZ40)
2623.E4634 Le Maugeois, Henry, 1903- (Table P-PZ40)
2623.E474 Lemonnier, Léon (Table P-PZ40)
2623.E48 Lenéru, Marie, 1875-1918 (Table P-PZ40)
2623.E52 Lenormand, Henri René, 1882- (Table P-PZ40)
2623.E569 Lerberghe, Charles van, 1861-1907 (Table P-PZ40)
2623.E58 Le Rouge, Gustave, 1867-1938 (Table P-PZ40)
2623.E6 Leroux, Gaston, 1868-1927 (Table P-PZ40)
2623.E63 Le Roux, Hugues, 1860-1925 (Table P-PZ40)
2623.E635 Leroux, Jules, 1880-1915 (Table P-PZ40)
2623.E9 Level, Maurice, 1875-1926 (Table P-PZ40)
Lévy, Jacob see PQ2609.D5
2623.E95 Lévy, Jules, b. 1857 (Table P-PZ40)
2623.I4 Lichtenberger, André, 1870- (Table P-PZ40)
2623.O47 Lombard, Jacques (Table P-PZ40)
2623.O7 Lorde, André de, 1870- (Table P-PZ40)
2623.O8 Louÿs, Pierre, 1870-1925 (Table P-PZ40)
2623.O9 Loyson, Paul Hyacinthe, 1873-1921 (Table P-PZ40)
Lubin, Armen, 1903-1974 see PQ2637.H3
2623.U37 Lucchini, Pierre, 1889- (Table P-PZ40)
2625 M
2625.A13 Machard, Alfred, 1887- (Table P-PZ40)

Modern French literature
Individual authors
1900-1960
M -- Continued

2625.A14 Machard, Raymonde (Table P-PZ40)
2625.A16 MacOrlan, Pierre, 1882- (Table P-PZ40)
2625.A25 Maël, Pierre (Table P-PZ40)
Maeterlinck, Maurice, 1862-
2625.A3 Collected works
2625.A31 Selected works
2625.A32 Selections. Anthologies
Translations
2625.A33 English
2625.A34 German
2625.A35 Italian
2625.A36 Spanish
2625.A37-.A39 Other. By language (Alphabetically)
2625.A4A-Z Separate prose works; essays, etc.
Poems
2625.A43 Collected
2625.A45 Separate
Drama
2625.A47 Collected
2625.A48 English translations
2625.A49 Other translations. By language, A-Z
2625.A5 Separate plays, A-Z
2625.A5A8 Les aveugles
2625.A5F5 Les finançailles
2625.A5I5 L'intruse
2625.A5M3 Marie Magdeleine
2625.A5M7 Monna Vanna
2625.A5O5 L'oiseau bleu
2625.A5O6 English translations
2625.A5P4 Pelléas et Mélisande
2625.A53 Translations of foreign works, by Maeterlinck
2625.A59 Journal, memoirs, etc.
2625.A6 Biography. "Life and works"
2625.A61 Criticism
2625.A67 Magre, Maurice, 1877 (Table P-PZ40)
Maizeroy, René see PQ2452.T6
2625.A7124 Mallet-Joris, Françoise, 1930- (Table P-PZ40)
2625.A72 Mandelstamm, Valentin, 1876- (Table P-PZ40)
Marbo, Camille see PQ2603.O625
2625.A784 Margueritte, Éve Paul (Table P-PZ40)
2625.A787 Margueritte, Lucie Paul (Table P-PZ40)
Margueritte, Paul and Victor see PQ2347.M3
Marie, André, 1919- see PQ2623.A834

Modern French literature
Individual authors
1900-1960
M -- Continued

2625.A823 Martin du Gard, Roger, 1881 (Table P-PZ40)
Maryan see PQ2607.E68
2625.A87 Mathéma (Table P-PZ40)
2625.A9 Mauclair, Camille, 1872- (Table P-PZ40)
2625.A92 Mauclère, Jean, 1887- (Table P-PZ40)
2625.A927 Maurey, Max, 1868- (Table P-PZ40)
2625.A93 Mauriac, François, 1885- (Table P-PZ40)
2625.A95 Maurois, André, 1885- (Table P-PZ40)
2625.A954 Maurras, Charles Marie Photius, 1868- (Table P-PZ40)
2625.E45 Mendès, Jane Catulle (Table P-PZ40)
2625.E52 Mercier, Louis, 1870- (Table P-PZ40)
2625.E525 Méré, Charles, 1883- (Table P-PZ40)
2625.E53 Mérouvel, Charles, 1832-1920 (Table P-PZ40)
Méténier, Oscar see PQ2364.M27
2625.E86 Meunier, Lucien Victor, 1857-1930 (Table P-PZ40)
2625.I53 Mille, Pierre, 1864- (Table P-PZ40)
2625.I58 Miomandre, Francis de, 1880- (Table P-PZ40)
2625.I7 Mirza Riza Khan-Arfa, princesse (Table P-PZ40)
Moinaux, Georges see PQ2605.O7677
Monlaur, Marie, Reynès see PQ2635.E93
2625.O39 Montesquiou-Fezensac, Robert, comte de, 1855-1921 (Table P-PZ40)
2625.O4 Montfort, Eugène, 1877- (Table P-PZ40)
2625.O45 Montherlant, Henry de, 1896- (Table P-PZ40)
2625.O67 Morand, Paul, 1888- (Table P-PZ40)
2625.O715 Morax, René, 1873- (Table P-PZ40)
2625.O76 Morice, Charles, 1861-1919 (Table P-PZ40)
2625.O77 Mortier, Aurélie (de Faucamberge), 1882- (Table P-PZ40)
2625.O8 Moëzy-Éon, André, 1880- (Table P-PZ40)
2625.O9148 Mousseron, Jules, 1868- (Table P-PZ40)
2625.Y3 Mycho, André (Table P-PZ40)

2627 N

2627.A17 Nabonne, Bernard (Table P-PZ40)
2627.A2 Nadaud, Marcel, 1889- (Table P-PZ40)
Nazelle, Alainde, 1919- see PQ2623.A834
2627.E56 Ner, Henri, 1861-1938 (Table P-PZ40)
Nesmy, Jean see PQ2637.U7
Nibor, Yann, pseud. see PQ2376.N35
2627.I3 Niccodemi, Dario (Table P-PZ40)
2627.I378 Nicole, b. 1895 (Table P-PZ40)
Pseudonym of Georges Duplaix
2627.I7 Nion, François, comte de, 1854-1923 (Table P-PZ40)

Modern French literature
Individual authors
1900-1960
N -- Continued

2627.O17 Noailles, Anna Elisabeth (de Brancovan), comtesse de, 1876-1933 (Table P-PZ40)
Nothomb, Paul, 1914- see PQ2637.E335
Nouveau, Germain, 1851-1920 see PQ2376.N88

2629 O
2629.F4 Offel, Horace van, 1876 (Table P-PZ40)
2629.R4 Orliac, Jehanne d' (Table P-PZ40)
2629.U5 Oulmont, Charles, 1883- (Table P-PZ40)

2631 P
2631.A4 Paillot, Fortuné (Table P-PZ40)
Parquin, Jean, 1919- see PQ2623.A834
2631.E25 Péguy, Charles Pierre, 1873-1914 (Table P-PZ40)
2631.E36 Pérochon, Ernest, 1885- (Table P-PZ40)
Perse, Saint-John, 1889-1975 see PQ2623.E386
Pert, Camille see PQ2635.O94
2631.E3795 Pesquidoux, Joseph de, 1869-1946 (Table P-PZ40)
Petitjean de la Rosière see PQ2607.E32
2631.E4 Pettit, Charles, 1875- (Table P-PZ40)
2631.H5 Philippe, Charles Louis, 1874-1909 (Table P-PZ40)
2631.I34 Picard, André, 1874- (Table P-PZ40)
2631.I4 Piéchaud, Martial (Table P-PZ40)
2631.I65 Pitray, Paul de (Table P-PZ40)
2631.I68 Pitt, Sylvain, 1860-1919 (Table P-PZ40)
Pougy, Liane de, 1869-1950 see PQ2613.H47
2631.O977 Pozzi, Catherine, 1882-1934 (Table P-PZ40)
2631.R63 Proust, Marcel, 1871-1922 (Table P-PZ40)
2631.U3 Puaux, René, 1878- (Table P-PZ40)
Puliga, Henriette Consuelo (Samson), contessa di see PQ2383.P9
2631.Y5 Pylkänen, Hilma (Table P-PZ40)

2633 Q
2633.U74 Quoirez, Françoise, 1935-2635 (Table P-PZ40)

2635 R
Rachilde see PQ2643.A323
2635.A25 Radiguet, Raymond, 1903-1923 (Table P-PZ40)
2635.A3 Rageot, Gaston, 1872- (Table P-PZ40)
Rameau, Jean see PQ2385.R3
2635.A34 Ramel-Cals, Jeanne, 1893- (Table P-PZ40)
2635.A35 Ramuz, Charles Ferdinand, 1878-1947 (Table P-PZ40)
Randau, Robert see PQ2601.R615
Randon de Saint-Amand, Gabriel see PQ2635.I38
2635.A376 Rapisarda, Antonio, 1900 (Table P-PZ40)
For works written in Italian see PQ4839.A7

Modern French literature
Individual authors
1900-1960
R -- Continued

	Ray, Jean, 1887-1964 see PQ2621.R35
2635.E22	Reboux, Paul, 1877- (Table P-PZ40)
2635.E34	Régnier, Henri Franois Joseph de, 1864-1936 (Table P-PZ40)
2635.E35	Régnier, Marie Louise Antoinette de Herdia de, 1875-1963 (Table P-PZ40)
2635.E48	Renard, Jules, 1864-1910 (Table P-PZ40)
2635.E53	Renaud, Jean, 1881 (Table P-PZ40)
2635.E8	Réval, Gabrielle (Table P-PZ40)
2635.E9	Rey, Étienne, 1879- (Table P-PZ40)
2635.E92	Rey de Villette, Marguerite (Table P-PZ40)
2635.E93	Reynès-Monlaur, Marie (Table P-PZ40)
2635.H3	Rhaïs, Elissa (Table P-PZ40)
2635.I17	Ribaux, Adolphe, 1864- (Table P-PZ40)
2635.I23	Richard, Gaston Charles, 1875- (Table P-PZ40)
2635.I2315	Richard, Jean Marius, 1905- (Table P-PZ40)
2635.I25	Riche, Daniel, 1864- (Table P-PZ40)
2635.I3	Richepin, Jacques, 1880- (Table P-PZ40)
2635.I33	Richet, Charles Robert, 1850-1935 (Table P-PZ40)
2635.I38	Rictus, Jehan, 1867-1933 (Table P-PZ40)
	Rim, Carlo, 1905- see PQ2635.I2315
2635.I75	Ripert, Émile, 1882- (Table P-PZ40)
2635.I87	Rivière, Jacques, 1886-1925 (Table P-PZ40)
2635.I92	Rivoire, André, 1872-1930 (Table P-PZ40)
2635.O17	Robert, Louis de, 1871- (Table P-PZ40)
2635.O42	Roland, Marcel, 1879- (Table P-PZ40)
2635.O5	Rolland, Romain, 1866- (Table P-PZ40)
2635.O52	Romains, Jules, 1885- (Table P-PZ40)
2635.O559	Rosny, J.H. (Table P-PZ40) Pseudonym of the Boëx brothers
2635.O56	Rosny, J.H. aîné (Table P-PZ40) Pseudonym of J.H.H. Boëx
2635.O562	Rosny, J.H., jeune (Table P-PZ40) Pseudonym of S.J.F. Boëx
	Rostand, Edmond, 1868-1918
2635.O58	Collected works. By date
2635.O6A-.O6Z	Selected works. By editor, A-Z
2635.O61-.O69	Translations. By language, A-Z
2635.O64N7	English translation by Norman
2635.O7	Separate works, A-Z
2635.O7A3	L'Aiglon
2635.O7C4	Chantecler
2635.O7C9	Cyrano de Bergerac

Modern French literature
Individual authors
1900-1960
R
Rostand, Edmond, 1868-1918
Separate works, A-Z -- Continued
2635.O7D5 La dernière nuit de Don Juan
2635.O7D8 Deux Pierrots, ou, Le souper blanc
2635.O7P6 La princesse Lointaine
2635.O7R7 Les romanesques
2635.O8 Biography. "Life and works"
2635.O81 Criticism
2635.O815 Rostand, Jean, 1894- (Table P-PZ40)
2635.O82 Rostand, Maurice, 1891- (Table P-PZ40)
2635.O9 Rouff, Marcel, 1877- (Table P-PZ40)
2635.O94 Rougeul, Hortense (Grille), 1865- (Table P-PZ40)
2635.O957 Roupnel, Gaston, 1871-1946 (Table P-PZ40)
2635.O96 Rouquette, Louis Frédéric, 1884-1926 (Table P-PZ40)
2635.O9628 Roux, Paul, 1861-1940 (Table P-PZ40)
Ruffieux, Cyprien, 1859-1940 see PQ2639.O32
2637 S
Sagan, Françoise, 1935- see PQ2633.U74
2637.A2512 Saint-Acère, Yan (Table P-PZ40)
Saint-Amand, Gabriel Randon de see PQ2635.I38
2637.A28 Saint-Georges de Bouhélier, (Table P-PZ40)
Saint-John Perse see PQ2623.E386
Saint-Laurent, Cecil, 1919- see PQ2623.A834
Saint-Palais, Marc de, 1919- see PQ2623.A834
2637.A36 Saint-Paul, Georges, 1870- (Table P-PZ40)
Saint-Pol-Roux, 1861-1940 see PQ2635.O9628
2637.A55 Salmon, André, 1881- (Table P-PZ40)
2637.A575 Samat, Jean Toussaint, 1865- (Table P-PZ40)
Samivel, 1907- see PQ2613.A93
Samuel, Pierre see PQ2609.D5
2637.A6 Sandy, Isabelle, 1886- (Table P-PZ40)
2637.A95 Savignon, André (Table P-PZ40)
2637.E3 Sée, Edmond, 1875- (Table P-PZ40)
2637.E335 Segnaire, Julien, 1914- (Table P-PZ40)
2637.E35 Ségur, Nicolas (Table P-PZ40)
2637.E9 Séverin, Fernand, 1867- (Table P-PZ40)
2637.H3 Shahnowr, Shahan, 1903-1974 (Table P-PZ40)
Sheridan see PQ2609.D5
2637.I45 Silvestre, Charles (Table P-PZ40)
Sinibaldi, Fosco see PQ2613.A58
2637.O68 Soulié, Charles Georges, 1878- (Table P-PZ40)
2637.O83 Soupault, Philippe, 1897- (Table P-PZ40)
2637.O84 Souvestre, Pierre, 1874-1914 (Table P-PZ40)

Modern French literature
Individual authors
1900-1960
S -- Continued

2637.O85 Soy, Emmanuel (Table P-PZ40)
2637.P27 Spalikowski, Edmond, 1874-1951 (Table P-PZ40)
2637.P7 Spitzmuller, Georges, 1867-1926 (Table P-PZ40)
2637.U2 Suarès, André, 1868-1948 (Table P-PZ40)
Sudy, Alainde, 1919- see PQ2623.A834
2637.U6 Supervielle, Jules, 1884- (Table P-PZ40)
2637.U7 Surchamp, Henry, 1876- (Table P-PZ40)
2637.Y5 Sylvane, André, 1851- (Table P-PZ40)
2639 T (Table P-PZ40)
2639.A3 Taboureau, Jean, 1879- (Table P-PZ40)
2639.A5 Tailhade, Laurent, 1854-1919 (Table P-PZ40)
Talmeyr, Maurice, 1884- see PQ2449.T4
2639.E5 Tendron, Marcel, 1884- (Table P-PZ40)
2639.E7 Téramond, Edmond Gautier, called Guy de, 1869- (Table P-PZ40)
2639.H13 Tharaud, Jérôme, 1874- (Table P-PZ40)
2639.H18 Thérive, André, 1891- (Table P-PZ40)
2639.I5 Tinayre, Marcelle, 1877- (Table P-PZ40)
2639.I75 Titaÿna (Table P-PZ40)
2639.O32 Tobi di-j-èlyudzo, 1859-1940 (Table P-PZ40)
2639.O87 Toudouze, Georges Gustave, 1877- (Table P-PZ40)
2639.O88 Toulet, Paul Jean, 1867-1920 (Table P-PZ40)
2639.O94 Toussaint, Franz, 1879- (Table P-PZ40)
Tousseul, Jean, 1890-1944 see PQ2607.E2
2639.R26 Traz, Robert de, 1884- (Table P-PZ40)
Trilby, T. see PQ2607.E28
2639.S5 T'Serstevens, Albert, 1886- (Table P-PZ40)
2641 U
2641.N55 Unik, Pierre (Table P-PZ40)
2643 V
2643.A12 Vacarescu, Elena, 1868-1947 (Table P-PZ40)
2643.A125 Vaché, Jacques (Table P-PZ40)
2643.A15 Vaillat, Léandre, 1878- (Table P-PZ40)
2643.A23 Valdagne, Pierre, 1854- (Table P-PZ40)
2643.A26 Valéry, Paul, 1871- (Table P-PZ40)
2643.A323 Vallette, Marguérite (Eymery), 1860- (Table P-PZ40)
2643.A35 Vandérem, Fernand, 1864- (Table P-PZ40)
Varenne, Albéric, 1919- see PQ2623.A834
2643.A56 Variot, Jean James, 1881- (Table P-PZ40)
2643.A7 Vaudoyer, Jean Louis, 1883 (Table P-PZ40)
2643.A743 Vaulet, Clément, 1876-1954 (Table P-PZ40)
2643.E3 Veber, Pierre Eugène, 1869- (Table P-PZ40)
2643.E34 Veber, Serge (Table P-PZ40)

Modern French literature
Individual authors
1900-1960
V -- Continued
Vercours, 1902- see PQ2603.R924
2643.E55 Verneuil, Louis, 1893- (Table P-PZ40)
2643.I158 Vibert, Paul, 1851-1918 (Table P-PZ40)
2643.I3 Vielé-Griffin, Francis, 1864- (Table P-PZ40)
2643.I4 Vignaud, Jean, 1875- (Table P-PZ40)
Vignes-Rouges, Jean des see PQ2639.A3
2643.I43 Vildrac, Charles, 1882- (Table P-PZ40)
2643.I5 Villetard, Pierre, 1874- (Table P-PZ40)
2643.I575 Vincy, René (Table P-PZ40)
2643.I9 Vivien, Renée, 1877-1909 (Table P-PZ40)
2645 W
2645.A3 Wahl, René, 1870- (Table P-PZ40)
2645.E4 Wenz, Paul (Table P-PZ40)
2645.E7 Werth, Léon, 1879- (Table P-PZ40)
Wild, Herbert see PQ2607.E54
2645.O6 Wolff, Pierre, 1865-1947 (Table P-PZ40)
2647 X
Xanrof, Leon see PQ2611.O8
2649 Y
2649.A6 Yamata, Kikou (Table P-PZ40)
Yver, Colette see PQ2615.U8
2651 Z
2651.A4 Zamacoïs, Miguel, 1866- (Table P-PZ40)
2651.A8 Zavie, Émile, 1884- (Table P-PZ40)
2651.E6 Zenda, Pierre (Table P-PZ40)
1961-2000
The author number is determined by the second letter of the name
Subarrange each author by Table P-PZ40 unless otherwise indicated
Including usually authors beginning to publish about 1950, flourishing after 1960
2660 Anonymous works (Table P-PZ28)
2661 A
Aury, Dominique see PQ2678.E2
2662 B
2662.A376 Baleine, Philippe de (Table P-PZ40)
Barrot, Jean see PQ2664.A87
2662.E64 Berg, Jeanne de (Table P-PZ40)
2662.R792 Bruller, Jacqueline (Table P-PZ40)
2663 C
Casamayor, 1912- see PQ2663.A795
2663.A795 Casamayor, Louis, 1912- (Table P-PZ40)

Modern French literature
Individual authors
1961-2000
C -- Continued

2663.L32445 Clauteaux, Rodolphe (Table P-PZ40)
2663.O7224 Corticchiato, Toussaint, 1927- (Table P-PZ40)
Cruysmans, Philippe see PQ2673.A6
Cyrille see PQ2678.O9

2664 D
2664.A87 Dauvé, Gilles, 1947- (Table P-PZ40)
Dauxois, Jacqueline see PQ2662.R792
Davidson, Albert, 1925- see PQ2678.E6
Delacorta see PQ2675.D5
Delsol, Chantal, 1947 see PQ2673.I3374
Dexet, André, 1921- see PQ2676.A464
2665 E
2665.N385 Engel, Vincent, 1963- (Table P-PZ40)
2666 F
Fuster, Serge, 1912- see PQ2663.A795
2667 G
Grobéty, Hélène see PQ2668.O786
2668 H
2668.E652 Herman, Jean, 1933-
2668.O786 Houlmann-Grobéty, Hélène (Table P-PZ40)
Hurst, Jean-Louis see PQ2673.A818286
2669 I
2670 J
Jacquemard-Sénécal see PQ2670.A249
2670.A249 Jacquemard, Yves (Table P-PZ40)
Japrisot, Sébastien, 1931- see PQ2678.O72
Jean, Bernard, 1950- see PQ2682.U48
Jonas, Philippe de see PQ2662.A376
Jury, Maurice, 1933- see PQ2680.O829
2671 K
2671.A69 Karénine, Vim (Table P-PZ40)
2671.E6759 Kerlan, Richard (Table P-PZ40)
2672 L
Lindbergh, Alika, 1929- see PQ2683.A78
2672.O7 Loriot, Noelle (Table P-PZ40)
2673 M
Magma, Julius see PQ2686.U33
Malroux, Claire see PQ2678.O88
2673.A6 Marceliaire, Philippe (Table P-PZ40)
Martinidesz, Ladislasz von see PQ2663.L32445
2673.A818286 Maurienne (Table P-PZ40)
Medine Shango, Toussaint, 1927- see PQ2663.O7224
2673.I3374 Millon-Delsol, Chantai, 1947- (Table P-PZ40)

Modern French literature
Individual authors
1961-2000
M -- Continued
Morgan, Baptiste, 1963- see PQ2665.N385
2674 N
2675 O
2675.D5 Odier, Daniel, 1945- (Table P-PZ40)
Oriol, Laurence see PQ2672.O7
2676 P
2676.A464 Panazô, 1921- (Table P-PZ40)
2677 Q
2678 R
2678.E2 Réage, Pauline (Table P-PZ40)
2678.E6 Reouven, René (Table P-PZ40)
Robbe-Grillet, Catherine, 1932- see PQ2662.E64
Roche, Jean-Jacques see PQ2671.E6759
2678.O72 Rossi, Jean Baptiste, 1931- (Table P-PZ40)
2678.O88 Roux, Claire Sara (Table P-PZ40)
2678.O9 Rovelli, Thérèse (Table P-PZ40)
Rufer, Ernest see PQ2680.U72
2679 S
Sussan, René, 1925- see PQ2678.E6
2680 T
Thiollier, Marguerite-Marie, 1908-2001 see PQ2680.H4893
2680.H4893 Thiorix, Agnès, 1908-2001 (Table P-PZ40)
2680.O829 Tournier, Maurice, 1933- (Table P-PZ40)
2680.U72 Turesne, Frère (Table P-PZ40)
2681 U
2682 V
Vautrin, Jean, 1933- see PQ2668.E652
Vial, Antoine de see PQ2671.A69
2682.U48 Vuillème, Jean-Bernard, 1950- (Table P-PZ40)
2683 W
2683.A78 Watteau, Monique, 1929- (Table P-PZ40)
2684 X
2685 Y
2686 Z
2686.U33 Zufferey, Jean-Gabriel
2001-
The author number is determined by the second letter of the name
Subarrange each author by Table P-PZ40 unless otherwise indicated
2700 Anonymous works (Table P-PZ28)
2701 A

Modern French literature
Individual authors
2001- -- Continued

2702 B
2703 C
2704 D
Delvig, Lou see PQ2722.I43
2705 E
2706 F
2707 G
2708 H
2709 I
2710 J
2711 K
2712 L
2713 M
2714 N
2715 O
2716 P
2717 Q
2718 R
2719 S
2720 T
2721 U
2722 V
2722.I43 Vigan, Delphine de (Table P-PZ40)
2723 W
2724 X
2725 Y
2726 Z

Provincial, local, colonial, etc.
Class here literary history, biography, criticism, and collections of the literature of provinces, regions, islands, and places belonging to France
Including countries with French literature outside of France: Belgium, Switzerland, etc.
Including French colonies and French literature outside of Europe
For the works, biography and criticism of individual European authors, see PQ1411-2686; for colonial and non-European authors, see PQ3897-3999
For Southern French or Provençal literature see PC3201+

3800 General
France
3801 By region
3803.A-Z By state, province, etc., A-Z
Including Alsace and Lorraine
By place

Provincial, local, colonial, etc.
France
By place -- Continued
3805 Paris
3807.A-Z Other, A-Z
French literature outside of France
3809 General
Europe
Belgium
Including general surveys of all Belgian literature
History and criticism
3810 Periodicals. Societies. Congresses
3811 Encyclopedias. Dictionaries
3812 Study and teaching
3813 Biography of teachers, critics, and historians
History
3814 General
General special
3816 Relations to history, civilization, culture, etc.
Relations to other literatures
3817 General
3818 Translations (as subject)
3819.A-Z Other special topics, A-Z
3819.N38 Naturalism
3819.P76 Proletarian literature
3819.R6 Romanticism
3819.S62 Socialism
3819.S86 Surrealism
3819.S9 Symbolism
Biography
3822 Collected
Individual see PQ1410.2+
3823 Special classes of authors, A-Z
3823.W6 Women
By period
3824 Origins. Medieval
Including history of poetry, drama, etc.
(3825) Modern
see PQ3814+
3826 Poetry
Medieval see PQ3824
3830 Drama
Medieval see PQ3824
3832 Prose. Fiction
Medieval see PQ3824
Other prose forms
3834 Oratory. Letters. Essays

Provincial, local, colonial, etc.
French literature outside of France
Europe
Belgium
History and criticism
Other prose forms -- Continued
3836 Wit and humor
Folk literature see GR185+
(3838) Treatises
(3839) Texts
Local see PQ3855+
Collections
3840 General
3841 Medieval
Including poetry, drama, etc.
3843 Poetry
3846 Drama
3848 Prose. Prose fiction
Other prose forms
3850 Oratory. Letters. Essays
3853 Wit and humor
Local
3855.A-Z By region, province, county, etc., A-Z
3856.A-Z By place, A-Z
3856.1 Outside of Belgium
Individual authors
see PQ1411+
3858.A-Z Translations from French into other languages, A-Z
3860 Netherlands
3861 Germany
3862 Great Britain
3863 Italy
3865 Russia
3867 Scandinavia
3870-3887 Switzerland (Table P-PZ23 modified)
Individual authors or works
see PQ1411+
3890.A-Z Other European countries, A-Z
Subarrange each by Table P-PZ26
Colonies and countries other than European
General
3897 History and criticism
3899 Collections
3900-3919.3 Canada, French Canadian literature (Table P-PZ23 modified)

Provincial, local, colonial, etc.
French literature outside of France
Colonies and countries other than European
Canada, French Canadian literature -- Continued

3919.A-Z Individual authors to 1960, A-Z

Subarrange each author by Table P-PZ40 unless otherwise specified

e. g.

3919.A5 Angers, Félicité (Table P-PZ40)

3919.A78 Aubert de Gaspé, Philippe, 1814-1841 (Table P-PZ40)

Barry, Robertine, 1863-1910, see PQ3919.F68

3919.B29 Beauchemin, Nérée, 1850-1931 (Table P-PZ40)

3919.B35 Beaugrand, Homoré, 1849-1906 (Table P-PZ40)

3919.B362 Béliveau, Louis-Joseph, 1874-1960 (Table P-PZ40)

3919.B387 Bessette, Arsène, 1873-1921 (Table P-PZ40)

3919.B693 Boucherville, George Boucher de (Table P-PZ40)

3919.B695 Bourassa, Napoléon, 1827-1916 (Table P-PZ40)

3919.B793 Buies, Arthur, 1840-1901 (Table P-PZ40)

3919.C56 Clapin, Sylva, 1853-1928 (Table P-PZ40)

3919.C7 Crémazie, Octave, 1827-1916 (Table P-PZ40)

3919.D25 Daignault, Pierre, 1925- (Table P-PZ40)

3919.D35 Delahaye, Guy, 1888-1969 (Table P-PZ40)

3919.D463 Desjardins, Henry,1874-1907 (Table P-PZ40)

3919.D7 Doutre, Joseph, 1825-1880 (Table P-PZ40)

3919.D8 Dubè, Rodolphe, 1905- (Table P-PZ40)

3919.F2 Faucher de Saint-Maurice Narcisse Édouard, 1844-1897 (Table P-PZ40)

3919.F42 Féron, Jean, 1881-1946 (Table P-PZ40)

3919.F68 Françoise, 1863-1910 (Table P-PZ40)

3919.F7 Fréchette, Louis Homoré, 1839-1908 (Table P-PZ40)

3919.G3 Gaspé, Philippe Aubert de, 1786-1871 (Table P-PZ40)

3919.G4 Gérin-Lajoie, Antoine, 1824-1882 (Table P-PZ40)

3919.G72 Grignon, Joseph-J. (Joseph-Jérôme), 1863-1930 (Table P-PZ40)

Hertel, François, 1905- see PQ3919.D8

3919.L215 Laberge, Albert, 1871-1960 (Table P-PZ40)

Lahaise, Guillaume, 1888-1969 see PQ3919.D35

Lebel, Joseph-Marc-Octave, 1881-1946 see PQ3919.F42

3919.P27 Panneton, Philippe, 1895-1960 (Table P-PZ40)

3919.P47 Petitjean, Léon, 1869-1923 or 4 (Table P-PZ40)

3919.R5 Riel, Louis David, 1844-1885 (Table P-PZ40)

Ringuet, 1895-1960 see PQ3919.P27

Saurel, Pierre, 1925- see PQ3919.D25

3919.S87 Sulte, Benjamin, 1841-1923 (Table P-PZ40)

Provincial, local, colonial, etc.
French literature outside of France
Colonies and countries other than European
Canada, French Canadian literature
Individual authors to 1960, A-Z -- Continued
3919.T3 Tardivel, Jules Paul, 1851-1905 (Table P-PZ40)
3919.2.A-Z Individual authors or works, 1961-2000, A-Z
Subarrange each author by Table P-PZ40 unless otherwise specified
Anne-Claire see PQ3919.2.V47
3919.2.A926 Auger, Marie, 1964- (Table P-PZ40)
Dutrisac, Billy Bob, I961- see PQ3919.2.D877
3919.2.D877 Dutrizac, Benoît, I961- (Table P-PZ40)
Fisher, Mark, 1953- see PQ3919.2.P575
3919.2.F6 Forcier, Louise Maheux (Table P-PZ40)
Girard, Mario, 1964- see PQ3919.2.A926
Laurier, Anne, 1953- see PQ3919.2.L3335
3919.2.L3335 Lavigne, Nicole, 1953- (Table P-PZ40)
Maheux-Forcier, Louise see PQ3919.2.F6
3919.2.P575 Poissant, Marc André, 1953- (Table P-PZ40)
Somain, Jean-Francois, 1943- see PQ3919.2.S6
3919.2.S6 Somcynsky, Jean-Francois, 1943- (Table P-PZ40)
3919.2.V47 Vickers, Nancy (Table P-PZ40)
3919.3.A-Z Individual authors or works, 2001- , A-Z
Subarrange each author by Table P-PZ40 unless otherwise specified
3920-3939 United States (Table P-PZ23 modified)
3937.A-Z Local, A-Z
3937.L7-.L8 Louisiana
3937.L7 History of the literature
3937.L8 Collections
3939.A-Z Individual authors, A-Z
Subarrange each author by Table P-PZ40 unless otherwise specified
3939.L28 La Houssaye, Sidonie de (Table P-PZ40)
3939.M5 Mercier, Alfred, 1816-1894 (Table P-PZ40)
3939.R55 Rouquette, Adrien, 1813-1887 (Table P-PZ40)
3940-3949.3 West Indies (Table P-PZ24 modified)
3949.A-Z Individual authors or works to 1960, A-Z
Subarrange individual authors by Table P-PZ40 unless otherwise specified
Subarrange individual works by Table P-PZ43 unless otherwise specified
e. g.
3949.B62 Bonneville, René, ca. 1870-1902 (Table P-PZ40)
3949.C492 Chauvet, Henri, 1863-1928 (Table P-PZ40)
3949.C6 Coicou, Massillon, 1867-1908 (Table P-PZ40)

Provincial, local, colonial, etc.
French literature outside of France
Colonies and countries other than European
West Indies
Individual authors or works to 1960, A-Z -- Continued
3949.F3 Faubert, Pierre, 1806-1868 (Table P-PZ40)
3949.L5 Lhérisson, Justin, 1873-1907 (Table P-PZ40)
3949.M3 Marcelin, Frédéric, 1848-1917 (Table P-PZ40)
3949.S287 Salavina, b. 1866 (Table P-PZ40)
3949.V52 Vieux, Isnardin, 1865-1941 (Table P-PZ40)
3949.V53 Vilaire, Etzer, 1872-1951 (Table P-PZ40)
3949.2.A-Z Individual authors or works, 1961-2000, A-Z
Subarrange individual authors by Table P-PZ40 unless otherwise specified
Subarrange individual works by Table P-PZ43 unless otherwise specified
e. g.
3949.2.A66 Apollon, Georges (Table P-PZ40)
3949.2.C52 Charles, Christophe, 1951- (Table P-PZ40)
Etienne, Franck see PQ3949.2.F7
3949.2.F7 Franketienne (Table P-PZ40)
Love, Christopher, 1951- see PQ3949.2.C52
3949.2.P39 Perfey, Liza (Table P-PZ40)
Sachy see PQ3949.2.A66
Zéphir, Lydia see PQ3949.2.P39
3949.3.A-Z Individual authors or works, 2001- , A-Z
Subarrange individual authors by Table P-PZ40 unless otherwise specified
Subarrange individual works by Table P-PZ43 unless otherwise specified
3950-3959.3 South America, Mexico, and Central America (Table P-PZ24 modified)
3959.A-Z Individual authors or works to 1960, A-Z
Subarrange individual authors by Table P-PZ40 unless otherwise specified
Subarrange individual works by Table P-PZ43 unless otherwise specified
3959.G74 Groussac, Paul, 1848-1929 (Table P-PZ40)
3959.2.A-Z Individual authors or works, 1961-2000, A-Z
Subarrange individual authors by Table P-PZ40 unless otherwise specified
Subarrange individual works by Table P-PZ43 unless otherwise specified

Provincial, local, colonial, etc.
French literature outside of France
Colonies and countries other than European
South America, Mexico, and Central America -- Continued

3959.3.A-Z Individual authors or works, 2001- , A-Z
Subarrange individual authors by Table P-PZ40 unless otherwise specified
Subarrange individual works by Table P-PZ43 unless otherwise specified

3960-3979.3 Asia (Table P-PZ23 modified)

3979.A-Z Individual authors to 1960, A-Z
Subarrange each author by Table P-PZ40 unless otherwise specified

3979.2.A-Z Individual authors, 1961-2000, A-Z
Subarrange each author by Table P-PZ40 unless otherwise specified

3979.3.A-Z Individual authors, 2001- , A-Z
Subarrange each author by Table P-PZ40 unless otherwise specified

3980-3989.3 Africa (Table P-PZ24 modified)

3989.A-Z Individual authors or works to 1960, A-Z
Subarrange individual authors by Table P-PZ40 unless otherwise specified
Subarrange individual works by Table P-PZ43 unless otherwise specified
e. g.

3989.D36 Dayot, Eugène, 1810-1852 (Table P-PZ40)

3989.L47 L'Homme, Léoville, 1857-1928 (Table P-PZ40)

3989.2.A-Z Individual authors or works, 1961-2000, A-Z
Subarrange individual authors by Table P-PZ40 unless otherwise specified
Subarrange individual works by Table P-PZ43 unless otherwise specified

3989.2.A96 Aziza, Mohamed (Table P-PZ40)

Badian, Seydou, 1928- see PQ3989.2.K6

Ben Jelloun, Tahar Ben, 1944- see PQ3989.2.J4

3989.2.J4 Jelloun, Tahar Ben, 1944- (Table P-PZ40)

Kateb Yacine see PQ3989.2.Y28

3989.2.K6 Kouyate, Seydou Badian, 1928- (Table P-PZ40)

Nadir, Chems see PQ3989.2.A96

3989.2.N4625 Ngandu, Pius, 1946- (Table P-PZ40)

Pius Ngandu Nkashama, 1946- , see PQ3989.2.N4625

3989.2.Y28 Yacine, Kateb, 1929-1989 (Table P-PZ40)

Provincial, local, colonial, etc.
French literature outside of France
Colonies and countries other than European
Africa -- Continued

3989.3.A-Z Individual authors or works, 2001- , A-Z

Subarrange individual authors by Table P-PZ40 unless otherwise specified

Subarrange individual works by Table P-PZ43 unless otherwise specified

3990-3999 Oceania (Table P-PZ24)

Italian literature
Literary history and criticism
In the case of combined literature and language, prefer PC1001+
4001 Periodicals. Societies. Congresses
Collections
Texts. Sources see PQ4201+
Chrestomathies see PC1112.9+
4003 Monographs. Studies
4004.A-Z Collections in honor of a particular person or institution, A-Z
4005 Collected works of individual authors
Cf. Collected essays, studies, etc. PQ4029 PQ4046 also special periods and forms
4006 Encyclopedias. Dictionaries
4007 Theory of the study of Italian literature. Philosophy. Psychology. Esthetics
(4009) History of Italian literary history
see PQ4013+
For biography, see PQ4023
Study and teaching
4013 General
4014 General special
By period
4015 Middle ages to 1600
4016 17th to 18th century
4017 19th century
4018 20th century
4019 21st century
4021.A-Z By country, A-Z
4022.A-Z By school, A-Z
Biography of teachers, critics, and historians
4022.5 Collective
4023.A-Z Individual, A-Z
Subarrange each by Table P-PZ50
Criticism
Cf. PN80+ Literature (General)
(4024) Periodicals
see PN80+
4025 Treatises. Theory. Canon
Cf. PN81+ Literature (General)
4026 Essays. Lectures
4027 History
4028 Special topics (not A-Z)
e.g. Textual criticism
4029 Collections of essays in criticism
Cf. PQ4005, PQ4046 and special subjects
By period
4031 Medieval to 1600

Literary history and criticism
Criticism
By period -- Continued
4032 17th to 18th century
4033 19th century
4034 20th century
4034.2 21st century
Authorship see PN101+
History of Italian literature
General
4035 Early works (published before 1800)
Recent works (1800-)
4037 Italian
4038 English
4039 French
4040 German
4041 Other
Compends
4042 Italian
4043 English
4044 Other
4045 Outlines. Quizzes. Tables. Charts
4046 Collected essays, studies, etc.
Cf. PQ4005 Collected works of individual authors
4047 Lectures, addresses, pamphlets, etc.
4047.5 Awards, prizes
4048.A-Z Individual, A-Z
4048.A56 Premio Antico Fattore
4048.B35 Premio Bagutta
4048.B37 Premio Basilicata
4048.G75 Premio Grinzane Cavour
4048.N37 Premio Napoli
4048.P69 Premio letterario Pozzale-Luigi Russo
4048.R37 Premio Rapallo Carige
4048.R43 Premio Riccione
4048.S55 Premio Sila
4048.S7 Premio Strega
4048.V5 Premio Viareggio
4049 Relations to history, civilization, etc.
Relations to foreign literature
4050.A2 General
4050.A3 Ancient
4050.A5-Z Special countries, A-Z
e. g.
4050.E5 England
4050.F5 France
4050.S7 Spain

Literary history and criticism
Relations to foreign literature -- Continued
Medieval poetry see PQ4094+
Italian authors in relation to foreign countries (Individual authors) see PQ4265+
4051 Translations (as subject)
4051.5 Italian literature by foreign authors
General works only. Individual authors classed in the same manner as native authors
(4051.8) Foreign literature by Italian authors
see the special foreign literature, PA, PQ-PT
4052 Various aspects, forms, etc.
e.g. Psychology, esthetics, evolution of the different forms, poetry, drama, etc.
4053.A-Z Special subjects, A-Z
Cf. PQ4129.A+ Poetry
(4053.A54) America
see PQ4054.A5
4053.A68 Art
4053.A7 Arthurian legends
Cf. PQ4066 Special subjects
4053.A87 Autobiography
4053.B56 Biography (as a literary form)
4053.B58 Blondes
4053.B64 Body, Human
(4053.B75) Brigands and robbers
see PQ4055.B75
4053.C3 Capitalism
(4053.C47) Charon (Greek mythology)
see PQ4056.C47
4053.C49 Childhood
4053.C5 Christianity
4053.C55 Cities and towns
4053.C56 Communism
4053.C57 Conversation
4053.C6 Country life
4053.D4 Death
4053.D43 Deception
4053.D45 Dialects
4053.D5 Diseases
4053.E74 Ermetismo
4053.E75 Erotic literature
4053.E94 Exempla
4053.F35 Fantastic literature
4053.F57 Folklore
4053.F58 Food
4053.F6 Fortune

Literary history and criticism
Special subjects, A-Z -- Continued

4053.F73 Freemasonry
4053.F87 Futurism
4053.G37 Gardens
4053.G6 Golden age (Mythology)
4053.H47 Heroines
4053.H57 History
Human body see PQ4053.B64
4053.H86 Hunting
Imprisonment see PQ4053.P76
4053.I54 Industries
4053.I6 Invective
(4053.J48) Jews
see PQ4054.J4
4053.L36 Landscape
4053.L38 Laughter
4053.L53 Life cycle, Human
4053.L54 Light and darkness
4053.L6 Local color
4053.M32 Magic
4053.M35 Marriage
(4053.M37) Mazzini, Giuseppe
see PQ4056.M37
4053.M45 Mental illness
4053.M53 Mimesis
4053.M56 Mirrors
4053.M66 Monsters
4053.M98 Myth
4053.N28 Names
4053.N29 National characteristics
4053.N3 Nature
4053.N64 Noon
(4053.N86) Nuns
see PQ4055.N8
4053.P37 Parodies
4053.P42 Periodization
4053.P45 Philologists. Critics
4053.P65 Point of view
Including first person narrative, etc.
4053.P67 Polemics
4053.P69 Political satire
4053.P7 Politics
4053.P73 Popular literature
4053.P76 Prisons. Imprisonment
4053.P8 Psychoanalysis
4053.P85 Pulp literature

Literary history and criticism
Special subjects, A-Z -- Continued

4053.Q47 Questione della lingua
4053.R34 Realism
4053.R35 Reason
4053.R36 Regionalism
4053.R4 Religion
4053.S18 Satire
4053.S23 Science
4053.S25 Science fiction
4053.S43 Seduction
4053.S48 Setting
4053.S54 Sleep
4053.S65 Solitude
4053.S68 Soul
4053.S7 Sports
4053.S94 Suicide
4053.T7 Tragedy
4053.T75 Travel
4053.U5 Underground movements. Resistance
4053.U76 Utopias
4053.V47 Verism
(4053.V57) Virgil
see PQ4056.V55
4053.W37 War
4053.W56 Wine
(4053.W6) Women
see PQ4055.W6
4053.W65 World War I
4054.A-Z Special countries and races, A-Z
4054.A5 America
4054.I53 India
4054.J4 Jews
4055.A-Z Special classes, A-Z
4055.B75 Brigands and robbers
4055.E94 Exiles
4055.N8 Nuns
4055.P7 Priests
4055.P75 Prisoners
4055.W6 Women
4056.A-Z Special persons or characters, A-Z
4056.C47 Charon (Greek mythology)
4056.C64 Columbus, Christopher
4056.F73 Francis, of Assisi, Saint
4056.G66 Gonnella
4056.M34 Mary, Blessed Virgin, Saint
4056.M37 Mazzini, Giuseppe

Literary history and criticism
Special persons or characters, A-Z -- Continued
4056.V55 Virgil
Biography
4057 Collective
Cf. PQ4023.A+ Study and teaching
Individual see PQ4265+
4058 Memoirs. Letters. Interviews
4060 Iconography: Portraits, monuments, etc.
4061 Literary landmarks. Homes and haunts of authors
4063 Women authors. Literary relations of women
Cf. PN471+ Literature (General)
4063.5.A-Z Other classes of authors, A-Z
4063.5.P64 Political prisoners
By period
Medieval
General to 1500/1600
4064 Treatises. Compends
4065 Collected essays, studies, etc.
Cf. PQ4005, PQ4046, etc.
4066 Special subjects (not elsewhere provided for under forms, etc.)
Prefer PQ4052+ for subjects not peculiar to the period
4067 "Letteratura cavalleresca"
Franco-Italian poetry see PQ4097
Troubadours see PC3304+
Special
4069 Origins. "Il duecento"
Cf. PQ4096 Sicilian school
Tuscan period. The age of Dante, Petrarca and Boccaccio. "Il trecento"
4071 General
4072 Collected essays, studies, etc.
4073 Special topics
4075 Renaissance, 1375 to 1500 (or 1600). "Il quattrocento"
Cf. PN715+ Literature (General)
Modern
4077 General
Prefer PQ4035-4037
By period
16th century. "Il cinquecento"
4079 General works
4080 Special
17th century. "Il seicento" (including treatises on the period of decline, ca. 1575 to 1750). "Secentismo"
4081 General works
4082 Special

Literary history and criticism
By period
Modern
By period -- Continued
18th century. "Il settecento"
4083 General works
4084 Special
19th century. "Il ottocento" (including treatises on the revival of Italiation literature, ca. 1750 to 1870)
4085 General works
4086 Special
20th century. "Il novecento"
4087 General works
4088 Special
Poetry (including treatises confined to lyric poetry)
Technique of Italian poetry
Philosophy, aesthetics see PN1031
History
General
4091 Treatises. Compends
4092 Collected essays, studies, etc.
Cf. PQ4005 Collected works of individual authors
4093 Special topics
Prefer PQ4052-PQ4055
By period
Medieval to 1400 (or 1500)
4094 General
Special
Italian troubadours see PC3309
Provençal poetry in Italy see PC3310
4096 The Sicilian school, i.e. the entire lyric poetry of Italy before Dante
Cf. Flamini, History of Italian literature, p. 10
4097 Franco-Italian poetry. Canzoni di gesta, canzoni franco-veneti, etc.
Cf. PQ151+ PQ4117
4098 The new Florentine School. "Dolce stil nuovo" of Dante
4099.A-Z Other special, A-Z
Cf. PQ4126.A+
4099.A46 Aesthetics
4099.A6 Allegorical-didactic
4099.E45 Ekphrasis
4099.H5 Historical
4099.L68 Love
4099.M9 Mythology
Popular see PQ4121

Literary history and criticism
Poetry (including treatises confined to lyric poetry)
History
By period
Medieval to 1400 (or 1500)
Special
Other special, A-Z -- Continued

4099.R4 Religious. Franciscan, etc.
Cf. PQ4128.L3 Laude, Devozioni
4099.S26 Satire
4099.T4 Tenzoni
4101 15th century. "Il quattrocento"
Cf. PA8040 Modern Latin literature
4103 16th century. "Il cinquecento"
16th century. "Il cinquecento" see PQ4126.S2
4105 17th century (including period of decline to ca. 1750). Marinism. Secentism
4107 18th century
4109 19th century (ca. 1750 to 1870/80)
Cf. PQ4126.H6 Historical and political poetry
4113 20th century
4115 21st century
4117 Epic and narrative poetry
Popular poetry
4119 General
4120 Special
4120.2 By period
4121 Origins. Medieval
Cf. PQ4094+ General
Modern see PQ4119+
4122.A-Z By region, locality, A-Z
e. g.
4122.N7 Noto
4122.V4 Venice
4123.A-Z By subject, A-Z
4126.A-Z Other, A-Z
e. g.
4126.B53 Blank verse
4126.D48 Dialect poetry
4126.D5 Didactic
4126.F5 Fidenzian
Cf. PQ4634.S25 Scroffa
4126.H4 Heroicomic
4126.H6 Historical. Patriotic. Political
4126.P2 Parody. Travesty
4126.P5 Pastoral
4126.R4 Religious and moral

Literary history and criticism
Poetry (including treatises confined to lyric poetry)
Other, A-Z -- Continued
4126.S2 Satirical (Pasquinades)
4128.A-Z Minor forms
e. g.
4128.B3 Ballata
Barzelletta see PQ4128.B3
4128.C2 Cantari
4128.C4 Canto carnascialesco
Cf. PQ4128.B3 Ballata
4128.C6 Canzone
Canzone a ballo see PQ4128.B3
4128.C8 Capitolo
Ciciliana see PQ4128.S7
Devozioni see PQ4128.L3
Discordo see PQ4128.C6
4128.D5 Ditirambo
4128.F7 Frottola (Motto confetto)
Cf. PQ4128.S4 Serventese
Cf. PQ4137 Sacre rappresenatazioni
4128.L3 Laude
Cf. PQ4137
4128.M3 Madrigale
Mandriale see PQ4128.M3
Motto confetto see PQ4128.F7
Napolitana see PQ4128.S7
4128.N6 Nona rima
4128.O3 Ode
4128.O7 Ottava rima
4128.R5 Rispetto
4128.R76 Rondels
Satira see PQ4126.S2
Satira in terza rima see PQ4128.T4
4128.S4 Serventese
Cf. PQ4128.F7 Frottola
Sesta rima (sestina, serventese, ritornellato) see PQ4128.C6
4128.S5 Sonetto
Stanza see PQ4128.C6
4128.S6 Stornello
4128.S7 Strambotto (Siciliana or Napolitana)
4128.S8 Strenne nuziali
4128.T3 Tenzoni
Cf. PQ4099.T4 Medieval to 1400
4128.T4 Terza rima (terzina)
Cf. PQ4126.S2 Satirical poetry

Literary history and criticism
Poetry (including treatises confined to lyric poetry)
Minor forms -- Continued
4128.V58 Visual poetry
4129.A-Z By subject: Treatment, etc., A-Z
4129.E76 Erotic
4129.M46 Metaphysics
4129.P7 Prayer
4129.R84 Ruins
4130.A-Z Special classes of persons, characters, etc., A-Z
Prefer PQ4055
(4131) Special characters
see PN57, PN1103
Drama
Technique see PN1660+
History and study of the Italian stage see PN2670+
History
General
Treaties and compends
4133 Early to 1800
4134 Later, 1801-
4135 Collected essays, studies, etc.
Cf. PQ4005 Collected works of individual authors
4136 Special topics (not A-Z)
By period
4137 Medieval. Origins
Laude
see PQ4126.R4; PQ4128.L3
Devozioni see PQ4128.L3
Sacre rappresentazioni and other medieval plays
4138 Modern
General see PQ4133+
Farce (Commedia dell' arte, etc.) see PQ4155+
Folk-drama see PQ4160
Pastoral drama see PQ4153.P2
Political drama see PQ4153.P6
4139 Renaissance. 15th-17th centuries
Cf. PA8073+ Latin drama
4141 (17th-) 18th century
4143 (18th-) 19th century
4145 20th century
4146 21st century
4147 Tragedy
4149 Comedy ("Commedia erudita")
Commedia dell' arte see PQ4155+
4153.H3 Historical drama

Literary history and criticism
Drama -- Continued
(4153.I2) Intermezzo (Intermedio)
see subclass ML
(4153.M2) Melodrama
see sublcass ML
(4153.O6) Opera
see subclass ML
(4153.O7) Opera buffa
see subclass ML
4153.P2 Pastoral drama
Cf. PQ4155+ Commedia dell' arte
4153.P6 Political drama
4153.R23 Radio plays
4153.R3 Romantic drama
Farce. Commedia dell' arte. Farsa dialettale, satirica, cavaiola
The latter ridiculing the inhabitants of Cava de' Tirreni (Turri, Dizionario storico)
4155 General
Special
Characters
General see PQ4155
4157.A-Z Special, A-Z
e. g.
4157.A8 Arlecchino
4157.C7 Colombina
4157.P9 Pulcinella
4158 Other
e.g. Congrega dei Rozzi
4159.A-Z By region, locality, etc., A-Z
4160 Folk drama
Prose
General
4161 Treatises. Compends
4162 Collected essays, studies, etc.
Cf. PQ4005 Collected works of individual authors
4163 Special topics
Short story (Novella) see PQ4177+
By period
4164 Medieval
Modern
General see PQ4161+
4165 Renaissance (1400-1600)
4166 17th and 18th centuries
4167 19th centuries
4168 20th centuries

Literary history and criticism
Prose -- Continued
Special
Prose fiction
Technique see PN3355+
General
4169 Treatises. Compends
4170 Collected essays, studies, etc.
By period
4171 Medieval (to 1400/1500)
4172 Renaissance to 1700
Modern
4173 18th and 19th centuries
4174 20th century
4175 21st century
Special
4177 Novella (Short story)
4179 Other
4181.A-Z Special forms and topics, A-Z
4181.A38 Adventure stories
4181.A87 Autobiographical fiction
4181.D4 Detective and mystery stories
4181.E65 Epistolary fiction
4181.F36 Fantastic fiction
4181.F48 Feuilletons
4181.H55 Historical fiction
4181.H65 Homosexuality
4181.L36 Landscape
4181.L68 Love stories
4181.P64 Political fiction
4181.S35 Science fiction
4181.W65 Women
4183.A-Z Minor forms, A-Z
4183.D5 Dialogues
4183.E8 Essays
(4183.F2) Fables
see PN986
4183.L4 Letters
4183.O7 Oratory
4183.W5 Wit and humor
4185 Miscellaneous
Folk literature
For general works on and collections of folk literature, see GR175+
(4186) Periodicals. Societies. Collections
History
(4187) Treatises. Compends

Literary history and criticism
Folk literature
History -- Continued
(4188) Essays, pamphlets, etc.
By period
4190 Origins. Medieval
(4191) Modern
By form
Poetry see PQ4119+
Drama see PQ4160
Collections of texts
(4193) General
Poetry see PQ4217+
4195 Chapbooks
(4196.A-Z) Special localities, regions, etc., A-Z
(4197) Special characters: heroes, fairies, etc.
(4197.9) Legends of Christ, saints, etc.
(4198) Individual tales
(4199.A-Z) Translations, by language, A-Z
4199.5 Juvenile literature (General)
For special genres, see the genre
For special subjects, see the subject
Collections of Italian literature
General (Comprehensive, not confined to any one period or form)
4201.A2 Early to 1800
4201.A5-Z 1801-
4202 Selections. Anthologies, etc.
4203 Selections from women authors
4203.5.A-Z Special classes of authors, A-Z
4203.5.C5 Child authors
4203.5.H65 Homosexuals, Male
4203.5.I55 Immigrants
4203.5.J48 Jewish authors
By period
4204.A3 To 1500
4204.A5 16th century (Cinquecento)
4204.A6 17th century (Seicento)
4204.A7 18th century (Settecento)
4204.A8 19th century (Ottocento)
4204.A9 20th century (Novecento)
4204.2 21st century
By region, place, etc. see PQ5901+
Translations from foreign literature see PN6041+
Translations of Italian literature into foreign languages
4205.A2 Polyglot collections
4205.E5 English

Collections of Italian literature
Translations of Italian literature into foreign languages -- Continued
4205.F5 French
4205.G5 German
4205.P5 Portuguese
4205.S5 Spanish
4206.A-Z Other. By language, A-Z
Poetry (General and lyric)
General
4207.A2 Early to 1800
4207.A5-Z 1801-
4208 Selections. Anthologies, etc.
Special classes of authors
4209 Women
4209.5.A-Z Other, A-Z
4209.5.H65 Homosexuals
4209.5.M35 Mentally ill
4209.5.M56 Minorities
4209.5.P75 Prisoners
4209.5.Y68 Youth
4210 Concordances, dictionaries, indexes, etc.
4211 Commentaries (without text)
By period
Early to 1500-1600
4212.A2 Reprints of manuscript collections
Critical editions, with modern editions, .A5-Z
4212.A2R79 Rome, Vatican, Codex 3793
4212.A3 Collections published before 1801
4212.A5-Z Modern editions, 1801-
By centuries
Including collections limited to special schools or forms
4213.A2 12th-13th centuries (Duecento). Sicilian school. Bolognese school
4213.A3A-.A3Z3 14th century (Trecento). Florentine school. Petrarchism
4213.A3Z5 Franco-Italian poetry
General collections only
For collections of Chansons de geste popularized in Italian idiom see PQ1310.5
For collections of French poems by Italian authors of the period see PQ1320
4213.A4 15th century (Quattrocento)
4213.A5 16th century (Cinquecento)
4213.A6 17th century (Seicento)
4213.A7 18th century (Settecento)
4213.A8 19th century (Ottocento)
4214 20th century (Novecento)

Collections of Italian literature
Poetry (General and lyric)
By period
By centuries -- Continued
4214.2 21st century
By form
General collections only
For collections of special periods see PQ4212+
Epic and narrative poetry
4215 General
(4216) Special
Heroicomic poems see PQ4220.H4
Novelle in verse see PQ4220.N5
Popular poetry (Folk-songs)
4217.A2 General
4217.A3 Selections. Anthologies
4218.A-Z By region or place, A-Z
e. g.
4218.C6 Corsica
4218.L8 Lucca
4218.N3 Naples
4218.P5 Piedmont
4218.R7 Rome
4218.S3 Sardinia
4218.T8 Tuscany
4218.V4 Velletri
4218.V5 Venice
4219.A-Z By subject, A-Z
4219.A45 Alexius, Saint
4219.E44 Emigration and immigration
4219.G95 Gypsies. Romanies
Immigration see PQ4219.E44
Marine see PQ4219.S43
4219.P6 Political. Protest
4219.R5 Religious (Laude, Devozioni)
4219.S43 Sea. Marine
Lyric see PQ4207+
4220.A-Z Other, A-Z
4220.B8 Burlesques
4220.D48 Dialect poetry
4220.D5 Didactic. Gnomic
4220.E5 Epigrams
4220.F2 Fables
4220.H34 Haiku
4220.H4 Heroicomic poems
4220.N5 Novelle in verse
4220.P2 Parodies. Travesties

Collections of Italian literature
Poetry (General and lyric)
By form
Other, A-Z -- Continued
4220.P5 Pastoral
4220.R8 "Rusticali"
4220.S2 Satirical (Pasquinades)
4220.V57 Visual poetry
Minor forms
4221 Sonetti
Class here collections of sonetti of all or several periods of Italian poetry
Collections of sonetti and canzoni are classed with PQ4207-4208; collections by period are classed with the period, PQ4212-4214
4222.A-Z Other, A-Z
For list of Cutter numbers, see PQ4128.A+
4223.A-Z By subject, A-Z
4223.B7 Brigands and robbers
4223.E7 Erotic
4223.F45 Feminism
4223.G37 Gardens
4223.H5 Historical. Patriotic. Political
4223.L7 Love
4223.M6 Military
4223.N3 Nature
4223.R4 Religious. Moral
Cf. PQ4219.R5 Laude; Devozioni
Revolutionary see PQ4223.H5
Robbers see PQ4223.B7
4223.R67 Roses
4223.S43 Sea
4223.W65 World War I
Translations
(4224) From foreign poetry into Italian
From Italian poetry into foreign languages
4225.A2 Polyglot collections
4225.A5-Z By language, A-Z
e. g.
4225.E5-.E8 English
Subarrange by title or editor
4225.E5 General
Special
4225.E6 Sonnets
4225.E7 Other forms or subjects
4225.E8A-.E8Z By translator, A-Z

Collections of Italian literature
Poetry (General and lyric)
Translations
From Italian poetry into foreign languages
By language, A-Z -- Continued

4225.F5-.F8 French
Subarrange by title or editor
4225.F5 General
Special
4225.F6 Sonnets
4225.F7 Other forms or subjects
4225.F8A-.F8Z By translator, A-Z
4225.G5-.G8 German
Subarrange by title or editor
4225.G5 General
Special
4225.G6 Sonnets
4225.G7 Other forms or subjects
4225.G8A-.G8Z By translator, A-Z

Drama
General
4227.A2 Early (published before 1801)
4227.A3-Z 1801-
4228 Selected plays. Anthologies
Special
By period
Medieval
4229 General
4230 Individual plays
Modern
General see PQ4227.A2+
By century
4231.A5 16th century (Cinquecento)
4231.A6 17th century (Seicento)
4231.A7 18th century (Settecento)
4231.A8 19th century (Ottocento)
4231.A9 20th century (Novecento)
(4231.Z9) Miscellaneous uncataloged (single) plays
(4231.Z99) Plays in typewritten form
4231.2 21st century
By form
4232 Tragedies
4233 Comedies (Commedia erudita)
Cf. PQ1231.I5 Comédie italienne
4234.A-Z Drama. By subject, A-Z
4234.H5 Historical and political
4234.P2 Pastoral

Collections of Italian literature
Drama
Special
By form
Drama. By subject, A-Z -- Continued

4234.R6 Romantic
(4235) Melodramas
see class M
4236 Farces (Commedia dell'arte)
4238 Local. By region (Commedia dialettale)
(4239) Intermezzi (Intermedii)
see class M
4240 Amateur drama
(4241) Juvenile plays
see PZ47
(4242) Puppet plays
see PN1981
4243.A-Z Other forms, A-Z
4243.R34 Radio plays

Translations
4244.A2 Polyglot collections
English
4244.E5 General
4244.E6A-.E6Z By translator, A-Z
French
4244.F5 General
4244.F6A-.F6Z By translator, A-Z
German
4244.G5 General
4244.G6A-.G6Z By translator, A-Z
Spanish
4244.S5 General
4244.S6A-.S6Z By translator, A-Z
4245.A-Z Other languages, A-Z
Under each language:
.x General
.x2A-.x2Z By translator, A-Z

Prose
General
4247.A2 Early (published before 1801)
4247.A5-Z 1801-
4248 Selections. Anthologies
4248.5.A-Z Special classes of authors, A-Z
4248.5.S4 School children
By period
4249.A2 Early to 1500
4249.A5 16th century (Cinquecento)

Collections of Italian literature
Prose
By period -- Continued

4249.A6 17th century (Seicento)
4249.A7 18th century (Settecento)
4249.A8 19th century (Ottocento)
4249.A9 20th century (Novecento)
4249.6.A-Z By subject, A-Z
4249.6.A3 Adolescence
4249.6.A5 Animals
4249.6.C45 Christian life
4249.6.D45 Detective and mystery stories
4249.6.E75 Erotic stories
4249.6.F34 Fantastic fiction
4249.6.G39 Gays
4249.6.H56 History
4249.6.H66 Horror tales
4249.6.I77 Istria (Croatia and Slovenia)
Mystery stories see PQ4249.6.D45
4249.6.R34 Regionalism
4249.6.R4 Revolutionaries
4249.6.S34 Science fiction
4249.6.S4 Sea stories
4249.6.S53 Sicily
4249.6.T73 Travel
4249.6.T73 Winter
4249.6.T75 Trieste (Italy)
4249.6.T8 Turin
4249.6.U6 Underground movements. Resistance
4249.6.V4 Venice
4249.6.W37 War stories
4249.6.W58 Witches
4250.A-Z Translations from Italian into foreign languages, A-Z
(4250.5) Translations from foreign literature into Italian

Prose fiction
General
4251.A2 Early (published before 1801)
4251.A5-Z 1801-
4252 Selections. Anthologies
By period
4253.A2 Early to 1500
Il novellino. Cento novele antiche
4253.A3 Italian texts
4253.A44 Translations, by language, A-Z
4253.A45 Criticism
4253.A5 16th century
4253.A6 17th century

Collections of Italian literature
Prose
Prose fiction
By period -- Continued
4253.A7 18th century
4253.A8 19th century
4253.A9 20th century
4253.2 21st century
Short stories. Novelle
4254.A2 Serial collections
4254.A3-Z Other collections
By period see PQ4253.A2+
Folk tales see GR175+
Other special see PQ4249.6.A+
4257.A-Z Translations from Italian into foreign languages, A-Z
(4257.5) Translations from foreign literatures into Italian
4258 Oratory
4259 Letters
4260 Essays
(4261) Fables in prose
see PN986
Fables in verse see PQ4220.F2
4262 Wit and humor
For minor works, prefer PN6203-6205
4263 Miscellaneous
Individual authors
Individual authors and works to 1400
Subarrange each by Table P-PZ40 or Table P-PZ43 unless otherwise specified
Anonymous works
see the title
4265.A4 Aesopus. Early Italian texts
4265.A45 Alexander the Great (Poems and romances)
4265.A5 Alfani, Gianni, 13th cent. (Table P-PZ40)
4265.A55 Alighieri, Jacopo di Dante, 14th cent. (Table P-PZ40)
4265.A57 Alighieri, Piero di Dante, d. 1364 (Table P-PZ40)
4265.A6 Andrea da Barberino, b. ca. 1370. (Table P-PZ40)
Andrea di Jacopo da Barberino di Valdelsa see PQ4265.A6
Andrea Monte see PQ4474.M68
4265.A62 Angioleri, Cecco, b. ca. 1258 (Table P-PZ40)
4265.A64 Anonimo cumano (Table P-PZ40)
4265.A65 Anonimo genovese, 13th cent. (Table P-PZ40)
4265.A67 Antonio da Ferrara, 1315-ca. 1371 (Table P-PZ40)
4265.A7 Apollonius of Tyre (Romance) (Early Italian texts)
4265.B15 Bambaglioli, Graziolo de', ca. 1291-ca. 1340 (Table P-PZ40)
Barberino, Andrea de see PQ4265.A6

Individual authors
Individual authors and works to 1400 -- Continued

4265.B3 Barberino, Francesco da, 1264-1348 (Table P-PZ40)
4265.B34 Barlaam e Giosaffatte (Table P-PZ40)
4265.B343 Barsegape, Pietro da, fl. 1264 (Table P-PZ40)
Berta dai gran pié see PQ1431.B2+
4265.B347 Bestiary. Italian
4265.B35 Betrico da Reggio, fl. 1320 (Table P-PZ40)
4265.B4 Bianco da Sienna, fl. 1367 (Table P-PZ40)
Bindo, Bonichi see PQ4299.B3
4265.B54 Binduccio, dello Scelto (Table P-PZ40)
Boccaccio, Giovanni, 1313-1375
4266.A1 Collected works, by date
(4266.A11) Critical and annotated editions. By editor, A-Z
4266.A15 Selected works. By editor
4266.A2 Miscellaneous (Italian and Latin)
4266.A3 Selections. Anthologies. By editor
Latin works see PQ4274.A2+
4266.A5 Collected poems
4266.A6 Collected novels (with or without the Decameron)
Separate works (Italian)
Decameron
Editions
4267.A1 Manuscripts reproduced in facsimile
Printed editions
4267.A2 Comprehensive. By date
4267.A3 Selected stories. By editor (or date)
4267.A4 School (and other expurgated) editions. By editor (or date)
4268.A-Z Separate stories. By title of story, A-Z
e.g. Abram Ciudeo Ciappeleto
Cf. Bacchi della Lega, pp. 83-97
(4269) Criticism and interpretation
see PQ4287, PQ4288
4270.A-Z Other works, A-Z
4270.A2 Ameto (Pastoral romance in prose interspersed with verses)
4270.A5 Amorosa visione (Poem in terza rime)
Caccia di Diana see PQ4275.C3
Commento sopra la Commedia see PQ4437+
4270.C7 Corbaccio (Story in prose. The false title "Laberinto d'amore" does not occur till the 16th century)
4270.F2 Fiammetta (Novel in prose).
4270.F5 Filocolo (Filocopo, story in prose).
4270.F7 Filostrato (Story in verse).
Laberinto d'amore see PQ4270.C7
4270.N2 Ninfale fiesolano (Pastoral poem in ottava rima).

	Individual authors
	Individual authors and works to 1400
	Boccaccio, Giovanni, 1313-1375
	Separate works
	Other works, A-Z
	Rime see PQ4266.A5
4270.T4	Teseide (Story in ottava rima).
	Vita di Dante see PQ4338
	Translations
	Class here translations of Italian works only
	For translations of the Latin works see PQ4274.A2+
	For translations of the spurious works see PQ4275.A+
	Italian dialects
4272.A1	Collections. By date
4272.A1A-.A1Z	By dialect, A-Z
4272.E5	English (Table PQ2)
4272.F5	French (Table PQ2)
4272.G5	German (Table PQ2)
4272.P5	Portuguese (Table PQ2)
4272.S5	Spanish (Table PQ2)
4273.A-Z	Other European languages, A-Z
4273.B3	Basque
4273.C2	Catalan
	Celtic
4273.C3	Breton
4273.C4	Cornish
4273.C5	Gaelic
4273.C6	Irish
4273.C7	Manx
4273.C8	Welsh
4273.D8	Dutch
4273.F4	Finnish
4273.G5	Greek
4273.H8	Hungarian
4273.L3	Latin
4273.P7	Provençal
4273.R8	Romanian
	Scandinavian
4273.S21	Danish. Dano-Norwegian
4273.S22	Icelandic
4273.S23	Swedish
	Slavic
4273.S3	Bohemian
4273.S4	Bulgarian
4273.S5	Croatian
4273.S53	Latvian

Individual authors
Individual authors and works to 1400
Boccaccio, Giovanni, 1313-1375.
Translations.
Other European languages.
Slavic. -- Continued

4273.S55 Lithuanian
4273.S6 Polish
4273.S7 Russian
4273.S75 Ruthenian
4273.S8 Serbian
4273.S82 Slovak
4273.S84 Slovenian
4273.S85 Wendic
4273.5.A-Z Other languages, A-Z
4273.6.A-Z Artificial languages, A-Z
4273.7 Dramatizations
Prefer classification under author
4273.8 Imitations. Adaptations. Parodies
Prefer classification under author
4273.9 Illustrations
Portfolios, etc. without text, and illustrations with quotations
Illustrated editions
see PQ4267+ PQ4274, PQ4275
History of Boccaccio portraits and of illustration of works see PQ4282
Latin works (including translations)
4274.A2 Comprehensive editions. By date
4274.A3 Selections
4274.A44-.Z2 Separate works
Africa
see Pro Africa Petrarchae
4274.B7-.B8 Bucolicon
4274.B7 Editions. By date
4274.B7A-.B7Z Translations. By language and date
4274.B8 Criticism
4274.C3 Carmen de Dante
4274.D1-.D3 De casibus virorum illustrium
4274.D1 Editions. By date
Translations
4274.D1A-.D1Z Italian. By translator, A-Z
4274.D2A-.D2Z Other. By language and date
4274.D3 Criticism
4274.D4-.D6 De claris mulieribus
4274.D4 Editions. By date
Translations
4274.D4A-.D4Z Italian. By translator, A-Z

Individual authors
Individual authors and works to 1400
Boccaccio, Giovanni, 1313-1375.
Latin works (including translations).
Separate works
De claris mulieribus
Translations -- Continued

4274.D5A-.D5Z	Other. By language and date
4274.D6	Criticism
4274.D7-.D9	De montibus, sylvis, fontibus, lacubus, fluminibus, stagnis et paludibus et de nominibus maris
4274.D7	Editions. By date
	Translations
4274.D7A-.D7Z	Italian. By translator, A-Z
4274.D8A-.D8Z	Other. By language and date
4274.D9	Criticism
	Eclogae see PQ4274.B7+
	Epistolae see PQ4278.A3
4274.G5-.G7	Genealogia deorum
4274.P8	Pro Africa Petrarchae
4274.Z2	Minor poems (Zibaldone)
4274.Z3	Criticism, interpretation, etc.
4275.A-Z	Spurious works, A-Z
4275.A8	Ava maria (Poem)
	Birria e Geta see PQ4275.G4
4275.C3	Caccia di Diana (Poem)
	Cenni intorno a Tito Libio (Brit. mus.) see PA6459.A2
	Chiose sopre Dante see PQ4437
4275.D5	Dialogo d'amore
	Ecatomfila see PQ4562.A6
4275.F5	Fiorio e Biancifiore
	Fioretti di antica storia romana
4275.G4	Geta e Birria
4275.P3	Papessa Giovanni
4275.P4	Passione del N.S. Gesu Cristo
4275.S8	Storia del Calonacho da Siena
4275.U7	Urbano
4275.Z5	Zibaldone
(4276)	Dramatization. Translation. Illustration (as subject) see PQ4273.9 PQ4284+ Cf. PQ4273.7, PQ4273.8, PQ4282
	Criticism, biography, etc.
	Bibliography see Z8106
4277.A2-.A39	Periodicals. Societies. Collections
4277.A4	Dictionaries. Encyclopedias Cf. PQ4297
4277.A5-.Z4	General works (Literary biography. Life and works)

Individual authors
Individual authors and works to 1400
Boccaccio, Giovanni, 1313-1375.
Criticism, biography, etc. -- Continued

4277.Z5 Lectures. Addresses. Essays
Special
4278.A1 Sources. Documents
Last will see PQ4278.A9
4278.A25 Autobiographical and biographical allusions
4278.A27 Letters
Cf. G. Koerting, Boccaccio, 1880, pp. 45-49
4278.A3 Collections and selections
4278.A33 Translations
4278.A35 Spurious letters.
4278.A4 Individual letters, A-Z, by addressee
4278.A49 Letters addressed to Baccaccio
4278.A49A5-.A49Z By author, A-Z
4278.A49.A2 Collections
4278.A5 Criticism
4278.A57 Family. Ancestry. Name
4278.A6 Birth. Early life. Education
4278.A7 Relation to women. "Fiammetta" (Maria d'Aquino)
4278.A75 Political activity
Prefer PQ4293.H5
(4278.A77) Study of classical literature
see PQ4293.L4
(4278.A79) Study of Dante
see PQ4346, PQ4358, PQ4382
4278.A8 Later years. Death
4278.A9 Last will
4279 The age of Boccaccio. Relation to contemporaries
Cf. PQ4283.A1+ Authorship, Literary relations
4279.A2 General
4279.A5-Z Individual
Boccaccio and Chaucer see PR1912.A5+
4280 Homes and haunts
4281 Anniversaries. Celebrations
4281.A2 General
4281.A25 Particular celebrations, by date and place
Use date-letters
4281.F75 1875
4281.G13 1913
4282 Iconography. Portraits. Monuments
4282.5.A-Z Museums. Relics. Exhibitions. By place, A-Z
(4282.9) Fiction, drama, etc., based upon Boccaccio's life
Prefer classification with special authors
Boccaccio in England, Germany, etc. see PQ4284+

Individual authors
Individual authors and works to 1400
Boccaccio, Giovanni, 1313-1375.
Criticism, biography, etc.
Authorship
Manuscripts. Autographs
(4283.A1) Facsimiles. By date
see Z115
4283.A2 Discussions of autographs
4283.A4 Sources
4283.A6 Precursors
(4283.A7) Associates. Followers. Circle. School
Prefer PQ4071-4073
4283.A8 Allusions
Prefer PQ4278.A25 for biography
4283.A9 Chronology of works
4283.5 Censorship
Criticism and interpretation
History of the study and appreciation of Boccaccio
Include the history of dramatizations, translations, imitations, parodies, etc.
Cf. PQ4282
4284 General and in Italy
4284.5 General special
Influence of Boccaccio in Italy and elsewhere (General)
Special countries see PQ4285.A+
Special authors or persons
see the authors or persons
Influence on literature see PQ4293.L2+
4285.A-Z Special. By country, A-Z
e. g.
4285.G5 Germany, Boccaccio in
4285.5.A-Z Special. By individual, A-Z
Treatises
4286 General
Decameron (mainly)
4287 General
4287.A2 Works before 1800
4288.A-Z Particular stories, A-Z (By original title)
Special
(4289) Philosophy, esthetics
see PQ4286
4290 Technique
Cf. PQ4295
4291 Characters

Individual authors
Individual authors and works to 1400
Boccaccio, Giovanni, 1313-1375.
Criticism, biography, etc.
Criticism and interpretation
Treatises
Special
Characters
4291.A2 General
Prefer PQ4286 or PQ4287
4291.A3 Groups. Classes
e. g.
4291.A3W7 Women
4291.A5-Z Individual persons, A-Z
4293.A-Z Treatment and knowledge of special subjects, A-Z
4293.A2 Art: Painting, sculpture, etc.
4293.A76 Arthurian romances
4293.C65 Contradiction
4293.D55 Dinners and dining
4293.F35 Fantasy
4293.H5 History. Politics
Cf. PQ4278.A75 Political activity
Literature
4293.L2 General
Cf. PQ4283.A1+
4293.L3 Boccaccio's library
Special
4293.L4 Classical
Prefer PA85
(4293.L7) Dante
see PQ4346, PQ4382, PQ4437
4293.L72 Love
4293.N17 Naples
4293.N2 Nature
4293.P4 Philosophy. Religion. Ethics
Cf. PQ4289
4293.S3 Science
4293.W65 Women
Cf. PQ4291.A3W7 Women characters
4293.2 Textual criticism. Interpretation. Running commentaries
Prefer PQ4286+
4294 General. General special. Decameron
Special topics see PQ4293.A+
4295 Language. Style
4295.2 General
4295.6 Grammar

Individual authors
Individual authors and works to 1400
Boccaccio, Giovanni, 1313-1375.
Criticism, biography, etc.
Criticism and interpretation
Language. Style -- Continued
4295.8 Prose
4296 Versification
4297 Dictionaries. Concordances
Cf. PQ4277.A4
Bonagiunta da Lucca see PQ4299.B8
Boncompagno da Signa see PA8295.B5
4299.B3 Bonichi, Bindo di Bonico, d. 1337 (Table P-PZ40)
Bono, Giamboni see PQ4471.G4
Bonvesin da Riva see PQ4554.R55
Bosone de' Raffaelli da Gubbio see PQ4554.R15
4299.B6 Bovo d'Antona (Table P-PZ40)
Cf. PQ1431.B25+ Old French
4299.B7 Brendan, Saint. Legend
Brunetto, Latini see PQ4473.A1+
4299.B77 Buccio di Ranallo, d. 1363 (Table P-PZ40)
4299.B8 Buonagiunta da Lucca, b. ca. 1220 (Table P-PZ40)
Buovo d'Antona see PQ4299.B6
Busono da Gubbia see PQ4554.R15
4299.C14 Canigiani, Ristoro, d. 1380 (Table P-PZ40)
Cantari di Fiorabraccia e Ulivieri see PQ4471.F37
4299.C16 Carduino (Table P-PZ40)
4299.C17 Catonis disticha (Early Italian texts)
4299.C18 Cavalca, Domenico, d. 1342 (Table P-PZ40)
4299.C2 Cavalcanti, Guido, d. 1300 (Table P-PZ38)
Cf. PQ4410.C4 Dante on Cavalcanti
4299.C25 Cecco d' Ascoli, 1269-1327 (Table P-PZ38)
4299.C3 Ceffi, Filippo, fl. 1324 (Table P-PZ40)
Cento novelle antiche see PQ4253.A3+
Chanson de Roland see PQ1517+
Chiaro Davanzati see PQ4471.D3
4299.C4 Cielo d' Alcamo, 12th cent. (Table P-PZ40)
4299.C5 Cino da Pistoia, 1270-1337 (Table P-PZ40)
4299.C7 Colonne, Guido delle, 13th cent. (Table P-PZ40)
Possibly identical with the author of the Historia trojana
Not doubted by Bertoni, Il duecento, p. 74
Cf. Gaspary, History of early Italian literature, p. 58
For his works in Latin see PA8310.C6
4299.C8 Compagni, Dino ca. 1260-1324 (Table P-PZ40)
Cf. DG737.2
Conti di antichi cavalieri see PQ4253.A3+
4299.C84 Conto di Corciano

Individual authors
Individual authors and works to 1400 -- Continued
Dante Alighieri, 1265-1321
Complete works
4300.A1 By date
(4300.A2) By editor
4300.A3A-.A3Z Partial editions. Selected works, by editor, A-Z
4300.A4 Selections. Anthologies, etc., by editor
Cf. PQ4308 Minor works
Cf. PQ4311 Latin works
4300.A5 Selections: Almanacs. Birthday books. Thoughts, etc. By editor
Separate works
Divina commedia
Comprehensive editions
4301 Manuscript
4301.A1 Editions reproduced in facsimile
(4301.A2) Editions, reproduced in print, classed by date
4302 Printed editions
Subarrange by date (date letters)
Early to 1500
Incunabula, placed with Library of Congress collection of incunabula, are represented in the Dante Collection by block dummies
Facsimiles of incunabula are placed with the Dante collection
4302.A1-.A7 Collection of facsimiles of several editions
4302.A72 Foligno, Numeister, 1472
4302.A72f Facsimiles or reprints, numbered ...
4302.A721 Mantova, Giorgio, and Paolo, 1472.
4302.A721f Facsimiles or reprints, numbered ...
4302.A722 Jesi, Federico Veronese, 1472
4302.A722f Facsimiles or reprints
4302.A74 Napoli, Reussinger, 1474/75
4302.A74f Facsimiles or reprints.
4302.A77 Venezia, Vendelin da Spira, 1477
Commentary by Benevenuto da Imola (in reality that of Jacopo della Lana)
4302.A77f Facsimiles or reprints
4302.A771 Milano, Paolo Nido beato, 1477
4302.A771f Facsimiles or reprints
4302.A772 Napoli (Martino Morano?), 1477
4302.A772f Facsimiles or reprints
4302.A78 Venezia, Filippo, 1478
4302.A78f Facsimiles or reprints
4302.A81 Firenze, N. di Lorenzo della Magna, 1481
Commentary by C. Landino

Individual authors
Individual authors and works to 1400
Dante Alighieri, 1265-1321
Separate works
Divina commedia
Comprehensive editions
Printed editions.
Early to 1500.
Firenze, N. di Lorenzo della Magna, 1481

4302.A81f	Facsimiles or reprints
4302.A84	Vinegia, Octaviano Scoto da Monza, 1484 Commentary by C. Landino
4302.A84f	Facsimiles or reprints
4302.A87	Brescia, D. de Boninis, 1487 Commentary by C. Landino
4302.A87f	Facsimiles or reprints
4302.A91	Venezia, Benali, and Matthio da Parma, 1491 Commentary by C. Landino
4302.A91f	Facsimiles or reprints
4302.A911	Vinegia, Petro Cremonese dito Veronese, 1491 Commentary by C. Landino
4302.A911f	Facsimiles or reprints
4302.A93	Venezia, Matteo di Chodoca da Parma, 1493 Commentary by C. Landino
4302.A93f	Facsimiles or reprints
4302.A97	Venetia, Piero de Zuanne, 1497 Commentary by C. Landino
4302.A97f	Facsimiles or reprints
	Later editions
4302.B00-.B99	Editions of the 16th century, 1500-1599
4302.C00-.C99	Editions of the 17th century, 1600-1699 (only 3 ed.)
4302.D00-.D99	Editions of the 18th century, 1700-1799
4302.E00-.E99	Editions of the 19th century, 1800-1899
4302.F00-.F99	Editions of the 20th century, 1900-1999
4302.G00-.G99	Editions of the 21st century, 2000-2099
(4302.Z3A-.Z3Z)	Critical and annotated editions, by editor or commentator, A-Z
(4302.Z4)	School editions With PQ4302 if complete; if not, with PQ4303
4303.A-.Z3	Selections. Anthologies. Extracts, etc. (including school editions, if not complete), by editor, A-Z3
4303.Z5	Prospectus of editions, not published
4304	Editions of two parts
	Editions of parts
4305	L'Inferno

Individual authors
Individual authors and works to 1400
Dante Alighieri, 1265-1321
Separate works
Divina commedia
Comprehensive editions
Printed editions
Editions of parts.
L'Inferno

4305.A1 Complete editions. By date
4305.A3 School editions
4305.A4 Selections. anthologies. Extracts
4305.A5 Editions of several cantos
4305.C01-.C34 Editions of particular cantos. By number of canto
Canto I = PQ4305.C01; Canto II = PQ4305.C02; etc.
Subarrange by date
4305.Z2 Particular passages, episodes
4306 Purgatorio
4306.A1 Complete editions. By date
4306.A3 School editions
4306.A4 Selections. anthologies. Extracts
4306.A5 Editions of several cantos
4306.C01-.C33 Editions of particular cantos. By number of canto
Canto I = PQ4306.C01; Canto II = PQ4306.C02; etc.
Subarrange by date
4306.Z2 Particular passages, episodes
4307 Paradiso
4307.A1 Complete editions. By date
4307.A3 School editions
4307.A4 Selections. anthologies. Extracts
4307.A5 Editions of several cantos
4307.C01-.C33 Editions of particular cantos. By number of canto
Canto I = PQ4307.C01; Canto II = PQ4307.C02; etc.
Subarrange by date
4307.Z2 Particular passages, episodes
4308 Minor works
General
4308.A1 Comprehensive editions. By date
4308.A2A-.A2Z Editions of several works. By editor
Cf. PQ4311 Latin works
4308.A3A-.A3Z Selections. Quotations. Thoughts. By editor

Individual authors
Individual authors and works to 1400
Dante Alighieri, 1265-1321
Separate works
Minor works.
General. -- Continued
4308.A5-.Z3 Criticism (of minor works in general)
4308.Z5 Concordances, indexes, etc.
Separate works
4309 Poems (Rime. Canzoniere)
4309.A1 Collections and selections. By date
4309.A2 Particular selections. By editor
e.g. from Convito or Vita nuova
(4309.A3) Posthumous poems see PQ4309.A1
4309.A4 Particular poems (By first word of poem, then by author)
4309.A6 Spurious poems
Cf. PQ4326.P6
4309.A7-.Z3 Criticism
4310 Il convito (Il Convivio. Amoroso Convivio)
4310.C2 Editions
Separate editions of poems see PQ4309+
4310.C4 Criticism
Cf. PQ4403+ Astronomical treatises
Sette salmi see PQ4326.S2
La vita nuova
4310.V2 Editions
4310.V4 Criticism
4311 Latin works
4311.A1 Collections and selections. By date
4311.A2 Translations into Italian
Other languages see PQ4314
Criticism
4311.A3 General
4311.A4 Special
e.g. Language
4311.A5 Concordances, indexes, etc.
Separate works
De monarchia
4311.D2 Editions. By date
4311.D3 Italian translations
Other languages see PQ4313+
4311.D4 Criticism
De vulgari eloquentia
4311.D6 Editions. By date
4311.D7 Italian translations
Other languages see PQ4313+

Individual authors
Individual authors and works to 1400
Dante Alighieri, 1265-1321
Latin works
Separate works
De vulgari eloquentia -- Continued
4311.D8 Criticism
Eclogae
4311.E2 Editions. By date
4311.E3 Italian translations
Other languages see PQ4313+
4311.E4 Criticism
4311.E6-.E8 Epistolae
4311.E6 Editions. By date
4311.E6A-.E6Z Individual letters. By addressee, A-Z
4311.E8 Criticism, including discussion of spurious letters
Quaestio de aqua et terra see PQ4326.Q2
(4312) Texts with translations
Prefer in general PQ4300-4311
For translations other than English, French, or German, prefer PQ4314-4324
Translations
4313.A-Z Polyglot translations. By editor, A-Z
4314 Italian
(4314.A2A-.A2Z) Modern Italian (including prose versions) see PQ4327
Translations of Latin works see PQ4311
4314.A5-Z Dialects, A-Z
4315 English (Table PQ3)
4316 French (Table PQ3)
4317 German (Table PQ3)
4318 Spanish (Table PQ3)
4319 Portuguese (Table PQ3)
Other languages
Other European languages
4320.A-Z Non-Slavic, A-Z
4320.B3 Basque (Table PQ1)
4320.C2 Catalan (Table PQ1)
Celtic
4320.C3 Breton (Table PQ1)
4320.C4 Cornish (Table PQ1)
4320.C5 Gaelic (Table PQ1)
4320.C6 Irish (Table PQ1)
4320.C7 Manx (Table PQ1)
4320.C8 Welsh (Table PQ1)
4320.D2 Dutch (Table PQ1)

Individual authors
Individual authors and works to 1400
Dante Alighieri, 1265-1321
Translations.
Other languages.
Other European languages
Non-Slavic, A-Z -- Continued

4320.F5 Finnish (Table PQ1)
4320.G2 Greek (Table PQ1)
4320.H8 Hungarian (Table PQ1)
4320.L2 Latin (Table PQ1)
4320.P7 Provençal (Table PQ1)
4320.R8 Romanian (Table PQ1)
Scandinavian
4320.S2 Danish. Dano-Norwegian (Table PQ1)
4320.S4 Icelandic (Table PQ1)
4320.S6 Swedish (Table PQ1)
4320.Y53 Yiddish (Table PQ1)
4321.A-Z Slavic, A-Z
4321.B3 Bohemian. Czech (Table PQ1)
4321.B6 Bulgarian (Table PQ1)
4321.C3 Croatian (Table PQ1)
4321.L3 Latvian (Table PQ1)
4321.L7 Lithuanian (Table PQ1)
4321.P3 Polish (Table PQ1)
4321.R2 Russian (Table PQ1)
4321.R7 Ruthenian. Ukrainian (Table PQ1)
4321.S2 Serbian (Table PQ1)
4321.S6 Slovakian (Table PQ1)
4321.S8 Slovenian (Table PQ1)
Ukrainian see PQ4321.R7
4321.W2 Wendic (Table PQ1)
Languages other than European
4322.A-Z Asian languages, A-Z
Subarrange each by Table PQ1
4323.A-Z Oceanic, African, or American Indian languages, A-Z
Subarrange each by Table PQ1
4324.A-Z Artificial or mixed (Pidgin or creole) languages, A-Z
Subarrange each by Table PQ1
(4325) Artificial languages (Esperanto, Ido, etc.)
see PM8001-8099
4326 Doubtful or spurious works
4326.A1 Comprehensive collections
Separate works
Catechismo cattolico see PQ4326.C8

Individual authors
Individual authors and works to 1400
Dante Alighieri, 1265-1321
Doubtful or spurious works
Separate works -- Continued

4326.C8 Credo (Professione di fede)
Poem in terza rima, beginning "Io scrissi gia d'amor"
4326.C9 Nuovo credo
Beginning "Credo in un solo omnipotente Dio"
(4326.D4) Detto d'amore
see PQ4471.D4
(4326.E2) Epistolae
see PQ4311.E6-8
(4326.F5) Il fiore
see PQ4471.F397
4326.L2 Laude in onore di Nostra Donna
Nuovo credo see PQ4326.C9
(4326.P6) Poems
see PQ4309.A6
Professions di fede see PQ4326.C8
4326.Q2 Questio de aqua et terra
4326.Q4 Criticism
4326.S2 Sette salmi penitenziali
4326.S4 Criticism
Tenzone di Dante con Forese Donati see PQ4556.T317
4327 Modern Italian versions
Including prose versions
4327.3 Dramatizations
4327.5 Adaptations, imitations, etc.
Cf. PQ4315.9, PQ4316.9, etc., Popular and juvenile adaptations
4327.8 Parodies. Travesties
4328 Translations and translators (as subject)
4328.A2 General
4328.A3-Z By language, A-Z
Under each:
.x *General*
.x2A-.x2Z *By translator, A-Z*
4328.5 Dante and art
4329 Illustrations
Illustrated editions, see texts, with added entry for notable illustrators
For history of Dante portraits, illustrations, etc. see PQ4366+
Dante's knowledge of art see PQ4430

Individual authors
Individual authors and works to 1400
Dante Alighieri, 1265-1321 -- Continued
(4329.8) Dante and music
see ML80.D2
Librettos based upon Dante's works
see ML
Music composed in honor of Dante
see M
Music composed for Dante's works
see M
Biography and criticism
(4330) Bibliography
see Z8215
4331 Periodicals and societies
Use successive cutter numbers for special periodicals or societies under each language
4331.A1-.A29 Italian
Societá "Dante Alighieri" see DG402
4331.A3-.A39 English and American
4331.A4-.A49 French
4331.A5-.A59 German
4331.A7-Z Other
4331.5 Congresses
4332 Collected papers, essays, studies, etc.
Collections for special anniversaries see PQ4363
4332.Z5 Pamphlet collections. By date-letters
e. g.
4332.Z5E64 1864
4332.Z5F21 1921
Collections of individual authors
see PQ4390, or special subject
4333 Dictionaries, indexes, etc.
Class here general encyclopedic dictionaries only
Special dictionaries with subject
Concordances with language dictionaries see PQ4464
Dictionaries of historic characters see PQ4424
Dictionaries of proper names see PQ4464
Dictionaries of quotations
see PQ4303, PQ4308.A3 PQ4315.17, etc.
4334 Manuals, introductions, etc.
Cf. PQ4335+
General works
4335 English
4336 French
4337 German

Individual authors
Individual authors and works to 1400
Dante Alighieri, 1265-1321
Biography and criticism
General works -- Continued
Italian

4338 Early to 1800
4338.A2 Collections. By date
4338.A2A-.A2Z Translations. By language
4338.A3-Z Individual authors
4339 1801-
4340 Other languages. By author
4341 Addresses, essays, lectures
Collections see PQ4332
Biography
General see PQ4335+
4342 Miscellaneous details, etc.
Sources. Documents, etc.
4343 General and miscellaneous
Early biographies to 1800 see PQ4338
4344 Compilations of autobiographical and contemporaneous allusions
(4345) Letters
see PQ4311.E6+, PQ4315.65, etc.
4346 Treatises on sources, including early biographies
Cf. PQ4382 History of Dante studies to 1600
4347 Family. Ancestry. Name. Arms
4348 Birth (date and place)
4349 Youth. Education
4350 Love. Marriage. Relation to women
4350.A2 General
Cf. PQ4409.W8
4350.A5-Z Special
For individual characters, prefer PQ4410
(4350.D7) La donna gentile
see PQ4410.D7
4350.G4 Gemma Donati (wife of Dante)
4350.G5 Gentucca
Matelda see PQ4410.M3
4351 Public life
4351.2 Military service. Political missions, etc.
Cf. PQ4422
4352 Banishment. Exile
4353 Homes and haunts. Travels
4353.A1 General
4353.A2 Italy in general, contemporary Italy
4353.A5-Z Other places, regions, etc., A-Z

Individual authors
Individual authors and works to 1400
Dante Alighieri, 1265-1321
Biography and criticism
Biography
Homes and haunts. Travels
Other places, regions, etc., A-Z -- Continued
Avellana, Fonte (Monastery) see PQ4353.C4
Benaco (Lago) see PQ4353.G3
4353.B7 Bologna
4353.C2 Calabria
4353.C3 Catona
4353.C4 Catria, Monte
Cf. Paradiso, XXI, 106-110
4353.C7 Corvo, Santa Croce del (Monastery)
Cf. PQ4353.L8
4353.F6 Florence
4353.F7 Forli
4353.G3 Garda, Lado di
4353.L3 Lagarina, Val
4353.L6 Lucca
4353.L7 Luni
4353.L8 Lunigiana
see also Corvo
4353.P2 Padua
4353.P4 Paris
4353.P5 Pisa
4353.P7 Pola
4353.R3 Ravenna
Cf. PQ4355
4353.S5 Siena
4353.T8 Tuscany
see also Florence
4353.U3 Udine
4353.V4 Venice
4353.V5 Verona
4355 Last years. Death
Cf. PQ4353.R3 Ravenna
4355.2 Tomb at Ravenna
4355.6 Treatment of his remains
4355.8 Epitaphs
4356 Legends and traditions concerning Dante's life
4356.5 Age of Dante. Renaissance. Florence and Italy
Cf. PQ4353 Homes and haunts
Relations to contemporaries
4357 General works

Individual authors
Individual authors and works to 1400
Dante Alighieri, 1265-1321
Biography and criticism
Biography
Relations to contemporaries -- Continued

4358.A-Z Individual, A-Z
Subarrange each by Table P-PZ50
4358.P4 Petrarca
4360 Personality. Character
4360.A1 Outward appearance
Cf. PQ4366+ Iconography
4360.A2 Physical qualities. Eyesight, etc.
4360.A3 Character. Pride, etc.
Other qualities
(4360.A4) Dante as patriot
Prefer PQ4422-PQ4424, Dante's knowledge and treatment of politics and history
(4360.A5) Dante as a statesman
Prefer PQ4351, Political missions
Cf. PQ4422 Political and social views
(4360.A6) Dante as a scholar
Prefer PQ4427-4429, Dante's knowledge of literature and languages
(4360.A7) Dante as a soldier
Prefer PQ4351, Dante's military service
4360.A8 Dante as a teacher
(4360.A9) Dante as a lawyer
Prefer PQ4432.L3, Dante's knowledge of law
Anniversaries. Celebrations
4362 History and description
4362.A1 General
4362.A15 Special. By date
Prefer PQ4363, Publications
4362.A2 Early before 1821. By date
4362.A21-.A99 1821-1899
4362.B00-.B99 1900-1999
4363 Publications in honor of special anniversaries
4363.A2 Early to 1821. By date
4363.A21-.A99 1821-1899
Under each:
.xA-.xZ29 *By society, institution or title*
.xZ3-.xZ99 *By individual author, alphabetically*
For collections of Dante studies, see PQ4332

Individual authors
Individual authors and works to 1400
Dante Alighieri, 1265-1321
Biography and criticism.
Biography.
Anniversaries. Celebrations.
Publications in honor of special anniversaries
4363.B00-.B99 1900-1999
Under each:
.xA-.xZ29 By society, institution or title
.xZ3-.xZ99 By individual author, alphabetically
4364 Memorials. Testimonials to Dante's genius other than centennial
Poetry
4364.A2 Collections, including collections of both poetry and prose
4364.A5-Z Individual authors or titles
Prefer PQ-PT for well known authors
(4365) Prose
Prefer PQ4332, PQ4341, PQ4390
Iconography
4366 General works. History and criticism of illustrations of Dante's works
For illustrated editions of Dante see PQ4301+
Collections of illustrations alone see PQ4329
(4366.9.A-Z) Illustrations by special artists, A-Z
4367 Portraits
4367.A2 General works
4367.A7-Z Special portraits. By artist, A-Z
e. g.
4367.G5 Giotto
4367.T7 Torrigiani bust and death mask
4368 Monuments
4368.A2 General
4368.A5-Z By place
4368.9 Medals and medallions
4369.A-Z Museums. Relics. Exhibitions. By place, A-Z
Exhibitions by place and date
(4370) Fiction, drama, etc., based upon Dante's life
Prefer classification by author
Dante in England, Germany, etc. see PQ4385.A+
4371 Study and teaching
Authorship
4372 General
4373 General special
4373.5 Autographs. Manuscripts
Discussion of value of manuscripts see PQ4435+

Individual authors
Individual authors and works to 1400
Dante Alighieri, 1265-1321
Biography and criticism
Authorship
Autographs
Catalogs and lists of manuscripts see Z8215
4374 Special topics (not A-Z)
e.g. title of the Divina commedia; for originality of the conception, see PQ4392 Origin and genesis of Divina commedia
Sources see PQ4393+
4375 Precursors
(4376) Associates. Followers. School
Prefer: PQ4357+
Cf. PQ4071+ History of Italian literature: Tuscan period
(4377) Allusions
Prefer PQ4344, Sources of biography: Autobiographical and other contemporaneous allusions
4378 Chronology of works and Divina commedia
Cf. PQ4404 Chronology of Dante's vision
Criticism and interpretation
History of the study and appreciation of Dante
Cf. PQ4331+ PQ4362+
4380 General (including Dante studies in Italy)
4381 General special
4381.2 Influence of Dante in Italy and elsewhere
Special countries see PQ4385.A+
Special subjects see PQ4411.2+
By period
4382 Early to 1600 (including history, criticism, and biography of early commentators)
4382.A-.Z3 General
4382.Z5A-.Z5Z Individual (Italian only)
For criticism of particular commentators see PQ4437+
Dante on his own works see PQ4344
Foreign scholars see PQ4385.A+
4383 Later, 1600-
4383.A-.Z3 General
4383.Z5A-.Z5Z Individual (Italian only)
For criticism of particular commentators see PQ4437+
Dante on his own works see PQ4344
Foreign scholars see PQ4385.A+

Individual authors
Individual authors and works to 1400
Dante Alighieri, 1265-1321
Biography and criticism
Criticism and interpretation
History of the study and appreciation of Dante -- Continued

4384.A-Z Special regions or places in Italy, A-Z
e. g.
4384.F5 Florence
4384.V5 Venice
4385.A-Z By country, A-Z
For Italy see PQ4380+
4385.F8 Dante in France
4385.F8A-.F8Z3 General
4385.F8Z5-.F8Z9 Special scholars (alphabetically)
4385.G7 Dante in Great Britain
4385.G7A-.G7Z3 General
4385.G7Z5-.G7Z9 Special scholars (alphabetically)
4386 Special points of view
e.g. Humanists, Clergy, etc.
Special topics
(4388) Criticism of particular commentaries or Dante students
see the commentators, PQ4437+
4389 Other

Treatises
Dealing with all the works of Dante or confined to the Divina commedia, provided that they are exclusively or prevailingly devoted to criticism, appreciation, or interpretation
Commentaries with text are classed with the editions; references are to be made in the respective chronological divisions provided for the commentators
For treatises on the Minor works in general, see PQ4308; on any particular works, see PQ4309+
For works combining biography and literary criticism see PQ4335+
General
4390.A2 Early (written before 1800)
Cf. PQ4382+
4390.A5-Z Recent, 1800-
Relation to and comparison with other authors
4391.A1 Collective
4391.A2-Z Individual, A-Z

Individual authors
Individual authors and works to 1400
Dante Alighieri, 1265-1321
Biography and criticism.
Criticism and interpretation.
Treatises. -- Continued
(4391.9) Outlines, summaries, arguments, etc.
See PQ4390 and PQ4402.Z7
Special
4392 Origin and genesis of the Divina commedia
Cf. PQ4372+ Authorship
Cf. PQ4404 Chronology of the vision
Sources
4393 General
4394 Special
e.g. Medieval visions, Celtic and other sources and parallels
Philosophical sources see PQ4413
Theological sources see PQ4417
Purport. Scope. Unity
(4395) General
See PQ4390
4396 Special
(4397) Philosophy. Esthetics
see PQ4390
Cf. PQ4412+
Technique. Structure. Mechanism
Cf. PQ4401+ Cosmography
4398 General
4399 Special
Cosmography. Topography. Itineraries
4401 General
Cf. PQ4326.Q2
Special
4402 Itineraries
4402.A-.Z3 General
(4402.Z4) Inferno
see PQ4443
(4402.Z5) Purgatorio
see PQ4447
(4402.Z6) Paradiso
see PQ4451
4402.Z7 Tables
Astronomical treatises
4403 General
Prefer PQ4401
Cf. PQ4310.C4

Individual authors
Individual authors and works to 1400
Dante Alighieri, 1265-1321
Biography and criticism.
Criticism and interpretation.
Cosmography. Topography. Itineraries.
Special.
Astronomical treatises -- Continued
Special
4404 Chronology of the Vision
4405 Other
e.g. Southern cross
Symbolism. Allegory
4406 General
4407.A-Z Special, A-Z
Cf. PQ4410 Individual characters and persons
4407.F8 Furies (Erinyes)
4407.N8 Numbers
4407.T5 Three beasts
4407.T73 Travel
4407.T76 Tree of life
4407.V4 Il veltro (The greyhound)
Characters and persons
General see PQ4390.A2+
4409.A-Z Groups, classes, A-Z
4409.A6 Angels
4409.C6 Clergy
4409.F37 Fathers
4409.H3 Heretics
(4409.H5) Historical
see PQ4424
4409.H9 Hypocrites
4409.I5 Infidels
4409.L9 Lustful
4409.M6 Monsters
(4409.M9) Mythological
see PQ4421
4409.N62 Nobility
4409.P3 Pagans
4409.P64 Poets
(4409.P7) Popes
see PQ4424.P7
4409.W8 Women
Cf. PQ4350 Relation to women
4410 Individual characters and persons
e. g.
4410.B3 Beatrice

Individual authors
Individual authors and works to 1400
Dante Alighieri, 1265-1321
Biography and criticism
Criticism and interpretation
Characters and persons
Individual characters and persons -- Continued

4410.B5 Beccheria
4410.B57 Bertran, de Born
Buonconte da Montefeltro see PQ4410.M6
4410.C2 Cacciaguida
4410.C3 Cato
4410.C4 Cavalcanti
4410.C7 Celestinus V., pope
4410.D7 Donati
4410.F7 Folquet de Marseille
4410.F8 Francesca de Rimini
4410.F84 Francis, of Assisi, Saint, 1182-1226
Gherardesca, Ugolino, conte della see PQ4410.U5
4410.G5 Giuseppe della Scala
Guido da Montefeltro see PQ4410.M6
4410.L7 Lucia, Saint
4410.L8 Lucifer
4410.M2 Malaspia family
4410.M27 Manfred, King of Naples and Sicily
Mary, Virgin see PQ4419.M2
4410.M3 Matelda
4410.M6 Montefeltro, Guido, Conte, and Buonconte Montefeltro
4410.P3 Pargoletta
4410.P554 Pia de' Tolomei
4410.P585 Pier delle Vigne
4410.P6 Pier Pettinagno
4410.P62 Pilate, Pontius
4410.S3 Satan
4410.U3 Uberti, Farinati degli
4410.U5 Ugolino, Conte
4410.U7 Ulysses (Ulisse)
4410.V3 Vanni Fucci bestia
4410.V5 Virgil

Relation to special subjects
Treatment, knowledge, influence, etc.
General or miscellaneous see PQ4390.A2+
Philosophy. Ethics. Psychology

4412 General
Cf. PQ4310.C4 Criticism of Convivio

Individual authors
Individual authors and works to 1400
Dante Alighieri, 1265-1321
Biography and criticism
Criticism and interpretation
Relation to special subjects
Philosophy. Ethics. Psychology -- Continued

4413 Special
e.g. Sources: Aristoteles, Thomas Aquinas, etc.
Cf. PQ4393, PQ4417

4414 Ethics
For moral system of Inferno or Purgatorio, see PQ4443, PQ4447
For Dante's doctrine of sin, hell, or purgatory see PQ4418

Theology. Religion. Mysticism

4416 General

4417 Special
e.g. Sources and relation to the Theologians: Dante and St. Paul; Dante and Thomas Aquinas; Dante and St. Bernard

4418 Special doctrines
Prefer, wherever possible, PQ4443-PQ4444, PQ4447-PQ4448, PQ4451-PQ4452

4419.A-Z Other special, A-Z
4419.A65 Apocalypse
4419.B5 Bible
4419.C4 Church and state
Prefer PQ4423-4424
4419.C64 Conversion
4419.D4 Deadly sins
4419.D42 Death
4419.D47 Desire
4419.E33 Eden
4419.E7 Eschatology
4419.F87 Future life
4419.G45 Generosity
4419.G65 Good
4419.G73 Grace
4419.L65 Love (Theology)
4419.M2 Mary, Virgin
4419.M7 Monasticism
4419.O34 Occultism
4419.P47 Perseverance (Theology)
Popes
see PQ4422 and PQ4424.P7
Individual popes see PQ4410

Individual authors
Individual authors and works to 1400
Dante Alighieri, 1265-1321
Biography and criticism
Criticism and interpretation
Relation to special subjects
Theology. Religion. Mysticism
Special
Other special, A-Z
4419.P74 Prophecies
4419.R4 Renouncement
4419.R47 Retribution
4419.T74 Trinity
Mythology. Folklore
4421 General
(4421.Z5) Particular characters
see PQ4410
4422 Political and social views (including theory of church and state, imperialist doctrines, temporal power of the popes, etc.)
Cf. PQ4311.D4 De monarchia (Criticism)
Cf. PQ4351 Political missions
History
4423.A2 General
4423.A3 Ancient
4423.A5-.Z3 Contemporaneous (Times of Dante)
4424 Persons
4424.A2 General
4424.A5-.Z3 Particular groups, A-Z
e. g.
4424.P7 Popes (Historical sketches or discussions of popes figuring in the Divina commedia)
For theory of church and state see PQ4422
(4424.Z5) Particular persons (Popes, emperors, etc.)
see PQ4410
Geography
4425 General
4425.5 Special
Prefer PQ4352+ Life in exile, journeys
For treatment and knowledge of specific places see PQ4432.A+
4427 Literature
4427.A2 General
4427.A5-Z Special, A-Z
4427.C53 Classical literature
4427.P7 Provençal (Troubadours)

Individual authors
Individual authors and works to 1400
Dante Alighieri, 1265-1321
Biography and criticism
Criticism and interpretation
Relation to special subjects
Literature
Special, A-Z
Provençal ... -- Continued
Particular troubadours see PQ4410

4429 Languages
4429.A2 General
Cf. PQ4311.D6+ De vulgari eloquentia
Cf. PQ4456+ Dante's language and style
4429.A5-Z Special
4429.A5 Arabic
4429.G5 Greek
4429.H5 Hebrew
4429.L5 Latin
4429.P7 Provençal
Dante and art
4430 Painting, sculpture, etc.
Cf. PQ4329 Illustrations of Dante's works
Cf. PQ4366+ Iconography
(4431) Music
see ML80.D2
4432.A-Z Other, A-Z
4432.A6 Alchemy (Chemistry)
Astronomy see PQ4401+
4432.A8 Astrology
4432.B7 Botany
4432.C37 Casentino (Italy)
4432.C45 Chivalry
4432.C5 Citizenship
Crafts see PQ4432.T4
Darkness see PQ4432.L5
4432.D74 Dreams
4432.E2 Economics
4432.E9 Eye (The human)
4432.F53 Florence
4432.F55 Flowers
4432.F75 Friendship
4432.G6 Geology
Geometry see PQ4432.M3
4432.H4 Heraldry
4432.I57 Intellect
4432.L3 Law

Individual authors
Individual authors and works to 1400
Dante Alighieri, 1265-1321
Biography and criticism
Criticism and interpretation
Relation to special subjects
Other, A-Z -- Continued

4432.L5 Light and darkness
4432.L6 Love
4432.M25 Magic
4432.M3 Mathematics
4432.M5 Medicine
4432.M56 Metaphysics
4432.N3 Nature
4432.N4 Naval art and science
4432.N8 Numbers. Symbolism of numbers
4432.O68 Optics
4432.O74 Orient
4432.P37 Paradox
4432.P4 Physics
4432.P7 Prophecies
4432.S3 Science
4432.S44 Self
4432.S46 Senses and sensation
4432.S52 Sicily
4432.S55 Silence
4432.S6 Spain
4432.T4 Technical arts
4432.T55 Time
4432.V5 Visions
4432.Z7 Zoology
4433 Miscellaneous

Textual criticism. Interpretation

4435 General

4435.A2 Discussion of value of manuscripts and early editions

Cf. PQ4329 Illustrations of Dante's works
Cf. PQ4430+ Dante and art
Cf. Z8215 Catalogs and lists of manuscripts

Special manuscripts

Special libraries under place, with successive cutter numbers for particular libraries if there are several, e.g. Manuscripts of Florence, .F2-7; Biblioteca Baldonetti, .F21

For discussion of variant readings in interpretation of particular passages, see PQ4442, PQ4446, PQ4450, PQ4454

Individual authors
Individual authors and works to 1400
Dante Alighieri, 1265-1321
Biography and criticism
Criticism and interpretation
Textual criticism. Interpretation
General
Discussion of value of manuscripts and early editions
Special manuscripts -- Continued

4435.A5-.Z3 Italian
Subdivide by place, A-Z
4435.Z5E2-.Z5E9 English
4435.Z5F2-.Z5F9 French
4435.Z5G2-.Z5G9 German
4435.Z9A-.Z9Z Other. By country, A-Z

Interpretation
Running commentaries, or notes without text, on all the works, or the Divina commedia alone.
Commentaries with texts, see PQ4300-PQ4311

4437 14th-16th centuries
Cf. PQ4390.A2 Earlier general treatises on Dante
(4437.A2) Criticism of early commentators in general
see PQ4382
4437.A5-Z Particular commentators or works, A-Z
Under each:
.x Editions. By date
.xA2-.xA49 Translations. By language and date
.xA7-.xZ Criticism
For history of study and appreciation of Dante by individual scholars, see PQ4382, PQ4383, PQ4385
4437.A58 Aligieri, Jacopo, 14th cent.
4437.A6 Alighieri, Pietro di Dante, d. 1364
4437.A7 Anonymo Fiorentino
4437.B53 Biblioteca ambrosiana. Manuscript. S.P.5
4437.G8 Guido, da Pisa, 14th cent.
4437.O8 L'ottimo commento
4438 17th-18th centuries
19th-20th centuries
4439 General
Brief expositions, summaries, arguments, etc.
see PQ4390.A2+
Cf. PQ4402.Z7
(4439.9) Commentaries for schools
see PQ4439

Individual authors
Individual authors and works to 1400
Dante Alighieri, 1265-1321
Biography and criticism
Criticism and interpretation
Textual criticism. Interpretation
Interpretation
19th-20th centuries -- Continued

(4440) Controversial literature
see PQ4390
4441 Particular cantos (not confined to a special part of the Divina commedia)
4442 Particular passages (not confined to a special part of the Divina commedia)
Inferno
Including exposition of moral system of Inferno
4443 General (comprising all or several cantos)
4444 Special subjects (not A-Z)
Prefer PQ4398+
For exposition of cantos or passages devoted to special characters see PQ4410
4445 Special cantos, arranged by number and commentator
e. g.
4445 1st .C3 Casini, Il canto I dell' Inferno
4446 Particular passages. By author
Purgatorio
4447 General (comprising all or several cantos)
4448 Special subjects (not A-Z)
Prefer PQ4398+
For exposition of cantos or passages devoted to special characters see PQ4410
4449 Special cantos, arranged by number and commentator
e. g.
4449 10th .C3 Campanini, Il canto X del Purgatorio
4450 Particular passages. By author
Paradiso
4451 General (comprising all or several cantos)
4452 Special subjects (not A-Z)
Prefer PQ4398+
For exposition of cantos or passages devoted to special characters see PQ4410

Individual authors
Individual authors and works to 1400
Dante Alighieri, 1265-1321
Biography and criticism
Criticism and interpretation
Textual criticism. Interpretation
Interpretation
19th-20th centuries
Paradiso -- Continued

4453 Special cantos, arranged by number and commentator
e. g.
4453 8th .R6 Rocca, Il canto VIII del Paradiso
4454 Particular passages. By author
Minor works see PQ4308
(4455) Tables. Outlines. Graphic illustrations
see PQ4402.Z7
Language. Style
4456 General
4457 Special topics (not A-Z)
e.g. Figures, similes, etc. Use of works
Grammar
4458 General
4459 Special (not A-Z)
e.g. Phonology, Word-order, Latinisms, etc.
4461 Dialect
4462 Versification. Rime, etc.
4463 Prose
4464 Dictionaries of language, concordances, indexes, quotations
Including dictionaries of proper names.
Cf. PQ4308.Z5, PQ4311.A5, PQ4333
4471.D1 Dante da Maiano, fl. 1290 (Table P-PZ40)
Genuineness of poems disputed
4471.D3 Davanzati, Chiaro, 13th cent. (Table P-PZ40)
De Barllam et de Jossaffa see PQ4265.B34
4471.D35 De Galerijs, Giovanni, 14th cent. (Table P-PZ40)
4471.D37 Del Bene, Sennuccio, d. 1349 (Table P-PZ40)
Del Pecora, Jacopo, da Montepulciano, 14th cent. see PQ4474.P5
4471.D4 Detto d'amore
Adaptation of the Roman de la rose; by some authorities ascribed to "Duranti" or "ser Duranti" author of Il fiore
Cf. PQ4471.F397
4471.D42-.D423 Detto gel gatto lupesco (Table P-PZ43)
Dino Compagni see PQ4299.C8
Dino Frescobaldi see PQ4471.F8

Individual authors
Individual authors and works to 1400 -- Continued

4471.D5 Disponsazione e feste della Nostra Donna
4471.D66 Dondi dell'Orologio, Giovanni, 1318?-1389 (Table P-PZ40)
(4471.D8) Durante, Ser. Il fiore
see PQ4471.F397
4471.E5 Enselmino, of Treviso, 14th cent. (Table P-PZ40)
Supposed author of Plainte de la Vierge.
Entrée de Spagne
Composed late in the 13th century by an anonymous author from Padua; written in the Franco-Italian dialect, revised and completed by Niccolò de Verona during the first half of the 14th century
see PQ1459.E74+
4471.E6 Enzo, King, 1225-1272 (Table P-PZ40)
4471.E75 Espo toscano
4471.F2 Faitinelli, Pietro, d. 1349
4471.F25 Fatti di Cesare
For French translation (Faits des Romaine) see PQ1461.F19+
Fazio degli Uberti see PQ4556.U2
4471.F35 Febusso e Breusso
4471.F36 Festa et storia di Sancta Caterina
Federico II see PQ4471.F97
4471.F37 Fierabraccia e Ulivieri (Metrical romance)
Fierabras see PQ1461.F3+
4471.F375 Figghiu du mercanti
4471.F38 Filippo da Siena, fra, d. 1422? (Table P-PZ40)
Fiorabraccia e Ulivieri see PQ4471.F37
4471.F39 Fioravante (Prose romance)
4471.F397 Il fiore
Adaptation of the Roman de la rose by Durante or "Ser Durante," who is considered by some authorities as identical with Dante.
4471.F4 Fiore di virtu
Original by Tomasso Gozzadini, 13th century; revised in the 14th century
Fiorentino, Ser Giovanni see PQ4472.G2
Fioretti di San Francesco see BX4700.F63
4471.F45 Fiori e vita di filosafi e d'altri savi
4471.F5 Fiorio e Biancofiore (Metrical romance)
4471.F6 Folgore da San Gimignano, fl. 1309-1317
Francesco d'Assisi, Saint see BX4700.F6+
4471.F74 Francesco Novello e la reconquista di Padova
Francesco da Barberino see PQ4265.B3
4471.F8 Frescobaldi, Dino, d. 1300 (Table P-PZ40)
4471.F9 Frescobaldi, Matteo, d. 1348 (Table P-PZ40)

Individual authors
Individual authors and works to 1400 -- Continued
4471.F95 Frezzi, Federigo, d. 1416 (Table P-PZ40)
4471.F97 Friedrich II, Emperor of Germany, 1194-1250 (Table P-PZ40)
4471.G12 Garzo, ca. 1167-ca. 1271 (Table P-PZ40)
4471.G14 Gentile da Ravenna, d. 1404 (Table P-PZ40)
Gherardo Pattechio see PQ4474.P4
4471.G2 Giacomino Pugliese, fl. 1239-1246 (Table P-PZ40)
4471.G3 Giacomo da Lentini, 13th cent. (Table P-PZ40)
4471.G4 Giamboni, Bono, fl. 1264 (Table P-PZ40)
Cf. BJ1241+ Ethics
Gianni, Alfani see PQ4265.A5
4471.G46 Gianni, Lapo, fl. 1298-1328 (Table P-PZ40)
4471.G5 Gianni dei Ricevuti, Lapo, fl. 1328 (Table P-PZ40)
4472.G17 Giovanni dalle Celle, 14th cent. (Table P-PZ40)
4472.G2 Giovanni Fiorentino, 14th cent. (Table P-PZ40)
Imitator of Boccaccio in his collection of tales called Il Pecorone, one of which is the source of Shakespeare's Merchant of Venice
Gozzadini, Tommaso see PQ4471.F4
Gui de Nanteuil see PQ1477.G6+
Guido delle Colonne see PQ4299.C7
Guido Guinicelli see PQ4472.G5
Guido Orlandi see PQ4474.O7
4472.G4 Guilelmus, Apuliensis, 12th cent. (Table P-PZ40)
4472.G5 Guinizelli, Guido, d. 1276 (Table P-PZ38)
4472.G7 Guittone d'Arezzo, d. 1294 (Table P-PZ40)
4472.I43 Inghilfredi, 13th cent. (Table P-PZ40)
4472.I5 Intelligenza (Poem), 13th cent.
4472.J3 Jacopone da Todi (Jacopo dei Benedetti), 1230-1306 (Table P-PZ38)
4472.L2 Lamento della sposa padovano, 13th cent.
4472.L3 Lancellotto (Poem)
4472.L4 Lancia, Andrea, ca. 1280- ca. 1360 (Table P-PZ40)
Cf. PQ4437 Dante commentators
Lapo Gianni die Ricevuti see PQ4471.G5
Lapo Gianni die Ricevuti see PQ4471.G5
Latini, Brunetto, 1220-1295
4473.A1 Collected works. By date
Il tesoro. Li livres dou tresor see AE2
4473.A2 Il tesoretto (Poem)
4473.A3 Il favolello (Poem didattico)
Spurious works
4473.A4 Fiore di filosofi
4473.A5-.A59 Other
4473.A5 Il pataffio

Individual authors
Individual authors and works to 1400
Latini, Brunetto, 1220-1295
Spurious works.
Other.
4473.A55 Mare amoroso
4473.A6-.A79 Translations
4473.A8-Z Biography and criticism
4474.L42 Leggenda di Santa Maria egiziaca
4474.L44 Leggenda di Vergogna (Poem)
Libro dei sette savi see PQ4556.S4
Libro di novelle di bel parlar gentile (Il novellino) see PQ4253.A3+
4474.L8 Lusignacca (Novella in verse)
4474.M27 Matteo dei Libri
4474.M3 Mazzei, Lapo, d. 1412 (Table P-PZ40)
4474.M4 Mezzani, Menghino, 14th cent. (Table P-PZ40)
4474.M68 Monte, Andrea, 13th cent. (Table P-PZ40)
4474.M7 Montemagno, Buonaccorso da, fl. 1364 (Table P-PZ40)
4474.N35 Nadal, Giovanni Girolamo, ca. 1334-ca. 1382 (Table P-PZ40)
4474.N5 Nicola da Verona, fl. 1343 (Table P-PZ40)
Prise de la Pampelune
see Entrée de Spagne
4474.N8 Novella d'un barone di Faraona
Il novellino see PQ4253.A3+
4474.N83 Novelletta del mago e del Guideo
4474.N9 Novello, Girardo, 13th cent. (Table P-PZ40)
4474.O5 Onesto da Bologna (Table P-PZ40)
4474.O7 Orlandi, Guido (Table P-PZ40)
4474.O85 Orlando (Poem), ca. 1380
Source of Pulci's "Morgante"
4474.P13 Pagliaresi, Neri, d. 1406 (Table P-PZ40)
4474.P16 Pannuccio dal Bagno, 13th cent. (Table P-PZ40)
4474.P2 Panziera, Ugo, fl. 1312 (Table P-PZ40)
4474.P3 Passavanti, Jacopo, ca. 1297-1357 (Table P-PZ40)
4474.P35 La passione (Poem), 14th cent.
4474.P4 Patecchio, Gherardo (Geraldo), fl. 1230 (Table P-PZ40)
4474.P5 Pecora, Jacopo del, fl. 1385-1405 (Table P-PZ40)
4474.P7 Pegolotti, Nanni, fl. 1364-1431 (Table P-PZ40)
Petrarca, Francesco, 1304-1374

Individual authors
Individual authors and works to 1400
Petrarca, Francesco, 1304-1374 -- Continued
4475.A1 Collected works
Of the five editions quoted in bibliographies under the head of collected works ("opera omnia") only two: Basileae 1554 and 1581, contain both the Italian works and the Latin works
The editions Basileae, 1496; Venetiis, 1501 and 1503 contain the Latin works only
Poetical works
4475.A2 Comprehensive editions (Italian and Latin works)
4475.A3 Selected works
Italian works
4476 Comprehensive editions
Title varies: Petrarca'a autograph collection (Codice vaticana latino 3195) entitled "Rerum vulgarium fragmenta," and "Triumphi"; in later editions the titles "Rime" or less frequently "Canzoniere" comprised both the Canzoniere proper and the poem Trionfi. The Canzoniere comprising 317 sonetti, 29 canzoni, 9 sestine and 7 ballate was divided by Petrarca into two parts, by later editors (Vellutello 1525 and Mansard 1819) in three or four parts respectively): 1. Sonetti e canzoni in vita di Madonna Laura; 2. Sonetti e canzoni in morte di Madonna Laura; 3. Sonetti e canzoni sopra vari argomenti or 1. and 2. as above; 3. Trionfi in vita ed in morte di Madonna Laura; 4. = 3. as above
4476.A1 Manuscript
Reproductions in facsimile, by date
Reproductions in print classed below by date-letters
4476.A72-.G Printed editions
Subarranged by date-letters and last two figures of date
4476.A72-.A99 1472-1499
see Incunabula
4476.B00-.B99 1500-1599
4476.C00-.C99 1600-1699
4476.D00-.D99 1700-1799
4476.E00-.E99 1800-1899
4476.F00-.F99 1900-1999
4476.G00-.G99 2000-2999
(4476.Z5A-.Z5Z) Critical and annotated editions. By editor or commentator, A-Z
4476.Z6 School editions
4476.Z7 Selections. Anthologies

Individual authors
Individual authors and works to 1400
Petrarca, Francesco, 1304-1374
Italian works -- Continued
Separate works
Letters see PQ4507.Z5
Poetical works
Canzoniere (proper) see PQ4476+
4477.A1-.A19 Canzoni
4477.A1 Complete editions. By date
4477.A12A-.A12Z Selected canzoni. By editor, A-Z
4477.A19A-.A19Z Particular canzoni, By title, A-Z
4477.A2-.A29 Sonetti
4477.A2 Complete editions. By date
4477.A22A-.A22Z Selected sonetti. By editor, A-Z
4477.A25A-.A25Z Selections. Anthologies, etc. By editor, A-Z
4477.A29A-.A29Z Particular sonetti. By title, A-Z
e.g. Italia mia, Spirto gentil
4477.A3 Trionfi
4477.A4 Rime estravaganti (i.e. poems excluded by Petrarca from his collection)
(4477.A5) Posthumous poems
see selected works under individual types of poetry
e.g., canzoni, see PQ4477.A12A+
4477.A6 Spurious and doubtful poems
4477.A9 Adaptations. Parodies
4477.A95 Note sull' orticultura
Commentaries. Interpretation. Textual criticism
For interpretation confined to the poetical works in Italian
Criticism and interpretation of Petrarca's works in general, see PQ4504-PQ4494; or of his Latin works, see PQ4491-PQ4494
4478 General
4478.A2 Early works to 1800
4479 General special
4480 Special topics (not A-Z)
e.g., Chronology of poems
4481 Particular canzoni
4482 Particular sonetti
4483 Trionfi
Language, style, etc.
4484 General
Cf. PQ4541 Technique
4485 Special topics (not A-Z)
e.g. Figures, similes, etc.
4486 Grammar
4487 Versification

Individual authors
Individual authors and works to 1400
Petrarca, Francesco, 1304-1374
Italian works -- Continued
4488 Dictionaries. Concordances
Latin works
4489.A1 Comprehensive editions. By date
4489.A2 Selections. Anthologies, etc. By editor
4489.A3 Selected works. By date
For Italian and Latin see PQ4475.A3
4489.A4 Poetical works. By date
4489.A5 Prose works
Cf. PA2027 Opuscula historica et philologica
(4489.A6A-.A6Z) Posthumous poems and treatises
see PQ4489.A4 (Poetry)
see PQ4489.A5 (Prose)
(4489.A7) Translations
Italian see PQ4495
Other
see PQ4496+
4490.A-Z Separate works, A-Z
4490.A4 Africa
4490.A6 Apologia contra cuiusdam anonymi Galli calumnias
4490.A7 Arenga facta in civitate Novarie, 1356
4490.A8 Arenga facta Mediolani, 1354
Arenga facta Veneciis, 1353 see PQ4499.A7
4490.B8 Bucolicum carmen
4490.C3 Carmen in laudem beati Hieronymi
4490.C4 Carmina XXXVI ob laudem Mariae Magdalenae
4490.C6 Collatio inter Scipionem, Alexandrum, Annibalem et Pyrhum
De contemptu mundi see PQ4490.S3
De insigne obedientia et fide vxoria Griseldis
see Historia Griseldis
4490.D2 De ocio religiosorum
4490.D3 De officio et virtutibas imperatoris (Epistolae seniles IV, 1)
4490.D4 De remediis utriusque fortunae
De rebus memorandis
see Rerum memorandarum libri IV
4490.D6 De republica optime administranda (Epistolae seniles XIV, 1)
De secreto conflictu curarum suarum
see Secretum
4490.D8 De sui ipsius et multorum aliorum ignorantia
De vera sapientia see PQ4499.D4
4490.D9 De vita solitaria

Individual authors
Individual authors and works to 1400
Petrarca, Francesco, 1304-1374
Latin works
Separate works, A-Z -- Continued
Eclogae
see Bucolicum carmen
Epistolae
For letters in Italian see PQ4507.Z5
4490.E2 Comprehensive editions
4490.E21 Selections. Anthologies
Partial editions (as grouped by Petrarca)
4490.E22 Epistolae metricae
4490.E23 Epistolae familiares
4490.E24 Epistolae seniles
4490.E25 Epistolae variae
4490.E26 Epistolae sine titulo
Other selections
4490.E4 By subject (not A-Z)
e.g. To the classic authors, or Epistolae XVI ... de pontificatu ... et de Romana curia. Argentoirati, 1555
By addressees
4490.E6 Groups
e.g., Statesmen
4490.E61-.E69 Individuals (alphabetically)
4490.E62 Boccaccio
(4490.E7) Particular letters
Separate editions of works in the form of letters are listed with works in their alphabetical order, e.g. De officio et virtutibus imperatoris, PQ4490.D3; Historia Griseldis, PQ4490.H4
Epistola ad posteros see PQ4507.A2
4490.E8 Spurious or doubtful letters
Cf. PQ4499 Spurious works
4490.E85A-.E85Z Letters to Petrarca. By author, A-Z
4490.E9 Criticism and interpretation
4490.H4 Historia Griseldis
Translation from Boccaccio
4490.I5 Invecta contra guendam Gallum innominatum, sed in dignatate positum
Published as Appendix in Vatasso's I codici Petrarcheschi della Biblioteca Vaticana
Invectiva in Gallum see PQ4490.A6
4490.I6 Invectivae contra medicum quemdam
Novem psalmi confessionales see PQ4499.N7
4490.O8 Orations (Prayers)

PQ4001-5999

Individual authors
Individual authors and works to 1400
Petrarca, Francesco, 1304-1374
Latin works
Separate works, A-Z -- Continued

4490.P8 Psalmi poenitentiales
4490.R4 Rerum memorandarum libri IV
4490.S3 Secretum (De contemptu mundi; De secreto conflictu curarum suarum)
4490.S45 Senilium rerum libri
Testamentum see PQ4514

Criticism, interpretation, etc.
For criticism and interpretation of Latin works only
For criticism and interpretation of Italian works, see PQ4478+

4491 General
4492 General special
4493 Special topics (not A-Z)
e.g. Chronology of Latin works

Criticism of special works
see the works

4494 Language. Style
4494.A-.Z3 General
4494.Z5 Grammar
4494.Z7 Versification
4494.Z9 Dictionaries. Concordances

Translations
4495 Italian
Translation of Latin works
4495.A2 Collections and selections. By editor, A-Z
4495.A5-.Z3 Separate works. By original title and translator, A-Z
4495.Z5 Translations into Italian dialects, A-Z
Subarranged by translator, using successive cutter numbers

4496.E2-.E29 English (Table PQ9)
4496.F2-.F29 French (Table PQ9)
4496.G2-.G29 German (Table PQ9)
4496.P2-.P29 Portuguese (Table PQ9)
4496.S2-.S29 Spanish (Table PQ9)
4497.A-Z Other European languages, A-Z
4497.B2 Basque
4497.C2 Catalan
Celtic
4497.C3 Breton
4497.C4 Cornish
4497.C5 Gaelic
4497.C6 Irish

Individual authors
Individual authors and works to 1400
Petrarca, Francesco, 1304-1374
Translations
Other European languages, A-Z
Celtic -- Continued

4497.C7 Manx
4497.C8 Welsh
4497.D2 Dutch. Flemish. Frisian
4497.F5 Finnish
4497.G7 Greek (both ancient and modern Greek)
4497.H8 Hungarian
4497.L2 Latin
4497.R8 Romanian
Scandinavian
4497.S2 Danish. Dano-Norwegian
4497.S4 Icelandic
4497.S6 Swedish
4498.A-Z Slavic
4498.B2 Bohemian
4498.B6 Bulgarian
4498.C2 Croatian
4498.L2 Latvian
4498.L4 Lithuanian
4498.P2 Polish
4498.R2 Russian
4498.R6 Ruthenian
4498.S2 Servian
4498.S4 Slovakian
4498.S6 Slovenian
4498.W2 Wendic
(4498.5) Languages of Asia, Africa, Oceanica, etc.
see PJ+
(4498.8) Mixed languages, Yiddish, etc.
see PJ5281+ PM801+ etc.
(4498.9) Artificial languages, Esperanto, Ido, etc.
see PM8001+
4499 Doubtful or spurious works
4499.A1 Collections and selections
4499.A5-.Z3 Separate works
4499.A7 Arengua facta Veniciis, 1353
4499.C3 Caso di amore (title in manuscript: Refrigerio de' miseri)
4499.C4 Chronica delle vite de pontifici et imperatori romani

Individual authors
Individual authors and works to 1400
Petrarca, Francesco, 1304-1374
Doubtful or spurious works
Separate works -- Continued

4499.D4 De vera sapientia
Two dialogues, mainly the work of Nicolaus Cusanus; part of the first dialogue extracted from Petrarca's De remediis utriusque fortunae, dialogus XII

4499.D6 Dialogus Pyladis et Orestis de miseria curiae romanae

Lettere volgare a L. Beccamuggi see PQ4490.E8

4499.N7 Novem psalmi confessionales

Refrigerio de' miseri
see Caso d'amore

Sonetti see PQ4477.A6

4499.Z5 Criticism

4500 Imitations, paraphrases, adaptations
For paraphrases, etc. of poems see PQ4477.A9

4501 Translations as subject (Comparative studies, etc.)

4501.A1 General

4501.A3-Z Special. By language, A-Z
Under each language:
.x General
.x2A-.x2Z By translator, A-Z
Cf. PQ4537.A+ Criticism and interpretation

4502 Illustrations
Illustrated editions classed with texts
For iconography, portraits, etc. see PQ4524

4503 Petrarca and music
see PQ4549.M8
For music and musical history and criticism, see M, ML

4504 Biography and criticism
Bibliography see Z8676

4504.A2 Periodicals and societies
Cf. PQ4534+ History of Petrarca studies

Collected papers, essays

4504.A5-.Z3 By several authors
Cf. PQ4522 Centennial publications

(4504.Z5) By individuals
see PQ4505-4550

Individual authors
Individual authors and works to 1400
Petrarca, Francesco, 1304-1374
Biography and criticism -- Continued
4504.Z7 Dictionaries, indexes, etc.
General encyclopedic dictionaries only
Special dictionaries with subject
For Concordances and language dictionaries, see PQ4488, PQ4494.Z9
For Dictionaries of proper names, see PQ4488, PQ4494.Z9
General works (Literary biography, Life and works)
4505.A2 Early to 1800
4505.A5-.Z4 1801-
4505.Z5 Addresses, essays, lectures
Biography
General
Treatises see PQ4505.A2+
4506 Minor works, miscellaneous details, etc.
e.g. Chronology of Petrarca's life
Special
4507.A1 Sources and documents
General and miscellaneous
Autobiography
4507.A2 Epistola ad posteros
Secretum see PQ4490.S3
4507.A3-.Z4 Autobiographical and biographical allusions. By editor, A-Z
Cf. PQ4538.A2 Petrarch on his own works
4507.Z5 Letters (in Italian only), by date of publication
Latin letters see PQ4490.E2+
4508 Family. Ancestry. Name
Including parents, brother, children, grandchildren, name
4509 Youth. Education. Birth (Date and place)
Love. Marriage. Relation to women
4510 General
Special
4511 Laura (de Noves, wife of H. de Sade (?))
Including family, marriage, death, tomb, portraits
4511.5 Poetry written by her
4512 Other
Manhood. Later years and death
General see PQ4505.A2+
4513 Special events
Including Minor orders (Canonry at Florence), Coronation at Rome

Individual authors
Individual authors and works to 1400
Petrarca, Francesco, 1304-1374
Biography and criticism
Biography
Special
Manhood ...
Special events
Journeys see PQ4518+
Political missions
Cf. PQ4544 Knowledge and treatment of politics, history
Literary activity
Prefer PQ4545-4548, Learning and scholarship
4514 Death
Including last will, remains, tomb
Eulogies and obituaries. Inscriptions
Prefer PQ4523
Relation to contemporaries. Age of Petrarca
4515 General
Prefer PQ4505
4516.A-Z By groups, A-Z
e. g.
4516.P7 Popes
4516.P8 Princes and statesmen
Special families see PQ4517.A+
4517.A-Z By individuals or families, A-Z
e. g.
4517.C3 Carraresi family
(4517.C4) Chaucer
see PR1912.P4
(4517.D3) Dante
see PQ4358.P4
Cf. PQ4546.Z7D3 Petrarca's knowledge of Dante's works
4517.V5 Visconti family
Homes and haunts. Journeys
4518 General
4519.A-Z Special, A-Z
4519.A7 Arezzo
4519.A8 Arqua
4519.A9 Avignon
4519.P15 Padua
4519.P2 Parma
4519.P5 Pisa
4519.V3 Vancluse
4519.V4 Venice

Individual authors
Individual authors and works to 1400
Petrarca, Francesco, 1304-1374
Biography and criticism
Biography
Special
Homes and haunts. Journeys
Special, A-Z -- Continued
4519.V44 Ventoux Mountain
4520 Personality. Character
Including mysticism, "accidia" (inertia), melancholy, misanthropy, fondness of solitude, patriotism, character, moral conduct
For religious and moral views see PQ4543
Outward appearance. Physical qualities
Cf. PQ4524 Iconography
Anniversaries and celebrations
4521 History and description
4521.A1 General
Special
Prefer PQ4522 for Publications
4521.A2 Early to 1874. By date
4521.A74-.A99 1874-1899
4521.B00-.B99 1900-1999
4522 Publications in honor of particular anniversaries
Prefer special subject or PQ4504
4522.A2 Early to 1874. By date
4522.A74-.A99 1874-1899
Under each date-letter:
.xA-.xZ29 By society, institution, or title
.xZ3-.xZ99 By individual author, alphabetically
4522.A74 1874. 500th anniversary of Petrarca's death
4522.B00-.B99 1900-1999
Under each date-letter:
.xA-.xZ29 By society, institution, or title
.xZ3-.xZ99 By individual author, alphabetically
4522.B04 1904, 600th anniversary of Petrarca's birth
4522.C00-.C99 2000-2099
Under each date-letter:
.xA-.xZ29 By society, institution, or title
.xZ3-.xZ99 By individual author, alphabetically
4523 Memorials. Testimonials to Petrarca's genius (Other than centennial)
Poetry
Prose see PQ4505.Z5
4524 Iconography. Portraits. Monuments

Individual authors
Individual authors and works to 1400
Petrarca, Francesco, 1304-1374
Biography and criticism
Biography
Iconography. Portraits. Monuments -- Continued
4524.A-.Z3 General works, history, etc., of illustrations of the works
Illustrated editions of the works
see PQ4475+ PQ4489+ PQ4495+
Collections of illustrations, portfolios, albums, prints, etc. see PQ4502
4524.Z5 Portraits
Cf. Masséna's Pétrarque, ses études d'art, ses portraits
4524.Z6 Monuments
4525 Museums. Relics. Exhibitions
(4526) Fiction, drama, etc., based upon Petrarca's life
See the author
Petrarca in England, Germany, etc. see PQ4537.A+
(4527) Study and teaching (Theory, methods)
see PQ4505; PQ4534+ PQ4540
Authorship
4528 General
4529 Autographs. Manuscripts
For discussion of value of manuscripts, see PQ4478+ PQ4491+
Catalogs and lists of manuscripts see Z8676
Cf. PQ4548 Petrarca's library
4530 Sources
Discussion of value of manuscripts, see PQ4478+ PQ4491+
4531 Forerunners. Associates. Followers. School
Cf. PQ4101 and PQ4103
4532 Allusions
Prefer PQ4507
4533 Chronology of works
Criticism and interpretation
History of the study and appreciation of Petrarca
Cf. PQ4504.A2 Periodicals, etc.
4534 General (and in Italy)
4535 General special
Influence of Petrarca in Italy and elsewhere (General)
Influence of Petrarca in special countries see PQ4537.A+

Individual authors
Individual authors and works to 1400
Petrarca, Francesco, 1304-1374
Biography and criticism
Criticism and interpretation
History of the study and appreciation of Petrarca
General special -- Continued
Influence of Petrarca on particular authors or persons
see the author or persons
Prefer PQ4515-4517, Relations to contemporaries
Influence of Petrarca on literature
Prefer PQ4546
Influence of Petrarca on art
see PQ4549.A8
Cf. PQ4524 Iconography, etc.

(4536) By period
Prefer PQ4534 or PQ4540
(4536.A2) Early to 1800
(4536.A5-Z) 1800-
4537.A-Z By country, A-Z
Cf. PR1912.A5+ Petrarca and Chaucer
4538 By individual authors or persons
4538.A2 Petrarca on his own works
4538.A5-Z Others
4539 Special topics

Treatises
Dealing with both the Italian and Latin works of the author, provided that they are exclusively or prevailingly devoted to criticism, appreciation, or interpretation
For treatises confined to the Italian works see PQ4478+
For treatises confined to the Latin works see PQ4491+
For works combining biography and literary criticism see PQ4505.A2+

4540 General
4540.A2 Early to 1800
4540.A5-Z 1801-
Special
Philosophy, esthetics
see PQ4540 or PQ4542
4541 Technique

Relation to special subjects
Including treatment and knowledge, influence, etc.
4542 Philosophy. Ethics. Psychology

Individual authors
Individual authors and works to 1400
Petrarca, Francesco, 1304-1374
Biography and criticism
Criticism and interpretation
Relation to special subjects -- Continued

4543 Religion. Theology
Including the Catholic Church, Popes, monasticism, St. Augustine
Cf. PQ4544

4544 Politics. History
Cf. PQ4513 Political missions

Learning. Scholarship. Relation to Renaissance

4545 General

Special

4546 Literature

4546.A1 General

4546.A2-.Z3 Ancient and Latin

4546.Z4 Particular authors
e. g.

4546.Z4C5 Cicero

4546.Z7 Modern authors, A-Z
e. g.

4546.Z7D3 Dante

4547 Languages

4548 Petrarca's library
Cf. Z989, Z997, Bibliography

4549.A-Z Other special subjects, A-Z

4549.A8 Art

4549.E4 Education

4549.G46 Geography

4549.L38 Law

4549.M54 Mnemonics

4549.M8 Music

4549.M94 Mythology

4549.N3 Nature. Petrarca and the Alps

4549.S3 Science

4549.V57 Visions

4550 Language. Style. Versification

(4552.P2) Pier delle Vigne, 1190?-1249
see DG531.8.P5

Pietro da Barsegapè see PQ4265.B343

4552.P3 Pieri Paolino, fl. 1300-1305 (Table P-PZ40)

4552.P4 Pigna, Giovanni Battista Nicolucci, called 1529-1575 (Table P-PZ40)

4552.P5 Piramo e Tisbe (Metrical romance)
Cf. PQ1501.P9+ Pyrame et Thisbé (Old French)

Individual authors
Individual authors and works to 1400 -- Continued

4552.P55 Ponzela Gaia (Poem)
(4552.P6) Prise de Pampelune
see L'Entree de Spagne, PQ1459.E75
Cf. PQ4474.N5 Nicola, da Verona
4553 Pucci, Antonio, d. 1388 (Table P-PZ39)
Cf. PQ4299.C16 Carduino
4554.P85 Pugliese, Giacomino, 13th cent. (Table P-PZ40)
4554.Q57 Quirini, Giovanni, ca. 1295-1333 (Table P-PZ40)
4554.R15 Raffaelli, Bosone de', da Gubbio, fl. 1337 (Table P-PZ40)
4554.R2 Rainardo e Lesengrino (Epic poem)
4554.R26 Ramo Corsi, Girolama, 14th cent. (Table P-PZ40)
Reali di Francia see PQ4265.A6
Reggimento e costumi di donne see PQ4265.B3
4554.R45 Rinaldino da Montalbano (Prose romance)
4554.R46 Rinaldo d'Aquino, 13th cent. (Table P-PZ40)
4554.R464 Rinaldo da Monte Albano (Verse romance)
4554.R47 Rinuccini, Cino, d. 1417 (Table P-PZ40)
4554.R474 Rinuccino, da Firenze, fl. 1289-1299 (Table P-PZ40)
4554.R5 Ristoro d'Arezzo, 13th cent. (Table P-PZ40)
4554.R53 Ritmo cassinese (Fragment)
4554.R55 Riva, fra Bonvesin da, fl. ca. 1300 (Table P-PZ40)
4554.R6 Rossi, Adriano de', 14th cent. (Table P-PZ40)
4554.R65 Rossi, Nocolò de', ca. 1290-ca. 1340 (Table P-PZ40)
4554.R8 Rusticianoda Pisa
4554.R85 Rustico di Filippo, 13th cent. (Table P-PZ40)
4555 Sacchetti, Franco, ca. 1330-ca. 1400
4555.A3 Collected poems
4555.A5 Novelle
4555.A6-.A79 Separate works. By title
4555.A8A-.A8Z Translations. By language, A-Z
4555.A9 Biography and criticism
4556.S14 Sacchetti, Giannozzo, 14th cent.
4556.S2 San Giovanni Boccadore (Metrical romance)
4556.S25 San Torpè (Legend)
4556.S3 Sercambi, Giovanni, 1347-1424 (Table P-PZ40)
4556.S4 Sette savi di Roma
4556.S5 Soldanieri, Niccolò di Neri, 14th cent. (Table P-PZ40)
Sordello di Goito, 13th cent. see PC3330.S6
Stabili, Francesco see PQ4299.C25
4556.S88 Storia di Mosè
Tavola ritonda o L'istoria di Tristano see PQ4556.T6
4556.T3 Tedaldi, Pieraccio, d. ca. 1350
4556.T317 Tenzone di Dante con Forese Donati
4556.T32 Testa, Arrigo, d. 1247
4556.T35 Tobia e Tobiolo

Individual authors
Individual authors and works to 1400 -- Continued

4556.T38 Tommaso, di Giunta, fl. 1336-1353 (Table P-PZ40)
4556.T4 Tommasuccio da Folignò, 1309-1377 (Table P-PZ40)
4556.T45 Torini, Agnolo, 14th cent. (Table P-PZ40)
Tristan (Romance)
4556.T5 La prima prodezza di Tristano
4556.T6 La tavola ritonda o L'istoria di Tristano
4556.T65 Tristano Panciatichiano
4556.T7 Tristano Riccardiano
Edited by E.G. Parodi
Collezione di opere inedita or rara, v. 74
4556.T75 Tristano veneto
4556.T85 Tristano e Lancielotto (Poem)
4556.T92 Tup, tup Cu'esti iocu?
4556.U2 Uberti, Fazio degli, ca. 1310-ca. 1370 (Table P-PZ40)
4556.U4 Uggeri, Apugliese, 13th cent. (Table P-PZ40)
4556.U5 Ugoçon da Laodho (Uguccione di Lodi), 13th cent. (Table P-PZ40)
4556.V3 Vannozzo, Francesco di, 14th cent. (Table P-PZ40)
4556.V4 Velluti, Donato, 1320-1370 (Table P-PZ40)
4556.V5 Vergogna e Rosana (Metrical romance)
4556.V53 Veronese riddle (Indovinello veronese)
4556.V6 Virtu e vizio (Poem)
4556.V7 Visconti, Bruzio, 14th cent.

Individual authors, 1400-1700
Subarrange each author by Table P-PZ40 unless otherwise specified

4561 Anonymous works (Table P-PZ28 modified)
4561.A1A-.A1Z Works without any indication of author, either by symbol or initial. By title, A-Z
4561.A1A74 Ardelia
4561.A1A87 Aurelia
4561.A1B3 Barunissa di Carini.
4561.A1B7 Il Breviario di Papa Galeazzo
4561.A1C27 Il Cancioniere, attributed to Alessandro Sforza, 1409-1473
4561.A1C28 Cancioniere, attributed to Anonimo, da Tulmegio, 16th cent.
4561.A1C56 Commedia degli Zanni
4561.A1D57 La Discontenta
4561.A1E34 Egloga pastorate di Morel
4561.A1G76 Griselda (Drama)

Individual authors
Individual authors, 1400-1700
Anonymous works
Works without any indication of author, either by symbol or initial. By title, A-Z -- Continued

4561.A1I16 Gl' ingannati
Title of 1538 edition: Commedia del sacrificio de gli intronati da Siena. First performed in 1531. Shakespeare's Twelfth night said to have been based on a Latin adaptation
4561.A1J48 Jhesus via de lo Paraiso
4561.A1J94 Il Judicio de la fine del mondo
4561.A1M37 La Masséra da bé
4561.A1N7 Novella del Grasso legnajuolo
4561.A1N74 Novella di Lionora de Bardi e Ippolito Buondelmonte
4561.A1P38 Passione de Revello
4561.A1P8 Pulon Matt
4561.A1R4 Refugio de'miseri
4561.A1T35 Tariffa delle puttane di Venezia
4561.A1V4 La Veniexiana
4562.A2 Abati, Antonio, d. 1667 (Table P-PZ40)
4562.A25 Acciano, Giulio, 1651-1681 (Table P-PZ40)
4562.A3 Accolti, Bernardo, d. 1535 (Table P-PZ40)
4562.A32 Achillini, Claudio, 1574-1640 (Table P-PZ40)
4562.A33 Achillini, Giovanni Filoteo, 1466-1538 (Table P-PZ40)
4562.A4 Adimari, Lodovico, 1644-1708 (Table P-PZ40)
4562.A45 Agostini, Agostino, 17th cent. (Table P-PZ40)
4562.A458 Agostini, Ludovico, 1536-1609? (Table P-PZ40)
4562.A46 Agostini, Niccolò degli, 16th cent. (Table P-PZ40)
4562.A48 Alamanni, Antonio, 1464-1528 (Table P-PZ40)
4562.A5 Alamanni, Luigi, 1495-1556 (Table P-PZ40)
4562.A55 Albéri, Giovan Battista, 1585-1648 (Table P-PZ40)
4562.A58 Alberti, Antonio degli, 15th cent. (Table P-PZ40)
4562.A6 Alberti, Leone Battista, 1404-1472 (Table P-PZ40)
4562.A63 Alione, Giovanni Giorgio, ca. 1460-ca. 1521 (Table P-PZ40)
4562.A64 Allegretti, Antonio, b. ca. 1512 (Table P-PZ40)
4562.A65 Allegri, Alessandro, 1560-1620 (Table P-PZ40)
Pseudonym: Parrida Pozzolatico
4562.A653 Almerici da Pesaro, Raniero (Table P-PZ40)
4562.A66 Alticozzi, Niccolò (Table P-PZ40)
4562.A665 Amanio, Nicolò, 15th/16th cent. (Table P-PZ40)
4562.A67 Ambra, Francesco d', d. 1558 (Table P-PZ40)
4562.A69 Andreini, Francesco, 1548-1624 (Table P-PZ40)
4562.A7 Andreini, Giovanni Battista, b. 1578 (Table P-PZ40)
4562.A72 Andreini, Isabella, 1562-1604 (Table P-PZ40)

Individual authors
Individual authors, 1400-1700 -- Continued

4562.A74 Anguillara, Giovanni Andrea dell', ca. 1517-1565 (Table P-PZ40)
4562.A76 Antodari, Giovanni Antonio, 16th cent. (Table P-PZ40)
Aquilano Serafino see PQ4619.C5
4562.A83 Aquino, Carlo d', fl. 1654 (Table P-PZ40)
4562.A9 Aragona, Tullia d', ca. 1506-1556 (Table P-PZ40)
4562.A95 Araolla, Girolamo, fl. 1543-1597 (Table P-PZ40)
4563-4564 Aretino, Pietro, 1492-1556 (Table P-PZ36)
Arienti, Giovanni Sabadino degli, d. 1510 see PQ4632.S3
Ariosto, Lodovico, 1474-1533
4566.A1 Collected works
(4566.A12) Editions. By editor, A-Z
4566.A3 Selections. Anthologies
4566.A4 Passages, thoughts, quotations
4566.A5 Selected works
Cf. PQ4578.A1
Separate works
4567 Orlando furioso
Editions
4567.A1 Facsimiles
(4567.A12) Reproductions in print
see PQ4567.A2
4567.A2 Printed editions. By date
(4567.A3) Annotated and critical editions. By editor, A-Z
4567.A4 I cinque canti
4567.A5 School editions. Expurgated editions. By editor, A-Z
4567.A6 Selections. Anthologies
Cf. PQ4566.A3
(4567.A7) Passages. Thoughts, etc.
see PQ4566.A4
Criticism and interpretation
4568 Early (to 1800)
For early controversial literature on the merits of Ariosto and Tasso see PQ4656
4569 Recent, 1801-
4570 Special topics
e.g. Unity of the poem and the episode; Purpose of the poem (Glorification of the House of Este); Comparison with Bojardo's Orlando innamorato; Madness of Orlando; The marvellous features
Cf. PQ4602.A+
4572 Characters
General see PQ4572
4572.A3 Special groups, A-Z
e.g., Christians, Saracens, Women

Individual authors
Individual authors, 1400-1700
Ariosto, Lodovico, 1474-1533
Separate works
Orlando furioso
Criticism and interpretation
Characters -- Continued

4572.A5-Z Special characters, A-Z
e. g.
4572.C4 Charlemagne
Orlando see PQ4572.A5+
4572.R8 Ruggiero
4574 Sources
Classic literature; Medieval literature
4575 Textual criticism
(4576) Language. Style. Versification
see PQ4603
4577 Dictionaries. Concordances
Cf. PQ4603.Z8
4578 Minor works
4578.A1 Collections and selections
Special works
4578.A3 Comedie (Collected)
4578.C2 Cassaria
4578.L2 Lena
4578.N2 Negromante
4578.S5 Studenti (Scolastica; Imperfecta)
Completed by Ariosto's brother Gabriele and entitled "Scolastica." The unfinished parts as supplied by Ariosto's son Virginio, who chose the title "Imperfecta," are lost, except the prologue
4578.S8 Suppositi (based in part on Plautus' Captivi)
4579 Criticism and special works
(4580) Language. Style. Versification
see PQ4603
4581 Poems (Shorter works)
4581.A1 Collections and selections
Special
4581.A3 Rime
4581.A5 Satire
4581.A7 Poesie latine
4581.A8-Z Criticism
Translations
4582.A1-.A19 Italian dialects
Arrange alphabetically
4582.A1 Collections. By date
English

Individual authors
Individual authors, 1400-1700
Ariosto, Lodovico, 1474-1533
Translations
English -- Continued

4582.E5 Collected and selected works. By date
4582.E5A3-.E5A39 Orlando Furioso, by translator
4582.E5A5-.E5Z3 Minor works. By title, A-Z
Subarranged by translator alphabetically
4582.E5Z5-.E99 Spurious works

French
4582.F5 Collected and selected works. By date
4582.F5A3-.F5A39 Orlando Furioso, by translator
4582.F5A5-.F5Z3 Minor works. By title, A-Z
Subarranged by translator alphabetically
4582.F5Z5-.F99 Spurious works

German
4582.G5 Collected and selected works. By date
4582.G5A3-.G5A39 Orlando Furioso, by translator
4582.G5A5-.G5Z3 Minor works. By title, A-Z
Subarranged by translator alphabetically
4582.G5Z5-.G99 Spurious works

Portuguese
4582.P5 Collected and selected works. By date
4582.P5A3-.P5A39 Orlando Furioso, by translator
4582.P5A5-.P5Z3 Minor works. By title, A-Z
Subarranged by translator alphabetically
4582.P5Z5-.P99 Spurious works

Spanish
4582.S5 Collected and selected works. By date
4582.S5A3-.S5A39 Orlando Furioso, by translator
4582.S5A5-.S5Z3 Minor works. By title, A-Z
Subarranged by translator alphabetically
4582.S5Z5-.S99 Spurious works

4583.A-Z Other European languages, A-Z
For list of Cutter numbers, see PQ4273.A+
4583.5.A-Z Other languages, A-Z
4583.6.A-Z Artificial languages, A-Z
4584 Doubtful or spurious works
e.g. L'erbolata o sia de la nobilità dell' uomo
4585 Imitations. Adaptations. Parodies
4586 Dramatization. Translation. Illustration
4586.A2 Relation to the drama and the stage
4586.A5 Translations (as subject, comparative studies, etc.)
4586.A7 Illustrations
Cf. note to PQ(4276)

Individual authors
Individual authors, 1400-1700
Ariosto, Lodovico, 1474-1533 -- Continued

(4586.A9) Ariosto and music
Cf. note to PQ(4329.8)

Biography and criticism

(4587.A1) Bibliography
see Z8043

4587.A2-.A4 Periodicals. Societies. Collections

4587.A5-.Z3 General works. Literary biography. Life and works

4587.Z5 Lectures, addresses, etc.

Biography

4588 Sources

4588.2 Letters. Autobiographical and biographical illusions

General works see PQ4587+

4589 Early life. Education

4590 Love and marriage. Relations to women

4591 Later life and death

4592 Relations to contemporaries

4593 Homes and haunts
Prefer special periods, PQ4589-PQ4591

4594 Anniversaries. Celebrations

4595 Iconography. Portraits. Monuments

4595.5 Museums. Relics. Exhibitions

4596 Authorship. Manuscripts. Sources, etc.
Cf. PQ4574 Sources of Orlando Furioso

4597 Chronology of works

Criticism and interpretation

4598 History of study and appreciation of Ariosto
Cf. PQ4587.A2+

4598.A2 General and in Italy

4598.A5-Z Foreign countries, A-Z
e. g.

4598.E5 England

4598.F7 France

4598.G5 Germany

Treatises
For general works only
For criticism of Orlando Furioso see PQ4568+
For criticism of other works see PQ4578
For works combining biography and criticism see PQ4587+

4599 General

4599.A2 Early works to 1800

4599.A5-Z 1801-

Special

Individual authors
Individual authors, 1400-1700
Ariosto, Lodovico, 1474-1533
Biography and criticism
Criticism and interpretation
Treatises
Special -- Continued

(4600) Philosophy. Esthetics
see PQ4599

4601 Technique

4602.A-Z Relation to special subjects, A-Z
Treatment, knowledge, influence, etc.

4603 Language. Grammar. Style

4603.Z5 Versification

4603.Z8 Dictionaries. Concordances (of all the works)

4604.A5 Ariosto, Orazio, 1555-1593 (Table P-PZ40)

4605.A4 Arrivabene, Lodovico, 16th cent. (Table P-PZ40)

Arsiccio, Intronato, 1500 or 1501-1559 see PQ4664.V63

4605.A46 Artale, Giuseppe, 1628-1679 (Table P-PZ40)

4605.A6 Asinari, Federico, conte di Camerano, 1527-1576 (Table P-PZ40)
Cf. PQ4645.A1

4605.A65 Assarino, Luca, 1602-1672 (Table P-PZ40)

4605.A84 Aversa, Tommaso, 1623?-1663 (Table P-PZ40)

Baciocchi, Giovanni Tommaso see PQ4683.B11

Baffo, Giorgio see PQ4683.B13

4605.B27 Baiardo, Andrea, fl. 1500 (Table P-PZ40)

4605.B3 Baldi, Bernardino, 1553-1617 (Table P-PZ40)

4605.B5 Baldovino, Francesco, 1635-1716 (Table P-PZ40)

4605.B6 Balducci, Francesco, 1579-1642 (Table P-PZ40)

4605.B8 Banchieri, Adriano, d. 1634 (Table P-PZ40)
Pseudonym: Cammillo Scaliggeri dalla Fratta
Cf. ML, MT, Music

4606 Bandello, Matteo, 1480-1561 (Table P-PZ39)

4607.B26 Barbieri, Niccolò, 1576-1641 (Table P-PZ40)

4607.B3 Bardi, Pietro de', conte di Vernio, fl. 1643 (Table P-PZ40)
Pseudonyms: Beridio Darpe, Brivio Pieverdi

4607.B33 Bargagli, Girolamo, 1537-1587 (Table P-PZ40)

4607.B34 Bargagli, Scipione, d. 1612 (Table P-PZ40)

Baruffaldi, Girolamo see PQ4683.B23

4607.B43 Barracco, Maurizio, 1562-1599 (Table P-PZ40)

4607.B45 Barzizza, Antonio, 15th cent. (Table P-PZ40)

4607.B48 Basile, Domenico, 17th cent. (Table P-PZ40)

4607.B5 Basile, Giovanni Battista, ca. 1575-1632 (Table P-PZ40 modified)

4607.B5A61-.B5Z458 Separate works. By title

4607.B5P4 Il pentamerone, overo lo cunto de li cunti

Individual authors
Individual authors, 1400-1700 -- Continued
4607.B56 Basso, Antonio, ca. 1605-1648 (Table P-PZ40)
4607.B6 Battiferi, Laura, 1523-1589 (Table P-PZ40)
4607.B65 Belcari, Feo, 1410-1484 (Table P-PZ40)
4607.B7 Bellincioni, Bernardo, ca. 1450-1492 (Table P-PZ40)
4607.B8 Bellini, Lorenzo, 1643-1704 (Table P-PZ40)
4607.B84 Bello, Francesco, called Il Cieco, fl. 15th cent. (Table P-PZ40)
4608 Bembo, Pietro, cardinal, 1470-1547
Latin works see PA8475.B5
4608.A1 Collected works. By date
4608.A12 Selected works. Selections. By date
4608.A15 Poetical works. By date
4608.A19 Miscellaneous prose works. By date
4608.A6-.A79 Separate works
4608.A6 Gli Asolani
4608.A7 Letters
4608.A75 Motti
4608.A8-Z Biography and criticism
4610.B3 Bene, Bartolommeo del, b. 1514 (Table P-PZ40)
4610.B4 Benivieni, Girolamo, d. 1542 (Table P-PZ40)
4610.B45 Bentivoglio, Ercole, 1506-1573 (Table P-PZ40)
4610.B47 Beolco, Angelo, called Ruzzante, 1502?-1542 (Table P-PZ40)
4610.B5 Berni, Francesco, 1497 or 8-1535 (Table P-PZ38)
For his refacimento of Orlando Innamorato see PQ4612+
4610.B52 Bernini, Gian Lorenzo, 1598-1680 (Table P-PZ40)
4610.B53 Berrardo, Girolamo, fl. 1501 (Table P-PZ40)
4610.B55 Bertoldo con Bertaldino e Cacasenno (Table P-PZ40)
By several authors
A version of Bertoldo con Bertoldino, by G.C. Croce, and Cacasenno, by A. Banchieri
Cf. PQ4605.B8 and PQ4621.C8
4610.B57 Bianco, Bernardino, 17th cent. (Table P-PZ40)
Bibbiena, Bernardo Dovizi da see PQ4621.D8
4610.B58 Bigolina, Giulia, d. 1569 (Table P-PZ40)
4610.B6 Bini, Giovanni Francesco, d. 1556 (Table P-PZ40)
4610.B7 Biondi, Sir Giovanni Francesco, 1572-1644 (Table P-PZ40)
4610.B74 Bisaccioni, Maiolino, 1582-1663 (Table P-PZ40)
(4610.B8) Boccalini, Traiano, 1556-1613
see JC158.B6-7
Boiardo, Matteo Maria, 1440 or 41-1494 see PQ4612+
Bojardo, Matteo Maria, conte di Scandiano, 1434-1494
4612.A1 Collected works
Orlando innamorato

Individual authors
Individual authors, 1400-1700
Bojardo, Matteo Maria, conte di Scandiano, 1434-1494
Orlando innamorato -- Continued
4612.A3 Editions. By date
e. g.
4612.A3 1539 Venice, 1539
4612.A3 1539a Milan, 1539
4612.A3 1545B Bernini's refacimento
4612.A3 1545D Domenichi's refacimento
4612.A7 School editions, selections, etc. By editor, A-Z
4612.A8-Z Minor works
For Latin works see PA8477.B54
4612.A9 Amorum libri tres (in Italian)
4612.C3 Capitoli ed egloghe in terze rima
(4612.L2) Letters
see PQ4614.A2
4613 Translations. By language and translator
4613.E5R7 English translations by Rose
4614 Biography and criticism
4615.B2 Bolognetti, Francesco, ca. 1520-ca. 1576 (Table P-PZ40)
4615.B3 Bonarelli della Rovere, Guidubaldo, conte, 1563-1608 (Table P-PZ40)
4615.B32 Bonarelli della Rovere, Pietro, conte, d. 1669 (Table P-PZ40)
4615.B323 Bonarelli della Rovere, Prospero, conte, ca. 1588-1659 (Table P-PZ40)
4615.B33 Bonciani, Antonio, 15th cent. (Table P-PZ40)
4615.B35 Borghesi, Diomede, d. 1598 (Table P-PZ40)
4615.B357 Borra, Luigi, 1517-1545 (Table P-PZ40)
4615.B37 Botta, Ascanio, ca. 1486-1544 (Table P-PZ40)
4615.B38 Bozza, Francesco, b. ca. 1553 (Table P-PZ40)
4615.B386 Braca, Vincenzo, ca. 1566-ca. 1625 (Table P-PZ40)
4615.B39 Braccesi, Alessandro, 1445-1503 (Table P-PZ40)
4615.B4 Bracciolini, Francesco, 1566-1645 (Table P-PZ40)
4615.B413 Brammini, Lucillo, 16th cent. (Table P-PZ40)
4615.B42 Brevio, Giovanni, ca. 1480-ca. 1562 (Table P-PZ40)
4615.B43 Brignole Sale, Antonio Giulio, marchese di Groppoli, 1605-1665 (Table P-PZ40)
4615.B45 Bronzino, Angelo, 1502-1572 (Table P-PZ40)
4615.B467 Brunelleschi, Filippo, 1377-1446 (Table P-PZ40)
4615.B47 Bruni, Antonio, 1593-1635 (Table P-PZ40)
4615.B48 Bruni, Domenico, 16th cent. (Table P-PZ40)
4615.B49 Bruni, Leonardo, Aretino, 1369-1444 (Table P-PZ40)
4615.B5 Bruno, Giordano, 1548-1600 (Table P-PZ40)
Cf. B783 Philosophy
4615.B55 Brusantini, Vincenzo, 16th cent. (Table P-PZ40)

Individual authors
Individual authors, 1400-1700 -- Continued

4615.B56 Brusoni, Girolamo, b. 1610 (Table P-PZ40)
4615.B57 Brusonio, Giovangiacomo, fl. 1548-1554 (Table P-PZ40)
4615.B574 Bucciolini, Pier Angelo, d. 1436 (Table P-PZ40)
4615.B6 Buonarroti, Michel Angelo, 1475-1564 (Table P-PZ38)
Cf. N6923.B9 Art
4615.B7 Buonarroti, Michel Angelo, il giovane, 1568-1646 (Table P-PZ40)
4615.B74 Buonfanti, Pietro, da Bibbiena, 16th cent. (Table P-PZ40)
4615.B76 Buoinsegni, Francesco, 1605-ca. 1660 (Table P-PZ40)
4615.B8 Burchiello, Domenico di Giovanni, known as, 1404-1448 (Table P-PZ40)
4617.B2 Busenello, Giovanni Francesco, 1598-1659 (Table P-PZ40)
4617.B4 Buti, Francesco, d. 1682 (Table P-PZ40)
Cf. Mandosio, P., Bibliotheca romana
4617.C116 Caccia, Giovanni Agostino, 16th cent. (Table P-PZ40)
4617.C12 Cademosto, Marco, 16th cent. (Table P-PZ40)
4617.C13 Caggio, Paolo, d. 1562 (Table P-PZ40)
4617.C14 Calenzio, Elisio, 1430?-1503? (Table P-PZ40)
4617.C147 Calmeta, ca. 1460-1508 (Table P-PZ40)
4617.C15 Calmo, Andrea, ca. 1510-1571 (Table P-PZ40)
4617.C17 Camilli, Camillo, fl. 1585 (Table P-PZ40)
For his I cinque canti see PQ4638.Z7
4617.C2 Cammelli, Antonio, called "Il Pistoia," 1436-1502 (Table P-PZ40)
4617.C215 Campailla, Tommaso, 1668-1740 (Table P-PZ40)
4617.C23 Campanella, Tommaso, 1568-1639 (Table P-PZ40)
4617.C25 Campani, Niccolò, called "Strascino," 1478-1523 (Table P-PZ40)
4617.C27 Campeggi, Ridolfo, conte di Dozza, 1565-1624 (Table P-PZ40)
4617.C272 Campiglia, Maddalena, 1553-1595 (Table P-PZ40)
4617.C273 Cano, Antonio, d. 1478 (Table P-PZ40)
4617.C276 Capasso, Giosuè, 15th/16th cent. (Table P-PZ40)
4617.C279 Capilupi, Camillo, 1504-1548 (Table P-PZ40)
4617.C28 Capilupi, Lelio, 1497-1560 (Table P-PZ40)
4617.C3 Caporali, Cesare, 1531-1601 (Table P-PZ40)
4617.C33 Capello, Bernardo, 1498-1565 (Table P-PZ40)
4617.C36 Caracciolo, Pietro Antonio, 1475?-1555 (Table P-PZ40)
Pseudonym: Antonio Epicuro
4617.C38 Caravia, Alessandro, 1503-1568 (Table P-PZ40)
Cariteo see PQ4623.G25
4617.C39 Carli, Paolo Francesco, 1652-1725 (Table P-PZ40)
4617.C4 Caro, Annibale, 1507-1566 (Table P-PZ40)
4617.C6 Casa, Giovanni della, abp., 1503-1556 (Table P-PZ40)
4617.C613 Casaburi Urries, Pietro (Table P-PZ40)

Individual authors
Individual authors, 1400-1700 -- Continued
4617.C615 Casoni, Guido, 1575-1640 (Table P-PZ40)
4617.C617 Cassola, Luigi, d. ca. 1560 (Table P-PZ40)
4617.C626 Castellani, Castellano, 1461-1519? (Table P-PZ40)
4617.C63 Castelletti, Cristoforo, 16th cent. (Table P-PZ40)
4617.C65 Castiglione, Baldassare, conte, 1478-1529 (Table P-PZ40)
For biography see DG540.8.C3
Cf. BJ1600+ Il cortegiano
4617.C67 Castiglione, Sabba da, 1484-1554 (Table P-PZ40)
4617.C7 Caviceo, Jacopo, 1443-1511 (Table P-PZ40)
4617.C73 Cavretto, Pietro, b. ca. 1424 (Table P-PZ40)
4617.C75 Cebà, Ansaldo, 1565-1623 (Table P-PZ40)
4617.C8 Cecchi, Giovanni Maria, 1518-1587 (Table P-PZ40)
His Gl' incantesimi based upon cistellaria of Plautus
4617.C815 Cei, Francesco, 1471-1505 (Table P-PZ40)
4617.C817 Cellini, Benvenuto, 1500-1571 (Table P-PZ40)
4617.C82 Centorio, Ascanio, 16th cent. (Table P-PZ40)
4617.C83 Ceresara, Paride, 1466-1532 (Table P-PZ40)
4617.C84 Cerva, Elio Lampridio, 1460-1520 (Table P-PZ40)
4617.C9 Cesarini, Virginio, 1595-1624 (Table P-PZ40)
4618 Chiabrera, Gabriello, 1552-1638 (Table P-PZ39)
4619.C17 Christoforo Armeno (Table P-PZ40)
4619.C2 Ciampoli, Giovanni, 1590-1643 (Table P-PZ40)
4619.C3 Cicognini, Giacinto Andrea, 1606-1660 (Table P-PZ40)
Cf. ML, Music
4619.C32 Cicognini, Jacopo, fl. 1614-1633 (Table P-PZ40)
Father of Giacinto Cicognini
Cieco, da Ferrara see PQ4607.B84
4619.C5 Ciminelli, Serafino dei, Aquilano, 1466-1500 (Table P-PZ40)
4619.C55 Cinthio Scala, Bartolommeo, 16th cent. (Table P-PZ40)
Ciro di Pers see PQ4630.P27
4619.C7 Clemens IX, pope (Giulio Rospigliosi), 1600-1669 (Table P-PZ40)
Cf. BX1340 Biography
Coccaio, Merlino, pseud. see PQ4623.F3
4619.C8 Collenuccio, Pandolfo, 1444-1504 (Table P-PZ40)
4619.C9 Colonna, Francesco, d. 1527 (Table P-PZ40)
Author of Hypnerotomachia Poliphili
4620 Colonna, Vittoria, marchesa di Pescara, 1492-1547 (Table P-PZ37)
4621.C3 Conti, Giusto de', d. 1449 (Table P-PZ40)
4621.C4 Corbellini, Aurelio, fl. ca. 1610 (Table P-PZ40)
4621.C42 Corbinelli, Jacopo, fl. 1568-1580 (Table P-PZ40)
4621.C45 Corna da Soncino, Francesco, 15th cent. (Table P-PZ40)
4621.C47 Cornacchini, Domenico, fl. 1605 (Table P-PZ40)

Individual authors
Individual authors, 1400-1700 -- Continued

4621.C48 Cornaro Piscopia, Elena Lucrezia, 1646-1684 (Table P-PZ40)
4621.C5 Cornazzano, Antonio, ca. 1431-ca. 1500 (Table P-PZ40)
4621.C6 Corsini, Bartolomeo, 1606-1673 (Table P-PZ40)
4621.C69 Cortese, Giulio, 1530-1598 (Table P-PZ40)
4621.C7 Cortese, Giulio Cesare, b. ca. 1575 (Table P-PZ40)
4621.C73 Cosmico, Niccolò Lelio, 1420-1500 (Table P-PZ40)
4621.C74 Costa Margherita, 17th cent. (Table P-PZ40)
4621.C75 Costanzo, Angelo di, 1507?-1591 (Table P-PZ40)
4621.C76 Costo, Tonunaso, ca. 1560-ca. 1630 (Table P-PZ40)
4621.C77 Cremonino, Cesare, 1500-1631 (Table P-PZ40)
4621.C78 Cresci, Pietro (Table P-PZ40)
4621.C8 Croce, Guilio Cesare, 1550-1620? (Table P-PZ38)
4621.C83 Cucchetti, Giovanni Donato, 16th/17th cent. (Table P-PZ40)
Darpe, Beridio, pseud. see PQ4607.B3
4621.D14 D'Albizzotto Guidi, Jacopo, b. 1377 (Table P-PZ40)
4621.D15 D'Alibrando, Cola Giacomo, 16th cent. (Table P-PZ40)
4621.D16 Dati, Carlo Roberto, 1619-1675 (Table P-PZ40)
4621.D17 Dati, Gregorio, 1363-1436 (Table P-PZ40)
4621.D18 Dati, Leonardo, c. 1425 (Table P-PZ40)
4621.D184 Davanzati, Bartolomeo, b. 1460 (Table P-PZ40)
4621.D198 De Jacobiti, Aurelio Simmaco, 15th cent. (Table P-PZ40)
4621.D1984 De Jennaro, Pietro Jacopo, 1436-1508 (Table P-PZ40)
4621.D199 Del Carretto, Galeotto, d. 1531 (Table P-PZ40)
4621.D1995 Del Tufo, Gioan Battista, ca. 1548-ca. 1600 (Table P-PZ40)
4621.D2 Delfino, Giovanni, cardinal, 1617-1699 (Table P-PZ40)
Della Casa, Giovanni, 1503-1556 see PQ4617.C6
Della Porta, Giambattista, 1535?-1615 see PQ4630.P6
4621.D24 Della Valle, Federico, ca. 1560-1628 (Table P-PZ40)
4621.D243 Della Valle, Francesco, d. ca. 1627 (Table P-PZ40)
4621.D244 Dell'Uva, Benedetto, 1540-1582 (Table P-PZ40)
4621.D25 De Pacienza, Rogeri, 15th cent. (Table P-PZ40)
4621.D26 Di Natale, Giovanni, 1642-1718 (Table P-PZ40)
4621.D265 Di Northumberland Paleotti, Cristina, 1649 or 50-1719 (Table P-PZ40)
4621.D27 D'Isa, Francesco, 1572-1622 (Table P-PZ40)
4621.D3 Dolce, Lodovico, 1508-1568 (Table P-PZ40)
4621.D44 Domenichi, Lodovico, 1515-1564 (Table P-PZ40)
4621.D5 Doni, Antonio Francesco, 1513-1574 (Table P-PZ40)
4621.D53 Donno, Ferdinando, 1591-1649? (Table P-PZ40)
4621.D6 Dotti, Bartolomeo, 1651-1713 (Table P-PZ40)
4621.D7 Dottori, Carlo de, conte, 1618-1686 (Table P-PZ40)
4621.D8 Dovizi, Bernardo, da Bibbiena, cardinal, 1470-1520 (Table P-PZ40)

Individual authors
Individual authors, 1400-1700 -- Continued

4621.D83 Dragoncino, Giovanni Battista, b. ca. 1497 (Table P-PZ40)
Duonnu Pantu, 1664 or 5-1696 see PQ4630.P39
4621.D9 Durante, Piero, 16th cent. (Table P-PZ40)
Enea Silvio Piccolomini
see BX1308, and PA8556 Pius II pope
4621.E5 Epicuro, Marc' Antonio, 1472-1555 (Table P-PZ40)
4621.E6 Equicola, Mario, 1470-1525 (Table P-PZ40)
4621.E7 Erizzo, Sebastiano, 1525-1585 (Table P-PZ40)
4621.E74 Errico, Scipione, 1592-1670 (Table P-PZ40)
4621.F23 Fagiuoli, Giovanni Battista, 1660-1742 (Table P-PZ40)
4621.F25 Falugi, Giovanni, 16th cent. (Table P-PZ40)
4621.F265 Favagrossa, Ottaviano (Table P-PZ40)
4621.F38 Fiamma, Gabriele, 1533-1587 (Table P-PZ40)
Fidenzio Glottocrisio, pseud. see PQ4634.S25
4621.F4 Figari, Pompeo, fl. 1690 (Table P-PZ40)
4621.F49 Filelfo, Giovanni Mario, 1426-1480 (Table P-PZ40)
4621.F5 Filicaia, Vincenzo da, 1642-1707 (Table P-PZ40)
4621.F53 Filocalo, Giovanni, b. ca. 1490 (Table P-PZ40)
4621.F55 Finiguerri, Stefano, 1365?-1435? (Table P-PZ40)
4621.F8 Fiorillo, Silvio, fl. 1600 (Table P-PZ40)
Pseudonym: Capitan Mattamoros
4622 Firenzuola, Agnolo, 1493-ca. 1545 (Table P-PZ39)
4623.F3 Folengo, Girolamo, in religion Teofilo, d. 1544 (Table P-PZ40)
For his Maccaronea or Macaronica see PN1489.Z7
4623.F36 Fonte, Moderata, 1555-1592 (Table P-PZ40)
4623.F37 Forteguerri, Giovanni, d. 1582 (Table P-PZ40)
4623.F5 Fortini, Pietro, d. 1562 (Table P-PZ40)
4623.F57 Franco, Matteo, 1447-1494 (Table P-PZ40)
4623.F58 Franco, Niccolò, 1515-1570 (Table P-PZ40)
Cf. PQ4103 Petrarchism
4623.F6 Franco, Veronica, 1546-1591 (Table P-PZ40)
4623.F62 Franzesi, Mattio, 16th cent. (Table P-PZ40)
4623.F65 Fregoso, Antonio, d. 1515 (Table P-PZ40)
4623.F7 Frugoni, Francesco Fulvio, 17th cent. (Table P-PZ40)
4623.F87 Fuscano, Ioan Berardino, fl. 1524-1546 (Table P-PZ40)
4623.G13 Galeazzo, Domenico, 16th cent. (Table P-PZ40)
4623.G14 Galeota, Francesco, d. 1497 (Table P-PZ40)
4623.G15 Galilei, Galileo, 1564-1642 (Table P-PZ40)
Cf. QB3, QB36.G2, Astronomy
4623.G157 Galli, Angelo, ca. 1390-ca. 1459 (Table P-PZ40)
4623.G17 Gallo, Filenio, d. 1503 (Table P-PZ40)
4623.G2 Gambara, Veronica, 1485-1550 (Table P-PZ40)

Individual authors
Individual authors, 1400-1700 -- Continued

4623.G25 Gareth, Benedetto, called Cariteo, b. ca. 1450 (Table P-PZ40)
Catalan author
4623.G26 Garopoli, Girolamo, ca. 1605-1678 (Table P-PZ40)
4623.G27 Gaudenzio, Paganino, 1595?-1649 (Table P-PZ40)
4623.G3 Gelli, Giovanni Battista, 1498-1563 (Table P-PZ40)
4623.G4 Gelsi, Giovanni, b. 1592 (Table P-PZ40)
4623.G43 Gennari, Giuseppe, 1721-1800 (Table P-PZ40)
4623.G45 Gentilericcio, Pietro Girolamo, 1563-1640 (Table P-PZ40)
4623.G46 Genuzio, Andrea, 17th cent. (Table P-PZ40)
4623.G47 Gherardi, Giovanni, ca. 1367-ca. 1444 (Table P-PZ40)
4623.G5 Ghirardi, Boneto, 16th cent. (Table P-PZ40)
4623.G53 Giacomini Tebalducci Malespini, Lorenzo, d. 1599 (Table P-PZ40)
4623.G6 Giambullari, Bernardo, fl. 1500 (Table P-PZ40)
4623.G7 Giancarli, Gigio Artemio, 16th cent. (Table P-PZ40)
Giannotti, Antonia see PQ4630.P8
Gigli, Girolamo see PQ4692.G65
4623.G8 Giliberto, Onofrio, 17th cent. (Table P-PZ40)
Ginnesio Gavardo Vacalerio, pseud. see PQ4632.S5
4623.G84 Giovanetti, Marcello, 1598-1621 (Table P-PZ40)
Giovanni, Domenico di see PQ4615.B8
4624 Giraldi Cintio, Giovanni Battista, 1504-1573 (Table P-PZ39)
4625.G17 Giuffredi, Argisto, ca. 1535-1593 (Table P-PZ40)
4625.G18 Giussano, Giovanni Pietro, 1548-1623 (Table P-PZ38)
4625.G2 Giustiniani, Leonardo, ca. 1383-1466 (Table P-PZ38)
4625.G23 Giustiniani, Orsatto, 1538-1603 (Table P-PZ40)
4625.G32 Gonzaga, Curzio, 1536-1599 (Table P-PZ40)
4625.G35 Goselini, Giuliano, 1525-1587 (Table P-PZ40)
4625.G36 Gradenigo, Jacapo, fl. 1417-1420 (Table P-PZ40)
4625.G37 Grandi, Ascanio, 1567-1647 (Table P-PZ40)
4625.G38 Grandi, Marcu di, 15th cent. (Table P-PZ40)
4625.G4 Granucci, Niccolò, 1522-1603 (Table P-PZ40)
4625.G46 Grasso, Nicola, 16th cent. (Table P-PZ40)
4625.G47 Gratarolo, Bongianni, fl. 1556-1589 (Table P-PZ40)
4625.G48 Gravina, Giovanni Vincenzo, 1664-1718 (Table P-PZ40)
4625.G5 Graziani, Gerolamo, 1604-1675 (Table P-PZ40)
4625.G6 Grazzini, Antonio Francesco, called Il Lasca, 1503-1584 (Table P-PZ40)
4625.G7 Groto, Luigi, 1541-1585 (Table P-PZ40)
4625.G8 Gualterotti, Raffaello, 1543-1638 (Table P-PZ40)
Guardato, Masuccio see PQ4630.M26
4626 Guarini, Giovanni Battista, 1538-1612 (Table P-PZ39)
4627.G26 Guarnello, Alessandro (Table P-PZ40)
Guicciardini, Francesco, 1482-1540 see DG738.14.G9

Individual authors
Individual authors, 1400-1700 -- Continued

4627.G3 Guido, Carol Alessandro, 1650-1712 (Table P-PZ40)
4627.G48 Guidicciolo, Levanzio da, Mantovano, 16th cent. (Table P-PZ40)
4627.G5 Guidiccioni, Giovanni, 1500-1541 (Table P-PZ40)
4627.I54 Ingegneri, Angelo, 1550-ca. 1613 (Table P-PZ40)
4627.I8 Isa, Francesco d', 1572-1622 (Table P-PZ40)
Comedies written by Francesco, a canon of the church, appeared under the name of his brother, Ottavio d'Isa.
Isa, Ottavio d' see PQ4627.I8
4627.J34 Jacobilli, Vincenzo, 1561-1601 (Table P-PZ40)
4627.J7 Jonata, Marino, fl. 1455 (Table P-PZ40)
4627.L3 Landi, Ortensio, ca. 1512-ca. 1553 (Table P-PZ40)
4627.L315 Landino, Cristoforo, 1424-1504 (Table P-PZ40)
For Latin works see PA8540.L3
Lasca see PQ4625.G6
4627.L327 Lazzarelli, Giovanni Francesco, 1631-1694 (Table P-PZ40)
4627.L33 Lazzaroni, Giovanni Battista, 1626-1698 (Table P-PZ40)
4627.L35 Lemene, Francesco de, conte, 1634-1704 (Table P-PZ40)
4627.L36 Lenio, Antonino, b. ca. 1470 (Table P-PZ40)
4627.L38 Leonardo da Vinci, 1452-1519 (Table P-PZ40)
4627.L39 Leoni, Francesco, 15th/16th cent. (Table P-PZ40)
4627.L4 Leopardi, Girolamo, fl. 1613 (Table P-PZ40)
4627.L43 Leporeo, Lodovico, 1582-ca. 1655 (Table P-PZ40)
4627.L45 Liburnio, Nicolò, 1474-1557 (Table P-PZ40)
Limerno, Pitocco, pseud. see PQ4623.F3
4627.L5 Lippi, Lorenzo, 1606-1664 (Table P-PZ40)
4627.L6 Lodovici, Francesco, fl. 1535 (Table P-PZ40)
4627.L65 Lomazzo, Giovanni Paolo, 1538-1600 (Table P-PZ40)
4627.L7 Loredano, Giovanni Francesco, 1606-1661 (Table P-PZ40)
4627.L75 Lorenzini, Niccolò (Table P-PZ40)
4627.L77 Lori, Andrea, fl. 1556 (Table P-PZ40)
4627.L78 Lubrano, Giacomo, 1619-1693 (Table P-PZ40)
4627.L8 Luigini, Federico, 16th cent. (Table P-PZ40)
4627.L83 Lupis, Bisanzio, ca. 1478-1555 (Table P-PZ40)
4627.M2 Machiavelli, Niccolò, 1469-1527 (Table P-PZ40)
For biography see DG738.14.M2
Maffei, Scipione, 1675-1755 see PQ4712.M3
4627.M4 Magalotti, Lorenzo, conte, 1637-1712 (Table P-PZ40)
4627.M45 Maggi, Carlo Maria, 1630-1699 (Table P-PZ40)
4627.M47 Maia Materdona, Giovan Francesco, 1590-c. 1650 (Table P-PZ40)
4627.M497 Malaspina, Giovanni, 17th cent. (Table P-PZ40)
4627.M5 Malatesti, Antonio, d. 1672 (Table P-PZ40)
4627.M54 Malatesti, Malatesta, ca. 1368-1429? (Table P-PZ40)
4627.M6 Malispini, Celio, b. 1531 (Table P-PZ40)

Individual authors
Individual authors, 1400-1700 -- Continued
4627.M63 Malipiero, Girolamo, d. ca. 1547 (Table P-PZ40)
4627.M7 Manetti, Antonio, 1423-1497 (Table P-PZ40)
4627.M72 Manetti, Marabottino, b. 1435 (Table P-PZ40)
4627.M726 Manfredi, Lelio (Table P-PZ40)
4627.M73 Manfredi, Muzio, fl. 1593 (Table P-PZ40)
4627.M74 Mantelli, Giovanni de, 15th cent. (Table P-PZ40)
4627.M742 Mantegna, Giovanni Alfonso, fl. 1525-1585 (Table P-PZ40)
4627.M744 Mantova Benevides, Marco, conte, 1489-1582 (Table P-PZ40)
4627.M75 Manzini, Giovanni Battista, 1599-1664 (Table P-PZ40)
Maratii Zappi, Faustina see PQ4734.Z5
4627.M78 Marana, Giovanni Paolo, 1642-1693 (Table P-PZ40)
4627.M8 Marcellino, Evangelista, 1530-1593 (Table P-PZ40)
4627.M82 Marchetti, Alessandro, 1632-1714 (Table P-PZ40)
4627.M83 Mariano da Siena, fl. 1431 (Table P-PZ40)
4627.M84 Marinella, Lucrezia, 1571-1653 (Table P-PZ40)
4627.M9 Marini, Giovanni Ambrogio, 17th cent. (Table P-PZ40)
Marino, Giovanni Battista, 1569-1625
4628.A1 Collected works. By date
4628.A2 Selected works. By date
4628.A3-.Z29 Separate works
Translations
4628.Z3-.Z39 English
4628.Z3 Collected works. By date
4628.Z31-.Z39 Separate works. By title and date
4628.Z4-.Z49 French
4628.Z5-.Z59 German
4628.Z6-.Z69 Spanish
4628.Z7-.Z79 Other. By language
4628.Z8 Biography and criticism
4630.M15 Mariotti, Francesco, 17th cent. (Table P-PZ40)
4630.M16 Martelli, Lodovico, 1499-1527 (Table P-PZ40)
4630.M165 Martelli, Ludovico, 1503-ca. 1531 (Table P-PZ40)
4630.M17 Martelli, Niccolò, 1498-1555 (Table P-PZ40)
Martelli, Pier Jacopo see PQ4716.M55
4630.M22 Martelli, Vincenzio, d. 1556 (Table P-PZ40)
Introduced the alexandrine in drama
4630.M23 Martirano, Bernardino, 1490-1558 (Table P-PZ40)
4630.M237 Massolo, Pietro, 1520-1590 (Table P-PZ40)
4630.M24 Massucci, Niccolò, 16th cent. (Table P-PZ40)
4630.M26 Masuccio, Salernitano, 1420?-1500? (Table P-PZ40)
4630.M263 Matraini, Chiara, 1515-1604? (Table P-PZ40)
Mattamoros, Capitan, pseud. see PQ4621.F8
4630.M266 Maura, Paolo, 1638-1711 (Table P-PZ40)
4630.M27 Mauro, Giovanni, 1490-1536 (Table P-PZ40)

Individual authors
Individual authors, 1400-1700 -- Continued

4630.M28 Medici, Lorenzino de', 1514-1548 (Table P-PZ40)
4630.M3 Medici, Lorenzo de', called Il Magnifico, 1449-1492 (Table P-PZ40)
Cf. DG737.9 History
4630.M32 Meglio, Giovan Matteo di, 15th cent. (Table P-PZ40)
4630.M33 Mele, Domenico Antonio, b. 1647 (Table P-PZ40)
4630.M34 Melò, Persià, 17th cent. (Table P-PZ40)
4630.M35 Melosio, Francesco, fl. 1660 (Table P-PZ40)
4630.M4 Menzini, Benedetto, 1646-1704 (Table P-PZ40)
Merlin, Coccaio, pseud. see PQ4623.F3
Michelangelo, Buonarroti, 1475-1564 see PQ4615.B6
4630.M45 Mini, Paolo, 16th cent. (Table P-PZ40)
4630.M48 Minutolo, Ceccarella, fl. 15th cent. (Table P-PZ40)
4630.M5 Molino, Girolamo, 16th cent. (Table P-PZ40)
4630.M6 Molza, Francesco Maria, 1489-1544 (Table P-PZ40)
4630.M62 Molza, Tarquinia, 1542-1617 (Table P-PZ40)
4630.M67 Moneti, Francesco, 1635-1712 (Table P-PZ40)
4630.M7 Moniglia, Giovanni Andrea, d. 1700 (Table P-PZ40)
Prefer ML49.A2
4630.M72 Monitio, Cesare, 17th cent. (Table P-PZ40)
4630.M74 Montano, Marco, d. 1586 (Table P-PZ40)
4630.M76 Montemagno, Buonaccorso da, d. 1429 (Table P-PZ40)
Monteverdi, Claudio, 1557-1643
see ML
4630.M77 Monti, Scipione de', d. 1583 (Table P-PZ40)
4630.M78 Morando, Bernardo, 1589-1656 (Table P-PZ40)
4630.M8 Mori, Ascanio Pipino de', 1533-1591 (Table P-PZ40)
4630.M836 Moro, Mauritio (Table P-PZ40)
4630.M84 Morra, Isabella di, ca. 1520-1546 (Table P-PZ40)
4630.M9 Muscettola, Antonio, 17th cent. (Table P-PZ40)
4630.M93 Mussio, Antonio (Table P-PZ40)
4630.M96 Muzzarelli, Giovanni, 1486 or 7-1511 (Table P-PZ40)
4630.N3 Negri, Francesco, 1623-1698 (Table P-PZ40)
4630.N4 Neri, Ippolito, 1652-1709 (Table P-PZ40)
4630.N5 Niccolò da Correggio, 1450-1508 (Table P-PZ40)
4630.N55 Nicola da Montefalco, 15th cent. (Table P-PZ40)
4630.N7 Nomi, Federigo, 1633-1705 (Table P-PZ40)
4630.O4 Oddi, Sforza, 1540-1611 (Table P-PZ40)
4630.O65 Olimpo da Sassoferrato, 1486?-1540 (Table P-PZ40)
4630.O7 Ongaro, Antonio, ca. 1569-1599 (Table P-PZ40)
4630.O8 Orologi, Giuseppe, d. 1576 (Table P-PZ40)
4630.P116 Pagano, Nunziante, b. 1683 (Table P-PZ40)
4630.P13 Pallavicino, Ferrante, 1615-1644 (Table P-PZ40)
4630.P136 Palmario di Ancona, Francesco, 15th cent. (Table P-PZ40)

Individual authors
Individual authors, 1400-1700 -- Continued

4630.P14 Palombara, Massimiliano, marchese, 1614-1685 (Table P-PZ40)
4630.P15 Panciatichi, Lorenzo, 1635-1676 (Table P-PZ40)
4630.P17 Pandimo, Antonio, 1602-1647 (Table P-PZ40)
4630.P18 Panteo, Giovanni Antonio, 1446?-1496 (Table P-PZ40)
Pantu, Duonnu, 1664 or 5-1696 see PQ4630.P39
4630.P2 Parabosco, Girolamo, d. 1560 (Table P-PZ40)
Parri da Pozzolatico, pseud. see PQ4562.A65
4630.P22 Partenio, Bernardino, d. 1589 (Table P-PZ40)
4630.P225 Paruta, Filippo, 1550?-1629 (Table P-PZ40)
4630.P228 Pascoli, Gabriel (Table P-PZ40)
4630.P23 Pasqualigo, Luigi, 16th cent. (Table P-PZ40)
4630.P235 Passerini, Gaetana, 1670-1726 (Table P-PZ40)
4630.P24 Pauluccio, Sigismondo, 16th cent. (Table P-PZ40)
4630.P243 Pazzi, Alfonso de', 1509-1555 (Table P-PZ40)
4630.P245 Pazzi de'Medici, Alessandro, 1469-1535 (Table P-PZ40)
Author of Dido in Cartagine
4630.P25 Peri, Giovanni Domenico, 17th cent. (Table P-PZ40)
4630.P26 Perrucci, Andrea, 1651-1704 (Table P-PZ40)
4630.P27 Pers, Cirodi, 1599-1663 (Table P-PZ40)
4630.P28 Piacentini, Marco, 15th cent. (Table P-PZ40)
4630.P3 Piccolomini, Alessandro, 1508-1578 (Table P-PZ40)
Piccolomini, Enea Silvio
see Pius II, pope, BX1308 and PA8556
4630.P36 Pierfrancesco, da Camerino (Table P-PZ40)
Pieverdi, Brivio, pseud. see PQ4607.B3
4630.P374 Pigna, Giovan Battista, 1529-1575 (Table P-PZ40)
4630.P378 Pincetti, Ippolito, 1531-1595 (Table P-PZ40)
4630.P379 Pino, Bernardino, d. 1601 TABLE P-PZ40 (Table P-PZ40)
4630.P39 Piro, Domenico, 1664 or 5-1696 (Table P-PZ40)
4630.P4 Pisani, Baldassarre, 17th cent. (Table P-PZ40)
Pistoia, Antonio da see PQ4617.C2
Pius II, pope
see Pius II, pope, BX1308 and PA8556
4630.P435 Podiani, Mario, ca. 1501-ca. 1583 (Table P-PZ40)
Poggio-Bracciolini, 1380-1459 see PA8477.B76
4630.P5 Poliziano, Angelo Ambrogini, known as, 1454-1494 (Table P-PZ38)
Cf. PA8560+ Italian literature
4630.P53 Pollastra, Giovanni, 1465-1540 (Table P-PZ40)
4630.P55 Pona, Francesco, 1594-1654 (Table P-PZ40)
4630.P58 Porrino, Gandolfo (Table P-PZ40)
4630.P6 Porta, Giovanni Battista della, 1535?-1615 (Table P-PZ40)
4630.P65 Porto, Luigi da, 1486-1529 (Table P-PZ40)
Author of Giulietta e Romeo

Individual authors
Individual authors, 1400-1700 -- Continued
Pozzo, Modesta, 1555-1592 see PQ4623.F36
4630.P7 Preti, Girolamo, 1582-1626 (Table P-PZ40)
4630.P75 Prodenzani, Simone, 1355?-ca. 1433 (Table P-PZ40)
4630.P79 Pucciarini, Clemente, 16th cent. (Table P-PZ40)
4630.P8 Pulci, Antonia (Table P-PZ40)
Wife of Bernardo
4630.P82 Pulci, Bernardo, 1438-1488 (Table P-PZ40)
4630.P9 Pulci, Luca, 1431-1470 (Table P-PZ40)
4631 Pulci, Luigi, 1432-1484 (Table P-PZ39 modified)
4631.A61-.Z48 Separate works. By title
Subarrange each work by Table P-PZ43 unless otherwise specified
Il Morgante maggiore
4631.M3 Editions. By date
4631.M3A-.M3Z Translations. By language
4631.M4 Criticism
4632.Q38 Quattromani, Sertorio, 1541-1611 (Table P-PZ40)
Cf. PA8570.Q3 Latin literature
4632.Q43 Querenghi, Antonio, 1546-1633 (Table P-PZ40)
4632.R133 Rainerio, Antonio Francesco, 16th cent. (Table P-PZ40)
4632.R135 Rapi, Andriotta, 16th cent. (Table P-PZ40)
4632.R15 Razzi, Girolomo, fl. 1560 (Table P-PZ40)
In religion: Silvano
4632.R2 Redi, Francesco, 1626-1698 (Table P-PZ40)
4632.R23 Renaldini, Panfilo di, 16th cent. (Table P-PZ40)
4632.R25 Ricchi, Agostino, fl. 1529 (Table P-PZ40)
4632.R3 Ricciardi, Giovanni Battista, 1623-1686 (Table P-PZ40)
4632.R33 Riccio, Onofrio, d. 1656 (Table P-PZ40)
4632.R337 Rimbotti, Tommaso, 1565-1622 (Table P-PZ40)
4632.R34 Rinaldi, Cesare, 1559-1636 (Table P-PZ40)
4632.R4 Rinuccini, Ottavio, d. 1621 (Table P-PZ40)
"Restauratore del melodramma". Cf. ML
4632.R43 Rocco, Antonio, 1576-1653 (Table P-PZ40)
4632.R5 Rosa, Salvatore, 1615-1673 (Table P-PZ40)
Cf. ND623.R7
4632.R55 Roselli, Rosello, 1399-1432 (Table P-PZ40)
4632.R6 Rota, Bernardino, 1509-1575 (Table P-PZ40)
4632.R7 Rucellai, Giovanni, 1475-1525 (Table P-PZ40)
4632.R73 Rucellai, Orazio Ricasoli, 1614-1674 (Table P-PZ40)
4632.R8 Ruspoli, Francesco, 1572-1625 (Table P-PZ40)
Ruzzante see PQ4610.B47
4632.S3 Sabadino degli Arienti, Giovanni, 15th cent. (Table P-PZ40)
4632.S35 Sachella, Bartolomeo, b. ca. 1380 (Table P-PZ40)
4632.S5 Sagredo, Giovanni, 1616-ca. 1696 (Table P-PZ40)
Salernitano, Masuccio see PQ4630.M26

Individual authors
Individual authors, 1400-1700 -- Continued

4632.S65 Salvestro, cartaio (Table P-PZ40)
4632.S7 Salviati, Leonardo, 1540-1589 (Table P-PZ40)
Salvini, Antonio Maria see PQ4732.S2
4632.S8 Salvucci, Salvuccio, fl. 1591 (Table P-PZ40)
4632.S82 San Martino d'Agliè, Filippo, conte, 1604-1667 (Table P-PZ40)
4632.S84 Sandoval, Diego de, conde de Castro, ca. 1510-1546 (Table P-PZ40)
4633 Sannazaro, Jacopo, 1458-1530 (Table P-PZ39)
4634.S13 Santi, Giovanni, ca. 1435-1494 (Table P-PZ40)
4634.S14 Santinelli, Francesco Maria, marchese, 17th cent. (Table P-PZ40)
4634.S15 Sardi, Tommaso di Matteo, 1458-1517 (Table P-PZ40)
4634.S157 Sarnelli, Pompeo (Table P-PZ40)
4634.S163 Sarrochi, Margherita, ca. 1560-1617 (Table P-PZ40)
4634.S17 Sassetti, Filippo, 1540-1588 (Table P-PZ40)

4634.S22 Savonarola, Girolomo Maria Francesco Matteo, 1452-1498 (Table P-PZ40)
Cf. DG737.97
4634.S224 Scala, Flaminio, fl. 1620 (Table P-PZ40)
Scaliggeri dalla Fratta, Camillo, pseud. see PQ4605.B8
4634.S2254 Scalini, Cesare, fl. 1540-1550 (Table P-PZ40)
4634.S226 Scammacca, Ortensio, 1565-1648 (Table P-PZ40)
4634.S23 Scaramuccia, Angelita, fl. 1609 (Table P-PZ40)
4634.S24 Schettini, Pirro, 1630-1678 (Table P-PZ40)
4634.S25 Scroffa, Camillo, conte, d. 1565 (Table P-PZ40)
4634.S3 Secchi, Niccolò, 16th cent. (Table P-PZ40)
4634.S32 Segni, Bernardo, 1504-1558 (Table P-PZ40)
4634.S325 Sempronio, Giovan Leone, ca. 1603-1646 (Table P-PZ40)
4634.S33 Sergardi, Lodovico, 1660-1726 (Table P-PZ40)
4634.S35 Sermini, Gentile, 15th cent. (Table P-PZ40)
Sforza, Alessandro, 1409-1473, supposed author, Il Cancioniere see PQ4561.A1C27
4634.S37 Sgruttendio, Felippo, 17th cent. (Table P-PZ40)
4634.S38 Sigonio, Vicenzo, 16th cent. (Table P-PZ40)
Smarrito, 1619-1675 see PQ4621.D16
4634.S5 Soldani, Jacopo, 1579-1641 (Table P-PZ40)
4634.S53 Sommi, Leone di, ca. 1525-ca. 1590 (Table P-PZ40)
4634.S55 Spelta, Antonio Maria, 1559-1632 (Table P-PZ40)
4634.S6 Speroni degli Alvarotti, Sperone, 1500-1588 (Table P-PZ40)
4634.S63 Spezzani, Antonio, fl. 1581 (Table P-PZ40)
4634.S65 Stampa, Gaspara, 16th cent. (Table P-PZ38)
4634.S66 Stelando, Lorenzo, fl. 1643 (Table P-PZ40)
4634.S68 Stigliani, Tommaso, 1573-1651 (Table P-PZ40)

Individual authors
Individual authors, 1400-1700 -- Continued
4634.S7 Straparola, Giovanni Francesco, fl. 1540 (Table P-PZ40)
Strascino see PQ4617.C25
4634.S78 Strozzi, Alessandra (Macinghi), 1407-1471 (Table P-PZ40)
4634.S8 Strozzi, Giovanni Battista, il vecchio, 1504-1571 (Table P-PZ40)
4634.S82 Strozzi, Giovanni Battista, il giovane, 1551-1634 (Table P-PZ40)
4634.S83 Sullam, Sara Copia, 1592-1641 (Table P-PZ40)
4634.T3 Tansillo, Luigi, 1510-1568 (Table P-PZ40)
4634.T33 Tantillo, Antonino, d. 1659 (Table P-PZ40)
4634.T4 Tarsia, Galeazzo di, b. ca. 1476 (Table P-PZ40)
4634.T6 Tasso, Bernardo, 1493-1569 (Table P-PZ40)
4634.T8 Tasso, Ercole, 16th cent. (Table P-PZ40)
4634.T9 Tasso, Faustino, b. ca. 1541 (Table P-PZ40)
Tasso, Torquato, 1544-1595
4636.A1 Collected works. By date
(4636.A11) Collected works. By editor
(4636.A14) Posthumous works
see PQ4636.A3
4636.A3 Selections, anthologies, etc. By editor, A-Z
4636.A4 Quotations, passages, thoughts, etc.
Selected works
4636.A5 Miscellaneous. By editor
4636.A7 Dramatic works. By date
4636.A9 Minor epic poems. By date
4637.A1 Collected (Lyric) poems. Rime
4637.A2 Selected (Lyric) poems
4637.A21 Amori
4637.A22 Laudi ed encomi de' principe e delle donne illustri
4637.A23 Rime spirituali
4637.A24 Lagrime di Maria Vergine
4637.A25 Lagrime di Gesù Cristo
4637.A3 Latin poems
4637.A4 Minor collections: Almanacs, birthday books, thoughts, etc.
Prefer PQ4636.A3-4
(4637.A45) Posthumously published poems
see PQ4637.A2+
4637.A5 Spurious poems
Separate works other than prose
4638 La Gerusalemme liberata
Also published as Il Goffredo ovvero Gierusalemme liberata
Editions
4638.A1 Manuscript (Facsimiles)

Individual authors
Individual authors, 1400-1700
Tasso, Torquato, 1544-1595
Separate works other than prose
La Gerusalemme liberata
Editions
Manuscript (Facsimiles) -- Continued
(4638.A2) Reproductions of manuscripts in print
Printed editions
Dated editions. By date-letter
4638.A80-.A99 1580-1599
4638.A80 First (incomplete) edition, 1580
4638.B00-.B99 1600-1699
4638.C00-.C99 1700-1799
4638.D00-.D99 1800-1899
4638.E00-.E99 1900-1999
4638.F00-.F99 2000-2099
4638.Z3 Editions without date, by place, A-Z
(4638.Z35) Critical and annotated editions, by editor, A-Z
4638.Z4 School editions, by editor, A-Z
Prefer PQ4638.A-E
4638.Z5 Selected portions
(4638.Z55) Minor selections. Quotations. Thoughts, etc.
Prefer PQ4636.A4
4638.Z6 Special cantos
4638.Z7 Cinque canti di Camillo Camilli
Criticism and interpretation see PQ4656
4638.Z9 La Gerusalemme conquistata
Il Goffredo
see La Gerusalemme liberata
4639 Dramatic works and minor epic poems
Aminta (Pastoral drama)
4639.A2 Editions. By date
4639.A3 Criticism
Galealto, re di Norvegia see PQ4639.T5+
4639.G2 Genealogia di casa Gonzaga
4639.I2 Intrighi d'amore, comedia
4639.M2 Il mondo creato (Le sette giornate del mondo creato)
4639.M5 Il monte Oliveto
4639.R2 Rinaldo
4639.R5 Rogo amoroso (Pastoral dramatic poem)
Torrismondo (Tragedy)
Begun as Galealto, re di Norvegia, 1573 (Act I and part of act II, only)
Finished as Il re Torrismondo (5 acts), 1586-87
4639.T5 Text of Galealto. By date
4639.T6 Texts of Torrismondo. By date

Individual authors
Individual authors, 1400-1700
Tasso, Torquato, 1544-1595
Separate works other than prose
Dramatic works and minor epic poems
Rinaldo
Torrismondo (Tragedy) -- Continued

4639.T7 Criticism

4640 Prose works (Dialoghi, Discorsi, Orazioni, etc.).
In general, prefer classification here, not by subject

4640.A1 Collections. By date

4640.A2 Selections. Anthologies, etc.
Prefer PQ4636.A3

Selected works

4640.A4 Dialoghi. By date

4640.A5 Discorsi. By date
Cf. PQ4640.D89

Letters see PQ4647.A1

4640.A6 Orazioni. By date

4640.A7-Z Separate works

(4640.A8) Apoligia in difusa della sua Gierusalemme liberata

4640.B3 I bagni, o vero De la pieta (Dialogo)

4640.B4 Il Beltramo, o vero De la cortesia (Dialogo)

4640.C2 Il Cataneo, o vero Delle conclusioni (Dialogo)

4640.C3 Il Cataneo, o vero De gl' idoli (Dialogo)

4640.C4 La Cavalletta, o vero Della poesia toscana (Dialogo)

4640.C5 Il cavaliere amante e la gentildonna amata (Dialogo)

4640.C6 Cinquante conclusioni amorose

4640.C7 Conclusioni amorose

Le consideration sopra tre canzoni di M.G.B. Pigna, intitolate, Le tre sorelle see PQ4552.P4

4640.C9 Il conte, o vero De l'imprese (Dialogo)

4640.C92 Il Costantino, o vero De la clemenza (Dialogo)

4640.D14 Del amor vincendevole tra il padre e il figliuolo (Discorso)

(4640.D145) Del giudizio sovra La Gerusalemme
see PQ4656

4640.D15 Del giuramente falso (Discorso)

4640.D17 Del poema eroico (Discorso)

4640.D2 Dell' arte del dialogo (Discorso)

Dell' arte poetica (Discorsi) see PQ4640.D89

4640.D3 Dell' ufficio del siniscalco (Discorso)

4640.D4 Della dignita (Dialogo)

4640.D5 Della gelosia (Discorso)

4640.D55 Della precedenza (Dialogo)

4640.D6 Della virtu dei Romani (Orazione)

4640.D7 Della virtu eroica e della carita (Discorso)

Individual authors
Individual authors, 1400-1700.
Tasso, Torquato, 1544-1595
Prose works (Dialoghi, Discorsi, Orazioni, etc.).
Separate works -- Continued

4640.D8 Della virtu femminile e donnesca (Discorso)
4640.D89 Discorsi dell' arte poetica e del poema eroico
4640.D9 Discorsi del poema eroico
The Discorsi dell' arte poetica (etc.) enlarged to six books
4640.D93 Discorso intorno alla sedizione nata nel regno di Francia l' anno 1585
4640.D95 Discorso sopra due questioni amorose
4640.F5 Il Ficino, o vero De l'arte (Dialogo)
4640.F6 Il forestiero napolitano, o vero Della gelosia (Dialogo)
4640.F7 Il Forno, o vero De la nobilita (Dialogo)
4640.G4 Il Ghirlinzone, o vero L'epitafio (Dialogo)
4640.G5 Il Gianluca, o vero De la maschere (Dialogo)
4640.G6 Il Gonzaga, o vero Del piacere onesto (Dialogo)
4640.G7 Il Gonzaga secondo, o vero Del giuoco (Dialogo)
4640.M2 Il Manso, o vero Dell'amicizia (Dialogo)
4640.M4 Il Malpiglio, o vero De la corte (Dialogo)
4640.M5 Il Malpiglio secondo, o vero Del fuggir la moltitudine (Dialogo)
4640.M7 Il messaggiero (Dialogo)
4640.M8 Il Minturno, o vero De la bellezza (Dialogo)
4640.M9 La Molza, o vero De l'amore (Dialogo)
4640.N5 Il Nifo, o vero Del piacere (Dialogo)
4640.O4 Orazione fatte nell'aprirsi dell' Accademia Ferrarese
4640.O5 Orazione in lode della serenissima casa de' Medici
4640.O6 Orazione in morte di Barbara d'Austria
4640.O7 Orazione nella morte dell'illustrissimo cardinale Luigi d'Este
4640.O8 Orazione nella morte del Santino
4640.P3 Il padre di famiglia (Dialogo)
4640.P6 Il Porzio, o vero De la virtu (Dialogo)
4640.R3 Il Rangone, o vero de la pace (Dialogo)
4640.R5 Risposta di Roma a Plutarco
4640.R6 Il Romeo, o vero Del giuoco (Dialogo)
4640.S4 Il secretario
(4640.Z5) Works annotated by Tasso
see the author

Translations
4641 Italian dialects
4641.A2 Collections and selections, by date
Separate works
4641.A3 Gerusalemme liberata, by dialect and date

Individual authors
Individual authors, 1400-1700.
Tasso, Torquato, 1544-1595
Translations
Italian dialects.
Separate works -- Continued

4641.A4 L'Aminta, by dialect and date
4641.A5 Rime, by dialect and date
4641.A7 Other works, by original title, A-Z
4641.Z5 Italian translations of Latin poems, by translator, A-Z
4642 Western European languages
4642.E2-.E29 English (Table PQ4)
4642.F2-.F29 French (Table PQ4)
4642.G2-.G9 German (Table PQ4)
4642.P2-.P29 Portuguese (Table PQ4)
4642.S2-.S29 Spanish (Table PQ4)
4643.A-Z Other European languages, except Slavic, A-Z
For list of Cutter numbers, see PQ4497
4644.A-Z Slavic languages, A-Z
For list of Cutter numbers, see PQ4498
4644.5.A-Z Languages of Africa, Asia, Oceania, etc., A-Z
(4644.9) Artificial languages, Esperanto, Ido, etc.
see subclass PM
4645 Doubtful and spurious works
4645.A1 Collections. By date
4645.A1D5 Dialogo dei casi d'amore
4645.A1D6 La disperazione di Giuda (Poemetto)
La Gismonda
F. Asinari's tragedy "Il Tancredi" published in Paris in 1587, by B. Lombardi with title: La Gismonda, tragedia del signor T. Tasso
see PQ4605.A6
Letters see PQ4647.A6
4645.A1R3 Ragionamente di due gentilhuomini.
4645.A1V4 Veglie del Tasso
By G. Compagnoni; first published Paris, anno VIII.
4645.A2 Imitations. Adaptations. Parodies
4645.A3 Relation to the drama and the stage. Dramatizations
4645.A5 Translation (as subject; comparative studies, etc.)
4645.A6 Illustrations
Illustrated editions
see PQ4636+
History of Tasso portraits and illustrations of his works
see PQ4652
(4645.A7) Tasso and music
see M or ML or PQ4657.M8
Biography and criticism.

Individual authors
Individual authors, 1400-1700.
Tasso, Torquato, 1544-1595
Biography and criticism. -- Continued

4646 General.
(4646.A1) Bibliography
see Z8860
4646.A2-.A39 Periodicals. Societies. Collections
4646.A4 Dictionaries. Encyclopedias
Cf. PQ4661 Language dictionaries
4646.A5-.Z3 Treatises. Literary biography. Life and works
4646.Z5 Lectures, addresses, etc.
Special
4647.A1 Sources. Documents
4647.A2 Autobiographical and biographical allusions
Letters
4647.A3 General collections. By date
4647.A4 Selections. Posthumously published letters. By date
4647.A5 Special correspondents, A-Z
4647.A6 Spurious letters
4647.A7-Z Criticism
4648.A1 Birth. Early life. Education
Relations to women
4648.A2 General
4648.A3 Leonora d'Este
4648.A4 Others, A-Z
4648.A5 Insanity and confinement in Sant'Anna
4648.A9 Later years and death
4649 Relation to contemporaries
4650 Homes and haunts
Prefer special periods
4651 Anniversaries. Celebrations
Prefer subject or PQ4646.A2+
Memorial addresses. Poetry
Cf. PQ4522 Arrangement under Petrarca
4651.A2 Early, by date
4651.A44 1844
4651.A95 1895
4652 Iconography. Portraits. Monuments. Relics
(4652.9) Fiction, drama, dialogs, poetry, etc., based on Tasso's life
see the author
4653 Authorship
4653.2 Manuscripts, Autographs, Sources, Forerunners, Associates, Followers, Chronology of works
Allusions see PQ4647.A2
Criticism and interpretation

Individual authors
Individual authors, 1400-1700.
Tasso, Torquato, 1544-1595
Biography and criticism.
Criticism and interpretation. -- Continued

4654 History of the study and appreciation of Tasso
Cf. PQ4646.A2+ Periodicals, societies, etc.
4654.A2 General and in Italy
4654.A5-Z By country, A-Z
e. g.
4654.S7 Spain
Treatises
4655 General
4656 Gerusalemme liberata (mainly)
4656.A2 Contemporaneous and early works (to 1800)
Controversy on the merits of Ariosto and Tasso
4656.A22 Tasso's Apologia and other polemic treatises
4656.A5-Z Later works, 1801-
4657.A-Z Special topics, A-Z
4657.A47 Aesthetics
4657.A77 Art
4657.E4 Education
4657.H64 Holy, The
4657.M35 Marvelous, The
4657.M57 Mirrors
4657.M8 Music
4657.R4 Religion. Ethics
4657.U76 Utopias
4657.V45 Venice
4657.W65 Women
4658 Textual criticism. Interpretation. Running commentaries
Prefer PQ4646, General (including works on Gerusalemme liberata alone).
Special topics see PQ4657.A+
4659 Language. Style
Including works on grammar, prose, etc.
4660 Versification
4661 Dictionaries (Language). Concordances
Cf. PQ4646.A4 Dictionaries, encyclopedias
4663 Tassoni, Alessandro, 1565-1635 (Table P-PZ39 modified)
4663.A61-.Z48 Separate works. By title
Subarrange each work by Table P-PZ43
e.g.
4663.S4-.S43 La secchia (Table P-PZ43)
4664.T4 Tebaldeo, Antonio, 1463-1537 (Table P-PZ40)
Teofilo see PQ4623.F3

Individual authors
Individual authors, 1400-1700 -- Continued

4664.T45 Terracina, Laura, 16th cent. (Table P-PZ40)
4664.T47 Terza, Giovanni Battista, d'Azzia, marchese della , 16th cent. (Table P-PZ40)
4664.T475 Tesauro, Emanuele, conte, 1592-1675 (Table P-PZ40)
4664.T48 Testi, Fulvio, conte, 1593-1646 (Table P-PZ40)
4664.T5 Theoduli, Giuseppe, conte, 17th cent. (Table P-PZ40)
4664.T523 Tinucci, Niccolo, b. 1391 (Table P-PZ40)
4664.T53 Tolomei, Claudio, 1492-1555 (Table P-PZ40)
4664.T55 Tolosani, Giovanni Maria, d. 1550 (Table P-PZ40)
4664.T58 Torelli, Pomponio, conte di Montechiarugolo, 1539?-1608 (Table P-PZ40)
4664.T59 Tornabuoni, Lucrezia, 1425-1482 (Table P-PZ40)
4664.T7 Trissino, Giovanni Giorgio, 1478-1550 (Table P-PZ38)
4664.T8 Tromba, Francesco, fl. 1525 (Table P-PZ40)
4664.T86 Tubiolo, di Gielichi, 1610-1689? (Table P-PZ40)
Tullia d'Aragona see PQ4562.A9
4664.U34 Udine, Ercole, c. 1608 (Table P-PZ40)
Vacalerio, Ginnesio Gavardo, pseud. see PQ4632.S5
4664.V15 Vai, Stefano, 1592-1650 (Table P-PZ40)
4664.V17 Valentino, Giovanni Battista, 17th cent. (Table P-PZ40)
4664.V18 Valenziano, Luca, 15th cent. (Table P-PZ40)
4664.V2 Valvasone, Erasmo di, 1523-1593 (Table P-PZ40)
4664.V3 Varchi, Benedetto, 1503-1565 (Table P-PZ40)
4664.V312 Varese, Fabio, b. ca. 1570 (Table P-PZ40)
4664.V314 Veneziano, Antonio, 1543-1593 (Table P-PZ40)
4664.V3148 Venier, Lorenzo, 1510-1550 (Table P-PZ40)
4664.V315 Venier, Maffio, 1550-1586 (Table P-PZ40)
4664.V32 Veniero, Domenico, 1517-1582 (Table P-PZ40)
4664.V35 Verdizotti, Giovanni Mario, 1525-1600 (Table P-PZ40)
4664.V37 Vergerio, Pietro Paolo, 1498-1565 (Table P-PZ40)
4664.V38 Verità, Girolamo, fl. 1490 (Table P-PZ40)
4664.V43 Verucci, Vergilio, fl. 17th cent. (Table P-PZ40)
4664.V5 Vettori, Francesco, 1474-1539 (Table P-PZ40)
4664.V57 Vico, Giovanni Battista, 1668-1744 (Table P-PZ40)
4664.V63 Vignali, Antonio, 1500-1559 (Table P-PZ40)
4664.V66 Villani, Nicola, 17th cent. (Table P-PZ40)
4664.V7 Villifranchi, Cosimo, d. 1698 (Table P-PZ40)
4664.V72 Villifranchi, Giovanni, 17th cent. (Table P-PZ40)
4664.V75 Visconti, Gaspare, 1461-1499 (Table P-PZ40)
4664.Z36 Zane, Giacomo, 1529-1560 (Table P-PZ40)
Zipoli, Perlone, pseud. see PQ4627.L5
4664.Z65 Zoppio, Girolamo, d. 1591 (Table P-PZ40)
4664.Z9 Zuccolo, Lodovico, fl. 1613 (Table P-PZ40)
4664.Z96 Zuñiga, Diego de, 17th cent. (Table P-PZ40)

Individual authors -- Continued
Individual authors, 1701-1900
Subarrange each author by Table P-PZ40 unless otherwise indicated

4675	Anonymous works (Table P-PZ28)
4676.A27	Adami, Anton-Filippo, d. 1770 (Table P-PZ40)
4676.A33	Adriani, Placido, 1690 or 91-1766 (Table P-PZ40)
4676.A35	Affò, Ireneo, 1741-1797 (Table P-PZ40)
4676.A37	Aganoor Pompilj, Vittoria, 1855-1910 (Table P-PZ40)
4676.A4	Albergati Capacelli, Francesco, marchese, 1729-1804 (Table P-PZ40)
4676.A5	Alberti, Luigi, 1822-1898 (Table P-PZ40)
4676.A8	Aleardi, Aleardo, 1812-1878 (Table P-PZ40)
	Alfieri, Vittorio, 1749-1803
	Collections
4677.A1	Comprehensive works. By date
4677.A2	Selected works. By date
	Tragedies and comedies
4677.A3	Comprehensive collections. By date Including comprehensive collections of tragedies
4677.A4	Selected tragedies. By date
4677.A5	Comedies (Collected)
	Poetry
4677.A6	Collected works
4677.A7-.A79	Special forms: Canzoni. Epigrammi. Satire. Sonetti, etc.
4677.A77	Satire
4677.A8	Prose works (Collected)
4677.A85	Posthumous works (Collected)
4677.A9	Quotations. Passages. Thoughts, etc.
	Separate works
4678.A-Z	Tragedies and comedies, A-Z
4678.A2	Abele
4678.A3	Agamennone
4678.A4	Agide
4678.A5	Alceste
4678.A6	L'antidoto
4678.A7	Antigone
4678.A8	Antonio e Cleopatra
4678.B6	Bruto primo
4678.B7	Bruto secondo
4678.C6	La congiura de' Pazzi
4678.D5	Il divorzio
4678.D6	Don Garzia
4678.F3-.F4	Filippo II (Table P-PZ43a)
4678.F5	La finestrina
4678.M2	Maria Stuarda

Individual authors
Individual authors, 1701-1900
Alfieri, Vittorio, 1749-1803
Separate works
Tragedies and comedies, A-Z -- Continued

4678.M4 Merope
4678.M6 Mirra
4678.O6 Oreste
4678.O8 Ottavia
4678.P4 I pochi
4678.P5 I poeti
4678.P6 Polinice
4678.R7 Rosmunda
4678.S3 Saul
4678.S6 Sofonisba
4678.T5 Timoleone
4678.T7 I troppi
4678.U6 L'uno
4678.V5 Virginia
4679.A-Z Minor works, A-Z
4679.A6 L'America libra
Canzoni see PQ4677.A7+
4679.D5 Dialoghi
Epigrammi see PQ4677.A7+
4679.E7 Etruria liberata
4679.M5 Misogallo
4679.P4 Parigi sbastigliato
Sonetti see PQ4677.A7+
Vita see PQ4683.A2
4680 Translations
4680.A1-.A99 Italian dialects (alphabetically)
4680.B2 Basque (Table PQ5)
4680.C2 Catalan (Table PQ5)
Celtic
4680.C3 Breton (Table PQ5)
4680.C4 Cornish (Table PQ5)
4680.C5 Gaelic (Table PQ5)
4680.C6 Irish (Table PQ5)
4680.C7 Manx (Table PQ5)
4680.C8 Welsh (Table PQ5)
4680.D8 Dutch or Flemish (Table PQ5)
4680.E5 English (Table PQ5)
4680.F4 Finnish (Table PQ5)
4680.F5 French (Table PQ5)
4680.G5 German (Table PQ5)
4680.G8 Greek (Table PQ5)
4680.H5 Hungarian (Table PQ5)

Individual authors
Individual authors, 1701-1900
Alfieri, Vittorio, 1749-1803
Translations -- Continued

4680.L5 Latin (Table PQ5)
4680.P5 Portuguese (Table PQ5)
4680.R5 Romanian (Table PQ5)
Scandinavian
4680.S21 Danish. Dano-Norwegian (Table PQ5)
4680.S22 Icelandic (Table PQ5)
4680.S23 Swedish (Table PQ5)
Slavic
4680.S3 Bohemian (Table PQ5)
4680.S4 Bulgarian (Table PQ5)
4680.S5 Croatian (Table PQ5)
4680.S53 Lettish (Table PQ5)
4680.S55 Lithuanian (Table PQ5)
4680.S6 Polish (Table PQ5)
4680.S7 Russian (Table PQ5)
4680.S75 Ruthenian (Table PQ5)
4680.S8 Serbian (Table PQ5)
4680.S82 Slovak (Table PQ5)
4680.S84 Slovenian (Table PQ5)
4680.S85 Wendic (Table PQ5)
4680.S9 Spanish (Table PQ5)
(4680.Z5) Other languages (including artificial languages)
see PJ-PM
Biography and criticism
4681 General works. Literary biography. Life and works
4681.A11-.A19 Periodicals. Societies
4681.A2 Autobiography (Vita)
4681.A3 Translations. By language, A-Z
Subarrange by translator, alphabetically
4681.A3E56 English translation by Lester
4681.A4 Journals
4681.A5 Letters
(4681.A59) Bibliography
see Z8026.6
4681.A6-Z Other works
4682 Criticism
4682.A3-.Z3 General works
4682.Z5 Language. Grammar
4682.Z7 Versification
4682.Z9 Dictionaries. Indexes
4683.A2 Algarotti, Francesco, conte, 1712-1764 (Table P-PZ40)
4683.A26 Altavilla, Pasquale, 1806-1875 (Table P-PZ40)
Amarilli Etrusca see PQ4683.B178

Individual authors

Individual authors, 1701-1900 -- Continued

4683.A3 Amicis, Edmondo de, 1846-1908 (Table P-PZ40)

Anselmo, Rivalta, pseud. see PQ4687.C29

4683.A33 Angelini, Giovanni Battista, 1679-1767 (Table P-PZ40)

4683.A45 Antonio, Giovanni d', fl. 1788 (Table P-PZ40)

4683.A55 Archinti, Luigi, 1825-1902 (Table P-PZ40)

4683.A552 Ardizzone, Girolamo, 1824-1893 (Table P-PZ40)

4683.A555 Argondizza, Antonio, 19th cent. (Table P-PZ40)

Arrighi, Cletto, pseud. see PQ4730.R7

4683.A59 Asachi, Gheorghe, 1788-1869 (Table P-PZ40)

Cf. PC839.A82 writings in Romanian

Ascetti, Ardano, conte, pseud. see PQ4687.C275

4683.A6 Aste, Ippolito Tito d',1844- (Table P-PZ40)

4683.A65 Astori, Achille, 1843- (Table P-PZ40)

4683.A75 Aureli, Mariano, 19th cent. (Table P-PZ40)

4683.A8 Auteri Pomàr, Michaele, fl. 1872-1887 (Table P-PZ40)

4683.A9 Azeglio, Massimo Tapparelli, marchese d', 1798-1866 (Table P-PZ40)

For the author's memoirs, letters etc. see DG552.8.A985

4683.A97 Azzinnari, Alfonso, 1847-1866 (Table P-PZ40)

4683.B103 Bacaredda, Ottone, 1848-1921 (Table P-PZ40)

4683.B104 Bacaredda, Antonio, 1824-1908 (Table P-PZ40)

4683.B105 Baccini, Ida, 1850-1911 (Table P-PZ40)

4683.B11 Baciocchi, Giovanni Tommaso, 1668-1723 (Table P-PZ40)

4683.B12 Baffi, Vincenzo, 1832-1882 (Table P-PZ40)

4683.B13 Baffo, Giorgio, 1694-1768 (Table P-PZ40)

4683.B15 Balatri, Dionisio Filippo, 1672-1756 (Table P-PZ40)

4683.B16 Balbiani, Antonio, fl. 1863-1888 (Table P-PZ40)

4683.B17 Balbo, Cesare, conte, 1789-1853 (Table P-PZ40)

Cf. DG551.8.B24 Balbo as Italian statesman

4683.B173 Baldacchini-Gargano, Francesco Saverio, 1800-1879 (Table P-PZ40)

4683.B174 Balestrieri, Domenico, 1714-1780 (Table P-PZ40)

4683.B178 Bandettini-Landucci, Teresa, 1763-1837 (Table P-PZ40)

4683.B18 Bandi, Giuseppe, 1834-1894 (Table P-PZ40)

4683.B185 Barbi Cinti, Francesco, fl. 1874-1890 (Table P-PZ40)

4683.B19 Baretti, Giuseppe Marco Antonio, 1719-1789 (Table P-PZ38)

4683.B197 Barricelli, G., fl. 1873 (Table P-PZ40)

4683.B2 Barrili, Antonio Giulio, 1836-1908 (Table P-PZ40)

Barti, P.T., pseud. see PQ4683.B8

4683.B225 Bartolo, Domenico, 18th cent. (Table P-PZ40)

4683.B227 Bartoloni, Pietro Domenico, 18th cent. (Table P-PZ40)

4683.B23 Baruffaldi, Girolamo, 1675-1755 (Table P-PZ40)

4683.B25 Batacchi, Domenico, 1748-1802 (Table P-PZ40)

Individual authors

Individual authors, 1701-1900 -- Continued

4683.B3 Bax, Gerolama, 1689?-1740 (Table P-PZ40)

4683.B35 Bazzero, Ambrogio, 1851-1882 (Table P-PZ40)

4683.B37 Bazzoni, Giovanni Battista, 1803-1850 (Table P-PZ38)

4683.B39 Beccaria, Cesare, marchese di, 1738-1794 (Table P-PZ40)

4683.B43 Belli, Giuseppe Gioacchino, 1791-1863 (Table P-PZ40)

4683.B434 Bellini, Melchoirre, 1841-1917 (Table P-PZ40)

4683.B45 Belluso, Alfio, fl. 1886 (Table P-PZ40)

4683.B47 Benaglio, Ines (Castellani Fantoni), contessa, 1849-1897 (Table P-PZ40)

4683.B474 Benci, Antonio, 1783-1843 (Table P-PZ40)

4683.B48 Benedetti, Francesco, 1785-1821 (Table P-PZ40)

4683.B49 Bentivoglio d'Aragona, Marco Cornelio, 1668-1732 (Table P-PZ40)

4683.B5 Berchet, Giovanni, 1783-1851 (Table P-PZ40)

4683.B56 Bergalli, Luisa, 1703-1779 (Table P-PZ40)

4683.B7 Bersezio, Vittorio, 1830-1900 (Table P-PZ40)

4683.B74 Bertola, Aurelio de' Giorgi, 1753-1798 (Table P-PZ40)

4683.B77 Bettinelli, Saverio, 1718-1808 (Table P-PZ40)

4683.B8 Bettoli, Parmenio, 1835-1907 (Table P-PZ40)

4683.B84 Bevilacqua Lazise, Carlo, conte (Table P-PZ40)

4683.B845 Bianchi, Antonio, 18th cent. (Table P-PZ40)

4683.B85 Biava, Samuele, 1792-1870 (Table P-PZ40)

4683.B86 Bini, Carlo, 1806-1842 (Table P-PZ40)

4683.B865 Birago, Girolamo, 1691-1773 (Table P-PZ40)

4683.B87 Bizzoni, Achille, 1841- (Table P-PZ40)

Black, Capitano, pseud. see PQ4688.D34

4684.B23 Boito, Arrigo, 1842-1918 (Table P-PZ40)

4684.B25 Boito, Camillo, 1836-1914 (Table P-PZ40)

4684.B27 Bolstad, Jens Martin, 1858-1905 (Table P-PZ40)

4684.B3 Bon, Francesco Augusto, 1788-1858 (Table P-PZ40)

Bonacci-Brunamonte, Alinda see PQ4684.B7

4684.B4 Bondi, Clemente, 1742-1821 (Table P-PZ40)

4684.B45 Boner, Edoardo Giacomo, 1864-1908 (Table P-PZ40)

4684.B5 Boni, Curzio Reginaldo, fl. 1778 (Table P-PZ40)

4684.B52 Bonsignori, Giovanni, 1846-1914 (Table P-PZ40)

4684.B54 Borghini, Maria Selvaggia, 1656-1731 (Table P-PZ40)

4684.B56 Borsieri, Pietro, 1788-1815 (Table P-PZ40)

4684.B565 Bottari, Giovanni Gaetano, 1689-1775 (Table P-PZ40)

4684.B6 Breme, Ludovico di, 1780-1820 (Table P-PZ40)

4684.B62 Bresciani, Antonio, 1797-1862 (Table P-PZ40)

4684.B63 Bricco, Gian Giacomo (Table P-PZ40)

4684.B65 Brofferio, Angelo, 1802-1866 (Table P-PZ40)

4684.B7 Brunamonte Bonacci, Maria Alinda, 1841-1903 (Table P-PZ40)

4684.B73 Bruni, Antonio, 1593-1635 (Table P-PZ40)

Individual authors
Individual authors, 1701-1900 -- Continued

4684.B75 Buondelmonti, Giuseppe Maria, 1713-1757 (Table P-PZ40)
4684.B8 Buratti, Pietro, d. 1832 (Table P-PZ40)
4684.B85 Buttura, A. (Antonio), 1771-1832 (Table P-PZ40)
4684.C12 Cabianca, Jacopo, 1809-1878 (Table P-PZ40)
4684.C18 Caccia, Antonio, fl. 1848-1872 (Table P-PZ40)
4684.C2 Caccianiga, Antonio, 1823-1909 (Table P-PZ40)
4684.C3 Cagna, Achille Giovanni, 1847- (Table P-PZ40)
4684.C33 Calandra, Edoardo, 1852-1911 (Table P-PZ40)
Calcodontèo, Argino, pseud. see PQ4684.B5
4684.C35 Calenzuoli, Giuseppe, 1815-1883 (Table P-PZ40)
4684.C4 Caliari, Pietro, 1841- (Table P-PZ40)
4684.C42 Calleri, Celestino (Table P-PZ40)
4684.C425 Calsabigi, Ranieri de, 1714-1795 (Table P-PZ40)
4684.C43 Calvi, Felice, 1822-1901 (Table P-PZ40)
4684.C435 Calvo, Edoardo Ignazio, 1773-1804 (Table P-PZ40)
4684.C438 Camerana, Giovanni, 1845-1905 (Table P-PZ40)
4684.C44 Caminer Turra, Elisabetta, 1751-1796 (Table P-PZ40)
4684.C45 Cammarano, Salvatore, 1801-1852 (Table P-PZ40)
4684.C46 Camoletti, Luigi, fl. 1851-1877 (Table P-PZ40)
4684.C462 Campanini, Naborre, 1850-1925 (Table P-PZ40)
4684.C466 Canale, Michele Giuseppe, 1808-1890 (Table P-PZ40)
4684.C47 Canepa, Pietro, fl. 1861-1881 (Table P-PZ40)
4684.C475 Cannizzaro, Tonunaso, 1838-1916 (Table P-PZ40)
4684.C48 Cantoni, Alberto, 1841-1904 (Table P-PZ40)
4684.C5 Cantù, Cesare, 1804-1895 (Table P-PZ40)
4684.C52 Cantù, Ignazio, 1810-1877 (Table P-PZ40)
Capacelli, Francesco Albergati see PQ4676.A4
4684.C6 Capponi, Gino, 1792-1876 (Table P-PZ40)
Cf. DG405; DG552.5.C2 etc.
4684.C62 Capponi, Luca Maria, 1768-1837 (Table P-PZ40)
4684.C7 Capranica, Luigi, marchese, 1820-189 (Table P-PZ40)
4684.C8 Capuana, Luigi, 1839-1917 (Table P-PZ40)
4684.C85 Carboni, Raffaello, 1817-1875 (Table P-PZ40)
4684.C89 Carcano, Francesco, 1735-1794 (Table P-PZ40)
4684.C9 Carcano, Giulio, 1812-1884 (Table P-PZ40)
4684.C93 Cardone Gian Lorenzo 1743-1813 (Table P-PZ40)
Carducci, Giosue, 1835-1907
4685.A1 Collected works
4685.A14 Indedited works. By date
4685.A2 Collected poems. By date
4685.A25 Collected prose works. By date
4685.A3 Selected works (prose and poetry). Selections. Anthologies. By editor
4685.A4 Quotations. Passages. Thoughts
4685.A5-.Z2 Separate works, A-Z

Individual authors
Individual authors, 1701-1900
Carducci, Giosue, 1835-1907
Separate works, A-Z -- Continued
A Giuseppe Garibaldi: ode barbara
A Margherita regina d'Italia
A Satana: inno
A Victor Hugo: ode barbara
Alla citta di Ferrara: ode
Alla croce di Savoia i Toscani: canto
Alla figlia di Fr. Crispi: ode
Alla regina d' Italia: ode barbara
Alle fonti del clitumno
Anniversario dell' 8 agosto: ode
Bicocca di S. Giacomo: ode
Cadore: ode
Ca ira! (12 sonnets on French revolution)
Il canto dell' amore
Carlo Goldoni: sonetti
La chiesa di Polenta: ode
Confessioni e battaglie
Giambi ed epodi
Giuseppe Garibaldi: versi e prose
La Guerra: ode
Inno alla croce di Savoia
Juvenilia
Levia gravia
Il libro delle prefazioni
La Madre: ode
La moglie del gigante
Nuove odi barbare
Nuove poesie
Odi barbare
Per la morte di Eug. Napoleone: ode
Per 0. Corazzini: epodo
Piemonte: ode
Poesie
Rime
Rime e ritme
Rime nuove
Satana e polemiche sataniche
Sei odi barbdre
Terze odi barbare
Vite ritratti
Translations
English
4685.Z3 Collected and selected works. By date

Individual authors
Individual authors, 1701-1900
Carducci, Giosue, 1835-1907
Translations
English -- Continued

4685.Z31-.Z39 Separate works, by original title (alphabetically)
French
4685.Z4 Collected and selected works. By date
4685.Z41-.Z49 Separate works, by original title (alphabetically)
German
4685.Z5 Collected and selected works. By date
4685.Z51-.Z59 Separate works, by original title (alphabetically)
4685.Z6-.Z99 Others. By language
4686 Biography and criticism
4686.A1-.A29 Periodicals and societies
4686.A3 Dictionaries. Indexes
4686.A35 Autobiography. Journals. Memoirs
4686.A4 Correspondence (Collections)
4686.A45A-.A45Z Correspondence to and from particular individuals, A-Z
4686.A6-.Z3 General works
4686.Z5 Language
4686.Z6 Versification
4687.C21 Carlo, Luigi di, 1835- (Table P-PZ40)
4687.C23 Carol, Jean, 1848-1922 (Table P-PZ40)
4687.C25 Carrér, Luigi, 1801-1850 (Table P-PZ40)
Carteromaco, pseud. see PQ4688.F7
4687.C254 Carrus, Maurizio, 17th/18th cent. (Table P-PZ40)
4687.C26 Carusu, Carmunu, 1840-1914 (Table P-PZ40)
4687.C27 Carutti, Domenico, barone di Cantogno, 1821-1909 (Table P-PZ40)
4687.C274 Casanova, Giacomo, 1725-1798 (Table P-PZ40)
For biography, see D285.8.A+ ; for literary works in French, see PQ1959.C6
4687.C275 Casotti, Andrea, fl. 1734 (Table P-PZ40)
4687.C28 Cassoli, Francesco, 1749-1812 (Table P-PZ40)
4687.C283 Cassone, Giuseppe, 1843-1910 (Table P-PZ40)
4687.C285 Castagnola, Paolo Emilio, 1825-1898 (Table P-PZ40)
4687.C29 Castellazzo, Luigi, 1827-1890 (Table P-PZ40)
Castelnovo, Leo di, pseud. see PQ4730.P92
4687.C3 Castelnuovo, Enrico, 1839-1915 (Table P-PZ40)
Castelvecchio, Riccardo, pseud. see PQ4730.P9
4687.C4 Casti, Giovanni Battista, 1724-1803 (Table P-PZ40)
4687.C45 Castiglione, Giuseppe, 1804-1866 (Table P-PZ40)
4687.C5 Castro, Giovanni de, 1837-1897 (Table P-PZ40)
4687.C55 Catanzaro, Carlo, fl. 1871-1897 (Table P-PZ40)
4687.C6 Cattermole, Eva, 1849-1896 (Table P-PZ40)
4687.C7 Causa, Cesare, fl. 1873-1896 (Table P-PZ40)

Individual authors
Individual authors, 1701-1900 -- Continued

4687.C8	Cavallotti, Felice Carlo Emanuele, 1842-1898 (Table P-PZ40)
4687.C84	Cerlone, Francesco, 1722-ca. 1799 (Table P-PZ40)
4687.C85	Cerretti, Luigi, 1738-1808 (Table P-PZ40)
4687.C9	Cesari, Antonio, 1760-1828 (Table P-PZ40)
4687.C95	Cesarotti, Melchiorre, 1730-1808 (Table P-PZ40)
4687.C96	Ceva Grimaldi, Giuseppe, marchese di Pietracatella, 1776-1862 (Table P-PZ40)
4687.C98	Chelli, Gaetano Carlo, 1847-1904 (Table P-PZ40)
4687.C99	Chersa, Tommaso, 1782-1826 (Table P-PZ40)
4688.C2	Chiari, Pietro, 1711?-1785 (Table P-PZ40)
4688.C22	Chiari, Prospero (Table P-PZ40)
4688.C23	Chiarini, Giuseppe, 1833-1908 (Table P-PZ40)
4688.C235	Chimieni, Agostino, 1832-1902 (Table P-PZ40)
4688.C24	Chiossone, David, 1822-1873 (Table P-PZ40)
	Chirtani, pseud. see PQ4683.A55
4688.C247	Ciaia, Ignazio, 1766-1799 (Table P-PZ40)
4688.C25	Ciampoli, Domenico, 1855 (Table P-PZ40)
4688.C253	Ciampolini, Luigi, 1786-1846 (Table P-PZ40)
4688.C26	Cibrario, Luigi, conte, 1802-1870 (Table P-PZ40)
4688.C265	Cicci, Maria Luisa, 1760-1794 (Table P-PZ40)
4688.C27	Ciconi, Teobaldo, 1824-1863 (Table P-PZ40)
4688.C28	Cima, Camillo, fl. 1861-1896 (Table P-PZ40)
	Cimerio, Ticofilo, pseud. see PQ4683.B74
4688.C3	Cimino Folliera de Luna, Aurelia, 1827-1895 (Table P-PZ40)
4688.C32	Cimmino, Francesco, 1862-1939 (Table P-PZ40)
	Cioni, Caetano, supposed author see PQ4692.G75
4688.C34	Claps, Tommaso, 1871-1945 (Table P-PZ40)
	Clasio, pseud. see PQ4688.F5
4688.C39	Coffa, Mariannina, 1841-1878 (Table P-PZ40)
4688.C4	Coletti, Francesco, 1821-1873 (Table P-PZ40)
	Collodi, Carlo see PQ4712.L4
	Colombi, marchesa, pseud. see PQ4733.T7
4688.C5	Colpani, Giuseppe, 1739-1822 (Table P-PZ40)
4688.C52	Compagnoni, Giuseppe, 1754-1833 (Table P-PZ40)
4688.C53	Conti, Antonio, 1677-1749 (Table P-PZ40)
4688.C55	Conti, Giovanni Battista, conte, 1741-1820 (Table P-PZ40)
4688.C6	Corbellini, Piero, 1840- (Table P-PZ40)
4688.C613	Cordara, Giulio Cesare, 1704-1785 (Table P-PZ40)
	Corilla Olimpica see PQ4688.F35
	Corradini, Enrico see PQ4809.O6
4688.C62	Corradini, Rinaldo (Table P-PZ40)
	Opere drammatiche, 1826
4688.C624	Corsi, Domenico, 19th cent (Table P-PZ40)

Individual authors
Individual authors, 1701-1900 -- Continued

4688.C627 Corvo, Nicola, 18th cent. (Table P-PZ40)
4688.C629 Corzetto Vignot, Pietro, 1850-1921 (Table P-PZ40)
4688.C63 Cossa, Pietro, 1830-1881 (Table P-PZ40)
4688.C64 Costa, Enrico, 1841-1909 (Table P-PZ40)
4688.C65 Costa, Lorenzo, 1798-1861 (Table P-PZ40)
Several poems on Columbus classed in E120
4688.C66 Costa, Paolo, 1771-1836 (Table P-PZ40)
4688.C7 Costanzo, Giuseppe Aurelio, 1843-1913 (Table P-PZ40)
4688.C73 Costetti, Giuseppe, 1834- (Table P-PZ40)
4688.C75 Crispi, Francesco, 1819-1901 (Table P-PZ40)
4688.C8 Crudeli, Tommaso, 1703-1745 (Table P-PZ40)
4688.C9 Cuciniello, Michele, 1825-1889 (Table P-PZ40)
4688.C95 Cuoco, Vincenzo, 1770-1823 (Table P-PZ40)
4688.D3 Da Ponte, Lorenzo, 1749-1838 (Table P-PZ40)
4688.D33 D'Avino, Gennaro, b. 1724 (Table P-PZ40)
De Amicis, Edmondo, 1846-1908 see PQ4683.A3
4688.D34 De Dominicis, Giuseppe, 1869-1905 (Table P-PZ40)
De Marchi, Emilio, 1851-1901 see PQ4716.M3
4688.D425 Degli Angioli, Gherardo, 1705-1783 (Table P-PZ40)
4688.D43 Del Buono, Luigi, 1751-1832 (Table P-PZ40)
4688.D445 Della Sala Spada, Agostino, 1842-1913 (Table P-PZ40)
4688.D455 Di Brazza, Antonio, 1792-1826 (Table P-PZ40)
4688.D46 Di Giorgi, Ferdinando, 1869-1929 (Table P-PZ40)
4688.D48 Donati, Antonio, fl. 1867 (Table P-PZ40)
4688.D5 Donati, Cesare, 1826- (Table P-PZ40)
4688.D55 Dossi, Carlo, 1849-1910 (Table P-PZ40)
4688.E45 Emma, b. 1844 (Table P-PZ40)
4688.E72 Ercoliani, Lorenzo, b. 1806 (Table P-PZ40)
Etrusca, Amarilli see PQ4683.B178
4688.F14 Fabbri, Edoardo, conte, 1778-1853 (Table P-PZ40)
4688.F142 Fabri, Alessandro, 1691-1728 (Table P-PZ40)
4688.F144 Fabri, Domenico, d. 1761 (Table P-PZ40)
4688.F16 Faccioli, Carlo, 1840- (Table P-PZ40)
4688.F162 Faccioli, Dario Napoleone, fl. 1871-1883 (Table P-PZ40)
4688.F17 Fagiuoli, Giovanni Battista, 1660-1742 (Table P-PZ40)
4688.F18 Fambri, Paulo, 1827-1897 (Table P-PZ40)
4688.F2 Fanfani, Pietro, 1815-1879 (Table P-PZ40)
4688.F23 Fantastici, Agostino, 1782-1845 (Table P-PZ40)
Fantastici-Rosellini, Massimina see PQ4731.R35
4688.F25 Fantoni, Giovanni, 1755-1807 (Table P-PZ40)
4688.F3 Farina, Salvatore, 1846-1918 (Table P-PZ40)
4688.F314 Farrugia, Giacomo, d. 1716 (Table P-PZ40)
4688.F32 Fava, Onarato, 1859- (Table P-PZ40)
Federici, Camillo, pseud. see PQ4734.V67
Felsinea, Corinna see PQ4688.F435

Individual authors
Individual authors, 1701-1900 -- Continued

4688.F35 Fernandez, Maria Maddalena (Morelli), called Corilla Olimpica, d. 1800 (Table P-PZ40)
4688.F37 Ferraresi, Paolo, fl. 1883 (Table P-PZ40)
4688.F4 Ferrari, Paolo, 1822-1889 (Table P-PZ40)
4688.F43 Ferrari, Severino, 1856-1905 (Table P-PZ40)
4688.F435 Ferrari Bosi, Teresa, fl. 1857-1892 (Table P-PZ40)
Ferretti, Emilia, b. 1844 see PQ4688.E45
4688.F45 Festa, Francesco (Table P-PZ40)
4688.F5 Fiacchi, Luigi, called Clasio, 1754-1825 (Table P-PZ40)
4688.F53 Fichert, Luigi, fl. 1857-1896 (Table P-PZ40)
4688.F57 Fiorentino, Salomone, 1743-1815 (Table P-PZ40)
4688.F6 Fogazzaro, Antonio, 1842-1911 (Table P-PZ40)
Cf. Bibliography by S. Rumor
4688.F63 Fojanesi Rapisardi, Giselda, 1851-1946 (Table P-PZ40)
4688.F66 Fonseca Pimentel, Eleonora, 1752-1799 (Table P-PZ40)
4688.F69 Forteguerra, Alessandra (Table P-PZ40)
4688.F7 Forteguerri, Niccolò, 1674-1735 (Table P-PZ40)
4688.F75 Fortis, Leone, 1824-1896 (Table P-PZ40)
4688.F8 Foscarini, Jacopo Vincenzo, 1785-1864 (Table P-PZ40)
Foscolo, Ugo, 1778-1827
Works
4689.A1 Collected works. By date
4689.A12 Selections
(4689.A14) Posthumous works
see PQ4689.A12
4689.A17 Collected poems
4689.A19 Collected plays
4689.A6-Z Separate works, A-Z
4690.A-Z Translations. By language, A-Z
4691 Biography and criticism
4691.A3 Letters
4692.F115 Fracassini, Francesco (Table P-PZ40)
4692.F12 Fraccacreta, Matteo, 19th cent. (Table P-PZ40)
4692.F2 Franceschi, Enrico, fl. 1852-1892 (Table P-PZ40)
4692.F22 Franceschi, Goffredo, fl. 1863-1867 (Table P-PZ40)
4692.F23 Franceschi Ferrucci, Caterina, 1803-1887 (Table P-PZ40)
4692.F24 Franciosi, Antonio, 19th cent. (Table P-PZ40)
4692.F25 Franciosi, Giovanni, conte, 1843-1891 (Table P-PZ40)
4692.F3 Franco, Giovanni Giuseppe, 1824-1908 (Table P-PZ40)
4692.F35 Frediani, Pietro, 1775-1857 (Table P-PZ40)
4692.F4 Frugoni, Carlo Innocenzo, 1692-1768 (Table P-PZ40)
4692.F6 Fucini, Renato, 1843-1921 (Table P-PZ40)
Pseudonym: Neri Tanfucio
4692.F7 Fulgonio, Fulvio, 1832-1904 (Table P-PZ40)
4692.F85 Fusconi, Lorenzo, 1726-1814 (Table P-PZ40)

Individual authors
Individual authors, 1701-1900 -- Continued

4692.F9 Fusinato, Arnaldo, 1817-1888 (Table P-PZ40)
4692.G13 Galaverna, Domenico, 1825-1903 (Table P-PZ40)
4692.G14 Galeotti, Ettore, fl. 1864-1891 (Table P-PZ40)
4692.G16 Galiani, Ferdinando, 1728-1787 (Table P-PZ40)
For French letters see PQ1985.G33
4692.G18 Galli, Celestino, 1804-1869 (Table P-PZ40)
4692.G2 Gallina, Giacinto, 1852-1897 (Table P-PZ40)
4692.G22 Galluppi, Pasquale, 1770-1846 (Table P-PZ40)
Gandolin, pseud. see PQ4734.V35
4692.G24 Garelli, Federico, 1827-1885 (Table P-PZ40)
4692.G25 Gargallo, Tommaso, 1760-1842 (Table P-PZ40)
4692.G28 Gargiolli, Corrado, 1834-1885 (Table P-PZ40)
4692.G3 Gargiulli, Onofrio, d. 1815 (Table P-PZ40)
4692.G33 Garibaldi, Giuseppe, 1807-1882 (Table P-PZ40)
4692.G35 Gatteschi, Angelo, fl. 1752 (Table P-PZ40)
4692.G36 Gatteschi, Gattesco, 1857-1918 (Table P-PZ40)
4692.G37 Gattinelli, Gaetano, fl. 1850-1887 (Table P-PZ40)
4692.G38 Gazzoletti, Antonio, 1813-1866 (Table P-PZ40)
4692.G39 Ghedini, Fernando Antonio, 1684-1768 (Table P-PZ40)
4692.G4 Gherardi del Testa, Tonunaso, conte, 1818?-1881 (Table P-PZ40)
4692.G42 Ghiglione, Antonio, fl. 1835-1863 (Table P-PZ40)
4692.G45 Ghislanzoni, Antonio, 1824-1893 (Table P-PZ40)
Cf. ML, Opera librettos, Aida, etc.
4692.G5 Giacometti, Paolo, 1816-1882 (Table P-PZ40)
4692.G6 Giacosa, Giuseppe, 1847-1906 (Table P-PZ40)
4692.G614 Gianformaggio, Giovanni, 1859-1901 (Table P-PZ40)
4692.G617 Gianni, Francesco, 1750-1822 (Table P-PZ40)
4692.G62 Giannone, Pietro, 1792-1872 (Table P-PZ40)
4692.G65 Gigli, Girolamo, 1660-1722 (Table P-PZ40)
4692.G68 Giordani, Pietro, 1774-1848 (Table P-PZ40)
Giorgi, Ferdinando di, 1869-1929 see PQ4688.D46
4692.G7 Giovagnoli, Raffaele, 1838-1915 (Table P-PZ40)
4692.G73 Giovannetti, Giovanni Pietro, fl. 1866 (Table P-PZ40)
4692.G75 Giraldi, Giraldo, pseud. (Table P-PZ40)
4692.G8 Giraud, Giovanni, conte, 1776-1834 (Table P-PZ40)
4692.G85 Giuria, Pietro, 1816-1876 (Table P-PZ40)
4692.G9 Giusti, Giuseppe, 1809-1850 (Table P-PZ40)
4692.G92 Giustana, Alessandro Giuseppe, 1860- (Table P-PZ40)
4692.G95 Gnoli, Gomenico, conte, 1838-1915 (Table P-PZ40)
Goldoni, Carlo, 1707-1793
4693 Editions
4693.A1 Comprehensive, including collections of dramatic works. By date
Selected works

Individual authors
Individual authors, 1701-1900
Goldoni, Carlo, 1707-1793
Editions
Selected works -- Continued
Comedies (Collections and selections)

4693.A2 General. By date

Special

4693.A4 By form (Genre)

e.g. Comedies of character. Plays dealing with cicisbeism, villeggiatura, etc.

4693.A5 Other

e.g. Comedies in Venetian dialect, Comedies in prose, Comedies in verse

4693.A6 Tragedies

4693.A7 Tragicomedies

(4693.A8) Operas, light operas, and interludes

see subclass ML

(4693.A9) Cantatas and serenatas

see subclass ML

4694.A-Z Particular plays (Comedies and tragedies), A-Z

Editions, by date; criticism, by author, A-Z, unless otherwise indicated

For separate editions of particular operas, light operas and interludes, see subclass ML

4694.A4 L'adulatore
4694.A8 L'avvocato veneziano
4694.B3 Le baruffe chiozzotte
4694.B6 La bottega del caffè
4694.B7 Il bugiardo
4694.B8 La buona figliuola
4694.B85 La buona madre
4694.B9 Il burbero benefico
4694.C3 Il campiello
4694.C4 La casa nuova
4694.C5 Il Cavaliere e la dama
4694.C9 Un curioso accidente
4694.D3 La Dalmatina
4694.D5 Il Don Giovanni
4694.D6 La donna di garbo
4694.D7 Le donne curiose
4694.D8 Le donne de casa soa
4694.D85 I due gemelli veneziani
4694.E7 L'erede fortunata
4694.F2 La famiglia dell' antiquario
4694.F4 Le femmine puntigliose
4694.F5 Il filosofo inglese

Individual authors
Individual authors, 1701-1900
Goldoni, Carlo, 1707-1793
Particular plays (Comedies and tragedies), A-Z -- Continued

4694.G5	Il giocatore
4694.I5	L'impostore
4694.I6	Gl' innamorati
4694.L5	La locandiera
4694.M2	La madre amorosa
4694.M3	I malcontenti
4694.M4	La mascherata
4694.M45	Il matrimonio per concorso
4694.M5	Il medico olandese
4694.M59	La moglie saggia
4694.M6	Il Molière
4694.P25	Il Padre di famiglia
4694.P3	La Pamela fanciulla
4694.P4	La Pamela maritata
4694.P63	Il poeta fanatico
4694.P8	La putta onorata
4694.R3	Il raggiratore
4694.S4	La serva amorosa
4694.S5	Il servitore di due padroni
4694.S56	Sior Todero brontolon
4694.S7	Le smanie per la villeggiatura
4694.V3	La vedova scaltra
4694.V4	Il vero amico
4694.V5	La villeggiatura
	Translations
4695.A1-.A8	Italian dialects
	English
4695.E5	Collected and selected works. By date
4695.E5A3	Selections, passages, thoughts
4695.E5A5-.E5Z3	Separate works, by original title and translator
4695.F5	French
4695.G5	German
4695.P5	Portuguese
4695.S5	Spanish
4696	Other languages For list of Cutter numbers, see PQ4273
4697	Apocryphal, spurious works
	Biography and criticism
	Bibliography see Z8352
4698.A1-.A29	Periodicals. Societies. Collections

Individual authors
Individual authors, 1701-1900
Goldoni, Carlo, 1707-1793
Biography and criticism -- Continued
4698.A3 Dictionaries. Encyclopedias
General only
For dictionaries and concordances see PQ4701
Sources
4698.A4 Documents, etc. By editor, A-Z
Autobiography. Memoirs
4698.A5 Editions (in French) and Italian translations. By date
4698.A6 Translations (other than Italian). By language, A-Z
4698.A7 Letters
4698.A8 Translations. By language, A-Z
4699 General works (Literary biography. Life and works)
4700 Special topics
For criticism of particular plays, see the play
(4700.9) Goldoni in fiction, drama, poetry, etc.
Mainly for added entry
4701 Language. Grammar. Dialect
4702 Gol - Goz
4703 Gozzi, Carlo, conte, 1722-1806 (Table P-PZ39)
4704 Gozzi, Gasparo Cesare, conte, 1713-1786 (Table P-PZ39)
4705.G2 Gradi, Temistocle, 1824-1887 (Table P-PZ40)
4705.G3 Graf, Arturo, 1848-1913 (Table P-PZ40)
4705.G318 Gramegna, Luigi, 1846-1928 (Table P-PZ40)
4705.G32 Granelli, Giovanni, 1703-1770 (Table P-PZ40)
Grappolino, pseud. see PQ4705.G35
4705.G35 Grapputo, Tommaso, fl. 1800 (Table P-PZ40)
Grimaldi, Giuseppe Ceva see PQ4687.C96
4705.G55 Griselini, Francesco, 1717-1784? (Table P-PZ40)
4705.G57 Gristi, Vittorio, ca. 1714-1787 (Table P-PZ40)
4705.G6 Grossi, Tommaso, 1791-1853 (Table P-PZ40)
4705.G63 Guadagnoli, Antonio, 1798-1858 (Table P-PZ40)
4705.G65 Gualdo, Luigi, conte, 1847-1898 (Table P-PZ40)
4705.G667 Guarino, Carlo, 1825-1876 (Table P-PZ40)
4705.G67 Guastella, Serafino Amabile, 1819-1899 (Table P-PZ40)
4705.G7 Gubernatis, Angelo de, conte, 1840-1913 (Table P-PZ40)
4705.G75 Guerini, Federiga, fl. 1877-1886 (Table P-PZ40)
Guerrazzi, Francesco Domenico, 1804-1873
4705.G8A2-.G8Z9 Separate works. By title
4705.G9 Biography and criticism
4707.G3 Guerrini, Olindo, 1845-1916 (Table P-PZ40)
4707.I4 Imbriani, Vittorio, 1840-1886 (Table P-PZ40)
4707.I47 Imperiale, Vincenzo Maria, 1738-1818 (Table P-PZ40)
4707.I6 Interdonato, Stefano, 1845-1896 (Table P-PZ40)
Jarro, pseud. see PQ4730.P3

Individual authors
Individual authors, 1701-1900 -- Continued

4707.J47 Jerocades, Antonio, 1738-1803 (Table P-PZ40)
4707.K6 Klitsche de la Grange, Antonietta (Table P-PZ40)
4707.K74 Kreglianovich, Giovanni, 1777-1838 (Table P-PZ40)
4707.L2 Lamberti, Luigi, 1759-1813 (Table P-PZ40)
4707.L27 Lancetti, Vincenzo, 1767?-1851 (Table P-PZ40)
Lara, contessa, 1849-1896 see PQ4687.C6
4707.L28 Lassala, Manuel, 18th cent. (Table P-PZ40)
4707.L3 Lauzières, Achille de, fl. 1857-1892 (Table P-PZ40)
4707.L5 Leonardis, Giuseppe de, fl. 1863-1899 (Table P-PZ40)
4707.L6 Leoni, Michele, 1776-1858 (Table P-PZ40)
Leopardi, Giacomo, conte, 1798-1837
4708.A1 Collected works. By date
4708.A13 Selected works. By date
(4708.A14) Posthumous works
see PQ4708.A13
4708.A2 Collected poetry
4708.A3 Collected prose
4708.A35 Collected plays
4708.A5-Z Separate works, A-Z
(4708.Z9) Works edited or commented upon by Leopardi, by author, A-Z
4709.A-Z Translations. By language, A-Z
4709.E5 English
4709.F5 French
4709.G5 German
4709.S7 Spanish
4710 Biography and criticism
4710.A2 Autobiography, journals, memoirs. By title
4710.A3 Letters
4712.L2 Leopardi, Monaldo, conte, 1776-1847 (Table P-PZ40)
Liberi, Ausonio, pseud. see PQ4692.G92
4712.L27 Linares, Vincenzo, 1804-1847 (Table P-PZ40)
4712.L37 Lombardo, Nicolò, d. 1749 (Table P-PZ40)
4712.L38 Lombroso, Cesare, 1835-1909 (Table P-PZ40)
4712.L4 Lorenzini, Carlo, 1826-1890 (Table P-PZ40)
Pseudonym: Carlo Collodi
4712.L43 Lo Sapiò, Francesco Peolo, 19th cent. (Table P-PZ40)
4712.L45 Lotesoriere, Arcangelo, 1825-1897 (Table P-PZ40)
4712.L5 Lovatelli, Ersilia (Caetani), contessa, 1840-1925 (Table P-PZ40)
4712.L82 Lunelli Spinola, Benedetta Clotilde, 1700-1774 (Table P-PZ40)
4712.L84 Lupo, Adele, 1851-1927 (Table P-PZ40)
4712.L89 Luzzatto, Carolina C. (Carolina Coen), 1837 or 9-1919 (Table P-PZ40)

Individual authors
Individual authors, 1701-1900 -- Continued
Maddaloni, Proto Carafa Pallavicino, duca di see PQ4730.P86
4712.M29 Maffei, Andrea, 1798-1885 (Table P-PZ40)
4712.M3 Maffei, Francesco Scipione, marchese, 1675-1755 (Table P-PZ40)
4712.M4 Magherini-Graziani, Giovanni, fl. 1897 (Table P-PZ40)
4712.M5 Mameli, Goffredo, 1827-1849 (Table P-PZ40)
4712.M6 Mamiani della Rovera, Terenzio, conte, 1799-1885 (Table P-PZ40)
Mancini-Pierantoni, Grazia see PQ4730.P38
4712.M7 Manfredi, Eustachio, 1674-1739 (Table P-PZ40)
4712.M75 Manin, Romanello, 1672-1726 (Table P-PZ40)
4712.M8 Mantegazza, Paolo, 1831-1910 (Table P-PZ40)
Manzoni, Alessandro, 1785-1873
Editions
4713.A1 Comprehensive collections
4713.A2 Selected works
4713.A3 Selections. Quotations. Passages. Thoughts
4713.A4 Collected poetry
4713.A5 Collected prose
(4713.A55) Posthumous works
see PQ4713.A2
4713.A6-Z Separate works
e.g.
I promessi sposi
4713.P3 Editions, by date
4713.P35 Modernized editions
4713.P4 School editions
4713.P45 Parodies, by author, A-Z
4713.P5 Criticism
4714 Translations
Italian dialects classed with Italian works
English
4714.A1 Collections and selections. By translator or date
4714.A2 I promessi sposi. By translator or date
4714.A21-.A29 Other works. By original title, alphabetically
French
4714.A3 Collections and selections. By translator or date
4714.A4 I promessi sposi. By translator or date
4714.A41-.A49 Other works. By original title, alphabetically
German
4714.A5 Collections and selections. By translator or date
4714.A6 I promessi sposi. By translator or date
4714.A61-.A69 Other works. By original title, alphabetically
Spanish

Individual authors
Individual authors, 1701-1900
Manzoni, Alessandro, 1785-1873
Translations
Spanish -- Continued

4714.A7 Collections and selections. By translator or date
4714.A8 I promessi sposi. By translator or date
4714.A81-.A89 Other works. By original title, alphabetically
4714.A9-Z Other European languages
4714.B2-.B29 Basque (Table PQ10)
4714.C2-.C29 Catalan (Table PQ10)
Celtic
4714.C3-.C39 Breton (Table PQ10)
4714.C4-.C49 Cornish (Table PQ10)
4714.C5-.C59 Gaelic (Table PQ10)
4714.C6-.C69 Irish (Table PQ10)
4714.C7-.C79 Manx (Table PQ10)
4714.C8-.C89 Welsh (Table PQ10)
Dutch
4714.D2 Collections and selections. By translator or date
4714.D3 I promessi sposi. By translator or date
4714.D31-.D39 Other works. By original title, alphabetically
Finnish
4714.F2 Collections and selections. By translator or date
4714.F3 I promessi sposi. By translator or date
4714.F31-.F39 Other works. By original title, alphabetically
Greek
4714.G2 Collections and selections. By translator or date
4714.G3 I promessi sposi. By translator or date
4714.G31-.G39 Other works. By original title, alphabetically
Hungarian
4714.H2 Collections and selections. By translator or date
4714.H3 I promessi sposi. By translator or date
4714.H31-.H39 Other works. By original title, alphabetically
Portuguese
4714.P2 Collections and selections. By translator or date
4714.P3 I promessi sposi. By translator or date
4714.P31-.P39 Other works. By original title, alphabetically
Romanian
4714.R2 Collections and selections. By translator or date
4714.R3 I promessi sposi. By translator or date
4714.R31-.R39 Other works. By original title, alphabetically
Scandinavian
4714.S1-.S19 Danish. Norwegian (Table PQ10)
4714.S2-.S29 Icelandic (Table PQ10)
4714.S3-.S39 Swedish (Table PQ10)
Slavic

Individual authors
Individual authors, 1701-1900
Manzoni, Alessandro, 1785-1873
Translations
Other European languages
Slavic -- Continued

4714.S4-.S49 Bohemian (Table PQ10)
4714.S491-.S4919 Bulgarian (Table PQ10)
4714.S5-.S59 Croatian (Table PQ10)
4714.S6-.S69 Polish (Table PQ10)
4714.S7-.S79 Russian (Table PQ10)
4714.S791-.S7919 Ruthenian (Table PQ10)
4714.S8-.S89 Serbian (Table PQ10)
4714.5.A-Z Oriental, etc., languages, A-Z

Biography and criticism

4715.A3 Journals. Letters. Memoirs
4715.A5-Z By author, A-Z
4715.2 Family. Ancestry. Name

Maratti, Faustina see PQ4734.Z5

4716.M2 Marchese, Annibale, duca, 1685?-1753 (Table P-PZ40)
4716.M3 Marchi, Emilio de, 1851-1901 (Table P-PZ40)
4716.M35 Marcotti, Giuseppi, 1850- (Table P-PZ40)
4716.M39 Marenco, Carlo, 1800-1846 (Table P-PZ40)
4716.M4 Marenco, Leopoldo, 1831-1899 (Table P-PZ40)
4716.M45 Mario, Alberto, 1825-1883 (Table P-PZ40)
4716.M47 Marradi, Giovanni, 1852-1922 (Table P-PZ40)
4716.M48 Marsili, Giovanni, 1760-1795 (Table P-PZ40)
4716.M55 Martelli, Pier Jacopo, 1665-1727 (Table P-PZ40)
4716.M556 Martello, Francesco, 19th cent (Table P-PZ40)
4716.M6 Martini, Ferdinando, 1841-1928 (Table P-PZ40)

Pseudonym: Fantasio

4716.M64 Martini, Vincenzo, 1803-1862 (Table P-PZ40)
4716.M67 Marugj, Giovanni Leonardo, 1753-1836 (Table P-PZ40)
4716.M68 Marulli, Giacomo, 1822-1883 (Table P-PZ40)
4716.M7 Marzo, Antonio Gualberto de, fl. 1847- (Table P-PZ40)
4716.M8 Mascheroni, Lorenzo, 1750-1800 (Table P-PZ40)
4716.M816 Massimi, Petronilla Paolini, 1663-1726 (Table P-PZ40)
4716.M82 Mastriani, Francesco, 1819-1891 (Table P-PZ40)
4716.M823 Mastro Bruno, 1837-1912 (Table P-PZ40)
4716.M83 Mathias, Thomas James, 1754?-1835 (Table P-PZ40)

Cf. PR4987.M2 English literature

4716.M84 Mauro, Domenico, 1812-1873 (Table P-PZ40)
4716.M85 Mazza, Angelo, 1741-1817 (Table P-PZ40)
4716.M86 Mazzoldi, Angelo, 1799-1864 (Table P-PZ40)

Melegari, Dora see PQ4829.E5

4716.M87 Meli, Giovanni, 1740-1815 (Table P-PZ38)

Memini, pseud. see PQ4683.B47

Individual authors
Individual authors, 1701-1900 -- Continued

4716.M88 Mercantini, Luigi, 1821-1872 (Table P-PZ40)
4716.M89 Merlini, Lodovico, 1815?-1888 (Table P-PZ40)
Metastasio, Pietro, 1698-1782
4717 Editions
Before 1801
see subclass ML
4717.A1 Comprehensive. By date
4717.A12 Selected works (Miscellaneous). By date
4717.A15 Selected plays
4717.A17 Collected and selected poems
(4717.A19) Posthumous works
see PQ4717.A12+
4717.A2-Z Separate works, A-Z
4718 Translations
English
4718.A1 Collected and selected works. By translator, A-Z
4718.A11 Poems
4718.A12-.A29 Other. By original title and translator
Translations of letters see PQ4719.A2
4718.A3 French
4718.A5 German
4718.A7 Spanish
4718.A9-Z Other languages, A-Z
Biography and criticism
4719.A2 Journals. Letters. Memoirs
4719.A5-Z By author, A-Z
4720.M15 Mezzanotte, Antonio, 1786-1857 (Table P-PZ40)
4720.M153 Mezzanotte, Giuseppe, b. 1855 (Table P-PZ40)
4720.M17 Micheli, Benedetto, 18th cent (Table P-PZ40)
4720.M24 Misasi, Nicola, 1850-1923 (Table P-PZ40)
4720.M3 Mollo, Gaspare, 1754-1823 (Table P-PZ40)
4720.M37 Mondo, Domenico, 1723-1806 (Table P-PZ40)
4720.M4 Mondolfi, Rodolfo, 1842- (Table P-PZ40)
4720.M45 Montani, Giuseppe, 1789-1833 (Table P-PZ40)
4720.M5 Monti, Vincenzo, 1754-1828 (Table P-PZ40)
4720.M55 Morbilli, Carlo, duci di Sant' Angelo a Frosolonè, 18th cent. (Table P-PZ40)
4720.M57 Morgagni, Giovanni Battista, 1682-1771 (Table P-PZ40)
4720.M87 Musemeci Catalono, Giuseppe Maria, 18th cent (Table P-PZ40)
4720.M89 Musi, Carlo, 1851-1920 (Table P-PZ40)
4720.N2 Napoli-Signorelli, Pietro, 1731-1815 (Table P-PZ40)
4720.N23 Napollon-Margarita, Ernesta, 1840- (Table P-PZ40)
4720.N25 Nardini, Bartolomeo, fl. 1801 (Table P-PZ40)
4720.N253 Nardini, Vincenzo Maria, 19th cent (Table P-PZ40)

Individual authors
Individual authors, 1701-1900 -- Continued
4720.N254 Nardo, Giovanni Domenico, 1802-1887 (Table P-PZ40)
4720.N3 Navarro della Miraglia, Emanuele, conte, 1838- (Table P-PZ40)
Neera, pseud. see PQ4730.R2
4720.N37 Negro, Gian Carlo di, d. 1857 (Table P-PZ40)
4720.N5 Niccolini, Giovanni Battista, 1782-1861 (Table P-PZ40)
4720.N65 Nieri, Idelfonso, 1853-1920 (Table P-PZ40)
4720.N7 Nievo, Ippolitio, 1832-1861 (Table P-PZ40)
4720.N8 Nota, Alberta, 1775-1847 (Table P-PZ40)
4720.N88 Nuvoletti, Giulio, 1734-1811 (Table P-PZ40)
Olimpica, Corilla see PQ4688.F35
4720.O57 Oliva, Francesco, 18th cent (Table P-PZ40)
4720.O58 Onetti, Luigi (Table P-PZ40)
4720.O6 Ongaro, Francesco dall', 1803-1873 (Table P-PZ40)
4720.O7 Oriani, Alfredo, 1852-1909 (Table P-PZ40)
Ormeville, Carlo d'
see ML50, D'Ormeville, Carlo
4720.O8 Orti, Girolamo, conte, 1769-1845 (Table P-PZ40)
4720.P12 Padula, Vincenzo, b. 1819 (Table P-PZ40)
4720.P145 Palli-Bartolomei, Angelica, 1798-1875 (Table P-PZ40)
4720.P2 Pananti, Filippo, 1766-1837 (Table P-PZ40)
4720.P3 Panzacchi, Enrico, 1840-1904 (Table P-PZ40)
4720.P4 Paradisi, Agostino, 1736-1783 (Table P-PZ40)
4720.P42 Paradisi, Giovanni, 1760-1826 (Table P-PZ40)
4720.P5 Pariati, Pietro, 1665-1733? (Table P-PZ40)
Parini, Giuseppe, 1729-1799
Editions
4721.A1 General collections. By date
4721.A12 Selected works. By date
4721.A2 Collected poems. By date
4721.A25 Collected prose works. By date
4722.A-Z Translations. By language, A-Z
4723.A-Z Separate works. By title, A-Z
Biography and criticism
4724 General
4725 Special
4726.P3 Parzanese, Pietro Paolo, 1810-1842 (Table P-PZ40)
4726.P37 Pasini, Antonio, 1833-1897 (Table P-PZ40)
4726.P39 Patitari, Nicola, 1852-1898 (Table P-PZ40)
4726.P4 Patuzzi, Gaetano Lionello, 1841-1909 (Table P-PZ40)
4726.P63 Pecchia, Carlo, 1715-1784 (Table P-PZ40)
4726.P65 Pedevilla, Luigi Michele, 1815-1877 (Table P-PZ40)
4726.P7 Pellegrini, Giuseppe, 1797-1879 (Table P-PZ40)
Pellico, Silvio, 1788-1854
Editions

Individual authors
Individual authors, 1701-1900
Pellico, Silvio, 1788-1854
Editions -- Continued

4727.A1	Collected works
4727.A12	Selected works
4727.A17	Collected plays
4727.A19	Collected prose works
4727.A6-Z	Separate works
	e. g.
4727.M5	Le mie prigioni
4728	Translations
	English
4728.A1	Collections
4728.A2	Le mie prigioni, by translator, A-Z
4728.A21-.A29	Other works, alphabetically
	French
4728.A3	Collections
4728.A4	Le mie prigioni, by translator, A-Z
4728.A41-.A49	Other works, alphabetically
	German
4728.A5	Collections
4728.A6	Le mie prigioni, by translator, A-Z
4728.A61-.A69	Other works, alphabetically
	Spanish
4728.A7	Collections
4728.A8	Le mie prigioni, by translator, A-Z
4728.A81-.A89	Other works, alphabetically
4728.A9-.A99	Other languages, alphabetically
4729	Biography and criticism
4730.P134	Pelosini, N. F. (Narciso Feliciano), 1823-1896 (Table P-PZ40)
4730.P142	Pepe, Cristoforo, 1840-1906 (Table P-PZ40)
4730.P145	Pepe, Gabriele, 1799-1849 (Table P-PZ40)
4730.P15	Pepoli, Alessandro Ercole, conte, 1757-1797 (Table P-PZ40)
4730.P22	Percòto, Caterina, 1812-1887 (Table P-PZ40)
4730.P224	Perodi, Emma, 1850-1918 (Table P-PZ40)
4730.P226	Perotti, Armando, 1865-1924 (Table P-PZ40)
4730.P229	Perticari, Costanza Monti, 1792-1840 (Table P-PZ40)
4730.P23	Perticari, Giulio, conte, 1779-1822 (Table P-PZ40)
4730.P232	Peruzzi, Bindo Simone, 1696-1759 (Table P-PZ40)
4730.P234	Petito, Antonio, 1822-1876 (Table P-PZ40)
4730.P238	Petrocchi, Policarpo, 1852-1902 (Table P-PZ40)
4730.P24	Petronj, Stefano Egidio, 1770-1837 (Table P-PZ40)

Individual authors
Individual authors, 1701-1900 -- Continued

4730.P25 Petrucelli della Gattina, Ferdinando, 1816-1890 (Table P-PZ40)
Cf. PQ2380.P87 French literature
4730.P28 Piaggio, Martino, 19th cent. (Table P-PZ40)
4730.P29 Piazza, Antonio, 1742-1825 (Table P-PZ40)
4730.P3 Piccini, Giulio, 1849-1915 (Table P-PZ40)
4730.P33 Pichi, Giovanni Battista, fl. 1702 (Table P-PZ40)
4730.P35 Picone, Cesare, fl. 1884 (Table P-PZ40)
4730.P38 Pierantoni-Mancini, Grazia, 1843-1915 (Table P-PZ40)
4730.P386 Pieri, Mario, 1776-1852 (Table P-PZ40)
4730.P39 Pietracqua, Luigi, 1832-1901 (Table P-PZ40)
4730.P4 Pignotti, Lorenzo, 1739-1812 (Table P-PZ40)
4730.P46 Pilotto, Libero, d. 1900 (Table P-PZ40)
Pimentel, Eleonora Fonseca see PQ4688.F66
4730.P49 Pindemonte, Giovanni, 1751-1812 (Table P-PZ40)
4730.P5 Pindemonte, Ippolito, 1753-1828 (Table P-PZ40)
4730.P54 Pinelli, Giuseppe, fl. 1860 (Table P-PZ40)
4730.P6 Poerio, Alessandro, 1802-1848 (Table P-PZ40)
4730.P63 Polcenigo e Fanna, Giorgio Andrea, conte di, 1715-1784 (Table P-PZ40)
4730.P636 Polidori, Gaetano, d. 1764-1853 (Table P-PZ40)
4730.P647 Pompeati, Luigi Bernardo, 1799-1828 (Table P-PZ40)
4730.P65 Pompei, Girolamo, 1731-1788 (Table P-PZ40)
Ponte, Lorenzo da, 1749-1838 see PQ4688.D3
4730.P7 Porta, Carlo, 1775-1821 (Table P-PZ40)
4730.P78 Pratesi, Mario, 1842-1921 (Table P-PZ40)
4730.P8 Prati, Giovanni, 1815-1884 (Table P-PZ40)
4730.P85 Procacci, Giovanni, 1836-1887 (Table P-PZ40)
4730.P86 Proto Carafa Pallavicino, Marzio Francesco, duca di Maddaloni, 1815-1892 (Table P-PZ40)
4730.P87 Pucci, Domenico Serafino, fl. 1831 (Table P-PZ40)
4730.P9 Pullè, Giulio, conte, 1814-1894 (Table P-PZ40)
4730.P92 Pullè, Leopoldo, conte, 1835-1917 (Table P-PZ40)
4730.Q45 Quintana, Cesare, 17th cent. (Table P-PZ40)
4730.R2 Radius, Anna (Zuccari), 1846-1918 (Table P-PZ40)
(4730.R22) Rainerio, Antonio Francesco, 16th cent.
see PQ4632.R133
4730.R236 Ranieri, Antonio, 1806?-1888 (Table P-PZ40)
4730.R24 Rapisardi, Mario, 1844-1912 (Table P-PZ40)
4730.R25 Re, Zefirino, 1782-1864 (Table P-PZ40)
4730.R4 Renzis, Francesco de, 1836-1900 (Table P-PZ40)
4730.R5 Revere, Giuseppe, 1812-1889 (Table P-PZ40)
Rezzonico, Carlo Castone Gaetano della Toree, conte see PQ4733.T75
4730.R53 Riccardi di Lantosca, Vincenzo, 1829-1887 (Table P-PZ40)

Individual authors

Individual authors, 1701-1900 -- Continued

4730.R54 Ricci, Angelo Maria, 1776-1850 (Table P-PZ40)

4730.R7 Righetti, Carlo, 1830-1906 (Table P-PZ40)

Rinaldi, Pietro see PQ4692.G62

4731.R2 Rolli, Paolo, 1687-1765 (Table P-PZ40)

Romani, Felice, 1788-1865

see ML50, ML429

Rosa, Ludovico de, pseud. see PQ4732.S3

4731.R35 Rosellini, Massimina (Fantastici), 1789-1859 (Table P-PZ40)

4731.R4 Rosini, Giovanni, 1776-1855 (Table P-PZ40)

4731.R6 Rossetti, Gabriele Pasquale Giuseppe, 1783-1854 (Table P-PZ40)

4731.R63 Rossi, Giovanni Gherardo de, 1754-1827 (Table P-PZ40)

4731.R64 Rota, Giuseppe, 1720-1792 (Table P-PZ40)

4731.R65 Rotondi, Pietro, 1814- (Table P-PZ40)

4731.R7 Rovani, Giuseppe, 1818-1874 (Table P-PZ40)

4731.R8 Rovetta, Gerolamo, 1854-1910 (Table P-PZ40)

4731.R9 Ruffini, Giovanni Domenico, 1807-1881 (Table P-PZ40)

4731.R92 Ruggeri, Pietro, 1797-1858 (Table P-PZ40)

4732.S15 Saccenti, Giovanni Santi, d. 1749 (Table P-PZ40)

4732.S17 Sacchetti, Roberto, 1847-1881 (Table P-PZ40)

4732.S173 Sacchi, Defendente, 1796-1840 (Table P-PZ40)

4732.S175 Salerno, Niccola M. (Niccola Maria), b. 1675 (Table P-PZ40)

4732.S177 Salfi, Francesco Saverio, 1759-1832 (Table P-PZ40)

4732.S18 Salmini, Vittorio, 1832-1881 (Table P-PZ40)

4732.S2 Salvini, Antonio Maria, 1653-1729 (Table P-PZ40)

4732.S23 Salvini, Salvino, 1667-1751 (Table P-PZ40)

4732.S25 Sanctis, Giustino de, fl. 1881-1895 (Table P-PZ40)

4732.S26 Sangro, Francesco di, fl. 1790 (Table P-PZ40)

Cf. Class M

4732.S28 Sappa, Alessandro, 1717-1783 (Table P-PZ40)

4732.S3 Saredo, Luisa (Emanuel), d. 1896 (Table P-PZ40)

4732.S4 Savioli, Ludovico Vittorio, 1729-1804 (Table P-PZ40)

4732.S422 Scalici, Ernanuele, 1846-1904 (Table P-PZ40)

4732.S425 Scarfoglio, Edoardo, 1860-1917 (Table P-PZ40)

4732.S428 Scarpetta, Eduardo, 1853-1925 (Table P-PZ40)

4732.S43 Scarselli, Flaminio, 1705-1776 (Table P-PZ40)

4732.S44 Schiavi, Lorenzo, 1829-1911 (Table P-PZ40)

4732.S45 Schizzi, Folchino, conte, fl. 1825 (Table P-PZ40)

4732.S455 Schmidt, Giovanni, b. ca. 1775 (Table P-PZ40)

4732.S456 Schmitz, Elio, 1863-1886 (Table P-PZ40)

Sciosciammocca, Felice, pseud. see PQ4732.S428

4732.S465 Scrofani, Saverio, 1756-1835 (Table P-PZ40)

4732.S47 Selvatico, Riccardo, 1849-1901 (Table P-PZ40)

Individual authors
Individual authors, 1701-1900 -- Continued
Serao, Matilde see PQ4841.E7
4732.S5 Seriman, Zaccaria, 1708-1784 (Table P-PZ40)
4732.S512 Serio, Luigi, 1744-1799 (Table P-PZ40)
4732.S517 Serra, Luigi, 1757-1813 (Table P-PZ40)
4732.S52 Serra-Greci, A., fl. 1877- (Table P-PZ40)
4732.S55 Sestini, Bartolomeo, 1792-1825 (Table P-PZ40)
4732.S58 Sgricci, Tommaso, 1789-1836 (Table P-PZ40)
4732.S59 Simon, Domenico, 1758-1829 (Table P-PZ40)
4732.S6 Sindici, Augusto, 1837-1921 (Table P-PZ40)
4732.S65 Soave, Francesco, 1743-1806 (Table P-PZ40)
4732.S7 Sografi, Antonio Simeone, 1759-1818 (Table P-PZ40)
4732.S73 Somma, Antonio, 1809-1864 (Table P-PZ40)
4732.S75 Sorelli, Guido, 19th cent (Table P-PZ40)
4732.S78 Spagna, Arcangelo, fl. 1700 (Table P-PZ40)
4732.S8 Spolverini, Giovanni Battista, marchese, 1695-1762 (Table P-PZ40)
Spuches, Giuseppina (Turrisi Colonna) de see PQ4733.T9
Stecchetti, Lorenzo, pseud. see PQ4707.G3
4732.S83 Stevens, Sofia, 1845-1876 (Table P-PZ40)
4732.S89 Sugara, Luigi, 1857-1904 (Table P-PZ40)
4732.S93 Susi, Giambattista, 1818-1887 (Table P-PZ40)
4733.S97 Suzzara Verdi, Paride, d. 1879 (Table P-PZ40)
4733.T18 Tagliazucchi, Veronica (Cantelli) de', fl. 1765. Tanfucio, (Table P-PZ40)
Tanfucio, Neri, pseud. see PQ4692.F6
4733.T3 Tarchetti, Iginio Ugo, 1841-1869 (Table P-PZ40)
4733.T314 Taruffi, Pier Iacopo, 1725-1794 (Table P-PZ40)
4733.T32 Tempio, Domenico, 1750-1820 (Table P-PZ40)
4733.T34 Tenca, Carlo, 1816-1883 (Table P-PZ40)
Testa, Tommaso Gherardi del see PQ4692.G4
4733.T4 Tigri, Giuseppe, 1806-1882 (Table P-PZ40)
4733.T5 Tommaseo, Niccolò, 1802-1874 (Table P-PZ40)
4733.T6 Torelli, Achille, 1844- (Table P-PZ40)
4733.T7 Torelli-Viollier, Maria Antonietta (Torriani), 1846- (Table P-PZ40)
4733.T75 Torre di Rezzonico, Carlo Castone Gaetano, conte della, 1742-1796 (Table P-PZ40)
Torriani, Maria see PQ4733.T7
4733.T79 Torti, Francesco, 1763-1842 (Table P-PZ40)
4733.T8 Torti, Giovanni, 1774-1852 (Table P-PZ40)
4733.T83 Trinchera, Pietro, d. 1755 (Table P-PZ40)
Turra, Elisabetta Caminer see PQ4684.C44
4733.T9 Turrisi Colonna, Giuseppina, 1822-1848 (Table P-PZ40)
4734.U3 Uccelli, Domenico, fl. 1811 (Table P-PZ40)
4734.V3 Varano, Alfonso, 1705-1788 (Table P-PZ40)

Individual authors
Individual authors, 1701-1900 -- Continued
4734.V33 Varese, Carlo, 1792-1866 (Table P-PZ40)
4734.V35 Vassallo, Luigi Arnaldo, 1852-1906 (Table P-PZ40)
4734.V386 Venuti, Filippo, 1709-1769 (Table P-PZ40)
Verati, Lisimaco, pseud. see PQ4726.P7
4734.V4 Verdinois, Federigo, 1843?- (Table P-PZ40)
4734.V5 Verga, Giovanni, 1840-1922 (Table P-PZ40)
Vero, Ausonio, pseud. see PQ4730.P86
4734.V6 Verri, Alessandro, conte, 1741-1816 (Table P-PZ40)
4734.V64 Vettori, Vittore, 18th cent (Table P-PZ40)
4734.V67 Viassolo, Giovanni Battista, 1749-1802 (Table P-PZ40)
4734.V676 Vidua, Carlo, 1785-1830 (Table P-PZ40)
4734.V683 Villa, Giustiniano, 1842-1919 (Table P-PZ40)
4734.V686 Visconti, Ermes, 1784-1841 (Table P-PZ40)
4734.V688 Vittorelli, Jacopo, 1749-1835 (Table P-PZ40)
Vivanti, Annie see PQ4809.H25
4734.V69 Viviani, Niccolò, marchese, fl. 1794 (Table P-PZ40)
4734.V73 Vollo, Benedetto (Table P-PZ40)
4734.V75 Vordoni, Teresa (Albarelli), 1788-1868 (Table P-PZ40)
4734.W5 Willi, Andrea, 1733-1793 (Table P-PZ40)
4734.Z3 Zamboni, Filippo, 1827-1910 (Table P-PZ40)
4734.Z35 Zanbrini, Francesco Saverio, 1810-1887 (Table P-PZ40)
4734.Z36 Zanchi Bertelli, Antonio, fl. 1847 (Table P-PZ40)
4734.Z37 Zanella, Giacomo, 1820-1888 (Table P-PZ38)
4734.Z38 Zannoni, Gio. Batista, 1774-1832 (Table P-PZ40)
4734.Z39 Zanoia, Giuseppe, 1752-1817 (Table P-PZ40)
Zanoja see PQ4734.Z39
4734.Z42 Zanotti, Francesco Maria, 1692-1777 (Table P-PZ40)
4734.Z43 Zanotti, Giovanni Pietro Cavazzoni, 1674-1765 (Table P-PZ40)
4734.Z5 Zappi, Faustina (Maratti), d. 1745 (Table P-PZ40)
4734.Z52 Zappi, Giovanni Battista Felice, 1667-1710. (Table P-PZ40)
4734.Z58 Zena, Remigio, 1850-1917 (Table P-PZ40)
4734.Z6 Zeno, Apostolo, 1668-1750 (Table P-PZ40)
Zuccari Radius, Anna see PQ4730.R2
4734.Z65 Ziccardi, Michelangelo (Table P-PZ40)
Individual authors, 1900-1960
Subarrange each author by Table P-PZ40 unless otherwise specified
Except for d'Annunzio, the author number is taken from that part of the name beginning with the second letter
For Italian authors in the United States see PQ5984.A+
For juvenile literature see PZ41+
4800 Anonymous works (Table P-PZ28)
4801 A - Annunzio
4801.B3 Abbamonte, Salvatore, 1877- (Table P-PZ40)

Individual authors
Individual authors, 1900-1960
A-Annunzio -- Continued

4801.D3 Adami, Giuseppe, 1878- (Table P-PZ40)
4801.G3 Aganoor Pompilj, Vittoria, 1868-1910 (Table P-PZ40)
4801.L3 Albertazzi, Adolfo, 1865-1924 (Table P-PZ40)
Aleramo, Sibilla, pseud. see PQ4815.A3
4801.L8 Alvi, Ciro, 1879- (Table P-PZ40)
4801.M5 Amico, Silvio d', fl. 1913- (Table P-PZ40)
4801.N45 Andreis, Alberto, fl. 1919- (Table P-PZ40)
4801.N46 Andreoni, Antonio, 1859-1945 (Table P-PZ40)

Annunzio, Gabriele d', 1863-1938

Collected works
4803.A1 General collections. By date
4803.A12 Selected works. By date
4803.A15 Collected novels
4803.A16 Collected essays, miscellanies, etc.
4803.A17 Collected poems
4803.A19 Collected plays
4803.A3-.Z29 Separate works, A-Z

Translations
English
4803.Z3A1 Collected works. Selected works. By date
Including collected poems, essays, etc.
4803.Z3A3-.Z3Z Separate works. By Italian title, A-Z
Subarrange by date
4803.Z4-.Z49 French
4803.Z4A1 Collected works. Selected works. By date
Including collected poems, essays, etc.
4803.Z4A3-.Z4Z Separate works. By Italian title, A-Z
Subarrange by date
4803.Z5-.Z59 German
4803.Z5A1 Collected works. Selected works. By date
Including collected poems, essays, etc.
4803.Z5A3-.Z5Z Separate works. By Italian title, A-Z
Subarrange by date
4803.Z6-.Z69 Other languages, alphabetically
4803.Z7-.Z79 Adaptations, dramatizations, etc.

Biography and criticism
Cf. DG575.A6 Annunzio as an Italian statesman
4804.A2-.A39 Autobiography, journals, memoirs. By title
4804.A4 Letters (Collections). By date
4804.A41-.A49 Letters to and from particular individuals. By correspondent (alphabetically)
4804.A5-.Z5 General works
4804.Z9 Dictionaries. Concordances, etc.

4805 Annunzio - Az

Individual authors
Individual authors, 1900-1960
Annunzio-Az -- Continued

4805.N79 Antona-Traversi, Camillo, 1857- (Table P-PZ40)
4805.N8 Antona-Traversi-Grismondi, Giannino, 1860- (Table P-PZ40)
4805.N85 Antonelli, Luigi, 1882- (Table P-PZ40)
Ardens, Lucilla see PQ4841.A38
4805.V3 Avancini, Avancinio, 1866- (Table P-PZ40)
4807 B - Bz
4807.A2 Baccelli, Alfredo, 1863- (Table P-PZ40)
4807.A23 Bacchelli, Riccardo, 1891- (Table P-PZ40)
4807.A57 Balsamo-Crivelli, Riccardo, marchese, 1874- (Table P-PZ40)
4807.A6 Balzo, Carlo del, 1853-1908 (Table P-PZ40)
Banti, Anna see PQ4827.O635
4807.A74 Bartolini, Luigi, 1892- (Table P-PZ40)
4807.E45 Belli, Pietro, fl. 1911 (Table P-PZ40)
4807.E6 Beltremelli, Antonio, 1874-1930 (Table P-PZ40)
4807.E64 Benco, Silvio, 1874-1949 (Table P-PZ40)
4807.E7 Benelli, Sem, 1877- (Table P-PZ40)
4807.E75 Bernasconi, Ugo, 1874-1960 (Table P-PZ40)
4807.E76 Berrini, Nino, 1880- (Table P-PZ40)
4807.E78 Bertacchi, Giovanni, 1869-1942 (Table P-PZ40)
4807.I5 Bini, Sofia, fl. 1892-129 (Table P-PZ40)
4807.I7 Bisi, Sofia (Albini), 1856-1919 (Table P-PZ40)
Pseudonym: Donna Conny
4807.O3 Boccardi, Alberto, 1854- (Table P-PZ40)
4807.O4 Bodrero, Emilio, 1874- (Table P-PZ40)
4807.O65 Bontempelli, Massimo, 1878- (Table P-PZ40)
4807.O75 Borgese, Giuseppe Antonio, 1882- (Table P-PZ40)
4807.O8 Borgialli, Mario, fl. 1914 (Table P-PZ40)
4807.O85 Bosis, Adolfo de, d. 1924 (Table P-PZ40)
4807.R2 Bracco, Roberto, 1862- (Table P-PZ40)
4807.R6 Brocchi, Virgilio, 1876- (Table P-PZ40)
4807.R8 Brunati, Giuseppe, fl. 1907- (Table P-PZ40)
4807.U8 Butti, Enrico Annibale, 1868- (Table P-PZ40)
4807.U85 Buzzi, Paolo, d. 1956 (Table P-PZ40)
4809 C - Cz
4809.A514 Camaiti, Venturino (Table P-PZ40)
4809.A5334 Camponovo, Guglielmo, 1847-1932 (Table P-PZ40)
4809.A547 Capriglione, Raffaele, 1874-1921 (Table P-PZ40)
4809.A55 Caprin, Giulio, 1880- (Table P-PZ40)
Capuana, Luigi see PQ4684.C8
4809.A6 Carbonara, Francesco, 1895- (Table P-PZ40)
Pseudonym: Cilly
4809.E5 Cena, Giovanni, 1870- (Table P-PZ40)

Individual authors
Individual authors, 1900-1960
C-Cz -- Continued

4809.E7 Cesareo, Giovanni Alfredo, 1861- (Table P-PZ40)
4809.H25 Chartres, Mrs. Annie (Vivanti), 1870- (Table P-PZ40)
4809.H34 Chiarelli, Luigi, 1886- (Table P-PZ40)
4809.H37 Chiesa, Francesco, 1871- (Table P-PZ40)
4809.H4 Chiggiato, Giovanni, 1876- (Table P-PZ40)
4809.H45 Chirico, Andrea de, 1891-1952 (Table P-PZ40)
4809.I46 Cinelli, Delfino, 1889- (Table P-PZ40)
4809.I5 Cippico, Antonio, conte, 1877- (Table P-PZ40)
Conny, Donna, pseud. see PQ4807.I7
Cordelia, pseud. see PQ4843.R4
4809.O57 Corra, Bruno (Table P-PZ40)
4809.O6 Corradini, Enrico, 1868- (Table P-PZ40)
4809.O9 Cozzani, Ettore, 1884- (Table P-PZ40)
4809.R3 Cramp, Walter Samuel, 1867- (Table P-PZ40)
4809.R33 Creazzo, Pasquale, 1875-1963 (Table P-PZ40)
4809.R6 Crispolti, Filippo, 1857-4811 (Table P-PZ40)
4811 D - Dz
D'Annunzio, Gabriele, 1863-1938 see PQ4803+
4811.E6 Deledda, Grazia, 1872- (Table P-PZ40)
De Michelis, Eurialo, 1904- see PQ4829.I35
De Roberto, Federico, 1861-1927 see PQ4839.O3
4811.I2 Dias, Willy, 1872- (Table P-PZ40)
Di Giacomo, Giovanni Antonio, 1891-1960 see PQ4847.A4947
Di Giacomo, Salvatore, 1862-1934 see PQ4817.I2
4813 E - Ez
4815 F - Fz
4815.A2 Fabbri, Guglielmo, fl. 1909 (Table P-PZ40)
4815.A3 Faccio, Rina, 1878- (Table P-PZ40)
4815.A4 Fago, Vincenzo, 1870-1931 (Table P-PZ40)
4815.A56 Faldella, Giovanni, 1846-1928 (Table P-PZ40)
4815.A6 Falena, Ugo, 1874- (Table P-PZ40)
4815.A7 Fanciulli, Giuseppe, 1881- (Table P-PZ40)
Fava, Onorato see PQ4688.F32
4815.E6 Félyne, Ossip (Table P-PZ40)
4815.E672 Ferrara, Francesco, 1858-1944 (Table P-PZ40)
4815.E675 Ferrero, Guglielmo, 1871- (Table P-PZ40)
4815.E68 Ferrigni, Mario, 1878- (Table P-PZ40)
4815.E7 Ferruggia, Gemma, 1868- (Table P-PZ40)
4815.I27 Ficarelli, Amerigo, 1873-1938 (Table P-PZ40)
4815.I8 Fiumi, Maria Luisa, contessa (Table P-PZ40)
4815.L3 Flamma, Ario (Table P-PZ40)
4815.O6 Fonty Archer, Nicolau Alberto de, 1882- (Table P-PZ40)
Writings also in French and Portuguese

Individual authors
Individual authors, 1900-1960
F-Fz -- Continued

4815.O7 Forlani, Osvaldo (Table P-PZ40)
4815.O715 Formichi, Carlo, 1871-1943 (Table P-PZ40)
4815.O75 Forzano, Giovacchino, 1884- (Table P-PZ40)
4815.R3 Fraccaroli, Arnaldo, 1883- (Table P-PZ40)
4815.R35 Fracchia, Umberto, 1889- (Table P-PZ40)
4815.R38 Frisina, Antonino, 1832-1917 (Table P-PZ40)
4817 G - Gz
Galt, William, pseud. see PQ4831.A85
4817.A52 Gamberi, Antonio, 1864-1944 (Table P-PZ40)
Garlanda, Ada (Negri) see PQ4831.E4
Giacomo, Giovanni Antonio di, 1891-1960 see PQ4847.A4947
4817.I2 Giacomo, Salvatore di, 1862- (Table P-PZ40)
4817.I6 Giordana, Tullio, 1877- (Table P-PZ40)
4817.I735 Giovanni, Alessio di, 1872- (Table P-PZ40)
4817.I8 Giovanola, Luigi, fl. 1910 (Table P-PZ40)
4817.O63 Gori, Pietro, 1865-1911 (Table P-PZ40)
4817.O7 Gotta, Salvator, 1887- (Table P-PZ40)
4817.O8 Govoni, Corrado, 1882- (Table P-PZ40)
4817.R16 Granato, Fernando (Table P-PZ40)
4817.R2 Grandi, Orazio, 1851- (Table P-PZ40)
4817.R535 Grimaldi, Giulio, 1873-1910 (Table P-PZ40)
4817.U2 Guasti, Amerigo (Table P-PZ40)
4817.U22 Guberti, Eugenio, 1871-1944 (Table P-PZ40)
4817.U37 Guglielminetti, Amalia, 1881-1941 (Table P-PZ40)
4817.U4 Gugliuzzo, Salvatore (Table P-PZ40)
4819 H - Hz
4821 I - Iz
4821.N9 Invernizio, Carolina, 1860- (Table P-PZ40)
4823 J - Jz
Jolanda, 1864-1917 see PQ4829.A45
4825 K - Kz
4827 L - Lz
4827.A3 Labruto Laspada, Francesco, fl. 1890 (Table P-PZ40)
Lima, Archer de, pseud. see PQ4815.O6
4827.I5 Lipparini, Giuseppe, 1877- (Table P-PZ40)
4827.O6 Lombroso, Paola (Table P-PZ40)
4827.O635 Longhi Lopresti, Lucia (Table P-PZ40)
4827.O7 Lopez, Sabatino, 1867- (Table P-PZ40)
4827.U45 Lucini, Gian Pietro, 1867-1914 (Table P-PZ40)
4829 M - Mz
4829.A3 Macina, Luisa (Gervasio), 1872- (Table P-PZ40)
Pseudonym: Luigi di San Giusto

Individual authors
Individual authors, 1900-1960
M-Mz -- Continued
4829.A45 Majocchi-Plattis, Maria, marchesa, 1864-1917 (Table P-PZ40)
4829.A53 Manganella, Renato (Table P-PZ40)
Pseudonym: Lucio d'Ambra
4829.A568 Maradea, Francesco, 1865-1941 (Table P-PZ40)
Marcotti, Giuseppe see PQ4716.M35
4829.A76 Marinetti, Filippo Tommaso, 1876- (Table P-PZ40)
4829.A77 Mariscotti, Fortunato (Table P-PZ40)
4829.A775 Marolla, G.A (Table P-PZ40)
4829.A78 Martini, Fausto Maria, 1886-1931 (Table P-PZ40)
4829.A79 Martoglio, Nino, 1870-1921 (Table P-PZ40)
4829.A8 Marzo, Trionfo (Table P-PZ40)
Mascaretti, Carlo see PQ4841.C33
Maurus, pseud. see PQ4831.A85
4829.E5 Melegari, Dora, 1849-1924 (Table P-PZ40)
Cf. PQ2359.M35 French literature
4829.E525 Mellusi, Antonio, 1847-1925 (Table P-PZ40)
4829.E7 Messina, Maria (Table P-PZ40)
4829.I35 Michelis, Eurialo de, 1904- (Table P-PZ40)
4829.I5 Milanesi, Guido, 1872- (Table P-PZ40)
4829.O6114 Monterisi, Riccardo, 1868-1944 (Table P-PZ40)
4829.O62 Moravia, Alberto, 1907- (Table P-PZ40)
4829.O65 Moretti, Marino, 1885- (Table P-PZ40)
4829.O7 Morselli, Ercole Luigi, 1882-1921 (Table P-PZ40)
4829.O8 Motta, Luigi, 1881- (Table P-PZ40)
4829.U25 Mucelli, Luigi (Table P-PZ40)
4829.U7 Murri, Linda, 1871- (Table P-PZ40)
4829.U8 Mussolini, Benito, 1883- (Table P-PZ40)
Cf. DG575.M8
4829.Y67 Myosotis, Alma, 1870-1960 (Table P-PZ40)
4831 N - Nz
4831.A7 Napoli, Franco di, 1897- (Table P-PZ40)
4831.A85 Natoli, Luigi, 1857-1941 (Table P-PZ40)
4831.E4 Negri, Ada, 1870- (Table P-PZ40)
4831.I4 Niccodemi, Dario, 1877- (Table P-PZ40)
For his French works see PQ2627.I3
4831.O26 Nobili, Guido, 1850-1916 (Table P-PZ40)
4831.O76 Novaro, Angiolo Silvio, 1866- (Table P-PZ40)
4831.O8 Novelli, Augusto, 1867- (Table P-PZ40)
4833 O - Oz
4833.J4 Ojetti, Ugo, 1871- (Table P-PZ40)
Oriani, Alfredo see PQ4720.O7
4833.R8 Orvieto, Angiolo, 1869- (Table P-PZ40)
4833.S8 Osta, Amelia (Table P-PZ40)

Individual authors
Individual authors, 1900-1960 -- Continued
4835 P - Pz
4835.A15 Padovan, Adolfo, 1869- (Table P-PZ40)
4835.A2 Palmarini, Italo Maria, 1865- (Table P-PZ40)
4835.A23 Palmieri, Aurelio, 1870- (Table P-PZ40)
4835.A2316 Palminteri, Michele, 1867-1951 (Table P-PZ40)
4835.A246 Pansini, Vittore, 1875-1953 (Table P-PZ40)
4835.A25 Panzini, Alfredo, 1873-1939 (Table P-PZ40)
4835.A27 Papini, Giovanni, 1881- (Table P-PZ40)
4835.A28 Pascarella, Cesare, 1858-1940 (Table P-PZ40)
4835.A3 Pascoli, Giovanni, 1855-1912 (Table P-PZ40)
4835.A8 Pastonchi, Francesco, 1877- (Table P-PZ40)
4835.E24 Pedrazzini, Alberto, 1852-1930 (Table P-PZ40)
4835.I5 Pietravalle, Lina (Table P-PZ40)
Pincherle, Alberto see PQ4829.O62
4835.I7 Pirandello, Luigi, 1867-1936 (Table P-PZ40)
4835.L2 Placci, Carlo (Table P-PZ40)
4835.O7 Porreca Olivieri, Potito, 1868- (Table P-PZ40)
4835.R3 Praga, Marco, 1862-1929 (Table P-PZ40)
4835.R7 Provenzal, Dino, 1877- (Table P-PZ40)
4835.U3 Puccini, Mario, 1887- (Table P-PZ40)
4837 Q - Qz
4837.U4 Quercia-Tanzarella, 0 (Table P-PZ40)
4837.U5 Quintieri Miglio, Agnese (Simoni) (Table P-PZ40)
4839 R - Rz
4839.A377 Ragazzoni, Ernesto, 1870-1920 (Table P-PZ40)
4839.A38 Ragni, Giuseppe, 1867-1919 (Table P-PZ40)
4839.A7 Rapisarda, Antonio, 1900- (Table P-PZ40)
For his works written in French see PQ2635.A376
4839.A8 Ratti, Federico Valerio (Table P-PZ40)
4839.I3 Ricci, Corrado, 1858- (Table P-PZ40)
4839.I7 Ristori, Rodolfo Jacuzio (Table P-PZ40)
4839.I9 Rivalta, Ercole, 1875- (Table P-PZ40)
4839.I98 Rizzotto, Giuseppe, 1828-1895 (Table P-PZ40)
4839.O3 Roberto, Federico de, 1861- (Table P-PZ40)
4839.O35 Rocca, Gino, 1891- (Table P-PZ40)
4839.O66 Rossato, Arturo, 1882- (Table P-PZ40)
4839.O7 Rosselli, Amelia (Table P-PZ40)
4839.O8 Rosso di San Secondo, Piermaria, 1889- (Table P-PZ40)
4839.U7 Rusconi, Arturo Jahn (Table P-PZ40)
4839.U77 Russo, Ferdinando, 1868-1927 (Table P-PZ40)
4839.U79 Ruta, Enrico, 1869-1939 (Table P-PZ40)
4841 S - Sz
4841.A38 Salerno, Elisa, 1873-1957 (Table P-PZ40)
4841.A4 Salgari, Emilio, 1862-1911 (Table P-PZ40)
4841.A46 Salustri, Carlo Alberto, 1871-1950 (Table P-PZ40)

Individual authors
Individual authors, 1900-1960
S-Sz -- Continued

4841.A65 Santoro, Maddalena (Table P-PZ40)
4841.A7 Saponaro, Michele, 1885- (Table P-PZ40)
4841.A83 Satta, Sebastiano, 1867-1914 (Table P-PZ40)
Savinio, Alberto, 1891-1952 see PQ4809.H45
4841.C33 Scarlatti, Americo, 1855-1928 (Table P-PZ40)
4841.C482 Schmitz, Ettore, 1861-1928 (Table P-PZ40)
4841.C484 Scibona, Carmelo, 1865-1939 (Table P-PZ40)
4841.E5 Segre, Dino, 1893- (Table P-PZ40)
4841.E7 Serao, Matilde, 1856-1927 (Table P-PZ40)
4841.I5 Silvestri Falconieri, Francesco di (Table P-PZ40)
4841.I6 Simoni, Renato (Table P-PZ40)
4841.O6 Sonzogno, Riccardo (Table P-PZ40)
Steno, Flavia, pseud. see PQ4833.S8
4841.T57 Sto, 1886-1973 (Table P-PZ40)
4841.T84 Sturzo, Luigi, 1871-1959 (Table P-PZ40)
Svevo, Italo, pseud. see PQ4841.C482
4843 T - Tz
4843.A7 Tartufari, Clarice, 1870- (Table P-PZ40)
4843.A75 Tartufari, Filippo (Table P-PZ40)
Térésah, pseud. see PQ4845.B4
4843.E68 Terruzi, Regina, 1862- (Table P-PZ40)
4843.E69 Tessa, Delio, 1886-1939 (Table P-PZ40)
4843.E8 Testoni, Alfredo (Table P-PZ40)
4843.I75 Titta, Cesare de, 1862-1933 (Table P-PZ40)
Tofano, Sergio, 1886-1973 see PQ4841.T57
4843.O8 Tozzi, Federigo, 1883-1920 ' (Table P-PZ40)
4843.R4 Treves, Virginia (Tedeschi), 1855-1916 (Table P-PZ40)
Trilussa, pseud. see PQ4841.A46
4843.U4 Tumiati, Domenico, 1874- (Table P-PZ40)
4845 U - Uz
4845.B4 Ubertis-Gray, Corinna Teresa, 1877- (Table P-PZ40)
4847 V - Vz
4847.A35 Valcarenghi, Carlo, 1862- (Table P-PZ40)
4847.A437 Valera, Paolo, 1850-1926 (Table P-PZ40)
4847.A486 Vamba, 1860-1920 (Table P-PZ40)
4847.A4947 Vann'Anto, 1891-1960 (Table P-PZ40)
4847.A7 Varaldo, Alessandro, 1876- (Table P-PZ40)
4847.A75 Varè, Daniele (Table P-PZ40)
For works written in English see PR6043.A+
4847.A765 Varvaro, Giuseppe, 1872-1942 (Table P-PZ40)
4847.E7 Verona, Guido da, 1881- (Table P-PZ40)
4847.O5 Volpi, Maria, 1895- (Table P-PZ40)
4849 W - Wz
4851 Z - Zz

Individual authors
Individual authors, 1900-1960
Z - Zz -- Continued
4851.O7 Zorzi, Guglielmo (Table P-PZ40)
4851.U3 Zuccoli, Luciano, 1870-1929 (Table P-PZ40)
4851.U5 Zunini, Carlo (Table P-PZ40)
Individual authors, 1961-2000
The author number is determined by the second letter of the name
Subarrange each author by Table P-PZ40 unless otherwise specified
Here are usually to be classified authors beginning to publish about 1950, flourishing after 1960
4860 Anonymous works (Table P-PZ28)
4861 A
4862 B
4863 C
4864 D
De Giorgi, Elsa see PQ4867.I633
4865 E
4866 F
4867 G
4867.I633 Giorgi, Elsa De' (Table P-PZ40)
4868 H
4869 I
4870 J
4871 K
4872 L
4873 M
Marcone, Maria see PQ4878.I27
Masada, Ruve, 1939- see PQ4882.I284
4874 N
4875 O
4876 P
4877 Q
4878 R
4878.I27 Ricci Marcone, Maria (Table P-PZ40)
4879 S
4880 T
4881 U
4882 V
4882.I284 Vigevani, Roberto, 1939- (Table P-PZ40)
4883 W
4884 X
4885 Y
4886 Z

Individual authors -- Continued
Individual authors, 2001-
The author number is determined by the second letter of the name
Subarrange each author by Table P-PZ40 unless otherwise specified
4900 Anonymous works (Table P-PZ28)
4901 A
4902 B
4903 C
4904 D
4905 E
4906 F
4907 G
4908 H
4909 I
4910 J
4911 K
4912 L
4913 M
4914 N
4915 O
4916 P
4917 Q
4918 R
4919 S
4920 T
4921 U
4922 V
4923 W
4924 X
4925 Y
4926 Z
Regional, provincial, local, etc.
Literary history, biography, criticism and collections
Including countries with Italian literature outside of Italy, as Switzerland, France, America, Asia
Class works, biography and criticism of individual Italian authors, regardless of dialect, in PQ4265-4886
Italy
5901 General works
5902.A-Z Special regions or provinces, A-Z
Under each (except where otherwise indicated):
.x *Collections*
.x2 *History and criticism*
.x3 *Translations*
Calabria

Regional, provincial, local, etc.
Italy
Special regions or provinces, A-Z
Calabria -- Continued
5902.C29 Collections
5902.C3 History and criticism
5902.C32 Translations
5902.L85-.L853 Lucca
5902.P5-.P53 Piedmont
5904.A-Z Special cities, etc., A-Z
Under each:
.x Collections
.x2 History and criticism
.x3 Translations
Italian literature outside of Italy
5941 General
Special
5943 Austria
5944 Tyrol. Trentino
5947 Dalmatia. Istria
5949 France
5951-5951.9 Malta (Table P-PZ25)
5961-5961.9 Switzerland (Table P-PZ25)
5971-5971.9 Other European countries (Table P-PZ25)
Colonial
Africa
5975 Eritrea. Somaliland
5976 Tripoli. Cyrenaica
America
North America
History of literature
5981 General
5982.A-Z By state, region, place, A-Z
5983 Collections and selections
5984.A-Z Individual authors, A-Z
South America
History of literature
5985 General
5986.A-Z By state, region, place, A-Z
5987 Collections and selections
5988.A-Z Individual authors, A-Z
5989-5989.9 Australia (Table P-PZ25)
5990-5999 Asia (Table P-PZ24)

Spanish literature
Literary history and criticism
6001 Periodicals. Yearbooks
6002 Societies. Congresses
Collections
Texts. Sources see PQ6170+
Chrestomathies see PC4112.9+
6003 Monographs. Studies, etc., by several authors
6004.A-Z Collections in honor of a special person or institution, A-Z. "Homenajes"
6005 Collections by individual authors
Cf. Essays, studies, lectures, etc., e.g. PQ6027, PQ6039, PQ6059, PQ6101, PQ6132
6006 Encyclopedias. Dictionaries
6007 Theory of the study of Spanish literature (Philosophy. Psychology. Esthetics)
(6009) History of literary history
see PQ6013+ PQ6025
(6010) Bibliography
see Z2691+
Study and teaching
6013 General
6014 General special
By period
6015 Early to 1800
6016 Later, 1801-
6018.A-Z By region or country, A-Z
6019 By school
Biography of teachers, critics, and historians
6019.5 Collective
6020.A-Z Individual, A-Z
Subarrange each by Table P-PZ50
Criticism
Cf. PN80+
(6021) Periodicals
see PN80
6022 Treatises. Theory. Canons
6023 Essays. Lectures
Prefer PQ6007, PQ6040
6025 History
6026 Special topics
6027 Collections of essays in criticism
Prefer PQ6039
By period
6029 Early to 1800
6030 Later, 1801-
Authorship see PN101+

Literary history and criticism -- Continued
History of Spanish literature
6031 Early works through 1800
1801-
6032 Spanish
6033 English
6034 French
6035 German
6036.A-Z Other languages, A-Z
6037 Compends. Textbooks
6038 Outlines. Syllabi, etc.
6039 Collected essays, studies, etc.
6040 Individual lectures, addresses, pamphlets, etc.
Awards, prizes
6040.4 General works
6040.5.A-Z Individual, A-Z
6040.5.C35 Premio de Novela Café Gijon
6040.5.C47 Premio de Literatura en Lengua Castellana Miguel de Cervantes
6040.5.G8 Premio Guatemala
6040.5.L5 Premio Lope de Vega
6040.5.N34 Premio Nadal
6040.5.P55 Premio Planeta
Special topics
6041 Relations to history, civilization, culture, etc.
e.g. Spanish literature from a Protestant standpoint
6042 Relation to other literatures and countries
6042.A2 General
6042.A3 Ancient
6042.A4 Arabic
Jewish-Spanish see PQ6056
6042.A5-Z Modern, A-Z
e. g.
6042.A6 American
6042.D8 Dutch
6042.E5 English
6042.F5 French
6042.G5 German
6042.I5 Italian
6042.P8 Provençal
6042.R8 Russian
6044 Translations (as subject)
6044.5 Spanish literature by foreign authors. General works only
6044.8 Spanish authors of foreign literature. General works only
For special literatures, see the literature

Literary history and criticism
History of Spanish literature -- Continued
6045 Various aspects, forms, etc.
e.g. Romanticism, Psychology, Evolution of the different forms: poetry, drama, etc.
6046.A-Z Special subjects, A-Z
6046.A66 Apocryphal Gospels
6046.B5 Bible
6046.B54 Blindness
6046.C36 Carnival
6046.C4 Characters and characteristics
6046.C44 Christian pilgrims and pilgrimages
6046.C45 Christianity
6046.C65 Cookery
6046.C68 Country life
6046.D4 Death
6046.D53 Difference (Psychology)
6046.D7 Dreams
6046.E67 Erotic literature
6046.E7 Errors and blunders
6046.E75 Escorial
6046.F35 Fantastic literature
6046.H64 Homeland
6046.I8 Islands
6046.L38 Law
6046.L68 Love
6046.M29 Magic
6046.M34 Marginality, Social
6046.M4 Mental illness
6046.M56 Mirrors
6046.M65 Monsters
6046.M9 Mysticism
6046.N3 Nature
6046.O5 Olives
6046.R27 Race
6046.R35 Reality
6046.R4 Religion
6046.S49 Sex
6046.S66 Sports
6046.S8 Supernatural
6046.V56 Violence
6046.V7 Voyages
Including imaginary voyages
6046.W35 War
6047.A-Z Special countries, cities, and ethnic groups, A-Z
6047.A47 Africa
6047.A5 America

Literary history and criticism
History of Spanish literature
Special countries, cities, and ethnic groups, A-Z -- Continued

6047.A72 Aragon
6047.B3 Basques
6047.B37 Benelux countries. Low countries
6047.B5 Blacks
6047.B7 Breda (Spain)
6047.C3 Canary Islands
6047.E87 Estremadura
6047.F8 France
6047.G34 Galicia (Spain)
6047.G46 Gijon (Spain)
6047.G7 Granada
6047.G94 Gypsies. Romanies
6047.I53 India
6047.I74 Italy
6047.J4 Jews
Low countries see PQ6047.B37
6047.M7 Moors
6047.O7 Orihuela (Spain)
6047.P6 Portugal
Romanies see PQ6047.G94
6047.S24 Salamanca (Province)
6047.S4 Segovia (Spain)
6047.S65 Soria (Spain)
6047.V54 Vinaroz (Spain)
6048.A-Z Special classes, A-Z
e. g.
6048.K5 Kings
6048.P7 Priests
6048.S64 Soldiers
6048.W6 Women
6049.A-Z Special persons, A-Z
Amantes de Teruel see PQ6049.L68
6049.D52 Díaz, Jimena, ca. 1056-ca. 1114
6049.D64 Don Juan
6049.I36 Ignatius de Loyola, Saint, 1491-1556
6049.J83 Juana, la Loca, Queen of Castile, 1479-1555
6049.L68 Lovers of Teruel
6049.P33 Pedro I, King of Castile and Leon, 1334-1369
6049.R35 Raquel, fl. 12th cent.
Biography
6051 Collected
Individual see PQ6271+
6052 Memoirs. Letters

Literary history and criticism
History of Spanish literature
Biography -- Continued

6052.9	Relations to women. Love. Marriage, etc.
	Cf. PN481 PQ6055
6053	Iconography: Portraits, monuments, etc.
	Literary landmarks. Homes and haunts of authors
6054	General works
6054.5.A-Z	By place, A-Z
	e. g.
6054.5.M33	Madrid
6055	Women authors (General)
	Individual authors see PQ6271+
6056	Moorish-Spanish literature
	Including the Hispano-Arabic/Hispano-Hebraic muwashshah and special studies of their final verses, the kharjas.
	Cf. PC4811 Aljamia (Spanish written in Arabic characters)
	Cf. PC4813+ Jewish-Spanish (Ladino) language and literature
	Cf. PJ7542.M8 Muwashshah in Arabic language exclusively
	By period
6057	General works (on more than one period)
	Origins. Middle ages to 1500
	Including works treating mainly of poetry
	see also Portuguese literature of this period
6058	Treatises. Compends
6059	Collected essays, studies, lectures
	Cf. PQ6003+ PQ6039, PQ6045, etc.
6060	Special subjects, subjects not elsewhere specified
	Cf. PQ6046.A+ Special subjects
	Modern
(6061)	General
	see PQ6031+ PQ6057
6063	Renaissance (ca. 1406-1517)
	Classic period (siglo de oro), 1500-1700
6064	General
6065	Lectures, addresses, etc.
6066	Special topics (not A-Z)
	e.g. Gongorism (Cultismo, Culteranismo); Conceptism
	18th-19th centuries
6068	General
	Special periods
6069	18th century
6070	19th century

Literary history and criticism
History of Spanish literature
By period
Modern
18th-19th centuries -- Continued

6071 Special topics (not A-Z)
Cf. PQ6084 Poetry

19th-20th centuries

6072 General
6073.A-Z Special topics, A-Z
6073.A46 Alphabet
6073.A54 America
6073.A93 Authors as artists
6073.A95 Avila
6073.B64 Bohemianism
6073.B84 Bulls. Bullfights
6073.C25 Canary Islands
6073.C3 Casticismo
6073.C56 Cities and towns
6073.D4 Death
6073.D43 Decadence (Literary movement)
6073.E54 Emigration and immigration
6073.E76 Erotic literature
6073.E917 Exiles' writings
6073.E92 Exoticism
6073.E94 Experimental literature
6073.F36 Fascism
6073.F55 Flirting
6073.G64 Goya, Francisco, 1746-1828
6073.H57 History
6073.H63 Holy Week
6073.H65 Homosexuality
6073.H7 Humor
6073.I53 Industrialization
6073.L47 Lesbians
6073.M26 Madrid
6073.M43 Melancholy
6073.M45 Melodrama
6073.M47 Metaphor
6073.M52 Miners
6073.M6 Modernism
6073.M95 Mythology, Classical
6073.N3 National characteristics
6073.N6 Noventa y ocho
6073.P44 Peinador, Dolores, 1819-1894
6073.P45 Phenomenology
6073.P48 Philippines

Literary history and criticism
History of Spanish literature
By period
Modern
19th-20th centuries
Special topics, A-Z -- Continued

6073.P53 Picasso, Pablo, 1881-1973
6073.P6 Politics
6073.P64 Postismo (Literary movement)
6073.P76 Psychology
6073.R4 Realism
6073.R47 Revolutionary literature
6073.R66 Romanticism
6073.S33 Science
6073.S6 Sports
6073.S9 Surrealism
6073.S94 Symbolism
6073.T43 Technology
6073.T73 Trafalgar, Battle of, 1805
6073.W5 Wills
6073.W65 Women
6073.Z35 Zaragoza (Spain), Siege of, 1808-1809

21st century
6074 General
6074.5 Special topics, A-Z

Technique
Philosophy. Esthetics see PN1031+

Poetry
History
6075 Periodicals
6076 Treatises. Compends
6077 Collected essays, studies, etc.
Cf. PQ6003+ etc.
6078 Special topics (not A-Z)
Prefer PQ6045+

Special periods
(6079) Origins. Middle Ages
see PQ6058+
(6080) Renaissance
see PQ6063

Classic age. Siglo de oro
6081 General
(6082) Special
see PQ6066
Romances see PQ6089+

1701-1868. 18th-19th centuries
6083 General

Literary history and criticism
History of Spanish literature
Poetry
History
Special periods
1701-1868. 18th-19th centuries -- Continued
6084 Special
e.g. School of Salamanca; School of Seville
6085 1869- . 20th century
Special forms
6088 Epics
Romances
6089 General
6090 Special
6091 Popular poetry. Folk songs
6094 Lyric poetry
Prefer PQ6076+
6096.A-Z Special forms, A-Z
6096.A4 Albas
6096.A6 Anacreóntica
6096.C3 Canción
6096.C4 Cantinela
6096.C6 Coplas
6096.C8 Cuarteto
6096.D42 Decimas
6096.E6 Elegía
6096.E7 Epitalamio
6096.G56 Glosas (Poetry)
6096.H3 Haiku
6096.I6 Invención
6096.L34 Laments
6096.L4 Letrilla
6096.L5 Lira
6096.M2 Madrigal
6096.O3 Oda
6096.P3 Pareado
6096.Q5 Quintilla
Romance see PQ6089+
6096.S2 Seguidilla
6096.S37 Serranillas
6096.S4 Sextina
6096.S6 Silva
6096.S8 Soneto
6096.T4 Terceto
6096.V5 Villancico
6097.A-Z Other, A-Z
6097.D5 Didactic. Gnomic

Literary history and criticism
History of Spanish literature
Poetry
History
Special forms
Other, A-Z -- Continued

6097.E7 Epigram
6097.E94 Experimental
(6097.F2) Fable
see PN988
6097.P2 Parody. Travesty
6097.P5 Pastoral
6097.S3 Satirical
6097.V57 Visual
6098.A-Z By subject, A-Z
6098.A34 Africa, North
6098.A86 Autopoiesis
6098.B5 Birds
6098.B8 Bullfights
6098.C54 Children
6098.D4 Death
6098.E95 Existentialism
6098.F4 Festivals
6098.G62 God
6098.H36 Happiness
6098.H5 Historical. Patriotic. Political
6098.I32 Icarus
6098.I35 Identity (Psychology)
6098.I56 Insects
6098.I85 Israel-Arab conflicts
6098.L36 Landscape
6098.M3 Madrid
6098.M5 Military
6098.M57 Moncayo Mountains Region (Spain)
6098.M6 Moon
6098.M9 Mysticism
6098.M93 Mythology, Classical
6098.N3 Nature
6098.R4 Religious. Moral
6098.S4 Sea
6098.S46 Senses and sensation
6098.S7 Solitude
6098.T44 Technology
6098.T54 Time
6098.W34 Water
6098.W5 Wine
6098.W64 Women

Literary history and criticism
History of Spanish literature -- Continued
Drama
Technique see PN1660+
History of the Spanish stage see PN2780+
History
General (including the period 1500-1700)
6098.7 Periodicals
6099 Treatises
6100 Compends. Textbooks
6101 Collected essays, studies, lectures
6102 Special topics (by author)
For special places, Seville, Valencia, Madrid, etc. see PQ6129.A+
(6103) Controversial literature on Spanish drama and stage see PN2051
By period
6104 Origins and early history before 1500
Golden age. 16th-17th centuries
6105 General
6106 Special: Sources, documents, etc.
6107 Period of Lope de Vega
6109 Period of Calderón
6111 18th century (18th-19th centuries)
6113 19th century (19th-20th centuries)
6115 20th century
6116 21st century
Special
6119 Tragedy
Comedy
(6120.A2) General see PQ6099+
Special types, A-Z
6120.C2 Comedia de capa y espada
Prefer PQ6105+
6120.C3 Comedia de figurón
Comedia de santos see PQ6121.R2+
6120.C4 Comedia del teatro (de apariencias)
Prefer PQ6106+
6120.C6 Comedia heroica
Prefer PQ6106+
6121.H5 Historical drama
6121.M4 Melodrama
6121.P3 Pastoral drama
6121.P64 Political
Religious drama
6121.R2 General

Literary history and criticism
History of Spanish literature
Drama.
Special.
Religious drama. -- Continued
6121.R3 Auto sacramental
6121.R4 Comedia de santos
6121.R45 Jesuit drama
6121.R5 Representaciones
6121.R8 Romantic drama
Prefer period PQ6113
6121.V47 Verse drama
6125 Popular drama. Folk drama
6127.A-Z Minor forms, A-Z
Bailes see PQ6127.E6
6127.E6 Entremeses. One-act plays
Including bailes, mojigangas, pasos, sainetes.
6127.I6 Introitos
6127.L6 Loas
Mojigangas see PQ6127.E6
One-act plays see PQ6127.E6
Pasos see PQ6127.E6
Sainetes see PQ6127.E6
Zarzuelas
see class M
6129.A-Z Local, A-Z
e.g. Madrid, Seville, Valencia
Early drama to 1500, prefer PQ6104
Cf. PQ7011.A+ Local literature (General)
Prose
General
6131 Treatises. Compends
6132 Collected essays, addresses, lectures
6134.A-Z Special topics, A-Z
6134.A44 Allegory
6134.A97 Autobiography
6134.B56 Biography (as a literary form)
6134.B8 Bullfights
6134.F73 Francoism
6134.L37 Latin America
6134.M33 Madrid
6134.N86 Nuns
6134.R52 Rif Revolt
6134.S62 Spain
6134.T73 Travel
Special periods
6135 Origins to 1500

Literary history and criticism
History of Spanish literature
Prose
General
Special periods -- Continued
6136 Classic age, 1500-1700
6137 Modern, 1700-
Prose fiction
Technique see PN3355+
General works
6138 Treatises. Compends
6139 Collected essays, addresses, lectures
6140.A-Z Special topics, A-Z
6140.B85 Bullfighting
6140.C37 Castile (Spain)
6140.C45 Children
6140.C57 Civil War, 1936-1939
Classical mythology see PQ6140.M87
6140.C68 Courtship
6140.D42 Decadence
6140.D49 Devil
6140.D53 Dictators
6140.F33 Family
6140.H64 Homosexuality
6140.J48 Jews
6140.K55 Knights and knighthood
6140.M35 Manners and customs
6140.M45 Memory
6140.M63 Modernism
6140.M85 Murcia
6140.M87 Mythology, Classical
6140.P37 Paradox
6140.P42 Philosophy
6140.P45 Physicians
Politics see PQ6147.P64
6140.P67 Postmodernism
6140.P75 Proletariat
6140.R4 Religion
6140.R87 Rural-urban migration
6140.S42 Secularism
6140.S49 Sex role
6140.S63 Social realism
6140.W6 Women
Special periods
6141 Origins to 1500
6142 Classic age, 1500-1700
6144 Modern, 1700-

Literary history and criticism
History of Spanish literature
Prose
General
Prose fiction -- Continued

6147.A-Z Special kinds, A-Z
6147.A38 Adventure stories
6147.A87 Autobiographical fiction
6147.C5 Chivalresque novel
6147.D47 Detective and mystery stories
6147.D64 Domestic fiction
6147.E65 Epistolary fiction
6147.E75 Erotic stories
6147.F35 Fantastic fiction
6147.F4 Feuilletons
6147.H5 Historical fiction
6147.L68 Love stories
Mystery stories see PQ6147.D47
6147.N68 Novelle
6147.P3 Pastoral romance
6147.P5 Picaresque novel
Cf. PN3428+ Picaresque novel (General)
6147.P64 Political fiction
6147.S32 Science fiction
6147.S44 Sentimental novel
6147.S5 Short story

Minor forms
6148 Oratory
6148.5 Diaries
6149 Letters
6150 Essays
6151 Dialogue
6152 Wit and humor
Cf. PN6213+ General collections
6153 Miscellaneous

Folk literature
For general works on and collections of folk literature, see GR229+
(6155.A1-.5) Periodicals. Societies. Collections
History and criticism
(6155.A6-Z) Treatises. Compends
(6156) Essays. Pamphlets, etc.
Special periods
6157.A2 Origins. Middle Ages
(6157.A5-Z) Modern
Special forms
Poetry see PQ6091

Literary history and criticism
History of Spanish literature
Folk literature
History and criticism
Special forms -- Continued
Drama see PQ6125
6157.5 Chapbooks
Collections of texts
(6158) General
Folk songs see PQ6210
Folk drama see PQ6237
6159 Chapbooks
(6161) Legends. Tales
(6163) Fairy tales
(6165) Individual tales
(6167.A-Z) Translations. By language, A-Z
History of local literature see GR237.A+
6168 Juvenile literature (General)
For special genres, see the genre
Collections of Spanish literature
6170 Periodicals
6171 General
6171.A2 Early (to 1880)
Including editions of Biblioteca de autores españoles.
6171.A3-Z Recent, 1880-
6172 Selections. Anthologies, etc.
6173 Selections from women authors
6173.5.A-Z Special classes of authors, A-Z
6173.5.C45 Child authors
6173.5.J47 Jewish authors
6173.5.T44 Teenage authors
6174 Special periods
6174.A3 Early to 1500
6174.A5 Classic age, 1500-1800
6174.A7-Z Modern
Special regions, places, etc. see PQ7000+
6174.9 Other general special
e. g.
6174.9.A6 Aljamía
Poetry
6174.95 Periodicals
6175 General
Early collections to 1700 see PQ6179+
6176 Selections. Anthologies, etc.
Special classes of authors
6177 Women
6178.A-Z Other, A-Z

Collections of Spanish literature
Poetry
Special classes of authors
Other, A-Z -- Continued
6178.C55 Children
6178.C65 College students
6178.P74 Prisoners
Medieval and early modern (to ca. 1700)
6179 General
Special
Medieval (to 1500)
Contemporaneous collections
Manuscript collections (Cancioneros)
e.g. Cancionero de Juan Alfonso de Baena
The manuscript collections of the 15th century include songs in Portuguese, Galician, and Catalan. Complete collections are classed here. Separate editions of either Portuguese, Galician, or Catalan are classed with Portuguese or Catalan, PQ or PC
6180.A1 Facsimile reproductions
6180.A3-.Z3 Printed editions
6181 Later collections
e.g. Poetas castellanos anteriores; Cancionero castellano del siglo XV ordenado por R. Foulché-Delbosc
Classic age, 1500-1700
Contemporaneous collections. Cancioneros, romanceros, etc.
6182 Reprints from manuscript collections
e. g.
6182.A3 Academia de los nocturnos. Cancionero
6183 Printed collections (including reprints).
Arrange by date-letters of original edition: A00-A99, 1500-1599; B00-B99, 1600-1699; subarrange by date of reprint
For multiple works of same date, distinguish by adding initial of the author, compiler, or title
For works without original date, subdivide .Z2A-Z, by compiler or title
6183.A11 Castillo. Cancionero general, 1511
6183.A19 Cancionerode obras de burlas provocantes a risa, 1519
6183.A49 Cancionero espiritual, 1549
6183.A50 Silva de Romances, 1550-1551
6183.A50C Cancionero de romances, 1550
6183.A51 Cancionero llamado Vergel de amores, 1551

Collections of Spanish literature
Poetry
Medieval and early modern (to ca. 1700)
Special
Classic age, 1500-1700
Contemporaneous collections. Cancioneros, romanceros, etc.
Printed collections (including reprints) -- Continued

6183.A51S Sepúlveda. Romances nuevamente sacados de historias antiguas de la crónica de España, 1551
6183.A52 Segunda parte del cancionero general, 1552
6183.A54 Cancionero general de obras nuevas, 1554
6183.A56 Villancicos de diversos autores, 1556
6183.A62 Ramírez Pagán. Floresta de varia poesia, 1562
6183.A62C Cancionero llamado Flor de enamorados, 1562
6183.A83 Padilla. Romancero, 1583
6183.B00 Romancero general, 1600
6183.B05 Espinoza. Flores de poetas ilustres de España, 1605
6183.B21 Arias Pérez. Primavera y flor de romances, 1629
6183.B29 Segura. Primavera y flor de romances, 1629
6183.B37 Pinto de Morales. Maravillas del Parnaso, 1637
6183.Z2F4 Fernández de Costantina. Cancionero

Modern collections
6184.A2 1700-1870
6184.A5-Z 1871-
6185 18th century (or 18th-19th centuries)
6186 19th century (or 19th-20th centuries)
6187 20th century
6187.5 21st century

By form
Epic
6190 General
6191 Old Spanish to 1500
Cf. PQ6366+ El Cid Campeador
6192 Classic age, 1500-1700
6193 Modern

Romances. Ballads
(6194) Early manuscript and printed collections to 1700
see PQ6182+

Modern editions.
6195 General.
6196 Selections. Anthologies.

Special types
Historical
6197 Collections and selections

Collections of Spanish literature
Poetry.
By form.
Epic.
Romances. Ballads.
Special types

6198.A-Z Special themes, A-Z
6198.B4 Bernardo del Carpio
(6198.C5) El Cid
see PQ6366+
6198.F4 El conde Fernán Gonçález
Cf. PQ6420.P54+
6198.I6 Los infantes de Lara
Cf. PQ6400.I6+
6198.P4 El rey don Pedro
6198.R6 El rey don Roderigo
6199 Frontier (Romances fronterizos)
6200 Historical romances on non-Spanish themes
e.g. Greek and Roman subjects
6201 Chivalresque
6201.2 Carolingian cycle. Breton cycle
6202 Artistic (Novelesco)
6203 Moorish
6204 Other
Class here romances in Spanish America
Judeo-Spanish see PC4813+
6205.A-Z Individual romances (Anonymous ballads), A-Z.
Romances of the later period see PQ6210
Lyric
6206 General
Prefer PQ6175
Selections. Anthologies see PQ6176
Special periods see PQ6179+
6208.A-Z By subject, A-Z
6208.A37 Air
6208.A42 Alberti, Rafael, 1902-
6208.A6 Aleixandre, Vicente
6208.B5 Birds
6208.B7 Brevity
6208.B8 Bullfights
6208.B83 Bulls
6208.C25 Cats
6208.C4 Children
6208.C5 Christmas
6208.C6 Clocks and watches
6208.C7 Crime and criminals
6208.C8 Cuba

Collections of Spanish literature
Poetry
By subject, A-Z -- Continued

6208.D4 Death
6208.D44 Delgado, Pilar
6208.D66 Don Quixote
6208.E7 Erotic poetry
6208.F35 Falla, Manuel de
6208.F45 Feminism
6208.F5 Flowers
6208.F65 Food
6208.F83 Francis of Assisi, Saint, 1182-1226
6208.G37 García Lorca, Federico, 1898-1936
6208.G63 God
6208.G83 Guevara, Ernesto, 1928-1967
6208.H4 Hernández, Miguel
6208.H49 Hierro, José, 1922-
6208.H65 Homosexuality
6208.I82 Italica (Spain)
6208.J55 Jiménez, Juan Ramón, 1881-1958
6208.J64 John of the Cross, Saint, 1542-1591
6208.L3 Labor
6208.L4 Lepanto
6208.L6 Love
6208.M32 Madrid
6208.M34 Manolete, 1917-1947
6208.M36 Manrique, Jorge, 1440?-1479
6208.M38 Maria Luisa, 1934-1984
6208.M4 Medicine
6208.M44 Melilla (Morocco)
6208.M47 Menéndez y Pelayo, Marcelino
6208.M6 Mothers
6208.M65 Mountains
6208.N4 Neruda, Pablo
6208.N53 Nicaragua
6208.N68 Noventa y ocho
Piezas de títulos de comedias see PQ6106
6208.P5 Pirates
6208.P6 Political poetry
6208.P8 Puerto Rico
6208.R3 Railroads
6208.R4 Religious poetry
Cf. BV505+ Hymns
6208.R5 Revolutionary poetry
6208.S32 Science
6208.S4 Sea
6208.S44 Sex

Collections of Spanish literature
Poetry
By subject, A-Z -- Continued

6208.S5 Sierra Nevada (Spain)
6208.S6 Spain
6208.T74 Trees
6208.V44 Velazquez, Diego, 1599-1660
6208.W3 War
6208.W34 Water
6208.W5 Whitman, Walt
6208.W55 Wine
6208.Z3 Zamora
6209.A-Z Minor forms, A-Z
e. g.
6209.A4 Albas
6209.A6 Anacreontics
6209.C3 Canciones
Cf. PQ6180+ Medieval poetry
6209.C6 Coplas
6209.C8 Cuartetos
6209.E6 Elegías
6209.E8 Epitalamios
6209.G6 Glosas
6209.I6 Invenciones
6209.L4 Letrillas
6209.L5 Liras
6209.M3 Madrigales
6209.O3 Odas
6209.P3 Parcados
6209.Q5 Quintillas
Romances see PQ6190+
6209.S2 Seguidillas
6209.S4 Sextinas
6209.S6 Silvas
6209.S8 Sonetos
6209.T4 Tercetos
6209.V5 Villancicos
6210 Folk songs (Cantares populares)
6213 Didactic poetry
6215.A-Z Other, A-Z
6215.C7 Concrete poetry
6215.C8 Curiosa
(6215.F3) Fables in verse
see PN988
6215.H8 Humorous verse
6215.S27 Satirical poetry

Drama

Collections of Spanish literature
Drama -- Continued
Comprehensive collections (including collections confined to the siglo de oro)

6217.A2 Early to 1800
6217.A5-Z Collections published after 1800
6218 Selected plays. Anthologies
6218.5.A-Z Special classes of authors, A-Z
6218.5.W65 Women
By period
6219 Origins and early modern before Lope de Vega
Period of Lope de Vega and Calderón
see PQ6217+
6221 Period of Lope de Vega (ca. 1590-1635)
6222 Period of Calderón. 17th century
(6223.A-Z) Local, A-Z
see PQ7001+
6225 18th century (18th-19th centuries)
6226 19th century (19th-20th centuries)
6226.Z9 Minor works of individual authors (mainly uncataloged)
6226.Z99 Typewritten plays
6227 20th century
6227.Z9 Minor works of individual authors (mainly uncataloged)
6227.Z99 Typewritten plays
6228 21st century
Special
6231 Tragedy
6233 Comedy
6233.A2 General
For older comedia, see PQ6217+
6233.C2 Comedia de capa y espada
Comedia de santos see PQ6235.R4
6233.C4 Comedia del teatro (de apariencias)
The phase "comedia de ruido" refers to the machinery used in their exhibition; so that comedia de capa y espada, and especially comedia de santos, which often demanded a large apparatus, were not infrequently called comedia de ruido (de caso or de fabrica)
In the same way comedias de apariencias were plays demanding much scenery and scene-shifting.
6233.C6 Comedia heroica
6235.A-Z Other special, A-Z
6235.H5 Historical drama
6235.M4 Melodrama
6235.P3 Pastoral drama
Piezas de títulos de comedias see PQ6106

Collections of Spanish literature
Drama
Special
Other special, A-Z -- Continued
Popular drama see PQ6237
Religious drama
6235.R2 General
6235.R3 Auto sacramental
6235.R4 Comedia de santos
6235.R5 Representaciones
6235.R8 Romantic drama
Prefer PQ6225
6237 Popular drama. Folk drama
6239.A-Z Minor forms of drama, A-Z
For list of cutters see PQ6127.A+
(6241) Local
see PQ7001+
Prose
Comprehensive collections
6247.A2 Early (published before 19th century)
6247.A5-Z Later, 1801-
6248 Selections. Anthologies
Special periods
6249.A2 Medieval to 1500
6249.A5 Classic age, 1500-1700
6249.A7-Z Modern, 1701-
6250.A-Z By subject, A-Z
6250.A72 Aragon (Spain)
6250.B8 Bullfights
6250.M33 Madrid (Spain)
6250.M37 Markets
6250.M85 Music
Spanish Sahara see PQ6250.W47
Spanish West Africa see PQ6250.W47
6250.T47 Tétouan (Morocco)
6250.W47 Western Sahara. Spanish West Africa. Spanish Sahara
Prose fiction
6251 Comprehensive collections
6252 Selections. Anthologies
Special periods
6253 Early to 1800
6254 Modern, 1801-
6256.A-Z Special forms, A-Z
6256.C5 Chivalresque novels
6256.C56 Christmas stories
6256.D47 Detective and mystery stories
6256.E76 Erotic stories

Collections of Spanish literature
Prose
Prose fiction
Special forms, A-Z -- Continued
6256.F35 Fantastic fiction
6256.F48 Feuilletons
6256.G56 Ghost stories
6256.H5 Historical novels
6256.H66 Horror tales
6256.L67 Love stories
6256.P3 Pastoral novels
6256.P5 Picaresque novels
6256.P65 Political fiction
6256.R34 Railroad stories
6256.S34 Science fiction
6256.S4 Sea stories
6257 Short stories
Popular tales. Folk literature see GR229+
6258 Oratory
6259 Letters
6260 Essays
6261 Dialogues
(6262) Fables
see PN988
6263 Wit and humor
For minor works, prefer PN6213+ etc.
6264 Miscellaneous minor
Cf. PN6255, PN6265, etc.
Translations
(6265-6266) Translations from foreign literature into Spanish
see the original language
6267 Translations from Spanish into other languages
6267.A1 Polyglot
6267.E1-.E9 English (Table PQ6)
6267.F1-.F9 French (Table PQ6)
6267.G1-.G9 German (Table PQ6)
6267.I1-.I9 Italian (Table PQ6)
6267.P1-.P9 Portuguese (Table PQ6)
6269.A-Z Other languages, A-Z
Individual authors
Individual authors and works to 1700
Subarrange each author by Table P-PZ39 or Table P-PZ40 unless otherwise specified
Anonymous works
see the title
6271.A15-.A153 Abad de Ayala, Jacinto (Table P-PZ40)
6271.A17-.A173 Abarca de Bolea, Ana (Table P-PZ40)

Individual authors
Individual authors and works to 1700 -- Continued

6271.A2-.A23 El Abencerraje (Table P-PZ43)
6271.A24-.A243 Academia burlesca (Table P-PZ43)
6271.A27 Acevedo, Alonso de, 1550-ca. 1648 (Table P-PZ40)
6271.A28 Acevedo, Pedro Pablo de, 1522-1572 (Table P-PZ40)
6271.A3 Acuña, Fernando de, d. 1580 (Table P-PZ40)
6271.A4 Agreda y Vargas, Diego de, fl. 1616 (Table P-PZ40)
6271.A5 Aguilar, Gaspar Honorato de, 1561-1623 (Table P-PZ40)
Alarcón y Mendoza, Juan Ruiz de see PQ6431.R8
6271.A6 Alcalá Yañez y Rivera, Gerónimo, 1563-1632 (Table P-PZ40)
6271.A7 Alcázar, Baltasar del, 1530-1606 (Table P-PZ40)
6271.A8 Aldana, Francisco de, 1537-1578 (Table P-PZ38)
Alemán, Mateo, 1547-1614?
Editions
6272.A1 Complete works. By date
Guzmán de Alfarache
6272.A2 First part. By date
6272.A22 Second part. By date
6272.A3 Complete editions. By date
6272.A4 Abridged editions, selections
6272.A5 Spurious second part by Matheo Luxán de Sayavedra, supposed to be the pseudonym of one Juan Martí, possibly Juan José Martí, d. 1604
(6272.A55) Odas de Horacio
see PA6400
(6272.A57) Ortografía castellana
see PC4143
(6272.A6) San Antonio de Padua
see BX4700.A6
6272.A7-.Z3 Translations, by language, A-Z
6272.Z5 Biography and criticism
Alexandre (Alejandro), Poema de see PQ6397.A1+
6273.A2 Alfonso X, el Sabio, king of Castile and Leon, 1221-1284
For his poetry see PQ9189.A44
6273.A27 Alvarez de Ayllón, Pedro, fl. 1540 (Table P-PZ40)
Alvarez de Toledo, Gabriel see PQ6503.A57
6273.A28 Alvarez de Villasandino, Alfonso, ca. 1340-1424? (Table P-PZ40)
6273.A3 Alvarez Gato, Juan, 15th cent. (Table P-PZ40)
Amadís de Gaula
6274 Editions
6274.A1 Comprehensive editions. By date
6274.A11 Selections
6274.A13 Books I-IV. By date
6274.A14 Books III-IV. By date

Individual authors
Individual authors and works to 1700
Amadis de Gaula
Editions
Continuations
Collections see PQ6274.A1
Individual books
6274.A2 Book V, Esplandián, by García-Ordóñez de Montalvo
6274.A3 Book VI, Florisando, by Páez de Ribeira
6274.A4 Book VII, Lisuarte de Grecia, by Feliciano de Silva
6274.A5 Book VIII, Lisuarte de Grecia y Muerte d'Amadís, by Juan Diaz
6274.A6 Book IX, Amadis de Grecia, by Feliciano de Silva
6274.A7 Book X, Don Florisel de Niquea, by Feliciano de Silva, parts 1-2
6274.A8 Book XI, Don Florisel de Niquea, by Feliciano de Silva, parts 3-4 (Rogel de Grecia)
6274.A9 Book XII, Silves de la Silva (Author unknown)
6275 Translations, adaptations, etc.
6275.A2 Spanish (Modern versions)
6275.A4-Z Other languages, A-Z.
English.
6275.E1 Comprehensive editions.
6275.E12 Selections.
Individual books.
6275.E2 Books 1-4.
6275.E21-.E44 Books 1-24.
6275.E5 Modern versions, abridgements, etc., by translator or title, A-Z.
6275.F1-.F5 French
6275.F1 Comprehensive editions
6275.F12 Selections
Individual books
6275.F2 Books 1-4
6275.F21-.F44 Books 1-24
6275.F5 Modern versions, abridgements, etc., by translator or title, A-Z
6275.F5D8 Du Verdier, Le roman de romans, Paris 1626-29
6275.F5E8 Extrait des IV livres d'Amadís de Gaula, Amsterdam, 1750
6275.F5T8 Amadís de Gaula, par le comte de Tressan, Paris, 1779
6275.G1-.G5 German
6275.G1 Comprehensive editions
6275.G12 Selections
6275.G2-.G44 Individual books

Individual authors
Individual authors and works to 1700
Amadis de Gaula.
Translations, adaptations, etc.
Other languages, A-Z.
German.
Individual books
6275.G2 Books 1-4
6275.G21-.G44 Books 1-24
6275.G5 Modern versions, abridgements, etc., by translator or title, A-Z
6275.I1-.I5 Italian
6275.I1 Comprehensive editions
6275.I12 Selections
Individual books
6275.I2 Books 1-4
Books 1-24
6275.I5 Modern versions, abridgements, etc., by translator or title, A-Z
6276.A-Z Other languages, A-Z
6277 Criticism
6279.A36 Amaro Sánchez, José, fl. 1665-1700 (Table P-PZ40)
Amescua, Antonio de Mira see PQ6413.M7
6279.A56 Arboreda, Alejandro, 1650-1698 (Table P-PZ40)
6279.A58 Arce de Otálora, Juan, 16th cent. (Table P-PZ40)
6279.A584-.A5843 Arderique (Table P-PZ43)
Argensola, Bartolomé
see PQ6410.L5, and PQ6410.L52
Argensola, Lupercio Leonardo de
see PQ6410.L5, and PQ6410.L53
6279.A6 Arguijo, Juan de, 1567-1628? (Table P-PZ40)
6279.A63 Arias de Saavedra, Diego (Table P-PZ40)
6279.A65 Armendáriz, Julián de, d. 1614 (Table P-PZ40)
Asbage, Juana Inés see PQ7296.J6
6279.A69 Arroyo, José de, 17th cent. (Table P-PZ40)
6279.A77-.A773 Auto de la huida a Egipto (Table P-PZ43)
6279.A79-.A793 El Auto sacramental de la universal redempción (Table P-PZ43)
Avellaneda, Alonso de Fernández, pseud. see PQ6323.A4
6279.A8 Avellaneda de la Cueva y Guerra, Francisco, fl. 1660 (Table P-PZ40)
6279.A87 Avila, Francisco de, ca. 1573-1647 (Table P-PZ40)
6279.A88 Avila, Gaspar de (Table P-PZ40)
6279.A9 Avila, Juan de, Saint, 1499?-1569 (Table P-PZ40)
Ayala, Pedro López de see PQ6412.L2
Badajoj, García Sánchez de see PQ6431.S7
6279.B23 Baena, Juan Alfonso de, 1406-1454 (Table P-PZ40)

Individual authors
Individual authors and works to 1700 -- Continued
Baladro del sabio Merlín see PQ6413.M36+
Balbuena, Bernardo de see PQ6437.V2
6279.B25 Bances Candamo, Francisco Antonio, 1662-1709? (Table P-PZ40)
6279.B3 Barahona de Soto, Luis, 1548?-1595 (Table P-PZ38)
Barbadillo, Alonso Jerónimo de Salas see PQ6431.S2
Barco Centenera, Martin del see PQ7796.B3
6279.B33-.B333 Barlaam and Joasaph (Legend) (Table P-PZ42)
6279.B35 Barrios, Miguel de, 1635-1701 (Table P-PZ40)
6279.B4 Belmonte y Bermudez, Luis de, 17th cent. (Table P-PZ40)
Cf. PQ6388.D3 El diablo predicador
6279.B445 Beltran Hidalgo, Diego, b. ca. 1580 (Table P-PZ40)
Benavente, Luis Quiñiones de see PQ6425.Q3
6279.B447-.B4473 Beneficiado de Obeda (Table P-PZ43)
6279.B47 Bermúdez, Jeronimo, 16th cent. (Table P-PZ40)
6279.B48 Bernal, Fernando, fl. 1516 (Table P-PZ40)
6279.B49 Bernardo de Quirós, Francisco, d. 1668 (Table P-PZ40)
(6279.B5) Bible (or portions of Bible)
see BS298, etc.
6279.B52-.B523 Blancaflor y Filomena (Table P-PZ43)
Bidpai (Spanish version "Calila e Dimna") see PQ6321.C16+
6279.B53-.B533 Bocados de oro (Table P-PZ43)
6279.B54 Bocángel, Gabriel, ca. 1608-ca. 1658 (Table P-PZ40)
6279.B543 Bondía, Ambrosio, fl. 1628-1653 (Table P-PZ40)
6279.B544 Bonifacio, Juan, ca. 1538-1606 (Table P-PZ40)
6279.B55 Borja, Francisco de, principe de Esquilache, 1582-1658 (Table P-PZ40)
6279.B6 Boscan, Juan, d. 1542
6279.B7 Botelho de Moraes e Vasconcellos, Francisco, 1670-1747 (Table P-PZ40)
6279.B77 Buendía, Ignacio de (Table P-PZ40)
Burguillos, Tomé de, pseud. see PQ6438+
6279.C32 Cabra, Pedro de la, fl. 15th cent. (Table P-PZ40)
6279.C33 Cabrera de Córdoba, Luis, 1559?-1623 (Table P-PZ40)
6279.C35 Cairasco de Fiqueroa, Bartolome, ca. 1538-1610 (Table P-PZ40)
Calderón de la Barca, Pedro, 1600-1681
6280 Original editions and early reprints before 1760
6280.A1-.A9 Parts 1-9. By date
6280.B1-.B9 Modern facsimiles and reprints. By date
6280.C1 Collected or selections reprints. By date
Partial editions
6281 Collected works, 1760-

Individual authors
Individual authors and works to 1700
Calderon de la Barca, Pedro, 1600-1681
Collected works, 1760- -- Continued
6281.A1 Comprehensive editions (including collected dramas). By date
(6281.A11) Collections. By editor, A-Z
Partial editions
Comedias
i.e plays other than the religious plays, entremeses, etc. under PQ6287+
6281.A2 General collections. By date
6281.A3 Selected plays
6281.A8 Pamphlet collections
Arrange by title of first pamphlet, A-Z
6281.A9 Selections. Anthologies. Quotations. By date
Individual plays (Sueltas), A-Z
Early undated editions (before 1700) are to be placed at the beginning under each, marked, instead of date, undated, a, b, etc.
Facsimile reproductions to be placed with the originals
6282 A - M
6282.A4 El alcalde de Zalamea
6282.E7 La espanola de Florencia
6283 El mágico prodigioso
6283.A1 Editions. By date
6283.A3 School editions
6283.A7-Z Criticism
6284 M - V
6285 La vida es sueño
6286 V - Y
Autos sacramentales
6287.A1 Comprehensive editions
6287.A2 Selected works
6287.A5-Z Individual works, A-Z
Entremeses. Mojigangas. Loas, etc.
6288.A1 Comprehensive editions
6288.A2 Selected works
6288.A5-Z Individual works, A-Z
6289 Poems
6289.A2 Collections. By date
6290 Prose writings
Censuras, aprobaciones, etc.
6290.9.A2 Collections and selections. By date
6290.9.A5-Z By author criticized, A-Z
6291 Doubtful or spurious works
Translations

Individual authors
Individual authors and works to 1700
Calderon de la Barca, Pedro, 1600-1681
Translations -- Continued

6292 English
6292.A1 Collected and selected works. By translator, A-Z
6292.A2 Selections, anthologies, quotations. By date
6292.A3 Autos (Collected or selected)
6292.A4 Poems
6292.A5-Z Separate works. By original title, A-Z
Subarrange by translator
6292.A6 El alcalde de Zalamea
6292.M2 El mágico prodigioso
6292.V5 La vida es sueño
6293 French
6293.A1 Collected and selected works. By translator, A-Z
6293.A2 Selections, anthologies, quotations By date
6293.A3 Autos (Collected or selected)
6293.A4 Poems
6293.A5-Z Separate works. By original title, A-Z
Subarrange by translator
6293.A6 El alcalde de Zalamea
6293.M2 El magico prodigioso
6293.V5 La vido es sueno
6294 German
6294.A1 Collected and selected works. By translator, A-Z
6294.A2 Selections, anthologies, quotations. By date
6294.A3 Autos (Collected or selected)
6294.A4 Poems
6294.A5-Z Separate works. By original title, A-Z
Subarrange by translator
6294.A6 El alcalde de Zalamea
6294.M2 El magico prodigioso
6294.V5 La vida es sueno
6295.A-Z Other European languages, A-Z
6295.B2 Basque
6295.C2 Catalan
Celtic
6295.C3 Breton
6295.C4 Cornish
6295.C5 Gaelic
6295.C6 Irish
6295.C7 Manx
6295.C8 Welsh
6295.D8 Dutch. Flemish
6295.F8 Finnish
6295.G7 Greek (including Modern Greek)

Individual authors
Individual authors and works to 1700
Calderon de la Barca, Pedro, 1600-1681.
Translations.
Other European languages, A-Z. -- Continued
6295.H8 Hungarian
6295.I8 Italian
6295.L3 Latin
6295.P6 Portuguese
6295.P8 Provençal
6295.R6 Romansh
6295.R8 Romanian
Scandinavian languages
6295.S2 Danish. Dano-Norwegian
6295.S22 Icelandic
6295.S23 Swedish
Slavic languages
6295.S3 Bohemian
6295.S4 Bulgarian
6295.S5 Croatian
6295.S53 Lettish
6295.S55 Lithuanian
6295.S6 Polish
6295.S7 Russian
6295.S75 Ruthenian
6295.S8 Serbian
6295.S82 Slovakian
6295.S84 Slovenian
6295.S85 Wendic
6295.9.A-Z Other languages, A-Z
6296 Imitations, paraphrases, adaptations
Prefer the special author for prominent authors
6296.A2 Spanish
6296.A5-Z Other
6297 Parodies. Travesties
6297.A2 Spanish
6297.A5-Z Other
6298 Translations (as subject). Comparative studies, etc.
6299 Illustrations of Calderón
Illustrated editions with other editions
History of Calderón portraits, etc., and illustrations see PQ6306
6299.5 Calderon and music; texts to which music has been composed
Librettos based upon works of Calderón
see subclass ML

Individual authors
Individual authors and works to 1700
Calderon de la Barca, Pedro, 1600-1681.
Calderon and music; texts to which music has been composed. -- Continued
Music composed to his works
see class M
Calderón's knowledge of music see PQ6317.M8
Biography
(6300.A1) Bibliography
see Z8140.5
6300.A2-.A39 Periodicals. Societies. Collections
Cf. PQ6304+
6300.A4 Dictionaries. Indexes, etc.
General encyclopedic dictionaries only
For special dictionaries with subject, see PQ6314, Dictionaries of characters, PQ6319.Z9 Dictionaries of language
6300.A5-Z General works. Literary biography. Life and works
6301 Details of his life
6301.A1 Sources. By date of publication
6301.A2 Letters
6301.A5-Z Family. Ancestry. Name
Including early life, education, service in the Army, life as an ecclesiastic, relation to court, later life and death
Relations to contemporaries
6302.A2 General
Prefer PQ6300
6302.A5-Z Special
6303 Homes and haunts
Prefer PQ6301
6303.A2 General
6303.A5-Z By place, A-Z
6304 Anniversaries. Celebrations. "Homenajes"
Arrange by date-letters
Under each:
.xZ3-.xZ99 *Single addresses, essays, lectures, etc.*
6304.A00 1700 (100th anniversary of birth)
6304.A81 1781 (100th anniversary of death)
6304.B00 1800 (200th anniversary of birth)
6304.B81 1881 (200th anniversary of death)
6304.C00 1900 (300th anniversary of birth)
6304.C81 1981 (300th anniversary of death)
6304.D00 2000 (400th anniversary of birth)

Individual authors
Individual authors and works to 1700
Calderon de la Barca, Pedro, 1600-1681
Biography -- Continued
6305 Memorials. Testimonials to the genius of Calderón other than centennials
Prefer subject with added entry here
6305.A2 Collections (Prose or poetry)
6305.A5-.Z3 Individual authors - Prose
6305.Z5 Individual authors - Poetry
6306 Iconography. Museums. Exhibitions
6306.A2 General and miscellaneous
6306.A3 Portraits, medals, etc.
6306.A5 Monuments
Museums. Relics. Endowments. Exhibitions
6306.A7 General
6306.A8 Special. By place
For Calderón in France, England, etc. see PQ6311.A+
(6306.9) Fiction, drama, etc., based upon Calderon's life
See the author
6307 Study and teaching (Method)
Cf. PQ6309+
6308 Authorship
Including manuscripts, autographs, sources, forerunners, chronology of works
Associates. Followers. Circle. School
See PQ6099+ PQ6106+
Allusions
See PQ6310
Criticism and interpretation
History of the study and appreciation of Calderón
6309 General (and in Spain)
Special
6310.A2 Contemporaneous criticism and allusion
6310.A3 Later
6310.A5-Z Special persons, A-Z
6310.S5 Shelley
6311.A-Z By country, A-Z
6311.G5 Germany
6312 Treatises
Cf. PQ6300+ Life and works
Special topics
(6313) Philosophy. Esthetics, etc.
see PQ6312
6314 Characters

Individual authors
Individual authors and works to 1700
Calderon de la Barca, Pedro, 1600-1681.
Criticism and interpretation.
Special topics
Characters. -- Continued

6314.A2 General
Cf. PQ6312
Special
6314.A3 Groups. Classes
6314.A3W7 Women
6314.A5-Z Individual
For works limited to one play, class with the play
6315 Technique. Dramatic art
6316 Calderon and the stage. Representations
6316.A2 General
Cf. PQ6309+
6316.A5-Z Special. By place, A-Z
6317.A-Z Treatment and knowledge of special subjects, A-Z
6317.A7 Art
Cf. PQ6299 PQ6306
6317.B63 Body, Human
6317.E8 Esthetics
6317.F38 Faust
6317.F73 Free will
6317.H5 History. Politics, etc.
6317.H85 Humor
6317.I44 Illusion
6317.L3 Law
6317.L5 Literature
6317.M3 Marvelous, The
6317.M8 Music
6317.M84 Myth
6317.N3 Nature
6317.P5 Philosophy
6317.R4 Religion. Ethics
6317.S4 Science
6317.S7 Social life
6317.T7 The tragic
6318 Interpretation
Including running commentaries, textual criticism, variant readings, etc.
For interpretation of special works, see the works
6319 Language. Style
6319.A2 General
6319.A3 Grammar
6319.A5-.Z3 Versification

Individual authors
Individual authors and works to 1700
Calderon de la Barca, Pedro, 1600-1681.
Criticism and interpretation.
Special topics
Language. Style. -- Continued

6319.Z9 Dictionaries. Concordances

6321.C16-.C163 Calila y Dimna (Spanish version of Bidpai) (Table P-PZ43)

Calisto y Melibea, Tragicomedia de see PQ6426+

6321.C164 Calleja, Diego, 1638-1725? (Table P-PZ40)

6321.C167 Campillo de Bayle, Gines, fl. 1669-1691 (Table P-PZ40)

6321.C2 Cáncer y Velasco, Jeronimo, d. 1655 (Table P-PZ40)

6321.C23-.C233 Cancionero capitular de la Colombina (Table P-PZ43)

6321.C24-.C243 Carajicomedia (Table P-PZ43)

6321.C26 Caravajal, Baltasar de, fl. 1604 (Table P-PZ40)

Cárcel de amor see PQ6431.S4

6321.C265 Cardona, Juan de, ca. 1519-ca. 1609 (Table P-PZ40)

6321.C268 Caro, Ana (Table P-PZ40)

6321.C27 Caro, Rodrigo, 1573-1647? (Table P-PZ40)

6321.C28 Caro Mallén de Soto, Ana, fl. 1653 (Table P-PZ40)

6321.C29 Carrillo Cerón, Gines, fl. 1653 (Table P-PZ40)

6321.C3 Carrillo y Sotomayor, Luis, ca. 1583-1610 (Table P-PZ40)

6321.C32 Cartagena, Pedro de, 1456-1486 (Table P-PZ40)

6321.C33 Carvajal, 15th cent. (Table P-PZ40)

6321.C35 Carvajal, Miguel de, fl. 1520 (Table P-PZ40)

6321.C38 Carvajal y Saavedra, Mariana de, 17th cent. (Table P-PZ40)

6321.C39 Carvallo, Luis Alfonso de, d. 1630 (Table P-PZ40)

6321.C45 Cascales, Francisco de, 1564?-1642 (Table P-PZ40)

6321.C46 Castaña, Hieronimo Francisco (Table P-PZ40)

6321.C47 Castelblanco, Simón de, fl. 1680 (Table P-PZ40)

6321.C48 Castellanos, Juan de, 1522-1607 (Table P-PZ40)

6321.C49-.C492 Castigos e documentos (Table P-PZ43a)
Formerly ascribed to King Sancho IV

6321.C5 Castillejo, Cristobal de, d. 1550 (Table P-PZ40)

6321.C53 Castillo, Andres, Sanz del, fl. 1641 (Table P-PZ40)

6321.C55 Castillo Solórzano, Alonso de, 1584-1647? (Table P-PZ40)

6321.C7 Castro y Bellvis, Guillem de, 1569-1631 (Table P-PZ40)

6321.C75 Catalá de Valeriola, Bernardo, 1568-1608 (Table P-PZ40)

6321.C8-.C83 Catonis disticha (Old Spanish version) (Table P-PZ43)

Cavallero Cifar see PQ6388.C2+

La Celestina, tragicomedia de Calisto y Melibea see PQ6426+

Centenera, Martín del Barco see PQ7796.B3

Cepeda, Teresa de
see BX4700.T4 PQ6437.T3

Cervantes Saavedra, Miguel de, 1547-1616

	Individual authors
	Individual authors and works to 1700
	Cervantes Saavedra, Miguel de, 1547-1616 -- Continued
	Editions
6322	Collected works
6322.A1	Comprehensive collections. By date
6322.A2	Selected works. By date
6322.A3	Selections. Anthologies. Quotations, etc. By date Cf. PQ6323.A7
6322.A4	Collected prose works
	Collected plays see PQ6325
	Collected poems see PQ6326
6323	Don Quixote
6323.A1	Comprehensive editions. By date Including the 17th century editions of first or second parts, or their facsimiles, number f1, f2, etc., according to date
6323.A2	First part. By date
6323.A3	Second part. By date
6323.A35	Spanish translation of the continuation in French, by François Filleau de Saint Martin
6323.A4	Spurious second part. By date Published under the pseudonym of Lic. Alonso de Fernandez
6323.A5	Abridged editions. By editor, A-Z
6323.A6	Particular parts, tales, episodes, etc.
6323.A6C3	El Cautivo
6323.A7	Quotations. Passages. Thoughts. Proverbs, etc. By editor, A-Z
6323.A9	Dramatizations Prefer classification under special author
	Criticism see PQ6352+
6324	Novelas ejemplares
6324.A1	Comprehensive collections. By date
6324.A2	Selected novelas. By date
6324.A5-Z	Separate works
	El amante liberal
6324.A5	Editions
6324.A6	Criticism
	El casamiento engañoso
6324.C2	Editions
6324.C3	Criticism
	El celoso extremeño
6324.C4	Editions
6324.C5	Criticism
	El coloquio de los perros (Los perros de Mahudes)
6324.C6	Editions

Individual authors
Individual authors and works to 1700
Cervantes Saavedra, Miguel de, 1547-1616
Editions
Novelas ejemplares
Separate works
El coloquio de los perros (Los perros de Mahudes) -- Continued

6324.C7 Criticism

Las dos doncellas

6324.D7 Editions

6324.D8 Criticism

La española inglesa

6324.E7 Editions

6324.E8 Criticism

La fuerza de la sangre

6324.F7 Editions

6324.F8 Criticism

La gitanilla

Weber's Preziosa

6324.G5 Editions

6324.G6 Criticism

Historia del noble Ricardo y la hermosa Leonisa

Refacimento of El amante liberal

6324.H5 Editions

6324.H6 Criticism

La ilustre fregona

6324.I6 Editions

6324.I7 Criticism

El licenciado Vidriera

6324.L5 Editions

6324.L6 Criticism

Rinconete y Cortadillo

6324.R5 Editions

6324.R6 Criticism

La señora Cornelia

6324.S4 Editions

6324.S5 Criticism

La tia fingida

6324.T5 Editions

6324.T6 Criticism

6324.Z5 Criticism (General)

Criticism of a particular novela in .A5-Z4

6325 Dramatic works. Comedias, entremeses, etc.

6325.A1 Collected and selected plays. By date

Individual authors
Individual authors and works to 1700
Cervantes Saavedra, Miguel de, 1547-1616.
Editions.
Dramatic works. Comedias, entremeses, etc. -- Continued

6325.A5-Z Separate works, A-Z

Under each:

(1)	*Editions*
(2)	*Criticism*

e.g.

Los baños de Argel (Comedia)
6325.B3 Editions
6325.B4 Criticism

La cárcel de Sevilla (Extremés)
Authorship doubtful
6325.C2 Editions
6325.C3 Criticism

La casa de los celos y selvas de Ardenia (Comedia)
6325.C4 Editions
6325.C5 Criticism

Comedia de la soberana Virgen de Guadalupe
6325.C6 Editions
6325.C7 Criticism

La cueva de Salamanca (Entremés)
6325.C8 Editions
6325.C9 Criticism

La elección de los alcaldes de Daganzo (Entremés)
6325.E3 Editions
6325.E4 Criticism

La entretenida (Comedia)
6325.E6 Editions
6325.E7 Criticism

El gallardo español (Comedia)
6325.G2 Editions
6325.G3 Criticism

La gran sultana (Comedia)
6325.G4 Editions
6325.G5 Criticism

La guarda cuidadosa (Entremés)
6325.G7 Editions
6325.G8 Criticism

Los habladores (Entremés)
6325.H2 Editions
6325.H3 Criticism

Individual authors
Individual authors and works to 1700
Cervantes Saavedra, Miguel de, 1547-1616.
Editions.
Dramatic works. Comedias, entremeses, etc.
Separate works, A-Z. -- Continued
El hospital de los posridos (Entremés)
Authorship doubtful
6325.H6 Editions
6325.H7 Criticism
El juez de los divorcios (Entremés)
Authorship doubtful
6325.J7 Editions
6325.J8 Criticism
El laberinto de amor (Comedia)
Authorship doubtful
6325.L2 Editions
6325.L3 Criticism
Numancia (Tragedia)
Authorship doubtful
6325.N7 Editions
6325.N8 Criticism
Pedro de Urdemalas
Authorship doubtful
6325.P5 Editions
6325.P6 Criticism
El retablo de las maravillas (Comedia)
Authorship doubtful
6325.R3 Editions
6325.R4 Criticism
El rufián dichoso (Comedia)
Authorship doubtful
6325.R5 Editions
6325.R6 Criticism
El rufián viudo (Entremés)
Authorship doubtful
6325.R7 Editions
6325.R8 Criticism
El trato de Argel (Comedia)
Authorship doubtful
6325.T6 Editions
6325.T7 Criticism
El viejo celoso (Entremés)
Authorship doubtful
6325.V5 Editions
6325.V6 Criticism

Individual authors
Individual authors and works to 1700
Cervantes Saavedra, Miguel de, 1547-1616.
Editions.
Dramatic works. Comedias, entremeses, etc.
Separate works, A-Z. -- Continued
El vizcaíno fingido (Entremés)
Authorship doubtful
6325.V7 Editions
6325.V8 Criticism
6325.Z5 Criticism
Including treatises on the lost plays:
La Amaranta o la del mayo
La batalla naval
La bizarra Arsinda
El bosque amoroso
La confusa
El engaño a los ojos
La gran Turquesca
La Jersualem
La única
6326 Poems (Sonnets, Canciones, etc.)
6327.A-Z Other miscellaneous works, A-Z
Under each:
(1) Editions
(2) Criticism
e.g.
El canto de Calíope (Part of the Galatea)
6327.C3 Editions
6327.C4 Criticism
Filena (or Silena) (Lost poem)
6327.F4 Editions
6327.F5 Criticism
La Galatea (Pastoral romance)
6327.G2 Editions
6327.G3 Criticism
Persiles y Sigismunda (Prose romance)
6327.P4 Editions
6327.P5 Criticism
Viage del Parnoso (Poem)
6327.V4 Editions
6327.V5 Criticism
6328 Doubtful or spurious works
Cf. PQ6323.A4 PQ6354
6328.A1 Collections
6328.A12 Special works
El buscapié see PQ6512.C23

Individual authors
Individual authors and works to 1700
Cervantes Saavedra, Miguel de, 1547-1616.
Editions.
Doubtful or spurious works.
Special works.

6328.A3-.A8 Other works ascribed to Cervantes
6328.A9-Z Criticism (General)

Translations

6329 English (Table PQ7)
6330 French (Table PQ7)
6331 German (Table PQ7)
6332.A-Z Other European languages, A-Z
For list of Cutter numbers, see PQ6295.A+
6332.9.A-Z Other languages, A-Z
e. g.
6332.9.C5 Chinese
6333 Imitations, paraphrases, adaptations
Class here collections of adaptations, etc. and works about adaptations, etc.
For adaptations by individual authors, see the authors' numbers in class P
6333.A2 Spanish
Cf. PQ6323.A5 PQ6329.A3
6333.A5-Z Other languages, A-Z
(6333.5) Dramatizations
See the author, PQ-PT, for prominent authors
Cf. PQ6323.A9
(6333.9) Parodies. Travesties
See the author, PQ-PT, for prominent authors
6334 Translations as subject (Comparative studies, etc.)
Cf. PQ6347+
6335 Illustrations
Illustrated editions to be classed with other editions.
Illustrations by special artists, see subclass NC
For Cervantes' portraits, etc. see PQ6343.A2+
6336 Cervantes and music
Including texts to which music has been composed
Librettos based upon Cervantes' works
see subclass ML
Music composed to Cervantes' works
see class M
Cervantes' knowledge and references to music see PQ6358.M8

Biography

(6337.A19) Bibliography
see Z8158

Individual authors
Individual authors and works to 1700
Cervantes Saavedra, Miguel de, 1547-1616.
Biography. -- Continued

6337.A2-.A39 Periodicals. Societies. Collections
Cf. PQ6341+
6337.A4 Dictionaries, indexes, etc.
General encyclopedia dictionaries only
For special dictionaries, see the subject, e.g., Language, figures of speech, PQ6361
6337.A5-Z General works
Including literary biography, life and works
Details
6338.A1 Sources. By date of publication
6338.A2 Letters. By date of publication
6338.A3 Miscellaneous
6338.A4 Family. Name. Ancestry. Descendants. Place of birth. Early life. Education
6338.A5 Military service. Battle of Lepanto
6338.A6 Captivity in Algeria
6338.A65 Portuguese campaign
6338.A7 Imprisonments
6338.A8 Later life. Death
Relations to contemporaries. Milieu. Age of Cervantes
6339.A2 General
Prefer PQ6337
6339.A5-Z Special
Cervantes and Lope de Vega see PQ6473.C4
6340 Homes and haunts
Prefer PQ6338
6341 Anniversaries. Celebrations. "Homenajes"
Publications in honor of special anniversaries if general or miscellaneous may be entered here, using date-letters
Prefer classification by subject
6341.A00-A99 1800-1899
e.g.
6341.A61 First anniversary celebrated by the R. Academia española, in 1861
6341.A75 Anniversary celebrated in New York in 1875
6341.B00-B99 1900-1999
e.g.
6341.B05 300th anniversary of Don Quixote in 1905
6341.B16 300th anniversary of death of Cervantes
6341.C00-C99 2000-2099

Individual authors
Individual authors and works to 1700
Cervantes Saavedra, Miguel de, 1547-1616.
Biography.
6342 Memorials. Testimonials to the genius of Cervantes other than anniversary celebrations
Prefer special subject with added entry here
6342.A2 Collections (Prose or poetry)
6342.A5-.Z3 Individual authors - Prose
6342.Z5 Individual authors - Poetry
Iconography. Museums. Exhibitions
6343.A2 General and miscellaneous
6343.A3 Portraits. Medals, etc.
6343.A5 Monuments
Museums. Relics. Exhibitions. Endowments
6343.A7 General
6343.A8-Z Special. By place, A-Z
Cf. PQ6349.A+
(6343.9) Fiction, drama, etc., based upon Cervantes' life
Prefer classification under author
6344 Study and teaching
Cf. PQ6347+
6345 Authorship
Manuscripts. Autographs. Sources. Forerunners
Associates. Followers. Circle. School
Prefer PQ6099+
Allusions
Prefer PQ6348.A2
Chronology of works
Criticism and interpretation
History of the study and appreciation of Cervantes
6347 General (and in Spain)
Special
6348.A2 Contemporaneous criticism and allusion
Cf. PQ6339.A2+
6348.A3 Later criticism
6348.A5-Z Biography of Cervantes scholars, A-Z
6349.A-Z Special countries, A-Z
e. g.
6349.E5 England
6349.F7 France
6349.G5 Germany
Treatises
6351 General
Prefer PQ6337 for works not limited to criticism
Don Quixote (mainly)
6352 General

Individual authors
Individual authors and works to 1700
Cervantes Saavedra, Miguel de, 1547-1616.
Criticism and interpretation.
Treatises.
Don Quixote (mainly) -- Continued

6353 Special
6354 Criticism of Avellaneda's Quixote
Special topics
(6355) Philosophy. Ethics. Esthetics
Prefer PQ6351 or PQ6358
6356 Technique.
6357 Characters
6357.A2 General
Prefer PQ6351
Special
6357.A3A-.A3Z Groups. Classes
e. g.
6357.A3C3 Clergy
6357.A3P5 Pícaros
6357.A3W6 Women
6357.A5-Z Individual
Don Quixote or Sancho Panza see PQ6352+
6358 Relation to special subjects. Treatment, knowledge, influence, etc.
6358.A4 Algeria
6358.A6 America
6358.A63 Andalusia
6358.A65 Arms
6358.A7 Art
Cf. PQ6335 PQ6343
6358.B3 Barcelona
6358.B5 Bible
6358.C54 Chivalry
6358.C57 Civilization, Classical
6358.C62 Commerce
6358.C7 Crime and criminals
6358.D45 Desire
6358.E74 Ethics
6358.F5 Fiction
6358.F64 Folklore
6358.G4 Geography
6358.H5 History. Politics
6358.I43 Identity
6358.I74 Islam
6358.L3 Law
6358.L45 Liberty

Individual authors
Individual authors and works to 1700
Cervantes Saavedra, Miguel de, 1547-1616.
Criticism and interpretation.
Relation to special subjects. Treatment, knowledge, influence, etc. -- Continued

6358.L5 Literature
6358.M4 Medicine
6358.M42 Mediterranean Region
6358.M5 Mental illness
6358.M8 Music
6358.N3 Natural history
6358.N8 Numismatics
6358.P5 Philosophy
6358.P7 Psychology
6358.R4 Religion
6358.S3 Science
6358.S7 Social life
6358.T73 Travel
6359 Interpretation. Running commentaries. Textual criticism. Variant readings
Interpretation and criticism of special works, see the work
6361 Language. Style
6361.Z3 Grammar
6361.Z5 Versification
6361.Z9 Dictionaries. Concordances
6365.C2 Céspedes, Valentín Antonio de, fl. 1615 (Table P-PZ40)
6365.C3 Céspedes y Meneses, Gonzalo de, 1585?-1638 (Table P-PZ40)
6365.C4 Cetina, Gutierre de, 1518?-1554? (Table P-PZ38)
El Cid Campeador
6366.A1 Editions comprising all or several parts
Editions of separate parts of the Cid legend
6366.A15 Latin hymn on the Cid
6366.A17 Gesta Roderici Campidocti
Poema del Cid (Cantar de mio Cid)
6366.A19 Facsimile reproductions of the unique manuscript
6366.A2 Other editions. By date
6366.A3 School editions. By date
(6366.A39) Running commentaries without text
see PQ6381
6366.A4 Crónica rimada del Cid ("Poema de las mocedades del Cid", or "El Rodrigo")
6366.A5 Crónica particular del Cid
6366.A55 Crónica del Cid Ruy Díaz (Crónica popular del Cid)
Romances
Editions of the 17th century and reissues

Individual authors
Individual authors and works to 1700
El Cid Campeador.
Editions of separate parts of the Cid legend.
Romances.
Editions of the 17th century and reissues.
6366.A6 Escobar. By date
6366.A7 Metje, 1626. By date
6366.A8 Modern editions. By date
Translations
English
6367.E2 Editions comprising all or several parts
6367.E3 Poema del Cid
6367.E4 Crónica rimada
6367.E5 Crónica particular
6367.E6 Crónica popular
6367.E7 Romances
French
6367.F2 Editions comprising all or several parts
6367.F3 Poema del Cid
6367.F4 Crónica rimada
6367.F5 Crónica particular
6367.F6 Crónica popular
6367.F7 Romances
German
6367.G2 Editions comprising all or several parts
6367.G3 Poema del Cid
6367.G4 Crónica rimada
6367.G5 Crónica particular
6367.G6 Crónica popular
6367.G7 Romances
Italian
6367.I2 Editions comprising all or several parts
6367.I3 Poema del Cid
6367.I4 Crónica rimada
6367.I5 Crónica particular
6367.I6 Crónica popular
6367.I7 Romances
6368.A-Z Other languages, A-Z
6369 Paraphrases, adaptations, etc.
Juvenile works
see PZ8.1, PZ14.1, etc.
(6369.5) Dramatizations
See the author, PQ-PT, e.g. Castro y Bellvia; Corneille
6369.9 Parodies, travesties, etc.
Prefer the individual author for prominent writers.
6370 Translations as subject (Comparative studies, etc.)

Individual authors
Individual authors and works to 1700
El Cid Campeador.
Translations as subject (Comparative studies, etc.). -- Continued

6370.A2 General
6370.A3-Z Special languages, A-Z
6371 Illustrations
Illustrated editions classed with other editions
Criticism, interpretations, etc.
6372 Sources. Early biographies of the Cid, etc.
Cf. PQ6366 (6368)
Treatises
6373 General (including criticism or the Poema del Cid alone)
6374 General special
6375 Essays, lectures, etc.
Special
6376 Style. Composition. Technique
6377 Comparison with other epics
e.g. Chanson de Roland
(6378) History. Geography
Prefer PQ6373+
(6379) Civilization
Prefer PQ6373+
6380 Other special
Textual criticism. Interpretation
6381 General
6382 Special (including special passages)
6383 Linguistic treatises
6384 Metrics. Versification
Lexicography
6385 Indexes, concordances, glossaries
6386 Treatises
El Cid Campeadór (Romances)
see El Cid Campeador, PQ6366.A6+ PQ6367.E7 etc.
6388.C2-.C23 Cifar (Historia del cavallero Cifar) (Table P-PZ43)
6388.C25 Cigorondo, Juan, 1560-1609 (Table P-PZ40)
6388.C4 Claramonte y Corroy, Andrés de, d. 1626 (Table P-PZ40)
6388.C42-.C423 Clarián de Landanís (Table P-PZ43)
6388.C43 Clavero de Falces, Ceferino, ca. 1609-1670 (Table P-PZ40)
6388.C44 Clemente, Dionís, 16th cent. (Table P-PZ40)
6388.C5 Coello, Antonio, 1611-1652 (Table P-PZ40)
6388.C53 Collado del Hierro, Agustín, 17th cent. (Table P-PZ40)
Comedia de Calisto y Melibea (known as "Celestina") see PQ6426+

Individual authors
Individual authors and works to 1700 -- Continued

6388.C58-.C583 Comedia de las burlas y enredos de Benito (Table P-PZ43)
6388.C585-.C5853 Comedia de Nuestra Señora de la Candelaria (Table P-PZ43)
6388.C586-.C5863 Comedia pastoril española (Table P-PZ43)
6388.C587-.C5873 Comedia Serafina (Table P-PZ43)
6388.C588-.C5883 Comedia Thebaida (Table P-PZ43)
6388.C589-.C5893 Conquista de la Nueva Castilla (Table P-PZ43)
6388.C5894 Contreras, Jerónimo, 16th cent. (Table P-PZ40)
6388.C59-.C593 Coplas de la panadera (Table P-PZ43)
Coplas de Mingo Revulgo see PQ6413.M6+
6388.C6-.C602 Coplas del provincial (Table P-PZ43a)
6388.C608 Cordero, Jacinto, 1606-1646 (Table P-PZ40)
6388.C609 Córdoba, Alonso de, fl. 1461-1462 (Table P-PZ40)
6388.C61 Córdoba, Martín Alfonso de, 15th cent. (Table P-PZ40)
6388.C617 Cornejo, Damián (Table P-PZ40)
6388.C6175-.C61753 Corónica de Adramón (Table P-PZ43)
Corónica del Cid Ruy Díaz see PQ6366.A55
6388.C618 Corral, Gabriel de, b. 1588 (Table P-PZ40)
6388.C62 Corral, Pedro de, fl. 1443 (Table P-PZ40)
Correa Castelblanco, Rodrigo, pseud. see PQ6321.C47
6388.C65 Cortés de Tolosa, Juan, b. 1590? (Table P-PZ40)
6388.C66 Corvera, Juan Bautista (Table P-PZ40)
6388.C7 Cota, Rodrigo de, fl. 15th cent. (Table P-PZ40)
Cota de Maguaque, Rodrigo de see PQ6321.C7
6388.C73 Covarrubias Horozco, Sebastián de, fl. 1611 (Table P-PZ40)
Crónica del Cid Ruy Díaz see PQ6366.A55
6388.C74-.C743 Crónica del muy valiente y esforzado caballero Platir hijo del invencible emperador Primaleón (Table P-PZ42)
6388.C75-.C753 Crónica del rey Enrico Otavo de Ingalaterra (Table P-PZ43)
Crónica particular del Cid see PQ6366.A5
Crónica rimada, ó El Rodrigo see PQ6366.A4
Crónica Troyana see PQ6398.H5+
Cruz, Juana Inés de la see PQ7296.J6
Cruz, San Juan de la see PQ6400.J8
6388.C8 Cubillo de Aragón, Alvaro, d. 1661 (Table P-PZ40)
6388.C84 Cuéllar, Jerónimo de, fl. 1650 (Table P-PZ40)
Cuello, Antonio see PQ6388.C5
6388.C9 Cueva, Juan de la, 1550?-1610? (Table P-PZ40)
6388.D15-.D153 Danza de la muerte (Table P-PZ42)
6388.D185-.D1853 Décimas a la muerte, compuestas por un hidalgo de la ciudad de Cuenca (Table P-PZ43)
6388.D19 Delgado, João Pinto, d. 1653 or 4 (Table P-PZ40)

Individual authors
Individual authors and works to 1700 -- Continued

6388.D2-.D23 Delicado, Francisco, 16th cent. La lozana andaluza (Table P-PZ43)
6388.D26 Delitala y Castelví, José (Table P-PZ40)
6388.D3 El diablo predicador
A famous play based upon Fray Diablo, an unpublished play by Lope de Vega
For Belmonte y Bermúdez, supposed author see PQ6279.B4
6388.D3A-.D3Z3 Translations. By language
Subarrange by translator (alphabetically)
6388.D3F57 French translation by Rouanet
6388.D3Z5-.D3Z99 Criticism
6388.D35-.D353 Diálogo de Luçiano llamado Palinuro (Table P-PZ43)
6388.D4 Diamante, Juan Bautista, 1625-1687 (Table P-PZ40)
6388.D5 Díaz de Gámez, Gutierrre, ca. 1379-ca.1450 (Table P-PZ40)
6388.D53 Díaz Tanco, Vasco, 16th cent. (Table P-PZ40)
6388.D535 Dicastillo, Miguel de, 17th cent. (Table P-PZ40)
Diego de San Pedro see PQ6431.S4
6388.D55 Diego de Valencia de Léon, 1350?-1412? (Table P-PZ40)
6388.D6-.D63 Disputa del alma y el cuerpo (Table P-PZ43)
La doncella Teodor
see PQ6165.D7 Folk literature, and PQ6439.D7 Lope de Vega
6388.D86 Duque de Estrada, Diego, 1589-1647? (Table P-PZ40)
6388.E16-.E163 Enamorado y la muerte (Table P-PZ43)
Encina, Juan del, 1468-1529?
Editions
6388.E2 Collections and selections. By date
6388.E2A1-.E2A29 Separate works
6388.E2A3-.E2A69 Translations. By language and date
6388.E2A7-.E2Z Biography and criticism
6388.E3 Encinas, Pedro de, d. 1595 (Table P-PZ40)
6388.E35-.E353 Engaño en la victoria (Table P-PZ42)
6388.E42 Enríquez, Fadrique, 1460-1538 (Table P-PZ40)
6388.E49 Enríquez Cartagena, Juan (Table P-PZ40)
6388.E494 Enríquez de Guzmán, Feliciana (Table P-PZ40)
6388.E5 Enríquez Gómez, Antonio, 1602-1662? (Table P-PZ40)
6388.E64-.E643 Entremés de los romances (Table P-PZ43)
Enxemplos, Libro de los see PQ6431.S75
6388.E7-.E73 Epístola moral a Fabio (Table P-PZ43)
Erasto see PQ6433.S53+
6389 Ercilla y Zuñiga, Alonso de, 1533-1594
6389.A2 La Araucana. By date
6389.A22 Imitations, adaptations, etc.

Individual authors
Individual authors and works to 1700
Ercilla y Zuñiga, Alonso de, 1533-1594
6389.A5-Z Biography and criticism
6390.E3 Escobar y Mendoza, Antonio de, 1589-1669
6390.E3A2 Historia de la virgen madre de Dios María
Later published with title: Nueva Jerusalén María, poema heroico
6390.E3A4 San Ignacio de Loyola, poema heroico
6390.E4 Escriba, Juan, 15th cent. (Table P-PZ40)
6390.E56 Espinel, Vicente, 1550?-1624 (Table P-PZ40)
6390.E58 Espinola y Torres, Juan, b. 1596 (Table P-PZ40)
6390.E6 Espinosa, Pedro, 1578-1650 (Table P-PZ40)
Esquilache, Francisco de Borja, principe de see PQ6279.B55
Ezquerra de Rozas y Blancas, Gerónimo see PQ6393.G4
6390.F17 Fajardo y Acevedo, Antonio, ca. 1630-ca. 1700 (Table P-PZ40)
6390.F2-.F23 Farça a manera de tragedia (Table P-PZ43)
Fernán Gonçalez (Poem) see PQ6420.P54+
6390.F28 Fernández, Jerónimo (Table P-PZ40)
6390.F3 Fernandez, Lucas, 1474?-1542 (Table P-PZ40)
6390.F33 Férnandez de Andrada, Andrés (Table P-PZ40)
Fernández de Avellaneda, Alonso see PQ6354
Fernández de Avellaneda, Alonso, pseud. see PQ6323.A4
6390.F347 Fernández de Oviedo y Valdés, Gonzalo, 1478-1557 (Table P-PZ40)
6390.F35 Fernández de Ribera, Rodrigo, 1579-1631 (Table P-PZ40)
6390.F37 Ferruz, Jaime, d. 1594 (Table P-PZ40)
Figueroa, Cristóbal Suárez de see PQ6433.S8
6390.F4 Figueroa, Francisco de, 1536?-1620 (Table P-PZ40)
6390.F5 Figueroa y Córdoba, Diego, fl. 1654 (Table P-PZ40)
6390.F51 Figueroa y Córdoba, José, fl. 1654 (Table P-PZ40)
6390.F65 Flores, Antonio, fl. 1668 (Table P-PZ40)
6390.F67 Flores, Juan de, 15th-16th centuries (Table P-PZ40)
6390.F7-.F72 Flores y Blancaflor (Romance) (Table P-PZ43a)
Fragoso, Juan de Matos see PQ6412.M9
Frasso, Antonio de la see PQ7049.F8
6390.F74 Frías, Damasio de, 16th cent. (Table P-PZ40)
6390.G28 Gabaldón, Rodrigo, 17th/18th cent. (Table P-PZ40)
6390.G35 Galán, Diego, fl. 1589 (Table P-PZ40)
6390.G4 Gálvez de Montalvo, Luis, 1549?-1591? (Table P-PZ40)
Gámez, Gutierre Díaz de see PQ6388.D5
6390.G8 Garciá, Carlos, pseud.? fl. 1619 (Table P-PZ40)
6390.G84 Garciá, Lorenzo, fl. 1667 (Table P-PZ40)
Garcilaso de la Vega, 1503-1536
6391.A1 Collected works. By date

	Individual authors
	Individual authors and works to 1700
	Garcilaso de la Vega, 1503-1536 -- Continued
6391.A3-.A69	Translations, alphabetically by language
6391.A5	English
6391.A7-Z	Separate works, A-Z
6392	Biography and criticism
6393.G2	Garcilaso de la Vega, el Inca, 1539-1616 (Table P-PZ40)
	Prefer E-F, American history
	Gato, Juan Alvarez see PQ6273.A3
	Gatos, Libro de los see PQ6411.L63+
6393.G4	Gerónimo, de San José, 1587-1654 (Table P-PZ40)
	Name in religion of Ezquerra de Rozas y Blancas, Gerónimo
	Gesta de los infantes de Lara see PQ6400.I6+
6393.G54	Gil Enriquez, Andres, 1636-1673 (Table P-PZ40)
	Gil Polo, Gaspar see PQ6420.P7
6393.G6	Gnósopho, Christóphoro, pseud. (Table P-PZ40)
	El crotalón, 16th cent., attributed to Villalón, Cristóbal de
6393.G63	Godínez, Felipe, 1588-1624 (Table P-PZ40)
	Gómez, Antonio Enríquez see PQ6388.E5
6393.G64	Gómez de Castro, Alvar, 16th cent. (Table P-PZ40)
6393.G645	Gómez de Ferrol, Pero, 15th cent. (Table P-PZ40)
6393.G7	Gonçal'Eanes do Vinhal, d. 1285 (Table P-PZ40)
	Gonçalez, Fernán, Poema de see PQ6420.P54+
6393.G8	Gonçález, Gregorio (Table P-PZ40)
	Góngora y Argote, Luis de, 1561-1627
6394.A1	Collected works. By date
6394.A11-.A29	Selected works. By editor
6394.A3	Collected translations. By language, A-Z
6394.A7-Z	Separate works, A-Z
	e. g.
6394.S6	Soledades
6394.S6E5	English translations
	Biography and criticism
6395.A1-.A29	Periodicals. Societies. Collections
6395.A3	Dictionaries. Indexes
6395.A4	Autobiography. Journals. Memoirs
6395.A45	Letters. By date
6395.A5-Z	General works
	González, Esteban see PQ6498.V3+
	González de Bustos, Francisco, fl. 1665 see PQ8096.G7
	Gonzalo de Berceo, 13th cent.
6397.A1	Collected works. By date
6397.A6	Selected works. By date
6397.A7	Translations (Collected). By language, A-Z
6397.A8-.Z4	Separate works, A-Z
	e. g.

Individual authors
Individual authors and works to 1700
Gonzalo de Berceo, 13th cent.
Separate works, A-Z. -- Continued
6397.S2-.S3 El sacrificio de la misa
6397.Z5 Biography and criticism
Gracián y Morales, Baltasar, 1601-1658
6398.G3 Collected works. By date
6398.G3A6 Selected works. By date
6398.G3A7-.G3A79 Translations (Collected), by language alphabetically
6398.G3A8-.G3Z Separate works including translations
e. g.
6398.G3C7-.G3C9 El criticón
6398.G3D5-.G3D7 El discreto
6398.G3H4-.G3H6 El héroe
6398.G3O7-.G3O9 El oráculo manual
6398.G4 Biography and criticism
6398.G5-.G53 Gran conquista de Ultramar, 13th cent. (Table P-PZ42)
Granada, Luis de see PQ6412.L8
6398.G75 Gual, Antonio, 1594-1655 (Table P-PZ40)
Guevara, Antonio de, d. 1545
6398.G8 Editions. By date
6398.G8A14 Selected works
Separate works
6398.G8A2 Aviso de privados y dictrina de cortesanos
6398.G8A25 Cartas de Rhuá
(6398.G8A28) De los inventores del marear (de navigar)
see VK144
6398.G8A3 Década de Césares
Also published with title: Vidas de los emperadores romanos
Despertador de cortesanos
see Aviso de privados, etc.
Epístolas familiares
6398.G8A4 Primera parte (or Primera y segunda parte)
6398.G8A42 Segunda parte
6398.G8A5 Libro áureo. Libro áureo con el Relox de príncipes
6398.G8A6 Menosprecio de corte y alabança de aldea
Monte Calvario
6398.G8A7 Primera parte (or Primera y segunda parte)
6398.G8A72 Segunda parte
6398.G8A8 Oratorio de religiosos y exercicio de virtuosos
Relox (Reloj) de principes
see Libro aúreo
Vidas de los diez emperadores
see Década de Césares
6398.G9A8-.G9Z Biography and criticism

Individual authors
Individual authors and works to 1700 -- Continued

	Guevara, Luis Vélez de see PQ6496+
6398.G936	Guillén de Segovia, Pero, 1413-1474? (Table P-PZ40)
6398.G97	Gusmão Soares, Vicente de, 1606-1675 (Table P-PZ40)
	Cf. PQ9231.G9 as Portuguese author
6398.G98	Guzmán, Juan de, 16th cent. (Table P-PZ40)
6398.H2	Hermosilla, Diego de, fl. 1573 (Table P-PZ40)
6398.H23	Hernández, Alonso, fl. 1516 (Table P-PZ40)
6398.H24	Hernández, Pedro, 16th cent. (Table P-PZ40)
6398.H25	Hernando de Jesús, fl. 1632 (Table P-PZ40)
6398.H3	Herrera, Fernando de, 1534?-1597 (Table P-PZ40)
6398.H33	Herrera y Sotomayor, Jacinto de, d. 1644 (Table P-PZ40)
6398.H35	Hierro, Baltasar del, fl. 1561 (Table P-PZ40)
6398.H355-.H3553	Hijo de la Cuna de Sevilla (Table P-PZ43)
6398.H37-.H373	Historia de Apolonio (Table P-PZ42)
6398.H374-.H3743	Historia de Griseldis (Table P-PZ42)
6398.H375-.H3753	Historia de la donzella Teodor (Table P-PZ43)
	Historia de los siete Sabios de Roma see PQ6433.S53+
6398.H38-.H383	Historia de Segundo (Table P-PZ43)
6398.H4-.H43	Historia de Yuçuf (Poema de José) (Table P-PZ42)
6398.H45-.H453	Historia del Invencible cavallero don Polindo (Table P-PZ43)
	Historia lastimera d'el príncipe Erasto see PQ6433.S53+
6398.H5-.H53	Historia troyana (Table P-PZ43)
	Hita, Ginés Pérez de see PQ6419.P8
	Hita, Juan Ruiz, arcipreste de see PQ6430
6398.H6	Hojeda, Diego de, 1570?-1615 (Table P-PZ40)
6398.H65	Horozco, Sebastián de, fl. 1548-1572 (Table P-PZ40)
6398.H7	Hoz y Mota, Juan Claudio de la, d. 1714 (Table P-PZ40)
6398.H83	Huerta, Antonio de, 17th cent. (Table P-PZ40)
6398.H85	Huete, Jaime de (Table P-PZ40)
6398.H9	Hurtado de Mendoza, Antonio, 1586-1644 (Table P-PZ40)
6399	Hurtado de Mendoza, Diego, 1503-1575 (Table P-PZ39)
	For Lazarillo de Tormes (formerly ascribed to him) see PQ6407+
(6400.I4)	Ildefonso, Vida de San
	see PQ6498.V26
6400.I5	Imperial, Francisco, 14th-15th centuries (Table P-PZ40)
	Inés de la Cruz, Juana see PQ7296.J6
6400.I6-.I63	Los infantes de Lara (Gesta) (Table P-PZ42)
6400.J27	Jarava, Juan de, fl. 1540-1550 (Table P-PZ40)
6400.J3	Jáuregui y Aguilar, Juan de, 1583-1641 (Table P-PZ40)
	Jiménez de Enciso, Diego see PQ6498.X5
	Jiménez de Urrea, Pedro Manuel, ca. 1486-ca. 1530 see PQ6437.U8
6400.J6	José de Sigüenza, Father, ca. 1544-1606 (Table P-PZ40)

Individual authors
Individual authors and works to 1700 -- Continued
6400.J8 Juan de la Cruz, Saint, 1542-1591 (Table P-PZ40)
6400.J83 Juan de los Angeles, d. 1609 (Table P-PZ40)
Juan Lorenzo see PQ6412.L45
Juan Manuel, Infante of Castile, 1282-1347
El libro de Patronio; o El conde Lucanor
6401.A1 Editions. By date
6401.A5-.Z8 Translations. By language, A-Z
6401.Z85 Collected works. Selected works
Subarrange by editor, if give, or date
6401.5.A-Z Other works, A-Z
6402 Biography and criticism
6403 Juan - Laz
6403.J83 Juan Manuel II, ca. 1444-1543 (Table P-PZ40)
Juan Ruiz, arcipreste de Hita see PQ6430
Juana Inés de la Cruz see PQ7296.J6
La Hoz y Mota, Juan Claudio de see PQ6398.H7
Lara, Gesta de los infantes de see PQ6400.I6+
6403.L25 Laredo, Bernardino de, 1482-1545? (Table P-PZ40)
Lasso de la Vega, Gabriel see PQ6411.L78
Lazarillo de Tormes
Formerly ascribed to Diego Hurtado de Mendoza
6407.A1 Editions of 1st part. By date
6407.A2 Editions of 2d part. By date
6407.A3 Editions of 1st and 2d parts. By date
6407.A7 Adaptations, etc. By date
6408 Translations. By language and date
e.g.
6408.E5 English
6408.F5 French
6408.G4 German
6409 Criticism
6410.L2 Ledesma, Alonso de, fl. 1600 (Table P-PZ40)
6410.L25 Leiva Ramírez de Arellano, Francisco de, 1630-1676 (Table P-PZ40)
León, Luis Ponce de, 1528?-1591
Editions
6410.L3 Collections and selections. By date
6410.L3A1-.L3A21 Separate works
6410.L3A3-.L3A69 Translations. By language and date
6410.L3A7-.L3Z Biography and criticism
6410.L4 León Marchante, Manuel de, 1631-1680 (Table P-PZ40)
6410.L5 Leonardo y Argensola, Bartolomé and Lupercio (Table P-PZ40)
6410.L52 Leonardo y Argensola, Bartolomé Juan, 1562-1631 (Table P-PZ40)

Individual authors
Individual authors and works to 1700 -- Continued

6410.L53 Leonardo y Argensola, Lupercio, 1559?-1613 (Table P-PZ40)
Leyba Ramírez, Francisco de see PQ6410.L25
6411.L3-.L32 Libro de Alixandre (Table P-PZ43a)
By some authorities ascribed to Gonzalo de Berceo
Cf. PQ6397.A1+
6411.L4-.L43 Libro de Apollonio (Table P-PZ43)
Cf. PA3871.A8 Apollonius of Tyre
6411.L5-.L53 Libro de las batallas (Table P-PZ43)
6411.L55-.L553 Libro de los buenos proverbios (Table P-PZ43)
6411.L58-.L583 Libro de los çient capitulos (Table P-PZ43)
6411.L59-.L593 Libro del los engaños. From the Arabic (Table P-PZ43)
Libro de los enxemplos see PQ6431.S75
6411.L63-.L633 Libro de los gatos (Libro de los quentos) (Table P-PZ43)
Libro de los siete sabios de Roma see PQ6433.S53+
6411.L67-.L673 Libro de los tres reyes de Oriente (Table P-PZ43)
6411.L68-.L683 Libro de miseria de omne (Table P-PZ43)
Libro del cavallero Zifar see PQ6388.C2+
6411.L7 Liñan de Riaza, Pedro, 16th cent. (Table P-PZ40)
6411.L75 Liñan y Verdugo, Antonio, 17th cent. (Table P-PZ40)
6411.L77 Llerena de Rueda, Cristóbal de, ca. 1550-ca. 1645 (Table P-PZ40)
6411.L78 Lobo Lasso de la Vega, Gabriel, 1559-ca. 1615 (Table P-PZ38)
6412.L17 Lomas Cantoral, Jerónimo de, ca. 1540-ca. 1600 (Table P-PZ40)
Lope de Vega see PQ6438+
6412.L19 López, Jerónimo, fl. 1528 (Table P-PZ40)
6412.L2 López de Ayala, Pedro, 1332-1407 (Table P-PZ40)
6412.L23 López de Corella, Alonso, ca. 1510-1584 (Table P-PZ40)
López de Ubeda, Francisco. La pícara Justina, sometimes ascribed to him see PQ6420.P5+
6412.L28 López de Villalobos, Francisco, 1473-1549 (Table P-PZ40)
6412.L3 López de Zárate, Francisco, d. 1658 (Table P-PZ40)
6412.L36 López Maldonado, Gariel, fl. 1586 (Table P-PZ40)
6412.L4 López Pinciano, Alonso, fl, 1596-1627 (Table P-PZ40)
(6412.L45) Lorenzo Juan (or Juan Lorenzo Segura), copyist
see Libro de Alixandre, PQ6411.L3+
6412.L5 Lozano, Cristóbal, 1609?-1667 (Table P-PZ40)
6412.L7 Lucena, Luis de, fl. ca. 1497 (Table P-PZ40)
6412.L73-.L733 Lucidario (Table P-PZ43)
6412.L75 Lugo y Dávila, Francisco de, 17th cent. (Table P-PZ40)
6412.L8 Luis de Granada, 1504-1588 (Table P-PZ40)
6412.L84 Lujan, Pedro de, 16th cent. (Table P-PZ40)
6412.M17 Mal-Lara, Juan de, 1524-1571 (Table P-PZ40)

Individual authors
Individual authors and works to 1700 -- Continued

6412.M2 Malón de Chaide, Pedro, 1530-1589 (Table P-PZ40)
6412.M26 Maluenda, Jacinto Alonso, 17th cent. (Table P-PZ40)
6412.M3 Manrique, Gómez, 1413-1491
6412.M4 Biography and criticism
6412.M5 Manrique, Jorge, 1440?-1478
6412.M6 Biography and criticism
María Egipciaqua, Vida de Santa see PQ6498.V28+
Martí, Juan José, d. 1604
Supposed author of the spurious second part of Vida del pícaro Guzmán de Alfarache, see PQ6272.A5
6412.M625 Martín de la Plaza, Luis, 1577-1625 (Table P-PZ40)
6412.M627 Martínez de Burgos, Juan (Table P-PZ40)
6412.M63 Martínez de Cuéllar, Juan, fl. 1663 (Table P-PZ40)
6412.M65 Martínez de Meneses, Antonio, b. 1608 (Table P-PZ40)
6412.M7 Martínez de Toledo, Alfonso, 1398?-1466 (Table P-PZ40)
6412.M9 Matos Fragoso, Juan de, 1608-1688 (Portuguese) (Table P-PZ40)
6412.M95 Medinilla, Baltasar Elisio de, 1585-1620 (Table P-PZ40)
6413.M17 Medrano, Francisco de, fl. 1617 (Table P-PZ40)
6413.M174 Medrano, Julián de, ca. 1540 (Table P-PZ40)
Mejía, Pedro
see Mexía, Pedro
6413.M2 Mena, Juan de, 1411-1456 (Table P-PZ40)
Mendoza, Antonio Hurtado de see PQ6398.H9
Mendoza, Diego Hurtado de see PQ6399
6413.M25 Mendoza, Iñigo de, ca. 1424-ca. 1507 (Table P-PZ40)
6413.M28 Meneses, Leonor de, condessa de Atougia, ca. 1620-1664 (Table P-PZ40)
6413.M32 Mercader y Cervellón, Gasper, 1656-1686 (Table P-PZ40)
6413.M35 Merino, Hernando, 16th cent. (Table P-PZ40)
6413.M36-.M363 Merlín, Baladro del sabio (Table P-PZ43)
6413.M38 Mesa, Cristóbal de, 16th-17th centuries (Table P-PZ40)
Mexía, Pedro, 1496?-1552?
Editions
6413.M5 Collections and selections. By date
6413.M5A1-.M5A29 Separate works
6413.M5A3-.M5A69 Translations. By language and date
6413.M5A7-.M5Z Biography and criticism
6413.M6-.M63 Mingo Regulgo (Table P-PZ43)
Political satire ascribed to Cota de Maguaque
6413.M7 Mira de Amescua, Antonio, fl. 1600 (Table P-PZ40)
6413.M8-.M812 Misterio de los reyes magos (Table P-PZ43a)
6413.M815 Molina, Juan de, b. 1490 (Table P-PZ40)
Molina, Tirso de, pseud. see PQ6434+

Individual authors
Individual authors and works to 1700 -- Continued

6413.M817 Moncayo y Gurrea, Juan de, marqués de San Felices, b. 1614? (Table P-PZ40)
6413.M85 Monroy y Silva, Cristóbal de, 1612-1649 (Table P-PZ40)
6413.M9-.M93 El monstruo satírico (Table P-PZ43)
Montalván, Juan Pérez de see PQ6420.P3
Montalvo, Luis Gálvez de see PQ6390.G4
6414 Montemayor, Jorge de, 1520?-1561
Portuguese author
6414.A1 Collections and selections. By date
6414.A11-.A29 Separate works
For continuations of "La Diana," see PQ6419.P77 PQ6420.P7
6414.A3-.A69 Translations. By language and date
6414.A7-Z Biography and criticism
Montemor, Jorge de see PQ6414
6415.M7 Monteser, Francisco Antonio de, d. 1668 (Table P-PZ40)
6415.M75 Montesino, Ambrosio, Bp., d. 1514 (Table P-PZ40)
6415.M8 Montoro, Antón de, 1404-1480 (Table P-PZ40)
6415.M9 Montreal, Miguel de, fl. 1709 (Table P-PZ40)
6415.M95 Moreno, Miguel, 1596-1635 (Table P-PZ40)
Moreto y Cavana, Agustin, 1618-1669
6416.A2 Collected works. By date
6416.A3 Selected works. By date
6416.A4A-.A4Z Translations (Collected). By language, A-Z
6416.A5-Z Separate works, A-Z
6417 Biography and criticism
6418 Mor - Mz
6418.M58-.M583 La Mujer de Peribáñez (Table P-PZ43)
6418.M6 Muñon, Sancho de, fl. 1549 (Table P-PZ40)
Naharro, Bartolomé de Torres see PQ6437.T76
6419.N2 Navarrete y Ribera, Francisco de, fl. 1640 (Table P-PZ40)
6419.N4 Negueruela, Diego de, 16th cent. (Table P-PZ40)
6419.N5 Nierembuerg, Juan Eusebio, 1595-1658 (Table P-PZ40)
6419.N6-.N63 No hay desdicha que no acabe (Novel) (Table P-PZ43)
6419.N65-.N653 No me mueve, mi Dios, para quererte (Poem) (Table P-PZ43)
6419.N8 Núñez Alva, Diego, 16th cent. (Table P-PZ40)
6419.N84 Núñez de Reinoso, Alonso, d. 1579? (Table P-PZ40)
Ojeda, Diego de see PQ6398.H6
6419.O66-.O663 Las oposiciones (Comedia) (Table P-PZ43)
6419.O694 Orellana, Pedro de, fray, 1496-1561? (Table P-PZ40)
6419.O695 Ortega, Melchor de, 16th cent. (Table P-PZ40)
6419.O697 Ortí y Moles, José, 1650-1728 (Table P-PZ40)
6419.O7 Ortiz, Agustín, 16th cent. (Table P-PZ40)
6419.O73 Ortiz, Alonso, fl. 1639 (Table P-PZ40)

Individual authors
Individual authors and works to 1700 -- Continued

6419.O8-.O9 Ortúñez de Calahorra, Diego, 16th cent.
Author of first part of L'espejo de principles y cavalleros. Continuations by Pedro de la Sierra and Marcos Martinez
6419.O8 Editions. By date
6419.O8A3-.O8A69 Translations. By language and date
6419.O8A7-.O8Z Biography and criticism
6419.O85 Ovando, Gasper de, 17th cent. (Table P-PZ40)
6419.O86 Ovando y Santarén, Juan de, 1624-1706 (Table P-PZ40)
6419.O9 Oviedo y Valdés, Gonzalo Fernández de, 1478-1557 (Table P-PZ40)
6419.P16 Pablo de Santa Maria, Bishop of Burgos, ca. 1351-1435 (Table P-PZ40)
6419.P173 Pacheco de Narváez, Luis (Table P-PZ40)
6419.P2 Padilla, Juan de, 1468-1522? (Table P-PZ40)
Padrón, Juan Rodriguez del see PQ6425.R8
6419.P25 Palafox y Mendoza, Juande, 1600-1659 (Table P-PZ40)
6419.P27 Palau, Bartolomé, 16th cent. (Table P-PZ40)
6419.P3 Palencia, Alfonso Fernández de, 1423-1492 (Table P-PZ40)
Palmerin romances
6419.P4 Palmerin de Oliva
6419.P5 Primaleón
Libro del inuencible cauallero Primaleón hijo de Palmerín de Oliva. Libro segundo del emperador palmerín
For further continuations, see the romances "Platir" and "Fiotir," the latter of Spanish or Italian origin. See also Palmerín de Inglaterra (In Portuguese literature), PQ9231.P25
6419.P6 Criticism
6419.P625 Paravicino, Hortensio Félix, 1580-1633 (Table P-PZ40)
6419.P63-.P633 Paris e Viana (Legend) (Table P-PZ43)
6419.P635 Pastor, Juan, fl. 1528 (Table P-PZ40)
6419.P637-.P6373 Pastora de Mançanares y desdichas de Pánfilo (Table P-PZ43)
6419.P65 Pedraza, Juan de, fl. 1565 (Table P-PZ40)
6419.P7 Pedro, Constable of Portugal, 1429-1466 (Table P-PZ40)
6419.P75 El Peregrino de Puey Monçón, pseud. (Table P-PZ40)
6419.P77 Pérez, Alonso, fl. 1564 (Table P-PZ40)
Author of second part of La Diana
Cf. PQ6414 Montemayor, Jorge de
6419.P78 Pérez, Antonio, d. 1611 (Table P-PZ40)
6419.P785 Pérez de Culla, Vicente (Table P-PZ40)
6419.P79 Pérez de Guzmán, Fernán, 1376?-1460? (Table P-PZ40)
6419.P8 Pérez de Hita, Ginés, 1544?-1619? (Table P-PZ40)
6420.P3 Pérez de Montalván, Juan, 1602-1638 (Table P-PZ40)

Individual authors
Individual authors and works to 1700 -- Continued

6420.P35 Pérez de Montoro, José, 1627-1694 (Table P-PZ40)
6420.P4 Pérez de Oliva, Fernán, 1494?-1533 (Table P-PZ40)
6420.P46 Persio Bertiso, Felix, 17th cent. (Table P-PZ40)
6420.P467-.P4673 Philesbián de Candaria (Table P-PZ43)
6420.P5-.P513 La pícara Justina (Table P-PZ43a)
Authorship ascribed to Andrés Pérez de León and Francisco López de Ubeda
6420.P52 Piña, Juan Izquierdo de, 1566?-1643 (Table P-PZ40)
6420.P53-.P533 Poema de Alfonso Onceno (Table P-PZ43)
Poema de Fernán Gonçález
6420.P54 Texts. By date
6420.P54A-.P54Z Criticism.
Poema de José see PQ6398.H4+
6420.P63-.P633 Poética silva (Table P-PZ43)
6420.P66 Poggio Monteverde, Juan Bautista, 1623-1707 (Table P-PZ40)
6420.P7 Polo, Gaspar Gil, 1516?-1591? (Table P-PZ40)
Author of a continuation of Jorge de Montemayor's "Diana"
6420.P8 Polo de Medina, Salvador Jacinto, 1603-1676 (Table P-PZ40)
6420.P83 Prado, Andrés de, 16th cent. (Table P-PZ40)
Poet. Author of the farce "Cornelia"
6420.P84 Prado, Andrés de, fl. 1663 (Table P-PZ40)
Novelist
6420.P86 Prado y Tovar, Diego de, 17th cent. (Table P-PZ40)
Primaleón see PQ6419.P5
6420.P9 Pulgar, Hernando del, 1436?-1492 (Table P-PZ40)
Quentos, Libro de los see PQ6411.L63+
6420.Q47-.Q473 Question de amor (Table P-PZ43)
Quevedo y Villegas, Francisco Gómez de, 1580-1645
Editions
6421.A1 Collected works. By date
6421.A15 Selected works. By date
Special collections
6421.A2 Prose
Discursos satiríco-morales: Los sueños see PQ6422.A2
6421.A3 Discursos festivos (Collections)
6421.A4 Discursos crítico-literarios (Invectivos; Juicios, progos y advertencias; Censuras y aprobaciones)
Discursos políticos
see DP or J
Discursos filosóficos
see B

Individual authors
Individual authors and works to 1700
Quevedo y Villegas, Francisco Gómez de, 1580-1645
Editions
Special collections
Prose -- Continued
Discursos ascéticos
see subclass BX
6421.A5 Poetry
(6421.A7) Posthumous works
see PQ6421.A15
6421.A9 Selections. Quotations. Passages
6422 Separate works
Translations see PQ6423.A+
6422.A1 El Buscón (Historia de la vida del Buscón llamado Don Pablos de Segovia; also known as El gran Tracaño)
6422.A2 Los sueños
6422.A3-.Z3 Other works
6422.Z5 Collections and selections. By date
Spurious works
6422.Z5A-.Z5Z Separate works, A-Z
6423.A-Z Translations. By language, A-Z
6423.E5-.E58 English
6423.E5 Collections and selections. By date
6423.E51 El Buscón (Don Pablos)
6423.E52 Los sueños
6423.E53-.E58 Other
6423.F5-.F58 French
6423.G5-.G58 German
6423.I5-.I58 Italian
6424 Biography and criticism
6424.A1 Sources, documents. By date
6424.A2 Letters. By date
6424.A5-.Z3 Biography. Life and works
6424.Z5 Criticism
6425.Q3 Quiñones de Benavente, Luis, 1589?-1651 (Table P-PZ40)
6425.Q5 Quintana, Francisco de, fl. 1626 (Table P-PZ40)
6425.Q65 Quiroga Faxardo, Juan de, ca. 1591-1660 (Table P-PZ40)
6425.R23 Rabadan, Muhammad, fl. 1603 (Table P-PZ40)
6425.R246 Ramírez de Guzmán, Catalina Clara, 1611-ca. 1663 (Table P-PZ40)
6425.R27-.R273 Razón de amor (Table P-PZ43)
6425.R3 Rebolledo, Bernardino, conde de, 1597-1676 (Table P-PZ40)
6425.R34 Reinosa, Rodrigo de (Table P-PZ40)
6425.R36 Remón, Alonso, fl. 1616-1632 (Table P-PZ40)

Individual authors
Individual authors and works to 1700 -- Continued
Renaldos de Montalbán
6425.R374 Book I-II (by Luis Dominguez) (Table P-PZ43)
6425.R375 Book III (Table P-PZ43)
6425.R376 Book IV (Table P-PZ43)
6425.R38-.R383 Revelación de un ermitaño (Table P-PZ43)
6425.R4 Reyes, Matías de los, b. ca. 1575 (Table P-PZ40)
6425.R45 Ribera, Anastasio Pantaleón de, 1580-1629 (Table P-PZ40)
6425.R5 Rioja, Francisco de, 1583?-1659 (Table P-PZ40)
6425.R7 Rodríguez de Ardila, Pedro (Table P-PZ40)
6425.R8 Rodríguez de la Cámara, Juan (Rodríguez del Padrón) (Table P-PZ40)
Rojas, Fernando de, fl. 1510-1538
La Celestina, o tragicomedia de Calisto y Melibea
6426.A1 Editions
6426.A3 Abridged editions
6427.A-Z Translations. By language, A-Z
(6427.5) Adaptations, imitations, etc.
See the author
6428 Biography and criticism
6429.R3 Rojas Villandrando, Agustin de, 1572-1612? (Table P-PZ40)
6429.R5 Rojas Zorilla, Francisco de, 1607-1648 (Table P-PZ40)
6429.R55 Román, comendador, 15th century (Table P-PZ40)
6429.R58-.R583 Romance del rey don Alonso que ganó a Toledo (Table P-PZ43)
6429.R63 Romero de Cepeda, Joaquin (Table P-PZ40)
6429.R65-.R653 Roncesvalles (Chanson de geste) (Table P-PZ43)
6429.R66 Rosas de Oquendo, Mateo, b. 1559 (Table P-PZ40)
6429.R67 Rosel y Fuenllana, Diego (Table P-PZ40)
6429.R7 Rosete Niño, Pedro b. 1608 (Table P-PZ40)
6429.R75-.R753 Rrey Guillelme (Table P-PZ43)
6429.R8 Rueda, Lope de, d. 1565 (Table P-PZ40)
6429.R9 Rufo Gutiérrez, Juan, fl. 1584 (Table P-PZ40)
6430 Ruiz, Juan, arcipreste de Hita, fl. 1343
6430.A1 Libro de buen amor
Also published with title: Libro de cantares; comprises all the poems published by Ruiz
6430.A5 Translations. By language and date
6430.A7-Z Criticism
6431.R76 Ruiz Alceo, Juan, 17th cent. (Table P-PZ40)
6431.R8 Ruiz de Alarcón y Mendoza, Juan, d. 1639 (Table P-PZ40)
Sá de Miranda, Francisco de, ca. 1485-1558 see PQ9241+
6431.S13 Saavedra Fajardo, Diego de, 1584-1648 (Table P-PZ40)
6431.S16 Sacristán de Vieja Rúa, pseud. (Table P-PZ40)

Individual authors
Individual authors and works to 1700 -- Continued
6431.S2 Salas Barbadillo, Alonso Jerónimo de, 1580?-1635 (Table P-PZ40)
6431.S22 Salazar, Ambrosio de, b. ca. 1575 (Table P-PZ40)
6431.S23 Salazar, Eugenio de, b. ca. 1530 (Table P-PZ40)
6431.S24 Salazar y Torres, Agustin de, 1642-1675 (Table P-PZ40)
6431.S26 Salinas, Juan de, 1562?-1643 (Table P-PZ40)
6431.S28 Salinas y Lizana, Manuel de, b. 1616 (Table P-PZ40)
6431.S3 Salucio del Poyo, Damián, ca. 1550-1614 (Table P-PZ40)
6431.S34 Salvo y Vela, Juan, d. 1720 (Table P-PZ40)
San Juan de la Cruz see PQ6400.J8
6431.S4 San Pedro, Diego de, fl. 1500 (Table P-PZ40)
6431.S6 Sánchez, Diego, fl. 1525 (Table P-PZ40)
Sánchez, Garci see PQ6431.S7
6431.S65 Sánchez, Miguel, surnamed El Divino, 17th cent. (Table P-PZ40)
6431.S66 Sánchez, Pedro, fl. 1640 (Table P-PZ40)
6431.S68 Sánchez, Vicente, 1643-1682 (Table P-PZ40)
Sánchez de Badajoz see PQ6431.S6
6431.S7 Sánchez de Badajoz, Garci (Table P-PZ40)
6431.S73 Sánchez de Talavera, Ferrán (Table P-PZ40)
6431.S75 Sánchez de Vercial, Clemente, 1370?-1462 (Table P-PZ40)
Compiler of the Libro de los exemplos
Sánchez del Quintenar, Pedro see PQ6431.S66
6431.S8 Sancho IV, king of Castile and Leon, 1257-1295 (Table P-PZ40)
Cf. PQ6321.C45 Castigos e documentos
6432 Santillana, Iñigo López de Mendoza, marqués de, 1398-1458 (Table P-PZ39)
6433.S2 Santob, de Carrión de los Condes, ca. 1290- ca. 1369 (Table P-PZ40)
6433.S25 Santos, Francisco, fl. 1663 (Table P-PZ40)
6433.S27 Sarabia, Gabriel de, 16th cent. (Table P-PZ40)
Sayavedra, Matheo Luxán de, pseud. see PQ6272.A5
6433.S4 Scriva, Ludovico, fl. 1537 (Table P-PZ40)
6433.S445 Sedeño, Juan, fl. 1536-1587 (Table P-PZ40)
6433.S448-.S4483 Segunda parte de la vida del pícaro Guzmán de Alfarache (Table P-PZ43)
Segundo, Historia de see PQ6398.H38+
Segura, Juan Lorenzo (i.e. Juan Lorenzo, copyist) see PQ6411.L3+
Sem Tob see PQ6433.S2
6433.S5 Sepúlveda, Lorenzo de, fl. 1551 (Table P-PZ40)
6433.S53-.S533 Seven sages of Rome. Spanish (Table P-PZ43)
6433.S54 Sierra, Pedro de la (Table P-PZ40)

Individual authors
Individual authors and works to 1700 -- Continued
Siete sabios de Roma see PQ6433.S53+
6433.S55 Silva, Feliciano de, fl. 1530 (Table P-PZ40)
6433.S57 Silva y Mendoza, Diego de, conde de Salinus, 1564-1630 (Table P-PZ40)
6433.S6 Silveira, Miguel da, ca. 1576-1636? (Table P-PZ40)
6433.S65 Silvestre Rodriguez de Mesa, Gregorio, 1520-1570 (Table P-PZ40)
6433.S7 Solís, Antonio de, 1610-1686 (Table P-PZ40)
Solórzano, Alfonso de Castillo see PQ6321.C55
Soto, Luis Barahona de see PQ6279.B3
6433.S75 Soto de Rojas, Pedro, ca. 1585-1658 (Table P-PZ40)
6433.S78 Stúñiga, Lope de, 15th cent. (Table P-PZ40)
6433.S79 Suárez de Alarcón, Juan, 1579 or 80-1618 (Table P-PZ40)
6433.S793 Suárez de Deza, Vincente, 17th cent. (Table P-PZ40)
6433.S8 Suárez de Figueroa, Cristóbal, fl. 1613 (Table P-PZ40)
6433.S82 Suárez de Robles, Pedro (Table P-PZ40)
6433.S9-.S93 Sumas de historia troyana (Table P-PZ43)
6433.T27 Tapia, Juan de, 15th cent. (Table P-PZ40)
6433.T3 Tárrega, Francisco Agustin, 1554?-1602 (Table P-PZ40)
6433.T36 Taybili, Ybrahim, 16th/17th cent. (Table P-PZ40)
Téllez, Gabriel, 1570?-1648
Pseudonym: Tirso de Molina
6434 Editions
6434.A1 Collected works
6434.A2 Collected plays
6434.A3 Collected novels
6434.A5 Collected poems
6434.A6 Selected works. Selections
6434.A7-Z Separate works, A-Z
Subarrange each by Table P-PZ43
e. g.
6434.B8-.B83 El burlador de Sevilla (Comedia) (Table P-PZ43)
6434.C4-.C43 La celosa de si misma (Comedia) (Table P-PZ43)
6434.C5-.C53 Cigarrales de Toledo (Prose and verse) (Table P-PZ43)
6434.C57-.C573 El colmenero divino (Auto) (Table P-PZ43)
6434.C6-.C63 El condenado por desconfiado (Comedia) (Table P-PZ43)
6434.D7-.D73 Don Gil de las calzas verdes (Comedia) (Table P-PZ43)
6434.N7-.N73 No le arriendo la ganancia (Auto) (Table P-PZ43)
6434.P35-.P353 Panegirico a la casa de Sastago (Poema) (Table P-PZ43)
6434.P7-.P73 La prudencia en la mujer (Comedia) (Table P-PZ43)
6434.T7-.T73 Los tres maridos burlados (Novel) (Table P-PZ43)

Individual authors
Individual authors and works to 1700
Téllez, Gabriel, 1570?-1648.
Editions.
Separate works, A-Z. -- Continued

6434.V5-.V53 La villana de Vallecas (Comedia) (Table P-PZ43)
6435.A-Z Translations. By language, A-Z
6436 Biography and criticism
Teodora, La doncella
see PQ6165.D7 and PQ6439.D7
6437.T3 Teresa, Saint, 1515-1582 (Table P-PZ40)
Originally Teresa de Cepeda
In religion: Teresa de Jesús
Cf. BX890 BX4700.T4
6437.T5 Timoneda, Juan de, d. 1583 (Table P-PZ40)
6437.T6-.T63 Tirano rey Corbanto (Table P-PZ43)
Tirant lo Blanc see PC3937.A+
Tirso de Molina, pseud. see PQ6434+
Torquemada, Antonio de, fl. 16th cent.
6437.T7 Collections and selections. By date
6437.T7A1-.T7A29 Separate works
6437.T7A3-.T7A69 Translations. By language and date
6437.T7A7-.T7Z Biography and criticism
6437.T72 Torre, Alfonso de la, d. 1460? (Table P-PZ40)
6437.T73 Torre, Fernando de la, ca. 1416-ca. 1475 (Table P-PZ40)
6437.T74 Torre, Francisco de la, 1534?-1594 (Table P-PZ40)
Poems published by Quevedo and for a long time ascribed to him
6437.T747 Torres, Alonso de, 16th cent. (Table P-PZ40)
6437.T75 Torres, Jerónimo, fl. 1630 (Table P-PZ40)
6437.T76 Torres Naharro, Bartolomé de, fl. 1517 (Table P-PZ40)
6437.T77-.T773 Tratado de amor (Table P-PZ43)
Tratado de la doctrine see PQ6498.V14
6437.T8-.T813 Tristán de Leonis (Romance) (Table P-PZ43a)
6437.T83-.T833 Triste deleytaçión (Table P-PZ43)
Troyana historia see PQ6398.H5+
6437.T9 Turia, Ricardo de, pseud.? (Table P-PZ40)
6437.U3 Ubeda, Francisco López de (Table P-PZ40 modified)
6437.U3A61-.U3Z458 Separate works. By title
La pícara Justina see PQ6420.P5+
6437.U6 Ulloa y Pereira, Luis de, 1584-1674 (Table P-PZ40)
6437.U7 Urrea, Jerónimo de, 16th cent. (Table P-PZ40)
6437.U8 Urrea y Fernández de Híjar, Pedro Manuel Jiménez de, 1486?-1530 (Table P-PZ40)
6437.V2 Valbuena, Bernardo de, 1568-1627 (Table P-PZ40)
6437.V27 Valdés, Alfonso de, d. 1532 (Table P-PZ40)
6437.V3 Valdés, Juan de, d. 1541 (Table P-PZ40)

Individual authors
Individual authors and works to 1700 -- Continued
6437.V4 Valdivielso, José de, 1560?-1638 (Table P-PZ40)
6437.V6 Valera, Diego de, 1412-1487? (Table P-PZ40)
6437.V65 Valladares de Valdelomar, Juan, 1553-1618? (Table P-PZ40)
6437.V77 Vargas, Bernardo de (Table P-PZ40)
Vega Carpio, Lope Félix de, 1562-1635
Pseudonym: Tomé de Burguillos
6438.A1 Collected works. By date
6438.A2 Selected works. By date
6438.A3 Selections. Anthologies. Quotations
Special classes of works
Comedias
6438.A5 Collected works. By date
6438.A6 Selected plays. By date
6438.A7-.Z4 Special groups, A-Z
6438.C7 Crónicas y leyendas dramáticas de España
6438.M5 Comedias mitológicas e históricas
6438.N7 Comedias novelescas
6438.P3 Comedias pastoriles
6438.S3 Comedias de vidas de santos
(6438.Z5) Posthumously published plays
see PQ6438.A6
6439.A-Z Separate plays, A-Z
For additions to Rennert, see A. Hämel, Beiträge zur Lope de Vega bibliographie in Zeitschrift für romanischen philologie, 1920, pp. 624-633
Cf. H.A. Rennert, Life of Lope de Vega, 1904, p. 389: Deducting the conjectural and doubtful pieces, and those in the Peregrino, there remain 431 comedias that are actually known. A careful search in the public and private libraries of Spain will doubtless increase the number somewhat. List of plays ascribed to Lope in alphabetical order, pp. 490-548
Cf. also H.A. Rennert, Bibliography of the dramatic works of Lope. 2d ed., 1915
6439.A3 El acero de Madrid
6439.A6 Amar sin saber a quién
6439.B59 Las bizarrias de Belisa
6439.B7 El Brazil restituido
6439.B76 La buena guarda
6439.B8 Las burlas veras
6439.C3 El castigo del discreto
6439.C32 El castigo sin venganza
6439.D7 La doncella Teodor
6439.F8 La fuerza lastimosa

Individual authors
Individual authors and works to 1700
Vega Carpio, Lope Félix de, 1562-1635
Special classes of works
Comedias.
Separate plays, A-Z -- Continued
6439.G2 Galan Castrucho
6439.G75 Guanches de Tenerife y Conquista de Canaria
6439.L63 Locos de Valencia
6439.M4 El mejor alcalde, el rey
6439.M7 La moza de cántaro
6439.P6 Porfiar hasta morir
6439.V45 Vellocino de oro
Autos. Coloquios. Loas. Entremeses
6449.A1 Collections
6449.A2 Selected plays
6449.A3 Original editions (and reproductions)
6449.A4 Later editions
Special classes. By date
6449.A5 Autos
6449.A6 Entremeses
6449.A7 Loas
(6449.A9) Posthumously published plays
see PQ6449.A4
6450.A-Z Separate plays, A-Z
(6451) Doubtful or spurious plays
see PQ6458
Minor works
6455 Collections and selections
6455.A1-.A19 Original editions to 1634 (and reprints), A-Z
e. g.
La Circe con otras rimas y prosas
La Filomena, con otras diversas rimas, prosas y versos
La hermosura de Angélica, con otras rimas
Laurel de Apolo, con otras rimas
Rimas humanas y divinas. (Sonnets and Gatomaquia)
Triunfos divinos y otras rimas
6455.A2 Later editions (after 1634)
e.g. Colección de las obras sueltas, 1776-1779
Poems
6455.A3 Collections and selections
Cf. PQ6455
6455.A35 Special groups of poems, A-Z
e. g.
6455.A35R7 Romancero espiritual

	Individual authors
	Individual authors and works to 1700
	Vega Carpio, Lope Félix de, 1562-1635
	Special classes of works
	Poems
(6455.A4)	Posthumously published poems see PQ6455.A3
6455.A5-.A69	Special forms, alphabetically e.g. Epigrams, sonnets, etc.
	Separate poems see PQ6457
	Doubtful and spurious poems see PQ6458
6455.A8	Prose works. Novelas
6455.A9	Collections and selections
	Letters see PQ6470.A2
	Separate works see PQ6457
6457	Separate works other than plays (Comedies, autos, etc.)
	Amarillis (an Eclogue)
6457.A2	Editions
6457.A3	Criticism
	Angélica see PQ6457.H3+
	Arcadia (Prose and verse)
6457.A5	Editions
6457.A6	Criticism
	Arte nuevo de hazer comedias (Poem)
6457.A8	Editions
6457.A9	Criticism
	La Araucana
6457.A93	Editions
6457.A94	Criticism
	Castelvines y Monteses
6457.C2	Editions
6457.C21	Criticism
	La Circe For original edition see PQ6455.A1
6457.C3	Editions
6457.C4	Criticism
	Corona trágica. Vida y muerte de María Estuarda (Epic poem)
6457.C7	Editions
6457.C8	Criticism
	La desdicha por la honra
6457.D2	Editions
6457.D3	Criticism
	Discurso sobre la nueva poesía Cf. PQ6395.A1+ Góngora
6457.D4	Editions
6457.D5	Criticism

Individual authors
Individual authors and works to 1700
Vega Carpio, Lope Félix de, 1562-1635.
Separate works other than plays (Comedies, autos, etc.) -- Continued
La Dorotea, acción en prosa
6457.D6 Editions
6457.D7 Criticism
La Dragontea
Epic poem attacking Sir Francis Drake
6457.D8 Editions
6457.D9 Criticism
Égloga a Claudio
6457.E4 Editions
6457.E5 Criticism
Filis, égloga
6457.F2 Editions
6457.F3 Criticism
La Filomena
Original edition with title: La Filomena, con otras diversas rimas, prosas, y versos, see PQ6455
6457.F4 Editions
6457.F5 Criticism
Las fortunas de Diana
6457.F6 Editions
6457.F7 Criticism
La gatomaquia
Originally published with Lope's Rimas humanas y divinas, 1634
6457.G2 Editions
6457.G3 Criticism
Guzmán el Bravo
First published with Lope's La Circe con prosas, 1624
6457.G7 Editions
6457.G8 Criticism
La hermosura de Angélica (Epic poem)
6457.H3 Editions
6457.H4 Criticism
Hortelano era Bernardo (Poem)
6457.H5 Editions
6457.H52 Criticism
Huerto deshecho (Poem)
6457.H8 Editions
6457.H9 Criticism
Isidro (Poem)
6457.I6 Editions
6457.I7 Criticism

Individual authors
Individual authors and works to 1700
Vega Carpio, Lope Félix de, 1562-1635.
Separate works other than plays (Comedies, autos, etc.) -- Continued
Jerusalem conquistada (Narrative poem)
6457.J3 Editions
6457.J4 Criticism
Laurel de Apolo
Original edition: 1630, with title, Laurel de Apolo, con otras rimas; contains La selva sin amor (Pastoral eclogue)
6457.L3 Editions
6457.L4 Criticism
Pastores de Belén (Prosas y versos divinos)
6457.P3 Editions
6457.P4 Criticism
El peregrino en su patria (Novel)
6457.P5 Editions
6457.P6 Criticism
La prudente venganza
Cf. PQ6455.A1 La Circe, 1624
6457.P7 Editions
6457.P8 Criticism
Selva sin amor
6457.S3 Editions
6457.S4 Criticism
Soliloquios amorosos de un alma a Dios
6457.S7 Editions
6457.S8 Criticism
(6457.T5-.T6) Triunfo de la fee en los reynos de Japón
see BV3443
(6457.T7-.T8) Triunfos divinos
Original edition, with title: Triunfos divinos, con otras rimas, 1625, see PQ6455
6458 Doubtful or spurious works
6458.A1 Collections and selections
6458.A5-.Z3 Separate plays
6458.E8 La estrella de Sevilla
6458.Z4 Other works, A-Z
Don Quijote, 2d part, by Avellaneda (i.e. Lope de Vega?) see PQ6323.A4
Doubtful or spurious poems
6458.Z5 Collections. By date
6458.Z6 Single poems
6458.Z9 Criticism
Translations

Individual authors
Individual authors and works to 1700
Vega Carpio, Lope Félix de, 1562-1635
Translations -- Continued
English
6459.A1 Collected works. By date
6459.A2 Selected works. By date
6459.A3 Selections. By date
6459.A4 Poems. By date
6459.A5-Z Separate works (by original title), A-Z
French
6460.A1 Collected works. By date
6460.A2 Selected works. By date
6460.A3 Selections. By date
6460.A4 Poems. By date
6460.A5-Z Separate works (by original title), A-Z
German
6461.A1 Collected works. By date
6461.A2 Selected works. By date
6461.A3 Selections. By date
6461.A4 Poems. By date
6461.A5-Z Separate works (by original title), A-Z
6462.A-Z Other languages, A-Z
For list of Cutter numbers, see PQ6295.A+
6463 Imitations. Paraphrases. Adaptations
For prominent authors prefer classification under author
6463.A2 Spanish
6463.A5-Z Other
6465 Parodies. Travesties
For prominent authors prefer classification under author
6465.A2 Spanish
6465.A5-Z Other
6466 Translations as subject. Comparative studies, etc.
6467 Illustrations
Illustrated editions classed with other editions
History of Vega's portraits, and illustrations to his works see PQ6477
6468 Lope de Vega and music
Cf. PQ6336
Biography
(6469.A1) Bibliography
see Z8930
6469.A2-.A39 Periodicals. Societies. Collections
6469.A4 Dictionaries, indexes, etc.
General encyclopedic dictionaries only
For dictionaries of characters see PQ6487
For language dictionaries see PQ6492.Z9

Individual authors
Individual authors and works to 1700
Vega Carpio, Lope Félix de, 1562-1635
Biography -- Continued
6469.A5-Z General works. Literary biography. Life and works
Details
6470.A1 Sources. By date of publication
6470.A2 Letters. By date of publication
Miscellaneous
6470.A3 General
6470.A4 Special
Family. Ancestry. Name. Descendants
Cf. PQ6471
Early life. Education
6470.A5 Imprisonment. Exile. Service in the Armada
6471 Love. Marriage. Relation to women
6471.A2 General
6471.A5-Z Special
6471.A6 Antonio Clara (daughter)
6471.I7 Isabel de Alderete (fist wife)
6471.J8 Juana de Guardo (second wife)
6472 Priesthood. Later years and death. Treatment of remains
6473 Relations to contemporaries
6473.A2 General
Prefer PQ6469
6473.A5-Z Individual
6473.C4 Cervantes
6474 Homes and haunts
Prefer PQ6470+
6475 Anniversaries. Centennial celebrations
Cf. PQ6304
6476 Memorials. Testimonials to his genius (other than centennial)
6476.A2 Collections
6476.A5-.Z3 Individual authors - Prose
6476.Z5 Individual authors - Poetry
6477 Iconography. Museums. Exhibitions
6477.A2 General and miscellaneous
6477.A3 Portraits, Medals, etc.
6477.A5 Monuments
Museums. Relics. Exhibitions
6477.A7 General
6477.A8 Special. By place, A-Z
6478 Study and teaching
Cf. PQ6481+
6479 Authorship

Individual authors
Individual authors and works to 1700
Vega Carpio, Lope Félix de, 1562-1635
Biography
Authorship. -- Continued
Manuscripts. Autographs. Sources. Forerunners
Associates. Followers. Circle. School
Prefer PQ6064+ PQ6099+ PQ6106+
Allusions
Prefer PQ6481+
Chronology of works
Criticism and interpretation
History of the study and appreciation of Vega
6481 General (and in Spain)
Special
6482.A2 Contemporaneous criticism and allusions
6482.A3 Later (after 1700)
6482.A5-Z Particular authors and persons, A-Z
e. g.
6482.G8 Grillparzer
6483.A-Z By country, A-Z
e. g.
6483.G5 Germany
Treatises
6485 General
Special topics
(6486) Philosophy. Esthetics, etc.
6487 Characters
6487.A2 General
Prefer PQ6485
6487.A3 Groups or classes
e. g.
6487.A3W6 Women
6487.A5-Z Special, A-Z
e. g.
For characters in special plays, see the play
6487.G7 The "gracioso"
6487.5 Wit and humor
6488 Technique. Dramatic art
6489 Vega and the stage. Representation of Vega's plays on the stage
6489.A2 General
6489.A5-Z Special. By place, A-Z
Cf. PQ6481+ History
6490.A-Z Relation to special subjects, A-Z
Treatment and knowledge, influence, etc.

Individual authors
Individual authors and works to 1700
Vega Carpio, Lope Félix de, 1562-1635
Criticism and interpretation.
Treatises.
Relation to special subjects, A-Z
6490.A7 Art
Cf. PQ6467 PQ6477
6490.D43 Deception
6490.E25 Economics
6490.H5 History. Politics
6490.H7 Honor
6490.L3 Law
6490.L5 Literature
6490.M43 Medicine
6490.M8 Music
6490.M95 Mythology
6490.N3 Nature
6490.P4 Philosophy. Ethics
6490.P63 Poetry
6490.R4 Religion
6490.S3 Science
6491 Interpretation. Textual criticism, etc.
For interpretation and criticism of a particular work, see the work
6492 Language. Style
6492.A2 General
6492.A3 Grammar
6492.A5-.Z3 Versification
6492.Z9 Dictionaries. Concordances
Vega, Garcilaso de la see PQ6391+
Vega, Garcilaso de la, el Inca see PQ6393.G2
6495.V6 Velásquez, Baltasar Mateo, fl. 1626 (Table P-PZ40)
6495.V62 Velazquez de Castillo, Gabriel (Table P-PZ40)
6495.V8 Vélez de Guevara, Juan Crisóstomo, 1611-1675 (Table P-PZ40)
Vélez de Guevara y Dueñas, Luis, 1579-1644
6496.A1 Collected and selected works. By date
6496.A2 Collected and selected works. By editor, A-Z
e.g. Collected autos
6496.A3 Translations. By language, A-Z
6496.A4 Selections
6496.A5-Z Separate works, A-Z
6496.C45 Cerco de Roma por el rey Desiderio
6496.D5 El diablo cojuelo
Cf. PQ1997.D5+ Le Sage, Alain
6496.N6 Los novios de Hornachuelos

Individual authors
Individual authors and works to 1700
Vélez de Guevara y Dueñas, Luis, 1579-1644
Separate works, A-Z
6496.R3 Reinar después de morir
6496.R4 El rey en su imaginación
6497 Biography and criticism
6498.V14 Veragüe, Pedro de, 14th cent.
Author of "Doctrina de la discrición" (in verse) published in the Biblioteca de Autores españoles (vol. 57, pp. 373-378) as an anonymous work entitled "Tractado de la doctrina." It has been wrongly ascribed to Santob
6498.V15-.V153 Versión de Alfonso XI del Roman de Troie (Table P-PZ43)
6498.V16 Vezilla Castellanos, Pedro de la, 16th cent. (Table P-PZ38)
6498.V18 Viana, Antonio de, b. 1578 (Table P-PZ40)
6498.V2 Vicente, Gil, ca. 1470-ca. 1536
Class here only Spanish works762 P-PZ40
Cf. PQ9251+ Portuguese literature
6498.V23-.V233 Vida de San Alejo (Table P-PZ43)
6498.V24-.V243 Vida de San Eustaquio (Table P-PZ43)
6498.V26-.V263 Vida de San Ildefonso (Table P-PZ43)
6498.V28-.V283 Vida de Santa Maria Egipciaqua (Table P-PZ43)
6498.V29-.V293 Vida del Ysopet con sus fabulas hystoriadas (Table P-PZ43)
6498.V3-.V33 Vida y hechos de Estevanillo González (Table P-PZ42)
6498.V34 Vidal Salvador, Manuel, d. 1698 (Table P-PZ40)
6498.V38 Villalobos y Benavides, Diego de, fl. 1598 (Table P-PZ40)
Historian
6498.V4 Villalón, Cristóbal de, 16th cent. (Table P-PZ40 modified)
6498.V4A61-.V4Z458 Separate works. By title
El crotalón de Christóphoro Gnósopho see PQ6393.G6
6498.V43 Villamediana, Juan de Tassis y Peralta, conde de, 1582?-1622 (Table P-PZ40)
6498.V44 Villaviciosa, José de, 1589-1658 (Table P-PZ40)
6498.V45 Villaviciosa, Sebastián de, fl. 1645 (Table P-PZ40)
6498.V48 Villegas, Antonio de, fl. 1551 (Table P-PZ40)
6498.V5 Villegas, Esteban Manuel de, 1589-1669 (Table P-PZ40)
6498.V55 Villena, Enrique de Aragón, marqués de, 1384-1434 (Table P-PZ40)
Violante do Ceo, Sister, 1601-1693 see PQ9253.V6
6498.V7 Virués, Cristóbal de, 1550?-ca. 1614 (Table P-PZ40)
6498.X48 Ximénez Ayllón, Diego, 1530?-1590 (Table P-PZ40)
6498.X5 Ximenez de Enciso, Diego, 1585-1633 (Table P-PZ40)
Yáñez y Rivera, Gerónimo Alcalá see PQ6271.A6
Yepes y Alvarez, Juan, in religion San Juan de la Cruz see PQ6400.J8
6498.Y7-.Y73 Ypólita (Comedy), ca. 1521 (Table P-PZ43)

Individual authors
Individual authors and works to 1700 -- Continued
Zabaleta, Juan de, ca. 1610-1625 see PQ6498.Z4
6498.Z15 Zaida (Moorish poet) (Table P-PZ40)
6498.Z166 Zamora, Lorenzo de, d. 1614 (Table P-PZ40)
6498.Z2 Zapata, Luis, 16th cent. (Table P-PZ40)
6498.Z25 Zárate, Hernando de, fl. 1592 (Table P-PZ40)
Author of Paciencia cristiana, 1593
6498.Z3 Zárate y Catronovo, Fernando de, fl. 1660 (Table P-PZ40)
6498.Z4 Zavaleta, Juan de, b. 1625 (Table P-PZ40)
6498.Z5 Zayas y Sotomayor, María de, 17th cent. (Table P-PZ40)
Zorilla, Francisco de Rojas see PQ6429.R5
Individual authors, 1700-ca. 1868
Subarrange each author by Table P-PZ40 unless otherwise indicated
6500 Anonymous works (Table P-PZ28 modified)
6500.A1A-.A1Z Works without any indication of author, either by symbol or initial. By title, A-Z
6500.A1A44 Alabanza a don Pedro de Cevallos por su feliz expedición al Plata, 1776-77
Abenámar, pseud. see PQ6536.L5
6501.A4 Afán de Ribera, Antonio Joaquín, 1837-1906 (Table P-PZ40)
6501.A5 Afán de Ribera, Fulgencio, fl. 1729 (Table P-PZ40)
6501.A56 Aguilar, Cristóbal de, 1733-1828 (Table P-PZ40)
Aguilera, Ventura Ruiz see PQ6563.R8
6501.A59 Aguirre, Aurelio, 1833-1858 (Table P-PZ40)
6502 Alarcón, Pedro Antonio de, 1833-1891 (Table P-PZ39)
6503.A4 Alas, Leopoldo, 1852-1901 (Table P-PZ40)
Pseudonym: Clarín
6503.A415 Alba y Peña, Juan de (Table P-PZ40)
6503.A426 Alemany, Vicente, 1729-1817 (Table P-PZ40)
Alfonso, Luis see PQ6601.L4
6503.A428 Alenda y Mira, Jenaro, 1816-1893 (Table P-PZ40)
6503.A435 Ali Bey, 1766-1818 (Table P-PZ40)
Alfaro Lafuente, Manuel Ibo, 1828-1885 see PQ6529.I3
6503.A437 Almendros Aguilar, Antonio, 1825-1904 (Table P-PZ40)
6503.A45 Alonso Montejo, José Vicente, 1774-1841 (Table P-PZ40)
6503.A48 Altés y Casals, Francisco, d. 1838 (Table P-PZ40)
Alvarez, Gaspar María de Nava, conde de Noroña see PQ6549.N75
6503.A5 Alvarez, Miguel de los Santos, 1818-1892 (Table P-PZ40)
6503.A52 Alvarez de Cienfuegos, Nicasio, 1764-1809 (Table P-PZ40)
6503.A56 Alvarez de Sotomayor y Abarea, Miguel, 1767-1839 (Table P-PZ40)

Individual authors
Individual authors, 1700-ca. 1868. -- Continued

6503.A57 Alvarez de Toledo y Pellicer de Tovar, Gabriel Patricio, 1662-1714 (Table P-PZ40)
Alvarez Pérez, José see PQ6601.L785
6503.A62 Ana de San Gerónimo, Sister, 1696-1771 (Table P-PZ40)
6503.A64 Añorbe y Corregel, Tomás de, d. 1741 (Table P-PZ40)
6503.A6473 Aparisi y Guijarro, Antonio, 1815-1872 (Table P-PZ40)
6503.A6474 Arana, Vicente de, 1846-1890 (Table P-PZ40)
6503.A6475 Arana Goiri, Sabino de, 1865-1903 (Table P-PZ40)
6503.A649 Ariza, Juan de, 1816-1876 (Table P-PZ40)
6503.A65 Arjona, Manuel María de, 1771-1820 (Table P-PZ40)
6503.A67 Arnao, Antonio, 1828-1889 (Table P-PZ40)
6503.A68 Arolas, Juan, 1805-1849 (Table P-PZ40)
Arriala, Ramón, pseud. see PQ6533
6503.A7 Arriaza, Juan Bautista de, 1770-1837 (Table P-PZ40)
6503.A72 Asensi, Julia de (Table P-PZ40)
Avellaneda, Gertrudis Gómez de see PQ6524+
Avellanet Balaguer, José see PQ6601.V4
Ayala, Adelardo López de see PQ6535
Ayanque, Sim, pseud. see PQ8496.T4
6503.A94 Ayguals de Izco, Wenceslao, 1801-1873 (Table P-PZ40)
6503.A96 Aza, Vital, 1851-1912 (Table P-PZ40)
Badía y Leblich, Domingo see PQ6503.A435
6503.B16 Balaguer, Víctor, 1824-1901 (Table P-PZ40)
6503.B2 Balart, Federico, 1831-1905 (Table P-PZ40)
6503.B23 Baralt, Rafael María, 1810-1860 (Table P-PZ40)
Barranco y Caro, Mariano see PQ6603.A73
6503.B27 Barrantes y Moreno, Vicente, 1829-1898 (Table P-PZ40)
Bartrina, Joaquín María see PQ6603.A77
6503.B3 Bécquer, Gustavo Adolfo, 1836-1870 (Table P-PZ40)
6503.B457 Benegassi y Luxán, Joseph Joachin, 1707-1770 (Table P-PZ40)
6503.B5 Bermúdez de Castro, José (Table P-PZ40)
6503.B6 Bermúdez de Castro, Salvador, 1817-1883 (Table P-PZ40)
Blanco, José María see PQ6574.W5
6504 Blasco, Eusebio, 1844-1903 (Table P-PZ39)
Böhl de Faber, Cecilia Francisca Josefa see PQ6509
6505.B5 Bonilla y Sánchez, Jacinto (Table P-PZ40)
6505.B68 Botana, Crispín, 1838-1900 (Table P-PZ40)
6506 Bretón de los Herreros, Manuel, 1796-1873 (Table P-PZ39)
6508.B8 Burgos, Javier de, 1842-1902 (Table P-PZ40)
6508.C33 Caballero, Fermín Agosto, 1800-1876 (Table P-PZ40)
6509 Caballero, Fernán, pseud. (Cecilia Bohl de Faber, 1796-1877) (Table P-PZ39)
6510.C26 Cabanyes, Manuel de, 1808-1833 (Table P-PZ40)

Individual authors
Individual authors, 1700-ca. 1868. -- Continued

6510.C3 Cadalso, José, 1741-1782 (Table P-PZ40)
6510.C7 Campillo y Correa, Narciso, 1838?-1900 (Table P-PZ40)
6511 Campoamor y Campoosorio, Ramón María de las Mercedes de, 1817-1901 (Table P-PZ39)
6512.C14 Camprodón y Safont, Francisco, 1816-1870 (Table P-PZ40)
6512.C146 Cañizares, José de, 1676-1750 (Table P-PZ40)
Cano y Masas, Leopoldo see PQ6605.A725
6512.C149 Cánovas del Castillo, Antonio, 1828-1897 (Table P-PZ40)
6512.C15 Cansino y Casafondo, Ramón, fl. 1751 (Table P-PZ40)
6512.C16 Carnerero, José María de (Table P-PZ40)
Carillo, Alvaro, pseud. see PQ6512.C22
6512.C18 Castañiera, Ramón de (Table P-PZ40)
Pseudonym: César Romano
6512.C2 Castelar y Ripoll, Emilio, 1832-1899 (Table P-PZ40)
Castillo, Juan Ignacio González del see PQ6526.G6
6512.C22 Castillo, Rafael del 19th cent. (Table P-PZ40)
Pseudonym: Alvaro Carillo
Castro, Francisco de, fl. 1729 see PQ7296.C3
Castro, Francisco Sánchez de see PQ6563.S65
Castro, José Bermúdez de see PQ6503.B5
6512.C226 Castro, Rosalía de, 1837-1885 (Table P-PZ40)
Pseudonym: Alvaro Carillo
Castro, Salvador Bermúdez de see PQ6503.B6
6512.C23 Castro y Rossi, Adolfo de, 1823-1898 (Table P-PZ40)
6512.C24 Castro y Serrano, José de, 1829-1896 (Table P-PZ40)
Celenio, Inarco, pseud. see PQ6541+
6512.C27 Cerdá y Rico, Francisco, 1739-1800 (Table P-PZ40)
6512.C3 Céspedes y Monroy, Atanasio (Table P-PZ40)
Cienfuegos, Nicasio Alvarez de see PQ6503.A52
Clarín, pseud. see PQ6503.A4
6512.C55 Coello de Portugal y Pacheco, Carlos, 1850-1888 (Table P-PZ40)
6512.C6 Coll, Gaspar Fernando (Table P-PZ40)
6512.C628 Comella, Luciano Francisco, 1751-1812 (Table P-PZ40)
6512.C65 Córdova, Pedro Tomás de (Table P-PZ40)
6512.C67 Coronado, Carolina, 1823-1911 (Table P-PZ40)
6512.C7 Corsini y Fontaine, Luis, d. 1878 (Table P-PZ40)
6513 Cruz, Ramón de la, 1731-1794 (Table P-PZ39)
El curioso parlante, pseud. see PQ6539
6515.D3 Delgado, Antonio, 18th cent. (Table P-PZ40)
6515.D5 Díaz, José María, d. 1888 (Table P-PZ40)
Díez Serra, narciso Sáenz see PQ6566
Doncel, Carlos García see PQ6523.G2833
El duende satírico, pseud. see PQ6533

Individual authors
Individual authors, 1700-ca. 1868 -- Continued

	Echegaray, Miguel see PQ6609.C6
6516-6517	Echegaray y Eizaguirre, José, 1832 or 3-1916 (Table P-PZ36) Pseudonym (Anagram): Jorge Hayaseca. Author of El gran Galeoto.
6518	Ech - Eg
6519	Eguílaz y Eguílaz, Luis de, 1830-1874 (Table P-PZ39)
6520.E4	Eguílaz y Yanguas, Leopoldo de, 1829-1906 (Table P-PZ40)
6520.E5	Enciso Castrillón, Félix (Table P-PZ40)
6520.E58	Esacalante y Prieto, Amós de, 1831-1902 (Table P-PZ40)
6520.E6	Escóiquiz, Juan de, d. 1820 (Table P-PZ40)
6520.E7	Escosura, Patricio de la, 1807-1878 (Table P-PZ40)
6520.E9	Espinosa y Quesada (Table P-PZ40)
6521-6522	Espronceda, José de, 1808-1842 (Table P-PZ36)
	Espronceda y Lara, José see PQ6521+
6523.E7	Estébanez Calderón, Serafín, 1799-1867 (Table P-PZ40)
6523.F2	Farigola y Domínguez, Antonio (Table P-PZ40)
6523.F3	Feijóo y Montenegro, Benito Jerónimo, 1675-1764 (Table P-PZ40)
6523.F34	Felíu y Codina, José, 1839-1914 (Table P-PZ40)
6523.F345	Fenollosa, Amalia, 1825-1869 (Table P-PZ40)
	Fernán Caballero see PQ6509
6523.F36	Fernández Bremón, José, 1839-1914 (Table P-PZ40)
	Fernández de Moratín, Leandro see PQ6541+
	Fernández de Moratín, Nicolás see PQ6549.M2
6523.F3644	Fernández Flórez, Juan Francisco, d. 1886 (Table P-PZ40)
	Fernández Shaw, Carlos see PQ6611.E66
	Fernández Villegas, Francisco see PQ6611.E715
6523.F37	Fernández y González, Manuel, 1821-1888 (Table P-PZ40)
6523.F375	Ferrán y Forniés, Augusto, 1836-1880 (Table P-PZ40)
	Ferrari, Emilio, 1853-1907 see PQ6611.E74
	Fidel, Tío, pseud. see PQ6561.R6
	Fígaro, pseud. see PQ6533
6523.F385	Flores, Antonio, 1821-1865 (Table P-PZ40)
6523.F39	Flores Arenas, Francisco, 1801-1877 (Table P-PZ40)
6523.F4	Floridablanca, José Moñino y Redondo, conde de, 1728-1808 (Table P-PZ40)
6523.F5	Forner, Juan Bautista Pablo, 1756-1797 (Table P-PZ40)
6523.F54	Forteza, Guillermo, 1830-1873 (Table P-PZ40)
6523.F555	Foz, Braulio, 1791-1865 (Table P-PZ40)
6523.F6	Frávega, Antonio Angel de (Table P-PZ40)
6523.F7	Frontaura y Vásquez, Carlos, 1834-1910 (Table P-PZ40)
6523.F8	Fulgosio, Fernando, 1831-1873 (Table P-PZ40)

Individual authors
Individual authors, 1700-ca. 1868. -- Continued

6523.G22 Gallardo, Bartolomé José, 1776-1852 (Table P-PZ40)
6523.G23 Gallego, Juan Nicasio, 1777-1853 (Table P-PZ40)
6523.G245 Galvez, Maria Rosa, 1768-1806 (Table P-PZ40)
6523.G26 Gandarias, Perfecto (Table P-PZ40)
García, Juan, pseud. see PQ6520.E58
6523.G265 García Carreño, Leonardo (Table P-PZ40)
6523.G27 García de la Huerta, Vicente Antonio, 1734-1787 (Table P-PZ40)
García de Quevedo, José Heriberto, 1819-1871 see PQ8549.G28
6523.G28 García del Canto, Antonio, 1824-1886 (Table P-PZ40)
García del Real, Luciano see PQ6613.A757
6523.G2833 García Doncel, Carlos (Table P-PZ40)
6523.G2835 García Gutiérrez, Antonio, 1813-1884 (Table P-PZ40)
García-Herraiz, Luis, b. 1844 see PQ6563.R78
6523.G284 García Malo, Ignacio (Table P-PZ40)
6523.G287 García y Tassara, Gabriel, 1817-1875 (Table P-PZ40)
Gil Ricardo, 1855-1907 see PQ6613.I38
6523.G53 Gil y Carrasco, Enrique, 1815-1846 (Table P-PZ40)
Gil y Luengo, Constantino see PQ6613.I5
6523.G6 Gil y Zárate, Antonio, 1793-1861 (Table P-PZ40)
Gimeno de Flaquer, Concepción see PQ6613.I8
6523.G7 Goizueta, José María de (Table P-PZ40)
6524-6525 Gómez de Avellaneda y Arteaga, Gertrudis, 1814-1873 (Table P-PZ36)
Pseudonym: La peregrina. Born in Cuba, lived in Spain after 1836
6526.G3 González, Diego Tadeo, 1731-1794 (Table P-PZ40)
6526.G4 González de Tejada, José (Table P-PZ40)
6526.G6 González del Castillo, Juan Ignaco, 1763-1800 (Table P-PZ40)
6526.G7 González Villa-Amil, Antonio, 1842- (Table P-PZ40)
Gorostiza, Manuel Eduardo de, 1789-1851 see PQ7297.G7
6526.G75 Grassi, Angela, 1826-1883 (Table P-PZ40)
6526.G77 Gregoria Francisca de Santa Teresa, 1653-1736 (Table P-PZ40)
6526.G794 Guerrero, Manuel, 18th cent. (Table P-PZ40)
6526.G8 Guillén Buzarán, Juan, 1817-1892 (Table P-PZ40)
6526.G86 Gutiérrez de Alba, José María, 1822-1897 (Table P-PZ40)
6526.G9 Gutiérrez de Vegas, Fernando, 18th cent. (Table P-PZ40)
6527-6528 Hartzenbusch, Juan Eugenio, 1806-1880 (Table P-PZ36)
Hayaseca, Jorge, pseud. see PQ6516+
6529.H3 Hernández y Fernández, Esteban (Table P-PZ40)
Herreros, Manuel Bretón de los see PQ6506

Individual authors
Individual authors, 1700-ca. 1868 -- Continued
Huerta, Vicente García de la see PQ6523.G27
6529.H75 Húmara y Salamanca, Rafael (Table P-PZ40)
6529.H8 Hurtado, Antonio, 1825-1878 (Table P-PZ40)
For Romancero de Hernán Cortés (Poem) see F1230
Cf. PQ6550+ Núñez de Arce, his collaborator
6529.I3 Ibo, Alfaro Lafuente Manuel, 1828-1885 (Table P-PZ40)
6529.I5 Iglesias de la Casa, José, 1748-1791 (Table P-PZ40)
6529.I8 Iriarte y Oropesa, Tomás de, 1750-1791 (Table P-PZ40)
6530-6531 Isla, José Francisco de, 1703-1781 (Table P-PZ36)
Pseudonym: Is-salps, Joaquín Federico; Lobón de Salazar, Francisco.
6532.J7 Jovellanos, Gaspar Melchor de, 1744-1811 (Table P-PZ40)
6532.J83 Juan de la Anunciación, fray, 1691-1764 (Table P-PZ40)
6532.L2 Labaila y González, Jacinto, 1833-1895 (Table P-PZ40)
6532.L27 Lamarque de Novoa, José, 1828-1904 (Table P-PZ40)
Larmig, pseud. see PQ6538.M35
6532.L4 Larra, Luis Mariano de, 1830-1901 (Table P-PZ40)
6533 Larra, Mariano José de, 1809-1837 (Table P-PZ39)
Larrañaga, Gregorio Romero see PQ6563.R5
6534.L3 León y Mansilla, José, 18th cent. (Table P-PZ40)
6534.L4 Lista y Aragón, Alberto, 1775-1848 (Table P-PZ40)
6534.L45 Llanos y Alcaraz, Adolfo, 1834-1894 (Table P-PZ40)
6534.L5 Llofríu y Sagrera, Eleuterio, 1835-1894 (Table P-PZ40)
6534.L55 Llorente y Olivárez, Teodoro, 1836-1911 (Table P-PZ40)
6534.L6 Lobo, Eugenio Gerardo, 1679-1750 (Table P-PZ40)
Lobón de Salazar, Francisco, pseud. see PQ6530+
6534.L66 López, Bernardo, 1838-1870 (Table P-PZ40)
6535 López de Ayala, Adelardo, 1828-1879 (Table P-PZ39)
6536.L28 López de Ayala, Ignacio, fl. 1776 (Table P-PZ40)
6536.L29 López de Sedano, Juan José, 1729-1801 (Table P-PZ40)
6536.L3 López del Plano, Juan Francisco, 1758?-1808 (Table P-PZ40)
6536.L4 López Escovar y Carbonera, José (Table P-PZ40)
6536.L5 López Pelegrin, Santos, 1801-1846 (Table P-PZ40)
6536.L6 López Soler, Ramón, d. 1836 (Table P-PZ40)
Luceño, Tomás see PQ6621.U35
6536.L83 Lucas, Ventura (Table P-PZ40)
6536.L9 Luzán, Ignacio, 1702-1754 (Table P-PZ40)
La poética see PN1048
Macías Picavea, Ricardo see PQ6623.A35
6536.M25 Mañer, Salvador, Joseph, d. 1751 (Table P-PZ40)
6536.M3 Marchena, José, 1768-1821 (Table P-PZ40)
María do Ceo, Sister see PQ9231.M4
6536.M37 Mármol, Manuel María del, 1769-1840 (Table P-PZ40)
6536.M4 Marqués y Espejo, Antonio, b. 1762 (Table P-PZ40)

Individual authors
Individual authors, 1700-ca. 1868. -- Continued
6536.M6 Martínez Colomer, Vicente, 1763-1820 (Table P-PZ40)
Martínez de Eguílaz, Luis see PQ6519
6537 Martínez de la Rosa, Francisco, 1787-1862 (Table P-PZ39)
6538.M2 Martínez Monroy, José, 1837-1861 (Table P-PZ40)
6538.M3 Martínez Villergas, Juan, 1817-1894 (Table P-PZ40)
6538.M35 Martínez y Guertero, Luis Antonio, d. 1874 (Table P-PZ40)
6538.M37 Massanés, Josefa, 1811-1887 (Table P-PZ40)
6538.M4 Mata y Fontanet, Pedro, 1810?-1877 (Table P-PZ40)
6538.M46 Megía, Félix, d. 1853 (Table P-PZ40)
6538.M5 Meléndez Valdés, Juan, 1754-1817 (Table P-PZ40)
6539 Mesonero y Romanos, Ramón de, 1803-1882 (Table P-PZ39)
6540.M2 Miñano y Bedoya, Sebastián de, 1779-1845 (Table P-PZ40)
Miranda, Gregorio Pérez de, pseud. see PQ6536.L6
6540.M4 Moja y Bolívar, Federico, 1842-1897 (Table P-PZ40)
6540.M45 Molíns, Mariano Roca de togores, marqués de, 1812-1889 (Table P-PZ40)
6540.M47 Moncín, Luis (Table P-PZ40)
6540.M5 Monreal y Jiménez Embún, Julio, 1839-1890 (Table P-PZ40)
Monroy, José Martínez see PQ6538.M2
6540.M6 Montengón, Pedro de, 1745-1825? (Table P-PZ40)
6540.M63 Montero y Moralejo, Félix, 1820-1885 (Table P-PZ40)
6540.M66 Montiano y Luyando, Agustín de, 1697-1764 (Table P-PZ40)
6540.M7 Mor de Fuentes, José, 1762-1848 (Table P-PZ40)
6540.M8 Mora, José Joaquín de, 1783-1864 (Table P-PZ40)
6540.M9 Morales, Benigno, d. 1824 (Table P-PZ40)
Moratín, Leandro Fernández de, 1760-1828
Editions
6541.A1 Collected works. By date
6541.A12 Posthumous works. By date
6541.A2 Selected works. By date
6541.A3 Selections. Anthologies, etc. By date
6541.A5-.Z4 Separate works, A-Z
e. g.
6541.C6 La comedia nueva
6541.S5 El sí de las niñas
6541.Z5 Spurious or doubtful works, A-Z
(6541.Z7) Translations of foreign works. By author, A-Z
6542.A-Z Translations. By language, A-Z
Biography and criticism
6542.A2-.A39 Periodicals and societies
6542.A5-Z General works. Literary biography. Life and works

Individual authors
Individual authors, 1700-ca. 1868
Moratín, Leandro Fernández de, 1760-1828 -- Continued
Criticism and interpretation
6544 General
6545 Special
Sources
6545.A1 General
6545.A2 Individual, A-Z
e.g. Molière
6545.A5-.A7 Other
6546 Textual criticism
6548 Language. Grammar. Style
6548.Z5 Dictionaries. Indexes, etc.
6549.M2 Moratín, Nicolás Fernández de, 1737-1780 (Table P-PZ40)
Munguía, Juan Pérez de, pseud. see PQ6533
6549.M8 Muñoz, Antonio, fl. 1739 (Table P-PZ40)
Nava Alvarez, Gaspar María de, conde de see PQ6549.N75
6549.N33 Navarro, Francisca, fl. 1827-1829 (Table P-PZ40)
6549.N35 Navarro Villoslada, Francisco, 1818-1895 (Table P-PZ40)
6549.N4 Nenclares, Eustaquio María de (Table P-PZ40)
Niporesas, Andrés, pseud. see PQ6533
Nocedal y Romea, Ramón see PQ6625.O3
6549.N64 Nogues, Romualdo, 1824-1889 (Table P-PZ40)
6549.N7 Nombela y Tabares, Julio, 1836- (Table P-PZ40)
6549.N75 Noroña, Gaspar María de Nava Alvarez, conde de, 1760-1815 (Table P-PZ40)
6549.N8 Novo y Colson, Pedro de, 1846- (Table P-PZ40)
6550-6551 Nuñez de Arce, Gaspar, 1834-1903 (Table P-PZ36)
Cf. PQ6529.H8 Hurtado, Antonio, collaborator of Núñez in certain dramas
6552.O4 Olona Gaeta, José (Table P-PZ40)
6552.O5 Olona Gaeta, Luis, 1823-1863 (Table P-PZ40)
6552.O65 Orbegozo y Jugo, Matilde, 1837-1891 (Table P-PZ40)
6552.O7 Orellana, Francisco José de, 1820-1891 (Table P-PZ40)
Ortega Munilla, José see PQ7389.O75
6552.O8 Ortega y Frías, Ramón, 1825-1883 (Table P-PZ40)
6552.O87 Ossorio y Bernard, Manuel, 1839-1904 (Table P-PZ40)
6552.O89 Ossuna y Saviñon, Manuel (Table P-PZ40)
6553 Palacio, Manuel del, 1832-1906 (Table P-PZ39)
Palacio Valdés, Armando see PQ6629.A5
Pardo, Felipe see PQ8497.P28
6554.P2 Pardo de Figueroa, Mariano, 1828-1918 (Table P-PZ40)
6554.P215 Parreño, Florencio Luis (Table P-PZ40)
6554.P218 Pastor Díaz, Nicomedes, 1811-1863 (Table P-PZ40)
6554.P22 Pastorfido, Miguel, d. 1877 (Table P-PZ40)

Individual authors

Individual authors, 1700-ca. 1868. -- Continued

6554.P23 Patxot, Fernando, 1812-1859 (Table P-PZ40)

Pelegrín, Santos López see PQ6536.L5

6554.P3 Pereda, José María de, 1833-1906 (Table P-PZ40)

La peregrin, pseud. see PQ6524+

Pérez de Miranda, Gregorio, pseud. see PQ6536.L6

Pérez de Munguía, Juan, pseud. see PQ6533

6554.P5 Pérez del Camino, Manuel Norberto, 1783-1842 (Table P-PZ40)

6554.P6 Pérez Escrich, Enrique, 1829-1897 (Table P-PZ40)

Pérez Ferrara, Emilio see PQ6611.E74

6555 Pérez Galdós, Benito, 1845-1920 (Table P-PZ39)

6556.P23 Pérez Zaragoza, Agustín (Table P-PZ40)

Pilar Sinués, María del see PQ6567.S5

6556.P3 Pina Domínguez, Mariano, d. 1895 (Table P-PZ40)

6556.P4 Pinazo, Antonio, 1750-1820 (Table P-PZ40)

6556.P5 Polo y Peyrolón, Manuel, 1846-1918 (Table P-PZ40)

6556.P52 Ponz, D. Mariano (Table P-PZ40)

6556.P55 Porcel y Salablanca, José Antonio, 1715-1794 (Table P-PZ40)

6556.P6 Príncipe y Vidaud, Miguel Agustín, 1811-1863 (Table P-PZ40)

6556.P7 Puig Pérez, José, 1845-1897 (Table P-PZ40)

6556.P72 Puigblanch, Antonio, 1775-1840 (Table P-PZ40)

6556.P8 Pusalgas y Guerris, Ignacio Miguel (Table P-PZ40)

6556.Q6 Querol, Vicente Wenceslao, 1836-1889 (Table P-PZ40)

Quevedo, José Heriberto García de see PQ8549.G28

6557-6558 Quintana, Manuel José, 1772-1857 (Table P-PZ36)

Ramón de la Cruz y Cano see PQ6513

6559.R2 Ramos Carrión, Miguel, 1845-1915 (Table P-PZ40)

Cf. PQ6503.A96 Aza Vital, joint author

6559.R23 Rebollo Parras, Francisco, d. 1879 (Table P-PZ40)

6559.R24 Reinoso, Félix José, 1772-1841 (Table P-PZ40)

6559.R28 Retes, Francisco Luis de, 1822-1901 (Table P-PZ40)

6559.R4 Revilla y Moreno, Manuel de la, 1846-1881 (Table P-PZ40)

6559.R44 Rey, Fermín del, fl. 1773-1792 (Table P-PZ40)

6559.R45 Reynosa, Pedro de, fl. 1727 (Table P-PZ40)

6559.R5 Ribero y Larrea, Alonso Bernardo, 18th cent. (Table P-PZ40)

6559.R6 Riego y Núñez, Miguel del (Table P-PZ40)

Ripalda, Salvador Bermúdez de Castro y Díez, duque de see PQ6503.B6

6559.R8 Ripoll Fernández de Urueña Ponce de León, Domingo María, d. 1775 (Table P-PZ40)

6560 Rivas, Angel de Saavedra, duque de, 1791-1865 (Table P-PZ39)

Individual authors
Individual authors, 1700-ca. 1868. -- Continued

6561.R5 Rivas, Enrique Ramírez de Saavedra cueto Remírez de Baquedano y Ortega, 4. duque de, 1826-1914 (Table P-PZ40)
6561.R55 Rivera, Luis, 1826-1872 (Table P-PZ40)
6561.R6 Robello y Vasconi, Francisco (Table P-PZ40)
Roca de Togores, Mariano, marqués de Molíns see PQ6540.M45
6561.R64 Roda, Nicolás de, 1802-1878 (Table P-PZ40)
Rodriguez de Ureta, Antonia see PQ6633.O4
6562 Rodríguez y Díaz Rubí, Tomás, 1817-1890 (Table P-PZ39)
Romano, César de, pseud. see PQ6512.C18
6563.R5 Romero Larrañaga, Gregorio, 1815-1872 (Table P-PZ40)
6563.R73 Ros de Olano, Antonio, 1802-1887 (Table P-PZ40)
Rotalde, Nicolás Santiago de see PQ6563.S7
Rubí, Tomás Rodriguez y Díaz see PQ6562
6563.R78 Ruiz, Juan, b. 1844 (Table P-PZ40)
6563.R8 Ruiz Aguilera, Ventura, 1820-1881 (Table P-PZ40)
6563.R85 Ruiz y Pérez, Manuel (Table P-PZ40)
6563.S15 Sáez de Melgar, Faustina, 1834-1895 (Table P-PZ40)
6563.S2 Salas, Francisco Gregorio de, 1740-1808 (Table P-PZ40)
Salazar, Francisco Lobón de, pseud. see PQ6530+
6563.S25 Salazar y Hontiveros, Juan José de, 18th cent. (Table P-PZ40)
6563.S3 Saldueña, Alonso de Solís Folch de Cardona Rodríguez de las Varillas, conde de, fl. 1754 (Table P-PZ40)
6563.S4 Sallent, Mariana, 1665- (Table P-PZ40)
6563.S5 Samaniego, Félix María, 1745-1801 (Table P-PZ40)
6563.S6 Sánchez Barbero, Francisco, 1764-1819 (Table P-PZ40)
6563.S65 Sánchez de Castro, Francisco, 1847-1889 (Table P-PZ40)
6563.S7 Santiago de Rotalde, Nicolás, d. 1834 (Table P-PZ40)
Santos Alvarez, Miguel de los see PQ6503.A5
Santoval, Domingo de see PQ6635.A66
6564 Sanz, Eulogio Florentino, 1825?-1881 (Table P-PZ39)
6565.S3 Seco y Shelley, Manuel, d. 1877 (Table P-PZ40)
6565.S4 Selgas y Carrasco, José, 1822-1882 (Table P-PZ40)
Sellés, Eugenio see PQ6613.E7
6565.S5 Sepúlveda y Planter, Ricardo, 1846-1909 (Table P-PZ40)
6566 Serra, Narciso, 1830-1877 (Table P-PZ39)
6567.S25 Sierra Valenzuela, Enrique, 1845-1880 (Table P-PZ40)
6567.S3 Silió y Gutiérez, Evaristo, 1841-1874 (Table P-PZ40)
6567.S39 Silvela, Manuel, 1781-1832 (Table P-PZ40)
6567.S4 Silvela, Manuel, 1830-1892 (Table P-PZ40)
6567.S5 Sinués de Marco, María del Pilar, 1835-1893 (Table P-PZ40)
6567.S55 Solís, Dionisio, 1774-1834 (Table P-PZ40)

Individual authors
Individual authors, 1700-ca. 1868

	El solitario, pseud. see PQ6523.E7
6567.S7	Somoza y Muñoz, José, 1781-1852 (Table P-PZ40)
6567.S8	Suárez Bravo, Ceferino, 1825-1896 (Table P-PZ40)
	Taboada, Luis see PQ6637.A2
6568-6569	Tamayo y Baus, Manuel, 1829-1898 (Table P-PZ36)
6570.T2	Tapia, Eugenio de, 1776-1860 (Table P-PZ40)
6570.T3	Tárrago y Mateos, Torcuato, d. 1889 (Table P-PZ40)
	Tassara, Gabriel García y see PQ6523.G287
6570.T4	Terrín, Buenaventura, fl. 1736 (Table P-PZ40)
	Thebussem, Doctor see PQ6554.P2
6570.T46	Toca Velasco, José Ignacio de, fl. 1734 (Table P-PZ40)
6570.T464	Togores, Mariano Antonio, 1769-1808 (Table P-PZ40)
6570.T467	Torniello, Marcos del (Table P-PZ40)
6570.T5	Torre Marín, conde de, fl. 1555 (Table P-PZ40)
6570.T57	Torres, Tomás Hermenegildo de las (Table P-PZ40)
6570.T6	Torres y Villarroel, Diego de, 1693?-1770 (Table P-PZ40)
6570.T7	Trigueros, Cándido María, 1736-1801? (Table P-PZ40)
6570.T82	Trueba y Cosío, Joaquín Telesforo de, 1799?-1835 (Table P-PZ40)
6571	Trueba y la Quintana, Antonio Manuel María de, 1819-1889 (Table P-PZ39)
	Urrecha, Federico see PQ6639.R7
6572.V3	Valbuena y Gutiérrez, Antonio de, 1844-1929 (Table P-PZ40)
6573	Valera y Alcalá Galiano, Juan, 1824-1905 (Table P-PZ39)
6574.V2	Valladares y Garriga, Luis, 19th cent. (Table P-PZ40)
6574.V25	Valladares y Saavedra, Ramón de, 1824-1901 (Table P-PZ40)
6574.V26	Valladares y Sotomayor, Antonio, 18th cent. (Table P-PZ40)
6574.V29	Valverde y Perales, b. 1848 (Table P-PZ40)
6574.V295	Vargas Ponce, José, 1760-1821 (Table P-PZ40)
6574.V297	Vayo, Estanislao de Cosca, 1804-1864 (Table P-PZ40)
6574.V3	Vega, Ricardo de la, 1839?-1910 (Table P-PZ40)
6574.V33	Vega, Ventura de la, 1807-1865 (Table P-PZ40)
6574.V34	Velarde, Fernando, 1821-1880 (Table P-PZ40)
	Velarde, José, 1849-1892 see PQ6641.E55
6574.V36	Vicetto, Benito, 1824-1878 (Table P-PZ40)
6574.V4	Viedma, Juan Antonio de, 1831-1868 (Table P-PZ40)
6574.V42	Viera y Clavijo, José de, 1738?-1799 (Table P-PZ40)
6574.V425	Viera y Clavijo, María Joaquina, 1737-1819 (Table P-PZ40)
6574.V43	Vilaplana, Melchor, 1781-1835 (Table P-PZ40)
(6574.V45)	Villanueva y Ochoa, Dionisio see PQ6567.S55
	Villegas, Francisco Fernández see PQ6611.E715

Individual authors
Individual authors, 1700-ca. 1868 -- Continued
Villergas, Juan Martínez see PQ6538.M3
Villoslada, Francisco Navarro, 1818-1895 see PQ6549.N35
6574.V6 Virués y Spínola, José Joaquín de, 1770-1840 (Table P-PZ40)
6574.W5 White, Joseph Blanco, 1775-1841 (Table P-PZ40)
Originally José María Blanco y Crespo
6574.Y3 Yago, Pedro Manuel (Table P-PZ40)
6574.Z3 Zafra, Antonio Enrique de, d. 1875 (Table P-PZ40)
6574.Z4 Zamora, Antonio de, d. 1728 (Table P-PZ40)
6574.Z5 Zea, Francisco, 1825-1857 (Table P-PZ40)
6574.Z57 Zernadas y Castro, Diego Antonio, 1702-1777 (Table P-PZ40)
Zorrilla, José, 1817-1893 see PQ6575
6575 Zorrilla y Moral, José, 1817-1893 (Table P-PZ39)
6576.Z6 Zumel, Enrique, 1822-1897 (Table P-PZ40)
Individual authors, 1868-1960
Subarrange each author by Table P-PZ40 unless otherwise specified
The author number is determined by the second letter of the name. The names of many minor writers are omitted
6600 Anonymous works (Table P-PZ28)
6601 A - Az
6601.B3 Abati y Díaz, Joaquín (Table P-PZ40)
6601.C3 Acebal, Francisco López (Table P-PZ40)
6601.C4 Acevedo, José María (Table P-PZ40)
6601.C55 Acosta, José María de, 1881- (Table P-PZ40)
6601.G8 Aguilar Catena, Juan, 1888- (Table P-PZ40)
Alas, Leopoldo see PQ6503.A4
6601.L2 Alberti, Rafael, 1902- (Table P-PZ40)
6601.L25 Alcover y Maspons, Juan, 1854-1926 (Table P-PZ40)
6601.L4 Alfonso, Luis, 1845-1892 (Table P-PZ40)
6601.L7 Altamira y Crevea, Rafael, 1866- (Table P-PZ40)
Alvarez, Enrique García see PQ6613.A75
6601.L785 Alvarez Pérez, José, fl. 1875 (Table P-PZ40)
6601.L79 Alvarez Quintero, Joaquin, 1873- (Table P-PZ40)
6601.L8 Alvarez, Quintero, Serafin, 1871- (Table P-PZ40)
6601.M62 Amorós, Juan Bautista, 1856-1912 (Table P-PZ40)
6601.N3 Andrade, Juan Bautista (Table P-PZ40)
Andrenio, pseud. see PQ6613.O35
6601.N35 Andrés Alvarez, Valentin, 1891- (Table P-PZ40)
6601.N4 Andrés de Prada, José, 1892- (Table P-PZ40)
6601.N7 Antón del Olmet, Fernando de, marqués de Dos-Fuentes, 1872- (Table P-PZ40)
6601.N75 Antón del Olmet, Luis, 1886- (Table P-PZ40)
Aparicio, Manuel Ciges see PQ6605.I5

Individual authors
Individual authors, 1868-1960
A - Az -- Continued

6601.R3 Aranaz Castellanos, Manuel, 1875-1925 (Table P-PZ40)
6601.R37 Arderíus, Joaquín, 1888- (Table P-PZ40)
6601.R5 Arniches y Barrera, Carlos, 1866- (Table P-PZ40)
6601.R7 Arteaga y Pereira, Fernando de (Table P-PZ40)
6601.S45 Asensio Más, Ramón (Table P-PZ40)
6601.U2 Aub, Max (Table P-PZ40)
6601.V4 Avellanet Balaguer, José, fl. 1887 (Table P-PZ40)
6601.Z3 Azaña, Manuel, 1880- (Table P-PZ40)
Azorín, 1873-1967 see PQ6623.A816
6603 B - Bz
6603.A2 Bacarisse y Casulá, Mauricio, 1895-1931 (Table P-PZ40)
Barga,Corpus, 1887-1975 see PQ6613.A7569
6603.A7 Baroja, Pío, 1872-1956 (Table P-PZ40)
6603.A73 Barranco y Caro, Mariano, 1850- (Table P-PZ40)
6603.A75 Barrett, Rafael (Table P-PZ40)
6603.A77 Bartrina, Joaquín María, 1850-1880 (Table P-PZ40)
6603.A9 Bayo, Ciro, 1860- (Table P-PZ40)
6603.E4 Belda, Joaquín, 1883- (Table P-PZ40)
6603.E6 Benavente y Martínez, Jacinto, 1866- (Table P-PZ40)
6603.E7 Bergua, Juan Bautista (Table P-PZ40)
6603.E79 Betancourt Cabrera, José, 1874-1950 (Table P-PZ40)
6603.E8 Betanzo, Francisca (Table P-PZ40)
Bhér, Alejandro, pseud. see PQ6623.A94
6603.L2 Blasco Ibáñez, Vicente, 1867-1928 (Table P-PZ40)
6603.O7 Borrás y Bermejo, Tomás, 1891- (Table P-PZ40)
6603.R3 Bravo, Julio, 1894- (Table P-PZ40)
6603.U3 Bueno, Manuel, 1874-1936 (Table P-PZ40)
6605 C - Cz
6605.A29 Cabrera Ivars, Juan Bautista, 1837-1916 (Table P-PZ40)
6605.A4 Cadenas, José Juan, 1872- (Table P-PZ40)
6605.A55 Camba, Francisco (Table P-PZ40)
6605.A6 Camba, Julio, 1882- (Table P-PZ40)
6605.A65 Camín, Alfonso, 1892- (Table P-PZ40)
6605.A67 Camino Galicia, León Felipe, 1884-1968 (Table P-PZ40)
6605.A72 Canalejas, Leonor (Table P-PZ40)
6605.A725 Cano y Masas, Leopoldo, 1844-1934 (Table P-PZ40)
6605.A73 Cansinos Assens, Rafael, 1883- (Table P-PZ40)
6605.A76 Carrere, Emilio, 1881- (Table P-PZ40)
6605.A8 Carretero, José María, 1888- (Table P-PZ40)
Pseudonym: El caballero audaz
6605.A8428 Casero y Barranco, Antonio, 1874- (Table P-PZ40)
Casona, Alejandro, 1903-1965 see PQ6633.O37
6605.A85 Castillo, Emilio G. del (Table P-PZ40)
6605.A93 Cavia, Mariano de, 1855-1920 (Table P-PZ40)

Individual authors
Individual authors, 1868-1960
C - Cz -- Continued
Celaya, Gabriel, 1911- see PQ6623.U34
6605.I5 Ciges Aparicio, Manuel, 1873- (Table P-PZ40)
6605.O39 Coll y Britapaja, José, 1840-1904. (Table P-PZ40)
6605.O45 Coloma, Jesús Rubio (Table P-PZ40)
6605.O5 Coloma, Luis, 1851-1915 (Table P-PZ40)
6605.O743 Costa y Martínez, Joaquín, 1846-1911 (Table P-PZ40)
Crespo, Angel, 1926- see PQ6605.R45
6605.R45 Crespo y Pérez de Madrid, Angel (Table P-PZ40)
6605.U7 Curros Enríquez, Manuel, 1851-1908 (Table P-PZ40)
6607 D - Dz
6607.A5 Danvila y Burguero, Alfonso (Table P-PZ40)
Darío, Rubén see PQ7519.D3
6607.I15 Díaz-Caneja, Guillermo, 1876- (Table P-PZ40)
6607.I28 Dicenta, Joaquín, 1893- (Table P-PZ40)
6607.I3 Dicenta, Joaquín, 1862-1917 (Table P-PZ40)
6607.O585 Domingo, Soler, Amalia, 1835-1909 (Table P-PZ40)
6607.O6 Domínguez, Antonio (Table P-PZ40)
6609 E - Ez
6609.C6 Echegaray y Eizaguirre, Miguel, 1848- (Table P-PZ40)
6609.L6 Elola Guriérrez, José de, 1859- (Table P-PZ40)
6609.S5 Espina, Concha, 1869-1955 (Table P-PZ40)
6609.S7 Estelrich, Juan Luis, 1857-1923 (Table P-PZ40)
6609.S75 Estévanez, Nicolas, 1838-1914 (Table P-PZ40)
6609.S76 Estevarena, Concepción de, 1854-1876 (Table P-PZ40)
6609.S78 Estremera, Antonio, 1884- (Table P-PZ40)
6609.S8 Estremera, Wenceslao (Table P-PZ40)
6611 F - Fz
6611.E5 Fernández Ardavín, Luis, 1892- (Table P-PZ40)
6611.E52 Fernández Arias, Adelardo, 1880- (Table P-PZ40)
6611.E54 Fernández de Sevilla, Luis (Table P-PZ40)
6611.E55 Fernández del Villar, José, 1888- (Table P-PZ40)
6611.E57 Fernández-Flórez, Wenceslao (Table P-PZ40)
6611.E58 Fernández Grilo, Antonio, 1845-1906 (Table P-PZ40)
6611.E582 Fernández-Guerra y Orbe, Aureliano, 1816-1894 (Table P-PZ40)
6611.E584 Fernández Lepina, Antonio (Table P-PZ40)
6611.E66 Fernández Shaw, Carlos, 1865-1911 (Table P-PZ40)
6611.E7 Fernández Vaamonde, Emilio (Table P-PZ40)
6611.E715 Fernández Villegas, Francisco, 1856-1916 (Table P-PZ40)
6611.E74 Ferrari, Emilio, 1853-1907 (Table P-PZ40)
6611.R27 Francés, José, 1883- (Table P-PZ40)
6611.R83 Frutos Baeza, José, 1861- (Table P-PZ40)
6613 G - Gz

Individual authors
Individual authors, 1868-1960
G - Gz -- Continued
6613.A2 Gabriel y Galán, José María, 1870-1905 (Table P-PZ40)
6613.A5 Ganivet, Angel, 1865-1898 (Table P-PZ40)
6613.A6 García, Germán R. (Table P-PZ40)
6613.A7 García Alemán E. (Table P-PZ40)
6613.A75 García Alvarez, Enrique, 1873- (Table P-PZ40)
6613.A7569 García de la Barga y Goméz de la Serna, Andrex, 1887-1975 (Table P-PZ40)
6613.A757 Garcia del Real, Luciano, d. 1902 (Table P-PZ40)
García González de Nora, Eugenio see PQ6625.O6
6613.A76 García Iniesta, César (Table P-PZ40)
6613.A77 García Sánchiz, Federico, 1886- (Table P-PZ40)
6613.A7725 García Toreal, Alicio (Table P-PZ40)
6613.A8 Garrido, José María (Table P-PZ40)
6613.A87 Gaspar y Rimbau, Enrique, 1842-1902 (Table P-PZ40)
6613.E7 Gerona, Eugenio Sellés Angel de Castro, maarqués de, 1842-1926 (Table P-PZ40)
6613.I38 Gil, Ricardo, 1855-1907 (Table P-PZ40)
6613.I5 Gil y Luengo, Constantino (Table P-PZ40)
6613.I8 Gimeno de Flaquer, Concepción, 1860- (Table P-PZ40)
6613.O35 Gómez de Baquero, Eduardo, 1866-1929 (Table P-PZ40)
Pseudonym: Andrenio
6613.O4 Gómez de la Serna, Ramón, 1891- (Table P-PZ40)
6613.O44 Gómez-Moreno, Manuel, 1870-1970 (Table P-PZ40)
6613.O5 González Anaya, Salvador, 1879- (Table P-PZ40)
6613.O55 González-Blanco, Andrés, 1886-1924 (Table P-PZ40)
González Peña, Carlos see PQ7297.G63
6613.O65 Gorbea Lemmi, Eusebio de (Table P-PZ40)
6613.O7 Goy de Silva, Ramón, 1888- (Table P-PZ40)
6613.R2 Grande Baudesson, Luis (Table P-PZ40)
6613.R24 Grandmontagne, Francisco, 1866-1936 (Table P-PZ40)
6613.R3 Grau, Jacinto, 1877- (Table P-PZ40)
Grilo, Antonio Fernández see PQ6611.E58
6613.U8 Gutiérrez Gamero y de Romate, Emilio, 1844- (Table P-PZ40)
6615 H - Hz
Heliófilo, pseud. see PQ6621.O885
6615.O8 Hoyos y Vinent, Antonio de, marqués de Vinent, 1885- (Table P-PZ40)
6617 I - Iz
Ibáñez, Vicente Blasco see PQ6603.L2
6617.N8 Insúa, Alberto, 1883- (Table P-PZ40)
6617.T8 Iturribarría y Laucirica, Francisco de, 1863-1916 (Table P-PZ40)
6619 J - Jz

Individual authors
Individual authors, 1868-1960
J - Jz -- Continued

6619.A3 Jackson Veyán, José, 1852- (Table P-PZ40)
6619.A8 Jarnés, Benjamín, 1888- (Table P-PZ40)
6619.I4 Jiménez, Juan Ramón, 1881- (Table P-PZ40)
6619.U3 Juarros, César, 1879- (Table P-PZ40)
6620 K - Kz
6620.I4 Kiew, Dimas (Table P-PZ40)
6621 L - Lz
Larmig, pseud. see PQ6538.M35
6621.A67 Larra y Ossorio, Luis de. 1862-1914 (Table P-PZ40)
Lasso de la Vega, marques de Villanova, 1890-1959 see PQ6641.I615
6621.E6 León, Ricardo, 1877 (Table P-PZ40)
León, Felipe, 1884-1968 see PQ6605.A67
Lepina, Antonio F. see PQ6611.E584
6621.E7 Lerroux, Alejandro, 1864- (Table P-PZ40)
6621.I35 Linares Becerra, Luis, 1887-1931 (Table P-PZ40)
6621.I4 Linares Rivas, Manuel, 1867- (Table P-PZ40)
6621.I65 Lizana, José María de (Table P-PZ40)
6621.O7 López Allué, Luis María (Table P-PZ40)
6621.O716 López Bago, Eduardo (Table P-PZ40)
6621.O72 López Ballesteros, Luis, 1869- (Table P-PZ40)
6621.O73 López Barbadillo, Joaquin (Table P-PZ40)
6621.O74 López de Haro, Rafael, 1876- (Table P-PZ40)
6621.O743 López de Sáa, Leopoldo, 1870- (Table P-PZ40)
6621.O748 López Muñoz, Antonio López Muñoz, conde de, 1849- (Table P-PZ40)
6621.O75 López Pinillos, José, 1875-1922 (Table P-PZ40)
6621.O765 López Prudencio, José (Table P-PZ40)
6621.O78 López Roberts, Mauricio, 1873- (Table P-PZ40)
6621.O79 López Silva, José, 1861-1925 (Table P-PZ40)
López-Valdemoro y de Quesada, Juan gualberto, conde de las Navas see PQ6625.A8
6621.O85 Lorente, Juan José (Table P-PZ40)
6621.O885 Lorenzo y Díez, Félix, 1879- (Table P-PZ40)
6621.U3 Luca de Tena, Juan Ignacio (Table P-PZ40)
6621.U35 Luceño y Becerra, Tomás, 1844- (Table P-PZ40)
6621.U37 Lucio y López, Celso, 1865-1915 (Table P-PZ40)
6623 M - Mz
6623.A3 Machado y Ruiz, Antonio, 1875- (Table P-PZ40)
6623.A34 Machado y Ruiz, Manuel, 1875- (Table P-PZ40)
6623.A35 Macías Picavea, Ricardo, 1847-1899 (Table P-PZ40)
6623.A36 Mac-Kinlay, Alejandro (Table P-PZ40)
6623.A4 Madariaga, Salvador de, 1886- (Table P-PZ40)
6623.A45 Maestre, Estanislao, 1867- (Table P-PZ40)

Individual authors
Individual authors, 1868-1960
M - Mz -- Continued

6623.A454 Maeztu, Ramiro de, 1875-1936 (Table P-PZ40)
6623.A55 Manzano Mancebo, Luis (Table P-PZ40)
6623.A58 Maragall, Juan, 1860-1911 (Table P-PZ40)
Marín Gutiérrez, José, 1913-1935 see PQ6635.I446
6623.A642 Marín Martínez, José María, 1865-1936 (Table P-PZ40)
6623.A7 Marquina, Eduardo, 1879- (Table P-PZ40)
6623.A8 Martínez Barrionuevo, Manuel, 1857-1917 (Table P-PZ40)
6623.A814 Martínez Olmedilla, Augusto, 1880- (Table P-PZ40)
6623.A816 Martínez Ruiz, José, 1873- (Table P-PZ40)
6623.A82 Martinez Sierra, Gregoro, 1881- (Table P-PZ40)
Martínez y Güertero, Luis Antonio ("Larmig") see PQ6538.M35
6623.A84 Más y Laglera, José, 1885- (Table P-PZ40)
6623.A87 Mata, Pedro, 1875- (Table P-PZ40)
6623.A94 Mazas, Mariano de, 1864- (Table P-PZ40)
6623.E35 Medina, Tirso (Table P-PZ40)
6623.E4 Medina y Tomás, Vicente, 1866- (Table P-PZ40)
6623.E695 Menéndez Pelayo, Enrique (Table P-PZ40)
6623.E8 Mesa y Rosales, Enrique de, 1879-1929 (Table P-PZ40)
6623.I4 Millán Astray, Pilar (Table P-PZ40)
6623.I44 Millares Cubas, Luis, 1861-1925 (Table P-PZ40)
6623.I63 Miral y López, Domingo (Table P-PZ40)
6623.I7 Miró, Gabriel, 1879-1930 (Table P-PZ40)
6623.O5 Moncayo, Manuel, 1880- (Table P-PZ40)
6623.O6 Montero y Vidal, José (Table P-PZ40)
6623.O624 Montoto y Rautenstrauch, Luis, 1851- (Table P-PZ40)
6623.O64 Morales, Gustavo, 1852- (Table P-PZ40)
6623.O645 Morales, María Luz (Table P-PZ40)
6623.O65 Morales San Martin, Bernardo, 1864- (Table P-PZ40)
6623.O665 Morell y Casanova, Eudaldo (Table P-PZ40)
6623.O85 Moya, Miguel, 1856- (Table P-PZ40)
6623.U34 Múgica, Rafael (Table P-PZ40)
6623.U5 Muñoz Seca, Pedro, 1881- (Table P-PZ40)
6623.U6 Muñoz y Pabón, Juan Francisco, 1866-1920 (Table P-PZ40)
6625 N - Nz
6625.A8 Navas, Juan Gualberto López-Valdemoro y de Quesada, conde de las, 1855- (Table P-PZ40)
6625.O3 Nocedal y Romea, Ramón, 1842-1907 (Table P-PZ40)
6625.O4 Noel, Eugenio, 1885- (Table P-PZ40)
6625.O6 Noel, Eugenio de (Table P-PZ40)
6627 O - Oz
6627.C4 Ochoa, Juan, 1864-1899 (Table P-PZ40)

Individual authors
Individual authors, 1868-1960
O - Oz -- Continued

6627.L5 Oliver, Miguel Santos, 1864-1919 (Table P-PZ40)
Cf. PC3941.A+ Catalan works
6627.P5 Opisso y Vinyas, Antonia (Table P-PZ40)
6627.R7 Ors y Rovira, Eugenio d', 1882- (Table P-PZ40)
Ortega Munilla, José see PQ7389.O75
6627.R8 Ortega y Gasset, José, 1883- (Table P-PZ40)
6627.R82 Ortega y Gironés, Juan, d. 1900 (Table P-PZ40)
6627.T4 Oteyza, Luis de, 1883- (Table P-PZ40)
6629 P - Pz
6629.A4 Pajares, Nicasio (Table P-PZ40)
6629.A5 Palacio Valdés, Armando, 1853- (Table P-PZ40)
6629.A51 Palacios, Miguel de, 1863- (Table P-PZ40)
6629.A66 Paradas, Enrique (Table P-PZ40)
6629.A7 Pardo Bazán, Elilia, condesa de, 1852-1921 (Table P-PZ40)
6629.A74 Parellada, Pablo (Table P-PZ40)
6629.A8 Paso, Antonio, 1870-1906 (Table P-PZ40)
6629.A81 Paso, Antonio, 1895- (Table P-PZ40)
6629.E4 Pedroso de Arriaza, A. (Table P-PZ40)
6629.E53 Pemán, José María, 1897- (Table P-PZ40)
6629.E58 Peñaranda, Carlos, 1848-1908 (Table P-PZ40)
6629.E62 Pereda y Revilla, Vicente de, 1881- (Table P-PZ40)
6629.E63 Pérez Capo, Felipe, 1878- (Table P-PZ40)
6629.E64 Pérez de Ayala, Ramón, 1881- (Table P-PZ40)
6629.E642 Pérez de la Ossa, Huberto, 1897- (Table P-PZ40)
6629.E65 Pérez Fernandez, Pedro, 1885- (Table P-PZ40)
Pérez Ferrari, Emilio see PQ6611.E74
6629.E67 Pérez Lugín, Alejandro, 1870-1926 (Table P-PZ40)
6629.E7 Pérez y Pérez, Rafael (Table P-PZ40)
6629.E73 Pérez Zúñiga, Juan, 1860- (Table P-PZ40)
6629.E8 Perrin, Guillermo, 1857-1923 (Table P-PZ40)
6629.I2 Picabia, Juan Héctor (Table P-PZ40)
6629.I3 Picón, Jacinto Octavio, 1853- (Table P-PZ40)
6629.O7 Porras, Antonio (Table P-PZ40)
6631 Q - Qz
6631.U35 Queralt y Formigales, Pascual, 1848-1898 (Table P-PZ40)
Quesada, Alonso, 1886-1925 see PQ6633.O73
6631.U5 Quintero, Antonio (Table P-PZ40)
6633 R - Rz
6633.A6 Ramírez Angel, Emiliano, 1883- (Table P-PZ40)
6633.A64 Ramos Martín, José, 1892- (Table P-PZ40)
6633.E4 Reina, Manuel, 1856-1905 (Table P-PZ40)
6633.E6 Répide, Pedro de, 1882- (Table P-PZ40)

Individual authors
Individual authors, 1868-1960
R - Rz -- Continued
6633.E87 Rey Soto, Antonio, 1879- (Table P-PZ40)
6633.E872 Rey Stolle, Alejandro (Table P-PZ40)
6633.E876 Reyes, Arturo, 1864-1913 (Table P-PZ40)
6633.E9 Reyes Huertas, Antonio (Table P-PZ40)
6633.I3 Rica, José de la (Table P-PZ40)
6633.I6 Ríos de Lampérez, Blanca de los, 1862- (Table P-PZ40)
Rivas, Manuel Linares see PQ6621.I4
6633.O37 Rodríguez Alvarez, Alejandro, 1903-1965 (Table P-PZ40)
6633.O4 Rodríguez de Ureta, Antonia (Table P-PZ40)
6633.O45 Rodríguez Marín, Francisco, 1855- (Table P-PZ40)
6633.O65 Romea, Julián, 1848-1903 (Table P-PZ40)
6633.O73 Romero Quesada, Rafael, 1886-1925 (Table P-PZ40)
6633.O79 Roso de Luna, Mario, 1872- (Table P-PZ40)
6633.U16 Rubín Gonzalez, Miguel de los Santos, 1849-1915 (Table P-PZ40)
6633.U3 Rudeda y Santos, Salvador, 1857-1933 (Table P-PZ40)
6635 S - Sz
6635.A3 Salaverría, José María, 1873- (Table P-PZ40)
6635.A4 San José, Diego, 1885- (Table P-PZ40)
6635.A625 Santero, Xavier, 1848-1923 (Table P-PZ40)
6635.A66 Santoval, Domingo de (Table P-PZ40)
6635.A93 Sawa, Alejandro, 1862-1909 (Table P-PZ40)
6635.E8 Sevilla, Alberto, 1877- (Table P-PZ40)
6635.I446 Sijé, Ramón, 1913-1935 (Table P-PZ40)
Silva, José Asunción, 1865-1896 see PQ8179.S5
Silva, José López see PQ6621.O79
6635.O65 Solsona, Conrado, 1851-1916 (Table P-PZ40)
6635.U38 Suárez de Deza, Enrique (Table P-PZ40)
6637 T - Tz
6637.A2 Taboada, Luis, 1848-1906 (Table P-PZ40)
6637.O7 Torres del Alamo, Angel, 1880- (Table P-PZ40)
6637.R5 Trigo, Felipe, 1864-1916 (Table P-PZ40)
6639 U - Uz
6639.G3 Ugarte, Eduardo (Table P-PZ40)
6639.N3 Unamuno, Miguel de, 1864-1936 (Table P-PZ40)
6639.R2 Urabayen Félix, 1884- (Table P-PZ40)
6639.R7 Urrecha, Federico, 1855- (Table P-PZ40)
6641 V - Vz
6641.A47 Valle-Inclán, Ramón del, 1870-1936 (Table P-PZ40)
6641.A75 Vargas, Luis de, 1891- (Table P-PZ40)
Velarde, Fernando see PQ6574.V34
6641.E55 Velarde, José, 1849-1892 (Table P-PZ40)
6641.E6 Verdaguer, Mario, 1893- (Table P-PZ40)
6641.I6 Villaespesa, Francisco, 1877- (Table P-PZ40)

Individual authors
Individual authors, 1868-1960
V - Vz -- Continued
6641.I615 Villanova, Rafael Lasso de la Vega, marques de, 1890-1959 (Table P-PZ40)
6643 X - Xz
Xavier, Adro, 1910- see PQ6633.E872
6643.I6 Ximénez de Sandoval, Felipe (Table P-PZ40)
6645 Y - Yz
6645.R3 Yrayzos, Fiacro (Table P-PZ40)
6647 Z - Zz
6647.A5 Zamacois, Eduardo, 1873- (Table P-PZ40)
6647.O8 Zozaya, Antonio, 1859- (Table P-PZ40)
6647.U5 Zugazagoitia, Julián (Table P-PZ40)
Individual authors, 1961-2000
Here are usually to be classified authors beginning to publish about 1950, flourishing after 1960
6650 Anonymous works (Table P-PZ28)
6651 A
The author number is determined by the second letter of the name
Subarrange each author by Table P-PZ40 unless otherwise specified
6652 B
The author number is determined by the second letter of the name
Subarrange each author by Table P-PZ40 unless otherwise specified
Benito de Lucas, Joaquín, 1934- see PQ6662.U3
6653 C
The author number is determined by the second letter of the name
Subarrange each author by Table P-PZ40 unless otherwise specified
6654 D
The author number is determined by the second letter of the name
Subarrange each author by Table P-PZ40 unless otherwise specified
6655 E
The author number is determined by the second letter of the name
Subarrange each author by Table P-PZ40 unless otherwise specified

Individual authors
Individual authors, 1961-2000 -- Continued

6656 F
The author number is determined by the second letter of the name
Subarrange each author by Table P-PZ40 unless otherwise specified

6657 G
The author number is determined by the second letter of the name
Subarrange each author by Table P-PZ40 unless otherwise specified

6658 H
The author number is determined by the second letter of the name
Subarrange each author by Table P-PZ40 unless otherwise specified

6659 I
The author number is determined by the second letter of the name
Subarrange each author by Table P-PZ40 unless otherwise specified

6660 J
The author number is determined by the second letter of the name
Subarrange each author by Table P-PZ40 unless otherwise specified

6661 K
The author number is determined by the second letter of the name
Subarrange each author by Table P-PZ40 unless otherwise specified

6662 L
The author number is determined by the second letter of the name
Subarrange each author by Table P-PZ40 unless otherwise specified

6662.U3 Lucas, Joaquin Benito de (Table P-PZ40)

6663 M
The author number is determined by the second letter of the name
Subarrange each author by Table P-PZ40 unless otherwise specified

6663.O535 Montaña, Genio (Table P-PZ40)

Individual authors
Individual authors, 1961-2000 -- Continued

6664 N
The author number is determined by the second letter of the name
Subarrange each author by Table P-PZ40 unless otherwise specified

6665 O
The author number is determined by the second letter of the name
Subarrange each author by Table P-PZ40 unless otherwise specified

6666 P
The author number is determined by the second letter of the name
Subarrange each author by Table P-PZ40 unless otherwise specified

Puig García, Eugenio see PQ6663.O535

6667 Q
The author number is determined by the second letter of the name
Subarrange each author by Table P-PZ40 unless otherwise specified

6668 R
The author number is determined by the second letter of the name
Subarrange each author by Table P-PZ40 unless otherwise specified

Rodriquez Valdes-Alvarez, Luis see PQ6673.E75

6669 S
The author number is determined by the second letter of the name
Subarrange each author by Table P-PZ40 unless otherwise specified

6670 T
The author number is determined by the second letter of the name
Subarrange each author by Table P-PZ40 unless otherwise specified

6671 U
The author number is determined by the second letter of the name
Subarrange each author by Table P-PZ40 unless otherwise specified

Individual authors
Individual authors, 1961-2000 -- Continued

6672 V
The author number is determined by the second letter of the name
Subarrange each author by Table P-PZ40 unless otherwise specified

6673 W
The author number is determined by the second letter of the name
Subarrange each author by Table P-PZ40 unless otherwise specified

6673.E75 Weiss, Cesar (Table P-PZ40)

6674 X
The author number is determined by the second letter of the name
Subarrange each author by Table P-PZ40 unless otherwise specified

6675 Y
The author number is determined by the second letter of the name
Subarrange each author by Table P-PZ40 unless otherwise specified

6676 Z
The author number is determined by the second letter of the name
Subarrange each author by Table P-PZ40 unless otherwise specified

Individual authors, 2001-

6700 Anonymous works (Table P-PZ28)

6701 A
The author number is determined by the second letter of the name
Subarrange each author by Table P-PZ40 unless otherwise specified

6702 B
The author number is determined by the second letter of the name
Subarrange each author by Table P-PZ40 unless otherwise specified

6703 C
The author number is determined by the second letter of the name
Subarrange each author by Table P-PZ40 unless otherwise specified

Individual authors.
Individual authors, 2001- -- Continued
6704 D
The author number is determined by the second letter of the name
Subarrange each author by Table P-PZ40 unless otherwise specified
6704.I34 Diego-Somonte, Jesús, 1963- (Table P-PZ40)
6705 E
The author number is determined by the second letter of the name
Subarrange each author by Table P-PZ40 unless otherwise specified
6706 F
The author number is determined by the second letter of the name
Subarrange each author by Table P-PZ40 unless otherwise specified
6707 G
The author number is determined by the second letter of the name
Subarrange each author by Table P-PZ40 unless otherwise specified
González Fernández, Jesus see PQ6704.I34
6708 H
The author number is determined by the second letter of the name
Subarrange each author by Table P-PZ40 unless otherwise specified
6709 I
The author number is determined by the second letter of the name
Subarrange each author by Table P-PZ40 unless otherwise specified
6710 J
The author number is determined by the second letter of the name
Subarrange each author by Table P-PZ40 unless otherwise specified
6711 K
The author number is determined by the second letter of the name
Subarrange each author by Table P-PZ40 unless otherwise specified

Individual authors.
Individual authors, 2001- -- Continued

6712 L
The author number is determined by the second letter of the name
Subarrange each author by Table P-PZ40 unless otherwise specified

6713 M
The author number is determined by the second letter of the name
Subarrange each author by Table P-PZ40 unless otherwise specified

6714 N
The author number is determined by the second letter of the name
Subarrange each author by Table P-PZ40 unless otherwise specified

6715 O
The author number is determined by the second letter of the name
Subarrange each author by Table P-PZ40 unless otherwise specified

6716 P
The author number is determined by the second letter of the name
Subarrange each author by Table P-PZ40 unless otherwise specified

6717 Q
The author number is determined by the second letter of the name
Subarrange each author by Table P-PZ40 unless otherwise specified

6718 R
The author number is determined by the second letter of the name
Subarrange each author by Table P-PZ40 unless otherwise specified

6719 S
The author number is determined by the second letter of the name
Subarrange each author by Table P-PZ40 unless otherwise specified

6720 T
The author number is determined by the second letter of the name
Subarrange each author by Table P-PZ40 unless otherwise specified

Individual authors.
Individual authors, 2001- -- Continued
6721 U
The author number is determined by the second letter of the name
Subarrange each author by Table P-PZ40 unless otherwise specified
6722 V
The author number is determined by the second letter of the name
Subarrange each author by Table P-PZ40 unless otherwise specified
6723 W
The author number is determined by the second letter of the name
Subarrange each author by Table P-PZ40 unless otherwise specified
6724 X
The author number is determined by the second letter of the name
Subarrange each author by Table P-PZ40 unless otherwise specified
6725 Y
The author number is determined by the second letter of the name
Subarrange each author by Table P-PZ40 unless otherwise specified
6726 Z
The author number is determined by the second letter of the name
Subarrange each author by Table P-PZ40 unless otherwise specified

Provincial, local, colonial, etc.
Includes the literary history, biography, criticism and collections of the literature of provinces, regions, islands, places, belonging to Spain; Spanish literature outside of Spain
Spain
Cf. PC4701+ Provincial dialects
7000 Regional. General or several regions
Special regions see PQ7001.A+
7001.A-Z Special states, provinces, regions, etc., A-Z
e. g.
Cf. PC3899.2+ Catalan literature
Cf. PQ9450+ Gallegan literature
Almeria
7001.A5 History
7001.A52 Collections

Provincial, local, colonial, etc.
Spain
Special states, provinces, regions, etc., A-Z
Almeria -- Continued
7001.A53 Translations
Andalusia
7001.A6 History
7001.A62 Collections
7001.A63 Translations
Aragon
7001.A7 History
7001.A72 Collections
7001.A73 Translations
Asturias see PQ7001.O8+
Balearic Islands. Mallorca
7001.B3 History
7001.B32 Collections
7001.B33 Translations
Estremadura
7001.E7 History
7001.E72 Collections
7001.E73 Translations
Murcia
7001.M8 History
7001.M82 Collections
7001.M83 Translations
Oviedo
7001.O8 History
7001.O82 Collections
7001.O83 Translations
Santander
7001.S3 History
7001.S32 Collections
7001.S33 Translations
Seville (Province)
7001.S4 History
7001.S42 Collections
7001.S43 Translations
Valencia
7001.V3 History
7001.V32 Collections
7001.V33 Translations
7011.A-Z Special cities, etc., A-Z
e. g.
Barcelona
7011.B3 History
7011.B32 Collections

Provincial, local, colonial, etc.
Spain
Special cities, etc., A-Z
Barcelona -- Continued
7011.B33 Translations
Granada
7011.G7 History
7011.G72 Collections
7011.G73 Translations
Seville (City)
7011.S4 History
7011.S42 Collections
7011.S43 Translations
Spanish literature outside of Spain
7020 General
Special
Europe
7030-7039 Portugal (Table P-PZ24 modified)
7039.A-Z Individual authors or works, A-Z
Subarrange individual authors by Table P-PZ40 unless otherwise specified
Subarrange individual works by Table P-PZ43 unless otherwise specified
e. g.
7039.C34 Camões, Luis de, 1524?-1580 (Table P-PZ40)
Cf. PQ9195+ Portuguese literature
7040-7049 Italy (Table P-PZ24 modified)
7049.A-Z Individual authors or works, A-Z
Subarrange individual authors by Table P-PZ40 unless otherwise specified
Subarrange individual works by Table P-PZ43 unless otherwise specified
e. g.
7049.F8 Frasso, Antonio de lo, 16th cent. (Table P-PZ40)
7050-7059 Netherlands (Table P-PZ24)
7061.A-Z Other European countries, A-Z
America
7070-7079.3 United States and Canada (Table P-PZ24 modified)
For works by and about Mexican-American (Chicano) authors writing in English or mixed English-Spanish, see subclass PS
7079.A-Z Individual authors or works through 1960, A-Z
Subarrange individual authors by Table P-PZ40 unless otherwise specified
Subarrange individual works by Table P-PZ43 unless otherwise specified

Provincial, local, colonial, etc.
Spanish literature outside of Spain
Special
America
United States and Canada -- Continued

7079.2.A-Z Individual authors or works, 1961-2000, A-Z
Subarrange individual authors by Table P-PZ40 unless otherwise specified
Subarrange individual works by Table P-PZ43 unless otherwise specified

7079.3.A-Z Individual authors or works, 2001- , A-Z
Subarrange individual authors by Table P-PZ40 unless otherwise specified
Subarrange individual works by Table P-PZ43 unless otherwise specified

Spanish America
Cf. PQ7471+ Central America
Cf. PQ7551+ South America

7081-7087 General (Table PQ8)

7100-7298.436 Mexico (Table P-PZ20 modified)
For works by and about Mexican-American (Chicano) authors writing in English or mixed English-Spanish, see subclass PS

Individual authors or works

7296.A-Z To 1810/25, A-Z
Subarrange individual authors by Table P-PZ40 unless otherwise specified

7296.A1A-.A1Z Anonymous works. By title, A-Z

7296.A1S44 Segunda parte de los sonados regocijos de Puebla

7296.A5 Alegre, Francisco Javier, 1729-1788 (Table P-PZ40)

7296.A58 Anaya, José Lucas, 1716-1771 (Table P-PZ40)

7296.A95 Ayrolo Calar, Gabriel de, fl. 1624 (Table P-PZ40)

7296.B45 Becerril, Miguel de, 17th cent. (Table P-PZ40)

7296.B66 Bocanegra, Matíasde, 1612-1668 (Table P-PZ40)

7296.C26 Cabrera y Quintero, Cayetano, d. 1775 (Table P-PZ40)

7296.C3 Castro, Francisco de, fl. 1729 (Table P-PZ40)

7296.C54 Cigorondo, Juan, 1560-1609 (Table P-PZ40)

7296.G7 González de Eslava, Fernán, 16th cent. (Table P-PZ40)

7296.G8 Guevara, Miguel de, d. 1640 (Table P-PZ40)

7296.J6 Juana Inés de la Cruz, Sister, 1651-1695 (Table P-PZ40)

Provincial, local, colonial, etc.
Spanish literature outside of Spain
Special
America
Spanish America
Mexico
Individual authors or works
To 1810/25, A-Z -- Continued

7296.L66 Lopéz Avilés, José, fl. 1669-1684 (Table P-PZ40)
7296.M2 Martínez, Diego, fl. 1788 (Table P-PZ40)
7296.N2 Navarrete, Manuel, 1768-1809 (Table P-PZ40)
7296.O45 Olmos, Andrés de, ca. 1491-1570 or 71 (Table P-PZ40)
7296.O56 Quiroz Campo Sagrado, Manuel (Table P-PZ40)
7296.S3 Saavedra Guzmán, Antonio de, fl. 1599 (Table P-PZ40)
7296.S35 Sandoval Zapata, Luis de, 1620?-1671 (Table P-PZ40)
7296.S5 Siguenza y Gongora, Carlos de, 1645-1700 (Table P-PZ40)
7296.T74 Trejo, Pedro de, 16th cent. (Table P-PZ40)
7296.V3 Vasconcelos, José, 18th cent. (Table P-PZ40)
7296.V54 Villagrá, Gaspar Pérez de, d. 1620 (Table P-PZ40)
7297.A-Z 1810/25-1960, A-Z
Subarrange individual authors by Table P-PZ40 unless otherwise specified
7297.A1A-.A1Z Anonymous works. By title, A-Z
7297.A6 Altamirano, Ignacio Manuel, 1834-1893 (Table P-PZ40)
7297.A627 Alvarez del Castillo, Manuel, 1860-1887 (Table P-PZ40)
7297.A865 Atl, Dr., 1875-1964 (Table P-PZ40)
7297.A9 Azuela, Mariano, 1873- (Table P-PZ40)
7297.B2692 Barrios de los Ríos, José Maria, 1864-1903 (Table P-PZ40)
7297.B718 Brioso y Candiani, Manuel, 1859- (Table P-PZ40)
7297.C24 Calderón, Fernando, 1809-1845 (Table P-PZ40)
7297.C244 Camarillo de Pereyra, María Enriqueta, 1872-1968 (Table P-PZ40)
7297.C2597 Castera, Pedro, 1838-1906 (Table P-PZ40)
7297.C5 Chavero, Alfredo, 1841-1906 (Table P-PZ40)

Provincial, local, colonial, etc.
Spanish literature outside of Spain
Special
America
Spanish America
Mexico
Individual authors or works
1810/25-1960, A-Z -- Continued

7297.C5123 Chavez, Ezequiel Adeodato, 1868-1946 (Table P-PZ40)
7297.C62 Correa Zapata, Dolores, 1853-1924 (Table P-PZ40)
7297.C77 Cuéllar, José Tomás de, 1830-1894 (Table P-PZ40)
7297.D35 Delgado, Rafael, 1853-1914 (Table P-PZ40)
7297.D55 Díaz Mirón, Salvador, 1853-1928 (Table P-PZ40)
7297.E8 Estrada, Genaro, 1887- (Table P-PZ40)
7297.F37 Fernández de Lizardi, José Joaquín, 1776-1827 (Table P-PZ40)
Pseudonym: El Pensador Mexicano
7297.F75 Frías, Heriberto, 1870- (Table P-PZ40)
7297.G3 Gamboa, Federico, 1864- (Table P-PZ40)
7297.G3486 García de Arellano, Luís (Table P-PZ40)
7297.G523 Gómez Marín, Manuel, 1761-1850 (Table P-PZ40)
7297.G56 González, Celestino, 1802-1896 (Table P-PZ40)
7297.G615 González Martínez, Enrique, 1871- (Table P-PZ40)
7297.G63 González Peña, Carlos, 1885- (Table P-PZ40)
7297.G7 Gorositza, Manuel Eduardo de, 1789-1851 (Table P-PZ40)
7297.G772 Guido, Juan B., 1872-1933 (Table P-PZ40)
7297.G8 Gutiérrez Nájera, Manuel, 1859-1895 (Table P-PZ40)
7297.I3 Icaza, Francisco A. de, 1863-1925 (Table P-PZ40)
7297.I6 Inclán, Luis Gonzaga, 1816-1875 (Table P-PZ40)
7297.L588 López, Jesús F., 1830-1901 (Table P-PZ40)
María Enriqueta, 1872-1968 see PQ7297.C244
7297.M28535 Martínez de Castro, Luis, 1819-1847 (Table P-PZ40)
7297.M653 Montes de Oca y Obregón, Ignacio, Abp., 1840-1921 (Table P-PZ40)
Murillo, Geraldo see PQ7297.A865

Provincial, local, colonial, etc.
Spanish literature outside of Spain
Special
America
Spanish America
Mexico
Individual authors or works
1810/25-1960, A-Z -- Continued

7297.N5 Nervo, Amado, 1870-1919 (Table P-PZ40)
7297.O3 Ochoa, Alvaro Leonor, 20th cent. (Table P-PZ40)
7297.O45 Olaguibel, Francisco Modesto de, 1874-1924 (Table P-PZ40)
7297.O79 Othón, Manuel José, 1858-1906 (Table P-PZ40)
7297.P2 Pagaza, Joaquín Arcadio, 1839-1918 (Table P-PZ40)
7297.P28 Paz, Ireneo, 1836-1921 (Table P-PZ40)
7297.P36 Peón y Contreras, José, 1843-1907 (Table P-PZ40)
7297.P3643 Perez Maldonado, Anselmo, 1843-1876 (Table P-PZ40)
7297.P8 Prieto, Guillermo, 1818-1897 (Table P-PZ40)
7297.P85 Puig Casauranc, José Manuel, 1888- (Table P-PZ40)
7297.Q4 Quevedo y Zubieta, Salvador, 1859-1935 (Table P-PZ40)
7297.R2 Rabasa, Emilio, 1856-1930 (Table P-PZ40)
7297.R357 Rembao, Alberto (Table P-PZ40)
7297.R386 Reyes, Alfonso, 1889- (Table P-PZ40)
7297.R46 Riva Palacio, Vicente, 1832-1896 (Table P-PZ40)
7297.R49 Rivera, José María, 1822-1887 (Table P-PZ40)
7297.R66 Rosa, Luis de la, d. 1856 (Table P-PZ40)
7297.S3 Salado Alvarez, Victoriano, 1867-1931 (Table P-PZ40)
7297.S35 Sánchez Mármol, Manuel, 1839-1912 (Table P-PZ40)
7297.S393 Santacilia, Pedro, 1826-1910 (Table P-PZ40)
7297.S5 Sierra, Justo, 1848-1912 (Table P-PZ40)
7297.T35 Taracena, Alfonso, 1897- (Table P-PZ40)
7297.T518 Tijerina, Juan B., 1857-1912 (Table P-PZ40)
7297.T63 Torres Bodet, Jaime, 1902- (Table P-PZ40)
7297.U54 Ulica, Jorge, 1870-1926 (Table P-PZ40)
7297.U7 Urbina, Luis Gonzaga, 1868-1934 (Table P-PZ40)
7297.V28 Vasconcelos, José, 1882- (Table P-PZ40)

Provincial, local, colonial, etc.
Spanish literature outside of Spain
Special
America
Spanish America
Mexico
Individual authors or works
1810/25-1960, A-Z -- Continued

7297.V463 Verástegui, José C., d. 1894 (Table P-PZ40)
7297.V535 Villarello, Felipe N. 1853-1921 (Table P-PZ40)
7297.V56 Villaseñor Cervantes, José María (Table P-PZ40)
7298-7298.36 1961-2000 (Table P-PZ29)
7298.4-.436 2001- (Table P-PZ29a)
Former provinces now in the United States see PQ7070+
West Indies
7361 General
Special
7370-7392 Cuba (Table P-PZ23 modified)
Local
7387.A-Z States, regions, etc., A-Z
Subarrange each by Table P-PZ26
7388.A-Z Cities, towns, etc., A-Z
Subarrange each by Table P-PZ26
7389.A-Z Individual authors, through 1960, A-Z
Subarrange each by Table P-PZ40 unless otherwise specified
7389.A75 Armas y Cárdenas, José de, 1866-1919 (Table P-PZ40)
7389.A76 Armas y Céspedes, José de, 1834-1900 (Table P-PZ40)
Avellaneda, Gertrudis Gómez de see PQ6524+
7389.B22 Balboa, Silvestre de (Table P-PZ40)
7389.B35 Bernal, Emilia, 1884- (Table P-PZ40)
7389.B379 Betancourt, José Ramón de, 1823-1890 (Table P-PZ40)
7389.B7 Bobadilla, Emilio, 1862-1921 (Table P-PZ40)
7389.B75 Borrero Echeverría, Esteban, 1849-1906 (Table P-PZ40)
7389.C23 Cabrera, Raimundo, 1852- (Table P-PZ40)
7389.C266 Casal, Julián del, 1863-1893 (Table P-PZ40)
7389.C28 Castellanos, Jesús, 1879-1912 (Table P-PZ40)
7389.C75 Crespo y Borbón, Bartolomé José, 1811-1871 (Table P-PZ40)

Provincial, local, colonial, etc.
Spanish literature outside of Spain
Special
America
Spanish America
West Indies
Special
Cuba
Individual authors, through 1960, A-Z -- Continued

7389.D4 Del Monte, Domingo, 1804-1853 (Table P-PZ40)

Delmonte y Aponte, Domingo, 1804-1853 see PQ7389.D4

7389.F7 Fornaris, José, 1827-1890 (Table P-PZ40)

7389.F83 Frías, Juan Antonio, 19th cent. (Table P-PZ40)

7389.G2616 García, Celestino, b. 1832 (Table P-PZ40)

Gómez de Avellandea y Arteaga, Gertrudis see PQ6524+

7389.G8 Guell y Renté, José, 1819-1884 (Table P-PZ40)

7389.G83 Guerrero y Pallarés, Teodoro, 1820-1905 (Table P-PZ40)

7389.H3 Heredia, José María, 1803-1839 (Table P-PZ40)

7389.H33 Hernández Catá, Alfonso, 1885- (Table P-PZ40)

7389.I3 Iglesia y Santos, Alvaro de la, 1859-1940 (Table P-PZ40)

7389.L74 Loveira y Chirino, Carlos, 1882- (Table P-PZ40)

7389.M187 Manzano, Juan Francisco, 1797-1854 (Table P-PZ40)

7389.M2 Martí, José, 1853-1895 (Table P-PZ40)

7389.M3 Mendive y Daumy, Rafael María, 1821-1886 (Table P-PZ40)

7389.M43 Meza y Suárez Inclán, Ramón, 1861-1911 (Table P-PZ40)

7389.M47 Milanés, José Jacinto, 1814-1863 (Table P-PZ40)

Monte, Domingo del, 1804-1853 see PQ7389.D4

7389.O75 Ortega Munilla, José, 1856-1922 (Table P-PZ40)

7389.P48 Piña, Ramón, 1819-1861 (Table P-PZ40)

Provincial, local, colonial, etc.
Spanish literature outside of Spain
Special
America
Spanish America
West Indies
Special
Cuba
Individual authors, through 1960, A-Z -- Continued
7389.P54 Pita y Borroto, Santiago Antonia, d. 1755 (Table P-PZ40)
Plácido, 1809-1844 see PQ7389.V3
7389.R75 Rodríguez Garcia, José Antonio, 1864- (Table P-PZ40)
7389.S27 Sánchez Galarraga, Gustavo, 1892?- (Table P-PZ40)
7389.T4 Tejera, Diego Vicente, 1848-1903 (Table P-PZ40)
7389.V3 Valdés, Gabriel de la Concepción, 1809-1844 (Table P-PZ40)
Pseudonym: Plácido
7389.V333 Valerio, Juan Francisco, ca. 1829-1878 (Table P-PZ40)
7389.V39 Varona González, Tomasa (Table P-PZ40)
7389.V4 Varona y Pera, Enrique José, 1849-1933 (Table P-PZ40)
7389.V55 Villaverde, Cirilo, 1812-1894 (Table P-PZ40)
7389.Z3 Zenea, Juan Clemente, 1832-1871 (Table P-PZ40)
7390.A-Z Individual authors, 1961-2000, A-Z
Subarrange each author by Table P-PZ40 unless otherwise specified
González Toledo, Eleuterio, 1963- see PQ7390.T45
Navarro, Osvaldo, 1946- see PQ7390.N34
7390.N34 Navarro Santana, Osvaldo, 1946- (Table P-PZ40)
7390.T45 Telo, 1963- (Table P-PZ40)
7392.A-Z Individual authors, 2001- , A-Z
Subarrange each author by Table P-PZ40 unless otherwise specified
7400-7409.3 Dominican Republic (Table P-PZ24 modified)

Provincial, local, colonial, etc.
Spanish literature outside of Spain
Special
America
Spanish America
West Indies.
Special
Dominican Republic -- Continued

7409.A-Z Individual authors or works through 1960, A-Z
Subarrange individual authors by Table P-PZ40 unless otherwise specified
Subarrange individual works by Table P-PZ43 unless otherwise specified
e. g.

7409.D38 Deligne, Gastón Fernando, 1861-1913 (Table P-PZ40)

7409.F5 Fiallo, Fabio, 1865- (Table P-PZ40)

7409.G3 Galván, Manuel de Jesús, 1834-1911 (Table P-PZ40)

7409.G35 García Godoy, Federico, 1857-1924 (Table P-PZ40)

7409.L8 Lugo, Américo, 1870-1952 (Table P-PZ40)

7409.P4 Pérez, José Joaquín, 1845-1900 (Table P-PZ40)

7409.R43 Reyes, Juan de Jesús, 1872-1962 (Table P-PZ40)

7409.U6 Ureña de Henríquez, Salomé, 1850-1897 (Table P-PZ40)

7409.2.A-Z Individual authors or works, 1961-2000, A-Z
Subarrange individual authors by Table P-PZ40 unless otherwise specified
Subarrange individual works by Table P-PZ43 unless otherwise specified

Carmen Natalia, 1917-1976 see PQ7409.2.M3

7409.2.M3 Martínez Bonilla, Carmen Natali (Table P-PZ40)

7409.3.A-Z Individual authors or works, 2001- , A-Z
Subarrange individual authors by Table P-PZ40 unless otherwise specified
Subarrange individual works by Table P-PZ43 unless otherwise specified

7410-7419 Jamaica (Table P-PZ24)

7420-7442 Puerto Rico (Table P-PZ23 modified)

7439.A-Z Individual authors through 1960, A-Z
Subarrange each author by Table P-PZ40 unless otherwise specified

Provincial, local, colonial, etc.
Spanish literature outside of Spain
Special
America
Spanish America
West Indies
Special
Puerto Rico
Individual authors through 1960, A-Z

7439.A53 Alvarez Marrero, Francisco, 1847-1881 (Table P-PZ40)
7439.A6 Amadeo y Antomarchi, Jesús María (Table P-PZ40)
7439.B36 Benítez, María Bibiana, 1783-1873 (Table P-PZ40)
7439.B59 Bonafoux y Quintero, Luis, 1855-1918 (Table P-PZ40)
7439.B8 Brau, Salvador, 1837-1912 (Table P-PZ40)
7439.C22 Caballero, Ramón C.F. (Table P-PZ40)
7439.C366 Cardona de Quiñones, Ursula, 1836-1875 (Table P-PZ40)
7439.C55 Coll y Toste, Cayetano, 1850-1930 (Table P-PZ40)
7439.C7 Corchado y Juarbe, Manuel, 1840-1884 (Table P-PZ40)
7439.C72 Córdova Landrón, Arturo (Table P-PZ40)
7439.D3 Daubón, José Antonio (Table P-PZ40)
7439.D35 Dávile, Virgilio, 1869-1943. (Table P-PZ40)
7439.D5 Diego, José de, 1866-1918 (Table P-PZ40)
7439.G3 Gautier Benitez, José, 1848-1880 (Table P-PZ40)
7439.H8 Huyke, Juan Bernardo, 1880- (Table P-PZ40)
7439.M475 Méndez Quiñones, Ramón, 1847-1889 (Table P-PZ40)
7439.M48 Mercado, José, 1863-1911 (Table P-PZ40)
7439.R544 Rivera, Daniel de, 1822-1856. (Table P-PZ40)
7439.R7 Rodríguez de Tío, Lola, 1843-1924 (Table P-PZ40)
7439.T3 Tapia y Rivera, Alejandro, 1826-1882 (Table P-PZ40)
7439.Z4 Zeno Gandía, Manuel, 1855-1930 (Table P-PZ40)

7440.A-Z Individual authors, 1961-2000, A-Z

Subarrange each author by Table P-PZ40 unless otherwise specified

Provincial, local, colonial, etc.
Spanish literature outside of Spain
Special
America
Spanish America
West Indies
Special
Puerto Rico -- Continued

7442.A-Z Individual authors, 2001- , A-Z
Subarrange each author by Table P-PZ40 unless otherwise specified

7451.A-Z Other islands, A-Z

Central America

7471-7477 General (Table PQ8)

Special

7480-7489.3 Costa Rica (Table P-PZ24 modified)

7489.A-Z Individual authors or works through 1960, A-Z
Subarrange individual authors by Table P-PZ40 unless otherwise specified
Subarrange individual works by Table P-PZ43 unless otherwise specified

7489.A77 Argüello Mora, Manuel, 1834-1902 (Table P-PZ40)

7489.B7 Brenes Mesén, Roberto, 1874-1947 (Table P-PZ40)

7489.E3 Echeverría, Aquileo J., 1866-1909 (Table P-PZ40)

7489.F4 Fernández Guardia, Ricardo, 1867- (Table P-PZ40)

7489.G27 Gagini, Carlos, 1865-1929 (Table P-PZ40)

7489.G35 Garita, Juan, 1859-1914 (Table P-PZ40)

7489.G6 González Zeledon, Manuel, 1864-1936 (Table P-PZ40)

7489.V5 Víquez, Pío, 1848-1899 (Table P-PZ40)

7489.2.A-Z Individual authors or works, 1961-2000, A-Z
Subarrange individual authors by Table P-PZ40 unless otherwise specified
Subarrange individual works by Table P-PZ43 unless otherwise specified

Salguero, Miguel see PQ7489.2.Z8

7489.2.Z8 Zúñiga Díaz, Miguel (Table P-PZ40)

7489.3.A-Z Individual authors or works, 2001- , A-Z
Subarrange individual authors by Table P-PZ40 unless otherwise specified
Subarrange individual works by Table P-PZ43 unless otherwise specified

7490-7499.3 Guatemala (Table P-PZ24 modified)

Provincial, local, colonial, etc.
Spanish literature outside of Spain
Special
America
Spanish America
Central America
Special
Guatemala -- Continued

7499.A-Z Individual authors or works through 1960, A-Z
Subarrange individual authors by Table P-PZ40 unless otherwise specified
Subarrange individual works by Table P-PZ43 unless otherwise specified
e. g.

7499.A3 Aguilar, Sinforo ("Xavier de Ximénez") (Table P-PZ40)
7499.B3 Batres Montúfar, José, 1809-1844 (Table P-PZ40)
7499.C45 Cerna, Ismael, 1856-1901 (Table P-PZ40)
7499.D5 Diéguez, Juan, 1813-1866 (Table P-PZ40)
7499.G6 Gómez Carrillo, Enrique, 1873-1927 (Table P-PZ40)
7499.I7 Irisarri, Antonio José de, 1786-1868 (Table P-PZ40)
7499.L3 Landívar, Rafael, 1731-1793 (Table P-PZ40)
7499.M22 Maldonado y Paz, Juana de, sor, 1598-1666 (Table P-PZ40)
7499.M5 Milla, José, 1822-1882 (Table P-PZ40)

7499.2.A-Z Individual authors or works, 1961-2000, A-Z
Subarrange individual authors by Table P-PZ40 unless otherwise specified
Subarrange individual works by Table P-PZ43 unless otherwise specified

7499.3.A-Z Individual authors or works, 2001- , A-Z
Subarrange individual authors by Table P-PZ40 unless otherwise specified
Subarrange individual works by Table P-PZ43 unless otherwise specified

7500-7509.3 Honduras (Table P-PZ24 modified)

7509.A-Z Individual authors or works through 1960, A-Z
Subarrange individual authors by Table P-PZ40 unless otherwise specified
Subarrange individual works by Table P-PZ43 unless otherwise specified
e. g.

7509.G73 Guardiola, Gonzalo, 1848-1903 (Table P-PZ40)

Provincial, local, colonial, etc.
Spanish literature outside of Spain
Special
America
Spanish America
Central America
Special
Honduras
Individual authors or works through 1960, A-Z -- Continued

7509.R3 Reyes, José Trinidad, 1797-1855 (Table P-PZ40)

7509.T8 Turcios, Froilán, 1875- (Table P-PZ40)

7509.V3 Valle, Rafael Heliodoro, 1891- (Table P-PZ40)

7509.2.A-Z Individual authors or works, 1961-2000, A-Z
Subarrange individual authors by Table P-PZ40 unless otherwise specified
Subarrange individual works by Table P-PZ43 unless otherwise specified

7509.3.A-Z Individual authors or works, 2001- , A-Z
Subarrange individual authors by Table P-PZ40 unless otherwise specified
Subarrange individual works by Table P-PZ43 unless otherwise specified

7510-7519.3 Nicaragua (Table P-PZ24 modified)

7519.A-Z Individual authors or works through 1960, A-Z
Subarrange individual authors by Table P-PZ40 unless otherwise specified
Subarrange individual works by Table P-PZ43 unless otherwise specified
e. g.

7519.D3 Darío, Rubén, 1867-1916 (Table P-PZ40)

7519.M42 Medina, Félix, 1857-1943 (Table P-PZ40)

7519.2.A-Z Individual authors or works, 1961-2000, A-Z
Subarrange individual authors by Table P-PZ40 unless otherwise specified
Subarrange individual works by Table P-PZ43 unless otherwise specified

7519.3.A-Z Individual authors or works, 2001- , A-Z
Subarrange individual authors by Table P-PZ40 unless otherwise specified
Subarrange individual works by Table P-PZ43 unless otherwise specified

7520-7529.3 Panama (Table P-PZ24 modified)

Provincial, local, colonial, etc.
Spanish literature outside of Spain
Special
America
Spanish America
Central America
Special
Panama -- Continued

7529.A-Z Individual authors or works through 1960, A-Z
Subarrange individual authors by Table P-PZ40 unless otherwise specified
Subarrange individual works by Table P-PZ43 unless otherwise specified
e. g.

7529.A49 Aguilera de Santos, Luisita (Table P-PZ40)

Aguilera P., Luisita see PQ7529.A49

7529.D6 Domínguez Alba, Bernardo, 1904- (Table P-PZ40)

7529.H33 Herrera, Dario, 1870-1914 (Table P-PZ40)

7529.S33 Sánchez Borbón, Guillermo, 1924- (Table P-PZ40)

Sinan, Rogello, 1904- see PQ7529.D6

Solarte, Tristan, 1924- see PQ7529.S33

7529.2.A-Z Individual authors or works, 1961-2000, A-Z
Subarrange individual authors by Table P-PZ40 unless otherwise specified
Subarrange individual works by Table P-PZ43 unless otherwise specified

7529.3.A-Z Individual authors or works, 2001- , A-Z
Subarrange individual authors by Table P-PZ40 unless otherwise specified
Subarrange individual works by Table P-PZ43 unless otherwise specified

7530-7539.3 Salvador (Table P-PZ24 modified)

7539.A-Z Individual authors or works through 1960, A-Z
Subarrange individual authors by Table P-PZ40 unless otherwise specified
Subarrange individual works by Table P-PZ43 unless otherwise specified
e. g.

7539.A493 Alvarado, Hermógenes, 1845- (Table P-PZ40)

7539.D45 Díaz, Francisco, 1812-1845 (Table P-PZ40)

7539.G3 Gavidia, Francisco Antonio, 1864-1955 (Table P-PZ40)

7539.L3 Lardé de Venturino, Alice (Table P-PZ40)

7539.M3 Masferrer, Alberto (Table P-PZ40)

Provincial, local, colonial, etc.
Spanish literature outside of Spain
Special
America
Spanish America
Central America
Special
Salvador
Individual authors or works through 1960, A-Z.
7539.P4 Peralta Lagos, José María, 1873-1944 (Table P-PZ40)
7539.2.A-Z Individual authors or works, 1961-2000, A-Z
Subarrange individual authors by Table P-PZ40 unless otherwise specified
Subarrange individual works by Table P-PZ43 unless otherwise specified
7539.3.A-Z Individual authors or works, 2001- , A-Z
Subarrange individual authors by Table P-PZ40 unless otherwise specified
Subarrange individual works by Table P-PZ43 unless otherwise specified
South America
7551-7557 General (Table PQ8)
Special
7600-7798.436 Argentina (Table P-PZ20 modified)
Individual authors or works
7796.A-Z To 1810/25, A-Z
Subarrange individual authors by Table P-PZ40 unless otherwise specified
7796.A1A-.A1Z Anonymous works. By title, A-Z
7796.B3 Barco Centenera, Martín del, 1535-1602 (Table P-PZ40)
7796.L34 Lafinur, Juan Crisóstomo, 1797-1824 (Table P-PZ40)
7796.M6 Monteagudo, Bernardo, 1785?-1825 (Table P-PZ40)
7796.R58 Rivarola, Pantaleón, 1754-1821 (Table P-PZ40)
7796.R6 Rodríquez, Cayetano José, 1761-1832 (Table P-PZ40)
7796.T4 Tejeda, Luis de, 1604-1680 (Table P-PZ40)
7797.A-Z 1810/25-1960, A-Z
Subarrange individual authors by Table P-PZ40 unless otherwise specified
7797.A1A-.A1Z Anonymous works. By title, A-Z
7797.A5 Alberdi, Juan Bautista, 1810-1884 (Table P-PZ40)

Provincial, local, colonial, etc.
Spanish literature outside of Spain
Special
America
Spanish America
South America
Special
Argentina
Individual authors or works
1810/25-1960, A-Z -- Continued

7797.A57 Alvarez, José Sixto, 1858-1903 (Table P-PZ40)
7797.A59 Amorim, Enrique, 1900- (Table P-PZ40)
7797.A6 Andrade, Olegario Victor, 1841-1882 (Table P-PZ40)
7797.A7 Arrieta, Rafael Alberto, 1889- (Table P-PZ40)
7797.A8 Ascasubi, Hilario, 1807-1875 (Table P-PZ40)
7797.B29 Barletta, Leónidas (Table P-PZ40)
7797.B35 Barreda, Ernesto Mario, 1883- (Table P-PZ40)
7797.B4343 Benedetto, Antonio di (Table P-PZ40)
7797.B6 Blomberg, Héctor Pedro, 1890- (Table P-PZ40)
Booz, Mateo, 1881-1943 see PQ7797.C713
7797.B635 Borges, Jorge Luis, 1899- (Table P-PZ40)
7797.B7 Bufano, Alfredo R., 1895- (Table P-PZ40)
7797.B8 Bunge, Carlos Octavio, 1875-1918 (Table P-PZ40)
7797.B852 Burgos, Fausto, 1888- (Table P-PZ40)
7797.C23 Cambacérés, Eugenio, 1843-1890 (Table P-PZ40)
7797.C26 Campo, Estanislao del, 1834-1880 (Table P-PZ40)
7797.C268 Cané, Luis, 1897- (Table P-PZ40)
7797.C27 Cané, Miguel, 1851-1905 (Table P-PZ40)
7797.C28 Capdevila, Arturo, 1889- (Table P-PZ40)
7797.C34 Castellanos, Joaquín, 1861-1932 (Table P-PZ40)
7797.C7 Coronado, Martín, 1850-1919 (Table P-PZ40)
7797.C713 Correa, Miguel Angel, 1881-1943 (Table P-PZ40)
7797.D35 Dávalos, Juan Carlos, 1887- (Table P-PZ40)
7797.D4 Dessein Merlo, Justo G. (Table P-PZ40)

Provincial, local, colonial, etc.
Spanish literature outside of Spain
Special
America
Spanish America
South America
Special
Argentina
Individual authors or works
1810/25-1960, A-Z -- Continued

	Di Benedetto, Antonio, 1922- see PQ7797.B4343
7797.E297	Echevarría, Bernardo, d. 1866 (Table P-PZ40)
7797.E3	Echevarría, Esteban, 1805-1851 (Table P-PZ40)
7797.E8	Estrada, Angel de, 1872-1923 (Table P-PZ40)
7797.F3	Fernández, Francisco F., d. 1922 (Table P-PZ40)
7797.F312	Fernández, Macedonio, 1874-1952 (Table P-PZ40)
7797.F37	Fernández Moreno, Baldomero, 1886- (Table P-PZ40)
7797.F7	Franco, Luis Leopoldo, 1898- (Table P-PZ40)
7797.G24	Galíndez, Bartolomé, 1896- (Table P-PZ40)
7797.G25	Gálvez, Manuel, 1882- (Table P-PZ40)
7797.G3	García Mérou, Martín, 1862-1905 (Table P-PZ40)
7797.G4	Gerchunoff, Alberto, 1883- (Table P-PZ40)
7797.G58	González Arrili, Bernardo, 1892- (Table P-PZ40)
7797.G6	Gorriti, Juana Manuela, 1819-1892 (Table P-PZ40)
7797.G63	Granada, Nicolás, 1840-1915 (Table P-PZ40)
7797.G65	Groussac, Paul, 1848-1929 (Table P-PZ40)
7797.G7	Guido y Spano, Carlos, 1827-1918 (Table P-PZ40)
7797.G75	Guiraldes, Ricardo, 1886-1927 (Table P-PZ40)
7797.G79	Gutiérrez, Eduardo, 1851-1889 (Table P-PZ40)
7797.G9	Gutiérrez, Ricardo, 1836-1896 (Table P-PZ40)

Provincial, local, colonial, etc.
Spanish literature outside of Spain
Special
America
Spanish America
South America
Special
Argentina
Individual authors or works
1810/25-1960, A-Z -- Continued

7797.H3 Hernández, José, 1834-1886 (Table P-PZ40)

7797.J35 Jerusalem, Frau Else (Kotányi), 1877- (Table P-PZ40)

Lacau, Maria Hortensia see PQ7797.P282

7797.L28 Larreta, Enrique Rodríguez, 1875- (Table P-PZ40)

7797.L4 Leguizamón, Martiniano, 1858-1935 (Table P-PZ40)

7797.L45 Leumann, Carlos Alberto, 1887- (Table P-PZ40)

7797.L85 Lugones, Leopoldo, 1874- (Table P-PZ40)

7797.L88 Lynch, Benito (Table P-PZ40)

7797.M25 Marasso Rocca, Arturo, 1890- (Table P-PZ40)

7797.M27 Mármol, José, 1818-1871 (Table P-PZ40)

Martel, Julian, 1867-1896 see PQ7797.M477

7797.M275 Martínez Cuitiño, Vicente (Table P-PZ40)

7797.M28 Martínez Zuviría, Gustavo Adolfo, 1883- (Table P-PZ40)

Pseudonym: Hugo Wast

7797.M29 Méndez Calzada, Enrique, 1898- (Table P-PZ40)

7797.M477 Míro, José María, 1867-1896 (Table P-PZ40)

7797.M5 Mitre, Bartolomé, 1821-1906 (Table P-PZ40)

7797.N4 Nelke, Jorge (Table P-PZ40)

7797.O3 Ocantos, Carlos María, 1860- (Table P-PZ40)

7797.O9 Oyuela, Calixto, 1857- (Table P-PZ40)

7797.P26 Palacios, Pedro Bonifacio, 1854-1917 (Table P-PZ40)

Pseudonym: Almafuerte

7797.P282 Palisa Mujica de Lacau, María Hortensia (Table P-PZ40)

Provincial, local, colonial, etc.
Spanish literature outside of Spain
Special
America
Spanish America
South America
Special
Argentina
Individual authors or works
1810/25-1960, A-Z -- Continued

7797.P3 Payró, Roberto Jorge, 1867-1928 (Table P-PZ40)

7797.P5765 Pizarro, Nicolás, 1830-1895. (Table P-PZ40)

7797.Q5 Quiroga, Carlos Buenaventura (Table P-PZ40)

7797.R7 Rojas, Ricardo, 1882- (Table P-PZ40)

7797.R75 Roldán, Belisario, 1873-1923 (Table P-PZ40)

7797.S4 Schiaffino, Eduardo, 1858- (Table P-PZ40)

7797.S66 Sosa, Raúl (Table P-PZ40)

7797.S74 Storni, Alfonsina, 1892- (Table P-PZ40)

7797.U5 Ugarte, Manuel, 1878- (Table P-PZ40)

7797.V26 Varela, Juan de la Cruz, 1794-1839 (Table P-PZ40)

7797.V3 Vázquez Cey, Arturo, 1888- (Table P-PZ40)

Wast, Hugo, pseud. see PQ7797.M28

7797.W5 Wilde, Eduardo, 1844-1913 (Table P-PZ40)

7797.Z4 Zeballos, Estanislao Severo, 1854-1923 (Table P-PZ40)

1961-2000

Here are usually to be classified authors beginning to publish about 1950, flourishing after 1960

7798.1 A

The author number is determined by the second letter of the name

Each author is subarranged by Table P-PZ40, unless otherwise specified

7798.1.L937 Alvarez Forn, Hernán, 1926- (Table P-PZ40)

7798.12 B

The author number is determined by the second letter of the name

Each author is subarranged by Table P-PZ40, unless otherwise specified

Provincial, local, colonial, etc.
Spanish literature outside of Spain
Special
America
Spanish America
South America
Special
Argentina
Individual authors or works
1961-2000, A-Z -- Continued

7798.13 C
The author number is determined by the second letter of the name
Each author is subarranged by Table P-PZ40, unless otherwise specified

7798.14 D
The author number is determined by the second letter of the name
Each author is subarranged by Table P-PZ40, unless otherwise specified

7798.15 E
The author number is determined by the second letter of the name
Each author is subarranged by Table P-PZ40, unless otherwise specified

7798.16 F
The author number is determined by the second letter of the name
Each author is subarranged by Table P-PZ40, unless otherwise specified

7798.17 G
The author number is determined by the second letter of the name
Each author is subarranged by Table P-PZ40, unless otherwise specified

7798.18 H
The author number is determined by the second letter of the name
Each author is subarranged by Table P-PZ40, unless otherwise specified
Hormiga, Negra see PQ7798.1.L937

7798.19 I
The author number is determined by the second letter of the name
Each author is subarranged by Table P-PZ40, unless otherwise specified

7798.19.V6 Ivo Marrochi, Hector (Table P-PZ40)

Provincial, local, colonial, etc.
Spanish literature outside of Spain
Special
America
Spanish America
South America
Special
Argentina
Individual authors or works
1961-2000, A-Z -- Continued

7798.2 J
The author number is determined by the second letter of the name
Each author is subarranged by Table P-PZ40, unless otherwise specified

7798.21 K
The author number is determined by the second letter of the name
Each author is subarranged by Table P-PZ40, unless otherwise specified

7798.22 L
The author number is determined by the second letter of the name
Each author is subarranged by Table P-PZ40, unless otherwise specified

7798.23 M
The author number is determined by the second letter of the name
Each author is subarranged by Table P-PZ40, unless otherwise specified

Marrochi, Hector Ivo see PQ7798.19.V6

7798.23.O412 Molinari, Alina, 1938- (Table P-PZ40)

7798.24 N
The author number is determined by the second letter of the name
Each author is subarranged by Table P-PZ40, unless otherwise specified

7798.25 O
The author number is determined by the second letter of the name
Each author is subarranged by Table P-PZ40, unless otherwise specified

7798.26 P
The author number is determined by the second letter of the name
Each author is subarranged by Table P-PZ40, unless otherwise specified

Provincial, local, colonial, etc.
Spanish literature outside of Spain
Special
America
Spanish America
South America
Special
Argentina
Individual authors or works
1961-2000, A-Z -- Continued

7798.27 Q
The author number is determined by the second letter of the name
Each author is subarranged by Table P-PZ40, unless otherwise specified

7798.28 R
The author number is determined by the second letter of the name
Each author is subarranged by Table P-PZ40, unless otherwise specified

7798.29 S
The author number is determined by the second letter of the name
Each author is subarranged by Table P-PZ40, unless otherwise specified

7798.3 T
The author number is determined by the second letter of the name
Each author is subarranged by Table P-PZ40, unless otherwise specified

Tortosa, Alina, 1938- see PQ7798.23.O412

7798.31 U
The author number is determined by the second letter of the name
Each author is subarranged by Table P-PZ40, unless otherwise specified

7798.32 V
The author number is determined by the second letter of the name
Each author is subarranged by Table P-PZ40, unless otherwise specified

7798.33 W
The author number is determined by the second letter of the name
Each author is subarranged by Table P-PZ40, unless otherwise specified

Provincial, local, colonial, etc.
Spanish literature outside of Spain
Special
America
Spanish America
South America
Special
Argentina
Individual authors or works
1961-2000, A-Z -- Continued

7798.34 X
The author number is determined by the second letter of the name
Each author is subarranged by Table P-PZ40, unless otherwise specified

7798.35 Y
The author number is determined by the second letter of the name
Each author is subarranged by Table P-PZ40, unless otherwise specified

7798.36 Z
The author number is determined by the second letter of the name
Each author is subarranged by Table P-PZ40, unless otherwise specified

7798.4-.436 2001- (Table P-PZ29a)

7800-7822 Bolivia (Table P-PZ23 modified)
Individual authors and works

7819.A1A-.A1Z Anonymous works. By title, A-Z

7819.A2-Z Individual authors through 1960, A-Z
Subarrange each author by Table P-PZ40 unless otherwised specified
e. g.

7819.A53 Aguirre, Nataniel, 1843-1888 (Table P-PZ40)

7819.C5 Chirvéches, Armando, 1880- (Table P-PZ40)

7819.J25 Jamies, Julio Lucas, 1840-1910 (Table P-PZ40)

7819.J3 Jaimes Freyre, Ricardo, 1868-1933 (Table P-PZ40)

Marof, Tristan see PQ7819.N3

7819.M4 Mendoza, Jaime, 1873- (Table P-PZ40)

7819.M77 Mujía, María Josefa, 1812-1888 (Table P-PZ40)

7819.N3 Navarro, Gustavo Adolfo (Table P-PZ40)

7819.O2 Oblitas, Arturo, 1873-1921 (Table P-PZ40)

Provincial, local, colonial, etc.
Spanish literature outside of Spain
Special
America
Spanish America
South America
Special
Bolivia
Individual authors and works
Individual authors through 1960, A-Z -- Continued

7819.R4 Reyes Ortiz, Félix, 1828-1883 (Table P-PZ40)

7819.Z36 Zamudio, Adela, 1854-1928 (Table P-PZ40)

7820.A-Z Individual authors, 1961-2000, A-Z

Subarrange each author by Table P-PZ40 unless otherwise specified

e. g.

7820.C24 Camargo, Edmundo (Table P-PZ40)

Camargo Ferreira, Edmundo see PQ7820.C24

7820.V27 Vacano, Arturo von, 1938- (Table P-PZ40)

Von Vacano, Arturo, 1938- see PQ7820.V27

7822.A-Z Individual authors, 2001- , A-Z

Subarrange each author by table P-PZ40 unless otherwise specified

7880-7889.3 Brazil (Table P-PZ24 modified)

7889.A-Z Individual authors or works to 1960, A-Z

Subarrange individual authors by Table P-PZ40 unless otherwise specified

Subarrange individual works by Table P-PZ43 unless otherwise specified

e. g.

7889.A52 Anchieta, José de, 1534-1597 (Table P-PZ40)

7889.B6 Botelho de Oliveira, Manuel, 1636-1711 (Table P-PZ40)

7889.2.A-Z Individual authors or works, 1961-2000, A-Z

Subarrange individual authors by Table P-PZ40 unless otherwise specified

Subarrange individual works by Table P-PZ43 unless otherwise specified

7889.3.A-Z Individual authors or works, 2001- , A-Z

Subarrange individual authors by Table P-PZ40 unless otherwise specified

Subarrange individual works by Table P-PZ43 unless otherwise specified

Provincial, local, colonial, etc.
Spanish literature outside of Spain
Special
America
Spanish America
South America
Special -- Continued

7900-8098.436 Chile (Table P-PZ20 modified)
Individual authors or works
8096.A-Z To 1800, A-Z
Subarrange individual authors by Table P-PZ40 unless otherwise specified
Subarrange individual works by Table P-PZ43 unless otherwise specified
Bustos, Francisco de, 17th cent. see PQ8096.G7
8096.G7 González de Bustos, Francisco, fl. 1665 (Table P-PZ40)
8096.O5 Oña, Pedro de, b. ca. 1570 (Table P-PZ40)
8097.A-Z 1800-1960, A-Z
Subarrange individual authors by Table P-PZ40 unless otherwise specified
Subarrange individual works by Table P-PZ43 unless otherwise specified
8097.A53 Acevedo Hernández, Antonio, 1886- (Table P-PZ40)
8097.A738 Allende, Juan Rafael, 1848-1909 (Table P-PZ40)
8097.A749 Aranda, Rosa (Table P-PZ40)
8097.B36 Barrios, Eduardo, 1884- (Table P-PZ40)
8097.B363 Barros Grez, Daniel, 1834-1904 (Table P-PZ40)
8097.B5 Blest Gana, Alberto, 1831-1920 (Table P-PZ40)
8097.B77 Brieba, Liborio E., 1841-1897 (Table P-PZ40)
8097.C553 Concha, Manuel, 1834-1891 (Table P-PZ40)
8097.E2 Edwards Bello, Joaquín (Table P-PZ40)
Emar, Juan, 1893-1964 see PQ8097.Y2
8097.G3 Gana y Gana, Federico, 1867-1924 (Table P-PZ40)
8097.G6 Godoy Alcayaga, Lucila, 1889-1957 (Table P-PZ40)
8097.G7 Grez, Vicente, 1847-1909 (Table P-PZ40)
8097.H8 Huidobro, Vicente, 1893- (Table P-PZ40)

Provincial, local, colonial, etc.
Spanish literature outside of Spain
Special
America
Spanish America
South America
Special
Chile
Individual authors or works
1800-1960, A-Z -- Continued

8097.L28 Lastarria, José Victorino, 1817-1888 (Table P-PZ40)
8097.L32 Latorre, Mariano, 1886- (Table P-PZ40)
8097.M27 Marín del Solar, Mercedes, 1804-1866 (Table P-PZ40)
Mistral, Gabriela, 1889-1957 see PQ8097.G6
8097.M74 Moock, Bousquet Armando, 1884- (Table P-PZ40)
8097.N4 Neruda, Pablo, 1904- (Table P-PZ40)
8097.P77 Prieto, Jenaro, 1889- (Table P-PZ40)
8097.R75 Rodríguez Mendoza, Emilio, 1873- (Table P-PZ40)
8097.R862 Rosales, Justo Abel, 1855-1896 (Table P-PZ40)
8097.S26 Sanfuentes, Salvador, 1817-1860 (Table P-PZ40)
8097.S75 Solar, Alberto del, 1860- (Table P-PZ40)
8097.S77 Sotomayor de Concha, Graciela. (Table P-PZ40)
Pseudonym: Lohengrin, Soledad
8097.V25 Valderrama, Adolfo, 1834-1902 (Table P-PZ40)
8097.V33 Vega, Daniel de la, 1892- (Table P-PZ40)
8097.V53 Vial Solar, Javier, 1854-1935 (Table P-PZ40)
8097.W3 Walker Martínez, Carlos, 1842-1905 (Table P-PZ40)
8097.Y2 Yáñez Bianchi, Alvaro, 1893-1964 (Table P-PZ40)
8098-8098.36 1961-2000 (Table P-PZ29)
8098.4-.436 2001- (Table P-PZ29a)
8160-8180.436 Colombia (Table P-PZ23 modified)
8179.A-Z Individual authors to 1960, A-Z
Subarrange each author by Table P-PZ40 unless otherwise specified
8179.A819 Arboleda, Julio, 1817-1862. (Table P-PZ40)

Provincial, local, colonial, etc.
Spanish literature outside of Spain
Special
America
Spanish America
South America
Special
Colombia
Individual authors to 1960, A-Z -- Continued

8179.A88 Avella Mendoza, Temístocles, 1841-1914 (Table P-PZ40)

Barba Jacob, Porfirio, 1883-1942 see PQ8179.O715

8179.C169 Camargo, R.M., 1858-1926 (Table P-PZ40)

8179.C2 Caro, José Eusebio, 1817-1853 (Table P-PZ40)

8179.C24 Caro, Miguel Antonio, 1843-1909 (Table P-PZ40)

8179.C3 Carrasquilla, Tomás, 1858-1940 (Table P-PZ40)

8179.C322 Carrasquilla-Mallarino, Eduardo, 1887- (Table P-PZ40)

8179.C369 Castillo, Francisca Josefa de la Concepción de, 1671-1742 (Table P-PZ40)

8179.C45 Celedón , Rafael (Table P-PZ40)

8179.C77 Cuervo, Angel, 1838-1896 (Table P-PZ40)

8179.C78 Cuervo, Rufino José, 1844-1911 (Table P-PZ40)

8179.D54 Díaz Castro, Eugenio (Table P-PZ40)

8179.D58 Domínguez Camargo, Hernando, 1606-1659 (Table P-PZ40)

8179.E4 Echeverri, Camilo Antonio, 1828?-1887 (Table P-PZ40)

8179.F4 Fernández de Madrid, José Luis Alvaro Alvino, 1789-1830 (Table P-PZ40)

8179.G614 Gomez, Jorge Ricardo. (Table P-PZ40)

8179.G674 González Zafra, Leonida, 1856 or 7-1945 (Table P-PZ40)

8179.G85 Gutiérrez González, Gregorio, 1826-1872 (Table P-PZ40)

8179.I8 Isaacs, Jorge, 1837-1895 (Table P-PZ40)

8179.I9 Ivaney, Jusuf (Table P-PZ40)

8179.L33 Latorre, Gabriel, 1868-1935 (Table P-PZ40)

8179.M3 Marroquín, José Manuel, 1827-1908 (Table P-PZ40)

8179.M793 Muñoz Feijóo, Antonio, 1851-1890 (Table P-PZ40)

Provincial, local, colonial, etc.
Spanish literature outside of Spain
Special
America
Spanish America
South America
Special
Colombia
Individual authors to 1960
Neyva, José Ignacio see PQ8179.I9
8179.N8 Núñez, Rafael, Pres. Colombia, 1825-1894 (Table P-PZ40)
8179.O26 Obeso, Candelario, 1849-1884 (Table P-PZ40)
8179.O715 Osorio, Miguel Angel, 1883-1942 (Table P-PZ40)
8179.P23 Palacios, Eustaquio, 1830-1898 (Table P-PZ40)
8179.P24 Paramo y Cepeda, Juan Francisco de, 17th cent. (Table P-PZ40)
8179.P3 Peña, Belisario, 1836-1906 (Table P-PZ40)
8179.P39 Pereira Gamba, Próspero, b. 1825 (Table P-PZ40)
8179.P4 Pérez, Felipe, 1836-1891 (Table P-PZ40)
Piedrahita, Rocío Vélez de see PQ8179.V356
8179.P6 Pombo, Rafael, 1833-1912 (Table P-PZ40)
8179.S3 Samper, José María, 1828-1888 (Table P-PZ40)
8179.S37 Sanín Cano, Baldomero, 1861-1957 (Table P-PZ40)
8179.S5 Silva, José Asunción, 1865-1896 (Table P-PZ40)
8179.S53 Silva, Ricardo, 1836-1887 (Table P-PZ40)
8179.S59 Solés y Valenzuela, Pedro de (Table P-PZ40)
8179.U7213 Uribe Angel, Manuel, 1822-1904 (Table P-PZ40)
8179.V27 Valencia, Guillermo, 1873-1943 (Table P-PZ40)
8179.V3 Vargas Vila, José María, 1860- (Table P-PZ40)
8179.V356 Vélez de Piedrahita, Rocío (Table P-PZ40)
8180-8180.36 Individual authors, 1960-2000 (Table P-PZ29 modified)
8180.2 J
Jaramillo Escobar, Jaime, 1932- see PQ8180.34.Q5
8180.34 X

Provincial, local, colonial, etc.
Spanish literature outside of Spain
Special
America
Spanish America
South America
Special
Colombia
Individual authors, 1960-2000, A-Z
X. -- Continued

8180.34.Q5 X-Quinientor Cuatro (Table P-PZ40)
8180.4-.436 Individual authors, 2001- (Table P-PZ29a)
8200-8220.436 Ecuador (Table P-PZ23 modified)
8219.A-Z Individual authors through 1960, A-Z
Subarrange each author by Table P-PZ40 unless otherwise specified
8219.A38 Aguirre, Juan Bautista, 1725-1786 (Table P-PZ40)
8219.A48 Andrade, Roberto, 1851-1938 (Table P-PZ40)
8219.B25 Baquerizo Moreno, Alfredo, 1859-1951 (Table P-PZ40)
8219.C19 Cadena, Pedro de la (Table P-PZ40)
8219.E95 Evia, Jacinto de, fl. 1657-1675 (Table P-PZ40)
8219.F3 Fálquez Ampuero, Francisco J., 1877- (Table P-PZ40)
8219.M35 Matovelle, Julio, 1852-1929 (Table P-PZ40)
8219.M4 Mera, Juan León, 1832-1894 (Table P-PZ40)
8219.M42 Mery, N. (Table P-PZ40)
8219.M5 Montalvo, Juan, 1832-1889 (Table P-PZ40)
8219.O5 Olmedo, José Joaquín de, 1780-1847 (Table P-PZ40)
8219.R4 Rendón, Víctor Manuel, 1859- (Table P-PZ40)
8219.R485 Riofrío, Miguel, 1822-1879 (Table P-PZ40)
8219.T49 Tobar, Carlos R. (Carlos Rodolfo), 1854-1920 (Table P-PZ40)
8219.V38 Vázquez, Honorato, 1855-1933 (Table P-PZ40)
8219.V387 Veintimilla de Galindo, Dolores, 1829-1857 (Table P-PZ40)
8219.V42 Velasco, Juan de, 1727-1792 (Table P-PZ40)
8219.Z32 Zaldumbide, Julio, 1833-1877 (Table P-PZ40)
8220-8220.36 Individual authors, 1961-2000 (Table P-PZ29 modified)
8220.3 T
8220.3.R54 Trigo y Tierra (Writer) (Table P-PZ40)
8220.4-.436 Individual authors, 2001- (Table P-PZ29a)

Provincial, local, colonial, etc.
Spanish literature outside of Spain
Special
America
Spanish America
South America
Special -- Continued

8230-8239 Guiana (Table P-PZ24)

8250-8259.3 Paraguay (Table P-PZ24, modified)

8259.A-Z Individual authors or works through 1960, A-Z

Subarrange individual authors by Table P-PZ40 unless otherwise specified

Subarrange individual works by Table P-PZ43 unless otherwise specified

8259.A23 Abente y Lago, Victorino, 1846-1935 (Table P-PZ40)

8259.A38 Aguiar, Adriano M., 1849-1912 (Table P-PZ40)

8259.G6 González, Juan Natalicio, 1897-1966 (Table P-PZ40)

González, Natalicio see PQ8259.G6

8259.G78 Guanes, Alejandro, 1872-1925 (Table P-PZ40)

8259.T34 Talavera, Natalicio, 1839-1867 (Table P-PZ40)

8259.2.A-Z Individual authors or works, 1961-2000 , A-Z

Subarrange individual authors by Table P-PZ40 unless otherwise specified

Subarrange individual works by Table P-PZ43 unless otherwise specified

Chevalier París, Gastón see PQ8259.2.G59

8259.2.G59 González Alsina, Ezequiel (Table P-PZ40)

8259.3.A-Z Individual authors or works, 2001- , A-Z

Subarrange individual authors by Table P-PZ40 unless otherwise specified

Subarrange individual works by Table P-PZ43 unless otherwise specified

8300-8498.436 Peru (Table P-PZ20 modified)

Individual authors or works

8496.A-Z To 1810/25, A-Z

Subarrange individual authors by Table P-PZ40 unless otherwise specified

Subarrange individual works by Table P-PZ43 unless otherwise specified

8496.A4 Alecio, Adriano de, 17th cent. (Table P-PZ40)

Ayanque, Simón see PQ8496.T4

Provincial, local, colonial, etc.
Spanish literature outside of Spain
Special
America
Spanish America
South America
Special
Peru
Individual authors or works
To 1810/25, A-Z -- Continued

8496.B37 Barrenechea y Albis, Juan de, 1638 or 9-1707? (Table P-PZ40)

8496.B47 Bermúdez de la Torre y Solier, Pedro José, b. 1665 (Table P-PZ40)

8496.C3 Castillo, Francisco del, 1716-1770 (Table P-PZ40)

8496.D38 Dávalos y Figueroa, Diego, ca. 1550-ca. 1608 (Table P-PZ40)

8496.E7 Espinosa Medrano, Juan, fl. 1660 (Table P-PZ40)

8496.L46 Llamosas, Lorenzo de las, ca. 1665-ca. 1705 (Table P-PZ40)

8496.M4 Melgar, Mariano, 1790-1815 (Table P-PZ40)

8496.M5 Miramontes Zuázola, Juan de, fl. 1600 (Table P-PZ40)

8496.O4 Olavide, Pablo de, 1725-1803 (Table P-PZ40)

Oña, Pedro de see PQ8096.O5

8496.P3 Peralta Barnuevo Rocha y Benavides, Pedro de, fl. 1732 (Table P-PZ40)

8496.R83 Ruiz Cano y Saenz Galiano, Francisco Antonio, marqués de Soto Florido, 1732-1792 (Table P-PZ40)

8496.T4 Terralla y Landa, Esteban de, fl. 1790 (Table P-PZ40)

8496.V34 Valle y Caviedes, Juan del, 1652-1692 (Table P-PZ40)

8497.A-Z 1810/25-1960, A-Z

Subarrange individual authors by Table P-PZ40 unless otherwise specified

8497.A1A-.A1Z Anonymous works. By title, A-Z

Adán, Martín, 1908- see PQ8497.F83

8497.B323 Barreto, Federico, 1870-1929 (Table P-PZ40)

8497.B8 Bustamante y Ballivián, Enrique, 1883- (Table P-PZ40)

Provincial, local, colonial, etc.
Spanish literature outside of Spain
Special
America
Spanish America
South America
Special
Peru
Individual authors or works
1810/25-1960, A-Z -- Continued

8497.C3 Cabello de Carbonera, Mercedes, 1845-1909 (Table P-PZ40)
8497.C433 Cateriano, Mariano Ambrosio (Table P-PZ40)
8497.C5 Chocano, José Santos, 1875-1934 (Table P-PZ40)
8497.E3 Eguren, José María, 1874-1942 (Table P-PZ40)
8497.F83 Fuente Benavides, Rafael de la (Table P-PZ40)
8497.G258 Gamarra, Abelardo M., 1857-1924 (Table P-PZ40)
8497.G3 García Calderón, Ventura, 1886- (Table P-PZ40)
8497.G6 González Prada, Manuel, 1848-1918 (Table P-PZ40)
La Torre, Alfonso see PQ8497.T624
8497.L6 López Albújar, Enrique, 1872-1966 (Table P-PZ40)
8497.M3 Matto de Turner, Clorinda, 1852-1909 (Table P-PZ40)
8497.P23 Palma, Clemente, 1872-1944 (Table P-PZ40)
8497.P26 Palma, Ricardo, 1833-1919 (Table P-PZ40)
8497.P28 Pardo y Aliaga, Felipe, 1806-1868 (Table P-PZ40)
8497.P284 Paz Soldán y Unanue, Pedro, 1839-1895 (Table P-PZ40)
8497.S28 Sanz, Mariano José, b. 1810 (Table P-PZ40)
8497.S3 Sassone, Felipe, 1884- (Table P-PZ40)
8497.S4 Segura, Manuel Ascensio, 1805-1871 (Table P-PZ40)
8497.T624 Torre, Alfonso la (Table P-PZ40)
8498-8498.36 1961-2000 (Table P-PZ29)
8498.4-.436 2001- (Table P-PZ29a)
8510-8520.436 Uruguay (Table P-PZ24 modified)

Provincial, local, colonial, etc.
Spanish literature outside of Spain
Special
America
Spanish America
South America
Special
Uruguay -- Continued

8519.A-Z Individual authors or works through 1960, A-Z
Subarrange individual authors by Table P-PZ40 unless otherwise specified

8519.A1A-.A1Z Anonymous works. By title, A-Z

8519.A3 Acevedo Díaz, Eduardo, 1851-1921 (Table P-PZ40)

8519.A32 Acosta y Lara, Manuel (Table P-PZ40)

8519.A33 Acuña de Figueroa, Francisco, 1790-1862 (Table P-PZ40)

8519.A5 Agustini, Delmira, 1886-1914 (Table P-PZ40)

Alonso y Trelles, José see PQ8519.T8

Bobadilla, Simplicio, 1908- see PQ8519.G334

8519.F85 Frugoni, Emilio, 1881- (Table P-PZ40)

8519.G333 Garcia, Arthur N., 1906-1956 (Table P-PZ40)

8519.G334 Garcia, Serafin J., 1908- (Table P-PZ40)

8519.H4 Herrera y Reissig, Julio, 1875-1910 (Table P-PZ40)

8519.H5 Hidalgo, Bartolomé, 1788-1822 (Table P-PZ40)

8519.I3 Ibarbourou, Juana de, 1895- (Table P-PZ40)

8519.L9 Lussich, Antonio Dionisio, 1848-1928 (Table P-PZ40)

8519.M3 Magariños Cervantes, Alejandro, 1825-1893 (Table P-PZ40)

8519.M35 Maldonado, Horacio, 1884- (Table P-PZ40)

8519.M366 Martínez Arboleya, Joaquín (Table P-PZ40)

8519.M6 Montiel Ballesteros, Adolfo, 1888- (Table P-PZ40)

8519.O7 Oribe, Emilio, 1893- (Table P-PZ40)

8519.P3 Pereira, Antonio N. (Table P-PZ40)

8519.P4 Pérez Petit, Víctor, 1871- (Table P-PZ40)

8519.P45 Pérez y Curis, Manuel, 1884-1920 (Table P-PZ40)

8519.P7 Princivalle, Carlos María (Table P-PZ40)

8519.Q5 Quiroga, Horacio, 1879- (Table P-PZ40)

8519.R38 Reyles, Carlos, 1868- (Table P-PZ40)

8519.R6 Rodó, José Enrique, 1872-1917 (Table P-PZ40)

8519.R7 Roxlo, Carlos, 1860-1926 (Table P-PZ40)

Provincial, local, colonial, etc.
Spanish literature outside of Spain
Special
America
Spanish America
South America
Special
Uruguay
Individual authors or works through 1960, A-Z -- Continued

8519.S24 Sabat Ercasty, Carolos, 1887- (Table P-PZ40)
8519.S4 Sánchez, Florencio, 1875-1910 (Table P-PZ40)
Santicaten, 1900- see PQ8519.M366
8519.T8 Trelles, José Alonso y, 1860-1924 (Table P-PZ40)
8519.V4 Viana, Javier de, 1872-1927 (Table P-PZ40)
Wimpi see PQ8519.G333
8519.Z7 Zorrilla de San Martín, Juan, 1855-1931 (Table P-PZ40)
8520-8520.36 Individual authors, 1961-2000 (Table P-PZ29 modified)
8520.23 M
8520.23.A23 Maca, 1956- (Table P-PZ40)
8520.33 W
Wojciechowski, Gustavo, 1956- see PQ8520.23.A23
8520.4-.436 Individual authors, 2001- (Table P-PZ29a)
8530-8550.436 Venezuela (Table P-PZ23 modified)
8549.A-Z Individual authors through 1960, A-Z
Subarrange each author by Table P-PZ40 unless otherwise specified
8549.A67 Arcía, Juan E., 1872- (Table P-PZ40)
8549.B3 Bello, Andrés, 1781-1865 (Table P-PZ40)
8549.B5 Blanco-Fombona, Rufino, 1874- (Table P-PZ40)
8549.C284 Carvajal de Arocha, Mercedes, 1902- (Table P-PZ40)
8549.C85 Curiel, Elías David, 1871-1924 (Table P-PZ40)
8549.D5 Díaz Rodríguez, Manuel, 1871-1927 (Table P-PZ40)
8549.F4 Febres Cordero, Tulio, 1860-1938 (Table P-PZ40)
8549.G24 Gallegos, Rómulo, 1882- (Table P-PZ40)
8549.G28 García de Quevedo, José Heriberto, 1819-1871 (Table P-PZ40)

Provincial, local, colonial, etc.
Spanish literature outside of Spain
Special
America
Spanish America
South America
Special
Venezuela
Individual authors through 1960, A-Z -- Continued

	Gil, Pío, 1865?-1918 see PQ8549.M72
8549.G46	Gil de Hermoso, Virginia, 1856-1912 (Table P-PZ40)
8549.G5	Gil Fortoul, José, Pres. Venezuela, 1861-1943 (Table P-PZ40)
8549.G56	González, Juan Vicente, 1810-1866 (Table P-PZ40)
8549.H35	Hernández, Marcial, 1874-1921 (Table P-PZ40)
8549.L38	Lazo Martí, Francisco, 1869-1909 (Table P-PZ40)
8549.M43	Menotti Spósito, Emilio, 1891-1951 (Table P-PZ40)
8549.M72	Morantes, Pedro María, 1865?-1918 (Table P-PZ40)
	Palacios, Lucila, 1902- see PQ8549.C284
8549.P3	Pardo, Miguel Eduardo, 1868-1905 (Table P-PZ40)
8549.P375	Peraza, Clestino, 1850-1930 (Table P-PZ40)
8549.P392	Pérez Bonalde, Juan Antonio, 1846-1892 (Table P-PZ40)
8549.P475	Picón Febres, Gonzalo, 1860-1918 (Table P-PZ40)
	Spósito Díaz, Emilio Menotti, 1891-1951 see PQ8549.M43
8549.T64	Tosta García, Francisco, 1852-1921 (Table P-PZ40)
8549.U62	Urbaneja Achelpohl, Luis Manuel, 1873-1937 (Table P-PZ40)
8549.Y38	Yepes, José Ramón, 1822-1881 (Table P-PZ40)
8550-8550.36	Individual authors, 1961-2000 (Table P-PZ29 modified)
8550.12	B
8550.12.U79	Bustillo, Carmen (Table P-PZ40)
8550.32	V
	Vincenti, Carmen see PQ8550.12.U79

Provincial, local, colonial, etc.
Spanish literature outside of Spain
Special
America
Spanish America
South America
Special
Venezuela -- Continued

8550.4-.436 Individual authors, 2001- (Table P-PZ29a)

8560.A-Z Spanish American authors not identified with a special country, A-Z
Subarrange each author by Table P-PZ40 unless otherwise specified

8600-8619 Africa (Table P-PZ23)

Asia

8651-8657 General (Table PQ8)

8700-8897 Philippines (Table P-PZ20 modified)

Individual authors or works

8897.A-Z Authors or works of all periods, A-Z
Subarrange individual authors by Table P-PZ40 unless otherwise specified
Subarrange individual works by Table P-PZ43 unless otherwise specified
e. g.

8897.B87 Burgos, José Apolonio, 1837-1872 (Table P-PZ40)

8897.P3 Pan, José Felipe del (Table P-PZ40)

8897.R5 Rizal y Alonso, José, 1861-1896 (Table P-PZ40)

8900-8909 Other former colonies (Table P-PZ24)

8910-8919 Other parts of Asia (Table P-PZ24)

8920-8929 Australia and Pacific Islands (Table P-PZ24)

Portuguese literature
History and criticism
9000 Periodicals
(9001) Yearbooks
see PQ9000
9002 Societies
9003 Congresses
Collections
9004 Series. Monographs by various authors
9004.5.A-Z Collections in honor of a special person or institution, A-Z
9005 Collected works of individual authors
9006 Encyclopedias. Dictionaries
Study and teaching
9008 General
9009.A-Z Schools, A-Z
9009.5 Biography of scholars, teachers, etc.
9009.7 Criticism. History of literary history
History
General
9010 Early works to 1800
Later works, 1801-
9011 Treatises
9012 Compends. Textbooks
9013 Outlines, syllabi, questions, etc.
9014 Collected essays
9016 Lectures, addresses, essays
General special
9018 Relations to history, civilization, culture, etc.
9019 Relations to other literatures
9020 Translations
Treatment of special subjects, classes, etc.
9022.A-Z Special subjects, A-Z
9022.D58 Discoveries in geography
9022.E54 Emigration and immigration
9022.H65 Horror
9022.N65 Nostalgia
9022.P6 Portugal
9022.S68 Space
9022.T73 Travel
9022.U76 Utopias
9023.A-Z Special classes, A-Z
9024.A-Z Special persons, A-Z
9024.C37 Castro, Ines de, d. 1355
9024.F38 Faust, d. ca. 1540
9024.P65 Pombal, Sebastião José de Carvalho e`Melo, Marques de, 1699-1782
Biography

History and criticism
Biography -- Continued
9027 Collected
Individual see PQ9191+
9029 Memoirs. Letters, etc.
9031 Literary landmarks. Homes and haunts of authors
9033 Women authors. Literary relations of women
9034.A-Z Other classes of authors, A-Z
9034.B53 Black authors
9034.J4 Jewish authors
Negro authors see PQ9034.B53
By period
9035 Origins
Medieval
9038 Treatises. Compends
9039 Collected essays
9040 Special subjects
Modern
9041 Treatises. Compends
9042 Collected essays
9043 Special subjects
Renaissance
9044 Treatises. Compends
9045 Collected essays
9046 Special subjects
16th-18th centuries
9047 Treatises. Compends
9048 Collected essays
9049 Special subjects
(18th and) 19th century
9050 Treatises. Compends
9051 Collected essays
9052 Special subjects
20th century
9053 Treatises. Compends
9054 Collected essays
9055 Special subjects
21st century
9056 Treatises. Compends
9057 Collected essays
9058 Special subjects
Poetry
History
9061 General
Medieval see PQ9038+
9065 Modern
9067 16th-18th centuries

History and criticism
Poetry
History
Modern -- Continued
9069 19th century
9071 20th century
9073 21st century
Special
9077 Epic
9079 Lyric
9080 Popular poetry. Ballads, etc.
9081.A-Z Other, A-Z
9081.C45 Children's poetry
9081.P38 Pastoral poetry
9081.V57 Visual poetry
Drama
History
9083 General
9085 Early to 1800
9087 19th century
9089 20th century
9090 21st century
9093.A-Z Special forms, A-Z
9095.A-Z Special subjects, A-Z
Prose
9097 General works
Special periods
9099 Origins to 1800
9100 19th century
9101 20th century
9101.2 21st century
9102.A-Z Special topics, A-Z
9102.A87 Autobiography
9102.T73 Travel
Prose fiction
Technique see PN3355+
9104 General works
Special periods
9106 Origins to 1800
9107 19th century
9108 20th century
9108.2 21st century
9109.A-Z Special topics, A-Z
9109.B54 Bildungsromans
9109.F35 Fantasy fiction
9109.F38 Fathers
9109.H57 Historical fiction

History and criticism
Prose -- Continued
Minor forms
9111 Oratory
9113 Letters
9115 Essays
9117 Wit and humor
9119 Miscellaneous
Folk literature
For general works on and collections of folk literature, see GR238+
(9121.A2) Periodicals. Societies. Collections
(9121.A5-.Z3) Treatises. Compends
(9121.Z5) Essays, pamphlets, etc.
Collections of texts
(9122) General
Folk songs see PQ9160
Folk drama see PQ9170
9123 Chapbooks
(9124) By locality, region, etc.
(9125) Special characters: Heroes, fairies, etc.
(9126.A-Z) Individual tales, A-Z
(9128.A-Z) Translations by language, A-Z
9129 Juvenile literature (General)
For special genres, see the genre
Collections of Portuguese literature
General
9131 Early to 1800
9133 Modern, 1801-
9135 Selections. Anthologies
9136.A-Z Special classes of authors, A-Z
9136.C5 Child authors
9137.A-Z Translations. By language, A-Z
By period
9140 Medieval
9141 16th-18th centuries
9143 19th century
9144 20th century
9145 21st century
Local see PQ9400+
Poetry
General collections
9149 Early to 1800
9150 Modern
9151 Selections. Anthologies
9153 Women poets
By period

Collections of Portuguese literature
Poetry
By period -- Continued

9155 Medieval to 1500
9155.A2 Contemporaneous collections
e. g.
9155.A2C3 Cancioneiro da Ajuda
9155.A2C4 Cancioneiro Colocci-Brancuti
9155.A2D5 Diniz (or Denis), King of Portugal, Cancioneiro
9155.A3-Z Modern collections. By editor, A-Z
9156 16th-18th centuries
9156.A2 Contemporaneous collections
e. g.
9156.A2C5 Cancioneira d'Evora
9156.A3-Z Modern collections. By editor, A-Z
9157 19th century
9158 20th century
9159 21st century
Special, by form or subject
9160 Popular poetry, ballads, etc.
9161.A-Z Other, A-Z
Castro, Ines de, d. 1355 see PQ9161.I6
9161.C5 Christmas
9161.C55 Clesse, Isabel Xavier, d. 1772?
9161.C6 Concrete poetry
9161.H5 Historical, etc.
9161.I6 Inez de Castro
9161.L5 Lisbon
9161.L7 Love
9161.M3 Mary, Blessed Virgin, Saint
9161.P7 Prostitution
9161.R35 Railroads
9161.R4 Religious poetry (General)
9161.S7 Sonnets
9161.S73 Sports
9161.T34 Tagus River (Spain and Portugal)
9161.T74 Trees
9163.A-Z Translations. By language, A-Z
Drama
9164 General
9165 Minor
By period
9166 To 1800
9167 19th century
9168 20th century
9168.2 21st century
9169.A-Z Special A-Z (Tragedy, Comedy, etc.)

Collections of Portuguese literature
Drama
Special A-Z (Tragedy, Comedy, etc.) -- Continued
9169.O54 One-act plays
9169.V47 Verse drama
9170 Folk drama
Prose
General
9172 Early to 1800
9173 Modern
Fiction
9175 General
9176 Minor
9179 Oratory
9181 Letters
9183 Essays
9185 Wit and humor
9187 Miscellany
9188.A-Z Translations. By language, A-Z
Folk literature see GR238+
Individual authors
9189 Individual authors and works to 1500
Subarrange individual authors by Table P-PZ38 unless otherwise specified. Subarrange individual works by Table P-PZ43 unless otherwise specified
For medieval manuscript collections see PQ9155.A2
9189.A38 Airas, Joan (Table P-PZ38)
9189.A44 Alfonso X, el Sabio, King of Castile and Leon, 1221-1284 (Table P-PZ38)
Andrada, Miguel Leitáo de, 1553-1632 see PQ9231.L42
9189.B39 Baveca, Johan (Table P-PZ38)
9189.B64 Bolseyro, Juyao (Table P-PZ38)
9189.B65 Bonaval, Bernal de (Table P-PZ38)
9189.B74 Briteiros, João Mendes de (Table P-PZ38)
9189.C37 Carpancho, Ayras (Table P-PZ38)
9189.C76 Cronica troyana (Table P-PZ38)
9189.D55 Dinis, King of Portugal, 1261-1325 (Table P-PZ38)
9189.E48 Elvas, Estevan Fernandez d', 14th cent. (Table P-PZ38)
9189.E83 Esgaravunha, Fernan Garcia, 13th cent. (Table P-PZ38)
9189.G37 Garcia Burgales, Pero, fl. 1250 (Table P-PZ38)
9189.G54 Gil, Vasco, 13th cent. (Table P-PZ38)
9189.G65 Gómez Charino, Payo, ca. 1225-1295 (Table P-PZ38)
9189.G84 Guilhade, Joao Garcia de, 13th cent. (Table P-PZ38)
9189.M46 Meogo, Pero, 13th cent. (Table P-PZ38)
9189.M69 Moxa, Martin (Table P-PZ38)
9189.P28 Padrozelos, Martin de, 12th cent. (Table P-PZ38)
9189.P34 Paez de Tamalancos, 13th cent. (Table P-PZ38)

Individual authors
Individual authors and works to 1500 -- Continued

9189.P45 Pedro Afonso, conde de Barcelos, ca. 1285-1354 (Table P-PZ38)
9189.S25 Sanchez, Afonso, ca. 1288-ca. 1328 (Table P-PZ38)
9189.T67 Torneol, Nuno Fernandes, 13th century (Table P-PZ38)
9189.V37 Vasconcelos, Rodrigu'Eanes de, 13th cent. (Table P-PZ38)
9189.V45 Velho, Fernan (Table P-PZ38)

Individual authors and works, 1500-1700
Subarrange each author by Table P-PZ40 unless otherwise specified

9191 A - Cam
9191.A4 Agostinho da Cruz, Brother, 1540-1619 (Table P-PZ40)
9191.A5 Alcoforado, Marianna, 1640-1723 (Table P-PZ40)
For works limited to biography see BX4705.A+
For editions and criticism of Lettres portugaises see PQ1799.G795
9191.A57 Alvares do Oriente, Fernao d', 1540?-1595? (Table P-PZ40)
9191.A6 Andrade Caminha, Pedro de, d. 1589 (Table P-PZ40)
9191.A63 Anjos, Luis dos, d. 1625 (Table P-PZ40)
9191.B37 Bernardes, Diogo, 16th cent. (Table P-PZ40)
9191.B4 Bernardes, Manuel, 1644-1710 (Table P-PZ40)
Caminha, Pedro de Andrade, d. 1589 see PQ9191.A6

Camões, Luiz de, 1524?-1580
Cf. PQ7039.C34 Spanish literature

9195.A1 Collected works. By date
(9195.A11) Collected works. By editor
(9195.A14) Posthumous works
see PQ9195.A2
Posthumous poems see PQ9196.A2
9195.A2 Selected works (Miscellaneous)
9195.A3 Selections. Anthologies
9195.A5 Selections (Minor). Quotations. Passages. Thoughts, etc.
Cf. PQ9198.A7 Os Lusiadas

Poems
9196.A1 Comprehensive editions
9196.A2 Selections (Miscellaneous)
9196.A5-.Z4 Selections, by form, A-Z
e. g.
9196.L9 Lyrics
9196.S7 Sonnets
(9196.Z5) Posthumous poems
see PQ9196.A2
9196.Z7 Spurious or doubtful poems
9196.Z8A-.Z8Z Special poems, A-Z
e. g.

PQ9000-9999

Individual authors
Individual authors and works, 1500-1700
Camões, Luiz de, 1524?-1580
Poems
Special poems, A-Z -- Continued
9196.Z8A6-.Z8A7 Alma minha gentil (Nathercia)
9196.Z9 Criticism
Dramatic works
9197.A1 Comprehensive editions
Separate works
9197.E6 Enfatriões (Amphitryões)
9197.F5 Filodemo
9197.R5 Rei Seleuco
9197.Z5 Criticism (General and particular plays)
9198 Os Lusiadas
Editions
9198.A1 Manuscript copies in facsimile. By date
9198.A15 Other manuscript copies
9198.A2 Printed editions. By date
(9198.A25) Critical editions. By editor
For added entry only
9198.A3 School editions. By editor and date
9198.A5 Selected portions. By date
9198.A7 Minor selections. Quotations, etc. By date
Cf. PQ9195.A5 Selections
Particular cantos
9198.A9 Canto I
9198.A92 Canto II
9198.A93 Canto III
Translations
English
9199.A1 Collections and selections
Os Lusiadas
9199.A2 Complete
9199.A3 Portions
9199.A5 Poems
Dramatic works
9199.A7 Complete
9199.A8-Z Special plays, by original title, A-Z
French
9200.A1 Collections and selections
Os Lusiadas
9200.A2 Complete
9200.A3 Portions
9200.A5 Poems
Dramatic works
9200.A7 Complete

Individual authors.
Individual authors and works, 1500-1700
Camões, Luiz de, 1524?-1580.
Translations
French
Dramatic works. -- Continued
9200.A8-Z Special plays, by original title, A-Z
German
9201.A1 Collections and selections
Os Lusiadas
9201.A2 Complete
9201.A3 Portions
9201.A5 Poems
Dramatic works
9201.A7 Complete
9201.A8-Z Special plays, by original title, A-Z
Italian
9202.A1 Collections and selections
Os Lusiadas
9202.A2 Complete
9202.A3 Portions
9202.A5 Poems
Dramatic works
9202.A7 Complete
9202.A8-Z Special plays, by original title, A-Z
Spanish
9203.A1 Collections and selections
Os Lusiadas
9203.A2 Complete
9203.A3 Portions
9203.A5 Poems
Dramatic works
9203.A7 Complete
9203.A8-Z Special plays, by original title, A-Z
9204.A-Z Other European languages, except Slavic, A-Z
e. g.
9204.L3 Latin. By translator, A-Z
9205.A-Z Slavic languages, A-Z
Cf. PQ4498.A+
9206.A-Z Other languages, A-Z
Prefer PJ-PM for languages of Asia
9206.5 Polyglot
9207 Imitations. adaptations. Parodies
9208 Dramatizations
9209 Translations (as subject)

Individual authors
Individual authors and works, 1500-1700
Camões, Luiz de, 1524?-1580. -- Continued
9210 Illustrations
Illustrated editions classed with other editions
For history of portraits and illustrations of Camões see PQ9218
Camões and music see ML80.C25
Biography and criticism
9212.A2-.A29 Periodicals. Societies. Collections
Bibliography see Z8142
9212.A4 Dictionaries. Encyclopedias.
Cf. PQ9230 Language dictionaries and concordances
9212.A5-.Z3 General works. Literary biography. Life and works
9212.Z5 Lectures, addresses, essays
Collections. see PQ9212.A2+
Special biographical details
9213.A1 Sources, documents, etc.
9213.A2 Letters
9213.A4 Birth. Early life. Education
9214 Relations to women
9214.5 Later years and death. Burial. Tomb, etc.
9215 Relations to his contemporaries
9216 Homes and haunts
Anniversaries. Celebrations
Prefer special subject or collections PQ9212.A2+
9217.A00-A99 1600-1699
9217.B00-B99 1700-1799
9217.C00-C99 1800-1899
9217.C80 300th anniversary of his death.
9217.D00-D99 1900-1999
9217.E00-E99 2000-2099
9218 Iconography. Portraits, monuments, relics
(9219) Fiction, drama, etc., based upon Camoes' life
Authorship
9220.2 Manuscripts. Autographs
9220.3 Sources
9220.4 Forerunners. Associates. Followers
Prefer History of Portuguese literature PQ9010+
9220.6 Chronology of works
Criticism and interpretation
9222 History of the study and appreciation of Camões
9222.A2 General and in Portugal
9222.A5-Z By country, A-Z
e. g.
9222.G4 Germany

Individual authors.
Individual authors and works, 1500-1700
Camões, Luiz de, 1524?-1580.
Biography and criticism
Criticism and interpretation.
History of the study and appreciation of Camoes.
By country, A-Z -- Continued

9222.S6	Spain
	Treatises
9223	General
9224	Os Lusiadas (mainly)
9225.A-Z	Special topics, A-Z
9225.A56	Architecture
9225.A7	Astronomy
9225.G4	Geography
9225.H8	Humor
9225.L57	Lisbon
9225.L68	Love
9225.N3	Naval art and science
9225.P6	Politics
9225.T5	Theology
9225.W7	Women
9225.Z6	Zoology
9226	Textual criticism. Interpretation
9227	Language. Style
9228	Grammar
9229	Versification
9230	Dictionaries. Concordances Cf. PQ9212.A4 General
9231	Cam - Sa
9231.C32	Campos, Manuel Monteiro de, 17th cent. (Table P-PZ40)
9231.C76	Corte-Real, Jeronymo, 16th cent. (Table P-PZ40)
9231.C84	Crasto, Antonio Serrao de, b. 1610 (Table P-PZ40)
	Crisfal, Trovas de see PQ9243.T78
9231.C87-.C89	Crónica do Imperador Maximiliano (Table P-PZ43)
9231.D4-.D43	Demanda do santo graal (Table P-PZ43)
9231.D52	Dias, Baltasar (Table P-PZ40)
9231.F2	Falcão, Christovão, 16th cent. (Table P-PZ40) For Trovas de Crisfal, sometimes ascribed to him see PQ9243.T78
9231.F25	Fernandes Trancoso, Goncalo, 16th cent. (Table P-PZ38)
9231.F3	Ferreira, Antonio, 1528-1569 (Table P-PZ40)
9231.F4	Ferreira de Vasconcellos, Jorge, 16th cent. (Table P-PZ40)
9231.F75	Freire, Joao Nunes, I7th cent. (Table P-PZ40)
9231.G35	Garcia Mascarenhas, Bras, 1596-1656 (Table P-PZ40)

Individual authors
Individual authors and works, 1500-1700
Cam - Sa -- Continued
9231.G9 Gusmão Soares, Vicente de, 1606-1675 (Table P-PZ40)
Cf. PQ6398.G97 Gusmão Soares as a Spanish author
9231.J47 Jessurun, Rehuel, 1596-1660 (Table P-PZ40)
9231.L42 Leitáo de Andrada, Miguel, 1553-1632 (Table P-PZ40)
Lobo, Francisco Rodrigues, 17th cent. see PQ6398.G97
9231.M3 Machado, Simão, ca. 1570-ca. 1640 (Table P-PZ40)
9231.M4 Maria do Ceo, Sister, 1658-1753 (Table P-PZ40)
Portuguese literature
Cf. PQ9153
Mascarenhas, Bras Garcia de, 1596-1656 see PQ9231.G35
9231.M5 Mello, Francisco Manuel de, 1611-1666 (Table P-PZ40)
9231.M63 Mendes Pinto, Fernao, b. 1509 (Table P-PZ40)
9231.M715 Morais, Inácio de, 1500?-1580 (Table P-PZ40)
9231.M72 Moura, Francisco Child Rolim de, 1572-1640 (Table P-PZ40)
9231.N55 Nogueira, João, 1603-1643 (Table P-PZ40)
Oriente, Fernao Alvares do, b. 1540? see PQ9191.A57
9231.P23 Paiva de Andrade, Diogo de, 1576-1600 (Table P-PZ40)
9231.P25 Palmerin de Inglaterra (Table P-PZ40)
9231.P45 Pereira de Castro, Gabriel, 1571-1632 (Table P-PZ40)
9231.P6 Portugal, Manuel de, d. 1606 (Table P-PZ40)
9231.R25 Rebello, Gaspar Pires de (Table P-PZ40)
9231.R46 Ribeiro, Bernardim, 1482-1552 (Table P-PZ40)
For Trovas de Crisfal, sometimes ascribed to him see PQ9243.T78
9231.R7 Rodrigues Lobo, Francisco, 17th cent. (Table P-PZ40)
9241-9242 Sá de Miranda, Francisco de, ca. 1485-1558 (Table P-PZ36)
9243 Sa - Vi
9243.S63 Sousa, Frei Luiz de, 1555?-1632 (Table P-PZ40)
9243.S7 Sousa de Macedo, Antonio de, 1606-1682 (Table P-PZ40)
9243.T78 Trovas de Crisfal (Table P-PZ40)
Authorship attributed to Christovão Falcão or to Bernardim Ribeiro
Vasconcels, Jorge Ferreira de see PQ9231.F4
Vicente, Gil, ca. 1470-ca. 1536
For his Spanish works see PQ6498.V2
9251.A1 Collected works. By date
9251.A17 Collected poems. By date
9251.A6 Translations, by language, A-Z
9251.A7 Selected works. By date

Individual authors
Individual authors and works, 1500-1700
Vicente, Gil, ca. 1470-ca. 1536 -- Continued
9251.A8-Z Separate works, A-Z
e. g.
9251.E8 Exhortacao da guerra
9251.F4 Auto da festa
9251.I6 Farsa de Inez Pereira
9252 Biography and criticism
9253 Vicente - Vz
9253.V5 Vimioso, Francisco de Portugal, conde de, d. 1549 (Table P-PZ40)
9253.V6 Violante do Ceo, Sister, 1601-1693 (Table P-PZ40)
9255 W - Z
9261.A-Z Individual authors, 1701-1960, A-Z
Subarrange individual authors by Table P-PZ40 unless otherwise specified
9261.A1A-.A1Z Anonymous works. By title, A-Z
9261.A475 Agostinho, José, 1866-1938 (Table P-PZ40)
9261.A483 Albuquerque, António de, 1866-1923 (Table P-PZ40)
Almada Negreiros, José de, 1893-1970 see PQ9261.N345
Almeida, Fialho d', 1857-1911 see PQ9261.F5
9261.A496 Almeida, Jose Evaristo d' (Table P-PZ40)
9261.A575 Almeida Garrett, João Baptista da Silva Leitão de Almeida Garrett, 1. visconde de, 1799-1854 (Table P-PZ40)
9261.A6 Alorna, Leonor de Almeida Portugal Lorena e Lencastre, Marquesa de, 1750-1839 (Table P-PZ40)
9261.A7 Antunes, Acacio, 1853-1927 (Table P-PZ40)
9261.A75 Araujo, Joaquim de, 1858-1927 (Table P-PZ40)
9261.A769 Arcos, Henrique Belford Correia da Sila, Paço d', 1906- (Table P-PZ40)
9261.A85 Ayres de Magalhaes Sepulveda, Christovam, 1857-1930 (Table P-PZ40)
9261.B49 Bocage, Manuel Maria de Barbosa du, 1765-1805 (Table P-PZ40)
9261.B6 Botelho, Abel Acacio de Almeida, 1856-1917 (Table P-PZ40)
9261.B65 Braga, Alberto, 1851-1911 (Table P-PZ40)
9261.B68 Braga, Theophilo, 1843-1924 (Table P-PZ40)
9261.B7 Brandão, Raul, 1867-1930 (Table P-PZ40)
9261.B735 Breyner, Thomaz de Mello, Conde de Mafra, 1866-1933 (Table P-PZ40)
9261.B75 Brito Camacho, Manuel de, 1862-1934 (Table P-PZ40)
9261.B8 Bulhao Pato, Raymundo Antonio de, 1829-1912 (Table P-PZ40)
Caeiro, Alberto, 1888-1935. see PQ9261.P417
Camacho, Brito, 1862-1934 see PQ9261.B75

Individual authors
Individual authors, 1701-1960, A-Z -- Continued

9261.C234 Camara, João da, 1852-1908 (Table P-PZ40)
Campos, Alvaro de, 1888-1935 see PQ9261.P417
9261.C245 Campos, Francisco António de Novaes, b. 1739 (Table P-PZ40)
Carvalho, Romulo de see PQ9261.G37
9261.C3 Castello Branco, Camillo, 1825-1890 (Table P-PZ40)
9261.C34 Castilho, Antonio Feliciano de, 1800-1875 (Table P-PZ40)
9261.C4 Castro, Eugenio de, 1869- (Table P-PZ40)
Castro, Ferreira de see PQ9261.F37
Cesariny, Mário see PQ9261.V277
Chagas, Manuel Pinheiro, 1842-1895 see PQ9261.P54
9261.C5415 Coelho, Joaquim Guilherme Gomes, 1839-1871 (Table P-PZ40)
9261.C5417 Coelho, Trindade, 1861-1908 (Table P-PZ40)
9261.C6 Corrêa de Oliveira, Antonio, 1879- (Table P-PZ40)
9261.C832 Courinho, Vicente de Sousa, 1726-1792 (Table P-PZ40)
9261.D3 Dantas, Julio, 1876- (Table P-PZ40)
9261.D5 Deus, João de, 1830-1896 (Table P-PZ40)
Dinis, Júlio see PQ9261.C5415
9261.E3 Eça de Queiroz, José Maria de, 1845-1900 (Table P-PZ40)
9261.F27 Feijó, Antonio, 1859-1917 (Table P-PZ40)
9261.F3644 Ferreira, David Mourão (Table P-PZ40)
9261.F37 Ferreira de Castro, Jose Maria, 1898- (Table P-PZ40)
9261.F5 Fialho de Almeida, Jose Valentim, 1857-1911 (Table P-PZ40)
9261.F514 Ficalho, Francisco Manuel de Melo, conde de, 1837-1903 (Table P-PZ40)
9261.F52 Figueiredo, Candido de, 1846-1925 (Table P-PZ40)
9261.F55 Figueiredo, Manuel de, 1725-1801 (Table P-PZ40)
9261.F689 Forjaz, Joana Isabel de Lencastre, b. 1745 (Table P-PZ40)
Frias, David Correia Sanches de, Visconde de, 1845-1922 see PQ9261.S13
9261.G3 Gama, Arnaldo, 1828-1869 (Table P-PZ40)
Garrett, João Baptista da Silva Leitão de Almeida, visconde de Almeida Garrett see PQ9261.A575
9261.G37 Gedeão, António, 1906- (Table P-PZ40)
9261.G5 Gil, Augusto, 1873-1929 (Table P-PZ40)
9261.G58 Gomes, João Baptista, ca. 1775-1803 (Table P-PZ40)
9261.G59 Gomes, Manuel Teixeira, 1860-1941 (Table P-PZ40)
Gomes Junior, João Baptista see PQ9261.G58
9261.G64 Gomes Leal, Antonio Duarte, 1849-1921 (Table P-PZ40)
9261.G7 Grave, João, 1872- (Table P-PZ40)
9261.G8 Guerra Junqueiro, Abílio Manuel, 1850-1923 (Table P-PZ40)

Individual authors

Individual authors, 1701-1960, A-Z -- Continued

9261.H5 Herculano de Carvalho e Araujo, Alexandre, 1810-1877 (Table P-PZ40)

Ivo, Pedro, 1842-1906 see PQ9261.L56

Junqueiro, Abílio Manuel Guerra, 1850-1923 see PQ9261.G8

Leal, Gomes, 1848-1921 see PQ9261.G64

9261.L56 Lopes, Carlos, 1842-1906 (Table P-PZ40)

9261.L58 Lopes de Mendonça, António Pedro, 1826-1865 (Table P-PZ40)

9261.L6 Lopes de Mendonça, Henrique, 1856- (Table P-PZ40)

9261.L65 Lopes Vieira, Affonso Xavier, 1878- (Table P-PZ40)

9261.L76 Luís, Nicolau, 1723-1787 (Table P-PZ40)

9261.M2 Macedo, José Agostinho de, 1761-1813 (Table P-PZ40)

9261.M25 Machado, Julio Cesar, 1835-1890 (Table P-PZ40)

9261.M3 Magalhães, Luis de, 1859-1935 (Table P-PZ40)

9261.M54 Mesquita, Marcellino, 1856-1919 (Table P-PZ40)

9261.M6 Moderno, Alice, 1867-1946 (Table P-PZ40)

9261.M7467 Moraes, Amador de (Table P-PZ40)

9261.M747 Moraes, Wenceslau de, 1854-1929 (Table P-PZ40)

Mourão-Ferreira, David see PQ9261.F3644

9261.N345 Negreiros, Jose de Almada, 1893-1970 (Table P-PZ40)

9261.N6 Nobre, António, 1867-1900 (Table P-PZ40)

9261.O64 Oliveira Mascarenhas, Joaquim Augusto de, 1847-1918 (Table P-PZ40)

Ortigão, Ramalho, 1836-1915 see PQ9261.R28

Paço d'Arcos, Anrique, 1906- see PQ9261.A769

Palmeirim, L.A. (Luís Augusto), 1825-1893 see PQ9261.P3

9261.P3 Palmeirim, Luiz Augusto, 1825-1893 (Table P-PZ40)

Pascoaes, Teizeira de see PQ9261.V276

Passos, A.A. Soares de (Antonio Augusto Soares) see PQ9261.S6

Pato, Bulhao, 1829-1912 see PQ9261.B8

9261.P33 Penha, João, 1839-1919 (Table P-PZ40)

9261.P352 Pereira, José Maria dos Reis, 1901-1969 (Table P-PZ40)

9261.P416 Pessanha, Camilo, 1867-1926 (Table P-PZ40)

9261.P417 Pessoa, Fernando, 1888-1935 (Table P-PZ40)

9261.P47 Pimentel, Alberto, 1849- (Table P-PZ40)

9261.P54 Pinheiro Chagas, Manuel, 1842-1895 (Table P-PZ40)

9261.P5677 Pires, A. Thomaz (Antonio Thomas), 1850-1913 (Table P-PZ40)

9261.P5695 Plácido, Ana Augusta, 1831-1895 (Table P-PZ40)

Queirós, Eça de, 1845-1900 see PQ9261.E3

9261.Q4 Quental, Anthero de, 1842-1891 (Table P-PZ40)

9261.R28 Ramalho Ortigão, Jose Duarte, 1836-1915 (Table P-PZ40)

9261.R3 Ramos Coelho, Jose, 1832-1914 (Table P-PZ40)

Individual authors
Individual authors, 1701-1960, A-Z -- Continued
9261.R4 Rebello da Silva, Luiz Augusto, 1822-1871 (Table P-PZ40)
Régio, José, 1901-1969 see PQ9261.P352
Reis, Ricardo, 1888-1935 see PQ9261.P417
9261.R477 Ribeiro dos Santos, Antonio, 1745-1818 (Table P-PZ40)
9261.R536 Rocha, Adolfo, 1907- (Table P-PZ40)
9261.R54 Rocha, João da, 1868-1921 (Table P-PZ40)
9261.S13 Sanches de Frias, David Correia, Visconde de, 1845-1922 (Table P-PZ40)
9261.S47 Silva, Antonio José da, 1705-1739 (Table P-PZ40)
9261.S49 Silva Gayo, Antonio da, 1830-1870 (Table P-PZ40)
9261.S6 Soares de Passos, Antonio Augusto, 1826-1860 (Table P-PZ40)
Soromenho, Castro, 1910-1968 see PQ9261.S63
9261.S63 Soromenho, Fernando Monteiro de Castro, 1910-1968 (Table P-PZ40)
9261.S759 Souza, Diogo de, conde de Rio Pardo, 1755-1829 (Table P-PZ40)
9261.T36 Teixeira de Queiroz, Francisco, 1848-1919 (Table P-PZ40)
9261.T4 Teixeira de Vasconcellos, Antonio Augusto, 1816-1878 (Table P-PZ40)
Teixeira Gomes, Manuel, 1860-1941 see PQ9261.G59
Torga, Miguel, 1907- see PQ9261.R536
9261.T7 Troni, Alfredo, 1845-1904 (Table P-PZ40)
9261.V276 Vasconcelos, Joaquim Pereira Teixeira de, 1877-1952 (Table P-PZ40)
9261.V277 Vasconcelos, Mário Cesariny de (Table P-PZ40)
9261.V45 Verde, Cesario, 1855-1886 (Table P-PZ40)
9262-9288 Individual authors, 1961-2000
The author number is determined by the second letter of the name
Subarrange each author by Table P-PZ40 unless otherwise specified
Here are usually to be classified authors beginning to publish about 1950, flourishing after 1960
9262 Anonymous works (Table P-PZ28)
9263 A
A. Ruben see PQ9274.E343
9264 B
Braga, Maria Ondina see PQ9277.N3
9265 C
9266 D
9267 E
9268 F
9268.I42 Figueiredo, Nuno de, 1943- (Table P-PZ40)
9269 G

Individual authors.
Individual authors, 1961-2000 -- Continued
9270 H
9271 I
9272 J
9272.O83 Joselia, 1926- (Table P-PZ40)
9273 K
9274 L
9274.E343 Leitõao, Ruben Andresen. (Table P-PZ40)
9275 M
Marques, Alberto, 1943- see PQ9268.I42
Martins, Josélia das Dores, 1926- see PQ9272.O83
9276 N
9277 O
9277.N3 Ondina, Maria (Table P-PZ40)
9278 P
9279 Q
9280 R
Ruben, A. see PQ9274.E343
9281 S
9282 T
9283 U
9284 V
9285 W
9286 X
9287 Y
9288 Z
9300-9326 Individual authors, 2001-
The author number is determined by the second letter of the name
Subarrange each author by Table P-PZ40 unless otherwise specified
9300 Anonymous works (Table P-PZ28)
9301 A
9302 B
9303 C
9304 D
9305 E
9306 F
9307 G
9308 H
9309 I
9310 J
9311 K
9312 L
9313 M
9314 N

Individual authors.
Individual authors, 2001- -- Continued

9315 O
9316 P
9317 Q
9318 R
9319 S
9320 T
9321 U
9322 V
9323 W
9324 X
9325 Y
9326 Z

Provincial, local, colonial, etc.
Includes the literary history, biography, criticism and collections of the literature of provinces, regions, islands, places, belonging to Portugal; Portuguese literature outside of Portugal

Portugal (including North Atlantic islands, Azores, etc.)
Cf. PC5351+ Provincial dialects

9400 Regional (General or several regions)
9401.A-Z Special states, provinces, regions, etc., A-Z
9401.A8-.A83 Azores
9401.A8 History
9401.A82 Collections
9401.A83 Translations
9411.A-Z Special cities, towns, A-Z

Portuguese literature outside of Portugal
9421 General
Special
Europe
9424-9424.9 Great Britain (Table P-PZ25)
9427-9427.9 Switzerland (Table P-PZ25)
Spain
History
9431 General
9432 Special
Collections
9433 General
9434 Special
9450-9469.3 Galicia (Table P-PZ23 modified)
For Gallegan literature prior to 1500, see PQ9038+, PQ9155, etc.
9469.A-Z Individual authors through 1960, A-Z
Subarrange each author by Table P-PZ40 unless otherwise specified
e. g.

Provincial, local, colonial, etc.
Portuguese literature outside of Portugal
Special
Europe
Spain
Galicia
Individual authors through 1960, A-Z -- Continued

9469.A46 Añon, Francisco, 1812-1878 (Table P-PZ40)
9469.C25 Carballo Calero, Ricardo (Table P-PZ40)
Carvalho Calero, Ricardo see PQ9469.C25
Castelao see PQ9469.R6
9469.C3 Castro, Rosalia de, 1837-1885 (Table P-PZ40)
Cf. PQ6512.C226 Spanish literature
9469.C53 Chao Ledo, Xose Maria, 1844-1894 (Table P-PZ40)
9469.C84 Curros, Enríquez Manuel, 1851-1908 (Table P-PZ40)
Cf. PQ6605.U7 Spanish literature
9469.L27 Lago Gonzáles, Manuel, Abp., 1865-1925 (Table P-PZ40)
9469.L3 Lamas Carvajal, Valentín, 1849-1906 (Table P-PZ40)
9469.L4 Leiras Pulpeiro, Manuel, 1854-1912 (Table P-PZ40)
9469.L6 López Ferreiro, Antonio, 1837-1910 (Table P-PZ40)
9469.M26 Manoel-Antonio, 1900- (Table P-PZ40)
9469.O7 Otero Pedrayo, Ramon, 1888- (Table P-PZ40)
9469.P43 Pérez Placer, Heraclio (Table P-PZ40)
Perez Sanchez, Manoel-Antonio, 1900- see PQ9469.M26
9469.P48 Pintos Villar, Xoán Manuel, 1811-1876 (Table P-PZ40)
9469.P56 Pondal, Eduardo, 1835-1917 (Table P-PZ40)
9469.P7 Prado Rodríguez, Xavier (Table P-PZ40)
9469.R6 Rodríguez Castelao, Alfonso, 1886-1950 (Table P-PZ40)
9469.S32 Sarmiento, Martin, 1695-1772 (Table P-PZ40)
9469.2.A-Z Individual authors, 1961-2000
Subarrange each author by Table P-PZ40 unless otherwise specified
9469.3.A-Z Individual authors, 2001- , A-Z
Subarrange each author by Table P-PZ40 unless otherwise specified

America
9470-9479 United States and Canada (Table P-PZ24)
9500-9698.436 Brazil (Table P-PZ20 modified)

Provincial, local, colonial, etc.
Portuguese literature outside of Portugal
Special
America
Brazil -- Continued
Local

9691.A-Z By region, state, etc., A-Z
Subarrange each by Table P-PZ26
e. g.

9691.C4-.C42 Ceara
9691.C4 History
9691.C42 Collections
9691.S3-.S4 São Paulo
9691.S3 History
9691.S4 Collections

Individual authors or works

9696.A-Z To 1800, A-Z
Subarrange individual authors by Table P-PZ40 unless otherwise specified
Subarrange individual works by Table P-PZ43 unless otherwise specified

Alvarenga, Manuel Inácio da Silva, 1749-1814. see PQ9696.S5

9696.A5 Anchieta, José de, 1534-1597 (Table P-PZ40)
Class here collected works and multi-lingual or Portuguese literary works
For works on a particular subject, see the subject
For literary works in one language, other than Portuguese, see the appropriate literature, e.g. PA8450.A66, Latin
For general biography, see F2528

9696.A78 Aranha, Bento de Figueiredo Tenreiro, 1769-1811 (Table P-PZ40)

Barbosa, Domingos Caldas see PQ9696.C3

9696.C3 Caldas Barbosa, Domingos, d. 1800 (Table P-PZ40)

9696.C35 Cartas chilenas (Table P-PZ40)
By some authorities ascribed to Cláudio Manuel da Costa or to Tomas Antonio Gorzaga
Cf. PQ9696.C6 Costa, Cláudio Manuel da
Cf. PQ9696.G6 Gonzaga, Tomas Antonio

9696.C6 Costa, Claudio Manoel da, 1729-1789 (Table P-PZ40)
Cartas chilenas (by some authorities ascribed to him) see PQ9696.C35

9696.G3 Gama, Jose Basilio de, 1740-1795 (Table P-PZ40)

Provincial, local, colonial, etc.
Portuguese literature outside of Portugal.
Special.
America
Brazil
Individual authors or works
To 1800, A-Z

9696.G6 Gonzaga, Tomás Antônio, 1744-1807? (Table P-PZ40)
Cartas chilenas (by some authorities ascribed to him) see PQ9696.C35
Lereno see PQ9696.C3
Matos, Gregório de, 1636-1696? see PQ9696.M3
9696.M3 Mattos Guerra, Gregorio de, 1636-1696? (Table P-PZ40)
9696.O7 Orta, Teresa Margarida da Silva e, b. 1711 or 12 (Table P-PZ40)
9696.P4 Peixoto, Inácio José de Alvarenga, 1744?-1792 (Table P-PZ40)
9696.P46 Pereira, Nuno Marques, 1652-1718 (Table P-PZ40)
9696.S5 Silva Alvarenga, Manuel Inácio da, 1749-1814. (Table P-PZ40)
9696.T4 Teixeira, Bento, 16th cent. (Table P-PZ40)
9697.A-Z 1801-1960, A-Z
Subarrange individual authors by Table P-PZ40 unless otherwise specified
Subarrange individual works by Table P-PZ43 unless otherwise specified
9697.A3 Abreu, Casimiro Jose Marques de, 1839-1860 (Table P-PZ40)
9697.A354 Abreu e Castro, Bernardino Freire de Figueiredo, 1809-1871 (Table P-PZ40)
9697.A385 Adalcinda (Table P-PZ40)
Adonias Filho, 1915- see PQ9697.A4
9697.A4 Aguiar, Adonias, 1915- (Table P-PZ40)
Albuquerque, Medeiros e, 1867-1934 see PQ9697.M35
9697.A53 Alencar, José Martiniano de, 1829-1877 (Table P-PZ40)
9697.A555 Alencar Araripe, Tristõao de, 1848-1911 (Table P-PZ40)
9697.A58 Almeida, Guilherme de (Table P-PZ40)
Almeida Julia Lopes de, 1862-1934 see PQ9697.L74
9697.A6 Almeida, Manuel Antônio de, 1831-1861 (Table P-PZ40)

Provincial, local, colonial, etc.
Portuguese literature outside of Portugal.
Special
America
Brazil
Individual authors or works
1801-1960, A-Z -- Continued

9697.A6215 Almeida, Prisciliana Duarte de, 1867-1944 (Table P-PZ40)
Alves, Castro, 1847-1871 see PQ9697.C35
9697.A666 Ambrósio, Manoel, 1865-1947 (Table P-PZ40)
Anapurus, 1843-1899 see PQ9697.E7
Andrade, Maria Julieta Drummond de see PQ9697.D72
9697.A775 Aranha, Jose Pereira da Graca, 1868-1931 (Table P-PZ40)
9697.A792 Araújo Filho, Luiz, 1845-1918 (Table P-PZ40)
9697.A8 Arinos, Affonso, 1868-1916 (Table P-PZ40)
9697.A93 Azevedo, Aluizio, 1858-1913 (Table P-PZ40)
9697.A95 Azevedo, Arthur, 1855-1908 (Table P-PZ40)
9697.A965 Azevedo, Manuel Antônio Alvares de, 1831-1852 (Table P-PZ40)
Azevedo Castro, Ana Luíza de see PQ9697.I57
9697.B3278 Barandas, Ana Eurídice Eufrosina de, b. 1806 (Table P-PZ40)
9697.B3454 Barcellos, Ramiro Fortes de, 1851-1916 (Table P-PZ40)
Barreto, Paulo, 1881-1921 see PQ9697.R59
9697.B35 Barreto de Menezes, Tobias, 1839-1889 (Table P-PZ40)
9697.B37 Barroso, Gustavo, 1888- (Table P-PZ40)
9697.B55 Bilac, Olavo dos Guimaraes, 1865-1918 (Table P-PZ40)
9697.B725 Borges dos Reis, Solon, 1917- (Table P-PZ40)
9697.B82 Brazil, Zeferino, 1870- (Table P-PZ40)
Cabral, João Passos, 1900-1950 see PQ9697.P316
Camarao, Adalcinda see PQ9697.A385
9697.C2423 Camargo, Maria Cândida de Jesus, 1868-1949 (Table P-PZ40)
9697.C244 Caminha, Adolpho, 1867-1897 (Table P-PZ40)
9697.C254 Cardona, Ibrantina (Table P-PZ40)
9697.C2546 Cardoso, Fausto, 1864-1906 (Table P-PZ40)
Carmontaigne, 1843-1899 see PQ9697.E7
9697.C26727 Carvalho, Alvaro Augusto, 1829-1865 (Table P-PZ40)

Provincial, local, colonial, etc.
Portuguese literature outside of Portugal.
Special
America
Brazil
Individual authors or works
1801-1960, A-Z -- Continued

9697.C285 Castello Branco, Francisco Gil, 1848-1891 (Table P-PZ40)

Castro, Ana Luíza de Azevedo see PQ9697.I57

9697.C35 Castro Alves, Antonio de, 1847-1871 (Table P-PZ40)

9697.C35 Álvares, João Teixeira, 1858-1940 (Table P-PZ40)

9697.C37 Cearense, Catullo da Paizao, 1863-1946 (Table P-PZ40)

9697.C383 Claúdio, Affonso, 1859-1934 (Table P-PZ40)

9697.C42 Coelho Netto, Henrique, 1864-1934 (Table P-PZ40)

9697.C55 Correia, Raymundo, 1860-1911 (Table P-PZ40)

Corte Real, Sebastião, 1843-1899 see PQ9697.E7

9697.C595 Costa, Francisco Lobo da, 1853-1888 (Table P-PZ40)

9697.C62 Costa, Júlia da, 1844-1884 (Table P-PZ40)

9697.C7425 Coutinho, José Candido de Lacerda, 1842-1900 (Table P-PZ40)

9697.C75 Cruls, Gastõao (Table P-PZ40)

9697.C7545 Cruz, Eddy Dias da, 1907-1973 (Table P-PZ40)

9697.D4 Delfino dos Santos, Luiz, 1834-1910 (Table P-PZ40)

9697.D42 Délia, 1853-1895 (Table P-PZ40)

9697.D52 Dias, Antônio Gonçalves, 1823-1864 (Table P-PZ40)

Dinarte, Sílvio, 1843-1899 see PQ9697.E7

9697.D66 Dourado, Autran, 1926- (Table P-PZ40)

Dourado, Waldomiro see PQ9697.D66

9697.D72 Drummond de Andrade, Maria Julieta (Table P-PZ40)

9697.D753 Duarte, Rafael de Andrade, 1867-1958 (Table P-PZ40)

Dupré, Leandro, Sra. see PQ9697.D78

9697.D78 Dupré, Maria José (Table P-PZ40)

9697.D788 Duque Estrada, Luis Gonzaga, 1863-1911 (Table P-PZ40)

9697.E52 Eiró, Paulo, 1836-1871 (Table P-PZ40)

Elísio, Flávio, 1843-1899 see PQ9697.E7

Provincial, local, colonial, etc.
Portuguese literature outside of Portugal
Special
America
Brazil
Individual authors or works
1801-1960, A-Z -- Continued

9697.E7 Escragnolle Taunay, Alfredo de, 1843-1899 (Table P-PZ40)
9697.F2 Fagundes Varella, Luis Nicolau, 1841-1875 (Table P-PZ40)
Flag, Suzana see PQ9697.R66
9697.F658 Fontoura, Adelino, 1859-1884 (Table P-PZ40)
Fradique, Mendes see PQ9697.M2
9697.F74 França, Joaquim José da, 1838-1890 (Table P-PZ40)
França Junior, 1838-1890 see PQ9697.F74
9697.F82 Franco de Sá, Antônio Joaquim, 1836-1856 (Table P-PZ40)
9697.F8264 Freire, Luiz José Junqueira, 1832-1855 (Table P-PZ40)
Galeno, Juvenal see PQ9697.G25
9697.G25 Galleno da Costa e Silva, Juvenal, 1836-1931 (Table P-PZ40)
9697.G32 Gama, Luiz, 1830-1882 (Table P-PZ40)
Gonçalves Dias, Antônio see PQ9697.D52
9697.G753 Gonsalves Teixeira e Sousa, Antônio, 1812-1861 (Table P-PZ40)
Graça Aranha, José Pereira da see PQ9697.A775
9697.G885 Guimaraens, Afonso Henriques de, 1870-1921 (Table P-PZ40)
9697.G9 Guimarõaes, Bernardo, 1825-1884 (Table P-PZ40)
Henrique, Luís, 1925- see PQ9697.T223
9697.I57 Indigena do Ipiranga (Table P-PZ40)
Indygena de Ypiranga see PQ9697.I57
9697.I6 Inglez de Souza, Herculano Marcos, 1853-1918 (Table P-PZ40)
9697.J23 Jansen, Carlos, 1829-1889 (Table P-PZ40)
Juvenal, Amaro see PQ9697.B3454
9697.L24 Laet, Carlos de, 1847-1927 (Table P-PZ40)
Leonardos, Stella see PQ9697.L5423
9697.L54212 Lima, José Coriolano de Sousa, 1829-1869 (Table P-PZ40)
9697.L54217 Lima, Natividade, 1871-1897 (Table P-PZ40)

Provincial, local, colonial, etc.
Portuguese literature outside of Portugal.
Special
America
Brazil
Individual authors or works
1801-1960, A-Z -- Continued

9697.L5423 Lima, Stella Leonardos da Silva, 1923- (Table P-PZ40)
9697.L59 Lobato, José Bento Monteiro, 1883-1948 (Table P-PZ40)
9697.L7223 Lopes, João Simões, 1865-1916 (Table P-PZ40)
9697.L74 Lopes de Almeida, Julia, 1862-1934 (Table P-PZ40)
Lopes Neto, J. Simões (João Simões) see PQ9697.L7223
9697.L965 Lynce, Léo, 1884-1954 (Table P-PZ40)
9697.M15 Macedo, Joaquim Manuel de, 1820-1882 (Table P-PZ40)
9697.M18 Machado de Assis, Joaquim Maria, 1839-1908 (Table P-PZ40)
9697.M1897 Maciel, Pedro Nolasco, 1861-1909 (Table P-PZ40)
9697.M2 Madeira de Freitas, Jose, 1893-1944 (Table P-PZ40)
9697.M2214 Magalhõaes, Domingos José Gonçalves de, visconde de Araguaya, 1811-1882 (Table P-PZ40)
9697.M225 Magalhõaes, Valentim, 1859-1903 (Table P-PZ40)
9697.M2319 Magno, Carlos Hipólito de Santa Helena (Table P-PZ40)
Malheiros, Heitor, 1843-1899 see PQ9697.E7
9697.M246 Manso, Pacifico Pacato Cordeiro, 1865-1931 (Table P-PZ40)
9697.M27 Marques, Zavier, 1861-1942 (Table P-PZ40)
9697.M35 Medeiros e Albuquerque, José Joaquim de Campos da Costa, 1867- (Table P-PZ40)
Melo, Eugênio de, 1843-1899 see PQ9697.E7
9697.M4625 Melo, Rita Barém de, 1840-1868 (Table P-PZ40)
9697.M472 Mendes, Manuel Odorico, 1799-1864 (Table P-PZ40)
9697.M47427 Menezes, Agrário de, 1834-1863 (Table P-PZ40)
9697.M4745 Menezes, Emilio de, 1866-1918 (Table P-PZ40)
9697.M4774 Menezes e Souza, João Cardoso de, Barão de Paranapiacaba, 1827-1915 (Table P-PZ40)
9697.M48 Menotti del Picchia (Table P-PZ40)

Provincial, local, colonial, etc.
Portuguese literature outside of Portugal.
Special
America
Brazil
Individual authors or works
1801-1960, A-Z -- Continued

9697.M6835 Monteiro, Maciel, 1804-1868 (Table P-PZ40)
Mota, Dantas, 1913-1974 see PQ9697.M7384
9697.M7384 Motta, José Franklin Massena de Dantas, 1913-1974 (Table P-PZ40)
9697.M747 Moura, Caetano Lopes de, 1780-1860 (Table P-PZ40)
9697.N2184 Nascimento, João Afonso do, 1855-1924 (Table P-PZ40)
9697.O5 Oliveira, Alberto de, 1859- (Table P-PZ40)
9697.O514 Oliveira, Antônio de, b. 1874 (Table P-PZ40)
9697.P215 Paiva, Manoel de Oliveira, 1861-1892 (Table P-PZ40)
Paiva, Manuel de Oliveira, 1861-1892 see PQ9697.P215
Paranapiacaba, João Cardoso de Menezes e Souza, Barão de, 1827-1915 see PQ9697.M4774
9697.P316 Passos Cabral, João, 1900-1950 (Table P-PZ40)
9697.P32 Patrocinio, José do, 1853-1905 (Table P-PZ40)
9697.P35 Peixoto, Afranio, 1876- (Table P-PZ40)
Pena, Martins, 1815-1848 see PQ9697.P382
9697.P382 Penna, Luiz Carlos Martins, 1815-1848 (Table P-PZ40)
Perneta, Emiliano, 1866-1921 see PQ9697.P453
9697.P453 Pernetta, Emiliano, 1866-1921 (Table P-PZ40)
9697.P6 Pires, Cornelio (Table P-PZ40)
9697.P655 Pompéia, Raul, 1863-1895 (Table P-PZ40)
Ponte Preta, Stanislaw, 1923-1968 see PQ9697.P685
9697.P685 Porto, Sergio, 1923-1968 (Table P-PZ40)
9697.P69 Porto Alegre, Apolinario, 1844-1904 (Table P-PZ40)
9697.P7 Porto Alegre, Manuel de Araujo, 1806-1879 (Table P-PZ40)
Preta, Stanislaw Ponte, 1923-1968 see PQ9697.P685
9697.Q2 Qorpo-Santo, José Joaquim de Campos Leao, 1829-1883 (Table P-PZ40)
Rebelo, Marques, 1907-1973 see PQ9697.C7545
Reis, Sólon Borges dos, 1917- see PQ9697.B725

Provincial, local, colonial, etc.
Portuguese literature outside of Portugal
Special
America
Brazil
Individual authors or works
1801-1960, A-Z -- Continued

9697.R5 Ribeiro, Julio, 1845-1890 (Table P-PZ40)
9697.R59 Rio, João do, 1881-1921 (Table P-PZ40)
9697.R636 Rocha Pombo, José Francisco da, 1857-1933 (Table P-PZ40)
9697.R66 Rodriques, Nelson (Table P-PZ40)
9697.S2 Saldanha, José da Natividade, 1796-1830 (Table P-PZ40)
(9697.S214) Sales, Antônio, 1868-1940
see PQ9697.S25
9697.S25 Salles, Antonio, 1868-1940 (Table P-PZ40)
9697.S2593 Sampaio, Maria Clemência da Silveira, 1789-1862 (Table P-PZ40)
9697.S3648 Saraiva, Ovídio, 1787-1852 (Table P-PZ40)
9697.S4225 Schutel, Duarte Paranhos, 1837-1901 (Table P-PZ40)
Scoevola, Múcio, 1843-1899 see PQ9697.E7
9697.S642 Silveira, Valdomiro, 1873-1941 (Table P-PZ40)
9697.S6545 Siqueira Filho, José Jorge de, 1845-1870 (Table P-PZ40)
Sousa, Cruz e, 1861-1898 see PQ9697.S673
9697.S6675 Sousa Andrade, Joaquim de, 1832-1902 (Table P-PZ40)
Sousândrade see PQ9697.S6675
Souza, João Cardoso de Menezes e, Barão de paranapiacaba, 1827-1915 see PQ9697.M4774
9697.S673 Souza, João da Cruz e, 1861-1898 (Table P-PZ40)
9697.S85 Suzano, Azambuja, 1791-1873 (Table P-PZ40)
Taunay, Alfedo d'Escragnolle Taunay see PQ9697.E7
9697.T213 Tavares, Crispiniano, 1855-1906 (Table P-PZ40)
9697.T223 Tavares, Luís Henrique Dias (Table P-PZ40)
9697.T27 Távora, Franklin, 1842-1888 (Table P-PZ40)
9697.T43 Teixeira, Mucio Scoevola Lopes, 1857-1926 (Table P-PZ40)
9697.T495 Teófilo, Rodolfo, 1853-1932 (Table P-PZ40)
9697.T5 Theophilo, Rodolpho Marcos, 1853-1932 (Table P-PZ40)

Provincial, local, colonial, etc.
Portuguese literature outside of Portugal.
Special
America
Brazil
Individual authors or works
1801-1960, A-Z -- Continued

9697.T58 Titara, Ladislau dos Santos, 1801-1861 (Table P-PZ40)

Valle, Cyllenêo, Marques de Araūjo, 1884-1954 see PQ9697.L965

Varela, Luís Nicolau Fagundes, 1841-1875 see PQ9697.F2

Varella, Luiz N. Fagundes, 1841-1875 see PQ9697.F2

9697.V28 Várzea, Virgílio, 1863-1941 (Table P-PZ40)

9697.V2814 Vasconcellos, Diogo Pereira Ribeiro de, 1760-1812 (Table P-PZ40)

9697.V3 Veríssimo de Mattos, José, 1857-1916 (Table P-PZ40)

Vidal, André, 1843-1899 see PQ9697.E7

9697.V552 Vilela, Carneiro, 1846-1913 (Table P-PZ40)

1961-2000

Here are usually to be classified authors beginning to publish about 1950, flourishing after 1960

9698.1 A

The author number is determined by the second letter of the name

Each author is subarranged by Table P-PZ40, unless otherwise specified

Anisio Chico, 1931- see PQ9698.13.H55

Antônio Maria, 1921-1964 see PQ9698.23.O7193

9698.1.S78 Assis Brasil, Luiz Antonio, 1945- (Table P-PZ40)

9698.12 B

The author number is determined by the second letter of the name

Each author is subarranged by Table P-PZ40, unless otherwise specified

9698.12.A686 Barreto, Arriete Vilela Costa, 1949- (Table P-PZ40)

9698.12.E88 Bezerra, Francisco Sobreira, 1942- (Table P-PZ40)

Brasil, Luiz Antonio Assis see PQ9698.1.S78

Buarque de Hollanda, Chico see PQ9698.18.O35

Provincial, local, colonial, etc.
Portuguese literature outside of Portugal.
Special
America
Brazil
Individual authors or works
1961-2000, A-Z

9698.13 C

The author number is determined by the second letter of the name

Each author is subarranged by Table P-PZ40, unless otherwise specified

Ceccon, Claudius see PQ9698.13.L325

Celso, Antônio, 1938- see PQ9698.26.E68

Ceres, Heliônia see PQ9698.18.E35

9698.13.H55 Chico Anísio, 1931- (Table P-PZ40)

9698.13.L325 Claudius (Claudius Ceccon) (Table P-PZ40)

9698.13.O617 Cora Coralina (Table P-PZ40)

Coralina, Cora see PQ9698.13.O617

Costa, Arriete Vilela see PQ9698.12.A686

9698.14 D

The author number is determined by the second letter of the name

Each author is subarranged by Table P-PZ40, unless otherwise specified

9698.15 E

The author number is determined by the second letter of the name

Each author is subarranged by Table P-PZ40, unless otherwise specified

9698.16 F

The author number is determined by the second letter of the name

Each author is subarranged by Table P-PZ40, unless otherwise specified

9698.16.A45 Falcõao, Celso Almir Japiassu Lins, 1939- (Table P-PZ40)

Faustino, Mário, 1930-1962 see PQ9698.29.I46

Ferreira, Filho, João Antônio see PQ9698.2.O18

9698.16.R26 Fraga Filho, Cid Seixas (Table P-PZ40)

Fuentes, Mora see PQ9698.23.O7112

9698.17 G

The author number is determined by the second letter of the name

Each author is subarranged by Table P-PZ40, unless otherwise specified

Provincial, local, colonial, etc.
Portuguese literature outside of Portugal.
Special
America
Brazil
Individual authors or works
1961-2000, A-Z -- Continued

9698.18 H
The author number is determined by the second letter of the name
Each author is subarranged by Table P-PZ40, unless otherwise specified
9698.18.E35 Heliônia Ceres (Table P-PZ40)
9698.18.O35 Hollanda, Chico Buarque de. (Table P-PZ40)
9698.19 I
The author number is determined by the second letter of the name
Each author is subarranged by Table P-PZ40, unless otherwise specified
9698.2 J
The author number is determined by the second letter of the name
Each author is subarranged by Table P-PZ40, unless otherwise specified
Japiassu, Celso, 1939- see PQ9698.16.A45
9698.2.O18 João Antonio, 1937- (Table P-PZ40)
9698.21 K
The author number is determined by the second letter of the name
Each author is subarranged by Table P-PZ40, unless otherwise specified
Kuri, 1948- see PQ9698.29.O88
9698.22 L
The author number is determined by the second letter of the name
Each author is subarranged by Table P-PZ40, unless otherwise specified
Lichterfeld, Helena de see PQ9698.29.T38
9698.23 M
The author number is determined by the second letter of the name
Each author is subarranged by Table P-PZ40, unless otherwise specified
9698.23.E464 Melo, Virgínius da Gama e (Table P-PZ40)
9698.23.O7112 Mora Fuentes, Jose Luis, 1951- (Table P-PZ40)
9698.23.O7193 Morais, Antônio Maria Araújo de, 1921-1964 (Table P-PZ40)

Provincial, local, colonial, etc.
Portuguese literature outside of Portugal.
Special
America
Brazil
Individual authors or works
1961-2000, A-Z -- Continued

9698.24 N
The author number is determined by the second letter of the name
Each author is subarranged by Table P-PZ40, unless otherwise specified

9698.25 O
The author number is determined by the second letter of the name
Each author is subarranged by Table P-PZ40, unless otherwise specified
Oliveira Paula Filho, Francisco Anísio de see PQ9698.13.H55

9698.26 P
The author number is determined by the second letter of the name
Each author is subarranged by Table P-PZ40, unless otherwise specified
Paula Filho, Francisco Anísio de Oliveira see PQ9698.13.H55

9698.26.E68 Pereira, Antonio Celso Alves (Table P-PZ40)
Pinto, Ziraldo Alves see PQ9698.36.I7

9698.27 Q
The author number is determined by the second letter of the name
Each author is subarranged by Table P-PZ40, unless otherwise specified

9698.28 R
The author number is determined by the second letter of the name
Each author is subarranged by Table P-PZ40, unless otherwise specified

9698.29 S
The author number is determined by the second letter of the name
Each author is subarranged by Table P-PZ40, unless otherwise specified
Seixas Cid see PQ9698.16.R26

9698.29.I46 Silva, Mario Faustino dos Santos e, 1930-1962 (Table P-PZ40)
Sobreira, Francisco, 1942- see PQ9698.12.E88

Provincial, local, colonial, etc.
Portuguese literature outside of Portugal.
Special.
America
Brazil
Individual authors or works
1961-2000, A-Z
S
9698.29.O88 Souza, Maria Beatriz Farias de, 1948- (Table P-PZ40)
9698.29.T38 Steigleder, Gertraude Schultz. (Table P-PZ40)
9698.3 T
The author number is determined by the second letter of the name
Each author is subarranged by Table P-PZ40, unless otherwise specified
9698.31 U
The author number is determined by the second letter of the name
Each author is subarranged by Table P-PZ40, unless otherwise specified
9698.32 V
The author number is determined by the second letter of the name
Each author is subarranged by Table P-PZ40, unless otherwise specified
9698.33 W
The author number is determined by the second letter of the name
Each author is subarranged by Table P-PZ40, unless otherwise specified
9698.34 X
The author number is determined by the second letter of the name
Each author is subarranged by Table P-PZ40, unless otherwise specified
9698.35 Y
The author number is determined by the second letter of the name
Each author is subarranged by Table P-PZ40, unless otherwise specified
9698.36 Z
The author number is determined by the second letter of the name
Each author is subarranged by Table P-PZ40, unless otherwise specified
9698.36.I7 Ziraldo (Table P-PZ40)

Provincial, local, colonial, etc.
Portuguese literature outside of Portugal
Special
America
Brazil
Individual authors or works
9698.4-.436 2001- (Table P-PZ29a)
9900-9948.9 Africa
9900-9908 General (Table P-PZ24)
9920-9929 Angola (Table P-PZ24 modified)
Carvalho, Agostino Mendes de see PQ9929.X58
9929.A-Z Individual authors or works, A-Z
Subarrange individual authors by Table P-PZ40 unless otherwise specified
Subarrange individual works by Table P-PZ43 unless otherwise specified
Almeida, Roberto Victor de see PQ9929.R63
9929.B65 Bonavena, E. (Table P-PZ40)
9929.F47 Ferreira, Jose da Silva Maia (Table P-PZ40)
9929.P46 Pepetela Santos, Artur Carlos Mauricio Pestana dos (Table P-PZ40)
Pestana, Nelson see PQ9929.B65
9929.R63 Rocha, Jofre, 1941- (Table P-PZ40)
9929.X58 Xitu, Uanhenga, 1924- (Table P-PZ40)
9930-9939 Mozambique (Table P-PZ24 modified)
9939.A-Z Individual authors or works, A-Z
Subarrange individual authors by Table P-PZ40 unless otherwise specified
Subarrange individual works by Table P-PZ43 unless otherwise specified
Chongo, Cardoso Lindo, 1977- see PQ9939.O33
9939.O33 Okapi, Sangare, 1977- (Table P-PZ40)
9942-9942.9 Cape Verde islands (Table P-PZ25 modified)
9942.9.A-Z Individual authors or works, A-Z
Subarrange individual authors by Table P-PZ40 unless otherwise specified
Subarrange individual works by Table P-PZ43 unless otherwise specified
9942.9.T38 Tavares, Eugenio, 1867-1930 (Table P-PZ40)
9945-9945.9 Guinea-Bissau. Portuguese Guinea (Table P-PZ25)
9948-9948.9 Sao Tome and Principe (Table P-PZ25)
9950-9959 Asia (Table P-PZ24 modified)
9959.A-Z Individual authors or works, A-Z
Subarrange individual authors by Table P-PZ40 unless otherwise specified
Subarrange individual works by Table P-PZ43 unless otherwise specified

Provincial, local, colonial, etc.
Portuguese literature outside of Portugal
Special
Asia
Individual authors, A-Z -- Continued

9959.O7 Osorio de Castro, Alberta (Table P-PZ40)

9959.R38 Rebelo, Joaquim Filipe Neri Soares, 1873-1922 (Table P-PZ40)

9990-9999 Australia. Oceania (Table P-PZ24)

A1	Collected works. Selections. Quotations. By date
	Divina commedia
A11	General
A12	Inferno
A13	Purgatorio
A14	Paradiso
	Minor works
A15	Collections. Selections
A16	Poems
A17	Convito
A18	Vito nuovo
	Latin works
A191	De monarchia
A192	De vulgari eloquentia
A193	Eclogae
A195	Epistolae
	Qiaestio de aqua et terra see PQ4326.Q2
A199	Juvenile and popular adaptations

.x date	Collected and selected works. By date
	Decameron (Complete or selected stories)
.xA3	Anonymous. By date
.xA31-.xA39	By translator
.xA4-.xA79	Separate stories, by (original) title and date
.xA9-.xZ3	Other works, A-Z
	Spurious works
	see PQ4275.A+

0.A2A-.A2Z	Works. By translator, A-Z
0.A3A-.A3Z	Selected works. By translator, A-Z
	Divina commedia
0.A5-Z	Complete editions. By translator, A-Z
0.1.A-Z	Collections and selections of older (Medieval and early modern) translations. By editor, A-Z
0.12	Incomplete Class special parts, if complete, with Inferno, Purgatorio, or Paradiso
0.13	Two parts
0.15	Selections (longer passages)
0.17	Passages, thoughts, etc.
	Inferno
0.2.A-Z	Complete translations. By translator, A-Z
0.21	Incomplete or several cantos or parts of cantos
0.23	Selections. Passages. Thoughts
0.25	Particular cantos
0.27	Particular episodes
	Purgatorio
0.3.A-Z	Complete translations. By translator, A-Z
0.31	Incomplete or several cantos or parts of cantos
0.33	Selections. Passages. Thoughts
0.35	Particular cantos
0.37	Particular episodes
	Paradiso
0.4.A-Z	Complete translations. By translator, A-Z
0.41	Incomplete or several cantos or parts of cantos
0.43	Selections. Passages. Thoughts
0.45	Particular cantos
0.47	Particular episodes
	Minor works
0.5	Collections or selections
	Particular works
0.52	Poems
0.56	Sette salmi
0.57	Convito
0.58	Vita nuova
	Latin works
0.6	Collections or selections
	Particular works
0.62	De monarchia
0.63	De vulgari eloquentia
0.64	Eclogae
0.65	Epistolae
(0.67)	Quaestio de aqua de terra see PQ4326.Q2

0.9 Popular and juvenile adaptations

.x	Collections and selections
.x1	Gerusalemme liberata, by translator, A-Z Early translations called Godfrey of Bulloigne; Godfrey of Boulogne
.x2	L'Aminta
.x3	Rime
.x4-.x9	Other works (by original title)
.x7	Rinaldo

.xA1-.xA19	Collected and selected works, by translator or editor and date
.xA2	Collected poetry
.xA5-.xZ	Separate works. By title

1	General and miscellaneous
	Poetry
2	General, by various translators. By date
3.A-Z	General, by special translator, A-Z
	Special
4A-4Z	By form, A-Z
4B2-4B28	Ballads (Romances)
4C46-4C468	Children's poetry
4F7-4F78	Folk songs
5A-5Z	By subject, A-Z
5F45-5F459	Feminist poetry
5L6-5L69	Love
5W37-5W379	War
6	Drama
8	Prose. Prose fiction
9	Local

.A1	Collected and selected works. By date
.A15	Selections. Quotations, etc. By date
	Don Quixote
.A2	Comprehensive works. By date
.A2A-.A2Z	Undated works. By place, A-Z
(.A25)	Editions. By translator
.A28	Continuation by François Filleau de Saint Martin
.A29	Spurious second part. By date Published under the pseudonym of Alonso Fernández de Avellaneda
.A3	Abridged translations, including juvenile. By date
.A5	Selections. Quotations, etc.
.A6	Novels
.A7	Plays
.A75	Poems
.A8-.Z	Individual works. By date
	Don Quixote see PQ7 .A2+
	Doubtful or spurious works see PQ6328
.G2	Galatea
.R5	Rinconete y Cortadillo

	History and criticism
1.A1	Periodicals. Societies. Congresses. Collections
1.A2	Awards, prizes (not A-Z)
1.A3-Z	By individual author
1.3	Biography (Collective)
	For individual biography, see the country
1.5	Women authors. Literary relations of women
1.7.A-Z	Other classes of authors, A-Z
1.7.B55	Black authors
1.7.J49	Jewish authors
2.A-Z	Special forms, A-Z
2.A87	Autobiographical fiction
2.C48	Children's literature
2.D7	Drama
2.E74	Erotic literature
2.E8	Essay
2.F35	Fantastic literature
	Fiction (General) see PQ8 2.N7
2.H57	Historical fiction
2.N7	Novels. Fiction (General)
2.P7	Poetry
2.P76	Prose literature
2.R46	Reportage literature
2.S26	Satire
2.S34	Science fiction
2.S5	Short story
	Collections
2.5	Periodicals
3	General
4	Poetry
4.5	Drama
5	Prose
7.A-Z	Translations. By language, A-Z
7.A32	Afrikaans
7.B8	Bulgarian
7.C48	Chinese
7.D3	Danish
7.E5	English
7.F7	French
7.G4	German
7.G73	Greek, Modern
7.H8	Hungarian
7.I8	Italian
7.L57	Lithuanian
7.P6	Polish
7.R8	Russian

.x General collections
.x1 Selections
Italian works
.x3 Poetical works. Rime, sonetti, etc.
.x5 Trionfi
Latin works
.x7 Collections and selections. By date
.x9A-.x9Z Separate works. By original title, A-Z
Prefer PQ4507.A2 for autobiographical sourcew
Epistolae
.x9E2 Comprehensive editions
.x9E21 Selections. Anthologies
Partial editions (as grouped by Petrarca)
.x9E22 Epistolae metricae
.x9E23 Epistolae familiares
.x9E24 Epistolae seniles
.x9E25 Epistolae variae
.x9E26 Epistolae sine titulo
Other selections
.x9E4 By subject (not A-Z)
e.g. To the classic authors, or Epistolae XVI ... de pontificatu ... et de Romana curia. Argentorati, 1555
By addressees
.x9E6 Groups
e.g. Statesmen
.x9E61-.x9E69 Individuals (alphabetically)
.x9E62 Boccaccio
(.x9E7) Particular letters
Separate editions of works in the form of letters are listed with works in their alphabetical order, e.g. De officio et virtutibus imperatoris, PQ4490.D3; Historia Griseldis, PQ4490.H4
Epistola ad posteros
see PQ4507.A2
.x9E8 Spurious and doubtful letters
Cf. PQ4499 Spurious works

.x	Collected works
.x1-.x9	Individual works, alphabetically

.A1	Editions. By date
.A2	Editions. By editor
.A3	School editions. By editor
.A37	Adaptations
	Translations
.A4-.A49	English
.A5-.A59	German
.A6-.A69	Other. By language (alphabetically)
	e.g.
.A67	Spanish
.A7-.Z	Criticism

INDEX

INDEX

M

N

O

INDEX

GPO U.S. GOVERNMENT PRINTING OFFICE: 2008–340–014/60028